D1694315

Enterprise Information Management with SAP®

SAP PRESS is a joint initiative of SAP and Galileo Press. The know-how offered by SAP specialists combined with the expertise of the Galileo Press publishing house offers the reader expert books in the field. SAP PRESS features first-hand information and expert advice, and provides useful skills for professional decision-making.

SAP PRESS offers a variety of books on technical and business-related topics for the SAP user. For further information, please visit our website: *www.sap-press.com*.

Jocelyn Dart, Susan Keohan, Alan Rickayzen
Practical Workflow for SAP (3rd edition)
2014, 1089 pp., hardcover
ISBN 978-1-4932-1009-1

Haun, Hickman, Loden, Wells
Implementing SAP HANA (2nd edition)
2015, approx. 850 pp., hardcover
ISBN 978-1-4932-1176-0

Bjarne Berg and Penny Silvia
SAP HANA: An Introduction (3rd edition)
2014, 579 pp., hardcover
ISBN 978-1-4932-1164-7

Loren Heilig et al.
Migrating Your SAP Data (2nd edition)
2008, 373 pp., hardcover
ISBN 978-1-59229-131-1

Brague, Champlin, Densborn, Dichmann,
Felsheim, Keller, Kuppe, On, Stefani

Enterprise Information Management with SAP®

Bonn • Boston

Galileo Press is named after the Italian physicist, mathematician, and philosopher Galileo Galilei (1564 — 1642). He is known as one of the founders of modern science and an advocate of our contemporary, heliocentric worldview. His words *Eppur si muove* (And yet it moves) have become legendary. The Galileo Press logo depicts Jupiter orbited by the four Galilean moons, which were discovered by Galileo in 1610.

Editor Laura Korslund
Acquisitions Editor Kelly Grace Weaver
Copyeditor Julie McNamee
Cover Design Graham Geary
Photo Credit Shutterstock.com/208628608/© Amacistock
Layout Design Vera Brauner
Production Kelly O'Callaghan
Typesetting III-satz
Printed and bound in the United States of America, on paper from sustainable sources

ISBN 978-1-4932-1045-9

2nd edition 2014

Library of Congress Cataloging-in-Publication Data
Enterprise information management with SAP / Corrie Brague. -- 2nd edition.
pages cm
Includes index.
ISBN 1-4932-1045-9 (print) -- ISBN 978-1-4932-1046-6 (ebook) -- ISBN 978-1-4932-1047-3 (print and ebook)
1. Information resources management--Data processing. 2. Management information systems. 3. SAP ERP. I. Title.
T58.64.B689 2014
658.4'03801--dc23
2014028647

Contents at a Glance

PART I SAP's Enterprise Information Management Strategy and Portfolio

PART II Working with SAP's Enterprise Information Management Solutions

Dear Reader,

Managing all of a book's text in a clear, organized way can be quite the daunting task, especially when multiple people are writing a single resource. There are often inconsistencies in terms, abbreviations, and writing style that can be very difficult to unify. However, this book's massive author team did just that. During the editorial process, it was impossible to tell where one author's text and another's changes began or ended (which in publishing, is true information management). It's rare that a book comes together so seamlessly, but managed by Corrie Brague, the authors delivered some of the most clean, organized, and comprehensive information (without editorial prodding) that I've seen to date!

With such diligence and attention to detail on this project, I have the utmost confidence that this book's author team has presented the details and tools that you need to start achieving your own extraordinary information management. With updated information on evolving SAP tools and topics such as SAP HANA Cloud Integration, SAP PowerDesigner, and SAP Information Steward, this resource on SAP's EIM solutions are sure to excite you about the possibilities that exist for managing enterprise data, and send you confidently on your journey.

What did you think about the second edition of *Enterprise Information Management with SAP*? Your comments and suggestions are the most useful tools to help us make our books the best they can be. We encourage you to visit our website at *www.sap-press.com* and share your feedback.

Thank you for purchasing a book from SAP PRESS!

Laura Korslund
Editor, SAP PRESS

Galileo Press
Boston, MA

laura.korslund@galileo-press.com
www.sap-press.com

Contents

PART II Working with SAP's Enterprise Information Management Solutions

Introduction

Welcome to the second edition of *Enterprise Information Management with SAP*! The goal of this book continues to be to introduce readers to the concepts of Enterprise Information Management (EIM), provide examples of how SAP's EIM solutions are used today, and offer technical instructions on performing some of the most common EIM tasks in SAP. The second edition includes updates to chapters on SAP Data Services, SAP HANA, SAP Information Steward, SAP Master Data Governance, SAP Information Lifecycle Management, and SAP Extended Enterprise Content Management by OpenText, which are based on recent releases, as well as some new chapters on SAP Rapid Deployment solutions, SAP PowerDesigner, and SAP Hana Cloud Integration.

Target Groups of the Book

This book is intended for both experienced practitioners and those who are new to managing, governing, and maximizing the use of information that impacts enterprises. Specifically, it will be of use to business process experts, architects, data stewards, data owners, business process owners, analysts, and developers who are new to the topic of EIM in SAP. While there are several specific "how to build" and "how this works" sections, the book content requires no previous knowledge of EIM or SAP's solutions for EIM.

This book is also intended for existing information management experts who need to expand their skills from a specific EIM domain to broader information management strategies. This target group won't need to reference all chapters, but will be interested in new capability information provided in many (e.g., the latest release information and new products available).

Structure of the Book

This book is divided into two parts:

- **Part I: SAP's Enterprise Information Management Strategy and Portfolio**
  This part of the book starts by introducing EIM and its main concepts, including information governance and big data. After you understand the ideas behind

EIM, we move on to an overview of the solutions for EIM within SAP's portfolio, offering brief explanations of the main EIM solutions, as well as the rapid deployment paradigm for those solutions. Finally, Part I concludes with real-life examples of how SAP's EIM solutions are used by several different customers.

- **Part II: Working with SAP's Enterprise Information Management Solutions**
  This part of the book focuses on how to get started using SAP's solutions for EIM. Part II includes product details on topics ranging from understanding the current state of your data, to managing unstructured content and getting started with master data governance. This section focuses on select parts of SAP's EIM offerings with the goal of providing practical examples and step-by-step instructions for key SAP capabilities. You'll learn how to model your information landscape (SAP PowerDesigner), get started assessing and monitoring your data (SAP Information Steward), integrate both on-premise and cloud data sources (SAP Data Services and SAP HANA Cloud Integration), use data quality transforms (SAP Data Services), turn text data into data points (SAP Data Services), govern your master data (SAP Master Data Governance), manage structured and unstructured content that impacts business processes (SAP Extended Content Management by OpenText), and set retention rules and retire information (SAP Information Lifecycle Management).

With the division of the book into two major parts, you can read the different parts as you need them. Part I is critical to understanding EIM and the role it plays in SAP's strategy and portfolio. In Part II, you can access information and insight about the EIM capabilities that are most applicable to your projects, planning, and information management strategy.

More specifically, the book consists of the following chapters:

- **Chapter 1: Introducing Enterprise Information Management**
  This chapter provides an introduction to the concept of EIM. It defines EIM, discusses common use cases and business drivers for EIM, discusses the impact of big data on EIM, explains SAP's strategy for EIM, and discusses common user roles of people and organizations that are normally involved in EIM. You'll also get an introduction to NeedsEIM Inc., which is the fictional company used as a basis for examples throughout the book.
- **Chapter 2: Introducing Information Governance**
  Information governance is the practice of overseeing the management of your enterprise's information. It touches all aspects of EIM and must be considered in any EIM strategy. This chapter provides tips for developing your governance

standards and processes, and maps governance activities to technology enablers for these standards and processes.

- **Chapter 3: Big Data with SAP HANA, Hadoop, and EIM**
  This chapter introduces Big Data in the context of SAP's solutions for EIM. Specifically, it focuses on the role of SAP HANA and Hadoop.
- **Chapter 4: SAP's Solutions for Enterprise Information Management**
  This chapter describes SAP's solutions for EIM, introducing and providing overviews of specific products. After reading this chapter, you will be able to quickly identify which chapters in Part II are of the most interest to you.
- **Chapter 5: Rapid-Deployment Solutions for Enterprise Information Management**
  This chapter explains the rapid-deployment paradigm for EIM solutions with predefined best practices, setting a foundation for the deployment of SAP EIM solutions.
- **Chapter 6: Practical Examples of EIM**
  This chapter discusses specific examples of EIM application by various customers. Content discussed includes recommendations for your EIM architecture (written by Procter & Gamble), the evolution of SAP Data Services (written by National Vision), and tips for successful Enterprise Content Management projects (written by Belgian Railways). In addition, there are other customer-written sections on data migration, managing master data, data archiving strategy recommendations, and recommendations for positioning different SAP tools for data and process integration.
- **Chapter 7: SAP PowerDesigner**
  This chapter focuses on the discipline of enterprise information architecture, and how SAP PowerDesigner enables you to understand your current information landscape, align business information with technical implementation, and plan for change.
- **Chapter 8: SAP HANA Cloud Integration**
  Chapter 8 introduces SAP HANA Cloud Integration as SAP's solution for delivering integration between on-premise and cloud applications.
- **Chapter 9: SAP Data Services**
  Chapter 9 introduces SAP Data Services as a data foundation for EIM. It describes the components and architecture of SAP Data Services and walks you through specific examples of how to start doing data integration, data quality, and text data processing with SAP Data Services.

- **Chapter 10: SAP Information Steward**
  This chapter introduces SAP Information Steward, which can be used for profiling and getting to know the current state of your data. This chapter discusses cataloging your data assets, performing data profiling, and monitoring your data quality over time.
- **Chapter 11: SAP Master Data Governance**
  Chapter 11 describes how to get started using SAP Master Data Governance for your master data governance initiatives. It includes a description of SAP-provided master data governance processes and explains how to create custom governance processes. It also describes the use of SAP Business Workflow and BRFplus for governing master data. Finally, the chapter gives an example of using SAP Information Steward in conjunction with SAP Master Data Governance for monitoring and remediating master data.
- **Chapter 12: SAP Information Lifecycle Management**
  Chapter 12 provides background information on the concept of information lifecycle management. It then specifically introduces SAP Information Lifecycle Management, offering discussions of retention management, system decommissioning, and how SAP Information Lifecycle Management works to support the lifecycle of information.
- **Chapter 13: SAP Extended Enterprise Content Management by OpenText**
  Chapter 13 discusses the major features of SAP Extended Enterprise Content Management by OpenText, how it uses SAP ArchiveLink, and how it works with the SAP Business Suite.
- **Online Appendices**
  There are several appendices to assist you: Appendix A covers advanced data quality capabilities, Appendix B provides details on SAP's migration content, and Appendix C provides tips for your first data archiving projects. The appendices and an example spreadsheet for monitoring your data migration projects can be downloaded from the book's website at *http://www.sap-press.com/3666*.

Acknowledgments

This second edition would not have been possible without the incredible efforts of a diverse set of authors that contributed to the first edition of this book, guided to success by the spirited leadership of Ginger Gatling. They laid down a solid foundation to build upon.

The second edition brought back some familiar faces as well as some new, aspiring authors. Without exception, each brought fresh energy and commitment to provide valuable updates and new content to the book. It was a pleasure to work with each and every one of them, and I feel extremely appreciative for the extra time many put forth to make their updates meaningful and to keep the book on track. In addition, there were many other people that took time out of their already busy schedules to provide a fresh perspective or critical eye to the material. A special thank you to John Schitka, Ken Beutler, Marie Goodell, Connie Chan, Yingwu Gao, Bharath Ajendla, Anthony Hill, Michael Hill, and Niels Weigel—your willingness to contribute and provide feedback was truly appreciated. Finally, I would like to acknowledge my manager, Subha Ramachandran, for supporting this project as a priority for me and others in the organization.

All of the royalties from this book will continue to be donated to Doctors Without Borders (*Médecins Sans Frontières*). Your purchase of this book helps us support an international medical humanitarian organization that delivers emergency aid in many countries. Thank you for enabling us to provide financial support to this important organization and its critical mission.

I hope the book becomes a valuable resource to you and your understanding of Enterprise Information Management with SAP. Enjoy!

Corrie Brague
Enterprise Information Management Product Management
SAP Labs, LLC

PART I
SAP's Enterprise Information Management Strategy and Portfolio

This chapter introduces Enterprise Information Management, including common use cases and big data. It also provides an overview of SAP's strategy for Enterprise Information Management.

1 Introducing Enterprise Information Management

Cloud, big data, and social media are powering new opportunities for companies that can leverage information-driven insights in real time to respond to customer preferences, identify operational efficiencies, and in some cases, create completely new business models. To achieve transformative business results, best-run businesses treat information as a corporate asset. It's carefully managed, thoughtfully governed, strategically used, and sensibly controlled.

Effective management of enterprise information can help your organization run faster. As a result, you can achieve new business outcomes: understanding and retaining your customers, getting the most from your suppliers, ensuring compliance without increasing your risk, and providing internal transparency to drive operational and strategic decisions.

SAP helps businesses run better and more simply by enabling IT to more easily manage and optimize enterprise information. SAP solutions for *Enterprise Information Management* (EIM) provide the critical capabilities to architect, integrate, improve, manage, associate, and archive all information. This chapter introduces EIM and explains what it is, why it's important to organizations, how it fits into SAP's strategy, and some typical user roles. Finally, the chapter concludes by introducing NeedsEIM Inc., a fictional company that we'll use throughout the book to illustrate EIM principles.

1.1 Defining Enterprise Information Management

On Gartner's IT glossary page, Enterprise Information Management is defined as "an integrative discipline for structuring, describing and governing information assets across organizational and technological boundaries to improve efficiency, promote transparency, and enable business insight."[1]

EIM involves a strategic and governed execution of the following disciplines: enterprise architecture, data integration, data quality, master data management, content management, and lifecycle management. It addresses the management of all types of information, including traditional structured data, semi-structured and unstructured data, and content such as documents, emails, audio, video, and so forth.

To optimize the use and cost of managing information, we must first understand its lifecycle. The active management and governance of information helps in avoiding the costs that are associated with blind information hoarding. The risk of having too much information is just as real as not having enough when you need it.

Figure 1.1 shows a typical spend on information over time. This is a technology *and* resources spend curve. What may be surprising for most organizations is the increase in spend during the off-boarding phase. Many companies spend a lot of money maintaining information that is out of control. Is the information still used? In what systems? Can you decommission those systems? Are you managing pieces of information that are no longer used?

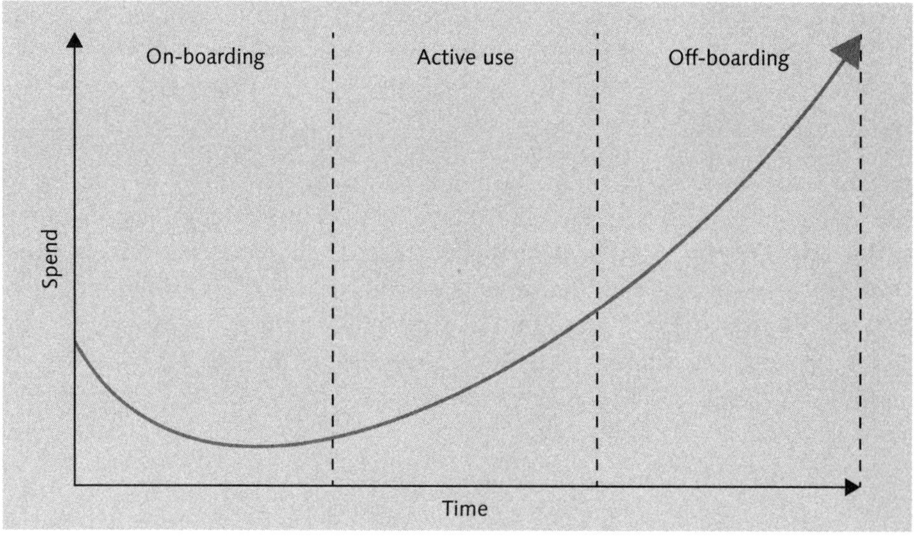

Figure 1.1 Typical Spend on Information Over Time

1 Source: *http://www.gartner.com/it-glossary/enterprise-information-management-eim/*

As illustrated in Figure 1.1, there's an associated cost in bringing information into an organization, using the information, and hopefully retiring the information after it's no longer producing value. The idea that organizations really just do three things with information—on-board, actively use, and then off-board—is powerful when thinking about EIM solutions.

After information is brought into your organization, it's required for many uses beyond its original purpose. Hence, it's advantageous to prepare the information for these manifold uses. That way, the effort to repurpose information during the active-use phase is greatly reduced. When the information is no longer required, it should be off-boarded or retired in a manner that meets your organization's legal and business requirements. The truth is that most organizations don't proactively consider the reuse and eventual off-boarding of information, which ends up costing millions in IT resources due to maintaining systems that are no longer used.

If you adopt an information strategy, the spend changes to what is shown in Figure 1.2.

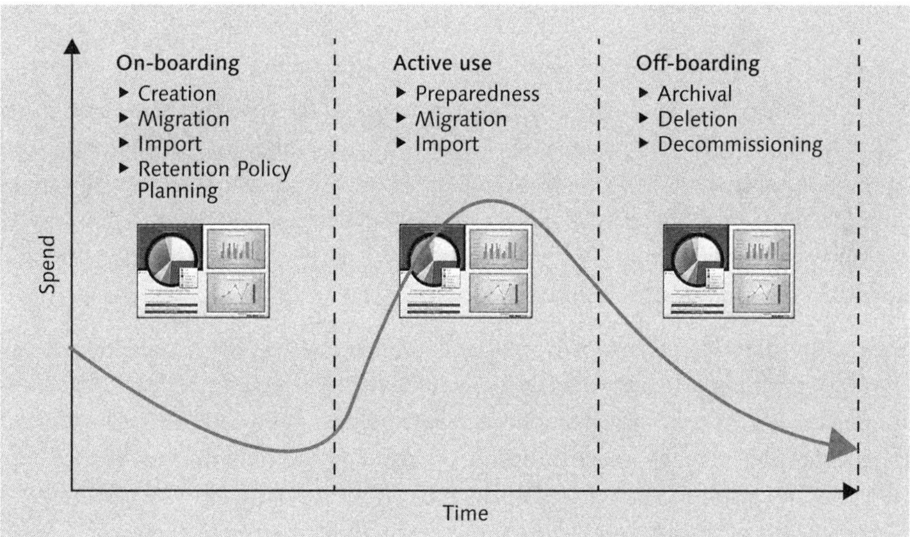

Figure 1.2 Spend on Information with an Enterprise Information Management Strategy

Figure 1.2 also provides detailed examples of the types of activities involved with EIM across the typical lifecycle of information. In the on-boarding phase, activities include the creation of information through online user creation, integration of processes that involves the creation of new information, import of information, and migration of information. Additionally, the on-boarding phase should include lifecycle planning (e.g., how long the information should be retained). Implementing governance and retention policies as the information is on-boarded dramatically lowers the cost of information over its effective lifetime. Notice that there is still some spend increase as information is actively used. This is from incrementally improving, enriching, and preparing information for alternative uses. The key to bending the cost curve down is understanding that information has tremendous value beyond its original purpose and proactively planning for that in your EIM strategy. The result is that the spend curve goes down over time in the active-use phase as information is simply repurposed. Again, this can be achieved because the incremental cost is just the provisioning of existing known and trusted information—as opposed to starting over for each new information initiative.

Next, we'll look at an example of information flow through a company and then discuss how this relates to information management.

1.1.1 Example of Information Flow through a Company

NeedsEIM Inc. is a fictional company that's based on real customer examples. We'll explain NeedsEIM Inc. in detail in Section 1.7 and again throughout Part II of the book when we describe how to use various EIM capabilities. For now, we want to introduce NeedsEIM and the types of information it must deal with, including how information flows through the company. This leads to a discussion about the types of information included in EIM.

Figure 1.3 depicts the business processes of NeedsEIM. It manufactures retail durable goods, and the majority of its manufacturing is outsourced. This business model results in a complex and diverse supplier network that impacts most departments. The major departments include finance, which must deal with supplier payments, and the engineering and contracts department, which must coordinate contracts and technical spec drawings with the manufacturers.

The IT department must deal with diverse systems, including SAP and non-SAP systems. The procurement department is responsible for the supplier relationships and ensuring the company gets the most from its suppliers. The sales department is always looking for new and creative sales channels, including opportunities in the supplier population.

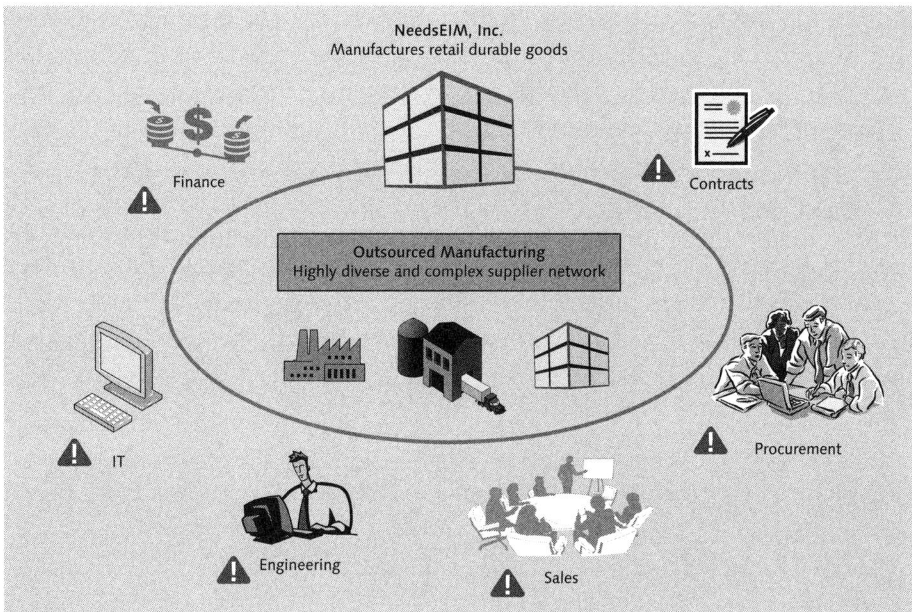

Figure 1.3 NeedsEIM Inc.

As an example of information flow through NeedsEIM Inc., let's look at the process of contract negotiations with a supplier:

1. The proposed supplier must be researched for due diligence, including type of products or services provided, similar customers serviced, reference calls with current customers, quality history, financial and credit ratings, reliability and trustworthiness, and general reputation.
   - This involves emails, online research, and getting information from external sources such as Dun & Bradstreet.
   - This information is shared among the finance, engineering, procurement, and contracts departments.
2. Assuming the due diligence indicates that the supplier is approved, the supplier master data needs to be created and distributed to related systems. The scope, projects, pricing, contracts, and legal documents must be created.
   - This involves most departments and includes sales if the durable goods price point might be impacted.
   - The supplier sends and receives legal, technical, financial, and other information.

3. After the contracts are negotiated, the supplier requires ongoing communication, including technical drawings, bills of materials, and other information required to do the work. In addition, financial documents such as invoices, purchase orders, and so on are exchanged.
   - This includes a lot of collaboration among engineering, contracts, procurement, and the supplier.

Figure 1.4 shows the information as it needs to flow through each department. Departments use the information with their perspective in mind: They store it, update it, download it, and ensure that it meets the requirements for their department's role with the supplier.

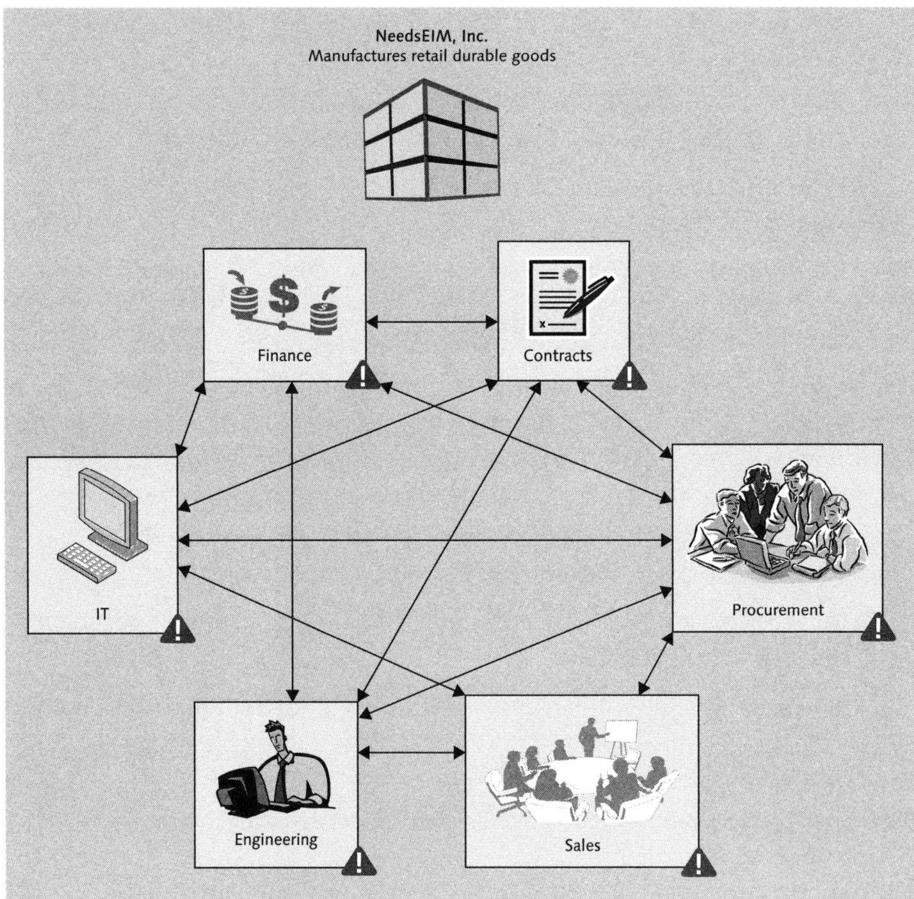

Figure 1.4 Example Information Flow for NeedsEIM Inc.

As you can see in Figure 1.4, the reality is that information is often required by many departments. Sometimes when the information doesn't move from one department to another due to application, political, and/or departmental silos, departments create their own "tribal" versions of the information, and each department has a different sense of its ownership of the information. (We'll talk more about tribal information in Section 1.3.2.)

Earlier, we mentioned several kinds of information needed for negotiations with a supplier. This includes detailed information on the supplier, external references for the supplier, pricing and detailed contract information, engineering documents of what the supplier will provide or build for NeedsEIM Inc., as well as billing, invoicing, and all the typical supplier interactions. The next section will break this down further into types of information that are required and how this information is included in EIM.

1.1.2 Types of Information Included in Enterprise Information Management

Figure 1.5 shows the types of information that are included in SAP solutions for EIM that will be covered in this book.

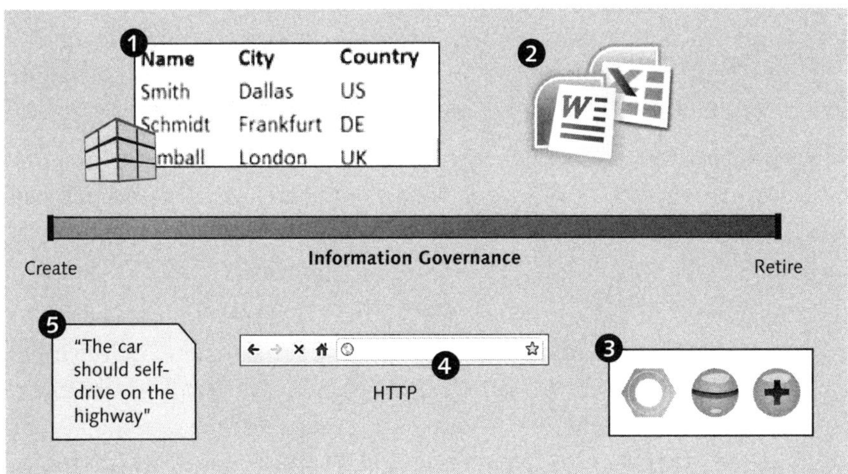

Figure 1.5 Types of Information Included in Enterprise Information Management

These information types are relevant for most companies, including NeedsEIM Inc. The following provides more information about these types:

❶ **Structured data**
This includes the familiar data that's used within an application system (e.g., customers, products, and sales orders); for example, supplier information such as name, address, credit information, contact information, and so on. This also includes all purchase orders, sales orders, and other data that's related to this supplier.

❷ **Desktop documents**
These include Microsoft Word, Microsoft Excel, Adobe Acrobat, and other desktop application documents. This data is stored across the enterprise on shared drives and laptops, which means that much of it isn't controlled at an enterprise level. This content may be critical to the application data, so you need to manage it with the same importance as the structured data in the database. Examples include purchasing documents (e.g., invoices), contracts with suppliers, legal documents, résumés, and HR documents, to name a few.

❸ **Pictures, scanned documents, videos, and other images**
These could be scanned invoices, videos, pictures of products that are sold in a catalog, and drawings of products that are being designed and built. These become part of the content that needs to be managed and related to the structured data when required. Managing content that's associated with a core business process is becoming increasingly important to process efficiency and regulatory compliance. Examples of such content include engineering documents that are to be shared with suppliers, pictures of raw materials, routine maintenance records in asset management, invoices, and expense report receipts.

❹ **Semi-structured data**
This is information such as RSS feeds, blogs and posts, emails associated with purchasing documents, and other semi-structured information that's important to the enterprise.

❺ **Text data**
In Figure 1.5, the piece of information that reads "The car should self-drive on the highway" may come from a survey or be a comment on a social media or other website and, by itself, might not be important. However, if you're looking at car design over the next five years, and 60% of the comments you receive include something about self-driving, this comment warrants further investigation. Information management includes looking into text you receive and analysis to determine sentiment, feedback, input, or actions that should be taken based on comments. Examples of text data include comments from supplier's

manufacturing process, feedback from internal departments, and comments on surveys and service tickets.

As you can see, EIM includes the support of traditional structured data and unstructured information, from the moment of creation through retirement. The retirement of data and information has the same value as creation. After information is no longer needed, it becomes a liability—a legal liability, a cost liability, or some other kind of liability. The entire life span of the data and information, and the governance of that information, is covered in EIM.

1.2 Common Use Cases for EIM

There are many use cases for EIM solutions. Three of the primary scenarios include the support of operational, analytical, and information governance initiatives.

1.2.1 EIM for Operational Initiatives

This scenario covers the use of EIM in the operation and execution of business processes and tasks that happen throughout the day. It has very broad applications, from ensuring that material replenishment data is set correctly, to customer data quality management, to migrating new data from a merger, to ensuring that all contracts and documents are available for the business process, to removing data that is no longer required.

SAP solutions for EIM provide trusted data to drive and deliver best practice business processes. This value includes the ability to holistically manage data within business processes, ensuring the quality and ability to reuse the data.

Here are a few examples of operational uses of EIM:

- **Cloud integration**
  As more business applications are running in the cloud, organizations need a way to integrate business processes and data between on-premise and cloud systems.
- **Data migration due to mergers, acquisitions, and global implementations across all industries**
  Information management lowers the risk of business and application disruption during mergers, acquisitions, and new application implementations.

- **Harmonized master data across line of businesses**
  Harmonized master data across disparate applications enables a single view of master data across the enterprise.
- **Compliance and regulations in the financial industry**
  The financial industry has requirements for financial risk-related data analysis. All data must meet quality levels and industry standards, and all associated content (e.g., documents and invoices) must be correctly associated to financial contracts.
- **Suspect tracking in public safety organizations**
  Federal, local, and state agencies must share information on criminal activity and suspect tracking. Information management ensures that each new suspect is compared to others to confirm that it's a unique suspect. Data quality rules can ensure that the most up-to-date information is available for suspect tracking.
- **Retaining and deleting information in the pharmaceutical industry**
  During the development of new medicines, all documents and government standards must be adhered to through various stages of research, development, trial, and release. When the compliance period has ended, information should be removed unless it's required for a legal hold.
- **Fraud detection in telecommunication and other industries**
  Telecommunications, media, high tech, and utilities share similar requirements for capturing, addressing, and mitigating fraudulent activity. Large volumes of data and real-time transactions place these industries at increased risk, as perpetrators can be "on and gone" before they are caught using traditional time-consuming software reporting methods provided by vendors today. Information management enables the filtering of diverse data to determine where the company is losing money across a broad spectrum of applications and business processes.
- **Plant maintenance compliance and data assessment**
  Ensuring that the virtual plant aligns with the physical plant, information management ensures that maintenance plans and documents are associated with each asset, asset tags are accurate, functional location information is complete, and all asset document and maintenance guides are available on the plant floor.
- **Data quality and data assessment in the retail industry**
  The retail industry requires high data quality; for instance, retailers must know article data throughout all stores where the articles are sold. For retailers, data

quality and assessment is an ongoing business process; it includes, for example, tracking articles that have not been maintained in required stores, articles missing valid sales price conditions, articles missing required procurement data, and articles with duplicate EAN codes.

Notice that many of these examples are focused on ensuring that information is managed, is available, is reliable, and serves the operational business process; the list can go on and on.

Chapter 6 provides more detailed real-world and practical scenarios for EIM.

1.2.2 EIM for Analytical Use Cases

EIM has a long history in business intelligence (BI) and analytics. If you look at some definitions of EIM online, you'll see statements saying that EIM drives decision-making analytics. Many of the operational use cases mentioned previously also fit into operational reporting and have some reuse for strategic reporting and analytics as well. Some examples of EIM for BI and analytics include the following:

- **Big data analysis**
  To unlock the potential of big data sources, EIM provides the capabilities to access and understand data from any source and variety, including Hadoop, and integrates it with existing data for better analysis of customer sentiment, fraud detection, new innovation opportunities, and competitive insights.
- **Analysis of supplier spend**
  Analysis of who are the top suppliers, how much they spend, and payment and credit issues can only be done if supplier records are transparent and harmonized, cleansed, and de-duplicated. When making decisions that are related to the supply network, the supplier data must be accurate and trusted.
- **True cost assessment of manufacturing goods in the manufacturing industry**
  Analyze total costs for making and delivering products. Crossing multiple business domains, data must be cleansed, duplicates removed, and correlations created to ensure that analysis provides accurate information.
- **Bring together timely, accurate, and actionable data to provide insights into the factors impacting sales and customer behavior**
  Silos of data sources and applications, limited business user access, and dependence on IT to create reports limits the ability of a business to gain insights on

sales and customer behavior. Information management brings together the data and provides data lineage and analysis so the users can create reports and know where the data is coming from.

- **Text mining to understand opinion and sentiment**
  Text and rich media content that's accessible on the web or on social media sites contain a lot of information that can be analyzed and used for sentiment analysis to get a better understanding of consumer opinions about a product or idea.

1.2.3 EIM for Information Governance

A primary use case for EIM is the management and governance of information as a strategic asset, usually referred to as *information governance*. Information governance is a discipline that oversees the management of your enterprise's information. Without it, there is no EIM. Information governance involves people, processes, policies, and technologies in support of managing information across the organization. It's advisable to have some degree of information governance in place for any EIM use case, analytical or operational, as this provides a framework for the enterprise to reuse policies, standards, and organizational best practices.

Information governance is the linchpin of EIM that empowers business users to own and manage data as a strategic asset, governs data in the business process to optimize operational performance and ensure compliance, and establishes trust in structured and unstructured information by ensuring data quality throughout its lifecycle.

Information governance will be a common thread throughout the book and will be covered in more detail in Chapter 2.

1.3 Common Drivers for EIM

Information can be a strategic weapon if an organization manages enterprise assets such as capital. Treating information as an organizational asset recognizes that it moves from a single-purpose use to something that must be managed for multiple uses.

Common business problems that require an EIM strategy often may not have the words *information, enterprise, management, data,* or *governance* in them. The business issues driving initiatives for EIM include (but are not limited to) trucks going out at the wrong weight, deliveries to the wrong location, hazardous products not in compliance with government standards, customer satisfaction issues, incorrect billing, misunderstood supplier networks, services that don't align with customer demand, lack of compliance with a government mandate that impacts payments or revenue, and so on. Many process issues are the result of a lack of an information management strategy—from poor-quality data to master data not being updated correctly, to not having the documents required for order processing, to financial documents not aligned with sales documents, to different parts of the organization using similar terms in different ways.

Adoption of EIM capabilities is usually driven by a few fundamental needs—responding to a growing set of compliance requirements, improved operational efficiency, and the strategic application of information to better manage your organization and gain competitive advantage.

Next, we discuss specific examples of issues as drivers of EIM adoption.

1.3.1 Operational Efficiency as a Driver of EIM

Operational efficiency includes many moving parts to ensure the company has an improved operational margin. From the EIM perspective, operational efficiency includes the provisioning and preparation of data so that it can be used to keep the business running well. The following subsections describe typical operational efficiency scenarios and the role of EIM.

Improving Payment Processing

The time that's taken to collect payments and the improvement of payment processing is critical in all industries, and is heavily impacted by the quality of the data. One example is the healthcare industry, in which it's critical to ensure that hospitals collect what they should from government agencies such as Medicare and Medicaid in the United States. Effectively provisioning data from disparate systems ensures data compliance with U.S. laws for Medicare and Medicaid and enables hospitals to receive their payments, having an impact in the millions of dollars.

Ensuring a Successful SAP ERP Go-Live

An SAP customer was implementing a new SAP system and had to migrate data from many non-SAP data sources. The customer was concerned about the large volumes of data to migrate from both the parent company and a variety of subsidiaries. It was critical that the entire business not be on hold during the migration, and the data from the migration had to be loaded accurately and safely. The requirement from the customer was a single, integrated application providing a high degree of visibility that could be easily rolled out to multiple subsidiaries, eliminating hours of custom coding to load data into the SAP system. SAP's EIM solutions were used to extract data from third-party applications and support a smooth transfer to a new environment. This automated approach saved valuable resources and expedited data migration processes, resulting in a smooth—and on-time—go-live, reducing the overall cost of the implementation.

Consolidating Systems to Improve Information Management and Reduce IT Spend

An SAP customer ran 80% of its business with several SAP systems and wanted to reduce IT costs and improve transparency of information across the systems. The company had 8 SAP systems when only 3 were needed and more than 400 non-SAP systems, most of which could be retired. EIM's role in this included the assessment, alignment, migration, and retirement of data and legacy systems and ensuring that the 3 remaining SAP systems had accurate and timely information.

Speaking the Same Language to Increase Operational Efficiency

Another SAP customer had issues where no one spoke the same language. For example, the term *margin* covered different realities depending on the department and employees concerned. To set things right, the company specified four objectives for itself: to centralize its data in a common environment; to secure the data; to make the data more reliable, especially for management access; and to standardize its vocabulary for indicators. EIM accelerates employee access to information and, as a result, saves significantly on the amount of time required to perform routine tasks. Teams made enormous gains in responsiveness. Where it previously took one week for data to be available after accounts were closed, the operation is now instantaneous.

1.3.2 Information as an Organizational Asset

All organizations have assets—capital, employees, materials, brands, and physical and intellectual property—that are all managed carefully. Information is similar, as it, too, is an asset that must be managed and protected. With the right EIM strategy, information can be leveraged and used as an organizational asset. We'll now discuss some specific examples of how actual companies use information as an organizational asset.

Improving Patient Care and Payer Response

An SAP customer is a large hospital conglomerate focused on first-class patient care and creating innovative ways to improve care. First-class patient care requires the management of information in large volumes and with daunting complexity. EIM was used to extract, transform, integrate, cleanse, load, and correlate patient records from many diverse systems for analysis by doctors and line managers. The cleansed and aligned data enabled line managers to improve operational efficiency (including aligning information across multiple hospitals). The project extended the use of information such that doctors now have the ability to "slice and dice" information as needed on patient groups and to provide recommended treatments and wellness programs based on trends, including re-admittance trends, long-term performance of different treatments, and so on. The other focus of the project was to ensure a high quality level of data provided to and by patients. The improved data quality improved patient service, which led to improved payments by payers, resulting in the collection of several million outstanding dollars.

Growing Past "Tribal Knowledge" to "Enterprise Information"

A large SAP customer had a wealth of information that was vitally needed across departmental lines, but the information—documents, spreadsheets, manuals—was locked up in information silos. Shared—or nonshared—hard drives, separate portals, and multiple content repositories held the data, with no central search or access capability. This resulted in "tribal knowledge;" the different departments could usually find the information that their employees created, but this information wasn't effectively shared with other departments. By implementing a strategic Enterprise Content Management (ECM) and global search capability, the customer was able to create a single enterprise information store that all employees could search and use, regardless of department.

Improving Data Quality for Customer Interactions

Another SAP customer had a goal to create a 360-degree view of customer data for sales, marketing, and service. EIM was used to consolidate heterogeneous data into a single database; integrate structures and processes across sales, marketing, and service; and ensure a systematic information exchange between field sales and sales support. Improved customer data quality strengthened dialogue with these customers and systematized customer-related processes across sales, marketing, and service. The data quality improvement and improved transparency drove a new structured quotation process. The new process provides time savings and fewer errors when creating quotations.

1.3.3 Compliance as a Driver of EIM

As governmental regulations and controls increase, and the cost of legal issues due to data issues rises, compliance plays a key role in most industries. Every company and its network of suppliers that produce a durable good that ends up in a shopping cart have compliance requirements. Other organizations, such as utilities, government agencies, security, and financial service providers, are also subject to regulatory and compliance issues. In addition to industries, countries have import and export regulations that impact the ability to do business globally.

In the following subsections, we discuss some general examples of compliance issues that indicate a need for an information management strategy.

Keeping Data Too Long

For regulatory compliance, companies must ensure that they keep retention-relevant data for a minimum period of time, as defined by retention laws. They must also ensure that certain data is purged from the system. For example, data privacy laws mandate the destruction of person-related data after a specified period of time. In Germany, companies must delete data from rejected job applicants in their HR systems not earlier than 6 months, but not later than 12 months, after the applicant was rejected. Failing to comply with these regulations may result in large fines for companies. Another example is a pharmaceutical company that must keep information related to a new clinical trial for a number of years. After that time has passed, the information should be deleted. Not deleting sensitive information after the required retention period increases the risk from potential lawsuits.

Building According to Specs

Remember the Mars probe? Launched in 1999, the Mars Climate Orbiter was designed to gather amazing data to help scientists better understand the universe. However, none of that amazing data was gathered from the $125 million venture because groups working across the globe failed to operate under similar units of measure. Specifically, the American units of measurement used in construction had to be converted to metric units for operation. Core information management principles could have helped alleviate this risk by documenting the data definitions and outlining use of that data throughout the data's lifecycle.

Maintaining Industry Standards for Data

Some external standards apply to entire industries. For example, global standards (GS1 standards) aim to help companies exchange information in the same format, thereby increasing the efficiency and visibility of supply and demand chains globally.[2] To participate, however, you not only need to understand the relevant GS1 standard, but you must also fully understand your data, the data model, and current data quality levels. Without this baseline understanding, your use of GS1 would be flawed at best, and you would miss golden optimization opportunities.

1.4 Impact of Big Data on EIM

It's well documented that the volume of data created in organizations is large and growing at an unprecedented velocity. Organizational datastores are now commonly measured in terabytes or even petabytes. There are many reasons for the unparalleled growth in datastores: social media, compliance and regulatory requirements, transactional data, sensory data (such as data from real-time shop floor sensors), multimedia content, mobile devices, RFID-enabled devices, the "internet of things" (connected devices), the never-ending quest to improve organizational effectiveness, and the list goes on. The fact is that data creation has become a by-product of nearly all individual and organizational activities.

Moreover, the reason data is preserved and reused is that it has value well beyond its original use. We dare to say that the value of the data created to automate business processes may in some cases be greater than the process itself. Today, the

2 Source: *http://www.GS1.org/about/overview*

market has christened the phenomena of organizations' desire to harness the great torrent of data, as well as the velocity, variety, and variability of information known as *big data*. Figure 1.6 is a representation of the volume, velocity, variety, and variability of data. It remains to be seen if the term *big data* will stick. However, as long as organizations can create value through data, the continued growth and importance of data will be immutable. Fortunately, advancements in computational power, storage capacity, information access and management, and analytics are progressing at an equally impressive rate. Two such advancements are Hadoop and SAP HANA (to be discussed further in Chapter 3). The combination of massively greater amounts of data with the tools and talent to analyze it promises to launch the next wave of innovation and productivity and even spawn new business models.

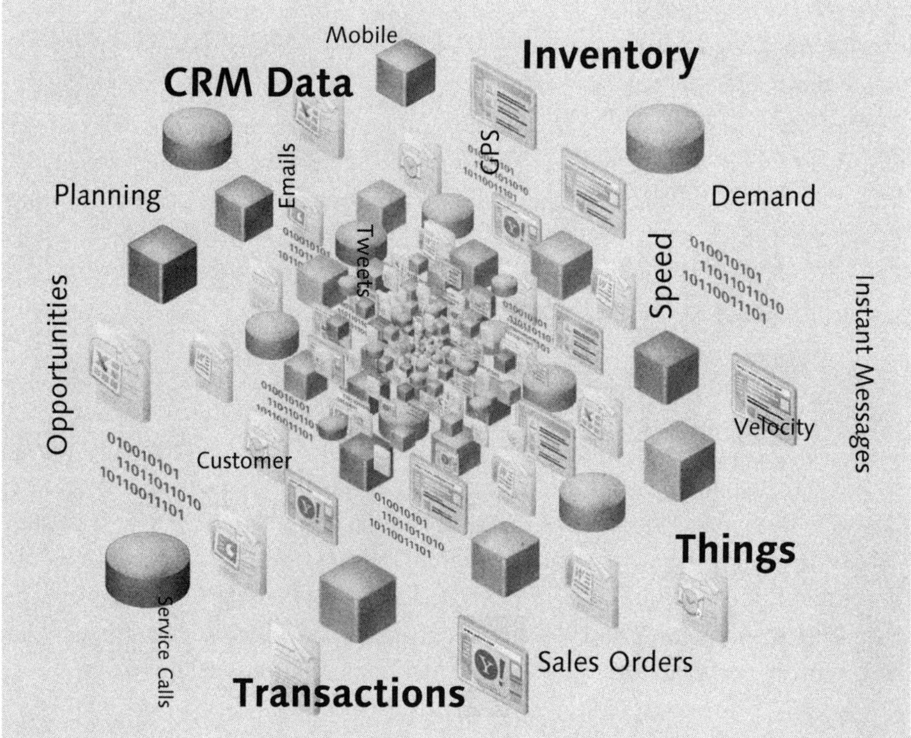

Figure 1.6 Information Growing in Volume, Velocity, Variety, and Variability

One example of new innovation provided by the ability to manage and analyze big data is in the healthcare industry, specifically related to the area of cancer treatment. The human genome contains 6 billion DNA base pairs; as the genome sequence for each patient will be decrypted in the near future, these billions of data points must be managed. Add to that documentation and features such as speech recognition, and you'll end up with 20 terabytes per patient.

The velocity of data collection is building daily, and you must manage and make sense of your data on the fly. You need to remain flexible through instability and change. You can't underestimate the pace of innovation, and you don't want to be playing catch-up with your competitors. If planning and implementing a coherent data management strategy seems daunting when your organization owns a few terabytes of data, how difficult will it be when you own thousands of terabytes?

The best way to realize the promise of big data, today and in the future, is to develop and adopt an EIM strategy. This strategy should cover your entire enterprise to take advantage of the benefits of sharing information and aggregating data across your organization. Typical topics that must be considered for an effective EIM strategy include interoperable data models, architectures for analytical and transactional data, integration architecture, analytical architecture, and information security and compliance. The goal is to have data that is shareable and can be leveraged over time within and across business units. The deployment of SAP solutions for EIM within a defined EIM strategy is a key starting point. The alternative is to have massive amounts of disintegrated and unreliable data analyzed fast.

"Garbage in, garbage out" is one of the oldest adages in information processing; when the volume of data reaches the big data stage, getting productive use of poorly managed information becomes the equivalent of searching for a priceless antique in a landfill.

1.5 SAP's Strategy for EIM

SAP recognizes the importance of maximizing the value of enterprise information in support of any data-driven analytical, operational, or governance initiatives. To achieve this, organizations need a comprehensive suite of solutions providing the capabilities from architect to archive. Figure 1.7 shows SAP solutions for EIM.

SAP solutions for EIM are comprehensive in functionality, including capabilities to support enterprise architecture, data integration, data quality, master data management, enterprise content management, and information lifecycle management.

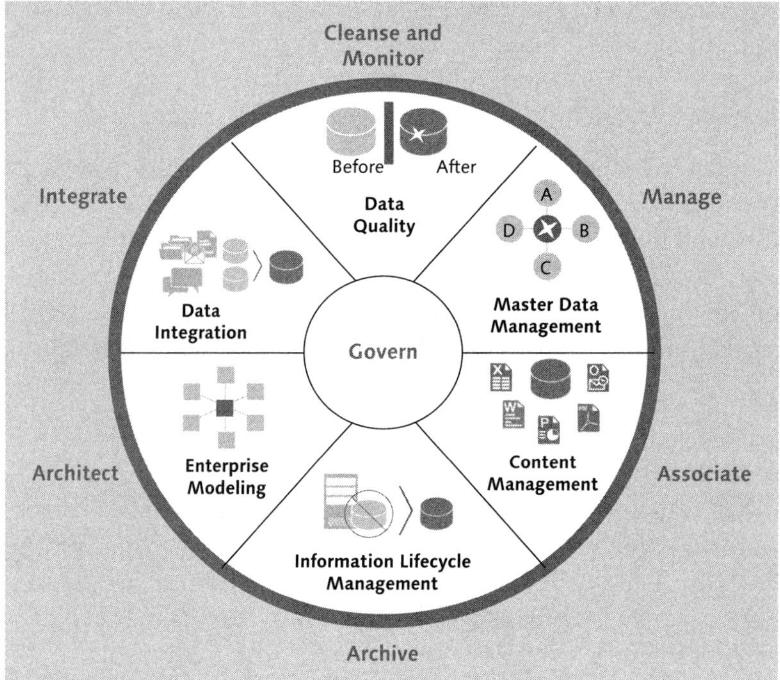

Figure 1.7 SAP Solutions for EIM

SAP solutions for EIM provide information across business applications, delivering complete and trusted information—both structured and unstructured—to your entire enterprise. SAP's investment in EIM is strong and will continue to grow as the requirement to provide data across many applications and databases on-premise and on the cloud grows. An overview of SAP solutions for EIM will be provided in Chapter 4.

1.6 Typical User Roles in EIM

Throughout the book, various user roles will be mentioned. The exact definition of EIM-related user roles varies by company; this section presents the common roles of people involved in EIM and the definitions assumed for this book. All these roles collaborate together for best results:

- **Data owner**
  A data owner role is accountable for the overall quality of a master data area. A

master data domain such as customer may have various cross-departmental contributors, but one individual will own a given master data area.

- **Data steward**
  A data steward understands data management practices and has domain knowledge for data and its impact on various business processes and business drivers. A data steward understands and develops policies and rules for data quality, text analytics, and information governance.
- **Global data manager/manager of master data**
  The global data manager manages the data governance program across IT and the business units. This person may also manage the data stewards, development teams, and migration activities.
- **Data analyst/IT analyst/business data analyst**
  The analyst performs data profiling and quality assessment, defines validation rules and data quality scorecards, determines cleansing requirements, and analyzes metadata impact and lineage.
- **Business process owner**
  A business process owner role is accountable for developing and implementing a strategy for a business area. The role is accountable for identifying improvements, driving standardization, and monitoring/measuring the process.
- **Business process manager**
  A business process manager role is responsible for developing various business processes per the strategy developed by the business process owner. The role is responsible for identifying improvements, driving standardization, and monitoring/measuring the process.
- **Chief data officer**
  A chief data officer (CDO) is a corporate officer responsible for information usage and governance as an asset. This role is increasingly prominent as organizations recognize the business potential for information.

1.7 Example Company: NeedsEIM Inc.

In this section (first mentioned in Section 1.1.1), we describe the fictional scenario that we'll refer to throughout the book. It depicts a company that needs an information strategy for its complex supplier network. This company is called NeedsEIM Inc.

NeedsEIM Inc. is a Fortune 500 company specializing in the manufacture of retail durable goods. It has outsourced the manufacturing to different contract manufacturers, but still has to deal with a vast supplier network in procuring finished goods, raw materials, and services to support the enterprise.

NeedsEIM Inc. has several business challenges, described in the following sections and shown in Figure 1.8.

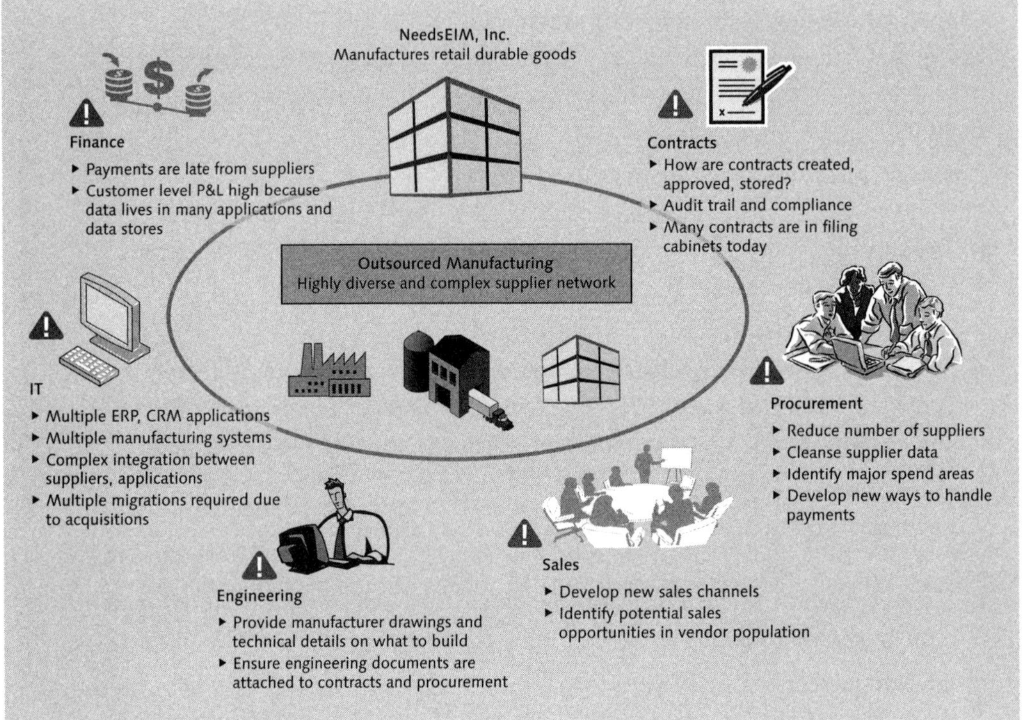

Figure 1.8 NeedsEIM Inc. Use Case

1.7.1 CFO Issues

Legal issues around vendor contracts have caused major disruptions in the past. The chief financial officer wants to get a handle on how contracts are created, approved, and stored so that the required audit trail and documentation is available in a timely manner.

1.7.2 Purchasing Issues

The vice president of purchasing has issued a different mandate: to decrease the number of suppliers, identify major spend areas, and develop new ways to handle payments to suppliers. There is a cost associated with paying a supplier through a credit card versus bank account ACH transaction versus check. The goal is to optimize the mix so that the payment costs are efficiently managed.

1.7.3 Sales Issues

The sales director is interested in developing new channels and identifying potential sales opportunities in the vendor population. Current processes are manual and time-consuming, consisting of spreadsheet analysis that compares all customers with vendors. Inconsistent data makes it hard to conduct any reliable and repeatable analysis. The sales director also faces a similar problem on contract management, where all documents are currently in filing cabinets, and any disputes or questions require staff poring over paper documents. In addition, it's hard to do any customer-level profit and loss analysis given the state of data. Multiple ERP, procurement, customer relationship management (CRM), and manufacturing systems make it that much harder to rationalize and do any type of analysis that can be actionable.

1.7.4 Engineering and Contracts Issues

The engineering department has received escalations of the products not being built to the correct specifications provided by engineering. The contracts and engineering departments are both trying to ensure that the legal contracts with the manufacturers have the correct drawings and technical details, and that all changes go through contracts back to the manufacturer.

1.7.5 Information Management Challenges Facing NeedsEIM Inc.

NeedsEIM Inc. is typical of a company with a diverse supplier network and outsourced manufacturing. None of the issues that were discussed earlier make it immediately obvious that the answer is a need for better information management, but as you examine the problems, it becomes clear. Notice, most importantly, that most of the issues are cross-departmental: The different organizations need information provided by another organization, or the organizations need to ensure that they are providing and making decisions based on the same information. Thus, while no one is screaming for an information management strategy, an information strategy is the building block to addressing the business concerns of NeedsEIM Inc. Key information management challenges facing NeedsEIM Inc. include the following:

- Identifying and managing customer, supplier, and analysis of master data
- Need for audit trail and workflow for contracts and unstructured data
- Ability to link unstructured data to master data
- Integration between disparate systems

Throughout the book, NeedsEIM Inc. will be referred to when we look at specific capabilities of EIM and how they can help address business issues.

1.8 Summary

In this chapter, we introduced you to Enterprise Information Management (EIM) and presented many real-world problems that EIM may address. It's likely that you or your company are already addressing these challenges, but without proper information governance, using disparate information management tools, and on an ad hoc basis. This is an expensive and unsustainable model for managing an ever-increasing volume of business-critical information across the entire organization. We're advocating that you, and all companies, prioritize the management of information as a strategic asset. As EIM is adopted, you can free your people to use information to solve big strategic problems instead of fighting daily data fires.

This chapter has looked at the key drivers for having an EIM strategy and introduced NeedsEIM Inc., which is the fictional company used as an example throughout the book. Subsequent chapters will examine information governance, EIM and SAP HANA, examples of EIM and how it's used today, and key parts of SAP solutions for EIM. We'll also provide concrete examples for getting you started using EIM.

By bringing together the right people, processes, policies, and metrics, an information governance discipline ensures trusted, consistent, and clear information throughout your organization.

2 Introducing Information Governance

Information governance is a discipline for treating your information as an asset for the enterprise. It provides oversight to ensure successful execution of your information initiatives and involves the management of people, technology, and processes based on policies, standards, and metrics, including the ongoing oversight necessary to manage information risks.

Information Governance versus Data Governance

The terms *information governance* and *data governance* are sometimes used interchangeably. SAP uses *information governance* because it's a broader term that indicates how the practice must expand beyond master data to include rich content (documents and PDFs), archiving and retention policies, and the business process context of that information.

By following the approaches that are outlined in this chapter, you'll learn how to establish an effective information governance program, so an information governance team can deliver information-driven projects both on time and without excessive rework. These new-found skills can also be reused for the next information project, which reduces cost.

The chapter begins by introducing information governance and then discusses the following topics:

- How to evaluate your existing information governance needs and resources, including establishing a plan for maturing your information governance policies.
- How to optimize existing infrastructure and resources to maximize the value of information governance.

- How to establish an information governance process by following a few key examples (creating a new reseller, supplier registration, and data migration).
- How to round out your information governance processes with key practices of identifying the impact of missing data, gathering metrics and key performance indicators (KPIs), and establishing a before-and-after view of your organization.

2.1 Introduction to Information Governance

Information governance touches all aspects of Enterprise Information Management (EIM), from information discovery, to data integration, to Enterprise Content Management (ECM), to retention and archiving policies. Figure 2.1 shows some of the key information-heavy use scenarios (scenarios where information provides critical elements, such as business analytics) where you should apply information governance principles.

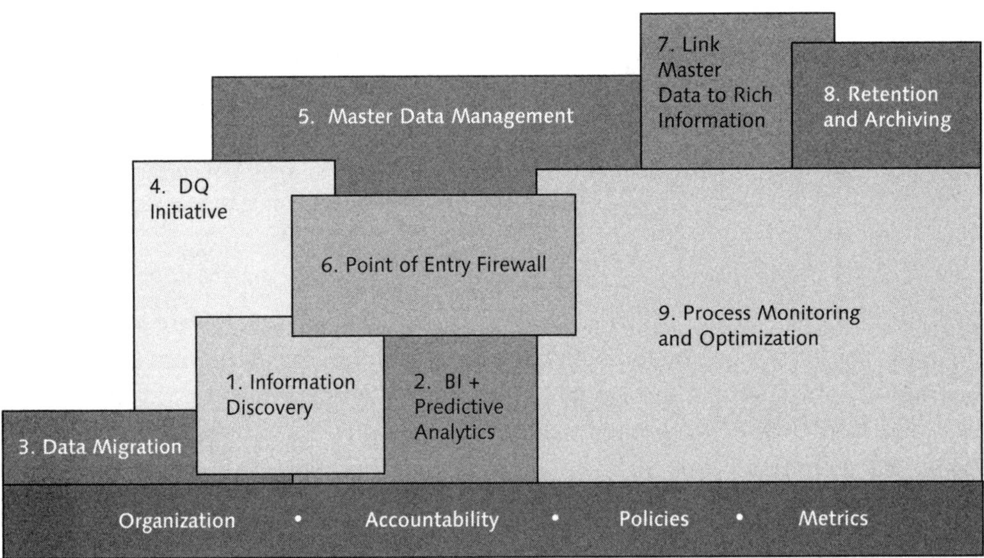

Figure 2.1 Information Governance Use Scenario Phasing

By now, most chief information officers (CIOs) have heard the phrase "information as a strategic asset" or "enterprise data assets." On the surface, this sounds really important. But how many organizations know what it means to tactically execute on information as an asset? Most corporations are just scratching the surface of which practices to put in place to support data as an enterprise asset. Whether you're part of management or of an IT department, it's important to move beyond this basic understanding and begin employing practical applications of the idea. If your company has any of the following characteristics, then providing governance of how information is managed or used is key to mitigating risks (operational and legal) and optimizing value:

- Legal requirements
- Regulatory and standards compliance
- Information-driven projects such as business process engineering, predictive analytics, and strategic initiatives

Several aspects of information can be governed:

- **People**
  - Informational ownership and accountability
  - Information access (who, when, where, what)
- **Processes**
  - Data handling (creating, updating, deleting)
  - Information storing (archiving, security)
- **Metrics**
  - Data quality levels
  - Reporting (who, when, what)
- **Policies and standards**
  - Data definitions
  - Allowable values
  - Information architecture

It's important not to underestimate how business processes rely on good information. To make this concept clear, let's consider an example from the airline industry.

Information as a Strategic Asset from the Airline Industry

Southwest Airlines had an issue with a Boeing 737-300, in which the Boeing experienced a ripped fuselage shortly after takeoff. Southwest then voluntarily canceled at least 600 flights in the week following the emergency landing.

After much analysis, the Federal Aviation Administration (FAA) issued an emergency directive requiring electromagnetic inspections of Boeing 737-300, -400, and -500 airplanes with a specific number of takeoff-and-landing cycles—more than 30,000 planes. The goal of these inspections was to proactively find signs of excessive wear.

Imagine the information governance that the FAA, Boeing, and individual airlines must have in place. First, the companies had to very quickly identify the causal issue, based on detailed maintenance logs, manufacturer data, and even the specific manufacturing processes involved. Next, the companies had to just as quickly do some predictive analytics to find where similar problems may be lurking to stop a disaster before it occurs. These predictive analytics had to be run across the individual airlines and had to take into account multiple parameters: manufacturer, manufacturing process, model numbers, inspection logs, and more. As if that wasn't enough, Southwest Airlines alone had to cancel flights, notify passengers, move aircraft around, and rebook at least 600 flights.

To track all of this information and react quickly, these organizations had to—in advance—clearly identify critical data elements that they needed to track (maintenance logs, manufacturing processes, etc.). They also had to document their information policies: how long to keep information, how to analyze information in maintenance logs, service-level agreements (SLAs) for notifying passengers of flight changes, and so on.

These business processes rely on clean, consistent information. If a model number isn't stored according to the defined data standard, quick access to that aircraft would not happen. In this case, the risk of *not* applying information governance principles is very clear and unacceptably high.

Information governance is a sustained activity that can be applied to one project, can be started with one data domain, and should be extended to the enterprise.

2.2 Evaluating and Developing Your Information Governance Needs and Resources

Now that you know what information governance is and how it can help, you can determine the shape of information governance at your company. In this section, we'll discuss the process of evaluating and developing your information governance needs and resources.

2.2.1 Evaluating Information Governance

Wait! Claim Success Immediately!

Yes, that's right. Before you even begin, you should recognize that you do have some information governance policies in place. Your business has information. Somehow you're shipping product to someone. Someone is creating that information. Someone is updating that information. Guess what? Those are information policies. Write them down. Document the policies—informal though they may be—that your company is practicing right now. Assemble them in a central place, and then publicize a few of the surprising policies you discovered. You haven't fixed any problems yet, but just gathering the policies in practice currently is a huge step forward for information governance.

When getting started with an information governance policy, many key questions need to be answered:

- Which information elements are absolutely critical?
- Which business processes depend on those information elements being of high quality?
- What does "high quality" mean to each individual business process?
- Which elements must be dealt with first?
- Who owns understanding the ramifications of poor governance and driving the information governance program forward?
- Does the business have an accurate assessment of current quality levels?
- Could the business quickly use predictive analytic techniques to proactively avoid large problems?
- Does the chief financial officer (CFO) have confidence enough to sign-off—on the threat of imprisonment or fines—that all the required regulations and organizational policies are being met while capturing and sharing this information?

Above all, to get started with an information governance policy, a company must understand how quality, timely information is critical to business function, value, and risk reduction.

Because information governance is most successful when practiced on an individual project (and thereafter sustained as an ongoing culture), there can't be a single best practice that fits most organizations. Instead, you need to evaluate your company along the following dimensions and develop a plan that works best for your needs:

- **Culture dimension** (Figure 2.2)
  How much change can your organization tolerate? Do you have lines of business or divisions that are used to working independently? Is the company process driven or action oriented?

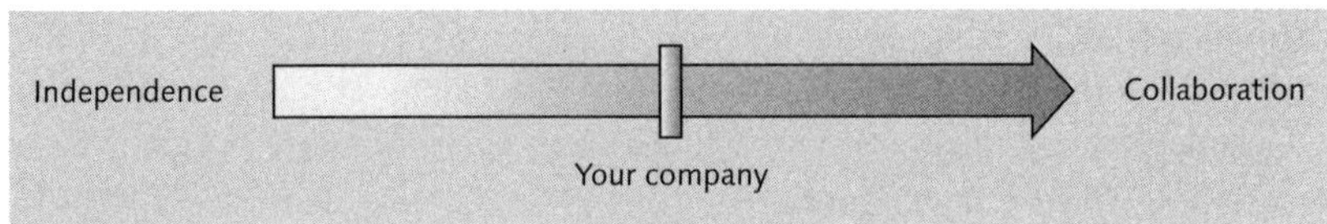

Figure 2.2 Culture Dimension of Information Governance

The farther your company falls to the left (independence), the more you'll need to focus on applying specific data standards on critical data elements. Don't immediately start a project to optimize information for order to cash, for instance. The kinds of sweeping change that information for business process optimization would require will be more than your organization can tolerate. The farther your company moves to the right (collaboration), the more you can focus on fit-for-use standards—and cleansing—for impactful business processes.

- **EIM maturity dimension** (Figure 2.3)
  Do you have any centers of excellence running around information (business intelligence, data quality, master data, etc.)? Do you operate in a shared services model? Do you have enterprise information architects that guide individual project decisions? Do you have a strategic information plan?

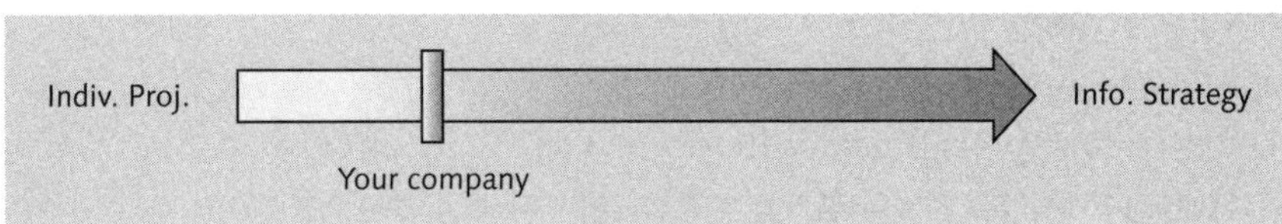

Figure 2.3 EIM Maturity Dimension of Information Governance

The farther your company falls to the left (individual projects), the more you'll need to focus on localized value first. Don't immediately start a project to manage vendor information globally, for instance. The farther your company moves to the right (information strategy), the more you can use executive sponsorship and more centralized decision making in your initial information governance efforts.

- **Management sponsorship dimension** (Figure 2.4)
  Who feels the most pain as a result of poor information? Do you have a senior executive (one with organizational clout) who understands the power of information? Would an executive sponsor be able to align all of the individual stakeholders to common goals and success metrics?

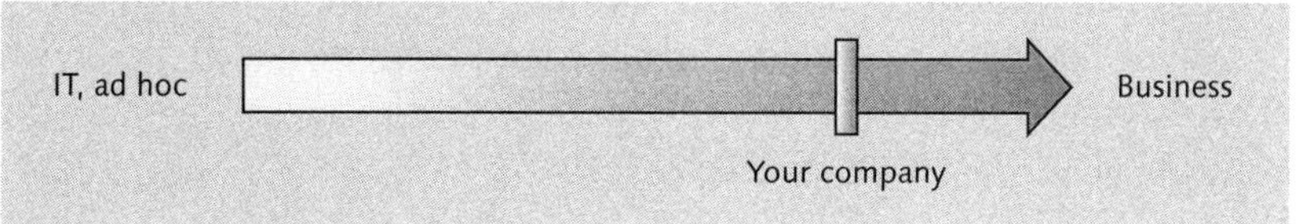

Figure 2.4 Management Sponsorship Dimension of Information Governance

  The farther your company falls to the left (IT, ad hoc), the more you'll need to focus on easy-to-interpret information projects, such as automated cleaning of address information according to governmental standards. Although the business would certainly need to understand the kind of cleansing happening with its data, the extent of business/IT collaboration is limited because external bodies have already made many of the fit-for-use decisions. The farther your company moves to the right (business), the more you can focus on projects where fit-for-use is very open to interpretation (e.g., classifying and attaining a single view of vendor information).

- **Data domains and process dimension** (Figure 2.5)
  Which business process or data domains are causing the most trouble in your organization? Which information is strategic? Which information is critical? Which information is shared across multiple business processes?

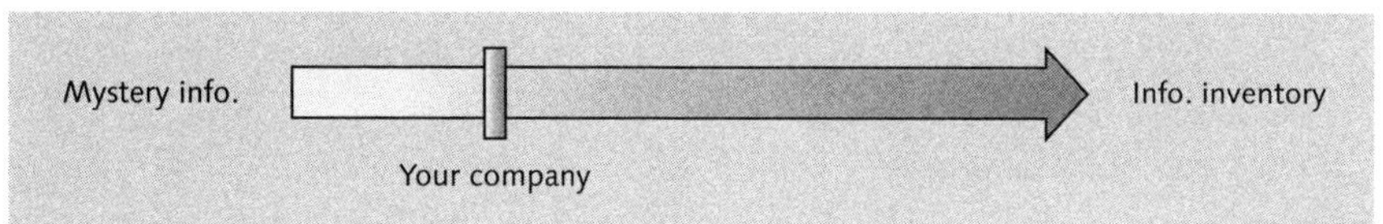

Figure 2.5 Data Domains Dimension of Information Governance

  The farther your company falls to the left (mystery information), the more you'll need to focus on finding, identifying, and tagging the information that has high business value for your chosen project. Without this first step, your fledgling information governance team will have no way to prove value or impact. In addition, your group won't be able to accurately target their work for high value or estimate the amount of work necessary to complete the project. The farther your company moves to the right (information inventory), the more you can use established baselines to set realistic, high-visibility metrics for your information stakeholders.

With answers to these questions in hand, you'll be able to domesticate your wild information. Business leaders and IT leaders can now collaborate on a working definition of information governance that is tailored to your company. One way to start tailoring your approach is with a capabilities assessment (self-assessment tools are available at *http://scn.sap.com/community/enterprise-information-management/blog/2014/07/08/new-information-governance-model-from-sap*). The capability assessment helps you to understand not only where your company is now (across multiple dimensions outlined in Figure 2.6), but also what solid improvement looks like.

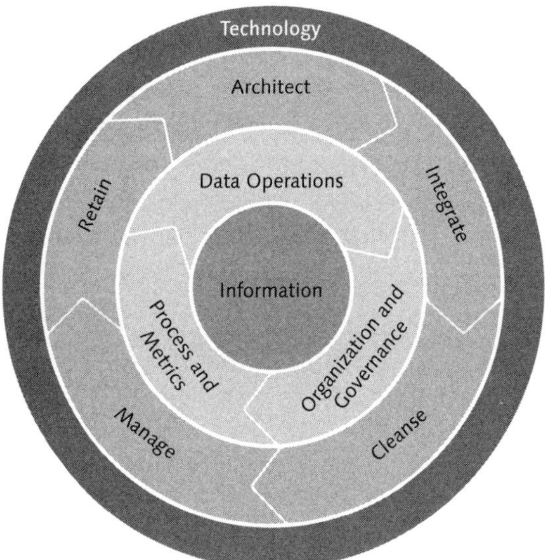

Figure 2.6 Information Governance Model

The dimensions shown in the figure are as follows:

- **Architect**
  Design of the information systems and interactions.
- **Integrate**
  Move and transform information with speed and reliability.

- **Cleanse**
  Clean, standardize, enrich, and find relationships among your information.
- **Manage**
  Manage stores of information, including access and workflow.
- **Retain**
  Archive and retain according to policies and regulations.
- **Data Operations**
  Establish high-priority information with metrics, establish programs for ongoing maintenance and cleansing, and create an incentive structure.
- **Organization and Governance**
  Establish resources, roles, responsibilities, standards, and business rules.
- **Process and Metrics**
  Establish global, consistent business processes for the most critical information (duplicate identification, allowable values, authorizations), and establish create/read/update/delete processes with improvement objectives.

After you tailor your governance approach to your company's quirks, you'll be ready to start talking resources. Although it may be tempting to start evaluating technology resources, the best first step is to figure out people resources, for example, people who modify information frequently and who decide what should be archived.

One great way to discover these hidden assets is with surveys. Send out a quick web survey that asks employees if they touch, enrich, or manage information. Then have the employees clarify which information they touch and what general actions they perform on that information (create, read, update, and delete). The survey results will show you the breadth of your information governance problem and will give you some idea of the direction you need to go.

Assessing Resources

One global company discovered that it had 92 people managing information, most certainly inconsistently. With this information (including the details of which information elements were touched and how), they were able to make a clear plan to centralize and standardize operations down to 19 employees.

After you have the employees and your executive sponsor in place, you need to define the scope of your first project. Keep in mind that managers and executives have the most to gain from high-quality data, so don't undersell your initiative. When choosing a project, make sure to consider which information elements are the most critical to govern. What does good governance look like for those key information elements? Then start working on documenting ownership and policies and standardizing important processes (e.g., can VENDOR CREATE use most of the same input form as CUSTOMER CREATE?). These activities can be as light or as heavy as you define in the tailoring step.

2.2.2 Developing Information Governance

You've defined a process and established both a rough organization and some basic tool requirements. Now, you need to make sure this information governance policy matures with time. Keep the following steps in mind:

1. Define a data strategy that supports the business strategy and goals.
2. Identify the critical data elements that support those business goals.
3. Quantify how managing those data elements increases value.
4. Establish a current baseline for those critical elements.
5. Create an improvement plan.
6. Align business and IT behind enterprise data standards, policies, and processes.
7. Create data standards and processes supporting end-to-end (E2E) business processes instead of ad hoc projects.
8. Achieve greater control over and visibility of the data.
9. Understand and manage the full data lifecycle (creation/acquisition to retirement/destruction).
10. Quantify results.
11. Do it again.
12. Manage the change cycle.

Keep in mind that any new critical projects can likely derail this project. Be prepared for these changes by using basic project management and tracking tools for your initial information governance project. (This is where starting out information governance as a smaller project really helps.) Use these tools to document owners, policies that the groups decided on, criticality, metadata inventory, and more. If you document/track wisely, you'll be able to pick up the project right where you left off. Also, you'll be able to easily extend some of the decisions you made to the *next* information governance project.

For most companies, the key is to start with a small, tactical project. Track a few simple metrics along the way, and then widely publicize the great results you attained (in terms of business value). For details, see Section 2.5.2.

2.3 Optimizing Existing Infrastructure and Resources

Companies need a systematic way of looking at the entire information landscape. Your company probably has a rough idea of that clear, orderly picture you would draw if you were starting from scratch. But because you've been managing information in an ad hoc manner for a while, you desperately need a system to help you figure out where to start.

Here are some of the criteria to factor into your plan:

- **Assessment/discovery**
  First, make sure your picture of your information landscape is accurate. Do you know how the business processes feed each other? Do you know which business intelligence (BI) and analytics systems depend on which datastores? Do you know when/how often you're getting data from external sources?
- **Nicely contained**
  One place to start might be where a system can be nicely contained. Not too many far-afield applications or processes depend on the information. In this way, a small, well-informed team can design, test, and deploy the new system.
- **High value**
  Your company may have a board-level initiative regarding customer information. If so, your project could be nicely attached to executive sponsorship and funding. However, even in customer information, you would have multiple projects to choose from. Choose a project that can show hard return on investment (ROI) through metrics you can reasonably track.
- **Remove an external service**
  Often, companies use external service bureaus for part of list processing—either in preparation for mailing or in purchased-list merging. Replacing these external providers with in-house processing is a natural, low-risk project. These projects are nicely contained, for one. Second, the cost is well defined because

you're paying the service provider. Third, somewhere you already have design specifications that you passed off to the service provider, so you have a jump-start.

- **Strategic impact**
  Don't pick an area that will undergo a lot of major, disruptive technical change in the next six months. If you're looking to start major changes such as big data or mobility in a specific area, don't spend your time implementing a technical solution where there will be major requirement/infrastructure changes. In some small cases, if you can implement quickly, then you may get automatically included in the disruptive project. It's up to you. That's more of a political decision.

As always, make sure you understand the roadmap and direction from your major technology partners. Without that information, you may box yourself in.

2.4 Establishing an Information Governance Process: Examples

You now have a good handle on what information governance is and why you need to apply those principles to all of your information-heavy projects. But as you set up your first information governance process, you need to recognize that there are two main types of information governance:

- **Preventative**
  Information governance enforces compliance before substandard information even enters your productive systems. For example, information may be cleansed and validated before it achieves *live* status in your business applications (e.g., SAP ERP).
- **Reactive**
  Information governance enforces compliance after information has made its way into your productive systems. For example, check for redundant information across different information silos.

To explore reactive information governance, let's look at an example where a homeowner in Omaha, Nebraska, received an erroneous water utilities bill for $13,499.02. The bill claimed that her residence used 4.5 million gallons of water in a month. Some possible causes for this localized billing error are listed here:

- The homeowner's bill was mistakenly merged with other bills, creating a larger cumulative total.
- The technician who read the homeowner's water meter mistakenly entered how many gallons she used.

Following good information governance principles, you'd start by performing solid root-cause analysis. For example, to prevent problems like this from occurring again, you could do the following:

- Require a review of merged records, where the types of records are different (e.g., residential and business).
- Provide last month's reading to the technician at the point of entry. Question the technician if the difference is greater than 50%.
- If you can't provide point-of-entry information or validation to the technician, at least run validations before the bills go out. Catch records where the difference in usage is more than 50%, and double-check the readings.

You can do these things by hand, manually scanning rows and rows of data. Better yet, use tools such as SAP Data Services (hereafter Data Services), SAP Information Steward (hereafter Information Steward), and SAP Business Process Management (SAP BPM) to automate this information governance workflow. (We'll discuss SAP's solutions for EIM in more detail in Chapter 4.) Or use Transaction EL27, which checks for implausible meter readings.

To finish the story, the utilities department did admit that the bill was wrong. A new one was sent in the mail. This example illustrates reactive information governance because an external event (in this case, a very public one) triggered an evaluation of the policies and processes governing information.

Now imagine this same story, but apply preventative information governance. In that case, you would follow these steps:

1. Upon creation of the billing business process, evaluate which key information elements support that process, such as meter reading.
2. Define what a good meter reading looks like: format, data type, completeness, freshness, and ownership.
3. Establish these policies, and build automation that enforces that policies at the point of entry.

4. Monitor compliance to the established policies to pinpoint information problems before an erroneous bill goes to a customer.

Notice that you can easily move from reactive information governance to preventative information governance—and in many cases, you can use the crisis of reactive information governance to gain support for a preventative information governance program.

In the next section, we provide some examples of how some companies got started with setting up an information governance policy.

2.4.1 Example 1: Creating a New Reseller

For this example, think about becoming a new customer of NeedsEIM Inc. (a manufacturer of retail durable goods who sells primarily to resellers of its equipment, introduced in Chapter 1). New customers/resellers require in-depth evaluation. NeedsEIM Inc. will be sending hundreds of thousands of dollars of inventory to these resellers, which tells you about the resellers' expectations.

Because of the price, the resellers will have high expectations for personal service. Often, the customer/reseller record may be created while sitting with the salesperson or by calling the company directly (perhaps based on a referral from another company). Therefore, it's a good idea to set up policy and procedures for how to handle this case. The following steps are one example of how the process might work:

1. The reseller identifies key suppliers and then calls account management to create a new customer record.
2. The account representative verifies reseller information.
3. The account lead verifies if the reseller is related to any other resellers the company already has: subsidiary, different division, parent corporation, and so on.
4. Account information is dispersed to the operational systems (customer and supplier relationship management systems, such as SAP Customer Relationship Management [SAP CRM], SAP Supplier Relationship Management [SAP SRM], logistics, engineering systems, and more).
5. Each operational system adds the account information necessary to complete the customer/reseller from their perspective. This completion cycle is predict-

able, repeatable, and well known. It follows a workflow that notifies users when it's their turn to add or approve information. Some of this information may include engineering drawings, aggregations, contracts, and more. The actual contract may not be stored with the master record, but a link to the transactional and associated metadata will be.

6. Each operation system feeds some of the new elements they added back to the customer/reseller definition of master data.
7. When enriching the master record with the data from separate operational systems, sometimes the user finds conflicts. Users must resolve these conflicts by working through a conflict resolution process. This predictable, repeatable, and well-known resolution process follows a workflow that notifies users when it's their turn to review or approve conflicts.
8. Every month, refresh the company/reseller information (such as Dun & Bradstreet data) to make sure changes are captured.
9. Every month, refresh the address data to make sure changes are captured.
10. Push company/reseller information (such as Dun & Bradstreet data) hierarchy number changes and address changes to the operational and reporting systems.

This is a heavyweight process, because creating a new business to work with has both high impact and low frequency. Mistakes that are caused by bad information are extremely expensive, so it's a good example of where an information governance policy should be established and followed.

2.4.2 Example 2: Supplier Registration

As a starting point, although not inclusive of all of the aspects and technologies of information governance, you could build a cross-system supplier self-service registration and approval process. This example takes some of the concepts in the example discussed in Section 2.4.1 and applies them to a similar scenario. In addition, this example provides a bit more technical tooling to build on what you've learned so far. (The SAP solutions mentioned here will be discussed in more detail in Chapter 4.) The steps in this process might be as follows:

1. A supplier registers via a website and enters some initial data such as company name, street, city, and postal code. These global attributes are stored in SAP NetWeaver Master Data Management (MDM) for further distribution to non-SAP systems.

2. When the master data specialist approves the supplier, a change request is automatically generated in SAP Master Data Governance (SAP MDG).
3. A workflow in SAP MDG ensures that all SAP ERP–specific attributes are maintained.
4. After final approval in SAP MDG, the new supplier is activated and distributed.
5. After activation, a notification is sent to the original requester.

For this example, assume that the following systems are part of this process (the systems can do much more than what is outlined here):

- SAP MDG: Maintain and distribute SAP ERP-specific attributes.
- Data Services: Clean address information and check for existing duplicates.
- SAP Extended Enterprise Content Management (ECM) by OpenText: Attach relevant supplier contracts.
- SAP NetWeaver MDM: Maintain and distribute global attributes.
- SAP Process Orchestration: Process runtime, workflows, and user interfaces, work lists, web service consumption and provisioning, business rules, and application integration.

This example process implements integrated master data maintenance. The process starts with the request by a supplier, which goes to a business user. That business user continues with processing and commenting by different expert users and stakeholders and finishes with approval or rejection by authorized experts.

Depending on the business use, different types of change requests are offered. In this example, the change request is a Create (meaning that the change is creating a new record, not an edit to an already-existing record). However, you could reuse much of this process for changing, blocking, or setting the flag for deletion. This reuse ensures that the correct information is maintained in the change request. The following list describes the process for creating, reviewing, and approving the new supplier's information:

1. The business user submits a request for creation in response to a call from the prospective supplier.
2. The master data specialist reviews the change request.
3. The business user completes the new supplier information, including cleansing and enriching the data, as well as checking for existing duplicates.

4. The master data specialist works with the knowledge worker to reference the correct supplier contract.
5. The master data specialist approves the create request.

The business value of this process is both fulfilled compliance requirements and improved information quality.

In our example, we assume that the process was implemented using SAP Process Orchestration for the design and execution of the cross-system process. The example also leverages the out-of-the-box governance process in SAP MDG for maintenance of SAP ERP-specific attributes. The process is highlighted in Figure 2.7.

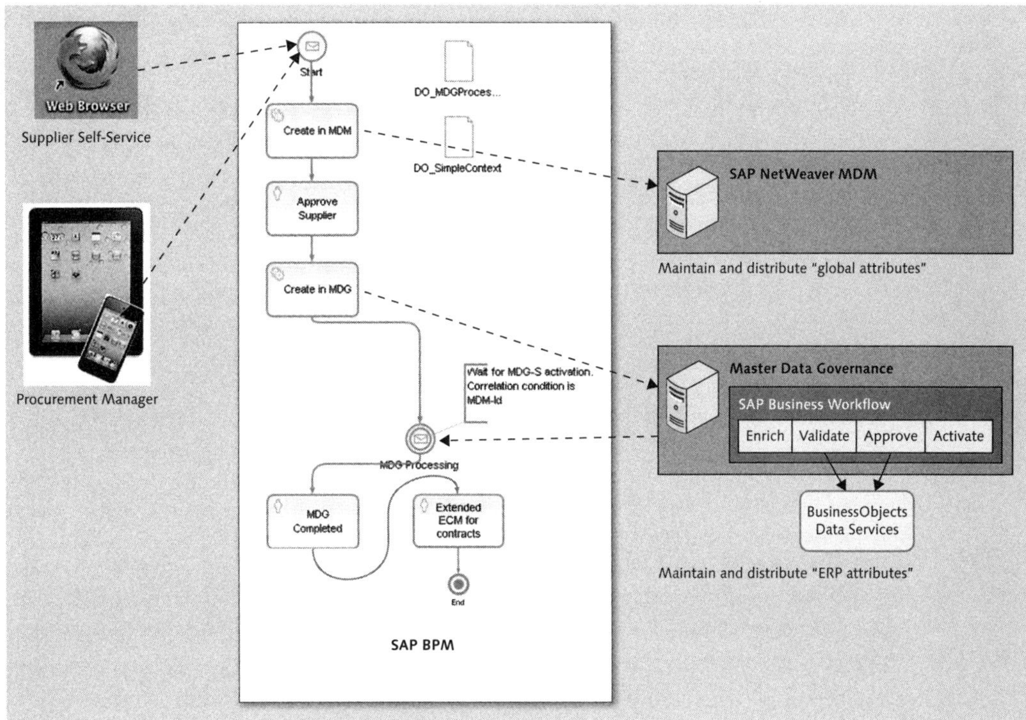

Figure 2.7 Supplier On-Boarding Process

The flow from a technical perspective is as follows:

1. The initial supplier registration web page triggers the start web service of the SAP BPM process.

2. The global attributes from the registration web page are used to create a new supplier record in SAP MDM.
3. In this human interaction step, a new supplier is being approved.
4. SAP Process Orchestration calls an SAP MDG service to create a change request with the initial supplier data. This also triggers SAP Business Workflow in SAP MDG.
5. SAP MDG triggers a web service call to Data Services to validate and automatically correct the address for the supplier. An additional web service call to Data Services uses matching to check if the supplier already exists in the MDG repository.
6. SAP MDG sends a message to SAP Process Orchestration so the flow can start.
7. SAP Process Orchestration uses the change request ID from SAP MDG to send an email to the original requestor. The email contains a link to the SAP Business Workflow log. Using this link, the original requestor can monitor the status of the change request in SAP MDG.
8. After sending an email, the SAP Process Orchestration process waits again for a message from SAP MDG. This time, SAP MDG sends a message at the end of the SAP Business Workflow process after the supplier has been finally approved and activated. The message includes the final ID of the business partner in the primary persistence.
9. The last step in the SAP Process Orchestration process informs the original requestor that the new business partner has been created and activated.
10. SAP MDG sends an email request to the knowledge worker to attach the appropriate contract documents from SAP Extended ECM to the master record.

This example of governance processes applied to the process of creating a supplier helps you understand how you can connect SAP software solutions to automate much of your information governance processes. These software solutions will be more thoroughly introduced in Chapter 4 and then discussed in detail throughout the book.

2.4.3 Example 3: Data Migration

Data migration projects are a good opportunity to start governance projects. One example is from a company that migrated from 4.6C to SAP ERP Central Component (ECC 6.0). Due to the 2009 financial crisis, executive management pushed the company to be a "break away" company by leveraging industry best practices and using as many standard processes as possible. The decision was to bring 60 countries online on the same day. The company was trying to minimize sequential go-live activities and reduce the amount of temporary interfaces between the old and new systems. The goal of the project was to use 90% standard SAP processes and 10% differentiating processes. Through a massive amount of coordination and hard work by the entire corporation, the organization was able to go live with the new system within 15 months.

Due to the complexity of this endeavor, there were risks from the master data management side. There were significant delays halfway into the project. To reduce the delays, management decided to move from cleansing 100% of the data to only cleansing critical fields. However, the project team performed the nominal checks needed to convert data from 4.6C to SAP ECC. After go-live, the organization had considerable global data issues, and the quality of customer data was degraded. In the worst case, certain sites were not able to ship for a few days, causing a task force to step in and identify all issues tied to the customer master. The task force manually addressed the issues.

This task force helped show the need for data quality. After surviving go-live issues, the company took a more holistic approach to enterprise information management with one key action: IT formed a data team to support the need for improved data quality. The new data team would take the existing SAP Business Warehouse (SAP BW)/reporting team and add Data Services and information governance to complete the new organization. This allowed the data team to become a complete center of excellence in extraction, transformation, and loading (ETL) for the SAP ERP system, as well as SAP BW. Also, this team led the corporate discussion of data quality and formed an information governance council for the first time in the company's history.

Figure 2.8 shows the team's model of how communication flows from the top down and bottom up. The information governance committee works as the glue holding together process and data quality. Such a committee should be formed with middle- to upper managers who become the strategic thinkers. When the committee approves certain processes and initiatives, these should be pushed down to global data stewards and IT/data management teams. The committee chair would need to discuss any issues not resolved by the information governance committee with an executive advisory board, which includes VP and senior director-level members.

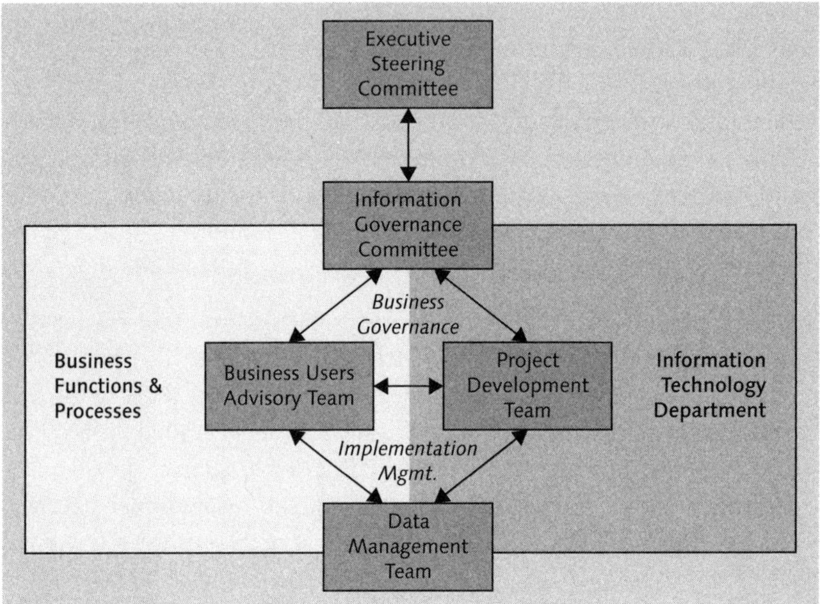

Figure 2.8 Organization for Information Governance

The information governance team quickly realized that although they were strong, forming the team wasn't enough. They immediately moved to formalizing team responsibilities and defining team interaction. The information governance committee also established a clear definition of success, including how to communicate that success.

Each team (executive advisory board, information governance committee, and data stewards/IT support team) had different roles in information governance. In general, responsibilities were divided as follows:

- The executive board was primarily responsible for company culture.
- The information governance committee was primarily responsible for strategic approaches.
- The data stewards/IT were primarily responsible for tactical execution.

The leader of the data team created a strategic three- to five-year plan and vision. This plan included topics such as data health metrics, master data strategy, and a rollout of an information governance program (customer, material, and vendor data cleansing, and data quality projects).

Because this was the first time the group had approached an information governance project, the data team leader used many resources to help design, build, and implement this strategic vision. Also, after building the first prototype, the leader worked with SAP experts in the EIM space to validate his work. After several iterations, the information governance strategy, plan, and package was presented to upper management and approved.

Takeaway

Go beyond building a roadmap. You need to also build a framework or structured methodology to help support sustainable growth. Part of an information governance framework should include (but not limit itself to) business process, definition, system, implementation, communication, and enforcement.

Table 2.1 shows the information governance framework that was derived from the example discussed in this section. It includes the definition, update, and enforcement of policies, and it ensures transparency so that everyone knows their role in information governance.

Category/Step	Data Governance Process
Business process	▸ Identify processes to match data set for cleansing rules. ▸ Establish decisions and accountability.
Define	▸ Define business rules from business users and IT. ▸ Define data. ▸ Specify data quality requirements. ▸ Leverage stewardship with business users and IT.
System	▸ Manage reporting, metrics, auto-cleansing functions. ▸ Deploy governance tools.
Implement	▸ Roll out business user roles. ▸ Perform monthly cleaning. ▸ Create de-duplication reports.
Data/communication	▸ Global data owner/IT data manager coordinate cleanup with regional owners. ▸ Communicate with stakeholders. ▸ Measure and report value.

Table 2.1 Example Information Governance Framework

Category/Step	Data Governance Process
Enforce	▸ Enforce policies via data governance committee and regional data owners. ▸ Align policies, requirements, and controls. ▸ Involve global and regional data stewards from business user groups.

Table 2.1 Example Information Governance Framework (Cont.)

2.5 Rounding Out Your Information Governance Process

As you get started with your first information governance process, in addition to the organization, tools, and processes to enforce compliance, you also want to ensure that you measure your success and also keep in mind the impact of data that you don't have but need. Often, these steps are forgotten; however, you must incorporate these aspects of information governance to be able to show success. To show the success of your initiative, you need to take a picture of where you are now, define what success looks like, and take a picture at the end of your efforts. And don't forget to look for information that has gone missing, too.

2.5.1 The Impact of Missing Data

Too often, all of our information governance efforts are focused on shaping, cleansing, and moving the most visible information. That work definitely needs to be done; however, keep in mind that missing information can significantly compromise your information governance success. This section not only highlights the impact of missing information, but also shows you how to spotlight areas where missing information negatively impacts your organization.

According to research from Vanson Bourne, one-third of large companies in the United Kingdom say they have lost customers and business because their data was missing.[1] According to 500 IT managers and CIOs in the United Kingdom:

1 Source: Savvas, Anthony. "Firms admit losing customers as a result of missing data," (July 19, 2011) *CIO*, *http://www.cio.co.uk/news/3292136/firms-admit-losing-customers-as-a-result-of-missing-data/?olo=rss*.

- 88% of businesses saw data as a strategic asset to their business.
- A third of large UK organizations admit to having lost a customer or new business due to missing data.
- More than half of the respondents (52%) said their biggest frustration was the complexity around managing multiple data sources.

You can make a few assumptions from these results:

- If businesses knew their data was missing or incomplete, they would do something about it.
- If businesses could somehow tie missing data to real business processes or sales losses, they would get real resources to do something about it.
- When pieces of data—meaningful to a single business process—are spread across multiple data sources, it's too hard to tell if data is missing or incomplete.

Think of a cooking analogy: Before cooking, you usually check about two cupboards for all of the ingredients. Imagine if you had to check five cupboards, and some ingredients were split across cupboards. You're much more likely to miss identifying an incomplete ingredient. Depending on the ingredient, you could compromise an entire meal. Information and business processes are much more complex.

When applied to information, you need a solution with the following capabilities to fix the problem:

- Access to multiple data sources at once
- Ability to associate a field to a business process
- Ability to check for nulls or blanks in a critical data field
- Ability to check for nulls or blanks when conditions arise across multiple data fields from multiple sources
- Ability to check for incomplete (or shorter than expected) data in a critical data fields
- Ability to check for incomplete data when conditions arise across multiple data fields from multiple data sources
- Ability to notice incomplete data before a transaction tries to complete
- Ability to require complete data at the point of entry

You don't have to lose customers or new business because of missing data or incomplete data. At the very least, you can start by identifying *where* you have critical, missing data.

2.5.2 Gathering Metrics and KPIs to Show Success

Establishing your first information governance process should feel like a great success. However, you undoubtedly need to show that the work (and resources) applied to the project had solid impact. Therefore, it's important to gather metrics and KPIs to show success.

Keep in mind that you have two key audiences that want this proof:

- **Executives**
  This audience wants to hear about increased business value, decreased cost, increased revenue, decreased risk, or quantifiable optimizations. Normally, this group also wants a more visual display of dashboards. For this group, gather *offensive KPIs*. Offensive KPIs show high-level value.
- **Cross-functional**
  This audience suspects that the business is running slower because of all of this new process. This group needs to hear about *service-level agreement* (SLA) compliance—including reverse SLAs. For this group, show detailed statistics on the quality and timeliness of data. At a high level, these metrics are categorized as *defensive metrics*. Defensive metrics help show—in excruciating detail—how specific lines of business, departments, or even individuals are supporting or hindering the information governance value.

SLAs are especially critical. Essentially, they define the expectations of the information provided to the data stewards or knowledge workers. Establish two kinds of SLAs when you start your information governance project:

- **Normal SLA**
  The normal SLA quantifies how quickly the data stewards or knowledge workers will complete their work in creating, updating, or flagging information for deletion. You should have different SLAs for each domain (material, customer, supplier, etc.). Depending on your company, there will be different expectations for the timeliness of each of these domains. For example, perhaps pricing change requests have a 1-month turnaround time, but a supplier has a 24-hour turnaround time.

- **Reverse SLA**
  The reverse SLA quantifies how good and complete the information is that's coming from the business users—including timeliness. Instead of quantifying how well your information governance team is meeting expectations, this SLA measures how well the organization is complying with the agreed-upon information governance policies. Without this reverse SLA, you'll frequently hear that *90% of the problems are with master data*. For example, determine how many rush requests you're getting for each domain and publish those results back to the business units. If 70% of your rush requests are coming from pricing (which must be established six months in advance), then your group can work collaboratively with pricing to solve this problem.

Determine these metrics and KPIs as you're defining your information policies. In this way, you can capture expectations and constraints as your working group is thinking deeply about what quality enterprise information actually means.

The KPIs generally fall into two camps:

- **Generic estimates of the cost of quality information**
  For this type, the business goes through a detailed process to assign a cost for each major type of error. For example, the executive steering committee may decide that the cost of an incorrect address is $100. Then you can gather metrics that say how much bad addresses are costing your business.
- **Specific costs for the specific errors found**
  For this type, use the open nature of your system landscape to tie specific values together. Instead of giving a generic cost estimate, you're giving the exact cost of the exact information that doesn't meet policy. For example, you can determine which master supplier records don't have a credit score. You can then look into the SAP ERP system to see how many open orders you have with that supplier. Add this to the other supplier records with significant errors, and you can publish the number of at-risk supplier inventory orders.

As with the rest of your information governance program activities, you can gather and publish these KPIs and metrics without sophisticated new tools. Some companies just use common email inboxes and manual logging of issues in spreadsheets. Perhaps this manual way helps you get the conversation going on acceptable metrics and KPIs.

However, you'll need to scale your efforts so you're not spending time on manual methods of aggregating information and building one-off dashboards. To this end, SAP products can be helpful. The following products help you automate not only the metrics around your data, but also the visualization of those metrics for appropriate audiences. Automation means you'll spend less time assembling data anecdotes and more time discussing the resulting business value. We'll discuss these products in more detail in Chapter 4 and throughout the course of the book.

- **SAP Information Steward**
  Establish drillable scorecards on each domain of information, letting the user go from a high-level score of "supplier is yellow" to which specific records aren't passing the threshold.
- **SAP Data Services**
  Move metric- and KPI-associated information into a data mart that the reporting system can access. Data Services also provides the quality metrics for numbers of duplicates; numbers of clean, shippable addresses; and so on.
- **SAP Process Orchestration and SAP Business Workflow**
  Provide details on how well the business processes are performing against their own SLAs. You can correlate these details to the quality of information for those specific business processes.
- **SAP BusinessObjects Business Intelligence (SAP BusinessObjects BI)**
  Provide multiple methods to visualize the metric and KPI information to your different audiences, including dashboards for your executives.

Sometimes the differences between offensive KPIs and defensive metrics or SLAs are difficult to visualize. And yet you must understand the difference so that you're reporting the right level of information to the appropriate audience. To help with that visualization, Figure 2.9 shows an example of a visualization that illustrates both defensive metrics and offensive KPIs.

Even without reading the numbers, the sheer detail and presentation of the numbers in Figure 2.9 make it clear that this report is for someone who cares deeply about the fine details of information readiness. The rush request pie chart in the figure shows defensive metrics while also nicely illustrating the concept of reverse SLAs. The Before ECC and After ECC pie charts highlight resource movement and whether those resource reassignments have met corporate targets after an initial

SAP ERP implementation, which involved significant business process reengineering. These pie charts represent offensive KPIs to use with executives.

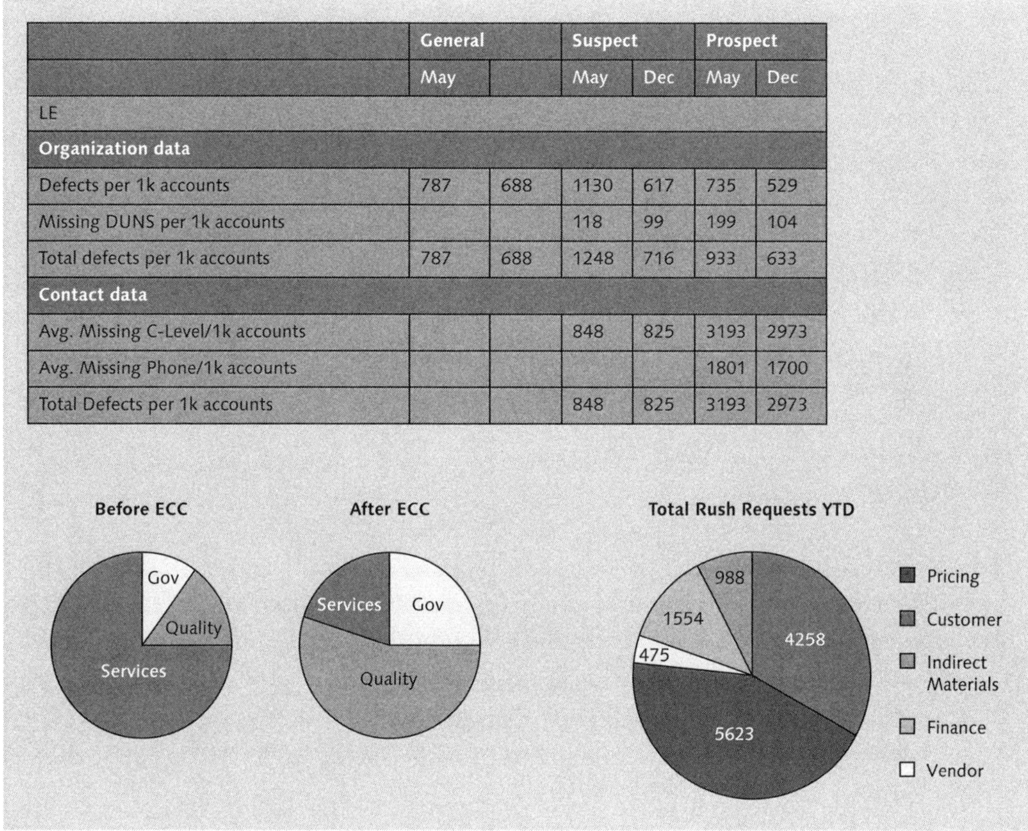

	General		Suspect		Prospect	
	May		May	Dec	May	Dec
LE						
Organization data						
Defects per 1k accounts	787	688	1130	617	735	529
Missing DUNS per 1k accounts			118	99	199	104
Total defects per 1k accounts	787	688	1248	716	933	633
Contact data						
Avg. Missing C-Level/1k accounts			848	825	3193	2973
Avg. Missing Phone/1k accounts					1801	1700
Total Defects per 1k accounts			848	825	3193	2973

Figure 2.9 Examples of SLA Metrics and KPIs

In conclusion, when evaluating the kinds of metrics and reports that you would provide to internal stakeholders, follow the advice summarized here:

- For executives, provide highly visual, business-value-based graphics (offensive KPIs).
- For cross-functional stakeholders, provide detailed information on SLA compliance, resourcing changes, and information quality. This information needs to be available both in simple charts and detailed data sheets.

2.5.3 Establish a Before-and-After View

Finally, know that to establish ongoing information governance resources—which is the best practice—you'll need to publish some kind of before-and-after view. To do this, you need to know what before looks like.

The only way to know what the before view looks like is to establish a baseline before you start any of your information governance work. Remember the scenario phasing shown earlier in Figure 2.1? Hopefully it's now clear that information discovery is an important phase. Information discovery includes cataloging what you already have and the basic information quality level of the critical information assets.

Without this step, you can't show the benefits of all of your work. It may seem like unnecessary busywork when you spot a problem and are intent on fixing the critical problems, but you must do it.

2.6 Summary

This chapter has provided some concrete and real examples on what information governance looks like, what you need to do to get started with your first governance process, and how the governance discipline impacts users, organizations, and software. The information governance discipline oversees the management of your enterprise's information. By bringing together the right people, processes, policies, and metrics, information governance delivers trusted, consistent, and clear information throughout your organization.

The 2000s saw the rise of "big data," a term coined by analysts to describe the massive amounts of data that come in varied types, at unprecedented speed, that businesses and other institutions began to store and process. This chapter discusses the enabling technological developments to deal with big data, including SAP HANA, Hadoop, and SAP's EIM solutions.

3 Big Data with SAP HANA, Hadoop, and EIM

The volume of data that's created in organizations is large and growing at a velocity that's unprecedented, and yet organizations struggle to make sense of data at that scale. Fortunately, advancements in computational power, storage capacity, information access and management, and analytics are progressing at an equally impressive rate. This chapter discusses two such advancements, SAP HANA and Hadoop, and how SAP's Enterprise Information Management (EIM) products complement these solutions to create an opportunity to harness big data as a foundation for better business decisions. This chapter provides a brief introduction to SAP HANA and then discusses its impact on SAP's EIM strategy. Additionally, this chapter introduces Hadoop as it relates to big data, SAP HANA, and EIM.

3.1 SAP HANA

SAP HANA was developed in response to SAP customers' requirements to get access to information *now*, to make sense of information *now*, and to make decisions *now*. Businesses and their employees must have quick access and the ability to analyze information quickly to make decisions. SAP HANA gives companies immediate insight into large volumes of data by placing real-time decision making in the hands of the business user.

SAP HANA combines both data management and application platform functionality into a single new innovative platform. The goal of SAP HANA is to simplify your business and technology landscape, while at the same time allowing your business to execute faster and react to changing conditions in real time. SAP's in-memory computing technology enables real-time computing by moving intensive computations to the data and bringing together Online Transaction Processing (OLTP) and Online Analytical Processing (OLAP) applications into a single platform. Combining the advances in hardware technology with in-memory computing empowers the entire business, from shop floor to boardroom, by giving real-time business processes instantaneous access to data. The alliance of these technologies can eliminate today's information lag for your business.

In this section, you'll learn about the business benefits of SAP HANA, basics of SAP HANA technology and how it works, its use for analytics, its use as an application platform, and SAP HANA and the cloud.

3.1.1 Business Benefits of SAP HANA

While SAP HANA is clearly a major technological advancement, how can it specifically benefit your business? The following subsections will provide the answers.

Make Better Decisions in Less Time

Technological advancements enable organizations to leverage SAP HANA as a single platform for both operational (OLTP) and analytical (OLAP) applications. This means that it's possible to gain real-time insights into your business directly on top of your operational applications running on SAP HANA. In Figure 3.1, you'll find the current common IT landscape with source operational system—extraction, transformation, and loading (ETL) with transformation of the data to an analytical data stored with a delay to gaining insight into that information. Many organizations have to wait hours or days to get access to this information through their analytics platforms.

SAP HANA provides a means for immediate analysis of the latest information. SAP provides SAP HANA Live for SAP Business Suite, which is a solution containing SAP HANA content that provides a virtual data model over the SAP Business Suite tables to enable quick reporting of the information in the SAP Business Suite (see *http://www.sap.com/pc/tech/in-memory-computing-hana/software/hana-live/index.html* for more information).

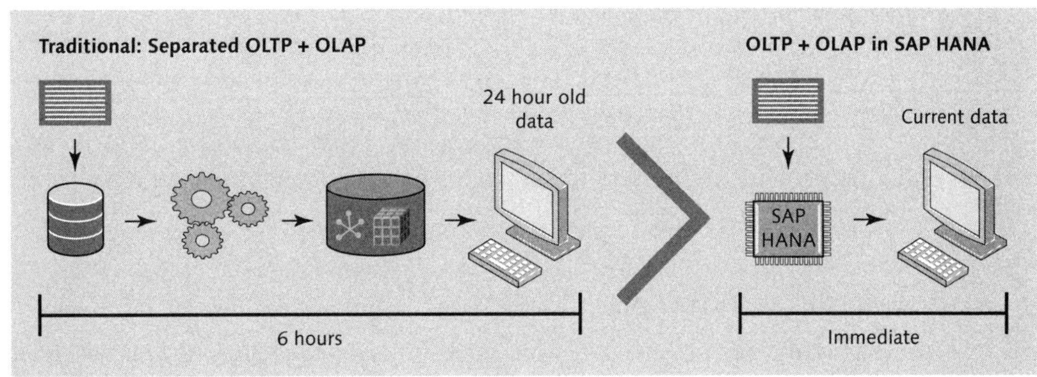

Figure 3.1 Combined Operational and Analytical Processing in SAP HANA

Reduce TCO

Leveraging SAP HANA as a single platform for both your operational and analytical applications can provide a greatly simplified IT landscape. You can reduce your data modeling and ETL development process. You may still need to move data to SAP HANA from outside applications, but these processes can be greatly simplified:

- **No aggregates**
  Due to the significant performance of SAP HANA's in-memory capabilities, you no longer need to calculate and persist aggregate information, because it can be calculated on the fly.
- **No or less data model transformation**
  You no longer need to change your data model purely for analytical performance reasons.
- **Built-in services**
  Built-in data integration services in SAP HANA simplify the technology stack.

You can significantly reduce the investment in independent data marts or even your data warehouse by consolidating onto the SAP HANA platform or performing operational reporting right on your applications that are running on SAP HANA. Doing so reduces the amount of hardware needed, as well as your overall design and development costs from a consolidated IT landscape.

SAP HANA provides an open architecture, including the use of industry technology standards such as SQL, MDX, ODBC/JDBC, OData, JSON, JavaScript, and HTML5.

Because of this, it's possible to port your existing applications over to use SAP HANA as a database platform to gain some immediate benefits.

SAP HANA is offered both on-premise and in the cloud, so you can choose the model that best suits your business and adapt accordingly. You can start with very low investment in the cloud to get experience and grow further in the cloud as needed, or use on-premise.

Enable New Innovative Applications

You can capitalize on the reinvention of enterprise software through the use of the SAP HANA platform. SAP offers many of its traditional applications on the SAP HANA platform such as the SAP Business Suite, SAP Business Warehouse (SAP BW), SAP Customer Relationship Management (SAP CRM), SAP Sales Pipeline Analysis, SAP Fraud Management, and many more. These applications are taking advantage of the performance and new capabilities that are available in the SAP HANA platform to provide more powerful features and performance than ever.

SAP HANA retains all data in-memory, and, due to its columnar nature, it provides significant data compression. This allows you to manage large volumes of data using less memory with massive performance and scalability, unlike any other application development platform that's available.

SAP HANA also comes with powerful modeling tools and a suite of capabilities that are only found through the use of many independent products and tools from other vendors. SAP HANA includes comprehensive text analysis, natural language processing, and search capabilities that allow you to gain insight into social media, customer support cases, and other unstructured information. SAP HANA includes an extensive library of predictive analytics algorithms and business functions for common data analysis problems. It also includes native, high-performance processing of spatial data in conjunction with traditional business data, enabling you to build geospatial analysis into your applications at unprecedented speeds.

SAP HANA provides more than just a database engine—it also has a complete application development infrastructure that revolutionizes application development. SAP provides built-in development tools and usage of common technologies such as SQL, JavaScript, and HTML5 for application development.

At the time of writing, there are new capabilities to drastically simplify and reduce time to value when developing software applications through its SAP River development environment. SAP River lets the application developer focus on building the data models and business logic and spend less time worrying about the infrastructure among the user experience, business logic, and data persistence. This development environment for the SAP HANA platform takes the complexity out of developing the data model, business logic, access control, and user interfaces (UIs). It does this by providing one language and set of tools that allow the developer to focus more on the intent of the application, its business objects and logic, and less on the technical architecture of the application, access control, and orchestration of activities.

These capabilities allow you to leverage SAP HANA's great functionality for existing applications as well as developing new applications, which will provide truly revolutionary performance and capabilities.

3.1.2 Basics of SAP HANA

SAP HANA combines SAP software components that have been optimized on hardware from SAP partners. It's based on SAP's in-memory technology, allowing it to process massive quantities of real-time transactional data in the main memory of the server.

Some of the SAP HANA capabilities that provide differentiating value include the following:

- **Data Locality Aware Processing**
  SAP HANA's optimizer is built to leverage the locality of data to the CPUs, their related caches, and the main memory to avoid cache hit misses.
- **Real-time OLTP and OLAP processing on a single shared copy of the data in column store**
  There's no need to keep copies of the data in different data models for OLTP versus OLAP type consumption. This is done using an in-memory column store providing high-performance data retrieval, aggregation, data compression, and advanced techniques to optimize performance for both types of applications.
- **Massively parallel processing on a shared nothing architecture leveraging Single Instruction, Multiple Data (SIMD) instructions**
  SAP HANA provides great vertical scalability leveraging many cores on a single host and massive horizontal scalability across many blades, increasing the volume of in-memory storage and CPU cores for processing. SAP HANA also

currently leverages common SIMD instruction set extensions on the platforms it supports.

- **A complete data foundation and application platform**
  SAP HANA is more than just a database. SAP HANA provides a complete data foundation, including data integration services for both physical and virtual data provisioning to SAP HANA and data modeling capabilities for physical and also virtual models. SAP HANA is also a complete application development platform, providing common software development technologies such as HTML5, JavaScript, OData/JSON support, SQL, and MDX interfaces.

As you can see, SAP HANA provides significant technological advancements, providing a revolutionary platform for the next generation of software applications.

3.1.3 SAP HANA Components and Architecture

Figure 3.2 shows the major architecture components of SAP HANA. An introduction to each major component is provided next.

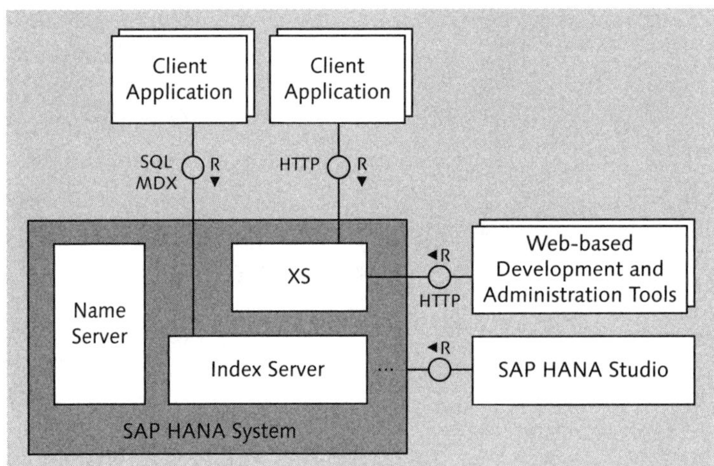

Figure 3.2 Major Architectural Components

SAP HANA also has many unique, built-in functional advantages and a wide variety of interfaces for developers to integrate the SAP HANA platform into their existing infrastructure or in development of new applications. Figure 3.3 depicts some of these capabilities.

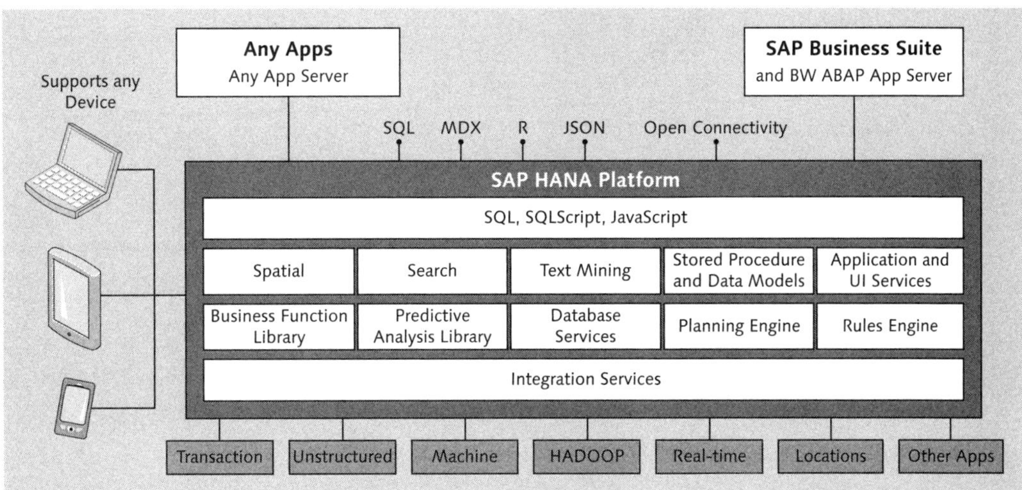

Figure 3.3 SAP HANA Functional Capabilities

Index Server

The index server process is the primary in-memory computing engine that you hear about first and foremost in discussions on SAP HANA. The index server process encompasses the primary capabilities for the following:

- **Connection, session, and transaction management**
- **Request processing and execution control**
  Handles execution of different types of requests to the core such as SQL, MDX, procedure execution, and so on. The index server also contains the calculation engine, which is used in many ways, including but not limited to execution model for stored procedures, graph processing, and calculation views.
- **Relational stores**
  Components for in-memory column store, and smart data access.
- **Repository**
  Where all design-time artifacts are persisted.
- **Persistence layer**
  Page management, logging, and other services related to persisting and accessing information on disk.

Note that there are other processes that make up the core SAP HANA "engine" that assist the index server in different ways. For example, the name server manages all the information about the topology of an SAP HANA system. In a distributed system, the name server knows where the components are running and which data is located on which server. There are also other components (which we won't discuss here), such as the preprocessor server, the compile server, and the script server.

SAP HANA Extended Application Services (XS Server)

The XS server is a web application server as part of the overall SAP HANA architecture. It allows clients to access the SAP HANA platform via HTTP. Application-specific services provided by the XS server are either created declaratively or by writing server-side application code. SAP also provides a UI toolkit called SAPUI5 (the open-source version is called OpenUI5), which is a JavaScript UI library consisting of a number of UI controls that make developing UIs on SAP HANA easier.

SAP HANA Studio

SAP HANA Studio is an integrated development environment, a data modeling utility, and an administration tool. It's a thick client application that is typically run on an end-user's PC. SAP HANA Studio users are system administrators, data modelers, and developers. System administrators use SAP HANA Studio, for example, to start and stop servers, to monitor the system, to configure system settings, and to manage users and security. Developers use SAP HANA Studio to create content such as data models (views), tables, JavaScript, HTML, stored procedures, and so on. These development artifacts are stored in the SAP HANA repository. SAP HANA Studio is based on the Eclipse platform.

Web-Based Development and Administration Tools

In addition to SAP HANA Studio, there is also a web-based version of the integrated development environment and a web-based administration tool. The server-side parts of these tools are system applications that run in the XS server. The web-based development tools can be used to perform many key development tasks in a browser versus using SAP HANA Studio.

Data Provisioning Services

Data Provisioning (referred to as Integration Services in Figure 3.3) is a key aspect of SAP HANA, as many use cases require that data originating in some OLTP system is transferred to SAP HANA for use in SAP BusinessObjects Business Intelligence (SAP BusinessObjects BI), SAP Predictive Analytics, or many various types of applications. SAP provides a variety of tools and capabilities for this situation. Some of these capabilities are built natively into SAP HANA and integrated into the user experience. Others are individual tools that are architecturally independent of SAP HANA. Also, depending on the SAP HANA package you've licensed from SAP, some may or may not be included with SAP HANA.

SAP Data Services (hereafter Data Services), SAP Replication Server (hereafter Replication Server), SAP Landscape Transformation Replication Server (SAP LT), and SAP HANA Cloud Integration (HCI) are covered in Section 3.2.2 as EIM tools available for data provisioning with SAP HANA. Other tools and capabilities include SAP HANA Direct Extractor Connection (DXC) and SAP Event Stream Processor.

Native Advanced Features

Many unique features are built into SAP HANA, which add to the functional uniqueness of the SAP HANA platform. These features can be leveraged easily by any application running on SAP HANA through standard interfaces such as SQL, stored procedure calls, or other interfaces provided to other development layers such as JavaScript in the XS server or in ABAP interfaces in the SAP NetWeaver stack.

Some of the advanced features that are provided natively include the following:

- SAP Predictive Analysis algorithms
- Business functions
- Spatial analysis (GIS functions)
- Text analysis to provide insight into free form text and documents
- Fuzzy search and matching
- Rules engine
- Data quality functionality

3.1.4 SAP HANA for Analytics and Business Intelligence

The first use case for SAP HANA is analytics and business intelligence (BI). This is particularly true for large amounts of data that are required to execute specific reports and analysis. SAP HANA is compelling for analytics and BI because it provides the following functions faster than the traditional SAP BW: reporting and analysis (query 10–100 times faster), decreased data latency (data loads 5–10 times faster), and accelerated integrated planning (calculations 5–10 times faster).

3.1.5 SAP HANA as an Application Platform

SAP HANA is a database and an application development platform. Over time, you'll see more and more applications running natively on SAP HANA. SAP HANA provides a new foundation for a new category of applications to significantly outperform current applications.

For developers of applications looking at SAP HANA, the platform provides the following:

- **Performance**
  Significant performance capabilities not found in other application development platforms. SAP HANA's in-memory column store technology delivers real-time analytics (OLAP) performance directly against transactional data (OLTP).
- **Common industry standards**
  SAP HANA supports SQL, JDBC/ODBC, MDX, OData, JavaScript, and HTML5.
- **Unique native functionality all in one box**
  A large selection of business functions, SAP Predictive Analytics algorithms, text analysis, data transformation, and spatial processing capabilities are included. All these features are easily accessible through standard SQL and stored procedure type interfaces.
- **Greatly simplified architecture**
  SAP HANA greatly reduces the number of solutions, integration points, and infrastructure needed to build a solution with these types of capabilities.
- **Cloud and on-premise**
  SAP offers a variety of consumption models to make it easy to get started and scale development efforts. SAP also has a world class community of developers, tutorials, and conferences to support new development efforts.

3.1.6 SAP Business Suite on SAP HANA

The SAP HANA applications that are available today include the SAP Business Suite, multiple rapid-deployment solutions from SAP, many accelerators, and SAP BW. In other words, the database for SAP BW is now SAP HANA.

With the SAP Business Suite on SAP HANA, you'll gain many immediate benefits, such as improved performance and the ability to perform analytics directly on your SAP Business Suite system to gain real-time insights. SAP also continues to enhance the SAP Business Suite with further SAP HANA-based optimizations, simplification, and improved user experiences. For example, the recently released SAP ERP Financials powered by SAP HANA solution provides many new optimizations based on SAP HANA as a platform, which greatly benefit the business:

- A common source of information for all regulatory and managerial accounting processes, eliminating the need for manual reconciliation
- New reporting and analytics capabilities for finance users with self-service access to all information, allowing instant insight-to-action
- On-the-fly capabilities for moving finance processing, such as month-end activities, from batch to real time

You should expect to see a continued stream of innovations from SAP in regards to the SAP Business Suite on SAP HANA.

3.1.7 SAP HANA and the Cloud

SAP's mission is to be the "cloud company powered by SAP HANA." Given this, SAP offers many types of solutions in the cloud anywhere from applications, to business network solutions, to a complete cloud platform. In this section, we'll focus purely on the current SAP HANA offerings around a cloud platform.

SAP HANA Enterprise Cloud

The SAP HANA Enterprise Cloud is the premier cloud service from SAP, which incorporates applications, platform, and maintenance. This offering provides complete management, subscription-based cloud service where experts can help you deploy, maintain, integrate, and extend SAP HANA applications in a private cloud environment. This solution provides a faster, easier transition to real-time business for those looking for a premier offering providing complete assistance. SAP HANA Enterprise Cloud is an enterprise-class managed cloud offering that provides infrastructure and managed services on a monthly subscription basis. SAP HANA Enterprise Cloud is ideally suited for applications such as SAP Business Suite and SAP BW, and for complex landscapes.

SAP HANA One

SAP HANA One provides a combination of the fastest in-memory platform along with a public cloud offering. This solution can provide you with a faster and more affordable way to get SAP HANA up and running. SAP HANA One provides a single instance of SAP HANA hosted in the Amazon Web Services (AWS) cloud.

SAP HANA Cloud Platform: Platform-as-a-Service (PaaS)

The SAP HANA Cloud Platform is SAP's Platform-as-a-Service (PaaS) offering. SAP HANA Cloud Platform is for customers who wish to do the following:

- Build, extend, and run next-generation applications on SAP HANA in the cloud
- Quickly deploy SAP HANA licenses and/or applications without hardware investment

The SAP HANA Cloud Platform includes the following:

- **SAP HANA Infrastructure Services**
  These services provide a way to quickly deploy and manage your pre-licensed SAP HANA instances without hardware investments and setup time. This is a subscription model that provides a scalable, affordable way to deploy your SAP HANA licenses in the cloud.
- **SAP HANA DB Services**
  These services provide an easy and low cost way to get up and running with an SAP HANA system in the cloud. This solution is offered as a monthly subscription that delivers fast provisioning of SAP HANA software and hardware, and includes a cloud management console for easy configuration and administration.
- **SAP HANA App Services**
  These services build on the capabilities of the SAP HANA DB Services offering by providing more advanced capabilities for developing consumer-grade applications and for the extension of cloud and on-premise applications. Whether your current applications are in the cloud or on-premise, these services enable you to quickly build additional functionality to meet your business needs. You can also easily publish and monetize your applications on the SAP HANA Marketplace. SAP HANA App Services includes support for integration, analytics, mobile, portals, security, and collaboration, and is available by purchasing license and infrastructure subscriptions in configurations from 128GB to 1TB. It also includes shared services for application management, systems management, administration, and monitoring.

3.2 SAP HANA and EIM

As a database application and cloud platform, SAP HANA doesn't fall into the SAP EIM family of solutions. However, it's tightly coupled with EIM. After all, what's the use of fast access to data if the data itself isn't good?

EIM's role with SAP HANA is to ensure that all data loaded into SAP HANA is correctly provisioned and ready for use in SAP HANA applications. This is especially important when loading data from diverse systems into SAP HANA. Normally, you don't want to just load the data without first assessing data quality levels, duplicates between the different systems, and other cleansing options that are discussed in Part II of this book.

The following sections provide details on how EIM solutions integrate with, complement, and are optimized for SAP HANA.

3.2.1 Data Modeling for SAP HANA

SAP PowerDesigner (hereafter PowerDesigner; see Chapter 7 for more details) is a tool that helps you understand information assets across the enterprise, within and outside of any given implementation. SAP HANA has a repository that's used for the development and implementation of data structures following SAP HANA-specific implementation concepts, and is optimized to help developers get the most out of SAP HANA's unique in-memory capability. PowerDesigner can write to the SAP HANA repository or read from it.

Reading the SAP HANA repository creates a physical data model (PDM) in PowerDesigner and can merge with an existing SAP HANA PDM, if it exists, to update the design view with changes made in development. PowerDesigner can also take objects modeled in the PDM as both standard SQL Schema objects, such as tables and views, and the SAP HANA-specific attribute and analytic views (taken from PowerDesigner's facts and dimensions in the dimensional diagram of a PDM) and can create new repository objects or merge with existing ones. PowerDesigner aligns with SAP HANA packages, making sure work is never written to the wrong location.

3.2.2 Data Provisioning for SAP HANA

This section provides a high-level overview of loading data into SAP HANA. And as you can see in Figure 3.4, you have a few different on-premise data movement options available to you. It's also important to note that there have been developments to enable the solutions to work together to support data provisioning use cases (see Chapter 4, Section 4.4.4 on Replication Server integration with Data Services). You'll see this same trend toward integration continue, especially as it relates to data provisioning for SAP HANA. SAP HANA Cloud Integration (HCI) is also available to cover your integration needs when cloud-based systems are involved (see Chapter 8 for more details).

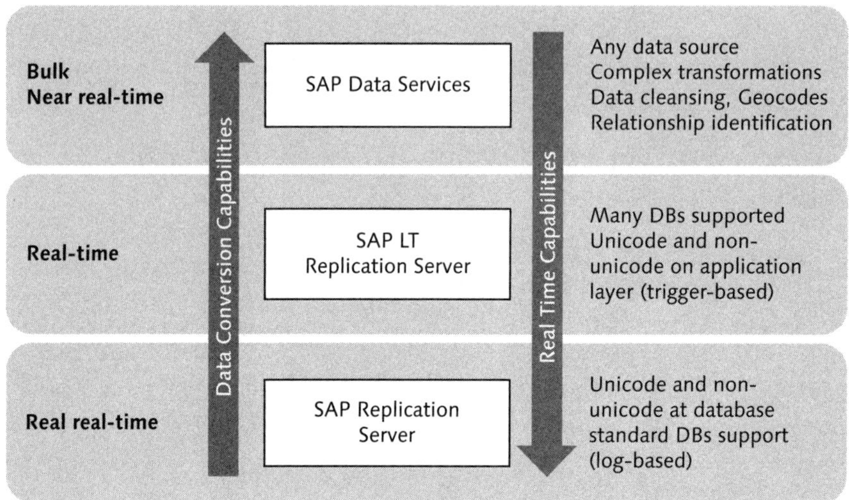

Figure 3.4 SAP Data Movement Options for SAP HANA

In the following subsections, we'll discuss some of the SAP data movement technology that's available to support data provisioning for SAP HANA.

SAP Data Services

Data Services is the leading data integration solution for high-performance batch loading of data into SAP HANA. Its highly-scalable engine supports the movement of large volumes of data into SAP HANA, and is integrated with SAP HANA's bulk-load interfaces to support parallel loading. Data Services' wide connectivity support of SAP and non-SAP data sources provides native, fast access to get the data you need into SAP HANA, including applications, RDBMSs, files, text, spatial data, XML, Hadoop, and so on. Data Services establishes a connection directly between a file or database and SAP HANA. With minimal interaction with the Data Services engine itself, data loads straight into SAP HANA without any transformation activity (extract and load, without the transformation).

Data Services also provides powerful transformation capabilities, which includes built-in support for data quality to ensure the right fit and quality of the incoming data. Data Services is optimized to push down processing to the SAP HANA database layer (E-L then the T) to improve performance for operations such as filters (where clause), aggregations (group by), sorting (order by), inner and outer joins, and various functions (aggregations, date, math, string, etc.). For SAP HANA, Data Services stages the data in SAP HANA and pushes the execution of transformations to SAP HANA by converting transformations to SAP HANA stored procedures using views and SQL.

The Data Services Workbench was specifically designed for quick and easy database replication. In just three steps within the UI, the ETL developer can deploy and execute database table replications to SAP HANA (see Figure 3.5). A quick replication wizard is also available to simplify the process even further. The Data Services Workbench additionally supports more complex data replication, jobs requiring data transformation, with a truly smart dataflow editor that guides the ETL developer with automatic table joins and mappings, expression macros, and dataflow lineage and transformed metadata.

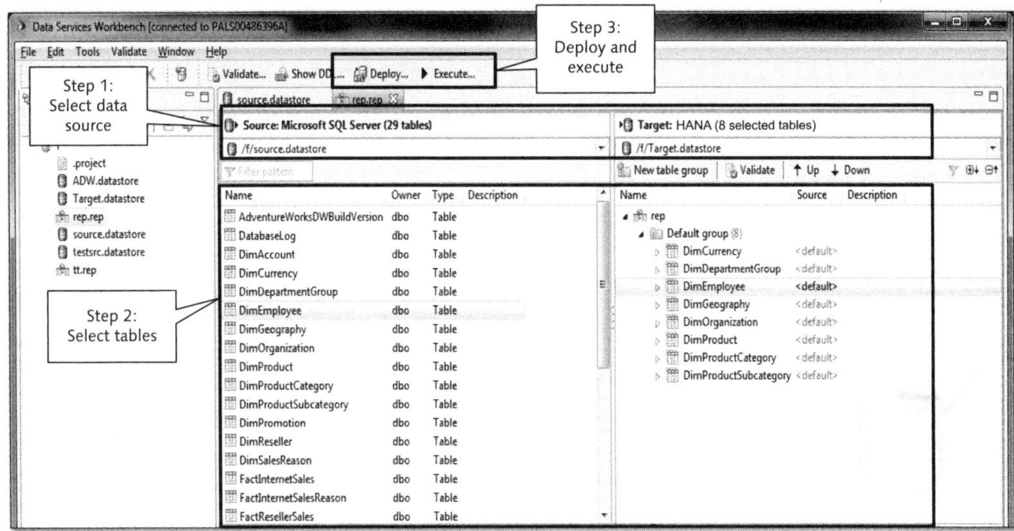

Figure 3.5 Quick Data Replication with the Data Services Workbench

Additional Facts about SAP Data Services and SAP HANA

- Migrating SAP Business Suite data to SAP HANA? Data Services supports 5000+ Business Content Extractors, with parallelized data extraction and simple drag-and-drop dataflow design.
- Is SAP HANA your data source in the ETL process? Data Services supports SAP HANA stored procedures and views (calculation, attribute, and analytical) as a data source.
- Migrating SAP BW data into SAP HANA? Data Services has optimized performance (10 times faster) for extracting SAP BW data to load into SAP HANA.
- SAP HANA is a supported repository for Data Services.

For more practical instructions, refer to Chapter 9, where we discuss Data Service's connection to data sources. Because SAP HANA is considered another data source in Data Services, the discussion in Chapter 9 also applies to SAP HANA, and no additional special configuration or development is required.

SAP Landscape Transformation Replication Server

SAP Landscape Transformation Replication Server (SAP LT) supports real-time, trigger-based replication from SAP and non-SAP sources into SAP HANA. SAP SLT is for customers who primarily need real-time data replication from ABAP-based SAP applications (with release coverage from SAP R/3 4.6C onward) to SAP HANA, including some basic data transformation capabilities such as filtering, enriching table structures, anonymization, and so on. SAP SLT is fully integrated with SAP HANA Studio's data provisioning and data modeler UIs. SAP SLT is also the default replication engine for all SAP HANA Live (sidecar) applications. There are also some advanced monitoring capabilities that are available via SAP Solution Manager and the SAP Replication Manager mobile application.

Note

SAP MaxAttention engagement support is required for initial certification of supported non-SAP data sources.

SAP Replication Server

Replication Server is a sophisticated transactional data movement product that moves and synchronizes data across the enterprise, without geographical distance limitation, to meet demanding requirements in the enterprise such as guaranteed data delivery, real-time BI, and zero operational downtime. Replication Server facilitates this by nonintrusively handling data (log-based) at the source and target, while ensuring high performance and transactional integrity. Replication Server is most commonly deployed in use cases that support high availability/disaster recovery, real-time reporting, and data distribution.

To provide high-performance real-time replication into SAP HANA, Replication Server leverages the native SAP HANA ODBC driver's bulk capabilities (such as bulk inserts and deletes, etc.) by using ExpressConnect for SAP HANA Database (ECH) technology. ECH is a library that can be loaded by Replication Server dynamically. It doesn't require a separate process for starting up, monitoring, or administering, unlike traditional Enterprise Connect Data Access (ECDA)-based technology.

The latest release of Replication Server included additional functionality to expand its SAP HANA replication support, including support for the following:

1. Database replication from SAP Business Suite applications that use cluster tables to SAP HANA
2. Data Definition Language (DDL) command replication into SAP HANA
3. Simplified installation and configuration of replication to SAP HANA using the Replication Management Agent (RMA)
4. SAP HANA as a source database

SAP HANA Cloud Integration

SAP HANA Cloud Integration (HCI) is SAP's Integration Platform as a Service (iPaaS) offering. iPaaS is comprised of a suite of cloud services that enables the development, execution, and governance of bidirectional integration flows between on-premise and cloud-based systems or cloud-to-cloud processes and services. HCI's secure and reliable integration middleware platform operates on the SAP HANA Cloud Platform (HCP). HCP resides on SAP's leading-edge SAP HANA in-memory DBMS. HCI is offered as a service solution with a strong focus on process and data integration across domains for SAP Business Suite applications, SAP HANA cloud applications, third-party cloud applications, databases (including SAP HANA), and files.

More details on HCI, including information on the architecture and getting started with the solution, are available in Chapter 8.

3.2.3 Data Quality for SAP HANA

Many SAP EIM solutions in support of data quality and information governance have been optimized to provide best-in-class support for SAP HANA. The following sections discuss how SAP Information Steward, SAP Data Quality Management, and SAP Master Data Governance both support and take advantage of SAP HANA as a part of your EIM landscape.

SAP Information Steward

SAP Information Steward (hereafter Information Steward) provides a single environment to discover, define, assess, and monitor enterprise data assets. Information Steward is a key tool in support of information governance, with the ability to monitor the quality of your data over time and centrally catalog the different data assets and business term definitions in your organization. The combination of these disciplines allows companies to identify bad data as well as see where the data is coming from (and where it's used in downstream processes).

Information Steward's Metadata Management module supports SAP HANA. The Information Steward/SAP HANA metadata integrator collects metadata information about server instances, databases, packages, views (attribute, analytic, and calculation), tables, columns, attributes/measures, variables, and so on. It also collets the metadata relationships between metadata objects within SAP HANA, as well as the relationships upstream and downstream of your SAP HANA instance for complete data impact and lineage analysis.

Information Steward views that are built on top of SAP HANA benefit from leveraging the Data Services engine, in that Data Services pushes down processing to the SAP HANA database to improve performance for operations such as filters (where clause), aggregations (group by), sorting (order by), and joins and various functions (aggregations, date, math, string, etc.). Similarly, when SAP HANA is the source, Information Steward profiling operations are pushed down to SAP HANA, which results in performance that is up to 1,000 (yes, that is three zeroes) times faster!

Additional information on Information Steward can be found in Chapter 10.

Data Quality Management, Version for SAP Solutions

SAP Data Quality Management, version for SAP Solutions (DQM for SAP) leverages the data quality capabilities in Data Services to provide real-time (point of entry) and batch cleansing, matching, and consolidation activities. DQM for SAP supports out-of-the-box integration with SAP ERP, SAP CRM, and SAP Master Data Governance (SAP MDG). When deploying this product onto a landscape for the SAP Business Suite powered by SAP HANA, the solution takes advantage of data quality functionality that is embedded natively inside SAP HANA, taking a dedicated install of Data Services out of the picture to overall lower the cost of ownership and increase the performance of the solution.

SAP Master Data Governance

SAP MDG allows you to keep master data consistent and accurate across your enterprise by using robust data governance functions to create, maintain, and replicate master data. SAP MDG includes support for the SAP Business Suite powered by SAP HANA.

In master data management, the data creation process typically starts with searching for existing data. The SAP HANA platform accelerates the process by supporting fuzzy search. This permits both freestyle Google-like searches (using search terms) as well as attribute-based searches (using dedicated thresholds for each search attribute). For all search hits, SAP HANA calculates a similarity rank and allows the result to be sorted by a weighted score across all attributes. The calculated similarity score speeds identification and sorting of potential duplicates.

SAP HANA also transforms the process of accessing master data. Because it's column-based and resides in memory, the SAP HANA database permits access to all different values of a master data attribute (e.g., all states in a selected country in all customers' addresses). To accomplish this, the SAP HANA database uses a column dictionary that lists all values for an attribute. Each individual database entry points to the dictionary. Because the dictionary resides in memory, information access (i.e., a display of all attribute values of all master data) occurs almost instantaneously, and drilldown and filtering by attribute values can be performed extremely fast. Multi-attribute drilldown enables filtering as well as analysis of intrinsic master data structures.

SAP MDG is covered in detail in Chapter 11.

3.3 Big Data and Hadoop

Chapter 1 discussed the market term *big data* to describe the growth in volume and complexity of information that must be managed today. This section discusses big data in relation to Hadoop, one of the most interesting and promising new technologies related to big data. By the end of this section, you'll have a basic understanding of how Hadoop compares to other available technologies and how to future-proof your EIM strategy.

3.3.1 The Rise of Hadoop

In this section, we'll go over the general conditions that have given rise to Hadoop.

The Rise of Parallel Processing Architectures

New tools, techniques, and strategies have been developed to manage ever-growing data volumes. There are two ways to scale a system so it can handle a larger workload: *scaling up*, which uses faster, more capable hardware, and *scaling out*, which adds more independent hardware. For example, adding RAM to a server is scaling up, while adding another server is scaling out. In the 2000s, it became clear that scaling out was the winning approach to scaling. In practical terms, this means computers can handle tasks faster when the tasks can be parallelized to run across multiple machines completely independently. Companies including Google and Yahoo! applied these parallel processing architecture concepts and developed a platform to work with mass amounts of largely unstructured web-related data that scales out by leveraging commodity hardware. This led to the Apache Hadoop project, which has spawned a number of subprojects related to Hadoop and NoSQL that are ideally suited to address some of the big data challenges.

NoSQL: A New Kind of Database

Taking advantage of the scalability offered by parallelization and the ability to deal with new types of data that doesn't come with predefined schemas requires a new kind of datastore. These new solutions are called *NoSQL datastores,* because they are nonrelational and therefore can't support full SQL semantics. The idea is that if you throw out the relations between pieces of data, then it's much easier to spread the data over multiple machines and therefore scale out. There is a range of NoSQL solutions with slightly different capabilities, depending on the exact trade-offs made in their design. Hadoop, which we'll discuss later, is one of these solutions.

To understand how the NoSQL solutions scale so well, we need to think about the two types of traditional database: Online Transactional Processing (OLTP) and Online Analytical Processing (OLAP). The OLTP, or operational database, is great for transactions and relational data, but those same useful characteristics make it difficult to scale out because each table may refer to many other tables, and retrieving a piece of information for an application may involve lots of intertwined tables. The information about an entity—say, a sales order—might live in several tables (product, customer, etc.), and those tables all need to be accessed to fulfill a request. OLAP databases scale out more effectively than OLTP databases because of optimizations such as aggregations that remove many of the size and speed roadblocks, but they still bog down at very large scales. This is largely due to the underlying relational database that makes it tricky to spread data across machines.

It's unlikely that NoSQL datastores will actually replace traditional databases. However, NoSQL datastores eliminate (or at least minimize) the relational aspect of relationship databases. Each piece of data that's stored has no specific relationship to any other piece of data stored. These systems are highly effective for certain applications such as crawling the web or analyzing log files, where each piece of data is logically independent of the others and where the ability to process large data volumes is more important than transactional integrity. Imagine storing a private copy of, say, one million web pages. Each one would have a unique identifier (the URL), a body, and perhaps a few other bits of information. It would be relatively easy to spread that information across many independent nodes, because no document has any particular relation to any other.

Most NoSQL datastores don't support schemas at all. Instead, each piece of data that's stored is unstructured from the datastore's perspective—simply a bunch of characters with no particular meaning and no relation to any other piece of data. The program that uses the data stored in them needs to make sense of what is retrieved. Clearly, this makes such solutions more difficult to work with in the EIM context. You may find that a programmer or data analyst with programming skills is needed to work with a NoSQL datastore. Also note that most EIM tools are designed to leverage SQL interfaces and to rely on the schema to define the semantics and structure of the data. If you plan to employ a NoSQL datastore, make sure you understand the implications and tools that are available for information management purposes.

Next, we'll define Hadoop, briefly explain how it works, and describe some key technologies that have been built on top of it. This isn't intended to be a comprehensive discussion, but rather a simple, high-level overview that will help you understand what Hadoop can and can't do. We encourage you to seek out more information sources online for this fast-developing space.

3.3.2 Introduction to Hadoop

Hadoop is free and open-source Java-based software that enables distributed, scalable, and reliable computing on clusters of inexpensive servers. Let's consider each of those characteristics separately.

Distributed

Hadoop runs on a coordinated group of machines that's known as a *cluster*, so that large amounts of RAM, storage, and CPU power can be brought to bear on big data sets. The Hadoop framework provides a high degree of automation for the core operations involved in running a distributed computing solution, such as partitioning, scheduling, dispatching, executing, communicating, failure handling, monitoring, reporting, and more.

A Hadoop cluster has several *worker nodes* and one *master mode*, which acts as the overall coordinator for the cluster. The master then keeps track of which workers have which data, so that programming jobs or "tasks" can be run against those data. When a task arrives at the master node, the master dispatches it to the worker nodes with the needed blocks of data, which then signal the master node after task execution is complete. Thus, programmers who use Hadoop don't have to concern themselves with the details of the location of data on which they want to perform operations.

Reliable

The Hadoop software is fault-tolerant, meaning it expects and handles hardware and software failures with as little human intervention as possible. One way in which Hadoop provides reliability is by automatically replicating data to physically different machines. If the master node detects that a worker node is out of service, the master node automatically instructs another worker node to create a copy of the data that was on the expired worker node. Furthermore, it instructs the new worker node to pick up any outstanding tasks that the worker node has not completed, all without human operators or programmers having to think about it.

Scalable

Hadoop is designed for a massive scale of processors, memory, and local attached storage. It's well known that Hadoop has been shown to scale up to 4,000 machines. To give you an idea of the size of the problems that Hadoop can tackle, consider that several businesses sprang up in the late 2000s that store a complete copy of the Internet on Hadoop clusters, which they also use to process that data.

3.3.3 Hadoop 2.0 Architecture: HDFS, YARN, and MapReduce

Any Hadoop 2.0 installation involves the modules that we discuss in this section: HDFS, YARN, and MapReduce. They are the core technologies that fulfill Hadoop's design goals of being distributed, scalable, and reliable.

Hadoop Distributed File System (HDFS) is the code that's responsible for storing data across potentially thousands of machines within a Hadoop cluster and retrieving it when needed. Behind the scenes, HDFS keeps track of where each piece of data is and ensures replication and data integrity. Because HDFS does all the work, programmers can use it almost as easily as they can use the file system on a single machine.

Yet Another Resource Negotiator (YARN) is the framework for job scheduling and resource management within a Hadoop cluster. The resource management capabilities were embedded within the MapReduce module in Hadoop 1.0. YARN has been introduced in Hadoop 2.0 architecture to enable multiple data processing engines that may support different interaction patterns for the data stored in HDFS beyond MapReduce to share the common resource management framework.

MapReduce is a programming model that allows programmers to use the processing and storage power offered by the Hadoop cluster. The idea behind MapReduce is to apply a "divide and conquer" approach to processing data. It has two explicit phases: map and reduce. In the map phase, a simple program is run over lots of independent pieces of data. Then, in the reduce phase, the results of the map phase are gathered from each independent worker and programmatically combined into a single result set.

Map Reduce

The term *map reduce* can refer to both a parallel programming model in general and to the specific MapReduce component in Hadoop that implements that programming model. Several other technologies, including IQ and the proprietary Google BigTable, have their own implementations of map reduce.

Let's consider an example to help understand how map reduce works. Imagine that the guests at a dinner party are asked to find all the instances of "white whale" in the book *Moby Dick*. This problem can be done in a map reduce paradigm. The map function would tear up the book into chapters, hand them around to each guest, and instruct them to write down every line number where the phrase is found. The reduce function would take all of the results from each guest and put them together into a single, ordered list of the line numbers where the word appears.

Note

Before we conclude this section, it's important to point out that Hadoop isn't just a place for storing data, but also provides a mechanism for processing the data that's stored in it. The end result is that instead of having to remove data from the database to process it, the processing can be done right where the data is stored. This *in situ* processing allows many steps to be chained together or, for recursive algorithms, the same step to be run over and over without moving the data over the network.

While MapReduce has served quite well as a core data processing model for Hadoop, it fundamentally addresses batch-oriented data processing needs. It doesn't provide an optimal solution for applications that need to interactively query the data from Hadoop. With Hadoop 2.0 architecture, Hadoop as a data processing platform has moved into its next phase. With the introduction of YARN, Hadoop has decoupled itself from MapReduce as the only programming framework for data processing and opened the opportunities for a new data processing framework to meet the challenges around real-time data access and higher throughput. Tez is a new framework based on YARN for near real-time big data processing. The MapReduce model constrains the programmers to express the problem via a set of map tasks followed by a set of reduce tasks. This typically results in multiple MapReduce jobs, which harm latency for short queries and throughput for large-scale queries. Tez provides a powerful framework that allows programmers to express a complex data processing task within a single application or job. For example, any given SQL query can be expressed as a single job using Tez. Tez allows projects within the Hadoop ecosystem to meet demands for faster response times as well as extreme throughput.

3.3.4 Hadoop Ecosystem

Hadoop is an open-source project that has a very active community contributing not only bug fixes, but also a considerable number of modules that provide additional capabilities to the Hadoop core. The Hadoop technology family is shown in Figure 3.6 and discussed in more detail in this section.

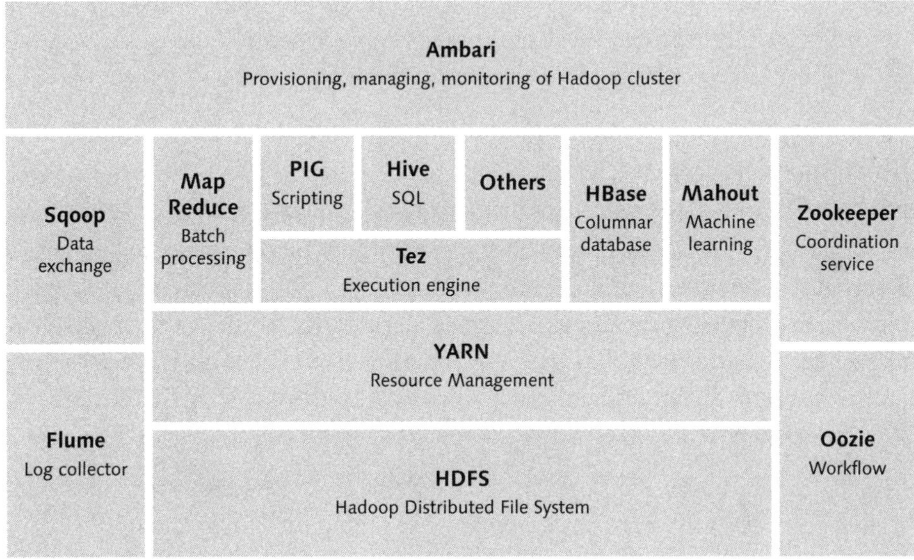

Figure 3.6 The Hadoop Ecosystem

Sqoop: Data Exchange with Relational Databases

Sqoop is designed to address the need for bulk data transfer between Hadoop and structured datastores such as relational databases. You can use Sqoop to move the data from a RDBMS system into Hadoop, process the data natively within

Hadoop, and then transfer it back to the RDMBS systems. Major Hadoop vendors have productized specialized Sqoop connectors for different RDBMS systems.

Note that Sqoop essentially addresses the data movement need for Hadoop, which is typically addressed by ETL tools within the enterprise landscape. Most of the enterprise class ETL tools, such as Data Services (see Chapter 9), already support data movement between Hadoop and RDBMSs. From an enterprise standpoint, these ETL tools are much more mature as compared to Sqoop, providing higher data transfer rates, complex data transformation capabilities, data lineage, traceability, and rich developer user experience. The enterprise also benefits from vendor support that comes with ETL tools.

Flume: Log Collector

Hadoop is ideally suited for processing unstructured data such as log data, which includes web logs, network logs, application logs, sensor data, and so on. Flume is a distributed, reliable, and scalable service for efficiently collecting, aggregating, and moving large amounts of log data into Hadoop.

Hive: SQL on Hadoop

Probably the most useful Hadoop project for the enterprise, *Hive*, is a data warehouse that provides an SQL interface on top of the Hadoop cluster, allowing programmers to interact with the Hadoop cluster like a gigantic database. Hive supports an extensive but incomplete set of SQL semantics. This has the advantage of allowing programmers and data analysts to analyze and slice and dice data using tools that are familiar to them, rather than having to write MapReduce jobs for even simple tasks.

In Hadoop 1.0, because all operations are done as MapReduce jobs behind the scenes, there is a rather large minimum processing time for any query due to job initialization and parallelization. Therefore, Hive was almost exclusively used for batch mode processing. As mentioned earlier, the introduction of YARN and Tez in Hadoop 2.0 enables Hive to optimize its execution model to deliver faster query response times. Note that even though Hive is moving toward supporting an interactive query scenario, at this time it's not expected to replace enterprise data warehouse systems, which are highly optimized for structured data and predefined schemas. Instead, it enables an organization to store unstructured or machine-generated data that doesn't fit nicely in their data warehouse, summarize it, aggregate it, and correlate it with data in their enterprise data warehouse to gain new insights.

HBase: NoSQL Datastore

HBase is a column-oriented, schemaless, distributed database modeled after Google's BigTable. It offers random, real-time read-write access to data. It's a NoSQL-type datastore as opposed to an RDBMS, so it lacks many of the features and data management capabilities of traditional databases. Unlike many other NoSQL distributed datastores, HBase offers strong consistency, meaning it can be used well for things such as high-speed counter aggregation (e.g., how many times has an ad been displayed on the web?).

At first glance, HBase seems like it would be extremely useful to the enterprise, but it really only makes sense with very large data sets involving either billions of rows or massive binary data sets such as photograph or video sharing sites might have; otherwise, HBase performs worse than similar technologies because of high initialization costs. Note also that the programming, management, and operations for HBase are quite specialized and can be tricky to achieve near real-time performance. In most cases, an enterprise would be better served using SAP HANA.

Pig: Scripting

Pig is a platform for manipulating and analyzing large data sets in Hadoop. It's primarily intended for data analysts, who can use its scripting language for manipulating and transforming data. Why do analysts have to program to work with data in Hadoop? Data that's stored in Hadoop isn't self-describing; that is, it's schemaless and may be untyped. Hadoop data also tends to be unstructured and may change over time. Because of this, analysts make sense out of the data using programs, which can be understood, reused, and tweaked by others. The result is that a greater than usual burden of understanding the data falls on the data analyst. Familiar tools for data analysts, including those based on SQL, either can't be used at all—or, if Hive is available—can be used to the extent that the tools support it. Pig helps fill this tool gap, but it has a significant learning curve.

Note

Both Hive and Pig are supported by Data Services. This is discussed in Chapter 9.

Mahout: Machine Learning

Mahout is a set of machine learning libraries for Hadoop that can leverage big data sets to provide recommendations, clustering, classification, and itemsets. Examples of machine learning include grouping related news stories or suggesting products that shoppers might want to buy. If you have a core business-differentiating service that runs in Hadoop, it may be worth leveraging machine-learning techniques to process that data more quickly and effectively. Otherwise, you may find that the built-in machine-learning capabilities in the SAP HANA Predictive Analytics Library offer easier management and faster performance.

Ambari: Provisioning, Managing, and Monitoring the Hadoop Cluster

Ambari is aimed at making Hadoop management simpler. It provides an intuitive, easy-to-use Hadoop management web UI for provisioning, managing, and monitoring Apache Hadoop clusters. Ambari also provides an Application Programming Interface (API) for application developers and system integrators to easily integrate Hadoop management capabilities into their own applications.

ZooKeeper: Coordination Service

ZooKeeper provides operational services for a Hadoop cluster. It provides a distributed configuration service, a synchronization service, and a naming registry for distributed systems. Distributed applications use ZooKeeper to store and mediate updates to important configuration information.

Oozie: Workflow

Oozie is a workflow scheduler system that's used to combine multiple Hadoop jobs sequentially into one logical unit of work. Oozie supports several types of Hadoop jobs out of the box such as MapReduce, Pig, Hive, and Sqoop. It can also be used to schedule system-specific jobs such as shell scripts.

> **Note**
>
> Ambari, ZooKeeper, and Oozie introduce enterprise class operational capabilities into Hadoop and in turn make Hadoop an enterprise-friendly data platform.

Now that you understand Hadoop concepts, let's apply them to common business requirements.

3.3.5 Enterprise Use Cases

In this section, we'll consider the most likely cases in which Hadoop might be used in an enterprise.

Hadoop for Preprocessing Raw Data

The most common use of Hadoop today is to store and process unstructured data such as log files stored in plain text, thereby turning them into structured information that can be read into a database or enterprise data warehouses for further analysis or consumption. This is also likely to be the number-one enterprise use case.

Although the phrase *log files* suggests highly technical information that's only of interest to a systems administrator, log files are actually used to store business information as well. For example, an e-commerce site may store its web access logs that show which IP addresses requested which resources on the site. With proper processing, those log files can be turned into information on which products were viewed, how long web visitors stayed on each page, and so on.

Hadoop tends to be useful for batch-style, exploratory data processing in which analysts sift through large volumes of data to find new patterns and relationships that weren't envisioned at the time the data was collected. There are two reasons why Hadoop is good for this.

First, processing raw information is computationally intensive. It's done by analyzing huge files, line by line, and organizing the information into a totally different form. Hadoop has this processing power right in the storage tier and can handle even highly recursive algorithms. By contrast, to process log files in a database, you first need to read the information into a program, process it, and then write each processed unit back into the database. In the past, this was precisely what people did, but as mentioned earlier, the larger such a system gets, the more prone it is to unexpected failures and the harder it is to keep running.

Second, unstructured information by definition doesn't follow a schema. Its format is unpredictable and may change over time. Hadoop's processing imposes meaning on this data *post hoc*, meaning analysts decide what information they want to pull out when the analysis is needed, instead of being stuck with whatever was specified when the application was built.

This doesn't mean that Hadoop should be used for all unstructured information handling. Unstructured data such as emails, documents, and presentations tend to be stored in disparate systems throughout an enterprise and are better handled by EIM. They are unlikely to be processed in Hadoop in an enterprise setting, especially if good information governance practices are followed.

Extended Archive Solution

Some enterprises leverage Hadoop as an online archive for storing and analyzing near-line data. That is, instead of backing up to tape or deleting old data, they offload it from their enterprise data warehouse to Hadoop for cost-effective online data storage. Unlike tape, which is almost exclusively used for disaster recovery, Hadoop makes it possible to query the data if it's needed, although it's slower than pulling it from an enterprise data warehouse or active database. This can also be done at low cost if the enterprise is large enough to take advantage of economies of scale. Obviously, the extended archive solution only makes sense if information doesn't need to be retired in accordance with information lifecycle management policies.

Advanced Scenarios

Complex information processing is needed in a wide variety of scenarios. This includes machine learning use cases that were mentioned earlier in this chapter, as well as more specialized uses such as video or image processing. Some real-world examples of this include using Hadoop for credit ratings, fraud detection, and risk assessment. In today's enterprise, such advanced scenarios are typically only seen when the Hadoop cluster provides a business differentiator or mission-critical service (e.g., computer vision algorithms applied to satellite maps by a mapping company or genome sequencing by a biomedical research firm).

The good news for the enterprise information manager who might be faced with an advanced Hadoop scenario is that qualified staff will almost certainly be available for a mission-critical scenario as part of the overall IT investment. These individuals need to be consulted to provide data for analytics. Typically, this data would be obtained using Pig or custom MapReduce jobs and then pulled in batch mode into an enterprise data warehouse, SAP HANA, or some other database. SAP recommends using Data Services for this purpose.

3.3.6 Hadoop in the Enterprise: The Bottom Line

As of the writing of this book, Hadoop use in the enterprise is in its early stages, but growing rapidly. The Hadoop developer community is enhancing Hadoop to meet enterprise demands. And software vendors, such Cloudera and Hortonworks, have emerged to further drive penetration of Hadoop within the enterprise. The market is realizing the opportunity represented by big bata and the ability to track new signals from digital noise that was once impossible to capture and make sense of. This section outlines some basic factors to keep in mind when considering Hadoop.

Hadoop is well suited for very large data storage and processing needs. It's a proven technology that has been used productively for many years by large companies. It can scale up to thousands of machines with a high degree of automation. Hadoop clusters are highly reliable and easy to operate (compared to alternatives). Hadoop also provides great flexibility. It's open source, so changes can be made as needed, such as organization-specific customizations or bugs fixes. Because Hadoop runs on commodity hardware and the software is free and open source, users can avoid vendor lock-in, driving down costs further.

However, all of those advantages do not mean that Hadoop is a must-have for the enterprise. There are many enterprise class data platforms, such as SAP HANA, that not only support storage of large volumes of data, but also support processing of that data to deliver real-time analytics. When it comes to choosing a big data solution, in many cases, there is no single answer. Hadoop can play a complementary role along with other big data platforms such as SAP HANA. An enterprise needs to consider several factors while determining whether Hadoop belongs in its solution architecture. First, although it's free and open source, Hadoop can be expensive to run, primarily because of the capital outlay that's necessary to establish the Hadoop cluster and the accompanying trained and qualified personnel. Hadoop needs to surpass a certain minimum size in terms of data volume and processing needs before it begins to outperform alternative solutions. Because Hadoop isn't efficient at small scales, it tends to only be used with lots of machines: no fewer than five but more likely tens or hundreds. The other cost driver is personnel. Hadoop requires highly skilled engineering, operations, and analysis resources. Because the technologies involved are still young, it can be difficult and costly to hire qualified people. Over time, this will likely change as Hadoop becomes more widespread.

The second factor limiting the spread of Hadoop is the immaturity of available tools. Few reporting and analytics tools interoperate well with Hadoop, and those that exist are less capable and user friendly than their traditional counterparts. This is true even if the Hadoop cluster uses Hive or Pig; Hadoop doesn't fully support SQL semantics. Although Hadoop is gaining traction within enterprise, so many traditional enterprise tool vendors are moving toward embracing Hadoop as an underlying data platform to minimize the learning curve for the end users.

Third, Hadoop doesn't currently support the type of role-based access that most enterprises rely on. Governance and security of data that's stored in Hadoop isn't as well understood as data stored in SQL. Typically, if someone has access to a Hadoop cluster, he also has access to all the data stored there. For the types of data traditionally stored in Hadoop—such as news stories, videos, or ad impression counters—this has not been a problem, but it's something to keep in mind when considering Hadoop for the enterprise.

Finally, remember that Hadoop is best for batch processing today. Real-time processing is possible for certain use cases, and technology is evolving but realistically beyond the reach of most enterprises at this time. Table 3.1 depicts the strengths and weaknesses of Hadoop. See the next section for a discussion of Hadoop and SAP HANA, where this topic is covered in more detail.

Strengths	Weaknesses
▸ Huge data volumes ▸ Unstructured data handling ▸ Batch processing ▸ Reliable ▸ Scalable ▸ Lowest cost ▸ Open source ▸ No hardware lock-in ▸ Excellent paid support available	▸ Requires skilled engineering, operations, and analysis resources ▸ Hiring qualified talent ▸ Less mature than SQL ▸ Governance ▸ Real-time challenges ▸ Not efficient at small scales

Table 3.1 Hadoop Strengths and Weaknesses

3.4 SAP HANA and Hadoop

In enterprises, there are many scenarios where SAP HANA is likely to be a better solution than Hadoop for big data needs. In this section, we'll discuss why this is so and consider why, in some cases, Hadoop may be a useful extension to SAP HANA's capabilities.

3.4.1 The V's: Volume, Variety, Velocity

Analysts have used the term *the V's* to refer to big data: volume (how much data?), variety (how uniform is the data?), and velocity (how quickly does the data arrive and how quickly do you need to process it?). The V's provide a simple framework for comparing Hadoop and SAP HANA. On volume, clearly Hadoop can handle more data, but SAP HANA can scale up to handle most big data use cases that an enterprise is likely to encounter. More accurately, Hadoop only makes sense when you're faced with many terabytes of data, whereas SAP HANA is also useful at smaller data volumes. Hadoop has the edge when it comes to handling a variety of data formats, including unstructured and nonrelational data. On velocity, SAP HANA is the clear winner, and for that reason, enterprise users may want to consider reading data processed in a Hadoop cluster into a SAP HANA box for faster consumption.

3.4.2 SAP HANA: Designed for Enterprises

Unlike Hadoop, SAP HANA was designed for enterprise use and is therefore easier to integrate with most organizations' available tools, personnel, and practices. Managing SAP HANA will be familiar to a database administrator; managing Hadoop requires a specialized skill set. Specialized programming knowledge is also required to write MapReduce jobs, which are almost always used on Hadoop even if the primary usage is via the SQL-like interface of Hive. Even the skills that are required by data analysts using Hadoop tend to be quite different from what is typically found in the enterprise.

3.4.3 Hadoop as an SAP HANA Extension

Hadoop is a part of the organizational data fabric that SAP can unify through the SAP HANA platform. Hadoop is an ideal place to store, preprocess, and perhaps even process the data, particularly unstructured data. Hadoop can be used as a data reservoir where data of unknown or low value can be held, mined, and explored, as well as where models can be trained and refined to help identify the valuable data. After the data that needs real-time action is identified, it can be moved into SAP HANA. Hadoop may be a useful complement to SAP HANA when unstructured data needs to be turned into structured data. Hadoop can be used to provide context to corporate data. Contextual data, which is typically unstructured, can be stored in Hadoop and used to enrich corporate data held in SAP HANA.

SAP HANA smart data access enables remote data that's located in heterogeneous data sources, including Hadoop, to be accessed as if they are local tables in SAP HANA, without copying the data into SAP HANA. It supports the development and deployment of the next generation of analytical applications that require the ability to access, synthesize, and integrate data from multiple systems in real-time regardless of where the data is located or what systems are generating it. Using this design pattern, processed data can be read out of the Hadoop cluster into SAP HANA or an enterprise data warehouse for further usage.

You'll know if you have a good candidate use case due to extreme data size, but there are other cases that might not be so easily identified. First, data processing on large unstructured data sets can often result in a situation where significant custom coding is needed for job scheduling to prevent users of the system from clashing over resources and to prevent stalled jobs. Highly recursive algorithms, algorithms that rewrite data regularly, or algorithms that can't easily be expressed as SQL may also be good candidates for use in Hadoop.

Hadoop can also be useful to keep information available at a lower cost, for example, offloading information that doesn't justify the expense of constant real-time availability.

3.5 EIM and Hadoop

While the uses of EIM and Hadoop have already been mentioned in this chapter, this section will focus on extraction, transformation, and loading (ETL) and Hadoop, as well as issues of governance and information lifecycle management with Hadoop.

3.5.1 ETL: Data Services and the Information Design Tool

SAP provides support for Hadoop using Data Services. Data Services is the single most important technology in SAP's solutions for EIM portfolio when it comes to Hadoop interoperability. Data Services is the primary technology component responsible for ETL (transferring data from one system into another, and possibly massaging it along the way). Rather than trying to access Hadoop clusters directly for reporting and analysis, most enterprises want to use Data Services to extract data from Hadoop in batch mode and store it in an enterprise data warehouse. From the data warehouse, analysts can access the data using familiar tools such as in the SAP BusinessObjects BI platform, or define universes using the Information Design Tool. Because Hadoop has high latency in retrieving data, it's unlikely that analytics tools would run well if they fetched their data directly from the Hadoop cluster.

3.5.2 Unsupported: Information Governance and Information Lifecycle Management

As will be described in more detail in Chapter 4, SAP's solutions for EIM include SAP Information Lifecycle Management (SAP ILM) and technologies to support information governance. Hadoop lacks the basic technology hooks that would enable a program to enforce governance on data stored in a Hadoop cluster. Also, the use case isn't quite right. You would not expect to find operational data of the type that is normally governed (e.g., master data domains such as customer data). This leaves uncertainty about what type of governance might be needed in this environment. Until these issues are cleared up, Hadoop as part of information governance is unlikely.

SAP ILM is also not likely to support Hadoop. SAP ILM performs the important function of obsoleting data that is no longer needed to reduce information overload and to mitigate legal risks. But again, this isn't a likely Hadoop cluster use case. On one hand, the types of data likely to be stored in a Hadoop cluster would not have a high probability of legal risk (as opposed to, say, company email or operational data). On the other hand, Hadoop is often inexpensive enough that organizations find it's more costly to identify which data needs to be purged than to simply add new machines to the Hadoop cluster. Besides, Hadoop tends to be used in cases where the business is deriving a core business advantage from having access to as much data as possible—more data than their competition—so they are unlikely to want to give any up.

3.6 Summary

This chapter has provided insight into SAP HANA and Hadoop, and how they fit in with your EIM strategy. Now that this and the previous two chapters have given you a big picture idea of the concepts and ideas behind EIM, you're ready to dive into the details. The next chapter provides specific information about SAP's solutions for EIM.

This chapter introduces you to SAP's solutions for Enterprise Information Management, allowing you to judge which products are of the most interest to you. Based on what you learn in this chapter, you can determine which chapters in Part II you should read first and where you need to start learning more.

4 SAP's Solutions for Enterprise Information Management

SAP's solutions for EIM have both great breadth and depth, spanning the full capabilities for managing information from its acquisition, through active use, until retirement and destruction. This chapter discusses all of the currently available products and solutions that SAP offers for EIM. The portfolio will continue to grow as SAP continues to make investments in this area.

Chapter 1 discussed EIM in SAP's overall portfolio; Figure 4.1 shows the same portfolio view, but also lists the EIM products, which are explored further in this chapter.

Figure 4.1 shows SAP's solutions for EIM in schematic form. At the top of the graphic are applications that depend on the data that the SAP solutions manage; at the bottom are the data sources and the types of data, which both feed the information management products and are managed by them. The middle of the graphic is dominated by the set of EIM solutions offered by SAP, all beneath a box labeled "Information Governance." (Information governance isn't a product, but a discipline that is supported by multiple products. It's discussed in more detail in Chapter 2.) The following products are included in SAP's solutions for EIM:

- SAP Data Services (hereafter referred to as Data Services)
- SAP Information Steward (hereafter referred to as Information Steward)
- SAP NetWeaver Master Data Management (SAP NetWeaver MDM)
- SAP Master Data Governance (SAP MDG)
- SAP Information Lifecycle Management
- Enterprise Content Management by OpenText (SAP ECM)

- SAP Replication Server (hereafter referred to as Replication Server)
- SAP PowerDesigner (hereafter referred to as PowerDesigner)

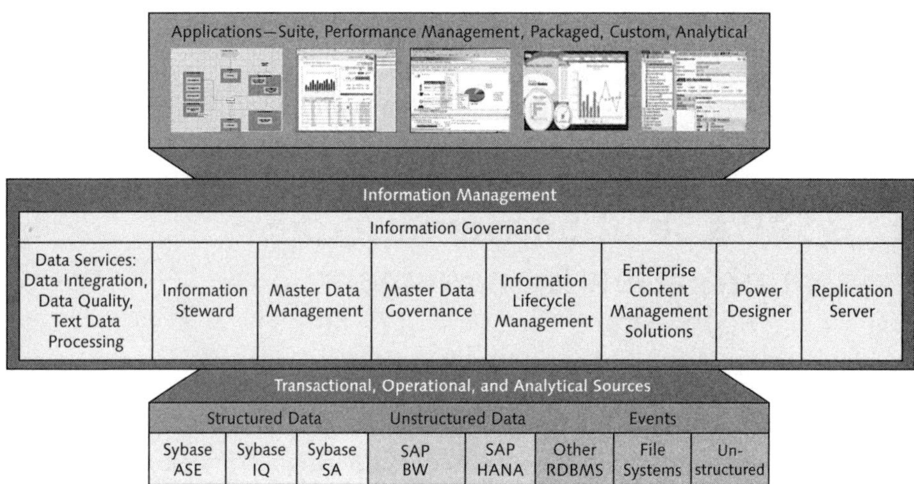

Figure 4.1 SAP's Solutions for EIM

In addition to the software products mentioned in this list, SAP also provides rapid-deployment solutions that are built on top of existing EIM products. These aren't listed in Figure 4.1 because they aren't standalone software. These solutions are covered in more detail in Chapter 5.

This chapter provides a brief introduction to SAP's capabilities for EIM, whether software products (such as Data Services, Information Steward, SAP MDG, etc.), solutions built on software products (such as data migration), or disciplines (such as information governance). Part II of the book will provide greater details on some of the capabilities; however, due to the extent of the capabilities, not all of them will be covered in depth.

Chapter 1 discussed the use of EIM for on-boarding, active use, and off-boarding of information. The following is a list of SAP's EIM capabilities for each area, all of which will be discussed in more detail in this chapter:

- **On-boarding**
  Includes Data Services, Information Steward, SAP ILM, SAP MDM, and SAP MDG, as well as the use of data migration and the on-boarding of content with SAP Extended ECM.

- **Active use**
  Includes Data Services, Information Steward, SAP MDM, SAP MDG, SAP Document Access by OpenText, and SAP Extended ECM.
- **Off-boarding**
  Includes Data Services, SAP Document Access by OpenText, SAP Extended ECM, and SAP ILM.

4.1 SAP PowerDesigner

PowerDesigner is an architecture and modeling platform that captures, designs, and communicates the current and planned state of enterprise information assets. It captures current state environments and easily, visually documents existing systems to understand what the business does today and how it's implemented in technology. PowerDesigner doesn't just draw the model of the business and technical environments—it also helps you easily capture the dependencies between these perspectives.

PowerDesigner starts with a business glossary to use a unified business language for all models in the environment, assisting in stewardship and governance during design-time. Next, it aligns the business language with an enterprise-wide conceptual data model that represents the information standards in pure business terms. The conceptual data model is aligned with other models that represent business processes, applications, physical databases, and many other viewpoints. Figure 4.2 depicts how all of these models work together to drive the future state plan for information with a real enterprise-wide impact analysis, from the business definitions to the technology and databases that implement it.

Full lifecycle design-time change management ensures easy implementation of proposed changes. By viewing changes that are proposed from architecture to execution, all stakeholders will collaborate more efficiently, leading to a plan that reduces the time, cost, and risk associated with any business transformation or change. Using the enterprise repository, users can share diagrams, navigate to information documentation, and recommend changes in both business and technical contexts.

Next, we'll introduce some of the different PowerDesigner models that are available.

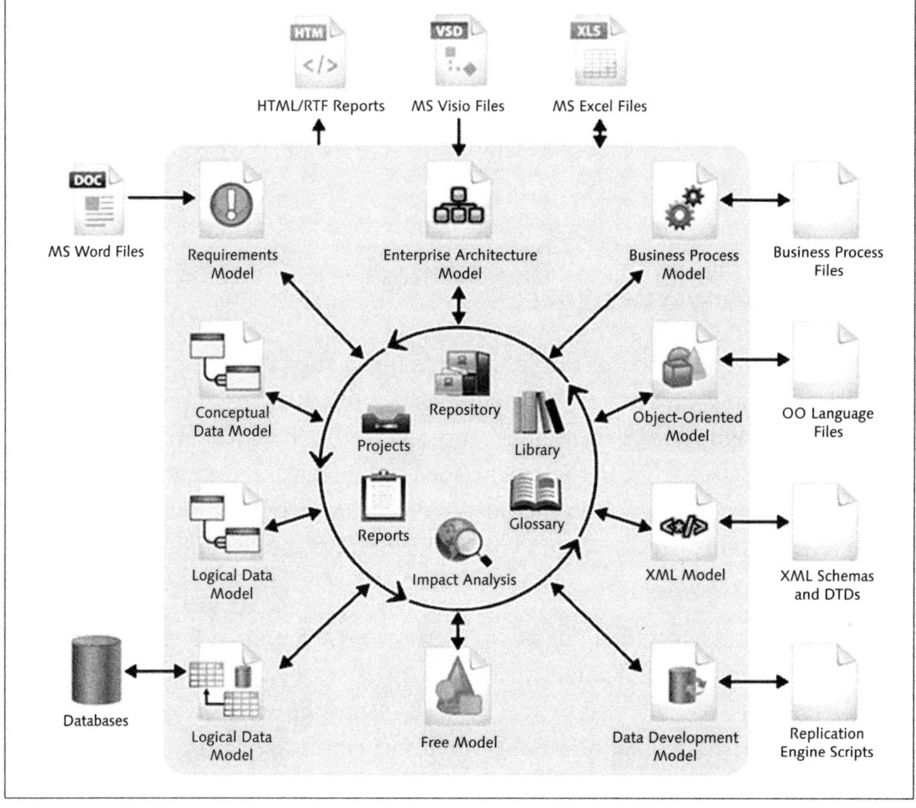

Figure 4.2 SAP PowerDesigner Capability Overview

Introduction to PowerDesigner Models

PowerDesigner's unique approach to information architecture starts with an enterprise conceptual data model (CDM), which is aligned with multiple logical and physical data models (LDMs and PDMs) that represent all the different information systems. The enterprise CDM defines all data sources, whether they ultimately are in relational, hierarchical, embedded object-oriented, or even unstructured storage formats. The enterprise CDM is a roll-up of information definitions for all sources and all business use cases, and it essentially serves as the enterprise standard blueprint for all implementations.

To define the implementation of a data system, we use the LDM and PDM, which represent the relational database management systems (RDBMSs) in our enterprise. PowerDesigner's unique data movement model (DMM) defines and describes data integration transformation and replication as a single logical landscape. For warehouse modeling and analytics systems, the PowerDesigner dimensional model can be used to define report structures independent of the physical database storing the measures and dimensions. This model can also synchronize with SAP BusinessObjects universes, or can be used to generate SQL queries for use with any OLAP-type reporting tool.

PowerDesigner can also document the entire application and technology landscape used for information systems, extending traceability from the definition of enterprise business data all the way to the interfaces in the runtime environments. See Figure 4.3 for an example of an enterprise architecture model.

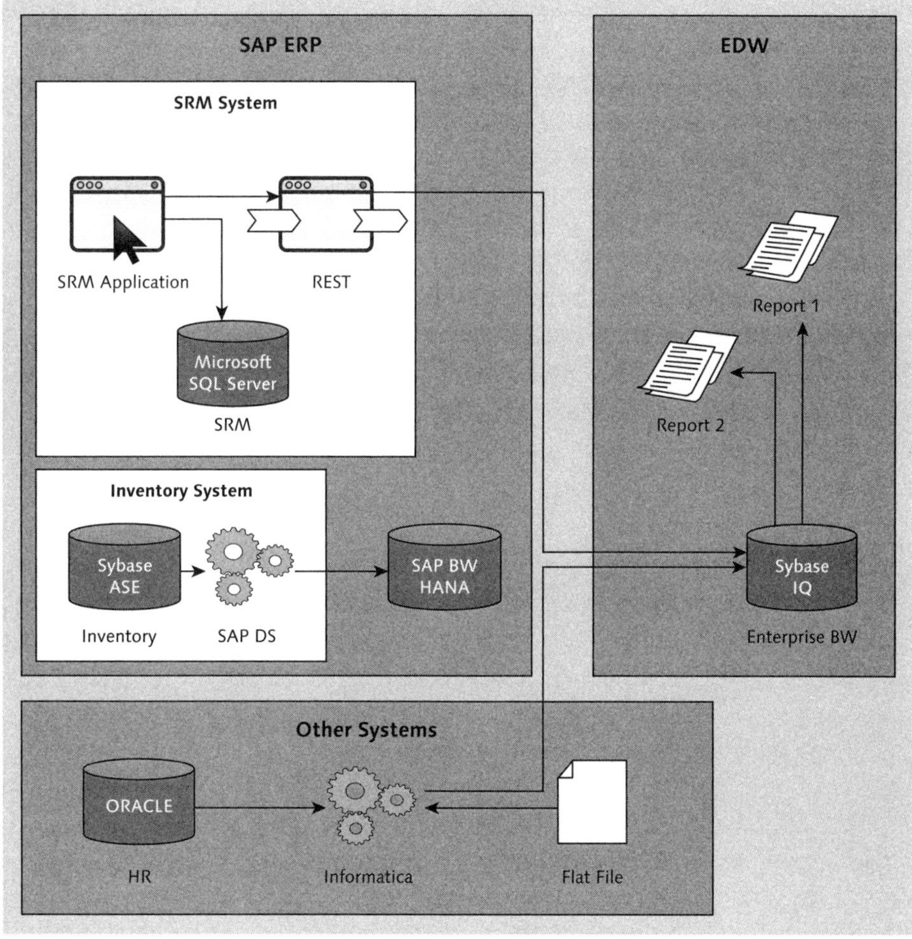

Figure 4.3 Enterprise Information Represented as Application Architecture

PowerDesigner is an open architecture tool, supporting all SAP and non-SAP elements of the enterprise. PowerDesigner's reverse engineering capabilities include support for more than 80 vendor/version RDBMSs (including IBM, Oracle, Microsoft, Teradata, and Netezza systems), standard process orchestration languages, and industry standard object-oriented code.

PowerDesigner is covered in detail in Chapter 7.

4.2 SAP HANA Cloud Integration

The cloud is here and is being quickly embraced by organizations to handle the rapidly changing times of users and businesses. As systems and data are moving very quickly to the cloud or to a hybrid landscape of on-premise and cloud systems, integration tools that offer a strategic discipline of connecting systems and data that were designed independently are a critical component for maximizing the value of moving data to the cloud or a hybrid landscape. This integration journey to incorporate the cloud into your system landscape can be filled with challenges (expensive and unsustainable challenges) of having disparate tools, hand-coded scripts, and manual procedures for managing the integration of data across on-premise and cloud environments. Through a strong corporate information management strategy and world-class integration tool, a company can leverage its combined data assets, including external data sources, throughout the business enterprise. After data are together, unified and easily accessible via the cloud, data can be quickly analyzed for opportunities and competitive advantage via the web.

SAP HANA Cloud Integration (HCI) is SAP's Integration Platform as a Service (iPaaS) offering (see Figure 4.4). iPaaS is comprised of a suite of cloud services that enable the development, execution, and governance of bidirectional integration flows for cloud to cloud and cloud to on-premise data integration and process orchestration. HCI's secure and reliable integration middleware platform operates on the SAP HANA Cloud Platform (HCP). HCP resides on the leading-edge SAP HANA in-memory database management system (DBMS). With a solution on HCP, a new user can be on a live system and working to integrate data in a matter of minutes. HCI is offered as a service solution with a strong focus on process and data integration across domains for SAP Business Suite applications, SAP HANA cloud applications, other SAP cloud applications (e.g., SuccessFactors and SAP Business ByDesign-based applications), third-party cloud applications, and on-premise databases (including SAP HANA) and files.

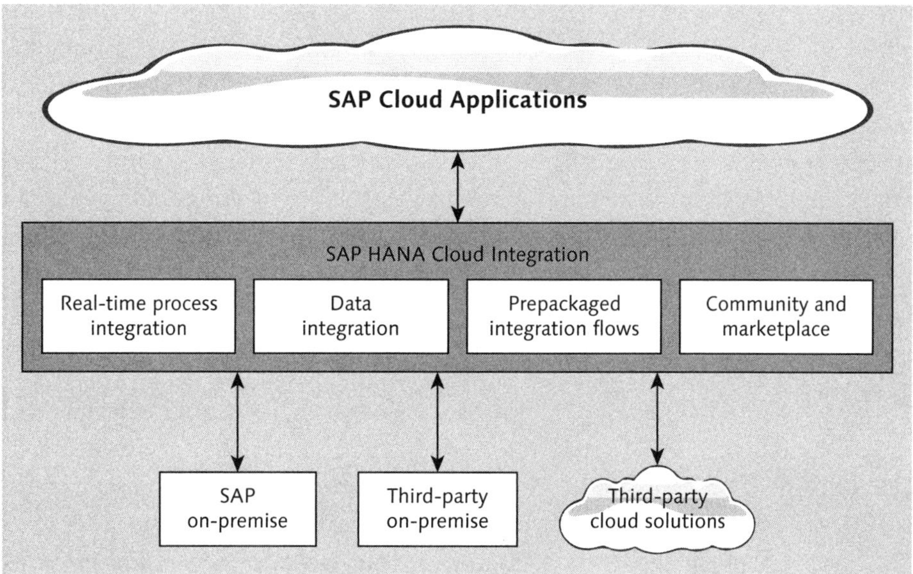

Figure 4.4 SAP HANA Cloud Integration

HCI facilitates the integration of business processes and data across on-premise and cloud applications. For process integration, HCI allows you to integrate business processes that span different companies, organizations, or departments within an organization. For data integration, HCI capabilities allow you to efficiently and securely use extract, transform, and load (ETL) tasks to move data reliably between on-premise systems and the cloud. Additionally, HCI provides a well-governed integration scheduling capability and full process logging.

In the following sections, we'll quickly overview the two options for cloud integration.

4.2.1 SAP HANA Cloud Integration for Process Integration

The SAP HANA Cloud Integration for process integration (HCI-PI) solution is designed to handle the real-time integration of systems data between on-premise and cloud-based systems. When data is changed in one system (e.g., a business transaction takes place in an on-premise SAP ERP system), the change event will be sent to HCI-PI, which will apply the necessary change in the corresponding cloud system in real time. HCI-PI is a critical solution if there is a requirement for real-time integration of processes that span on-premise and cloud environments where its users are making business decisions second-by-second and minute-by-minute based on that data. HCI-PI meets these requirements by capturing business objects triggered by an application event and loading the change captured to a cloud system in real time. HCI-PI offers prepackaged integration content as reference templates that allow customers to quickly realize new business scenarios. This drastically reduces integration project lead times and significantly lowers resource consumption.

4.2.2 SAP HANA Cloud Integration for Data Services

The SAP HANA Cloud Integration for data services (HCI-DS) solution is designed to handle bulk data loads between on-premise and the cloud systems, as well as cloud-to-cloud. The bulk data loads are on-demand or scheduled, in contrast to HCI-PI where data loads are triggered by an application event. The HCI-DS solution requires no expensive programming of integration scenarios and provides out-of-the-box content in support of best practices to quickly enable data integration scenarios between SAP Business Suite and SAP cloud solutions. HCI-DS offers additional integration content out-of-the-box via connectivity adapters for SuccessFactors and SAP ERP, as well as generic adapters for OData and technical systems (REST and SOAP web services, SFTP, etc.). In terms of accessing databases, HCI-DS can easily connect securely and natively to databases on-premise, including SAP HANA, IBM DB2, Oracle, MySQL, and Microsoft SQL Server. HCI-DS can also read data from files, including delimited files such as CSV files or XML files. HCI-DS provides a simple and straightforward web-based UI to create, configure, deploy, and monitor integration scenarios. Additional capabilities include version management, auditing, and alerts.

More details specifically on the HCI-DS solution are available in Chapter 8.

4.3 SAP Data Services

Data Services is the primary tool to extract, transform, and load data from one or more source systems into one or more target systems. Data Services lets you improve, integrate, transform, and deliver trusted data to critical business processes across the enterprise for both SAP and non-SAP systems. Data Services can be used in almost any scenario that requires you to move, enrich, transform, or cleanse data, and in this regard, it functions as the technology foundation for a coherent EIM strategy. The following sections provide an overview of the capabilities delivered with Data Services.

4.3.1 Basics of SAP Data Services

Data Services is used for data migration, systems migration, data synchronization, application data cleansing, loading data warehouses and data marts, and for query, reporting, analysis, and dashboard data provisioning. The three major capabilities of Data Services are data cleansing, data validation, and text data processing (TDP). The core of Data Services is the data services engine (see Figure 4.5, which shows Data Services' capabilities and typical uses). As mentioned previously, Data Services combines two products: Data Integrator for ETL and SAP Data Quality Management for data validation and data cleansing. The third major capability of Data Services is text data processing and is referred to simply as *text data processing*, or *TDP*.

The left side of Figure 4.5 shows the data sources supported by Data Services. Data Services can access data from a wide variety of applications and file sources and can consume almost every type of data—structured, semi-structured, and unstructured—from those sources. Data Services can be called in batch mode (e.g., to extract and deliver data for reporting in the data warehouses) or via client applications such as SAP ERP, SAP Customer Relationship Management (SAP CRM), or custom applications to perform data transformation and cleansing in real time.

Notice in the figure that Data Services shares a common technology layer with the SAP BusinessObjects Business Intelligence (SAP BusinessObjects BI) platform. This allows for common user provisioning; advanced user management; password and security policies; use of external authentication mechanisms such as Active Directory, Lightweight Directory Access Protocol (LDAP), or SAP Identity Management; and granular access control.

You can see in Figure 4.5 how Data Services can access many types of systems and applications and can work with many kinds of data and how that data can be profiled. The connectivity options and profiling capabilities of Data Services are described next.

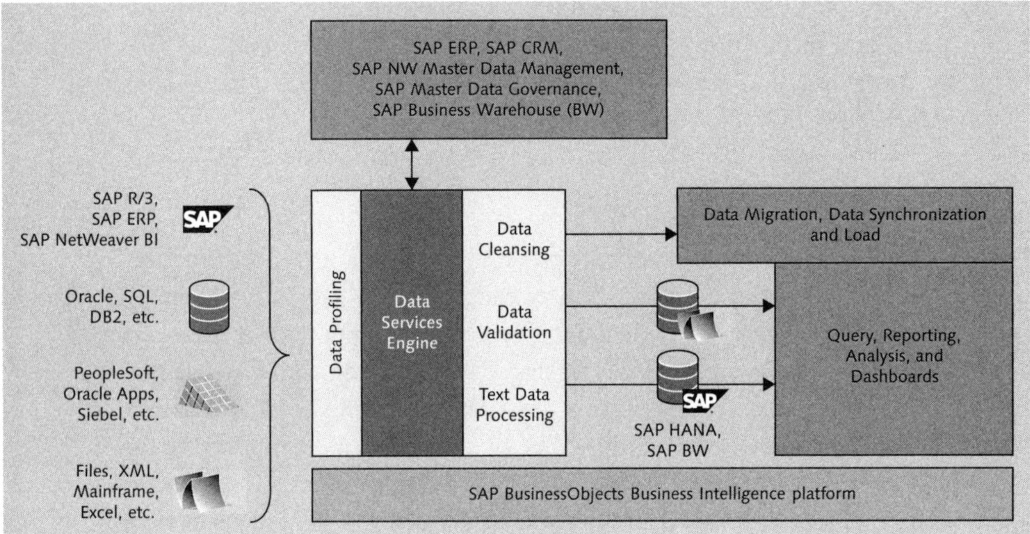

Figure 4.5 Data Services Architecture

Connectivity Options for SAP Data Services

Data Services supports many connectivity options for structured and unstructured data. These include SAP applications, databases, other vendor applications, and pure files (Excel, mainframe, etc.). Details of the connectivity options are discussed in Chapter 9.

Data Profiling in SAP Data Services

Data profiling is the practice of determining the overall quality of data and finding data anomalies. While Information Steward is the primary tool for data profiling, technical data profiling can be done directly in Data Services; you can go beyond simple viewing of the data to conduct an analysis of your data. You can build better jobs in Data Services by understanding the following types of information:

- Frequency distribution
- Distinct values
- Null values
- Minimum/maximum values

- Data patterns (e.g., Xxx Xxxx99, 99-Xxx)
- Comparison of values between data sets
- Drill-down to view specific records

The profiling in Data Services allows you to quickly assess the source data to discover problems and anomalies, such as the following:

- Of the employees in the Human Resources source system, 21% don't have a country associated with their ID.
- There are four genders entered: 60% are male, 30% are female, and the other 10% are either "unknown" or have a question mark in the GENDER field.
- Benefits are available for all new employees after one month of service, but 35% of three-month employees still have no benefit ID assigned to their HR records.

You can also quickly detect patterns, distinct values, and null values for zip codes, product codes, sales items, and other key data fields to better understand your data.

4.3.2 SAP Data Services Integration with SAP Applications

Data Services provides seamless integration with SAP applications as an integration and data quality tool. Specific examples include SAP CRM, SAP ERP, SAP MDM, SAP MDG, SAP Business Warehouse (SAP BW), and SAP HANA. Data Services is used as a service to the applications, called only to perform a specific function when needed. It can also be used to load data into the applications. Next, we discuss a few examples in a bit more detail.

SAP Data Services for SAP Data Quality Management with SAP ERP, SAP CRM, and SAP MDM

Figure 4.6 shows common uses of Data Services with the SAP Business Suite. One common use of Data Services with the SAP Business Suite is the deep integration with Business Address Services (BAS). BAS is an SAP NetWeaver capability embedded in the ABAP application server. BAS provides flexible dialog integration for standard functions such as creating, changing, displaying, and finding addresses. It's a reusable component across the SAP Business Suite that is used heavily in SAP ERP (such as SAP ECC 6.0) and SAP CRM. With Data Services integration to BAS, as addresses are updated, the data quality capabilities in Data Services are used to correct the addresses and check for duplicates. Figure 4.6 shows Data Services integration with BAS.

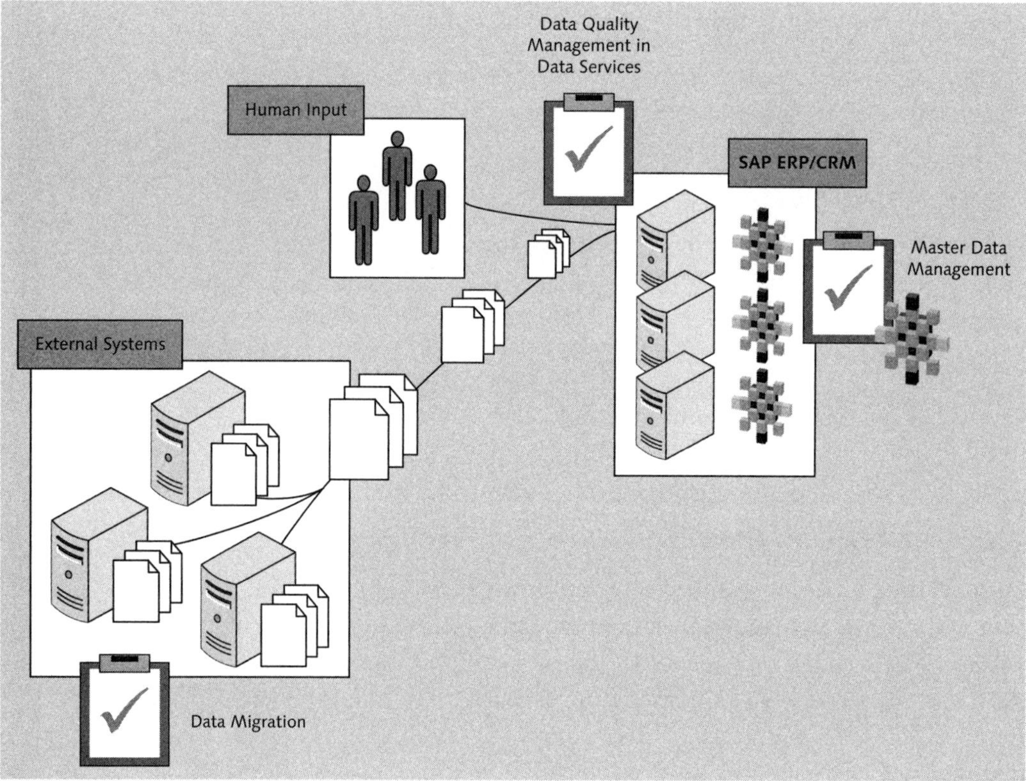

Figure 4.6 Data Services with SAP Applications

In Figure 4.6, notice that Data Services is used for data migration to the SAP Business Suite. SAP provides a robust data migration solution for mapping and validating source data against the SAP target system using Data Services. Data Services is used to migrate each application object (e.g., materials, sales orders, cost centers, etc.). For each object, the data is cleansed, validated against the required configuration in the SAP target system, and loaded into the SAP system. Reports are provided using SAP BusinessObjects Web Intelligence so users can monitor, remediate, and govern the data migration project.

Additional integration with Data Services for SAP applications includes integration with SAP MDM and SAP MDG. SAP MDM uses Data Services to load data, as well as cleanse names and addresses, de-duplication and automatic consolidation, and data validation. Data Services provides real-time cleansing, matching, and consolidation activities for SAP MDG, providing reusability between SAP MDM and SAP MDG. Figure 4.7 shows Data Services integration with SAP MDG. The SAP Data Quality Management, version for SAP Solutions, is covered in more detail in Section 4.5.

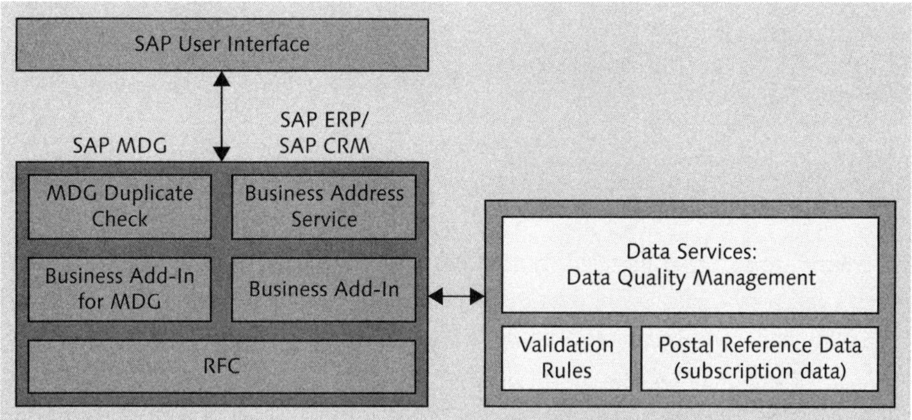

Figure 4.7 Data Services Integration with SAP MDG, SAP ERP, and SAP CRM

Next, we'll discuss how Data Services is used with SAP HANA, SAP BW, and the SAP BusinessObjects BI platform.

SAP Data Services for SAP HANA, SAP BW, and the SAP BusinessObjects BI Platform

A key strength of Data Services is its easy integration with data warehouses and databases for analytics. This is true for Data Services integration with SAP BW, SAP HANA, and the entire SAP BusinessObjects BI platform.

Data Services is the preferred tool for loading non-SAP data into SAP HANA. In fact, the data integration capabilities of Data Services are included with SAP HANA. Additionally, SAP is making major improvements for a seamless user interface (UI) between Data Services and SAP HANA. This is explained in more detail in Chapter 3. Figure 4.8 shows the integration of Data Services with SAP BW and SAP HANA.

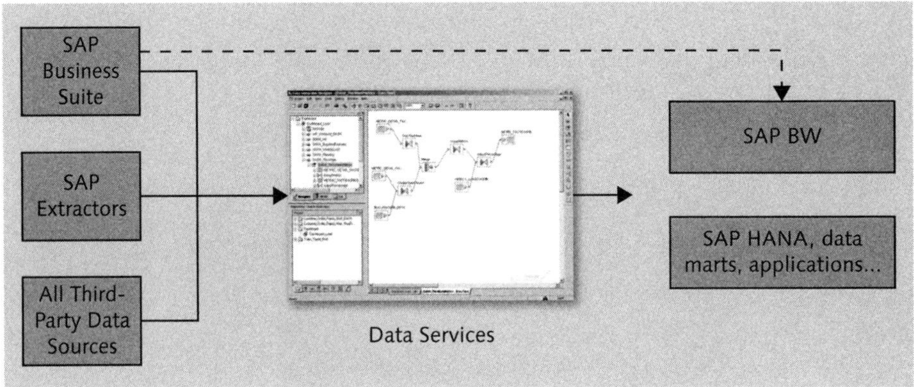

Figure 4.8 Data Services Integration with SAP BW and SAP HANA

Data Services can also be used to load data into SAP BW. Existing SAP BW customers can now easily apply data quality transformations when loading data into SAP BW. They can use one tool to define all extraction, validation, and cleansing rules to load all data (SAP and non-SAP) into SAP BW. This is important to understand because everyone faces data quality issues, and you don't want to re-implement your ETL jobs to add data quality. Non-SAP BW customers can get *native* access to the SAP Business Suite, including delta changes, without going through SAP BW.

In addition to integration with databases and data warehouses, Data Services also works natively with the SAP BusinessObjects BI platform. Data Services is used to provide data for reports, dashboards, ad hoc queries, online analytical processing (OLAP) analyses, and data exploration. Data Services provides access and integration of disparate data from virtually any data source, structured or unstructured. This data can be built up in a data warehouse or data mart to provide historical trending and analysis for more accurate decision making. Data Services also enables the understanding of information context (data lineage) to help you make more confident decisions. The integration with the SAP BusinessObjects BI platform is standard out-of-the-box functionality.

4.3.3 SAP Data Services Integration with Non-SAP Applications

Data Services has a much longer history of integration with non-SAP applications than it does with SAP applications. It started as a pure ETL tool that moved data from any source to any other source. It has grown into a full-scale data foundation that includes ETL, data quality, and TDP, with deep integration into SAP applications, while maintaining the ability to integrate into any application. In your enterprise, there could be a few or many non-SAP systems where integration, data quality, and data validation are required. Data Services is well equipped to meet the requirement of moving and transforming data between diverse non-SAP systems. Figure 4.5 showed the connectivity options for Data Services, ranging from Microsoft Excel spreadsheets to Oracle applications, to mainframe connectivity. Refer back to Figure 4.6 to also see the reference to data migration, data synchronization, and data loading. In this book, we'll focus on data migration to SAP target applications when we discuss data migration. When migrating to SAP applications, the target canonical data formats, field requirements, and so on, are delivered by SAP. However, Data Services can easily be used to migrate to a new home-grown application or some other niche application as well; in this case, however, you need to define the target structure.

Figure 4.6 also showed that external systems and human input are linked to the data quality capabilities in Data Services. This is very common for Data Services integration with non-SAP applications. One very specific example is the SAP Data Quality Management software development kit (SDK). SAP has many software partners who develop their own software but use part of SAP's solution within their solution. The SAP Data Quality Management SDK provides developers with a lightweight integration method to integrate the robust capabilities of the data cleansing and validation capabilities directly in their own custom applications.

Non-SAP integration with Data Services includes loading third-party data in SAP HANA and SAP BW, as well as extracting data to go in other data marts, data warehouses (such as Sybase IQ), and applications.

Data Services' native capabilities for dealing with both SAP and non-SAP data provide great flexibility so that Data Services can be embedded in SAP and non-SAP applications and used across the SAP family of solutions where data cleansing, validation, and integration are critical for the application.

4.3.4 Data Cleansing and Data Validation with SAP Data Services

SAP Data Quality Management is a key capability in Data Services and will be covered in detail in Chapter 9. Data quality capabilities include address cleansing, data standardization, data validation, data correction, data enrichment, and matching. Figure 4.9 shows an example of the entire data quality process.

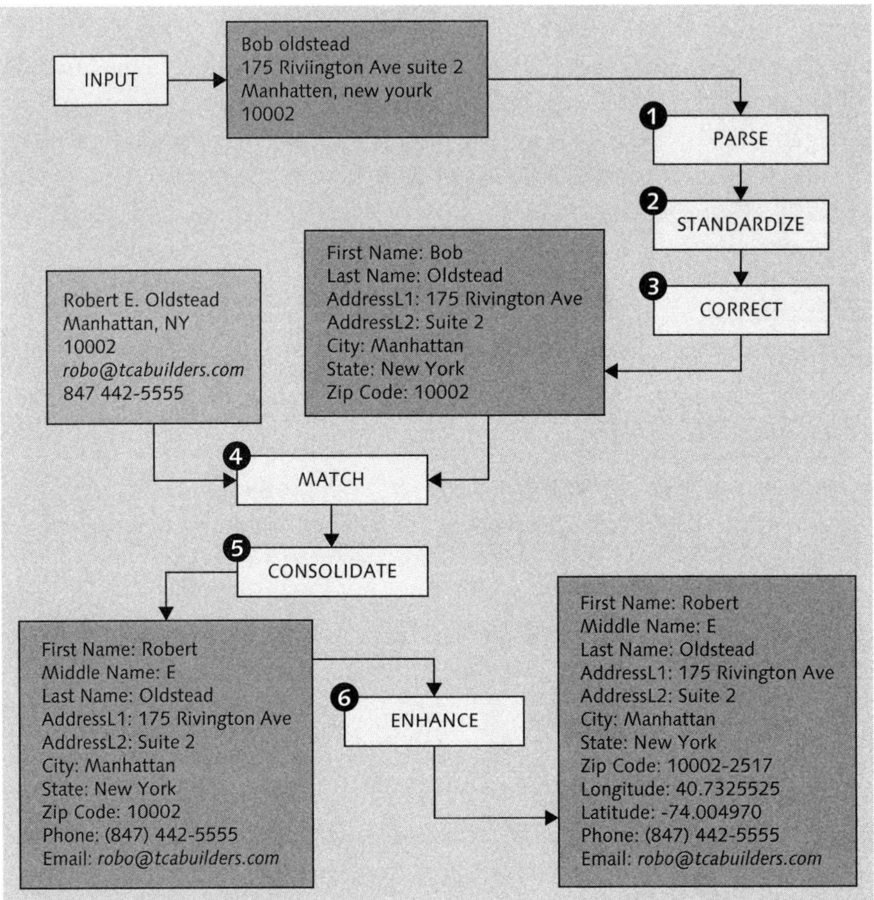

Figure 4.9 Example of the Data Quality Process

To begin, the input record is parsed into its component parts and standardized. Figure 4.9 shows the following example:

- First Name: Bob
- Last Name: oldstead

- Address1: 175 Riivington Ave
- Address2: Suite 2
- City: Manhatten
- State: new yourk
- Zip Code: 10002

Errors in the record are corrected; for instance, "Oldstead" is capitalized, and the street name, city, and state are edited. After this step, the record looks like this:

- First Name: Bob
- Last Name: Oldstead
- Address1: 175 Rivington Ave
- Address2: Suite 2
- City: Manhattan
- State: New York
- Zip Code: 10002

Data Services then searches for a matching record in the target application and finds the following match:

- Name: Robert E. Oldstead
- City, State: Manhattan, NY
- Zip Code: 10002
- Email: *robo@tcabuilders.com*
- Phone: 847 442-5555

The two records are consolidated:

- First Name: Robert
- Last Name: Oldstead
- Address1: 175 Rivington Ave
- Address2: Suite 2
- City: Manhattan
- State: New York
- Zip Code: 10002

- Phone: (847) 442-5555
- Email: *robo@tcabuilders.com*

Finally, the record is enhanced with a normalized zip code and geographical coordinates to provide a complete record:

- First Name: Robert
- Last Name: Oldstead
- Address1: 175 Rivington Ave
- Address2: Suite 2
- City: Manhattan
- State: New York
- Zip Code: 10002-2517
- Longitude: 40.7325525
- Latitude: -74.004970
- Phone: (847) 442-5555
- Email: *robo@tcabuilders.com*

Although this example focused on cleansing a customer record, the data quality process can be applied to business partners, material products, services, and many other types of data that need parsing, standardization, and data cleansing.

4.3.5 Text Data Processing in SAP Data Services

The text data processing (TDP) feature in Data Services unlocks unstructured text sources. With advanced linguistic and semantic capabilities, TDP knows the elements of human language, how these elements differ from language to language, and how their dependencies express the underlying salient information. It understands the meaning and context of information, not just the words themselves. Through core natural-language processing of the entity extraction transform, TDP extracts key information—the "who, what, where, when, and how" in text—revealing important relations and events occurring between these entities. Ultimately, it gives structure to unstructured text sources and disregards the noise, allowing for business analytics and reporting. The following are some common use cases for TDP:

- **Electronic discovery law**
  Discovery is a pretrial phase in a lawsuit in which each party makes information available to the other. TDP accelerates the process of analyzing documents for evidence.
- **Brand monitoring**
  A company wants to know what people are saying about its products and brands. Are they creating buzz? Is that buzz positive or negative, and how does it change over time?
- **Employee morale**
  Sentiment analysis of collaboration spaces and employee surveys can detect employee problems and feedback.
- **Customer service**
  Companies can optimize call centers by routing questions to the right person.

The following are several business examples of how TDP is used today:

- **Media company**
  - **Problem:** Records containing artist names, songs, and movie titles are stored in legacy repositories where they can't be queried, analyzed, or aggregated.
  - **Goal:** Integrate legacy records into a warehouse for a single source of truth for reporting.
  - **Solution:** TDP identifies artist names, titles, dates, and so on. Data quality normalizes names and titles. Integrated, trusted data is loaded into a data warehouse.
- **Law enforcement**
  - **Problem:** Agents need to link the common characteristics of crime scenes with suspects. Databases are incomplete, and important clues may be lost in the volumes of textual information in field notes, case documents, IM logs, emails, and so on.
  - **Goal:** Integrate content from unstructured sources into agency databases so it's available for investigations. Via analytical application, the agent queries for suspects, things, organizations, and locations, as well as links or co-occurrences between these.
  - **Solution:** TDP extracts person names, objects, locations, and other data of interest using public sector extraction rules. The extracted entities are

cleansed and normalized by data quality. Human review of the output occurs prior to database commit.

Optional Function for Law Enforcement

When joining results into the repository, the match function looks for similar persons, addresses, or other attributes that may resolve identities.

- **Maintenance and repairs**
  - **Problem:** A company doesn't know what repair issues are most common or why. Managers are under pressure to reduce maintenance-related costs. Technicians don't always select correct values in a database.
  - **Goal:** Analyze field technicians' repair logs and profile maintenance issues to drive predictive analytics for future maintenance problems. Identify root causes of costly warranty repairs and report back to engineering. Complete blank fields in structured data based on comments.
  - **Solution:** TDP recognizes concepts, part numbers, and problems. It matches cluster concepts, which reveal the most common issues. Models and part numbers can be normalized.

TDP extracts the text and clearly recognizes its meaning from a large number of words. One example is reporting on the most mentioned concepts. An output report created by analyzing comments about a car could result in the information in Table 4.1 (with drill-down capabilities to get more details).

Concept	Total Feedback	Negative Sentiments	Positive Sentiments	Requests
Handling	109	9	98	2
Maintenance	98	19	64	15
Brakes	66	20	43	3
Cup holder	51	27	20	4
Interior	50	4	42	4
Mileage	37	4	30	3

Table 4.1 Car Sentiment Report

From the car sentiment report, you can see that cup holder and brakes have the most negative sentiments and that handling has the most positive. This report can be used to drill down to collect feedback that can be used to support marketing and advertising or provide input into future designs of the car. TDP is covered in more detail in Chapter 9.

4.4 SAP Replication Server

SAP Replication Server supports the EIM environment by helping ensure that an organization's data is readily accessible to all who need it. Replication Server is a real-time data replication and synchronization solution that allows organizations to move and synchronize data across the extended enterprise. It was designed from the ground up to move and synchronize data from one or many primary database sources to one or many database targets in real time (meaning seconds or even fractions of a second) with virtually no performance effect on the primary source database(s). So transactional applications running on the source database never slow down, while all the data changes are being captured behind the scenes from the database log and quietly moved to a secondary site to support application high availability, mission-critical disaster recovery, real-time transactional reporting from a secondary site, and a variety of data distribution solutions.

In the following sections, we'll discuss the common use cases and basic components of Replication Server.

4.4.1 SAP Replication Server Use Cases

As just mentioned (and illustrated in Figure 4.10), the most commonly deployed use cases for Replication Server include the following:

- **High availability/disaster recovery to improve recovery, resumption times, and minimize downtime:**
  - Enables business continuity in the event of a site-wide disaster
  - Maintains application availability during planned/unplanned downtime
  - Enables failover to a secondary site and failback to a primary site when operations are restored (e.g., bi-directional replication)
  - Provides availability of a standby database for read-only report server
- **Real-time reporting to guarantee fresh data to enable timelier, more accurate decisions:**
  - Creates a copy of production systems for daily reporting

- Reduces information latency for reporting
- Optimizes available windows for batch reporting
- Runs resource-intensive reports on reporting servers without impacting performance of Online Transaction Processing (OLTP) systems

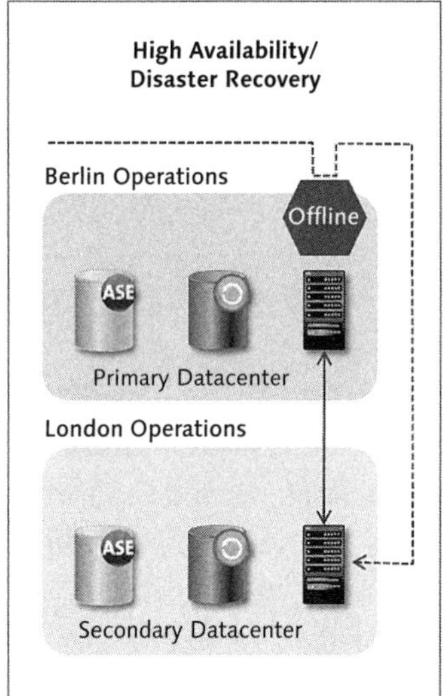

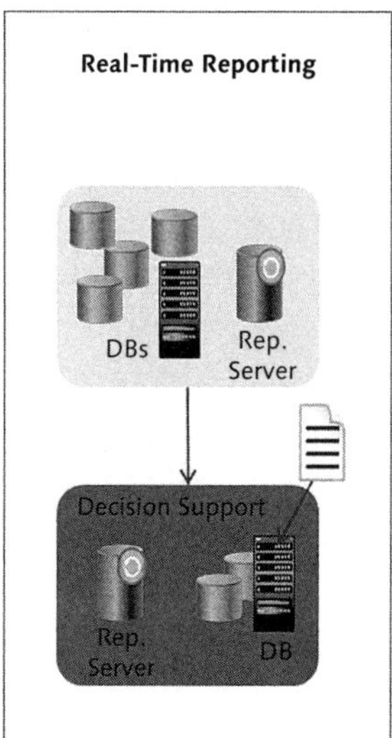

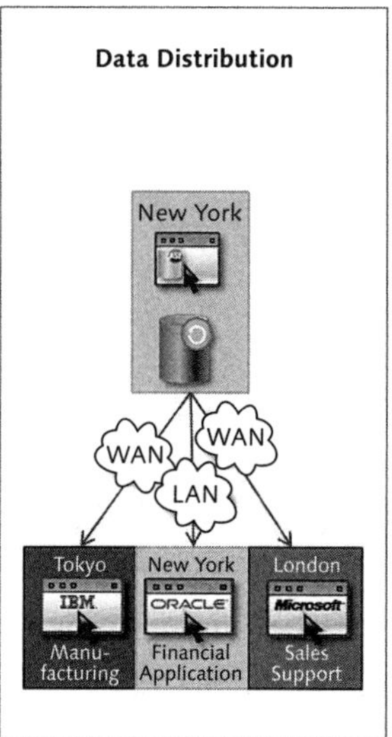

Figure 4.10 SAP Replication Server Common Use Cases

- **Data distribution to support real-time data sharing and synchronization:**
  - Facilitates decentralized business operations by moving centralized data to operations applications
  - Enables remote applications to access data locally for improved performance
  - Shares data between operational systems
  - Synchronizes and maintains consistency in overlapping data values
  - Supports database migration, moving from an older version of a database platform to a new one

4.4.2 Basics of SAP Replication Server

Replication Server uses a publish-subscribe model. As shown in Figure 4.11, the entity to be replicated is published on the primary side, and this can be subscribed to by one or more replicate databases. Such an entity can be an individual database table or an entire database. This includes the option to propagate data as received or with transformation support available via function strings.

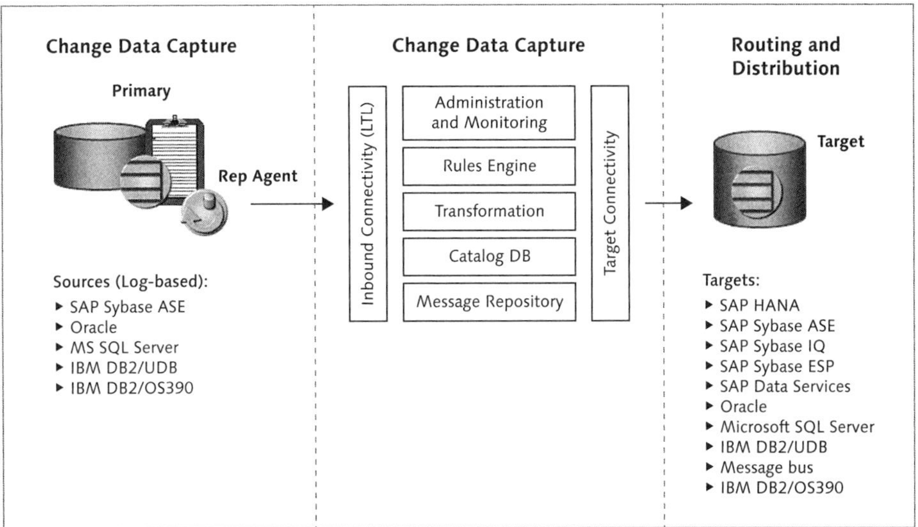

Figure 4.11 Basic Architecture of SAP Replication Server

Replication Server performs asynchronous replication, which means that when the database transaction in the primary database commits, it will be picked up and applied to the replicated database shortly afterward, decoupled from the primary transaction. In a well-designed and well-tuned replication system, latencies of no more than single-digit seconds are typical, even when the replicate database is on a wide area network (WAN).

Because the typical replication system operates in a networked environment, Replication Server is designed to accommodate the fact that network connections will fail temporarily and then come back into service. In this case, Replication Server will automatically keep retrying until the connection is back and then proceed with the replication where it left off.

Replication Server can access and replicate data from multiple databases vendors through log reading interfaces. The set of supported source databases includes SAP Sybase ASE, Oracle, IBM DB2/UDB, IBM mainframe UDB/OS390, and Microsoft SQL Server. Replication Server can replicate data to a variety of different databases (SAP HANA, SAP Sybase ASE, SAP Sybase IQ, Oracle, MS SQL

Server, IBM DB2/UDB/IBM mainframe DB2/OS390) and non-database targets, including message buses, Sybase SAP ESP, and SAP Data Services.

4.4.3 Data Assurance

To ensure consistency of distributed data, Replication Server also provides the Data Assurance utility. Replication Server's Data Assurance utility compares row data and schemas between two or more databases and reports any discrepancies. The Data Assurance utility allows the user to check for data discrepancies using a number of settings that determine which data is being compared and in what way.

Data Assurance is a scalable, high-volume, and configurable data comparison utility to run comparison jobs even during replication by using a "wait and retry" strategy that eliminates any downtime. If any machine or user errors cause data discrepancies between source and target databases, there is no need to reinitialize, which is a time-consuming process. Data Assurance can be used to identify and correct any discrepancies without interrupting the production system and inducing downtime.

4.4.4 SAP Replication Server Integration with SAP Data Services and SAP PowerDesigner

A combination of Replication Server and Data Services provides an end-to-end, real-time, and continuous change data capture (CDC) update with complex transformation and data quality for data-intensive projects.

Replication Server can be integrated with Data Services to provide complex transformation and data quality processing on the data before it's loaded into the target system (see Figure 4.12). Data Services retrieves the changed data captured by the Replication Server, which is stored within its internal data queue, and applies complex transformation and data quality operations before loading the data to the target system.

PowerDesigner can also be included as a part of the solution (see Figure 4.12). With PowerDesigner, the user can create and capture the metadata used to describe the replication topology and make changes to that topology rapidly and flexibly. The software will even generate many of the replication-logic definitions needed to set up the replication server for SAP Replication Server.

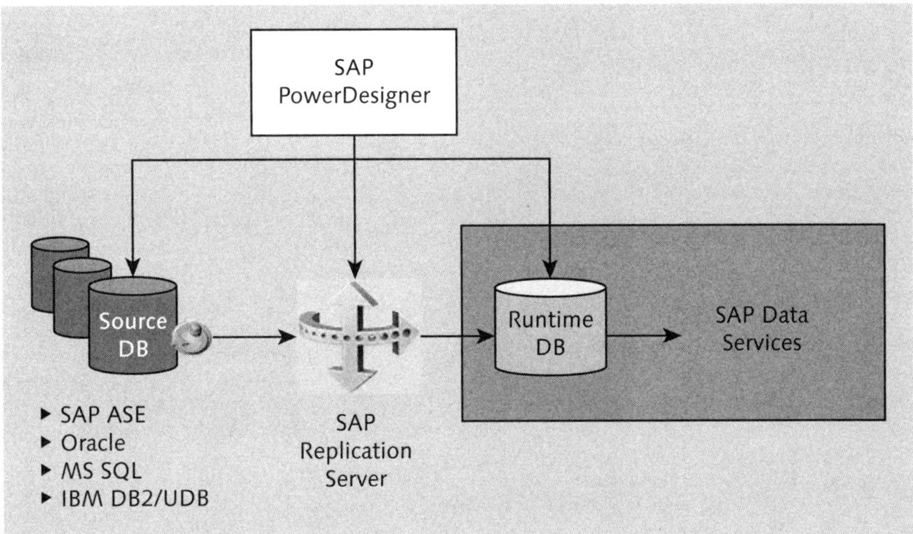

Figure 4.12 SAP Replication Server with SAP Data Services and SAP PowerDesigner

4.5 SAP Data Quality Management, Version for SAP Solutions

SAP Data Quality Management, version for SAP solutions, is a transparent, out-of-the-box data quality solution within SAP applications, specifically in SAP ERP, SAP CRM, and SAP MDG. The key capabilities include address cleansing, address enhancements, and duplicate checking. As you enter a new business partner in the SAP application, an immediate check is done to cleanse the address and check for duplicates. Figure 4.13 shows how the solution works. The solution is embedded in the Business Address Services (BAS) layer provided in SAP NetWeaver Application Server ABAP.

First, the user enters the address data, and then a check is done with the data quality capabilities in Data Services. This provides an immediate response to the user. A validated address is provided, and the user can decide to use the validated address or the original address. After the address validation is completed, a duplicate check is performed to identify any potential duplicates. The user can then open an existing business partner or select to create a new one based on the duplicate list.

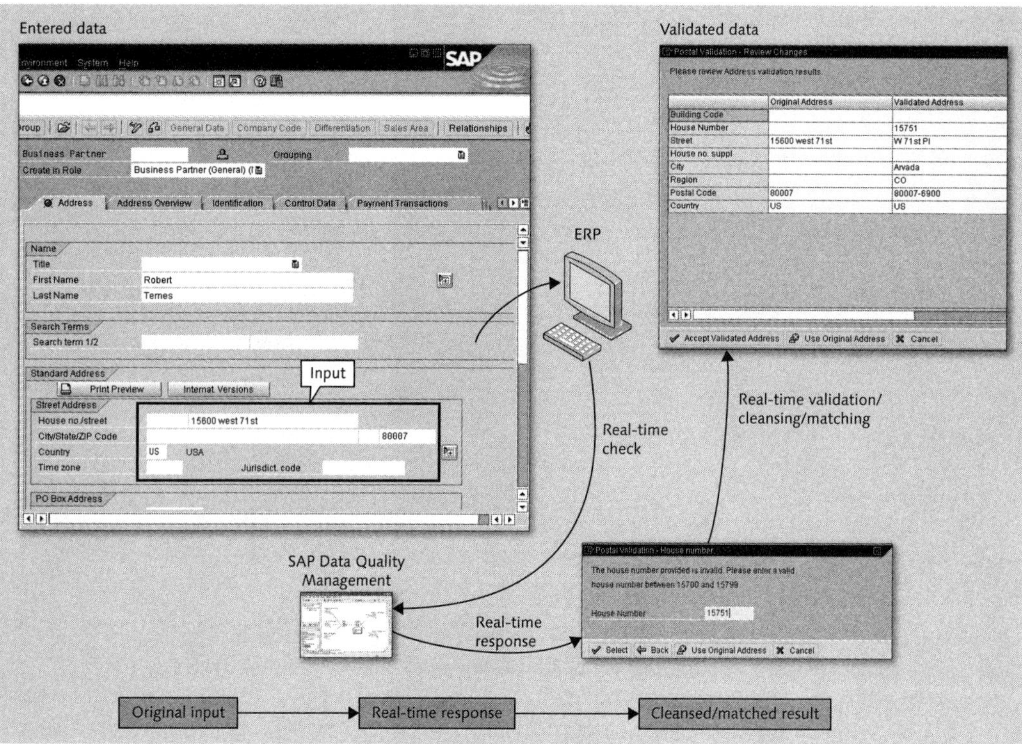

Figure 4.13 SAP Data Quality Management, Version for SAP Solutions

In addition to the data quality capabilities provided as the user enters the information, you can also perform data quality cleansing and matching in batch mode. This provides reports that identify potential duplicates, such as matching reports. Also, preexisting records can be detected during data loads. This can be especially helpful with SAP CRM if you're loading prospects from service bureaus or leads gathered during trade shows, webinars, or other marketing events. Additional support for marketing includes matching on marketing attributes such as age, hobbies, and salary.

SAP Data Quality Management also includes data quality in SAP MDG. You can customize which fields you want to match on, for example, plant data, material type, net weight for materials. This capability enables you to take advantage of robust data quality capabilities with the SAP CRM, SAP ERP, and SAP MDG native UIs.

4.6 SAP Information Steward

Information Steward delivers a single environment to discover, assess, define, and monitor the quality of your enterprise data. It's positioned as a key UI for governance, with the ability to monitor the quality of your data over time and centrally catalog the different data assets and business term definitions in your organization. The combination of these disciplines allows companies not only to identify bad data but also to see where the data is coming from (and where it's used in downstream processes).

Information Steward provides an environment that enables you to do the following:

- **Discover**
  Discover and understand enterprise data, including data profiling and metadata management. Information Steward gives your company the means to discover its data assets, visually assess its quality, isolate issues, and understand the impact they are having on your critical business processes. And in doing so, it provides a starting point for both business and IT users to collaborate on and improve data quality. It's an essential starting point for any information governance initiative.
- **Define**
  Define the data quality requirements and data quality business rules, as well as the common business term glossary centrally in one application. Information Steward provides a means to define ownership and accountability of critical business data assets and the ability to relate them to business terms in a business glossary. This helps establish a common understanding of the data and its meaning for key stakeholders of a governance program. In addition, Information Steward provides users with the ability to define validations rules to further assess the quality of the data. And as data quality issues become apparent, both business and IT users are able to define cleansing packages to address them.
- **Monitor**
  Monitor data quality over time, provide data quality scorecards in business user applications, and resolve data quality issues over time. With Information Steward, both business and IT users are empowered to monitor data quality throughout the enterprise via the use of standardized scorecards that are easy to access, intuitive to use, and allow the user to interactively drill down to the

data sources that have failed to meet defined validation rules. Business users can also access these same data quality scores in the environments they already work in. For example, an analyst viewing a report has the ability to see where the data in the report originated and the data quality score associated with the report sources. In addition, the analyst can leverage Information Steward's Business Value Analysis to demonstrate and monitor the financial impact of poor data quality to the business's bottom line.

In this section, we'll provide an overview of each major capability in Information Steward. Chapter 10 will provide more details on the profiling and data quality scorecards. In Information Steward, there are five major areas:

- **Data profiling and data quality monitoring**
  These are used to gain insight, assess data, and provide dashboards for monitoring data quality, including financial impact, over time.
- **Cleansing rules**
  Cleansing rules enable the creation of specific rules for cleansing data according to best practices, company policies, industry standards, and so on.
- **Match review**
  Match review supports the manual review and approval of the results of the automated matching and consolidation process.
- **Metadata analysis**
  Metadata analysis integrates and relates metadata from multiple systems in the company and allows transparency of the existing assets in the company and how they are related to each other.
- **Business term glossary**
  A business term glossary provides a central glossary for organizations to store business terms or definitions that have been approved by the responsible business experts.

Tip

The term *metadata*, when used with respect to Information Steward, refers to technical metadata regarding the structure of the data. The National Information Standards Organization defines metadata as "structured information that describes, explains, locates, or otherwise makes it easier to retrieve, use, or manage an information resource."

Each of these areas will be discussed next.

4.6.1 Data Profiling and Data Quality Monitoring

Data profiling and data quality monitoring are key capabilities of Information Steward. You can assess and monitor the data quality of a specific data domain for a specific purpose (e.g., customer quality assessment, sales system migration, or master data quality monitoring).

By measuring data quality and its financial impact along the core processes in your organization—from the point of entry down to the place of consumption—you can easily identify which business process is processing good data and the cost when they aren't. Ongoing data quality monitoring allows you to respond early to slight dips in your data quality level. With early detection, you can set up the necessary cleansing activities or processes, rather than identify data quality issues after they have negatively impacted your core business processes.

Figure 4.14 shows an example of a data quality scorecard that provides a quality score along specific data quality dimensions and cost information.

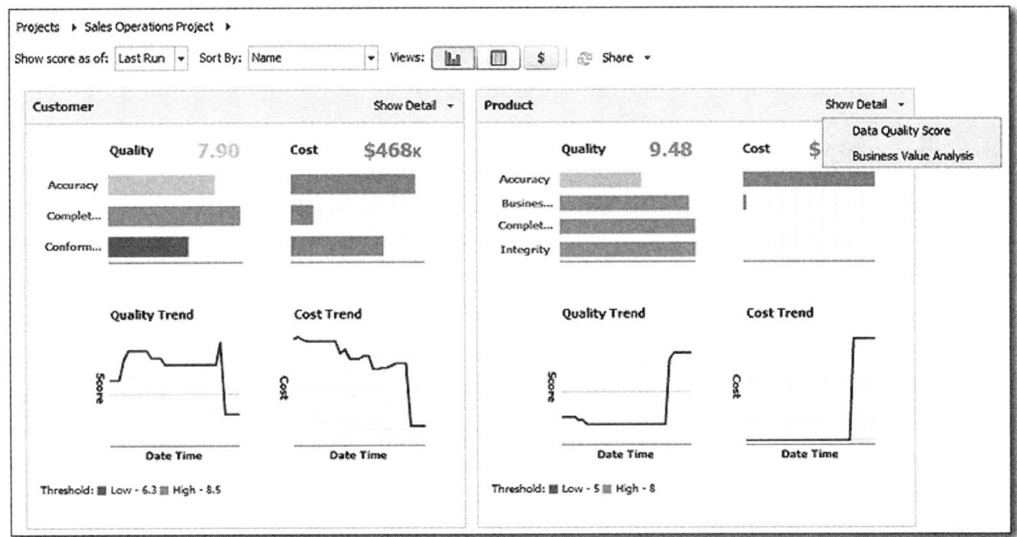

Figure 4.14 Example Data Quality Scorecard

The following are typical data profiling and data quality monitoring activities:

- **Adding tables to a project**
  For example, in a project to assess supplier master data, you would include tables and files that should be analyzed to assess supplier master data.

- **Profiling the data**
  You interactively execute data profiling steps to create statistical information on minimum values, maximum values, frequency distribution of values, pattern distribution of values, and so on. This is a first insight into the content of the data when the first outliers are identified. For example, with supplier master data, say you assess the data and notice that the pattern of the supplier name includes a high percentage of special characters. You can directly create validation rules from the profiling results area that the data steward later verifies and approves from a business perspective.
- **Setting up the data quality validation rules**
  You might have a great set of already documented or identified requirements based on policies, industry standards, or external regulations that you can transfer into validation rules. A typical validation rule for supplier master data validates that the name of the supplier doesn't contain any characters other than letters, numbers, and blanks.
- **Defining the cost per failure**
  You can optionally associate an itemized cost per failure to a validation rule, for example, the financial cost when inaccurate order information causes delayed or lost shipments.
- **Binding the validation rules to your data**
  Because the central validation rules are generic and can be reused for multiple tables, they are bound to the multiple tables in your company after their approval by the data steward. For example, a definition for a valid telephone number format is done once centrally by the data steward but is then bound to your employee, customer, and supplier data tables.
- **Executing the rule tasks**
  Apply the defined validation rules to the existing data in the tables, files, or applications that you've bound to your project to calculate the number of failed records for each rule.
- **Analyzing or reviewing the current data quality level from different perspectives**
  From a technical perspective, you can view the quality of the data based on specific tables or applications, for example, data quality in the completeness of sales orders tables for the sales application. Alternatively, the data quality level can be viewed from the perspective of a business user or data steward who is responsible for a specific data domain such as supplier master data. In this case,

you're only interested in the overall score of your key data domain; in other words, drill down from the data quality scorecard domain (such as supplier, product, or customer) to the data quality dimensions, to the individual rules set up for your data domain, and down to the individual tables where your data is stored. Business Value Analysis also enables business users or data stewards to connect the financial return-on-investment (ROI) aspect to their data quality and information governance initiatives.

- **Scheduling rule tasks for ongoing monitoring**
  Because data quality measurement isn't a singular activity, you can set up scheduled execution of your rule tasks using the internal scheduling capability.

Specific details on how to create a data quality dashboard are covered in Chapter 10.

4.6.2 Cleansing Rules

Information Steward also provides a capability called the Cleansing Package Builder. This enables the creation of custom cleansing rules that Data Services uses as a transformation step to cleanse and standardize your data. You can create custom parsing and standardization rules that can be used with the data cleanse transform (covered in Chapter 9) in Data Services. Information Steward also provides a feature called the Data Quality Advisor with the intelligence to analyze the data and the results of the profiling process to make recommendations in terms of cleansing rules that would improve the quality of customer and supplier data.

Cleansing Package Builder

Custom cleansing rules can be created to parse and standardize account numbers, product codes, product descriptions, purchase dates, part numbers, SKUs, dates, names, Social Security numbers, and so on.

The Cleansing Package Builder was created to empower the data steward or subject matter expert to develop a custom data cleansing solution, allowing the user to easily and quickly develop new data cleansing solutions for data domains not provided out of the box (e.g., product data in the pharmaceutical industry) and to customize the cleansing packages delivered by SAP.

The data steward defines how the data should be classified simply based on the desired output. After the desired output is created, the Cleansing Package Builder automatically creates the data dictionary, rules, and patterns that make up a cleansing package, which is then consumed by Data Services data cleanse transforms. The following example shows the input and output after using a custom cleansing rule developed using the Cleansing Package Builder:

Glove ultra grip profit 2.3 large black synthetic leather elastic with Velcro Mechanix Wear.

After the cleansing step executes, the parsed and standardized output would look like the information shown in Table 4.2.

Parsed Text Output	Standardized Text Output
Product Category	Glove
Size	Large
Material	Synthetic Leather
Trademark	Pro-Fit 2.3 Series
Cuff Style	Elastic Velcro
Palm Type	Ultra-Grip
Color	Black
Vendor	Mechanix Wear
Standard Description	Glove—Synthetic Leather, Black, Size: Large, Cuff Style: Elastic Velcro, Ultra-Grip, Mechanix Wear

Table 4.2 Parsed and Standardized Output from the Data Cleanse Transform

In the Cleansing Package Builder, the data steward can set up how to create a standard for parsed values, a standard description, and any punctuation. For example, the input includes the phrase "profit 2.3," but after the cleansing package executes, the description for the trademark attribute is "Pro-Fit 2.3 Series." You can also see that the standard description has appended multiple attributes together and added additional punctuation. Ultimately, the data steward can control how the data looks based on business requirements. The Cleansing Package Builder can be used to create custom cleansing rules for specific industry standards such as GS1 (Global Standards 1) and UNSPSC (United Nations Standard Products and Services Code). It can be used to create company-specific cleansing rules so that data is uniformly cleansed according to company policies and compliance requirements in diverse application systems.

Data Quality Advisor

The Data Quality Advisor guides data stewards to rapidly develop a solution to measure and improve the quality of their information assets. The Data Quality Advisor is integrated into Information Steward's Data Insight module. Following Figure 4.15, the advisor starts with the data. It first leverages data profiling to get an understanding of the data, including its content (identifying the context of the data in terms of its name, address, email, etc.), characteristics (qualities in terms of uniqueness, redundancy, word/value frequency, etc.) as well as anomalies (e.g., data outliers). The Data Quality Advisor then intelligently combines these findings with best practices per a data domain to make an initial recommendation to the data steward in terms of what his data validation, cleansing, and matching rules should be.

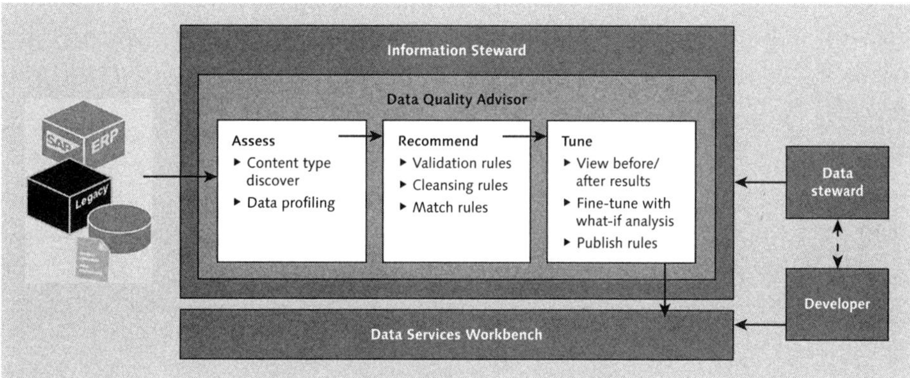

Figure 4.15 Information Steward's Data Quality Advisor

The data steward can review validation rule suggestions and select to apply them to the profiled data set via the Data Validation Advisor. He can also leverage the Data Cleansing Advisor to review as well as visualize the cleansing and matching rules in the context of the data itself. In other words, the rules are applied to the data, and the data steward has the opportunity to see the affect the cleansing and matching rules have on the data with a before and after view and filters to focus in on interesting records (e.g., match groups that have near matches or addresses where the primary street name was changed).

With the Data Cleansing Advisor, the data steward also has the option to tune the results to better meet business requirements with the support of an intuitive interface, including what-if analysis. When satisfied with the cleansing and matching results, the data steward can publish the data cleansing configuration to Data Services, allowing the IT developer to use or consume the solution within the context of a larger data set and ETL dataflow.

4.6.3 Match Review

In an enterprise landscape, duplicate records may exist in the same or different source systems; essentially the duplicates refer to the same entity but likely with some variations. The process of identifying and consolidating duplicate data is important because it delivers direct cost savings by eliminating redundant data in your systems to improve analytics and business process efficiency. For example, as a part of a marketing campaign, product catalogs are sent to your customer base. As a result of that campaign, if multiple copies of that catalog are sent to the same individual or family (with slight variations in the addressee's name or address), it not only increases your costs but also impacts the reputation of your company in minds of those customers (e.g., "How well does this company really know me?").

Typically, automated data quality processes are deployed to cleanse data and deduplicate matching records to avoid such problems (see Chapter 9, Section 9.10.3). However, manual intervention is unavoidable when the automated process can't determine the duplicate records with high enough confidence. Organizations need to determine whether to invest in further optimization of automated matching or to employ a manual inspection process for the suspect match results, especially when the accuracy target is high.

When manual inspection is the decision, Information Steward provides a business user-centric interface to review match groups that consist of duplicate or potentially duplicate records. The business user can easily navigate through match groups using standard filtering, sorting types of features. Based on their domain expertise, business users can confirm the results of the automated matching process or make changes, such as identifying the nonmatching records, reassigning the master record, and so on. In addition, the user can preconfigure best record strategies or survivorship rules to create a golden record to represent a single view of a match group. During the review process, users can also pick and choose fields from different records within the match group to fine-tune that preconfigured, consolidated best record. They can also annotate the records or add comments at the group level that may benefit fellow reviewers and approvers working on the same review task, thus promoting collaboration.

Match review supports governance through centralized task management and the ability to route the subsets of data to appropriate domain experts. An operational dashboard is available to monitor overall status, progress, and productivity of the match review process.

4.6.4 Metadata Analysis

Metadata analysis enables users to know what data assets exist in the company and the relationships between those data assets. For example, in the SAP BusinessObjects BI suite, users can track the source data that's used for a report, and they can see how a change in a source will impact a report. If you delete a column in one of your source systems, for instance, this might have a significant impact on your reports; it could result in missing data and erroneous calculations. Metadata analysis empowers users to do the following:

- Understand the entire BI environment.
- Trace a data lineage from a report to sources.
- Identify a change impact from a source to reports and users.
- Manage metadata from various data sources, data integration technologies, and BI systems.
- Lower the total cost of ownership by tracking usage and promote reuse of data and reports.
- Improve decision making and regulatory compliance.
- Provide root-cause and impact analysis of bad data in the system landscape.

Metadata analysis consolidates metadata from various sources, stores the metadata in a central metadata repository, and analyzes the dependencies and relationships between the different data assets. This consolidated and related metadata enables auditing, usage, change impact, and data lineage analysis. Metadata can be supplemented with custom attributes and annotations to add further information to the collected metadata, which in turn provides a full picture and understanding of the existing data assets. Figure 4.16 shows the integration with the central repository. The universe creation in the figure refers to the universe capability in the SAP BusinessObjects BI platform.

One of the most common use cases of the metadata management capabilities in Information Steward is the direct integration of the data lineage capabilities into the BI Launch Pad in the SAP BusinessObjects BI platform. In the BI Launch Pad, users can choose to view the lineage of a report that they're working on. The lineage offers a graphical representation of what data from which sources a report uses, and how the data is flowing into the report. In addition to knowing how much they can trust the data in the tables, users can also see the results of a data quality assessment on the source or data warehouse staging area tables. Leveraging the metadata analysis with the data quality assessment provides credibility to the report.

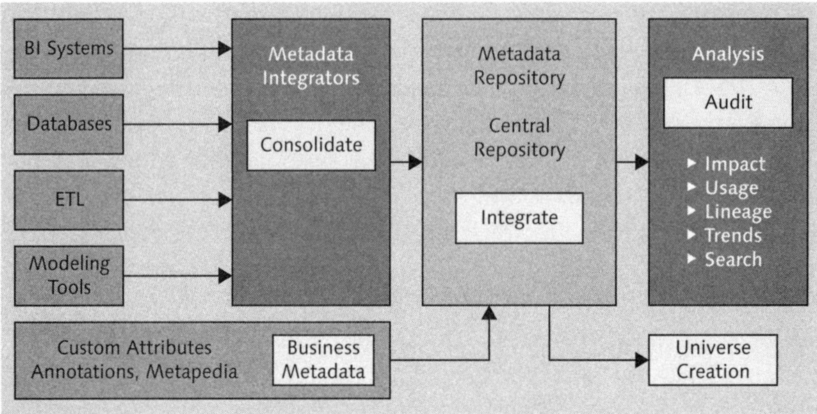

Figure 4.16 Consolidate, Integrate, and Audit Your Metadata

Another example of metadata analysis is to support data quality root-cause analysis and impact analysis. While you're reviewing the data quality results, you can drill into the failed data. When you drill down, you can directly call the metadata management functionality to see where the data in the assessed column is coming from. This enables you to evaluate the source of the error, as well as where the data is used in downstream reports. The linkage goes all the way to the business terms and linkage to the business process. This allows you to drill down from your business process name to the associated tables and contextualize the quality score for the table and the individual columns.

4.6.5 Business Term Glossary

If you ask five employees in your company what the term *revenue* means to them, you might get at least three different definitions. But for analysis and decision making, it's essential that everyone in the company be on the same page when talking about the same terms or policies. Information Steward provides *Metapedia* as a central location for the definition, maintenance, and approval of business terms; its goal is to promote proactive information governance with common understanding and agreement on business terms and concepts.

The application range for Metapedia is broad and ranges from descriptive explanations of terms (as in a simple dictionary) to central storage of calculation formulas, to technical terms, to business process descriptions that are associated with tables and data assets in business processes. Metapedia also enables business users to understand data attributes used in BI reporting environments with business user-oriented descriptions. In Metapedia, you can organize business terms into categories or hierarchies that align with business subject matter or lines of business.

Metapedia's searching capabilities let you search for not only the terms that have been created, but also synonyms that have been assigned to them. From the search results, you can easily trace the associated objects or their details into the categories and hierarchies the terms are linked to. In this way, Metapedia terms can be associated and linked to other technical objects in your Information Steward system. This is used to extend the central data assets repository with business terms. For example, you can define business names in Metapedia and assign them to the technical column names in your metadata management. If a business user searches for a business term such as *telephone number*, he can get a list of all table columns associated with that business term in the system landscape, including telephone number information, even if the column is labeled "PHNNR."

Metapedia is a helpful component to bridge the gap between IT and the business user, providing a common understanding of what information is available where in the company.

4.7 SAP NetWeaver Master Data Management and SAP Master Data Governance

Managing master data is critical to an enterprise-wide information management strategy. Every company and every line of business are impacted by master data. From financial close, to product development, to order management, to help desk support, to supplier management, every organization is impacted by master data—especially when the master data is incorrect, unclear, redundant, or conflicting. SAP's solutions for EIM include an integrated suite for managing and governing master data. These solutions include previously discussed capabilities, such as Data Services and Information Steward. Additionally, two other key capabilities for managing and governing master data include SAP NetWeaver Master Data Management (SAP NetWeaver MDM) and SAP Master Data Governance (SAP MDG).

The focus of SAP NetWeaver MDM is to consolidate and harmonize master data in application- and system-agnostic contexts (e.g., in analytical scenarios, to ensure trustworthy data for enterprise reporting). SAP NetWeaver MDM supports all domains for master data consolidation, harmonization, and stewardship, covering business initiatives such as mergers and acquisitions, divestitures, and supply chain optimization.

SAP MDG provides centralized master data creation, maintenance, and governance for the SAP Business Suite and beyond. In the standard version, this is prebuilt for selected data domains, such as the financial, material, supplier, and customer domains. It can be extended for additional domains. SAP MDG is focused on operational master data management. It's a natural extension of the business processes running in the SAP Business Suite, adding prebuilt master data creation, change, and distribution processes and stewardship.

4.7.1 SAP NetWeaver Master Data Management

SAP NetWeaver MDM enables you to manage master data across multiple domains and multiple systems. It's primarily used for master data consolidation and master data harmonization, as described next.

Master Data Consolidation

Master data consolidation aggregates master data across SAP and non-SAP systems into a centralized master data repository. After data is consolidated, you can search for data across linked systems, identify identical or similar objects across systems, and provide key mapping for reliable company-wide analytics and reporting.

Master Data Harmonization

Master data harmonization first consolidates the master data from heterogeneous systems, and then harmonizes the data to meet global quality standards. It ensures high-quality master data by distributing harmonized data that is globally relevant using distribution mechanisms. Subscribing applications can enrich master data with locally relevant information.

4.7.2 SAP Master Data Governance

SAP MDG provides centralized governance for selected master data domains that are based on SAP's standard data models and is extensible to custom-defined models. It performs native integration with the SAP Business Suite, using existing business logic and customer-specific configuration for validation of master data while it's being created. In addition, SAP MDG integrates with Data Services for data quality and enrichment. It uses the data quality engine mentioned previously to inform the user about duplicate data sets. It also uses Data Services' rich address enrichment features to support users in entering correct addresses for their business partners.

SAP MDG uses SAP Business Workflow for the governance process and allows you to design your own workflows for the central master data creation or maintenance process. These workflows typically involve multiple people adding their expertise to complex master data (e.g., one person edits a material's classification information, and another adds units of measurement and their conversions). The workflows also include workflow steps for approval of the changed data.

Note

For more information on SAP Business Workflow, refer to the book *Practical Workflow for SAP* (3rd edition, SAP PRESS, 2014).

Until the approval, inactive data is kept in a staging area, separate from productive master data, and it's only after approval that the data is posted to the master data tables in the SAP system and distributed to systems that subscribe to these master data changes. Through this process, SAP MDG delivers consistent definition, authorization, and replication to corporate systems such as SAP Business Suite and non-SAP systems. By tracking all changes and approvals, SAP MDG supports compliance and a complete audit trail.

SAP MDG provides master data maintenance capabilities through a role-based, domain-specific UI. In addition to central maintenance of master data in the SAP Business Suite, data from external sources is supported. For example, you can upload data into SAP MDG via a file or services and then further process (or enrich) the data in SAP MDG. SAP MDG provides governance for specific master data areas. The primary areas are discussed in the following subsections.

SAP Master Data Governance for Financial Master Data

SAP MDG provides governance processes for a broad set of financial master data, including charts of accounts, general ledger accounts, financial reporting structures, companies, consolidation units, profit centers and cost centers along with their hierarchies, and cost elements and cost element hierarchies.

SAP Master Data Governance for Supplier and Customer Master Data

SAP MDG supports the governance of customer master data creation and changes. The provided standard scope includes generic business partner attributes such as central data, address information, roles, and relationships; specific data for customers, such as general, company code, or sales area data; and specific supplier data, such as company code or purchasing data. For both customers and suppliers, SAP MDG supports the search, display, change, and creation of single master data sets as well as mass processing or changes to hierarchies.

Figure 4.17 shows an example of the master data governance process for supplier data. A requestor enters the initial supplier data and submits the master data record for approval. A specialist can review the request and return it to the requestor for additional information, reject the request, or approve the request. If additional data is required to enrich the record—for instance, purchasing data—then a domain specialist can perform this data enrichment. After the record is complete and has received final approval, it's created in the SAP ERP system and, if applicable, distributed to other systems that share the data. Prebuilt workflows are used to control the creation process at every step.

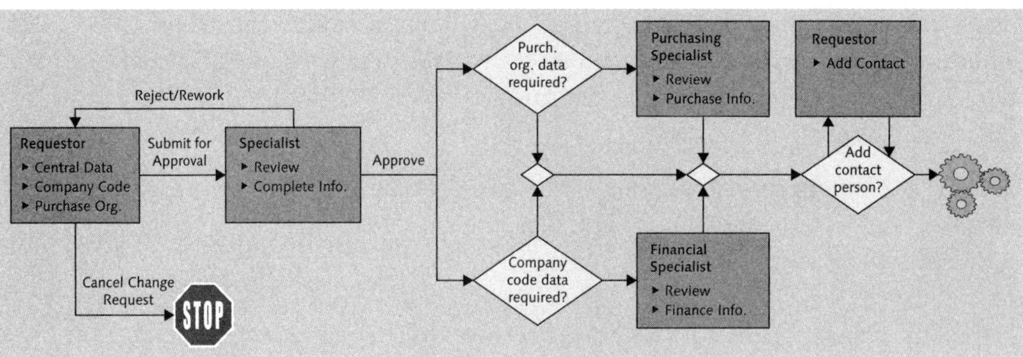

Figure 4.17 Example of SAP MDG Process for Supplier

SAP Master Data Governance for Material Master Data

SAP MDG allows for central creation and change processes for material master data. The broad data model provided in SAP MDG covers basic data such as descriptions, units of measure, and quality data; classification data; logistics data such as sales, plant, storage, and warehouse data; and valuation and costing data. Again, you can search, display, change, and create a single material master data element; perform mass processing; and upload files.

In addition to the governance processes provided, users can also create customized governance processes. Business process experts can define enhancements and checks (e.g., by enriching parts of data through assigning an enrichment spot, skipping unnecessary checks, or ensuring that validations occur by assigning checks), specify which fields are relevant and required at a certain step of the governance process, and assign a different UI in addition to the standard interface configured for the data model. All this allows a maximum of flexibility for each process step.

In addition to this flexibility at design time, power users or even end users can easily adapt the UI to their specific needs at runtime. For example, they can rearrange the screen layout or set default values on selected fields for their most-often-used screens. All this is based on the new UI design paradigm that has been adopted across SAP MDG's master data domains.

SAP Master Data Governance Integration with SAP Data Services and SAP Information Steward

Native integration among Data Services, SAP MDG, and Information Steward is critical to ensuring ongoing data quality, data remediation, duplicate prevention, validations, and data enrichment. Combined, these three applications provide a holistic solution for governing master data in the SAP Business Suite.

SAP MDG focuses on comprehensive master data governance ready for use in a company's business processes through ready-to-run governance processes for specific master data domains. In addition, the SAP MDG application foundation allows for custom-defined master data objects, processes, and UIs. SAP MDG provides prebuilt validation against SAP business logic and customers' configuration settings and can distribute master data to SAP and non-SAP applications.

Further details about SAP MDG are covered in Chapter 11.

4.8 SAP Solutions for Enterprise Content Management

Enterprise Content Management (ECM) is a broad area that includes the capturing, managing, preservation, and delivery of content and documents to organizations and business processes. ECM focuses on unstructured information. Some consider ECM to be a completely separate discipline from EIM, but SAP takes a different view; documents and other content are critical information assets that must be managed in a holistic information management strategy. ECM covers a wide range of technologies and use cases, extending EIM to unstructured content that is critical to the business. ECM delivers solutions that focus on the following business pain points:

- Inability or excessive effort to find and reuse relevant content
- Exponential growth of unstructured content
- Content fragmentation across applications and content silos
- "Tribal knowledge" versus enterprise information
- Need for long-term preservation and legal compliance
- Cost reduction and increased process efficiency via digitization of paper documents

These pain points reduce business efficiency as it relates to content and increase legal and compliance risk. *Reduced business efficiency* includes the inability to find what is needed to complete a business process. For example, before you sign a contract with a new vendor, a specific spreadsheet or email needs a final review, but where is it? Perhaps it's in an application that the user can't access or in a file share for which the user has no permissions, or the content has been fragmented, and parts are stored among several applications. There could also be paper documents that are difficult to tie to a digital process.

Increased legal and compliance risk includes content that was not kept for the legally required duration (e.g., someone got rid of an old file without realizing that some documents for a legal hold were inadvertently deleted as well), or content was kept longer than legally required. Additionally, regulation requires auditable content lifecycle records.

Table 4.3 depicts a list of concepts and activities typically considered to belong to the ECM solution space. SAP provides solutions for each of the ECM components listed in the table.

ECM Process	Key Features
Document Management	▸ Perform basic content handling capabilities such as retrieval, storage, versioning, and check-in/check-out. ▸ Handle metadata. ▸ Handle security. ▸ Use audit trails.
Input Management	▸ Capture manually created or scanned information (office documents, forms, or rich media). ▸ Capture application-created information (XML, financial applications, or e-forms). ▸ Recognize printed or written information (optical character recognition, bar code, or hand-printed character recognition).
Output Management	▸ Assemble documents from text fragments, data, or a clause library (based on simple rules or complete business logic). ▸ Make transformation (conversion, syndication, and compression). ▸ Perform security (digital rights management, watermark, and digital signatures). ▸ Distribute (Internet, intranet, email, fax, CD/DVD, or paper).
Records Management	▸ Manage enterprise information as a business record. ▸ Perform file plan classification (automatically and interactively). ▸ Fulfill compliant standards (such as U.S. Department of Defense (DOD) 5015.2 certification and International Standard Organization 15489 standard). ▸ Map classifications to retention rules and support of disposition management.
Web Content Management	▸ Create web content (manage content with template support). ▸ Include documents or social media/collaboration capabilities in web content. ▸ Manage web content lifecycle and publish content to different channels.
Digital Asset Management	▸ Support consuming, annotating, cataloging, storage, and retrieval of digital assets (photographs, videos, and music). ▸ Manage metadata for digital assets, copyrights, and distribution rights.
Email Management	▸ Perform email classification. ▸ Integrate emails into business processes or records.

Table 4.3 Scope of Enterprise Content Management Solutions Provided by SAP

SAP's ECM solutions provide end-to-end support for processing unstructured content, including activities such as capturing, managing, storing, preserving, sharing, and distributing content. Capabilities for managing unstructured content in SAP's ECM solutions include the following:

- **Content creation and capture**
  This produces new content with editing capabilities and handling of inbound information as content (e.g., content provided via email or scanning).
- **Content discovery, sharing, and collection**
  This covers all activities around finding and searching content and browsing through existing content repositories. Created content has to be shared and published. A typical example of sharing content is to create web content and publish the information in an intranet. Collaboration capabilities are crucial to working jointly on content.
- **Content governance and compliance**
  This is required to freeze content (e.g., via generating stable outputs in PDF) or to treat content as a record, which means fulfilling predefined compliance rules for the content. An example of a compliance standard is the U.S. DOD 5015.2 certification.
- **Content archiving and destruction**
  This process ensures a proper, total cost of ownership-minimizing end of life for content.

This section discusses the actual SAP products that are associated with the tasks of ECM. We begin by offering an overview of all the ECM solutions, and then dive into a more specific discussion of the most commonly used solutions: SAP Extended Enterprise Content Management by OpenText, SAP Document Access by OpenText, and SAP Archiving by OpenText.

4.8.1 Overview of SAP's ECM Solutions

To deliver on the full breadth of functionality and to offer an enterprise-grade ECM offering, SAP's extended and full-fledged ECM offerings include both SAP solutions and solutions provided by OpenText as solution extensions. The OpenText products have been tested to conform to the SAP product standards, can be purchased from SAP, and are maintained via SAP standard support mechanisms.

SAP's ECM Solutions Provided by OpenText

The following is a list of ECM solutions divided into SAP solutions provided by OpenText and SAP solutions provided by SAP:

- **SAP Document Presentment by OpenText**
  Automates document generation and personalization. Examples include billing statements, campaign execution, and customer-focused marketing messages.
- **SAP Digital Asset Management by OpenText**
  Provides optimized management of rich media assets, as well as the ability to integrate media into marketing communications; for example, images for a new washing machine that might be used on the web, for mobile devices, or printed on a brochure. These washing machine images could be part of a marketing campaign for new washing machines, with all images managed by brand and model.
- **SAP Invoice Management by OpenText (including optical character recognition)**
  Minimizes capture effort and human intervention and streamlines accounts payable processes (e.g., scanning invoices to create the invoice document in the SAP system).
- **SAP Travel Receipt Management by OpenText**
  Automates receipt handling and streamlines the expense management process.
- **SAP Employee Management by OpenText**
  In HR file administration, enables self-service scenarios such as a requests to see personnel files.
- **SAP Portal Content Management by OpenText**
  Manages version control, sharing, and collaboration of documents in SAP Enterprise Portal.
- **SAP Portal Site Management by OpenText**
  Manages web content in a company's SAP Enterprise Portal installation.
- **SAP Archiving by OpenText**
  Stores information, including scan and viewer technology. For example, SAP Archiving stores scanned images of invoices in the archive and links them to the invoice in the SAP ERP system.
- **SAP Document Access by OpenText (includes SAP Archiving by OpenText)**
  Offers 360-degree information access with SAP GUI context, meaning that from within SAP GUI, users can get a complete view of all content associated with a transaction, master data, or business process. For example, when you look at a

plant asset, such as a machine, all manuals and pictures associated with a physical asset on the plant floor are available in the SAP asset transaction. This includes the ability to check in and check out documents, get authorization and access rights, and search for documents.

- **SAP Extended ECM by OpenText (includes SAP Archiving by OpenText, SAP Document Access by OpenText, and SAP Portal Content Management by OpenText)**
  Connects unstructured content with SAP business processes—including document and records management, collaboration, archiving, scanning, information retrieval—that interconnect with SAP software and support core business processes. For example, you can associate a picture, résumé, or performance review with an employee.

Figure 4.18 shows several SAP ECM solutions provided by OpenText.

Non-SAP/ECM User

SAP User

Portal Site Management
Document Management and Collaboration embedded into SAP Enterprise Portal

Portal Content Management
Document Management and Collaboration embedded into SAP Enterprise Portal

Extended ECM
Attach content to SAP processes
Unique SAP Integration
Business workspaces with flexible UI
Records Management

Employee File Management
Automate HR File admin. and enable self-service scenarios

Travel Receipts Management
Automate receipt handling and streamline expense management process

Invoice Management and OCR
Minimize capture effort and human intervention
Streamline accounts payable processes

Digital Asset Management
Optimized management of rich media assets
Integrate media into marketing communications

Document Presentment
Automate document generation and personalization (e.g., billing statements)

Document Access
360-degree information access

Archiving
Secure, compliant, cost-efficient storage of information

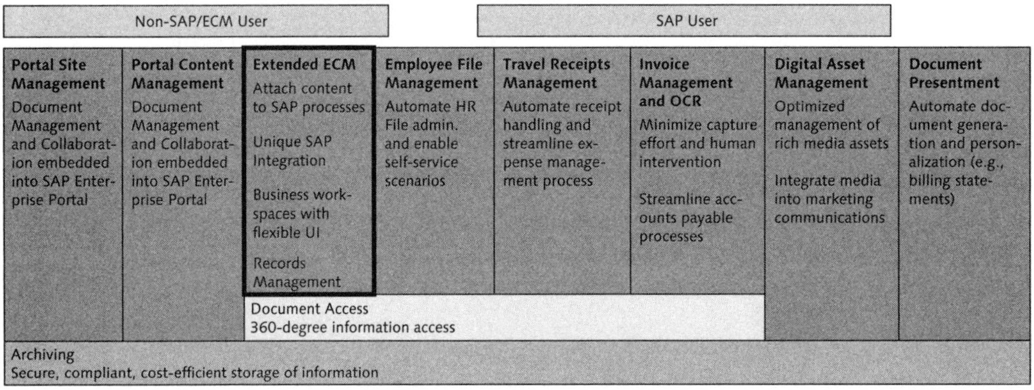

Figure 4.18 SAP's ECM Solutions Provided by OpenText

In Figure 4.18, notice that the bottom horizontal solution is archiving. All OpenText solutions use the archiving layer for secure, compliant, and cost-effective storage of all content. Notice Document Access above the archiving layer. Document Access is available in the SAP GUI to view content related to a business object; for example, a customer. Also notice at the top that all content is available to SAP and non-SAP users with security access to the content.

ECM Solutions Provided by SAP

In addition to the solution extensions provided by OpenText, SAP offers a range of products that provide content management capabilities:

- **SAP Product Lifecycle Management (PLM) Document Management System and SAP Easy Document Management**
Supports the scenarios delivered with SAP Product Lifecycle Management, including integration with computer-aided design (CAD) tools (which, for example, lets you store CAD files of a new engine in the SAP system and automatically create and update material master data in the SAP system based on the information maintained in CAD tools).
- **SAP cFolders**
Supports seamless collaboration on documents and material master data with external parties such as suppliers. This can be done without giving them access to your corporate system within the firewall.
- **SAP Folders Management**
Allows customers to build intuitive, structured views of diverse application data to boost business user productivity and support workflows on these folders and cases (e.g., to manage dispute cases or change cases).
- **CRM Content Management in SAP CRM**
Attachment service that allows users to attach documents to any SAP CRM object (e.g., a lead within the SAP CRM web interface).
- **E-mail Response Management System (ERMS) capability in SAP CRM**
Manages automatic replies to emails (e.g., a notification that your email was received and the recipient will get back to you as soon as possible).
- **SAP Enterprise Workspace for SAP Enterprise Portal**
Supports easy creation of collaboration spaces, workgroups, and teams via SAP Enterprise Portal.
- **Knowledge Management in SAP Enterprise Portal**
Supports basis document management functionality in the SAP Enterprise Portal frontend.
- **SAP Information Lifecycle Management (ILM)**
Manages retention and retirement of content associated with SAP via SAP ArchiveLink business processes in system decommissioning and retention management scenarios.
- **SAP StreamWork**
Content capability in the cloud for collaboration on documents and projects (e.g., writing an EIM book by collaborating with SAP and non-SAP authors).

- **SAP NetWeaver Enterprise Search**
  Has search capabilities for structured and unstructured content.
- **SAP Content Server**
  Content server delivered by SAP and supporting SAP ArchiveLink to support document storage.

4.8.2 SAP Extended Enterprise Content Management by OpenText

SAP Extended ECM is a full ECM suite (including document management, collaboration, capture, workflow, content access, records management, and archiving) that combines content management capabilities with deep SAP integration to provide content-enriched SAP business processes. It provides a new paradigm where content is managed *within* the business processes instead of *outside* the business processes, as shown in Figure 4.19.

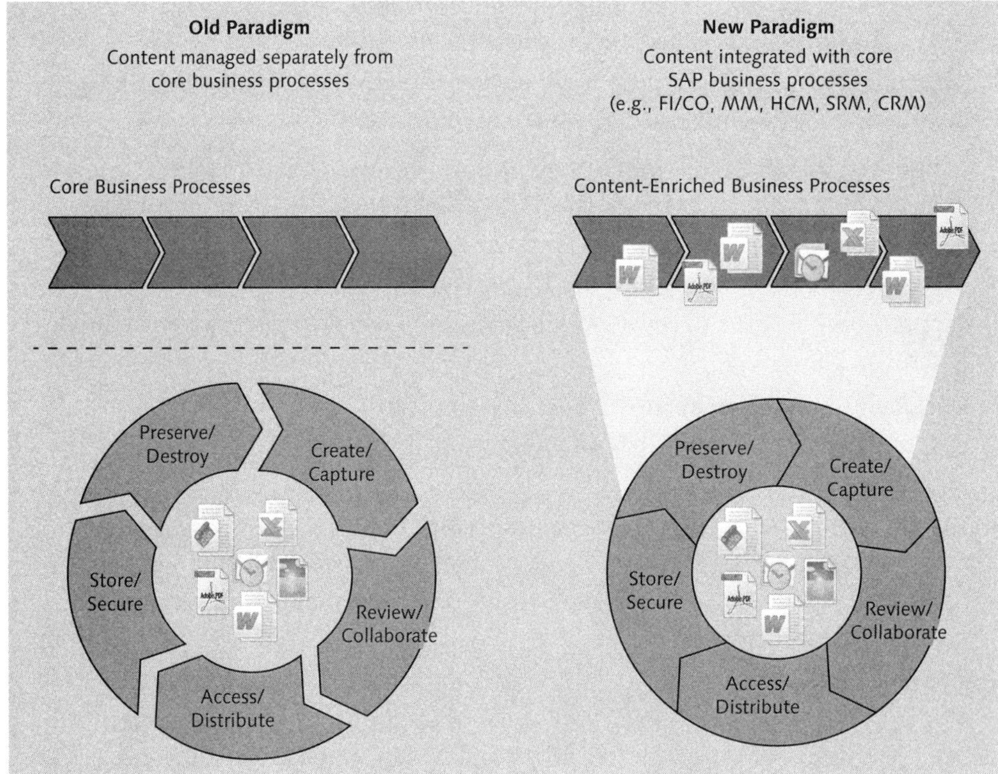

Figure 4.19 SAP Extended ECM Integrates Content with SAP Business Processes

Figure 4.19 depicts the integration of content and the business process with the content-enriched business processes on the right side of the figure. The integration between SAP systems and SAP Extended ECM is described next.

Deep Integration with SAP

The deep integration of SAP Extended ECM with other SAP systems includes workspaces that natively extend SAP processes. SAP Extended ECM is seamlessly integrated inside SAP applications such as the SAP Business Suite and SAP Enterprise Portal to enable SAP users to easily access content. In addition to accessing content in SAP's native UIs, content can be accessed from an SAP Extended ECM web UI, Microsoft Outlook, and Microsoft Windows Explorer. The support for many UIs allows for sharing of content between different stakeholders in an organization, independent from what applications the content originates or what a user's preferred UI may be.

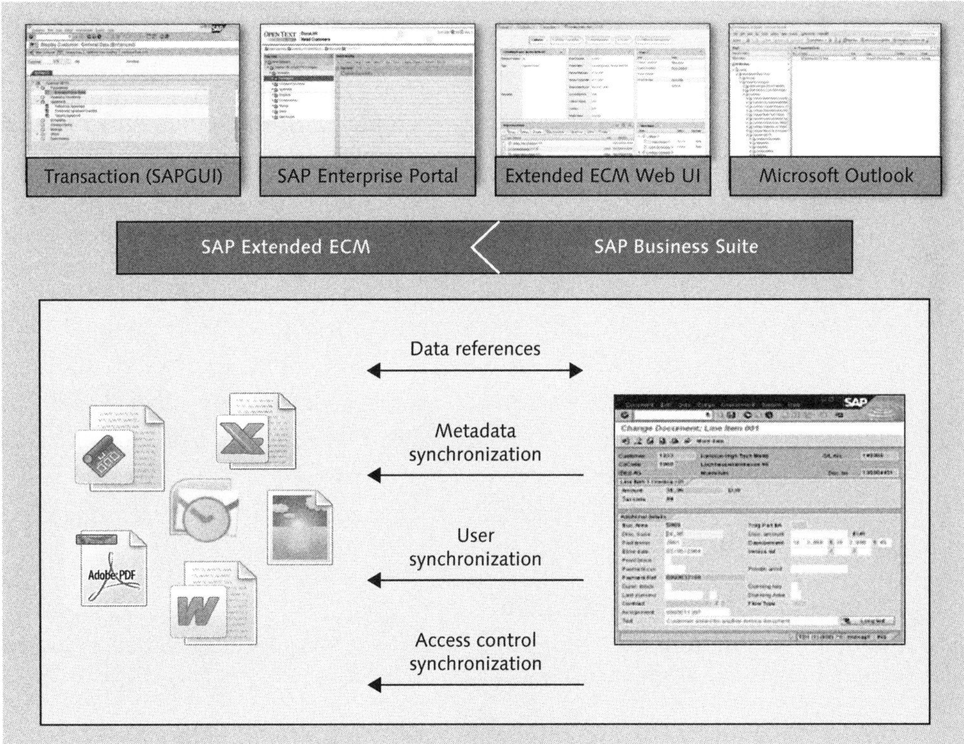

Figure 4.20 SAP Extended ECM Integration with SAP Business Suite

The deep connection with SAP extends beyond the UI to data, structures, roles, and permissions. Basically, everything customers have already standardized around SAP processes can be leveraged for ECM use cases. The impact is that SAP and ECM are always in sync. As shown in Figure 4.20, the SAP Business Suite is integrated in the frontend as well as in the backend by data referencing and data, user, and authorization synchronization, which supports SAP Single Sign-On (SSO).

In Figure 4.20, notice the constant synchronization of data references between SAP Extended ECM and the SAP Business Suite. Metadata synchronization, user synchronization, and access controls are driven from the SAP Business Suite to SAP Extended ECM, meaning that the security setup in your SAP system is inherited and applied to SAP Extended ECM. Also notice the variety of UIs in the figure. The content can be accessed from SAP GUI, SAP Enterprise Portal, an SAP Extended ECM UI, Microsoft Outlook, Lotus Notes, web browsers, and Windows Explorer (not included in the figure).

Examples of Content-Rich SAP Business Processes

SAP Extended ECM's deep integration provides very content-rich SAP business processes in the SAP Business Suite. Some examples of those content-enriched processes are project management, product lifecycle management, procurement, quality management, case and claims management, asset management, and customer relationship management. In each of these examples, the process is enriched due to the content.

One specific example is SAP Enterprise Asset Management (SAP EAM), which is used heavily in the Plant Maintenance (PM) module for processes such as equipment failure analysis, shutdown turnaround, and general change management. In this example, SAP Extended ECM leverages and extends SAP EAM for PM, providing content management and collaboration capabilities in every step related to the analysis and reporting the results to various stakeholders. The following is the process in the PM module:

1. **Create maintenance notification.**
   When the maintenance notification is created, a workspace is created in SAP Extended ECM that includes the notification documents. The workspace allows you to add additional content for sharing.

2. **Create work orders.**
   As the work order is created to investigate the problem, a failure analysis process is triggered in SAP Extended ECM. SAP Extended ECM collects failure data, scope, photographs, analysis, email correspondence with suppliers, and a final report for review.
3. **Schedule and fix.**
   As the technician is assigned and works on documents, all photos, manuals, and correspondence—that is, all content required for the repair—is provided via SAP Extended ECM.
4. **Complete the analysis.**
   The root-cause analysis can require updates to maintenance plans, equipment repair, and so on. All information is captured in the final analysis report managed by SAP Extended ECM.

Figure 4.21 shows an example of the content integrated in SAP EAM.

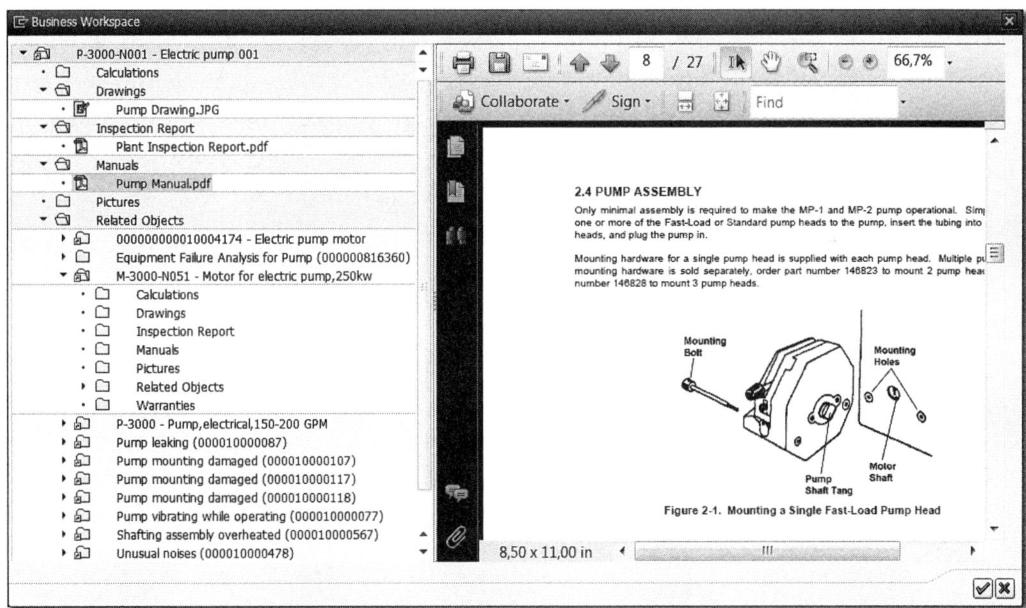

Figure 4.21 Example of Content Integrated in SAP Enterprise Asset Management

Figure 4.21 shows a workspace in PM where the user can access all content regarding a specific piece of equipment—in this case, an electric pump. The user can access the manuals, inspection reports, pictures, drawings, warranties, and so on required to maintain and fix the electric pump. (Workspaces will be discussed in more detail in Chapter 13.)

4.8.3 SAP Document Access by OpenText and SAP Archiving by OpenText

SAP Document Access by OpenText and SAP Archiving by OpenText are two key capabilities included in SAP Extended ECM that enable great flexibility when managing unstructured content. These capabilities are used heavily in both SAP Extended ECM and SAP ILM (covered in Section 4.9). SAP Document Access by OpenText and SAP Archiving by OpenText are discussed next in more detail.

SAP Document Access by OpenText

SAP Document Access by OpenText is powerful ECM software that integrates fully with your SAP applications. It allows you to store, manage, and retrieve documents across SAP transactions or applications such as SAP ERP or SAP CRM. Content can also originate from various sources such as host systems, legacy software, or customer-specific applications. SAP Document Access by OpenText provides three key features:

- **Ease of use**
  Enables even occasional users to quickly retrieve content by working with the intuitive, customizable navigation based on folder structures.
- **Ready access**
  Offers 360-degree views of SAP documents and SAP online and archived data.
- **Web interface**
  In addition to the SAP GUI interface, the web interface provides a convenient web UI that can be integrated into a customer portal or in the SAP Enterprise Portal component.

An example of using SAP Document Access by OpenText is providing front office employees with a complete view of all customer interactions (e.g., customer messages, emails, and letters written to the company), all brought together in one place so the employee can quickly gain insight into the customer's request.

SAP Archiving by OpenText

SAP Archiving by OpenText securely stores all types of documents and links them to SAP transactions via SAP ArchiveLink. SAP Archiving by OpenText also minimizes your database growth and improves performance, resulting in a lower total cost of ownership for your SAP software. Combined with SAP ILM, the archiving function lets you address the compliance requirements associated with electronic document retention regulations from government agencies (such as the U.S. Securities and Exchange Commission and the U.S. Food and Drug Administration) and mandates (such as the Sarbanes-Oxley Act and Germany's Principles of Due Operation of Electronic Bookkeeping Systems and Principles of Data Access and Auditing of Digital Documents).

What Is Archiving?

The term *archive* has two meanings:

- The relocation and removal of content from your systems (e.g., removing all closed purchase orders that are more than 10 years old and relocating them to a storage system)
- Associating content with data in your system (e.g., scanning invoices or emails associated with a vendor)

SAP Archiving by OpenText helps with both processes.

As you can see, ECM is a very large area. Chapter 13 focuses on SAP Extended ECM and how to get started using SAP Extended ECM in SAP ERP.

4.9 SAP Information Lifecycle Management

Information has a predictable lifecycle in which it's created, lives, and changes in databases, repositories, and software solutions. Information is then archived and eventually destroyed. A comprehensive strategy for information lifecycle management (ILM) focuses on maintaining a balance between total cost of ownership, risk, and legal compliance. It specifies steps to define, document, and introduce ways to better manage the information that exists across the organization. The ILM process includes knowing and categorizing your data, defining policies that govern what you do with the data, and setting up your system in such a way that you can apply these policies to your data. You then implement your information management strategy with the help of technology. The added value of

ILM compared to more conventional information management strategies is automation and completeness.

Several factors have converged to bring about a major change in the way companies manage data. For example, awareness of the unforeseen events that could occur—such as natural disasters, terrorist attacks, or financial meltdowns—has set in motion new efforts to protect consumer identity and privacy. This awareness has led to an explosion in legal requirements. There are currently thousands of regulations worldwide pertaining to the handling of electronic data, and the number of regulations continues to grow. Another factor that's becoming increasingly urgent is the management of legacy systems in both SAP software and non-SAP software landscapes. Not only are the aged systems generating ongoing and unnecessary costs through the consumption of electricity and the need for administration and maintenance effort, but they also pose a significant legal risk. The data they hold must be accessible and ready to be presented at relatively short notice (e.g., to an auditor in the event of a tax audit). However, as knowledge about the old systems gradually fades from the company, and the old hardware is physically removed, it's difficult to predict whether that data will be accessible when needed. The management and retention of information has become so important that traditional data management approaches are no longer sufficient. An effective ILM strategy is an essential part of an enterprise's overall strategy for dealing with the challenges of cost, compliance, and risk. SAP has developed an approach to ILM that meets the complex information management needs of today's organizations.

SAP ILM comprises the policies, processes, practices, and tools that are used to align the business value of information with the most appropriate and cost-effective IT infrastructure from the time information is created through its final destruction. The complete, flexible, and automated approach to ILM advanced by SAP gives you the support you need to adapt to constantly changing regulations. It helps you accomplish the following steps:

- Identify and categorize your data.
- Define policies that govern what you do with data.
- Leverage application and storage technology in such a way that you can apply these policies to your data.
- Implement your information management strategy.
- Shut down your legacy systems in a legally compliant manner.

Figure 4.22 shows the evolution from data archiving to retention management to systems decommissioning. This evolution is discussed next in more detail.

SAP Archiving by OpenText versus SAP Data Archiving

SAP Archiving by OpenText is a product that's used for the storage of content. For example, it's used to store scanned invoices in an SAP ERP system. SAP Archiving by OpenText is also used for the storage of those scanned invoices after they are retired from the SAP system. This product was discussed in Section 4.8.3 and isn't the focus of this section.

In this section, we talk about SAP Data Archiving, which refers to the *relocation* of business-complete data from the SAP application database to the *storage system*. The archived data can be accessed from the original system at any time for read-only activities, such as reporting, for example, the archiving of closed invoices older than 18 months.

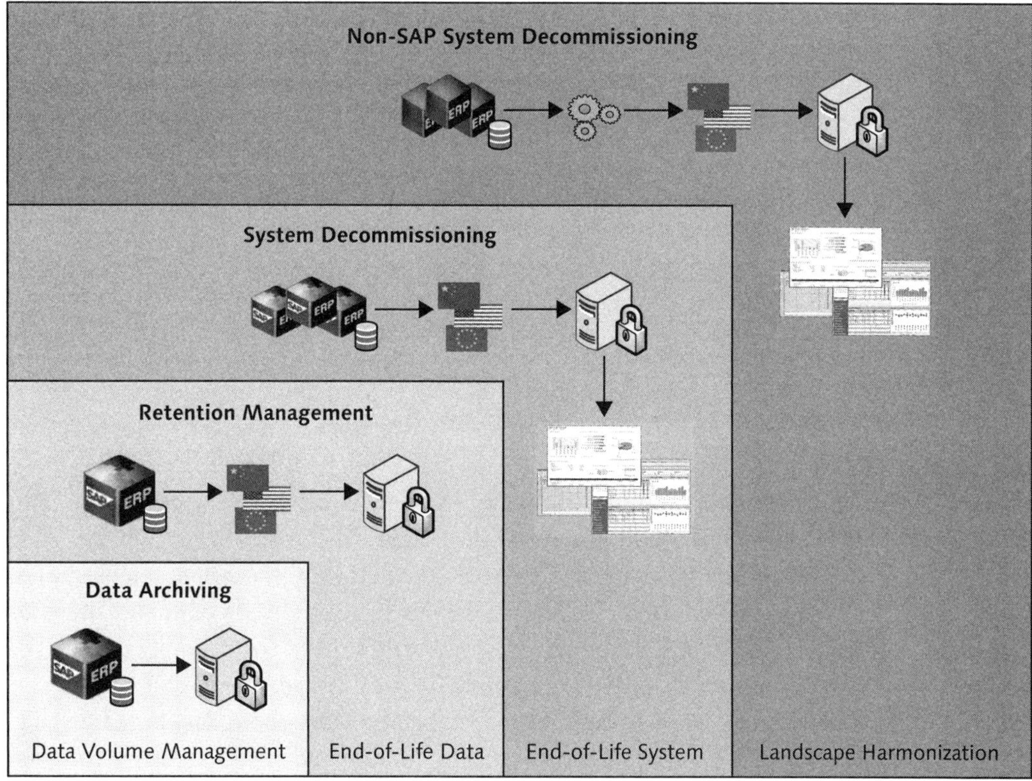

Figure 4.22 Evolution of Data Archiving

SAP ILM has evolved from a simple data archiving solution to a comprehensive solution for determining how long data should be kept, in what ways data should be kept, how data should be used, and which means to use for decommissioning SAP and non-SAP systems. It works with Data Services and SAP Archiving by OpenText for a complete ILM solution. SAP Data Archiving has been around for many years and lets you archive selected business objects from business-complete processes, relocating them from the database to an external storage system. Examples include closed purchasing documents, order history, and technical items such as intermediate documents (IDocs) and workflow work items. SAP Data Archiving has evolved into retention management, enabling you to proactively monitor how long you need to keep data in your system and placing legal holds as required on selected data. The further expansion of SAP ILM includes decommissioning of SAP and non-SAP systems that are no longer required.

SAP ILM provides three major use cases and scenarios for use:

- **SAP Data Archiving**
  Again, this data archiving should not be confused with SAP Archiving by OpenText. SAP Data Archiving is a tool that helps you to manage the data volumes in your live application database. As a core component of SAP ILM, it enables you to move business-complete data (transactional and master data) that is no longer required in everyday business from the database into long-term, less expensive storage. The data is still available to meet regulatory or other legal requirements when it's stored in the archive.
- **Retention management**
  SAP tools and technologies for SAP ILM provide retention policy management functions that support the complete information lifecycle from creation to retention to destruction. They enable you to enter different rules and policies that reflect various criteria, including where data is stored, the duration of data retention, and when data can be destroyed. The policies, usually based on external legal requirements or internal service-level agreements, can be applied to both structured and unstructured data stored on all types of media. Based on the rules, the data is automatically archived into the correct storage area and receives an expiration date. SAP ILM-aware storage integration means that your storage systems understand and can act on the stored data based on rules you define. At the end of the lifecycle, an automated destruction function permanently destroys the archived data when the expiration date has been

reached. SAP ILM includes functions that support legal-hold management and automated electronic discovery.

- **System decommissioning**
  SAP ILM provides a complete approach to shutting down legacy systems and bringing the data from both SAP and non-SAP software into a central SAP ILM retention warehouse. In the retention warehouse, the data is stored with the relevant expiration dates in SAP ILM-aware storage and can be viewed with different reporting options even after the original system has been shut down. Functions of SAP BW as well as local reporting functions are used to extend the SAP ILM retention warehouse with centralized auditing and reporting functions. Included are functions that enable you to create snapshots of master data and customizing data and provide on-demand analysis of archived data.

The major SAP ILM components that support these use scenarios are retention management and system decommissioning capabilities within SAP ILM, which are discussed next. Both these components integrate natively with SAP Archiving by OpenText and SAP Document Access by OpenText.

Note

SAP Archiving by OpenText is used in SAP Extended ECM by OpenText and SAP ILM. When removing data and content from SAP systems, SAP ILM manages all SAP-structured data and all associated content (e.g., scanned invoices, employee pictures, etc.) via SAP ArchiveLink. SAP Extended ECM manages the archiving of all non-SAP content, such as collaborative documents, emails, physical boxes of old documents not in an SAP system, or web images (e.g., used for a TV advertisement) not associated with an SAP system.

4.9.1 Retention Management

Retention management provides a range of dedicated tools and functions to help you adequately control the retention of your data along its entire lifecycle. This holds true for structured information, such as a sales documents posted in the SAP application, as well as for unstructured information such as scanned invoices. After a policy is set up and activated in the SAP ILM policy engine, data is protected against destruction until its expiration date has been reached. Retention management is based on SAP Data Archiving technology, so you don't have to start from scratch if you're already using SAP Data Archiving. You can use retention management functions directly within your SAP ERP application as of SAP ERP EHP5 or higher. Retention management includes the follow capabilities:

- Archiving data from open and completed business processes
- Storing archived information on an SAP ILM-certified server (to guarantee non-changeability of the information and protect from premature destruction)
- Determining and managing retention rules
- Inclusion of retention rules for stored information so the destruction is timely and in adherence with the retention periods required by law
- Using stored information to create reports for tax auditing and product liability
- Retrieving information for legal cases and defining legal holds
- Destroying stored information after the retention period has expired, assuming there is no legal hold

More details on these capabilities will be provided in Chapter 12.

4.9.2 System Decommissioning

System decommissioning enables you to consolidate multiple large legacy systems into a small single instance and retain on-demand access to data from legacy systems, as well as respond to tax audits and create reports. The legacy data is stored in the SAP ILM retention warehouse, which serves as a single repository for multiple systems. When the data is required for legal, audit, or tax purposes, it's exposed to a data warehouse such as SAP BW (and, in the future, SAP HANA) for flexible and modern reporting capability. The business knowledge and context is preserved during the decommissioning, even as retention policies are being enforced. After moving retention-relevant data from the legacy system to the SAP ILM retention warehouse, you can shut down the legacy system for good.

In a typical decommissioning scenario, you have one or more systems that will be shut down and a dedicated retention warehouse system that will receive the data you want to retain from the original systems. The retention warehouse consists of three pieces:

- A dedicated SAP ERP application running only SAP ILM
- A dedicated implementation of SAP BW
- Third-party SAP ILM-certified storage hardware

In the retention warehouse, data from decommissioned systems is organized according to audit areas and covered by the retention policies you define and manage using the software. This means retention times and legal holds apply to the data maintained in the retention warehouse, just as they do for non-decommissioned (or live) systems.

The system that is to be shut down is first emptied of its data using standard and SAP ILM-enhanced archiving objects and programs. You can archive all the business-complete data, and then use snapshot functionality to archive data from objects that aren't yet business-complete, as well as any related master and context data. Figure 4.23 shows the decommissioning of several systems to a single SAP ILM system and related storage.

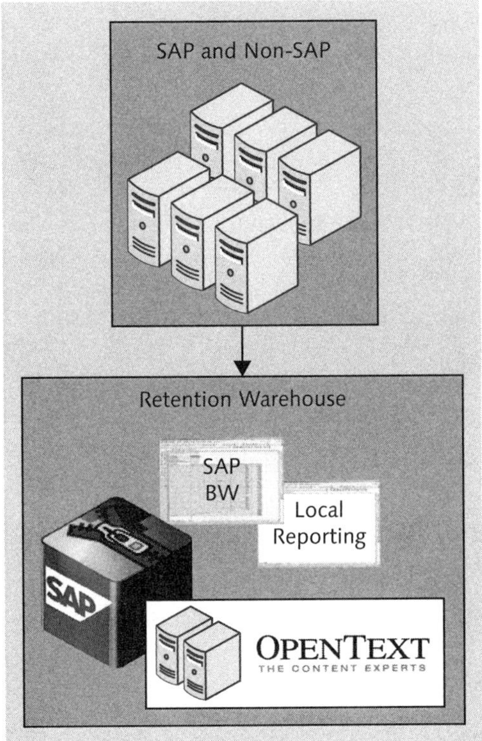

Figure 4.23 Decommissioning Systems Using SAP ILM

Next, we discuss a typical system decommissioning scenario and some of the required steps.

A Typical System Decommissioning Scenario

For a decommissioning project, there are multiple steps that can be roughly grouped into two categories: steps for the legacy system and steps for the retention warehouse in SAP ILM:

- **Steps for the legacy system**
  - Analyze the system.
  - Enable the legacy system for archiving.
  - Prepare the legacy system for shutdown.
  - Extract data from the legacy system.
  - Conduct testing and quality assurance.
- **Steps for the retention warehouse**
  - Install an SAP ERP application with only SAP ILM and SAP BW, and connect to an SAP ILM-aware storage system.
  - Set up the retention warehouse.
  - Set up audit areas, policies, and rules.
  - Move archived data to the retention warehouse system.
  - Convert and store the archive files and apply rules.
  - Generate SAP BW queries using archived data or run a local reporting option.

The following sections discuss several of the most important steps in more detail. You can find more details on SAP ILM in Chapter 12.

Analyze the Legacy System

It's not uncommon for IT departments to have only limited knowledge of their legacy systems, particularly with respect to the amount and types of data they contain. If you don't know what your legacy system "looks" like, you have the option of either moving everything over to the retention warehouse system or, after you run an analysis of your system, moving only the specific data you'll need later for auditing and reporting.

Enable the Legacy System for Archiving

After you've identified the data you need to retain and the tools you need to retain it, you can enable the legacy system for archiving. Because SAP ILM is delivered with SAP ERP, your older, legacy system has to receive the necessary SAP ILM functions. (SAP ILM natively supports legacy systems back to R/3 4.6c. For older releases, additional consulting is required.) This includes enhancements for archiving objects, snapshot functionality, and the context data extractor (CDE). The CDE functionality is preconfigured for tax reporting and product liability reporting.

Extract Data from Legacy Systems

After the legacy system and retention warehouse are prepared, you can extract the data from the legacy system. This includes enhanced data archiving functionality, such as the snapshot option (one of the archiving options), and the CDE functionality. After you've "emptied" the legacy system, moved data to the retention warehouse, and performed testing, you can shut the legacy system down.

SAP ILM provides a streamlined IT infrastructure and lowered costs through the safe and efficient decommissioning of redundant systems. It reduces risk by delivering full auditing and reporting functionality and rules-based enforcement of retention policies and preventing destruction of important data. This enables greater legal compliance by automatically managing the retention of data from your SAP applications, based on retention policies and rules you define.

Set Up the Retention Warehouse

After preparing your legacy system to be shut down, you can set up the retention warehouse to receive the data from the system you want to decommission. Your dedicated SAP ERP application should be set up and connected to a third-party storage system, which must be an SAP ILM-certified product. If you're using SAP Archiving by OpenText for your image and content storage, you can automatically use it for SAP ILM as well. (To find an SAP ILM-certified partner, visit *http://global.sap.com/community/ebook/2013_09_adpd/enEN/search.html*; search for "ILM".) In addition, you need to connect SAP BW. SAP recommends that you use a dedicated business warehouse system for your data retention warehouse. You'll find more details about SAP ILM in Chapter 12.

4.10 Information Governance in SAP

We introduced the discipline of information governance in Chapter 2. In this section, we review the concept and then explain how SAP solutions can assist with information governance. It's important to understand that all information management must include governance from both product capabilities and across all processes that update critical information in your enterprise. Information governance is a discipline that provides oversight to ensure successful execution of your information initiatives. It involves the management of people, technology, and processes; as well as policies, standards, and metrics, including the ongoing oversight necessary to manage information risks.

Information governance can be applied to one project, can be started with one data domain, and should be extended to the enterprise. Information governance is a sustained activity.

How do you know if problems you're seeing in your company can be attributed to a lack of information governance? The first step is always to listen. Words such as *mergers, risk, compliance, migration, acquisition, shared services, security,* and *Sarbanes-Oxley* can all point to information governance.

Case Study: New Driver's License in Indiana

In Indiana, 58,600 residents lost confidence in state IT practices when, as Chris Sikich noted in a *USA Today* article, the Bureau of Motor Vehicles (BMV) sent out a notice for drivers to renew their driver's licenses. The notices were intended as a proactive measure because the state was expecting 2.4 million people to renew their license. The state spent $247,450 to mail postcards to about 700,000 people with birthdays from January through August.

Of those 700,000 people, 58,600 (approximately 8.3 %) received incorrect information. Though, for many recipients, addresses and last names were correct, first names were not. For example, Rod Humphrey received a notice for Brandon Humphrey. Rod just threw out the renewal notice, effectively subverting the proactive measure taken by the BMV. The consequences of this are twofold:

- The renewal notices are more likely to be ignored, and therefore the proactive renewal-avoidance process is less effective.
- The mailing cost of those postcards was wasted. At a cost of 35 cents per mail piece, the postal cost of the error was approximately $20,510.

The next section discusses scenarios for how to get started with information governance.

4.10.1 Information Governance Use Scenario Phasing

The Indiana driver's license case study indicates a data quality problem. However, many other kinds of use scenarios can spur you to start an information governance project. Figure 4.24 highlights common use scenarios that your company may be approaching. The size of the squares indicates the relative complexity of each of the use scenarios, paying particular attention to the organizational change management and business process changes required to succeed in the individual use scenarios.

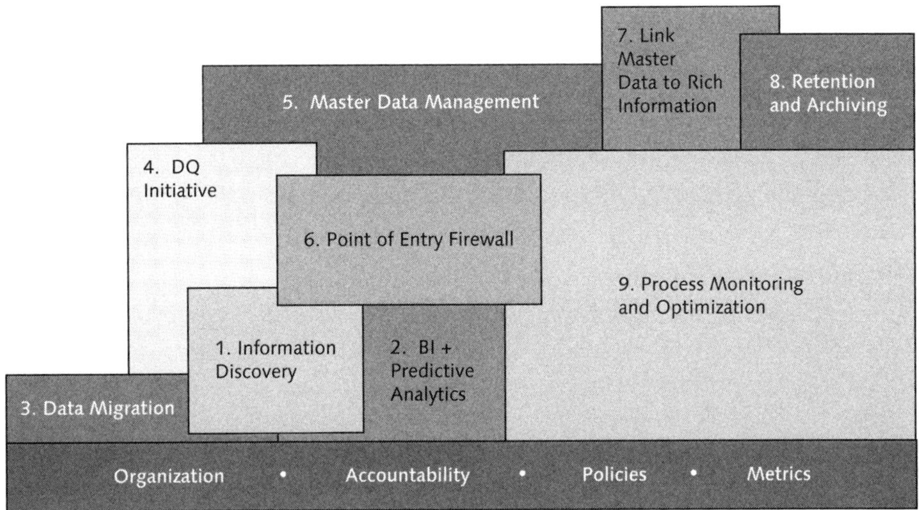

Figure 4.24 Information Governance Use Scenario Phasing

Notice that the use scenarios overlap. For example, if you do the work for an information discovery project, you can reuse some of that work for your BI and predictive analytics project. For a BI and predictive analytics project, you need to know the location of the best information (and the quality of that information) from which to drive the decision making. Information discovery includes activities such as knowing where the information is kept as well as quality-level base-lining.

The following list describes each of the use scenarios.

- **Information discovery**
  Finding all of the critical information sources in your company, including discovering (and documenting) quality levels, freshness, and timeliness of those information sources.
- **BI and predictive analytics**
  Using high-quality, fresh, and timely information to drive decision making throughout the enterprise.

- **Data migration**
  Moving and integrating data as you move from one system to another (e.g., moving data from a retiring system to a new version of SAP ERP), including aggregations and quality corrections.
- **Data quality initiative**
  Establishing policies to answer questions such as the following: What is a customer? What is a material? How can we create a single view of a material? Who needs to create and approve these master records?
- **Manage master data**
  Creating single points of reference for master data records, including setting up review and approval workflows for creating, changing, and flagging records for deletion.
- **Point-of-entry firewall**
  Proactively fixing and verifying information before it enters productive systems in a live state, including enrichment and verifying against third-party truth sources.
- **Link master data to rich information**
  Correctly linking rich information (documents, PDFs, videos, etc.) to the master data that needs the information, requiring accurate identification and tagging of both rich information and master data.
- **Retention and archiving**
  Establishing retention and archiving policies in compliance with both corporate and regulatory policies, including both enforcement and manifestation of the policies.
- **Process monitoring and optimization**
  Actively monitoring how well both business processes and information governance processes are performing, including where key bottlenecks are forming and recommendations for optimizing both business processes and information governance processes.

Refer to Chapter 2 for more on getting started with governance initiatives.

4.10.2 Technology Enablers for Information Governance

You can implement information governance without any new technology purchases. Many customers use standard software to facilitate their information governance project: email, departmental Microsoft SharePoint, and spreadsheets. You *should* start information governance this way because it helps you gain experience and perspective, as well as grow your information network.

However, keep in mind human nature. You can establish all of the good policies and standards in the world, and people can agree on the inherent goodness of these policies and standards. But if these policies and standards are inordinately difficult to comply with, people will find a way to get around them.

How do you make your information governance program easy to comply with? Technology is a great force multiplier here. Figure 4.25 ties in the EIM technologies mentioned in this chapter with information governance.

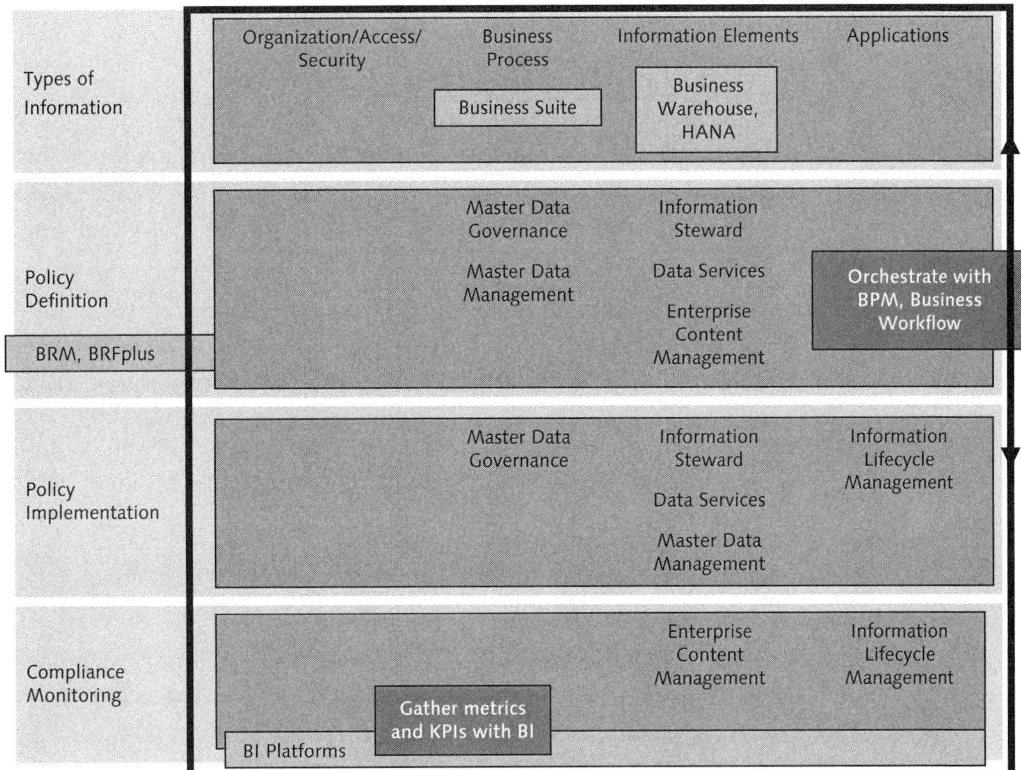

Figure 4.25 Enabling Information Governance Technologies

Figure 4.25 demonstrates that information governance doesn't only apply to master data. It applies to the organization, including governing user access and monitoring security. Information governance must be concerned with how the business processes use your enterprise information and where all of the data is stored.

Finally, which systems access, use, and update the business processes and data elements that truly are enterprise assets? For all of these kinds of information (organization, business process, data elements, and systems), you have the following kinds of activities:

- **Policy definition**
  What does "good" look like? How should this information behave? These policies are defined in plain language by the key business stakeholders. The following list mentions the major products where information policy definitions are created.
  - *Information Steward:* This is the place for data stewards to define policies for master data.
  - *SAP Extended ECM:* SAP Extended ECM supports the definition of retention policies, determining how long documents should be retained and how access rights should be changed over the lifespan of content. SAP Extended ECM is also able to use SAP data from the SAP Business Suite to define retention periods.
  - *SAP ILM:* SAP ILM supports the definition of retention policies, determining how long data and associated documents should be retained. It's possible to synchronize (to create, update, and delete) SAP ILM retention policies via Application Programming Interfaces (APIs) with SAP Extended ECM retention policies.
- **Policy implementation**
  How can you seamlessly implement and enforce the policies you defined—with as much collaboration and as little rewriting as possible? The following software and components can help:
  - *Data Services:* This is the place for IT developers to design, move, aggregate, and understand master data, transactional data, and text data. Also, data stewards and IT developers can collaborate on core questions such as how to define a unique customer at the global level.
  - *SAP NetWeaver MDM:* This is an environment for data stewards and IT developers to design and enforce master data storage, provisioning, and quality rules in analytical master data management scenarios.

- *SAP MDG:* Much like SAP NetWeaver MDM, this component takes advantage of the SAP ERP environment as a master data repository, business rule repository, and business workflow processing.
- *SAP Extended ECM:* Records management manages the retention and disposition of paper documents and digital content according to compliance requirements supporting international records management standards.
- *SAP ILM:* Establishes retention and policies for transactional data, master data, and rich content (such as documents), and enforces those policies.

- **Compliance monitoring**
  How can you prove that you're complying with the information policies defined previously? For a legal hold, can you prove that you're following industry standards when the audit department comes calling? The following software and components can help:
  - *SAP BusinessObjects BI platform:* Here you can organize information and package it in a way that allows the business users to make decisions based on that information.
  - *Information Steward and SAP MDG:* These enable you to monitor over time how well the data is complying with the business rules.

In addition to the software capabilities previously mentioned for policy definition, policy implementation, and compliance monitoring, SAP Business Process Management (SAP BPM), SAP Business Workflow, Business Rules Framework plus (BRFplus), and SAP Business Rules Management (SAP BRM) are software components that have a cross-functional role in information governance. They can be used to support policy definition, implementation, and compliance monitoring.

As you can see, information governance requires a holistic look at policies, processes, and procedures to ensure that you're provisioning trusted, relevant, and reliable information for business processes.

4.11 NeedsEIM Inc. and SAP's Solutions for EIM

Now that you understand the EIM solutions offered by SAP, let's take a high-level look at how these solutions may help NeedsEIM Inc. (We'll go into more detail about this fictional company in subsequent chapters of the book.)

Chapter 1 introduced NeedsEIM Inc. and discussed its business challenges. SAP technologies that can help address them are shown in Figure 4.26. (Note that this is only one possible solution. Depending on your specific landscape, there are other alternate options that can provide similar resolutions for your business challenges.)

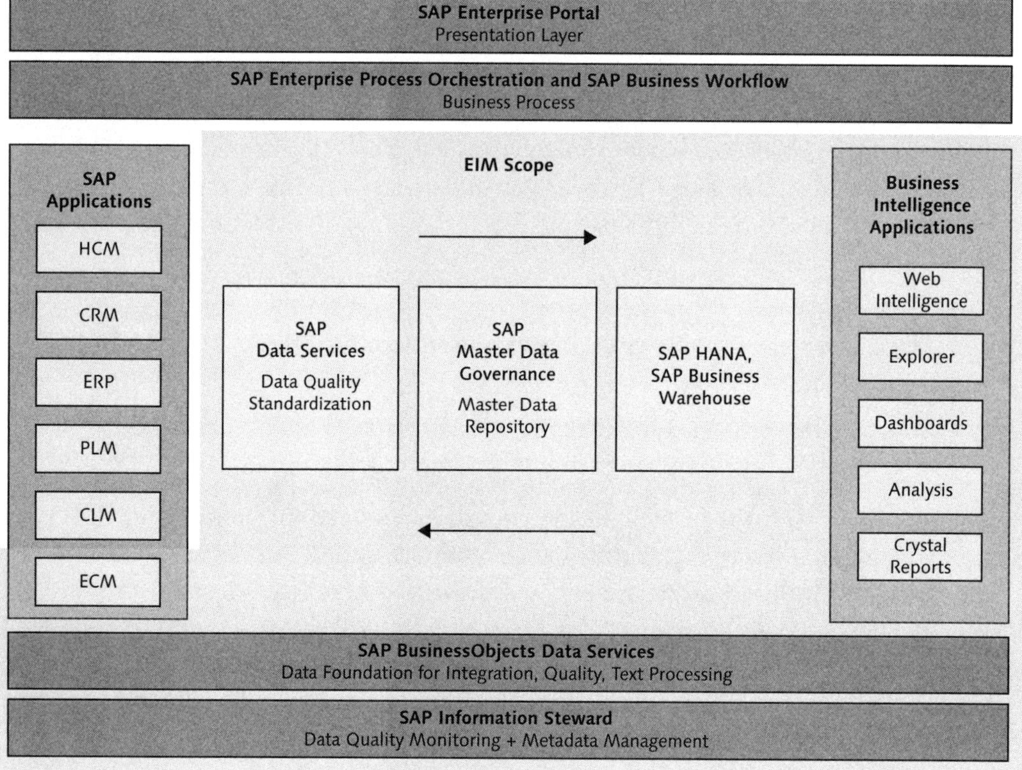

Figure 4.26 Sample Solution Architecture

Notice that the EIM components cover the cleansing and consolidation of information for both operational use in the applications and analytical use in the SAP BusinessObjects BI suite. Using SAP Enterprise Portal, SAP BPM, and SAP Business Workflow, a master data creation and updating process can be designed that provides clear audit trails of approval. The record is stored in the SAP MDM system, prior to which it goes through standardization, cleansing, and any enrichment processes using Data Services. The data can now be syndicated to subscribing systems such as SAP ERP, SAP CRM, and so on. If there is any unstructured content that has to be managed and attached to a master data record (such as a W-4, company financials, or a vendor record), the attachment can be triggered as part of the approval workflow, and the documents can be stored in a content repository along with requisite metadata. A one-time migration of existing master data from various systems includes cleansing, matching, de-duplicating, and enriching, which can all be done by using Data Services and SAP MDG.

The issue of contracts may require a complex contract lifecycle management (CLM) solution or a combination of workflow and ECM solutions along with integration between systems. The analysis that's required to identify supplier spending may need a combination of information from a vendor master data governance process and an application that tracks spending. This data can be housed in an analytic database such as SAP BW and/or SAP HANA for further analysis. A similar solution can be applied for customer-level profit and loss that would need all types of expense data collected from various applications such as SAP ERP Human Capital Management (SAP ERP HCM), SAP CRM, and SAP ERP, along with revenue data from SAP ERP to arrive at the comprehensive profit and loss figure by customer.

As you move through Part II of the book, you'll see how different capabilities within SAP's EIM portfolio can be used to address the major issues at NeedsEIM Inc.

4.12 Summary

This chapter provided an overview of all of SAP's solutions for EIM. It introduced PowerDesigner as an architecture and modeling platform to capture and communicate the current and future state of the information enterprise. Additional information on PowerDesigner is available in Chapter 7. The chapter also covered the various data provisioning capabilities available with SAP HANA Cloud Integration, Data Services, and Replication Server. It also introduced Data Services data quality, and text data processing capabilities. More details on SAP HANA Cloud Integration and Data Services can be found in Chapter 8 and Chapter 9, respectively. Information Steward was covered as a single environment to discover, assess, define, and monitor the quality of your information assets (more detail can be found in Chapter 10). You've also seen how managing master data includes both SAP MDM and SAP MDG as an embedded master data solution. SAP MDG is discussed in more detail in Chapter 11.

You now understand the breadth of ECM solutions offered by SAP and OpenText. SAP Extended ECM is the primary offering from OpenText and is discussed in more detail in Chapter 13. You understand that information is a risk if kept too long, so data archiving, retention policies, and systems decommissioning must be included in an information management strategy. Chapter 12 provides more detail on SAP ILM.

In addition to details on the specific software capabilities, in Chapter 5 and Chapter 6, you'll learn about SAP Rapid Deployment solutions and real-world applications of EIM that are being used today. Chapter 6 is provided by named and unnamed customers who describe how they are using EIM and SAP's solutions for EIM to solve specific business problems.

In this chapter, we'll explain the rapid-deployment paradigm for Enterprise Information Management solutions. The key is standardized and engineered implementation of predefined best practices as the foundation of every SAP EIM solution, based on SAP Rapid Deployment solutions.

5 Rapid-Deployment Solutions for Enterprise Information Management

Today more than ever, a company's software strategy is heavily influenced by the business, rather than by IT alone. Line-of-business leaders are in the driver's seat, and they care most of all about business outcomes of the solution—and about how fast and simply these can be achieved. Long projects with unpredictable post-implementation results and costs are no longer acceptable. Instead, both business and IT leaders want to know up front what they get, and get it fast and at predictable cost. This means that a new implementation methodology is required. The aim of this chapter is to give you an insight into this new implementation paradigm, as it applies in the EIM space.

SAP Rapid Deployment solutions enable a best practices methodology for the way we approach the implementation of SAP solutions today. In a nutshell, the new paradigm is based on the realization that it's faster and less risky to leverage available best business practices with SAP Rapid Deployment solutions, perform a fit/gap analysis, and restrict additional customizing, add-ons, and interfaces to only those areas of a company's operations where significantly more business value and differentiation can be achieved.

SAP Rapid Deployment solutions simplify the implementation of SAP solutions in the cloud, on-premise, or in hybrid landscapes by making the implementation faster, with less cost and predictable business outcomes. It includes best practices-based implementation content and proven risk-reducing implementation methodologies. This accelerates the deployment of new solutions with key technology and business capabilities to help companies solve business problems and go-live fast. Figure 5.1 shows how SAP Rapid Deployment solutions fit into the overall deployment model with its best business and implementation practices for faster time-to-value.

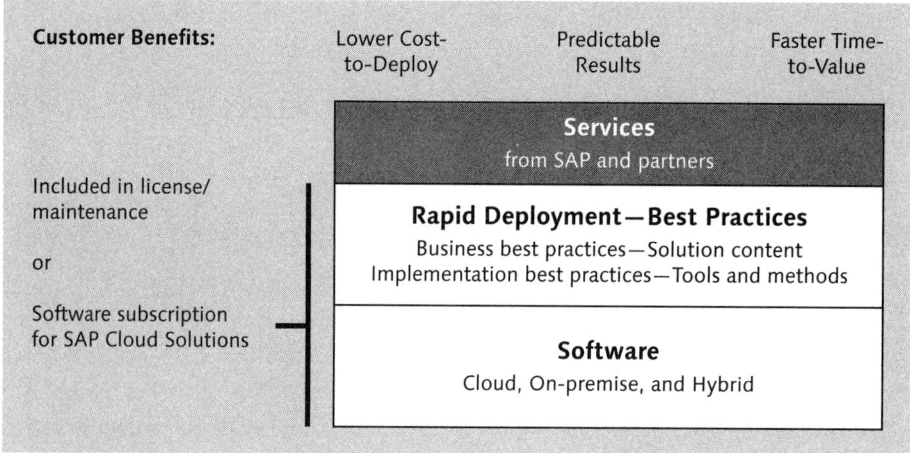

Figure 5.1 Best Practices for Faster Adoption with SAP Rapid Deployment Solutions

Customers quickly see proposed solutions via a comprehensive and seamless guidance from evaluation to go-live, with no surprises. Modular scope options enable the assembly of end-to-end solutions, helping companies easily adopt the right combination of best business practices and IT capabilities or extend where necessary to meet the customer's needs.

This chapter introduces the SAP Rapid Data Migration content that transforms the ETL-tool SAP Data Services into a data migration engine for SAP target systems, introduces a Data Migration accelerator, and describes the rapid-deployment solutions from SAP around SAP Master Data Governance and SAP Information Stewardship.

5.1 Rapid-Deployment Solutions for Data Migration

Migration projects are relevant for all types of companies, including those with SAP applications, those with non-SAP applications, those who are upgrading, and those who are migrating into the cloud. This list basically includes any company that needs to migrate data from one application to another, such as companies in the following situations:

- Acquiring or merging with other companies
- Expanding into new lines of business
- Moving parts of their applications into the cloud
- Migrating to SAP HANA
- Initiating green IT projects to reduce hardware and environmental and monetary costs
- Harmonizing data and processes across organizational boundaries
- Conducting a global SAP rollout

Because of this, data migration is often a first entry point with EIM, and it serves as a compelling use case for starting data management and information governance initiatives across the enterprise. Chapter 9 also discusses data migration as a typical use case for using data integration capabilities delivered with SAP Data Services (hereafter Data Services).

This section walks you through both the SAP products and migration content that SAP provides for data migration projects. Specifically, this section discusses use cases for data migration, describes solutions that are available for data migration, teaches you about migration content delivered by SAP to accelerate migration projects, walks you through a specific example of migrating customer data to SAP ERP, and finally, introduces you to the SAP Data Services Migration Accelerator by BackOffice Associates.

5.1.1 Introduction to Data Migration

Along with the business reasons for migrating data just mentioned, there are also technical reasons for data migration projects. Some common reasons include the following:

- **Implementing a new SAP application system**
  This includes any new SAP ERP or SAP Customer Relationship Management (SAP CRM) implementation, a line of business addition to an existing SAP application, or an industry implementation such as SAP for Utilities or SAP for Banking. This could also include a new data warehouse application from SAP.
- **Database vendor consolidation**
  Database vendor consolidation requires a data migration if companies want to reduce the number of databases they need to support; for example, a company

might migrate its existing SAP ERP systems to SAP HANA or SAP Sybase Adaptive Server Enterprise (SAP Sybase ASE).

- **System consolidation**
  System consolidation projects can be driven from a green-IT or sustainability project, by the business to simplify the business processes, or by IT to reduce the total cost of ownership through the reduction of systems that require maintenance and ongoing production support.

In all of these scenarios, you need to migrate data from one system to another. Data migration is often a first entry point to EIM. Normally, you need to do more than just relocate the data. You also need to cleanse, validate, de-duplicate, and possibly enrich the data. Additionally, data migration projects include a definition of rules for the quality of the data, and these rules can be reused for ongoing data integration as well as ongoing data assessment. The governance that's required in migration projects will hopefully evolve to ongoing information governance.

SAP has several solutions for data migration:

- **SAP Rapid Data Migration**
  SAP Rapid Data Migration (hereafter, Rapid Data Migration) is based on rapid-deployment solutions and uses Data Services and SAP Information Steward (hereafter Information Steward) to assess and migrate your data. This solution is the focus of this chapter and SAP's recommendation when migrating from non-SAP applications to SAP.
- **Legacy System Migration Workbench**
  LSMW is a data loader tool available in SAP NetWeaver Application Server ABAP. It's a tool for loading the data and doesn't extract, cleanse, govern, or provide data quality capabilities.
- **SAP Information Lifecycle Management (ILM)**
  For a system consolidation scenario, after you move to a central and harmonized system, you need to decommission your source data. From a data migration perspective, this includes a data migration of your source systems to SAP ILM.
- **SAP Landscape Transformation**
  SAP Landscape Transformation is used to migrate specific data from one SAP system to another SAP system. A common example is an older 4.6c system where you want to migrate one company code or one profit center to another SAP system. SAP Landscape Transformation performs these types of migrations for companies with multiple SAP systems.

- **SAP Data Services Migration Accelerator by BackOffice Associates**
  The Data Services Migration Accelerator extends the capabilities of Data Services and Rapid Data Migration by providing full migration project management capabilities in a single-pane-of-glass console, as well as simple web forms for conducting mapping and data construction activities within the context of the migration project.

Note

For those experienced with LSMW who want to also extract, cleanse, and get the full benefit from using Data Services, you can use Data Services for extraction and transformation, and then you can call LSMW to load the data.

Rapid Data Migration software is the focus of this section, because it includes migration of non-SAP data and migration from any target to any source. It offers (via Data Services) rich capabilities for extraction, cleansing, transformation, validation, and de-duplication of data prior to loading. The work done for data migration can be leveraged for ongoing integration, as well as ongoing data cleansing.

Using SAP's solutions for EIM in your data migration projects enables you to do the following:

- Profile and extract from diverse source systems.
- Map the source data to the target data structures, including simple and complex transformations of the data.
- Standardize, parse, cleanse, and validate data. This includes data validation against the target business context (i.e., the business rules of the target system, such as if plants are required or if the country codes are correct).
- Load data into the target system.
- Reconcile loaded data to know what was loaded versus what was expected to be loaded.

When referring to Rapid Data Migration software, we're specifically referring to Data Services and Information Steward, which are used for data migration projects.

5.1.2 Data Migration Rapid-Deployment Content

If all you needed for successful data migration projects was software tooling, we wouldn't provide a separate paragraph for data migration. The primary software products that you need for data migration are Data Services and Information Steward. Data migration projects require deep knowledge of and expertise in the target data structures: understanding what system you're migrating to, the requirements for the data in the new system, and the expectations for the data to be successful in the new system. When migrating to SAP applications, the source system is completely unknown to the Rapid Data Migration developers of the SAP Rapid Deployment solutions team. You could be migrating from a home-grown application, another vendor's software solution, a mainframe application, or any other datastores that were used prior to your SAP application. While SAP can't provide accelerators or deep knowledge of your legacy source systems, SAP can and certainly does provide details on your target system for data migration. This knowledge, provided for you as out-of-the-box migration content, accelerates your SAP implementation.

Migration content that accelerates data migration projects is provided as rapid-deployment solutions, which provide data migration best practices out of the box, referred to as Rapid Data Migration solutions. Many Rapid Data Migration packages are available today. A full list is available at *http://service.sap.com/rds-datamigration*. These Rapid Data Migration solutions provide migration content that is used with Data Services. In Section 5.1.3, we'll provide a specific example of using the migration content that will enable you to understand what the migration content is and what is delivered with the migration content.

The Rapid Data Migration content follows SAP's best practices methodology for data migration and gains functionality to manage and complete six distinct activities that are critical to the transformation and migration of data as illustrated in Figure 5.2.

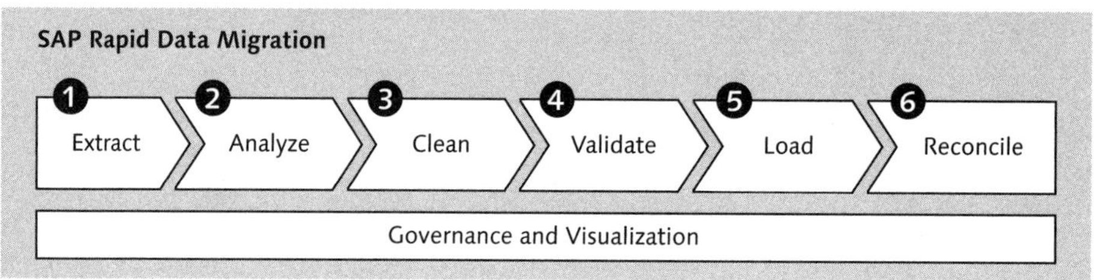

Figure 5.2 Rapid Data Migration Methodology

The six critical data migration activities are listed here:

❶ Analyze and profile the data from the source system(s).

❷ Extract the data from the source system.

❸ Clean the data records to achieve a high data quality.

❹ Validate the data against the target business context (i.e., the business rules of the target system, such as checking to identify if specific fields are required or if the country codes are correct).

❺ Load the data into the target SAP system.

❻ Reconcile the data between the target system and the source system.

SAP offers tools for governance and visualization to support the activities taking place in each of these stages. The governance solutions help ensure that only authorized individuals can make changes to the data or mappings and that an audit trail exists to capture each change. The visualization tools enable you to see just what is taking place with each step in the migration process.

Next, we discuss further details regarding the migration content and how data migration works with Data Services.

5.1.3 Getting Started with Rapid Data Migration Rapid-Deployment Content

When we refer to Rapid Data Migration content, we're referring to several things you can download from the SAP Service Marketplace and use with SAP software to accelerate your data migration projects. This migration content includes the following (discussed in more detail in the following subsections):

- Specific jobs, workflows, and cleansing packages provided in Data Services. For example, more than 100 jobs are provided in Data Services for different data domains in SAP, such as material, sales order, employee, and so on. Each job extracts, maps, and validates the data against the SAP business context. This will be explained in more detail in the next section.
- A tool called Migration Services that reads the SAP IMG configuration for mapping source to target values in a translation table (e.g., map U.S.A. in legacy system to US in target systems).
- SAP BusinessObjects Web intelligence reports for reporting on the progress of the migration.
- SAP BusinessObjects Dashboards reports for matching and merging duplicate records.
- Information governance project tracking for data migration projects.

As mentioned, the content is delivered for specific SAP data domains such as material, sales order, employee, and so on. While Appendix B (available for download from the book's page at *www.sap-press.com/3666*) provides a complete list of migration content, the following provides a few more details on migration content that's delivered by application area:

- **Migration content in Data Services for SAP ERP (including SAP HANA)**
  - Business partner content such as customer and vendor masters
  - Logistics content such as material master, bills of material (BOMs), purchasing documents, sales documents, employee information, and cost centers
  - Financial content such as receivables, payables, and cost elements
- **Migration content in Data Services for SAP ERP Human Capital Management (SAP ERP HCM) (including SAP HANA)**
  - Organizational management content such as org structure and employee groups
  - Personal administration content such as address data, basic pay, and family data
  - Additional content for benefits, payroll, compensation, and time
- **Migration content in Data Services for SAP Retail (including SAP HANA)**
  - Retail article master content, including material data at client level and international article numbers (EANs)
- **Migration content in Data Services for SAP CRM (including SAP HANA)**
  - Business partner content such as customer and vendor masters
  - Sales content such as activities, leads, opportunities, and contracts
- **Migration content in Data Services for SAP Billing for Utilities**
  - Content such as meter readings, move-in dates, equipment, and devices
- **Migration content in Data Services for Loans Management**
  - Content such as banking business partner and loan information
- **Migration content in Data Services for cloud solutions**
  - Content such as employee and foundation data for SuccessFactors Employee Central
  - Content such as business partner, opportunities, leads, and activities for SAP Cloud for Customer

- **Migration content in Data Services for SAP Business Warehouse (SAP BW)**
  - Analytical content such as sales, financials, purchasing, and manufacturing

Note

Because new migration content is added a few times each year, you should check *http://service.sap.com/rds-datamigration* and *http://service.sap.com/bp-datamigration* for additional data migration content. In addition to the migration content by object that includes integration and data quality transforms for some objects, there is also content for data remediation and for information governance for data migration projects.

Architecture of SAP Best Practices and Data Services for Data Migration to SAP Applications

Figure 5.3 shows how data migration works using the content provided with the Rapid Data Migration rapid-deployment solution packages.

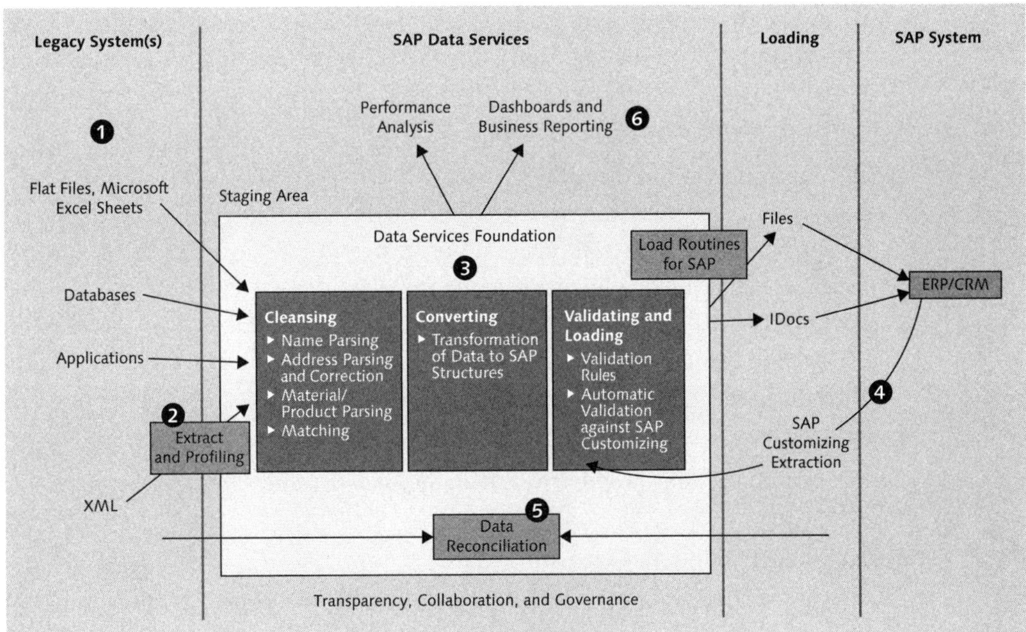

Figure 5.3 Architecture for SAP Best Practices for Data Migration

Each area in Figure 5.3 is explained in the following list:

- ❶ **Legacy data environment**
  The legacy data environment refers to the source systems for the migration. The legacy environment can be any source system that is supported by Data Services connectivity (connectivity options for Data Services are discussed in Chapter 9).
- ❷ **Extract and profile**
  Data is extracted from the source and placed in a staging area in Data Services. At this point, you can conduct technical profiling with Data Services. Additionally, you can start profiling very early on the source systems using Information Steward.
- ❸ **Cleanse, transform, and validate**
  This includes updating the data so that it meets specific patterns, mapping and transforming the data according to rules, and validating data against the SAP business context. This can involve combining two fields into one, splitting fields, updating the data in a field to match certain rules (e.g., telephone number formats), and validating data against required fields and lookup values from the SAP business context and configuration. Cleanse, transform, and validate processes are discussed in Chapter 9.
- ❹ **SAP configuration extraction**
  As part of an SAP implementation, the SAP system is configured with many values such as plants, material types and groups, and sales territories. Mapping of the source data normally requires mapping fields that comply with the SAP configuration. The extraction of SAP configuration data takes the settings in the SAP system so that the source data can conform to the required format in the target system.
- ❺ **Reconciliation**
  Reconciliation looks at what was actually loaded versus what was expected to be loaded.
- ❻ **Dashboards and business reporting**
  Throughout the process, dashboards are available for people involved with the project to stay informed about the status of the migration. Additionally, the migration project often sets data quality expectations and governance around data management.

Migrating Customer Data to SAP ERP

Now that you have an understanding of the solution, including the migration content, you're ready for an example of how to get started with data migration using Data Services and the migration content. Use the steps discussed next to get started with the software and the content.

Step 1: Download the Migration Content

To download the migration content to be used in Data Services, your first step is to go to *http://service.sap.com/rds-datamigration* (requires SAP Service Marketplace login credentials). There, you can explore the migration content of the existing Rapid Data Migration packages. In this specific example, we're using the rapid-deployment solutions package for SAP ERP and SAP CRM. The core migration content can be downloaded from the Software Download Center; a link to the download area is provided on the SAP Service Marketplace page for every single package.

After you complete the download and unzip the file, select the START.HTM or similar named HTML file. This brings up a page with access to the getting started guides and the documentation. The documentation provides quick guides for SAP ERP and SAP CRM and walks you through manually loading the migration content into Data Services.

At this point, even without the software installed, there are still key guides and places to start planning for the migration. The migration content has Word documents and Excel mapping templates for each of the objects in the SAP system (e.g., a document on materials, and another on customers). You can read the document to understand the object and use the Excel spreadsheet to start researching how the source data maps to the target.

Step 2: Install the Software

When it's time to install the software, get a temporary key from *http://service.sap.com/licensekey*. As mentioned previously, the download includes a configuration guide that walks you through the process of installing both the software and the migration content. (However, if you already have Data Services installed, you can use the documentation guides provided at *http://service.sap.com/bp-datamigration* to install the content manually into your existing Data Services installation.)

If you're new to Data Services, you might want to start by going through the Data Services tutorial that is included in the documentation when you install the product. You will also want to go through the examples provided in Chapter 9 on data integration and data quality.

Step 3: Review the Jobs in Data Services

After everything is installed, you can see a project called AIO_BPFDM_IDOC in Data Services. This project has jobs for each of the objects, including JOB_AIO_CUSTOMERMASTER_IDOC for the customer master and JOB_AIO_MATERIALMASTER_IDOC (see Figure 5.4).

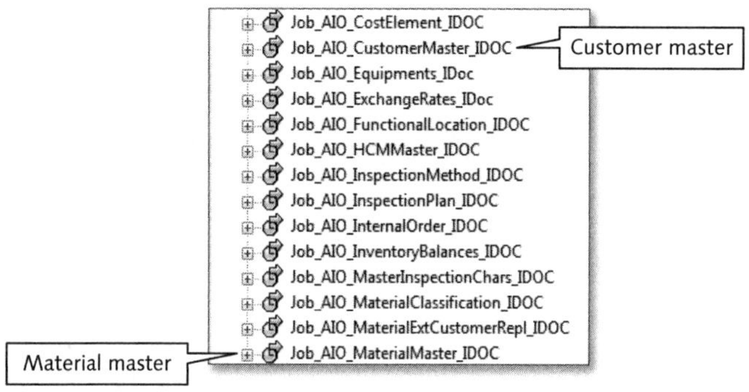

Figure 5.4 Migration Content in Data Services

Drill into the customer job to see the mapping and validation that takes place (see Figure 5.5). The validation is against required lookup fields in the SAP system, validating mandatory fields as well as the format (e.g., all phone numbers should have a country code; all U.S. zip codes should be in 5+4 format).

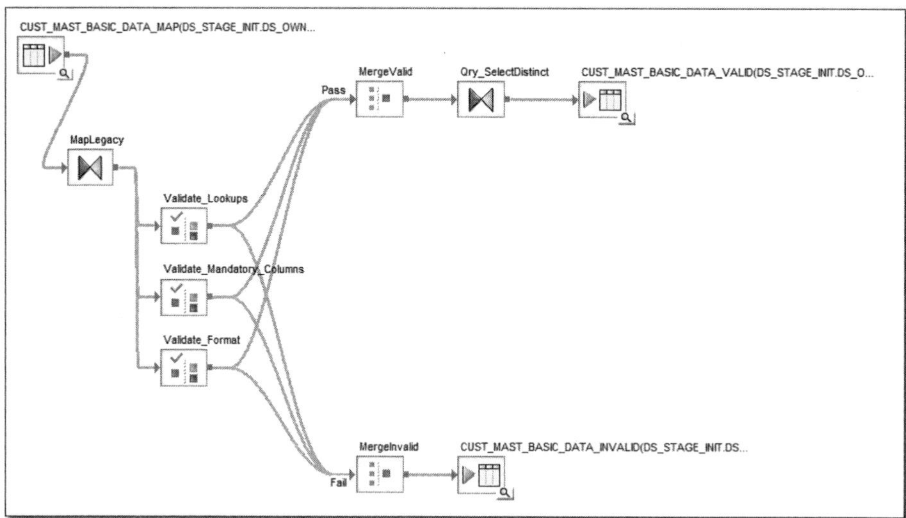

Figure 5.5 Mapping and Validation in the Customer Basic Data Job

The mapping within the job, as shown in Figure 5.6, has the source fields on the left and the target fields on the right. The pop-up screen is produced by double-clicking on MAPLEGACY. This example shows the mapping of the country from the source to the target.

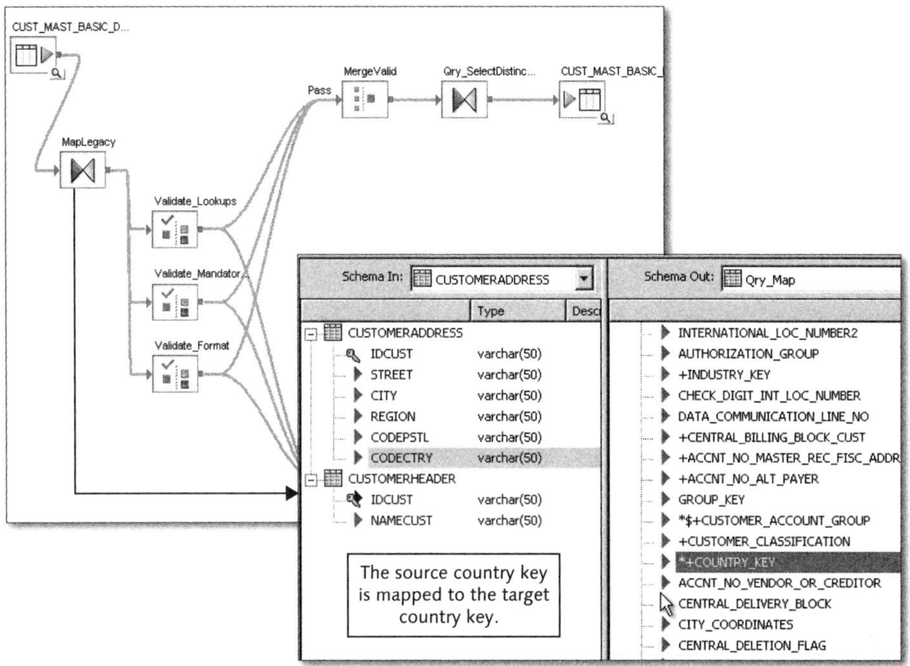

Figure 5.6 Mapping the Source Data to Target SAP Structures

The migration content includes Word documents that explain each intermediate document (IDoc), as well as spreadsheets for mapping the legacy customer data to the SAP IDoc structure. You can use the Excel template to start the mapping research of the source to the target (i.e., the source system table customer and FIRSTNAME field will be mapped to SAP Table KNA1 Name1) prior to the mapping in Data Services.

The other component that is important during the migration is the Migration Services tool. This tool reads the SAP system and extracts values that are then used to map source values to values required in the SAP system. In this example, USA, US, and Vereinigte Staaten von Amerika in the source system should map to U.S. in the target system (see Figure 5.7).

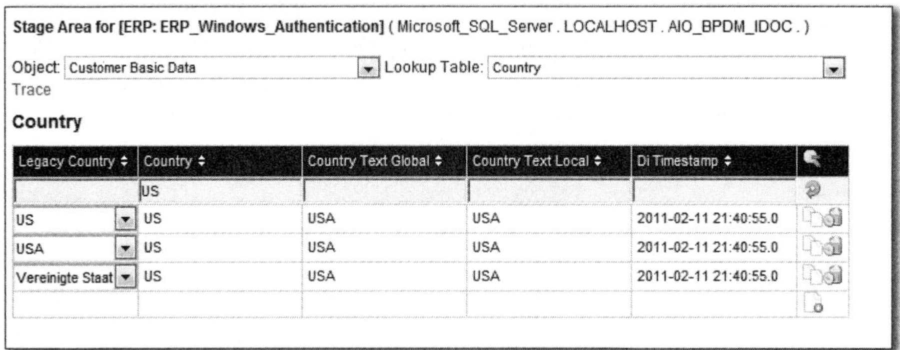

Figure 5.7 Migration Services Tool Provided by SAP Best Practices

Following these steps, you can start using the migration content and Data Services for your data migration project. For a complete demo of data migration, go to *http://service.sap.com/bp-datamigration* and select DEMO.

5.1.4 SAP Accelerator for Data Migration by BackOffice Associates

Customers who have large, complex, and frequent data migration needs, such as those driven by ongoing merger and acquisition activities, massive business transformation projects, or global consolidation from many systems, may find that they require a more comprehensive solution to manage the complexity of their data migration activities and to reduce the costs of the System Integrator, data consulting, and internal resources. For these customers, SAP has partnered with BackOffice Associates to deliver the SAP Data Services Migration Accelerator by BackOffice Associates.

While the focus of this chapter is on rapid-deployment solutions for EIM, and the Data Services Migration Accelerator isn't a rapid-deployment solution, we cover it here to complete the topic of Rapid Data Migration solutions from SAP. The Data Services Migration Accelerator is sold and supported by SAP, and it extends and augments the capabilities of Data Services and Rapid Data Migration. Specifically, it provides the In-Context Project Management Console, which is used to plan and track every aspect of the data migration project. These aspects include the following:

- Setting up the project hierarchy, including waves and process areas to organize the migration activities. Project waves can be defined by data domain, geographical region, business processes (such as Materials Management [MM] or Plant Maintenance [PM]), or by any other entity that makes sense. This helps to bring clarity and structure to the migration project.

- Creating users, granting rights, and assigning specific project tasks to those users.
- Managing worklists to keep migration tasks on track.
- Tracking the status of individual tasks, the overall migration project, and the migration analytics in role-based, customizable dashboards.
- User-friendly, browser-based mapping interfaces to allow data stewards and business experts to collaborate on field-level mappings for transforming source data to the target format. Users can specify, for instance, whether a target field should be mapped with a default value, a constant, or a direct copy of the source value; whether the field shouldn't be used; whether a Data Services rule should be applied (and what that rule should be); or whether data construction is required. Data construction is required when the data exists in the target system but doesn't exist in the source system.

The output of these mapping activities are Excel sheets with the specified mapping rules that are automatically entered into the worklist of the business user for approval and subsequent implementation in an Data Services job. Simple, browser-based data construction interfaces allow knowledgeable business users an easy way to enter the data that's required for the target system.

5.2 Rapid-Deployment Solutions for Information Steward

If you're planning to implement Information Steward to help guide your data quality initiatives, then good for you! After all, Information Steward gives you detailed insight into the quality of your master data. It's a business-focused solution that offers deep data profiling and data quality validation rules to determine the nature and depth of data quality defects, and it exposes the results of those rules in easy-to-read scorecards that graphically illustrate data quality metrics. (Of course, Information Steward does a great deal more than that, but we'll focus on these aspects in this section because they are the most relevant to the Information Steward rapid-deployment solution; you'll learn far more about all of the Information Steward capabilities in Chapter 10).

But how do you get started with Information Steward? How do you plan your implementation and realize quick value from the solution? How do you install, set up, and configure Information Steward to analyze your master data? What kinds of data profiling should you implement, and what are the validation rules you should define? How do you set up scorecards?

The best way to jump-start an Information Steward project is to use the Information Steward rapid-deployment solution. Like all rapid-deployment solutions, the Information Steward rapid-deployment solution combines expert, packaged service modules delivered by SAP or qualified partners, enablement materials, and prebuilt content that gets you up and running quickly. The solution delivers fast results, letting you focus on your data and your business, rather than on the details of the software; it also provides knowledge transfer to help you master those details in the context of your data quality initiatives. In other words, you become expert in using Information Steward not through theoretical cases or standardized examples, but by using it, with expert help, to analyze the data on which your critical business processes depend. The Information Steward rapid-deployment solution includes prebuilt content for three important master data domains: customer, supplier, and material. The content supports three main processes within the Information Steward environment:

1. Profile SAP ERP master data. Profiling tasks are created in Information Steward to examine ECC master data. This makes it possible to understand the content, structure, and data quality dependencies of the data.
2. Validate SAP ERP master data. Validation rules are executed using Information Steward to validate ECC master data. A validation rule is a specific type of business rule that checks whether the data complies with the business constraints and requirements.
3. Monitor SAP ERP master data quality. The data quality results, including quality trends and historical quality information, can be monitored in the data quality dashboard, which generates measurable health results.

In the next section, we'll take a closer look at the content that is delivered with the Information Steward rapid-deployment solution.

5.2.1 Information Steward Rapid-Deployment Solution Content

As stated in the previous section, the Information Steward rapid-deployment solution helps you profile, validate, and monitor three crucial master data domains:

customer, supplier, and material. The content is delivered in the form of a business content package for Information Steward, which was developed in line with the following key design principles:

1. Make it easier for users to adopt and use the Information Steward system with content deployed on it.
2. Reduce or eliminate training and learning time for new and advanced users by applying intuitive naming conventions, content organization structure, and organized packaging.
3. Provide as much functionality as possible in a ready-to-use package without sacrificing its generic nature.
4. Support content delivery with comprehensive documentation, such as configuration guides and business process documentation, so that users can work with the solution independently.
5. Reduce or eliminate the involvement of IT or technical users during deployment and use of the content provided, assuming an Information Steward system has already been made available for use.

The Information Steward business content was developed for a standard SAP ERP system to ensure that the content is generic and applicable across the widest possible range of customer scenarios. It was developed with the input and cooperation of SAP internal Information Steward developers and consultants, with the intention of delivering the highest value to the greatest number of customers. In most cases, the sequence of view elements is the same as the sequence in the corresponding data view within SAP ERP. This reduces the time needed by users who are familiar with the SAP ERP views to adapt the content to their specific needs. This also helps to reduce, and in some cases even eliminate, training costs normally associated with a new product.

Information Steward is designed to be used by business users, who know the data, to analyze and remediate data quality problems. As such, it presents data in business-oriented, rather than technical, data views.

Business-oriented data views and corresponding metadata descriptions represent subsets or combinations of data in the underlying source system (e.g., an SAP ERP system) within tables as fields. Technically, these are similar to database views of a connected source system's tables or data extractors (as in an SAP ERP system). Information Steward currently supports view definitions of tables as well as data extractors. Each view contains view elements. These represent the underlying database table field or an element in the data extractor. The Information Steward view definition makes it possible to see the original field name, description, and data type immediately upon connection for view definition (design time).

Domain-specific business data validation rules, aligned with SAP ERP and SAP Master Data Governance (SAP MDG), enable the business user to validate the master data records against the latest quality policies and execute business rule driven analysis. Although additional rules, with different classifications, can be defined, the delivered rules can be classified into five specific types:

- **Completeness rules**
  Check whether the data analyzed contains mandatory fields; for instance, determine whether a material has a base unit of measure associated with it.
- **Consistency rules**
  Check for data consistency in accordance with check tables or domain definitions within SAP ERP; for instance, ensure that the base unit of measure for a material exists in the check Table T006A.
- **Conformity rules**
  Check whether data adheres to a predefined form; for example, determine whether a Canadian customer's postal code matches the Canadian postal code format.
- **Rule bindings**
  Help to link the views with the rules so that data within the views can be validated against the rules.
- **Preconfigured dashboards**
  Provide measurable insight into data quality and quality improvement over time.

The delivered rules comprise a comprehensive basic package for validation of master data quality; for instance, the content for the material master domain includes more than 135 validation rules.

It's important to understand that Information Steward applies these rules to the master data residing in your SAP ERP or SAP MDG system (if present); it doesn't duplicate the master data into its own repository, but rather returns the rule results, including failed records. By leveraging this content, you can visually discover data defects in a matter of weeks, if not days, and begin correcting them more quickly. As you make progress at eliminating errors and improving data quality, you'll easily be able to track and measure your progress using scorecards, and will thus be able to demonstrate the effectiveness of your information governance initiative.

5.2.2 Getting Started with Information Steward Rapid-Deployment Solution Content

Assuming that an Information Steward system has already been made available for use (and that you have an SAP ERP system with master data to govern), installing the rapid-deployment solution content and using it to start profiling, validating, and monitoring your master data quality is fairly straightforward, even for users with little or no Information Steward experience. The process is extensively documented within the content package itself. To give you an idea of what tasks are required to get the solution functioning and delivering meaningful results, we give you a high-level view of these tasks in this section.

You can download the rapid-deployment solution content by pointing a browser to *http://service.sap.com/swdc* (SAP SMP login required) and then navigating to Installation and Upgrades • Browse Our Download Catalog • SAP Rapid Deployment Solutions • SAP Information Steward Rapid-Deployment Solution. Choose the latest (or appropriate) version of the rapid-deployment solution, download the .zip file, and save it to a local drive accessible to your Information Steward server.

The process for configuring and getting started with the rapid-deployment solution content is similar for all three data domains (material, customer, and supplier). Thus, we'll describe (at a high level) the process for material master data, purely for the purpose of giving you an understanding of the effort involved, and leave it to you to follow the documentation when it comes time to implement any of the included domains.

1. Create a system connection to the SAP ERP (or SAP MDG) system. This connection is used to look at the SAP master data within the SAP system, so this will be created as a connection type Application Connection with application type SAP Applications and connection parameters that make sense for such a connection (e.g., system number, client, and so forth).

Note

You must enter "SAP" as the connection name when creating the new connection, because that name is used throughout the business content and can't be overridden or changed. It's important to maintain the correct location for the working directory on the SAP server and the application shared directory values in the connection parameters to prevent errors during execution of the rules and profiling tasks.

It's also important that the users have read/write permissions for these directories, because temporary files are written here during execution of profiling tasks and rules, and execution will fail if these permissions are missing.

2. Create a new profiling project to serve as a placeholder for organizing all related content within the Information Steward workbench as shown later. To create the profiling project, right-click the project folder, and choose NEW • DATA INSIGHT PROJECT from the context menu.
3. Create a system connection for the failed records database for each data domain (material, customer, and supplier). This assumes that the databases are available in the database instance.
4. Import the Business Package Content. This business content is created to handle both SAP and non-SAP system. The SAP connection may provide direct access to ECC or go through to a staging database where direct access to the SAP system isn't available. Separate views are created for both the scenarios to access SAP data. For non-SAP sources, views may not be useful; however, most of the rules can be used as generic content.

After the downloaded content is available for use from a local or network location, based on the source system access, import the *IS_RDS_BusinessContent_v1.0.zip* to the Information Steward environment.

When these steps have been completed, configuration of the package is complete, and you can start working with the content in Information Steward. Open your project, select a view (e.g., VS_MATR_MAST_ACCOUNTING1), and click on the VIEW DATA button, which will fetch the data for the view from the source system. This should display data in the VIEW DATA window.

To profile your master data, select a view (e.g., ZB_G13_MATNR_ACCOUNTING1), and click on the COLUMN in the PROFILE drop-down menu. Create a column profile task, and click SAVE AND RUN NOW. After the task is completed, expand the view in WORKSPACE HOME to see the profile results.

To execute rule validation on your master data and calculate a score, in the RULE RESULT tab in the workspace, select a view (e.g., ZB_G13_MATNR_ACCOUNTING1), and click on the CALCULATE SCORE button.

Perform the following steps to validate the accuracy of views, rules, and the corresponding rule bindings:

1. In WORKSPACE HOME, choose the RULE RESULT tab, select the ZB_G13_MATNR_ACCOUNTING1 view, and click the CALCULATE SCORE pushbutton to create the rule task.
2. Enter a valid rule task name. You can also specify other parameters such as the email notification address and location for saving failed data.
3. Choose the SAVE AND RUN NOW button to execute the rule. Depending on the volume of data related to the view, rule execution can take a few minutes.
4. Review the results of the rules execution. You have access to failed records and trending, if the same rule or rules have been executed more than once.

You may set up scorecard dashboards to view and monitor quality trends. You can set up the data domain, quality dimension, rules, and rule bindings based on different business requirements; configure the scorecard to be able to track historical data quality changes; get insight on the data quality trending; and understand the overall data health. See Chapter 10 for more information on Information Steward and its capabilities for data assessment and monitoring.

5.3 Rapid-Deployment Solutions for Master Data Governance

Like the Information Steward rapid-deployment solution discussed in the previous section, the Master Data Governance rapid-deployment solution is designed to get you up and running quickly on SAP EIM software, as well as to support your data quality and information governance initiatives.

Note

SAP MDG was briefly introduced in Chapter 4 and will be covered in depth in Chapter 11. Just as a reminder, SAP MDG enables collaborative governance of master data through integrated workflows using a change request process.

Essentially, SAP MDG is an appliance that delivers a governed process for creating and maintaining master data. As such, it allows customers to leverage existing SAP capabilities, including SAP ERP data models, SAP Business Workflow, SAP Business Rules Framework, and the same data validation transactions that SAP ERP master data transactions use, thereby giving SAP customers a comfortable framework for implementing enterprise governance standards for master data. At the same time, SAP MDG is flexible enough to govern non-SAP master data within the existing framework.

The SAP MDG rapid-deployment solution puts customers on the fast track to adopting SAP MDG for supplier, material, finance, customer, and custom objects in the organization; to gain end-to-end insight into master data create, read, updated, delete (CRUD) processes across the landscape; and to remediate data quality challenges by integrating with Information Steward. In fact, customers who are implementing both Information Steward and SAP MDG can realize the greatest and fastest benefit from these solutions when they leverage both rapid-deployment solutions to quickly gain control of enterprise information governance initiatives.

From the services perspective, SAP offers a "build to suit" model for customers to select only the service options they require for their implementation. Of course, customers can then choose to add customized services for further development of their SAP MDG capabilities, but the modular services available offer customers predictable results at a predictable price.

5.3.1 Master Data Governance Rapid-Deployment Solution Content

All rapid-deployment solutions deliver prebuilt content to accelerate the successful implementations of SAP solutions, and the SAP MDG rapid-deployment solution is no exception. The rapid-deployment solution includes content developed for the following critical master data domains: customer, supplier, finance, material, and custom object master data. For each of these domains, the solution includes content to support the processes that we discuss in the following subsections.

Governance

The baseline implementation of SAP MDG includes all activities from installation to go live. To add additional value, the scope item provides additional workflow templates for sequential and parallel processing of master data change requests. To accelerate the implementation of additional customer-specific validation rules, a set of master data domain-specific business rules for BRFplus are provided that can be used as a baseline for implementing additional data policies and quality rules. The scope item also includes the optional configuration of the business context viewer content, which grants insight into the transactional relevancy of the master data object in the context of the master data object in the user's current activity scope. All in all, the scope item allows for a quick start and significant ROI, enabling customers to hit the ground running with SAP MDG.

Process Insight

This module supports end-to-end master data process monitoring across one or multiple target systems, including local and global processes. It allows customers to combine global and local workflow monitoring in the context of the master data process and distribution models and offers, as well as complete insight on process execution and distribution. It provides the possibility to audit down to individual processes making creations and updates.

Master Data Remediation

SAP MDG and Information Steward integrate to provide an essential piece for a successful information governance strategy, where the quality of master data is continuously monitored, and data quality issues of the master data are transparent to the user on the SAP MDG system. The remediation process can be initiated right from SAP MDG, and the changes are performed by the specialists on SAP MDG using the familiar interfaces and processes. This scope item provides an integrated solution for data quality analysis and remediation without media breaks, allowing users to track and visualize the improvement of quality over time (see Figure 5.8). For this scope item, the implementation of the Information Steward rapid-deployment solution is recommended in addition to the SAP MDG rapid-deployment solution (the functionality delivered in the Information Steward rapid-deployment solution must be implemented to use this capability, whether it's through the rapid-deployment solution or some other means).

For each of these included processes, the solution includes detailed business process documentation, configurations guides, and other content to get you up and running quickly with the solution.

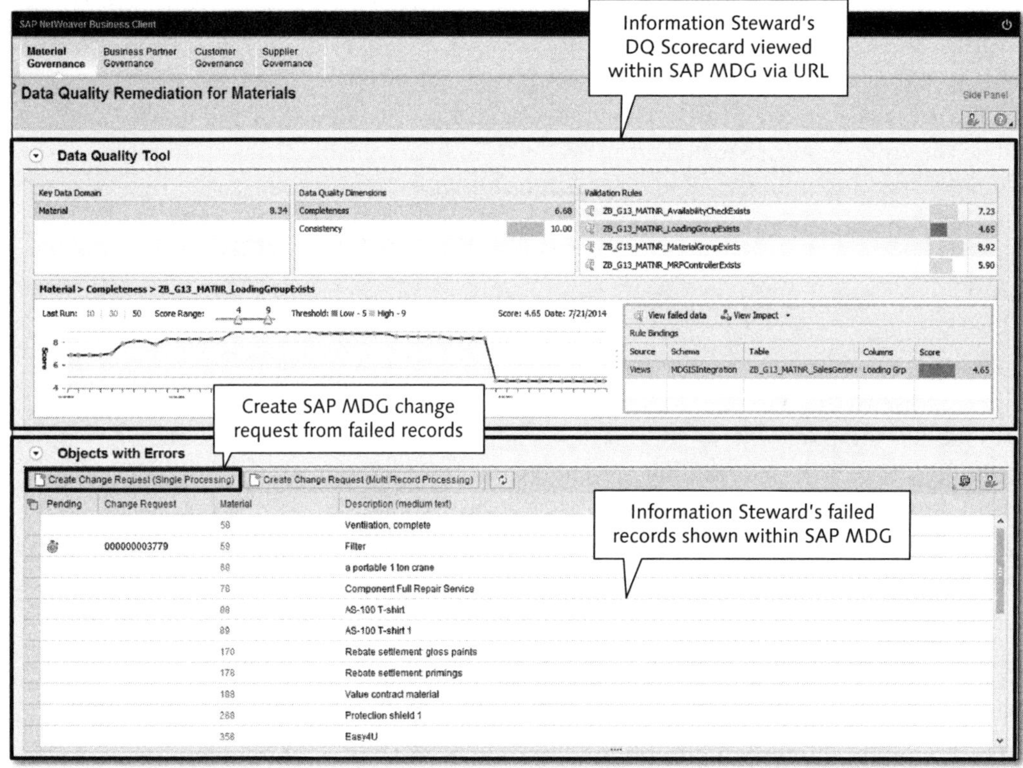

Figure 5.8 Managing Master Data with Remediation Processes from the Information Steward Dashboard

5.3.2 Getting Started with SAP Master Data Governance Rapid-Deployment Solution Content

As part of the rapid-deployment solution implementation, SAP consulting (or qualified partners) can install SAP MDG in your landscape. They can configure the system and get you launched with the solution. Of course, you may already have SAP MDG installed, in which case, you can proceed directly to scoping the particular domains and processes that will be part of your solution. If you'll be implementing the master data remediation scenario for any of the included master data domains, you must also have Information Steward installed and configured. As they are built to work hand-in-hand, SAP also recommends that you start with the Information Steward rapid-deployment solution and then proceed to the SAP MDG rapid-deployment solution.

The SAP MDG rapid-deployment solution requires that you have the following software in your environment:

- SAP ERP 6.0 EHP6 or EHP7, including SAP MDG 7.0
- SAP Information Steward 4.2 or higher (for remediation scope item)
- SAP Enterprise Search 7.1, version 45 or above (for material search scenario only)
- SAP Solution Manager 7.0+ (optional, but recommended)

The best way to get started with the SAP MDG rapid-deployment solution content is to download SAP Note 182165. This note includes the Quick Start guide, which describes how to download and activate the rapid-deployment solution content.

To download the content, point your browser to *http://service.sap.com/swdc*, and then navigate to INSTALLATION AND UPGRADES • BROWSE OUR DOWNLOAD CATALOG • SAP RAPID DEPLOYMENT SOLUTIONS • SAP SOLUTION MANAGER IMPLEMENTATION CONTENT • ST-RDS 100.

After you've downloaded the content, the Quick Start guide describes how you can load and activate the content.

5.4 Summary

In this chapter, you've learned how rapid-deployment solutions represent a new paradigm for implementing SAP solutions quickly at fixed scope and predictable cost. You've also learned about SAP's solutions for data migration, including the business drivers for data migration, the options SAP offers for supporting data migrations, and how you can leverage Rapid Data Migration to migrate legacy data to SAP solutions more easily. You've also learned how you can take your data migration capabilities to a higher level with the SAP Data Services Migration Accelerator by BackOffice Associates.

Finally, you learned how SAP Rapid Deployment solutions for Information Steward and SAP MDG can jump-start your implementation of these unique data governance solutions and get you up and running more quickly.

Now it's time to see some practical, real-world examples of EIM in action; for that, turn to the next chapter.

This chapter shows SAP's EIM solutions in action, and offers real-world experience and advice from actual SAP customers.

6 Practical Examples of EIM

This chapter focuses on actual examples of how enterprise information management is being used today by different companies. While there are real-world example scenarios in many of the chapters throughout this book, the goal of this chapter is to provide broad-based examples of EIM use across different scenarios and organizations. Examples range from managing data migration projects, to master data projects, to developing an architecture for information management. This chapter is best read by thinking of each section as its own chapter, because the topic for each section is different.

6.1 EIM Architecture Recommendations and Experiences by Procter and Gamble

An enterprise information architecture is ultimately intended to deliver the right content to the right end users. This means data that is in the right form, in the right level of quality, in the right level of granularity, and on the right timing.

To be successful in a business context, the architecture must be inclusive of classic architecture elements, most notably principles, guidelines, standards, inventories, and models, which give it focus and meaning within an enterprise. It must take into account the information-producing and information-consuming processes of the enterprise and all manners of interfaces. It must be supported by solid data governance, data stewardship, data maintenance, and logical and physical design. And throughout that set of considerations, information security must be a part of the equation.

To deliver a manageable and well-formed architecturc, we typically create three leveled views:

- Conceptual—the user's view
- Logical—the designer's view
- Physical—the builder's view

This section will focus on the framework and elements that need to go into such an architecture. The purpose of the architecture is to guide decision making for IT projects such that systems can:

- **Increase end-user productivity**
  - Eliminate time wasted looking for information
  - Simplifying knowledge generation
  - Increase time for analysis and decision making
  - Reduce effort in data/information manual rework
- **Reduce total operating costs**
  - Streamline the architecture, information lifecycle management, data marts
  - Eliminate and consolidate databases
  - Eliminate redundant data solutions
- **Increase speed to market**
  - Establish reusable data assets for solutions and applications to deploy
  - Establish a clearly defined set of rules for managing data that projects and organizations will use in their work

Next, we discuss the details of an EIM architecture. This includes the principles that are grounded on accepted industry practices, the scope of what the architecture should include, the types of structured data included in the architecture, what is required for unstructured data, data standards, governance, typical lifecycle information, and the role of enterprise information architecture in the organization.

6.1.1 Principles of an EIM Architecture

An EIM architecture must be based on principles that are grounded in accepted industry practices. Principles guide decision making in areas where there *are* viable alternatives, and you want to guide the organization consistently. To help with the understanding and adoption of those principles, they are generally created as follows:

- The *principle*, which is a statement of choice
- The *rationale*, which provides the basis for making that choice
- The *implications*, which call out the major consequences of making this choice so that the organization is clear on what this means

Principles

Several principles may be involved in information management. One example of such a principle might be:

There is one comprehensive, integrated, information architecture, and it encompasses all shareable content, whether structured or unstructured. This includes text, image, video, and voice data.

Rationale

Some examples of the rationale for an EIM architecture might be:

- The complexity introduced by the continued acceptance of multiple, local variations (for example, when each region has their own architecture), and/or solution-specific architectures is inconsistent with our corporate objectives of rapid response to business need, productivity break through, improved decision making, common solutions, simplification, and standardization.
- A single information architecture focuses resources on achieving meaningful results by reducing the opportunity for divergent project and technology efforts while reducing the complexity of support.
- A single information architecture enables the delivery of information that spans type (e.g., structured, text, image, etc.) using standard tools and techniques, as opposed to requiring each application to reinvent this increasingly needed functionality. Business users of our IT products and services and our own resources are consequently more productive.

Implications

Some examples of the implications of an EIM architecture might be:

- Application development teams, support staff, and business partners must define and be accustomed to work processes that allow them to effectively achieve their objectives while sharing the control and use of their resources on which they depend.

- Integration across data types (i.e., structured, text, image, etc.) will be driven by the business user's context—job, roles, and decision types. That experience will be designed following this single architecture.

It's suggested that you start with the first principle discussed here—one comprehensive integrated information architecture—and then add in the other handful of strategic choices that you need to make to deliver this "one architecture." Other principles may touch on the areas of:

- Data ownership
- Information as a shared asset
- The management of master data versus other types
- Lifecycle management

6.1.2 Scope of an EIM Enterprise Architecture

Data, *information*, and *content* should all be within the scope of information management. For the purposes of this discussion, these three terms are defined as follows:

- **Data**
  Content that is captured via a system process but has had no human intervention.
- **Information**
  Content that has had subsequent human thought processes applied to it.
- **Content**
  Unstructured content, including documents, video, image, and audio content. The term *content* is used in this section to imply any unstructured data or information.

A truly inclusive and comprehensive enterprise information architecture encompasses the following content scope:

- Operational data stores, data warehouses, data marts (centrally or locally)
- Internal and external content (e.g., the Internet)
- Local, regional, and corporate content with abilities to integrate

- Dimensional data (e.g., reference or master data), hierarchies, and taxonomies
- Key performance indicators (KPIs) or "measures" data at atomic and aggregate levels
- Metadata
- Purchased data, aggregator subscriptions (e.g., wire feeds, RSS, etc.)
- Behavioral data, performance data, preferences, and subscriptions
- Unstructured content types, including voice, video, and multimedia

6.1.3 Structured Data

A simple architectural view of structured data classifies the data as one of the following three types:

- Reference data
- Transactional data
- Management reporting data (including analytics)

Each of these classes of data has particular characteristics that need to be properly accounted for in a well-designed information architecture. Consider characteristics such as time, data volume, performance characteristics, numbers of users, and read-to-write profile, and it becomes clear that special handling is required to meet the variety of use cases. Let's define each of these classes in a little more detail.

Reference Data

Reference data provides the dimensional basis for transactions or events. Those dimensions typically include time, location, geography, organization, and parties involved, and are often characterized as "nouns" (e.g., customer, consumer, supplier, legal entities). It often includes objects involved in the transaction (e.g., product, services, raw material). This class of data is usually the object of master data management.

Transactional Data

Transactional data typically describes an event (the change as a result of an operation; for example, creating an order, initiating shipments, etc.) and is often described with action-oriented nouns (e.g., order, shipment, invoice). Transactional data always has a time dimension and a numerical value and refers to one or more objects (i.e., reference data).

The use of transactional data, in an event-reporting context, is referred to as operational reporting. Operational reporting is concerned with the reporting of transactional data, often at the discrete transaction level (e.g., a *single* invoice) produced at the time of the actual event. Operational reporting takes a very short time horizon, from as short as a single event, and does not aggregate from multiple applications. It is generally produced from the transactional system, using this lowest level of data. That lowest level—an individual transaction—is often referred to as *atomic data*.

Management Reporting

Management reporting is concerned with reporting data over longer periods of time or over larger sets of data (e.g., aggregates and summaries) than operational reporting systems support. It consequently takes operational data and applies further processing against it. This may be in the form of aggregations, historical collections, or integrating multiple measure types (e.g., shipments and consumption). It is this subsequently processed data that is typically managed in the data warehouse environment. For our purposes we include analytics use cases in this same class, including operational analytics.

6.1.4 The Dual Database Approach

A longstanding cornerstone of this kind of data architecture is based on a dual database strategy. The dual database strategy sources standard, shareable data from the operational environment (i.e., transactional systems) to the data warehouse environment each supported by a common "reference" capability that maintains standard reference/master data used in both capture and access environments.

Transactions are entered, processed, and ultimately formatted and sent to the data warehouse. Data is stored in a data warehouse complex at an elemental level according to data subject, where it may be further aggregated and summarized and accessed via any business intelligence use cases. Reference data capability consists of master data, reference data, and metadata and is available to interact with and support both types of processing through interactive and callable interfaces.

This framework is predicated on the following:

- An environment for single-sourced data, thereby eliminating the productivity problems caused by multiple sources. This is fundamental to achieving a single basis for truth, and for many of our information systems, a single version of the truth.
- Reference data (including master data and metadata that encompasses a data dictionary as well) that is managed distinct from a single application, representing the union of our requirements for that reference subject area.
- A data dictionary to be used by all systems, thereby reducing if not eliminating the problem of data credibility caused by the lack of consistency in data definition and content.

Implementing this single data architecture throughout the enterprise provides common processes to follow, with consistent data as the product. From creation, maintenance, extract, transform, load, all the way to end-user consuming processes, you can measure, control, predict, and improve the performance of your data capabilities. With such an architecture, you can reasonably expect to be able to access the data when needed, with assurance that it will be consistent and accurate.

Dual Database Strategy

With the advent of memory-based and solid-state appliances supporting a new class of data warehouse "appliances," some argue that the "dual database" strategy is dead. The following considerations cause us to propose that a dual strategy will remain viable in the short run:

- The scope of history held in the transactional environment may not meet the needs of what is retained separately in the data warehouse.
- As storage gets cheaper, the business desire to have more history online continues to grow. This further calls for a separate database for data warehousing, to preserve performance requirements in our operational databases. Therefore, we will generally move operational data into a distinct database for performing operational analytics.
- For management, availability, and recoverability, a single database may simply not make sense in many instances, requiring the isolation of workloads.

6.1.5 Typical Information Lifecycle

It's useful to consider the full lifecycle of information, its uses and characteristics, and an enterprise-wide strategy for how it needs to be managed. Taking this holistic view is uniquely within the purview of the enterprise information architect and, if neglected, can lead to detrimental and/or disastrous consequences for the enterprise. History and newspapers routinely recount the unfortunate choices companies have made that can be attributed to information stewardship neglect.

Figure 6.1 shows a very simple model, but certainly it's more complicated in real life. For example, development, quality assurance, and production instances may exist, but we are considering the simple cases for our purposes. The same principles would apply throughout a complete lifecycle of data warehouses.

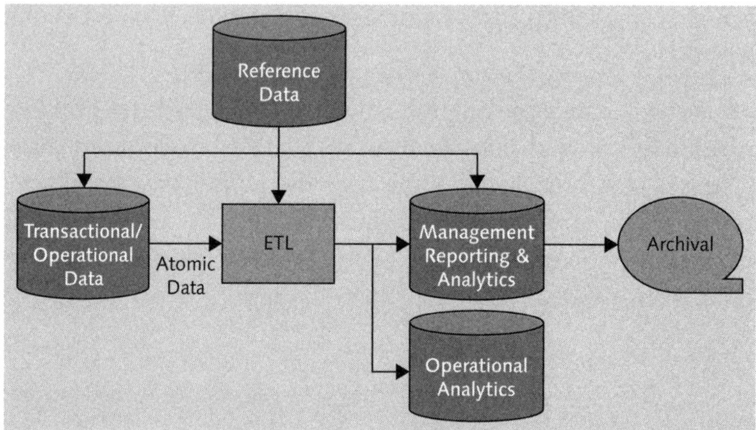

Figure 6.1 Typical Information Lifecycle

Each area of Figure 6.1 is described in the following sections in more detail.

Transactional/Operational Data

Operational data is captured in what's referred to as the system of record, which is the system responsible for the initial creation of the data in the transactional system. It should be captured in a well-formed system that has the following characteristics:

- Data standards for the data it is creating
- Standard master data, which is managed independent of this application

- Clear ownership of all data in scope
- Data retention clearly specified, at a minimum at a database level, as well as at a "record" or document level
- Backup and recovery requirements
- Security classifications as defined by the enterprise
- Access requirements and controls consistent with enterprise definition

Operational Analytics

It's often desirable to be able to perform analysis on data that's in the transactional system, looking for trends, anomalies, or solutions to specific problems. While it may be possible to do this directly against the operational environment, there may be circumstances that introduce performance considerations requiring that a separate environment for operational analytics be set up.

When that occurs, a separate, data warehouse-like environment can be created to prevent the sorts of I/O contention that typically occur, while providing for longer retention of data in the operational analytics that the transactional system can support. Statistical analysis over long periods of time and correlation across transactions are typically run here.

ETL

ETL (extraction, transformation, and loading) is a set of processes that are executed in support of formal data warehouse preprocessing, and is supported by formal tools that are designed for that specific purpose. Admittedly, enterprise application integration (EAI) tools may be used as a vehicle for feeding downstream data warehouses in a publish/subscribe fashion; however, we will present a traditional ETL approach to illustrate the flow of data.

Management Reporting and Analytics

In Figure 6.1, *management reporting and analytics* is a data warehouse providing management reporting and analytics capabilities by bringing data together from one or more operational systems. A data warehouse exists to provide the following kinds of capabilities:

- A longer time basis of data than the operational systems, for reporting beyond operational needs. For example, summaries by week, month, quarter, and year may be desirable.
- The ability to create multi-fact-type integration. Where the data scope of a transactional application may only cover a few transaction types, a data warehouse may source those transactions and provide an integrated view, enabling greater insight; for example, combining shipment, financials and market share.
- A shareable data asset that can meet the needs of many use cases and organizations beyond the scope of a single application; for example, a data service that provides customer information to be used by many applications.
- Scale, cost savings, and efficiencies over individual, redundant, point to point copies of data.
- A single source for reporting a single set of "official numbers."

Data Levels of the Data Warehouse

The well-formed data warehouse is based on atomic data, an integrated data layer, and then business views composed upon the integrated data layer. Let's look at these layers in more detail:

- **Atomic data**
  Atomic data is the lowest level of data granularity, based on a single transaction, whose source is preserved as originally captured. A data warehouse that's composed of atomic data can be used to "roll-up" data along many different dimensional lines; it can be reorganized from the atomic level, and different views can be created. This lowest-level, fundamental ingredient is the foundation upon which your data warehouse architecture should be constructed.
- **Integrated data**
  An integrated data layer is intended to serve the many needs of many divergent applications by providing multi-fact integration of many data types in a broadly shareable asset. It is this level of the data in the data warehouse that is the target for end-user and application access. This layer is typically centrally managed. Orders, shipments, services, inventory and account receivables (for example) can all be integrated.
- **Business views**
  Creating value-added business views on top of the integrated data layer provides an instantly usable asset to project teams, superior to creating additional

copies of the data and/or external data marts. The business views layer is composed of views (and potentially local data) that are owned by the various business areas and applications. It typically isn't managed centrally. For example, you may have a subset of orders, shipments, and inventory based on a designated time duration critical from a planning perspective.

Summaries and Aggregations

The data warehouse provides capabilities to support management reporting and analytics. While it's the goal of data warehouse designers to do as much work on-the-fly as possible, it often becomes clear that the warehouse needs to deliver an answer to an end user within a committed time frame (i.e., a service-level agreement; for example, a three-second response time for less than 1000 rows of data). When that occurs, summaries of data are precalculated to improve query performance.

Caution should be observed when creating summaries/aggregates to avoid, when possible, the inclusion of dimension types that are likely to change. When you include such dimensions, your aggregates take on new maintenance overhead and may have to be recalculated. If your data warehouse contains many years of history, recalculating that history can be costly.

Sample Data

The data warehouse environment can quickly "accrete" large quantities of data, which has positive and negative consequences. Long-running jobs not only frustrate the job owner, but may negatively impact other users of the shared environment. Creating sample sets, statistically valid representative samples of a broader population, may allow you to deliver an analytics result without having to process the entire population of data. This can save time, money, and aggravation.

Analytics Considerations

There has never been more data available, and it's growing at an alarming rate. As sources grow (e.g., the Internet), as types of data grow (e.g., geolocation), and as value in mining the data grows, we must increasingly look at different use cases for the data. Analytics is increasingly one of these use cases.

Simply retaining more data is not sufficient. As good stewards we should strive to process it in practical, efficient ways. Considerations include:

- Can I use sample data?
- Do I need to employ aggregates?

- Can I leverage tiered storage?
- Can I leverage analytics that are part of the data warehouse platform (i.e., can I directly "play the data" where it lies)?
- Are the scalar functions of the database management system (DBMS) sufficient, are additional functions or extended procedure libraries available, or do I have to move the data to an analytics server?

These are just a few of the considerations that the enterprise information architect must contend with. But increasingly, it is highly advantageous if you can leverage the data warehouse for use cases beyond traditional reporting; for example, ad-hoc queries, exploratory analytics, etc.

Data Warehouse Governance Considerations
You will want to build the rules of engagement for your data warehouse environment. Considerations should include a landscape strategy that defines how and where your databases will be located, sourcing strategies, staging, ETL, reference data design, fact data design by layers, and how applications interact with the centrally managed layers. You should also consider local data and its integration with other levels of data as well as overall governance of what can become a large, complex environment.

Archival

Archival strategies and storage tiers must be considered as part of the strategy. As you create your information management architecture, you assign retention limits and factor the cost and timings of retrieval needs into your tiered storage plans as part of a broader information lifecycle management strategy. Security considerations (e.g., security classifications by data subject area) should be identified and factored into the thinking.

6.1.6 Data Standards

Information management is predicated on having clear, effective, measurable data standards. We have defined data standards as being composed of three parts:

- **Business definition**
  - Definition of the data element in terms of its business use
  - Allowable values for a data element

  - Rules governing uniqueness (i.e., no two instances have the same code) and exclusivity (i.e., an instance has only code)
  - Rules governing assignment and reuse of codes
- **Organizational ownership and stewardship**
  - Business owner: Person and role accountable for developing and maintaining this data standard
  - Business process for creating and maintaining the data
  - Data administrator: Person and role accountable for the business process of maintaining data
  - Business unit scope: Business units to which this standard applies
- **Technical definition**
  - Official source system that produces the data
  - Number of instances
  - Canonical data structure agreed on and maintained as an enterprise standard, including attributes/fields associated with this subject area as well as data type and length of data elements
  - Format: Is there a specific format for storing or reporting this data? (For example, a date must include CCYYMMDD, a monetary amount must have three decimal places, and so on.)
  - Optional/mandatory (field by field)
  - Structure

6.1.7 Unstructured Data

Unstructured data includes documents, images, audio, video, and social content. It is the unstructured nature of this class of data or content that makes it much more difficult to find and beneficially apply in an enterprise. Consequently, metadata and accompanying metadata standards are required to give unstructured data the corresponding context that makes it findable and usable. We will examine the role of metadata more closely in subsequent sections.

To properly manage unstructured content, it's necessary to look at the continuum of processes that interact with the content, cradle to grave. Following this approach, we can zoom in on needs at particular steps along the way. Figure 6.2 depicts the overall lifecycle.

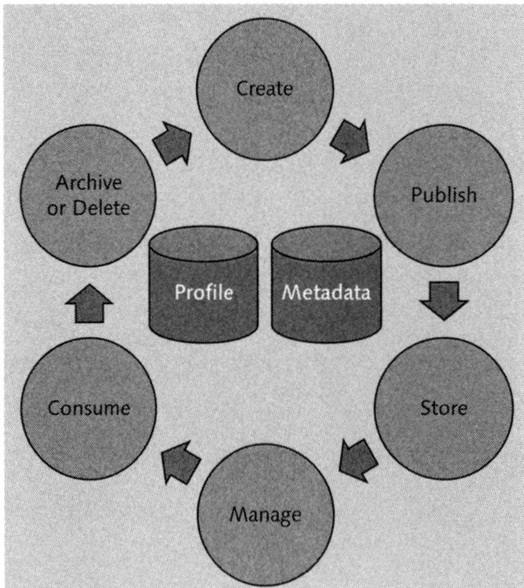

Figure 6.2 Unstructured Content Lifecycle

Create

In this step, content may be authored locally or in a shared authoring tool. Information management must be considered with the business processes and the kinds of content produced by those processes so that the appropriate metadata designs may be employed as that content is published.

Publish

Publishing is the act of formally releasing the content from the authoring/creation environment into a shareable environment. It is in this process that metadata can be beneficially applied; applying a few standard tags to assist in finding desired content may require one minute by the publishers, but without such tags, end users may spend many minutes searching for that exact content. The investment in applying tags in the publishing process can more than pay for itself and shows consideration for the content consumer's time.

Store

For completeness, we include this step of physically storing the content. Actual physical storage may trigger the automatic activities that can be considered as management processes.

Manage

Management processes applied on the stored content may include, but are not limited to, the following activities:

- Applying default retention rules
- Automated tagging
- Indexing of the content
- Triggering routing/approvals
- Applying analytics (e.g., tag clouds, usage, etc.)
- Managing site content—ensuring that the content meets quality standards, metadata and content standards, and security standards; versioning is appropriately applied; and so on
- Enterprise content management (discussed in Chapter 4 and Chapter 13)

Consume

For completeness, we include the step of consumption, defined as the act of end users physically accessing the content. This can occur via an enterprise search, direct navigation, routing, subscription, application search, and so on. Given the many ways that physical access (consumption) may occur, it should become clear that the architecture standards and management processes are essential to facilitating efficient consumption.

Archive/Delete

All content should have retention limits established when published. Those dates should be used to ensure that documents and content stores are moved to archival storage and/or deleted.

6.1.8 Governance

Governance is the capability that enables consistency of decision making through defined decision rights, in accordance with aligned policies and procedures. Organizations evolve in their ability to govern. The corporate culture plays a major role in how strong a first-generation governance model can be and how it will evolve. For example, if governance policies are too broad and too quickly deployed, adoption is very low. A balance of control, delivering stability and value, needs to be realized for the governance to become part of daily work.

Different organizations and their unique cultures, drivers, and strategies may dictate a different approach to governance. One size probably does not fit all in this realm, so the approach described here should not be taken as prescriptive, but instead should provide insight to one company's journey that you may be able to learn from.

Scope and Intent of Governance

At Procter and Gamble, the scope and intent of governance started with the dual database strategy in the late 1980s with a focus on managing the master data centrally, independent of the consuming applications, and enforcing a standard definition of keys in the core subject areas such as material, product, customer, and vendor. This evolved in the late 1990s to managing master data across all major platforms, including product lifecycle management, SAP ERP, and reporting/analytics. This was pursued as part of the journey to deliver a single version of the truth. Some of the lessons of that journey are defined next.

Harmonization of Keys and Single Version of the Truth

The first step in creating a single version of the truth in data is to have a standard definition, unique identification, and official sources from which to provide the information. In our first steps, business functions and country IT organizations separated their master data from the applications. The journey into data management began with a separation of duties for control purposes and managing data as an asset. The first value realized was globally and uniquely identifying key assets such as product, material, vendor, and customer.

Integrated Application Platforms

As the IT architecture evolved, integrated platforms were developed for managing the major application components supporting the supply chain. Thus was born the early stages of product lifecycle management, SAP ERP, and an integrated reporting and analytics capability. At this stage, central management of the primary key and basic data was insufficient. Governance was expanded to any master data that needed to be shared between transactional and/or reporting functionality. Successful governance of the global data with reliable data distribution laid the foundation for a central organization to deliver data to thousands of downstream systems with high reliability in a manner that supported the transactions from those applications to be sent to a common data warehouse for analytics.

End-to-End Process Management
As productivity and efficiency requirements continued to increase, the platform management was insufficient. End-to-end work processes needed to be addressed, and the silos of the platforms needed to be broken down. The application architecture and individual data owners were no longer sufficient to enable the required data governance.

Application Architecture Evolves to Data Governance

The dual database architecture provided a foundation for data management that served Procter and Gamble for 20 years, growing from a country and regionally organized company to a globally managed one. As the complexity of the global operations grew and the need to respond more quickly to changing business conditions grew, the application architecture was insufficient, and a business-led data governance capability was required.

Consequently, C-level sponsorship initiated a project to design and implement a new organizational capability delivering global data governance to enable an end to end supply chain capable of keeping pace with the rapidly changing requirements for data. The new organization is bringing executive-level governance to master data work processes and the quality requirements of the data. Data steward roles are being formalized with an expectation of leading business transformation to drive clarity of responsibility and designing system automation (workflow, validation rules, etc.).

Data Quality as Defined by the Consuming Business Process

As data governance is being defined, one of the overarching goal you can expect is to increase the quality of the data. However, without an agreed upon definition of quality, it is impossible to measure. The critical component of defining quality requirements is for all consuming processes to document their requirements. Not all requirements will necessarily be met, but without the complete list of requirements the data providers cannot report the effectiveness of their governancc in a context that reflects business value.

An industry study of this space typically shows that the components of data quality include:

- **Timeliness**
  Is the data available when the consuming processes require it?
- **Completeness**
  Is the data complete when consuming processes require it?
- **Consistency**
  Are related data elements logically consistent with each other? For example, does the individual item weight of an item in a case containing 12 items equal item weight times count (e.g., 12). If not, there is an error in the relationship between these fields.
- **Accuracy**
  Accuracy can be challenging to measure, as it often requires physical audits. A key element of accuracy for numerical data is the allowed tolerance. There may be tolerances for accuracy that vary by data item. Some may have zero tolerance, and others might have a tolerance range, for example, ±4%.

Data Quality Measures

Measuring governance and data quality is an evolving capability, just as is overall governance. First-generation measures are often activity-based. A metric may be deployed to track the effort it takes to keep operations at the current level. But with time, it may be determined that activity is not a measure of actual business needs, nor of the value, nor of the quality of the data being delivered.

Quality measurement often evolves to focus on timeliness, completeness, consistency, and accuracy. With this focus and additional scope, business impact may be inferred. Correlations to improvement in data quality can be linked to efficiency improvements in the business process. This "virtuous cycle" should drive greater data quality.

It may also be seen that there are linkages of quality metrics of the data with incident management, and data outages may be identified as root causes of specific business process performance or specific incidents. When such examples surface, make sure to factor in the true cost of poor data quality as being the business impact as well as the cost of the organizational capacity to resolve the errors.

Information Security

While it isn't the intent of this section to cover the breadth and depth of information security, we would be remiss to not at least touch on some of the essential elements, which are presented here independent of how a firm may organize around information governance and information security.

Information security should be a policy-driven approach to governance, covering information assurance, physical safety and security, and business continuity and disaster recovery. Such a policy is augmented by required standards and recommended guidelines, which specify in more detail how the requirements set forth in the policy are to be satisfied. Finally, operational units (IT and business) are expected to develop written procedures that enable security-related tasks to be performed in a defined, repeatable, and policy-compliant way.

The differences among policies, standards, guidelines, and procedures are outlined here:

- **Policies**
  Policies are general statements of direction and purpose. They outline specific high-level requirements or rules that must be met, but do not specify how that is to be done. Policies are for the most part non-technical in nature, and are intended to remain relatively static over long periods of time.
- **Standards**
  Standards are specific and, where applicable, technical documents that contain directives and specifications for implementing the requirements and rules set forth by policies. Compliance with standards is mandatory; their requirements must be met by everyone (although some standards may have documented exception processes). Standards are generally written using the verb "must," and to the extent possible, apply in all situations.
- **Guidelines**
  Guidelines are similar to standards, but advisory in nature. Guidelines represent suggestions for best practices, and while implementing these suggestions is not required, doing so is strongly recommended. Guidelines are generally written using the verb "should," and frequently apply to very specific situations.
- **Procedures**
  Procedures provide detailed instructions (usually step-by-step) for performing activities that are governed by the policies, standards, and guidelines. Procedures

are generally developed by each individual unit that is required to comply with a particular policy, and reflect the individual unit's particular business environment.

6.1.9 Role of the Enterprise Information Architecture Organization

The enterprise information architecture organization is responsible for delivering the following kinds of capabilities to the enterprise:

- The big picture. From a planning or strategic perspective, what does the information landscape look like? This can take the form of an enterprise data model and will find many uses as projects try to navigate this space.
- Roadmaps for the current state and future state assessments of the information capability, as well as roadmaps for driving improvements.
- Artifacts for the information domain, such as models, standards, designs, roadmaps, assessments, metrics, and so on.
- Impact analysis. When change is needed that spans organizations and geographies, the enterprise information architecture organization may be the only ones with the appropriate skills, scope, and vantage point.
- Metrics that indicate that the coverage of artifacts have been defined as required.

This section discussed information management architecture recommendations starting with a definition of principles for your architecture, the scope, the types of structured data, and the dual database approach. It discussed a typical information lifecycle for structured and unstructured data, data standards, governance, and the role of the enterprise information architecture organization. The next section provides recommendations for managing data migration projects.

6.2 Managing Data Migration Projects to Support Mergers and Acquisitions

Companies that are successful with merger and acquisition migration activity excel at managing their ability to map legacy data into the current business process and have a sustainable method for managing their data load activity. The secrets to this success include the ability to:

- Understand and build a specific scope of what needs to be loaded.
- Manage business rules and how incoming data is transformed.
- Create flexible and sustainable ETL programs using SAP Data Services (hereafter Data Services).
- Create a roadmap document that can be used to manage and govern the entire data load process from cradle to grave and be able to report to leadership on status.

Without doing this, major business processes could be impacted; for example, you cannot ship or receive goods. You could also have quality issues that are reflected in incorrect billing and payments, as well as poor customer service.

In this section, we discuss tips for scoping your data migration project, an example migration process flow, and the options for enriching data during a migration project.

6.2.1 Scoping for a Data Migration Project

The first step to a successful data migration project is to understand the scope of your data requirement. You need to work with many groups; for example, finance, controlling, plant maintenance, sales, supply chain, materials management, customer service, and so on, to understand what they need for a successful implementation. In the finance area, you might need to load elements such as accounts receivables and accounts payable open items, assets, bank master records, and so on. Also, you need to consider subcategories within the same data object; for example, a customer master record where some fields are in SAP ERP and other fields are in SAP Customer Relationship Management (CRM). While the use of customer data in SAP CRM and SAP ERP maybe be different, it's important for the migration to look holistically at all attributes required for the customer. Cross-functional meetings are the best place to detect and discuss the cross-use of data elements for the same object. One way to ensure that you capture the correct data requirement is by using a data plan. This is not the only way to do it, but the following outlines a data plan and how it can be used to ensure that data requirements are captured for a data migration project. The data plan is an Excel spreadsheet that captures the following information:

- **Priority**
  Priority of load. For example, master data comes before transactional data.

- **Team**
  Which specific team is responsible for the load (i.e., purchasing/supplier relationship management [SRM]).
- **Data type**
  Master data versus transactional data.
- **Conversion description**
  Object detail (i.e., accounts payable).
- **Source**
  Source of data you are extracting.
- **SAP load date**
  Estimated load.
- **Estimated hours to load**
  Estimated hours of runtime.
- **Load order**
  Overall job sequence to help with planning.

An example data migration spreadsheet is available for download from this book's page at *http://www.sap-press.com/3666*. The second tab in the data plan spreadsheet covers the data details. The data details provide the following nine subcategories that help manage the entire process holistically:

- **Source data**
  Database size and record count; used for production load.
- **Data mapping**
  Number of fields to be mapped, business owner, percentage complete.
- **Business rules**
  Number of fields to be mapped, business owner, percentage complete.
- **Data cleaning**
  Number of records cleaned per object, percentage complete.
- **Development/programming**
  Program name, tool (e.g., Data Services, ABAP).
- **Data extract**
  Date, extract option (e.g., Data Services), number of records extracted, number of rejected records, number of extracted versus total count.

- **Data extracts/loads into development system (unit testing)**
  Load date, number of records loaded, percentage of records loaded versus total count extracted.
- **Data extracts/loads into quality system**
  For advanced unit testing and integration testing: load date, number of records loaded, percentage of records loaded versus total count extracted.
- **Data extracts/loads into production system**
  Load date, number of records loaded, percentage of records loaded versus total count extracted.

6.2.2 Data Migration Process Flow

When preparing for a data migration project, it may be helpful to break the conversion into two phases: data cleansing and data loading. The data cleansing phase prepares you and your organization for cleaning and de-duplication of data. Once the data is cleansed, it is loaded. Figure 6.3 shows an example data migration process flow.

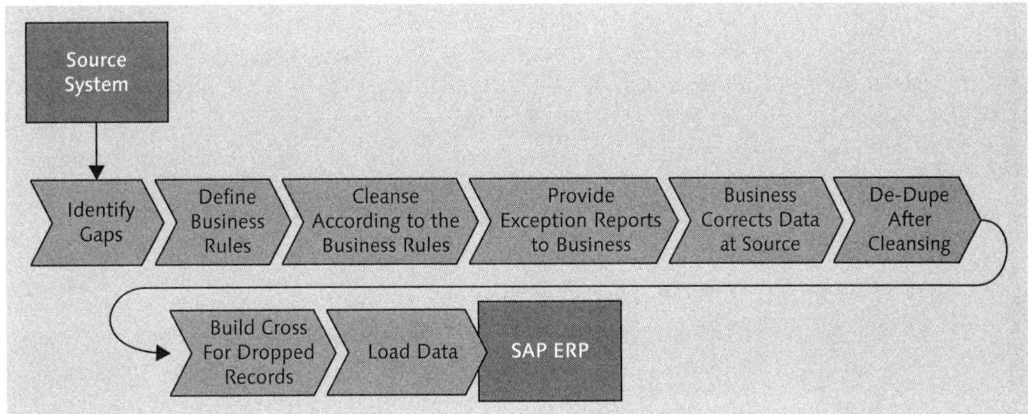

Figure 6.3 Example Data Migration Process

When loading SAP customer master data, you can take the approach of creating a super table that holds many field attributes that are contained within the sales view. Because the sales view of the customer master holds many SAP tables, it is good to have one staging table that is logically defined. If you use the SAP-delivered content for data migration (*http://service.sap.com/bp-datamigration*), there is already content provided for validating the fields. The SAP-provided migration content is discussed in Chapter 10.

Next, we discuss more details of the process flow that's shown in Figure 6.3. This includes identifying what data you want to cleanse, defining the business rules, cleansing, providing errors and exceptions to the business users, correcting the data, de-duplicating, building a cross-reference (or key mapping), and finally transferring all cleansed data to the target system.

Identify What Business Objects Need to be Cleansed

Identifying your cleansing objects may be one of the most important steps in your process. It is vitally important to identify what to clean and the scope for data governance. You'll want to start with something small; for example, you should look at cleaning a small part of a larger master data element or related master data areas, as in the sales view of the customer master. This allows you to begin crafting your approach of data quality and to provide your company with a visible win and promote the process of a reusable data quality project. Also, it's very important to have buy-in with the IT and business leaders on the scope of work and other follow-on projects.

SAP Information Steward (hereafter Information Steward) can be used to help you determine which objects you really need to cleanse. Data profiling of key objects will provide quick insight on the major data quality issues that require attention. Information Steward for data profiling is discussed in more detail in Chapter 10.

Define Business Rules

Once you've decided on the scope of work, you should move into the specific business rules. This step is as important as defining your scope of work. You should take three specific steps in this area.

First, conduct workshops with all parts of the company that have a responsibility in the area you want to clean. For example, if you are developing rules for the materials resource planning (MRP) view of the material master record, you should make sure people involved in your initial workshop are from production planning, purchasing, logistics/warehousing, and inventory management. Also, you need to make sure you align the proper IT counterpart in this workshop.

Second, it's good to have a data architect who can document all requirements and another person to lead discussions in each workshop. It is *critical* to have open dialog in the workshop and to allow all users to communicate all possible business rules. Allow the synergies of the collective group to help brainstorm and provide the best input possible.

Third, when you have all possible business rules provided by the team, these rules can be created in Information Steward. Creation of business rules is discussed in more detail in Chapter 10. Having these rules in Information Steward ensures reuse and the ability to clean data on an ongoing basis.

Cleanse According to the Business Rules

During your cleansing of the data per business rules, it's important to be holistic. When implementing a field to clean, you should make sure the field being cleaned has a standard definition globally, and the rule being applied should be considered a "global cleansing method" throughout your enterprise. When you start to design cleansing rules differently across countries and organizations, you add complexity and additional management needed to maintain your data governance organization. The cleansing is done using the cleansing transformations provided by Data Services. A detailed example of data cleansing and validation is provided in Chapter 9.

Provide Exception Reports to Business

Depending on how often you decide to clean your data, you need to work together with your business leaders to develop the correct time for each cleaning cycle. Typically, if you are cleaning customer master information on a global level, most companies look at processing the cleansing jobs once per month, or bimonthly. The cleansing jobs separate good from bad data. The good data is staged and isolated to ensure that no further handling is needed. The bad data is separated into two areas. The first subdivision of bad data is corrected based on the specific business rule. The second portion of bad data is sent on an "exception report" that key users in the business community need to review and then report on to their management and/or IT leadership for further correction and processing. The main reason for the data split is to support the business rules. Users back in the business definition phase determined that certain rules can be simply updated with the correct data and other bad data needs to be analyzed further, as it is exceptional. Part of the users' job is to review each exception and update the spreadsheet or system if it needs to be updated or to ignore the exception. If an exception is to be ignored, then you need to design the system to flag this item to not be considered in the future.

Correct Data at the Source

In some cases bad data needs to be corrected in the source application where the business rules are being checked. You need to take into consideration the replication of jobs systems. There are several ways to update your data. First, you can have local users update bad data from the exception reporting. Second, you can leverage Data Services to make updates in the source system to fix the bad data. You can also use a workflow or use SAP Master Data Governance (MDG) for key master data changes. SAP MDG is a good fit if your project is going to launch a centralized master data project. SAP MDG is discussed in Chapter 11.

Duplication after Cleansing

When identifying duplication and cleaning your system, most people focus on cleaning the specific duplicate record, such as sold-to or ship-to customer. This is fine, but you also need to look at the entire system if you want to clean in a holistic manner. For example, if you want to clean and remove duplicate sold-to customer numbers, you also need to look at all objects within your target system that link to the customer number. You need to consider things such as customer part numbers, customer info records, customer pricing records, customer hierarchies, all forms of sales documents (sales orders, sales contracts, sales schedule agreements), customer discount records, price lists, and so on. Timing is also important. For example, do you wait until your last delivery is shipped and then block customer B, or do you place a hard block on customer B and back all open orders and start with customer A? It's best to devise an action plan and sequence for proper de-duplication efforts. This action is not to be minimized, as you'll need a strong focus and commitment to make sure all steps per each duplicate record are cleansed and removed if required.

Build Cross-References for Dropped Records

Part of a successful de-duplication effort is the ability to record your dropped records. It's important to have your system maintain a historical master list of current and duplicate records. Some companies look at the ETL system maintaining a master file or database (i.e., staging table) that lists the object going through the duplication process and understand which one is the current versus duplicate record. For example, if you have five customer numbers for John Doe, you need to label which one is current and which ones are duplications. Then you use this information to point the duplicate records to the current one within your SAP ERP system. This process of keeping a master list applies until your SAP ERP system has holistically removed the reference of the duplicated customer number.

If you are using an application such as SAP MDG, you can build the cross-references using key mapping. This is discussed in Chapter 11.

Transfer the Cleansed Data for Migration to the Target System

As cleansed data is transferred to your target system, you should start to develop monthly KPIs or "health of the data" metrics for IT and the business units to measure and build accountability. For example, each month you process customer or material master cleansing, you should be able to gather the following data: number or records extracted, number of records in bad files, number of records sent to good files, number of records corrected from bad files, number of records not corrected due to loading issues. This type of data will help you transform simple data into powerful information. With this information, you can tell per sales organization if you have recurring data corrections every month. Perhaps you have 50 errors and then 50 corrections for the same business rule every month. This may be due to the same customer service representative making the same mistake, and you are simply running the cleansing jobs over and over. You don't gain anything with this data governance initiative if you aren't looking at these types of KPIs. However, if you pay attention to these types of issues, you can proceed with data mining and find you have a training issue that needs to be addressed. Historically, this data has been collected using spreadsheets, but Information Steward can be used for data quality trending over time.

6.2.3 Enrich the Data Using Dun and Bradstreet (D&B) with Data Services

In addition to the typical data migration process flow described in the previous section, data migration projects may also include data enrichment. While data enrichment is discussed in more detail in Chapter 9, it's worth mentioning that many companies use a DUNS (data universal numbering system) number to enrich SAP's customer hierarchy approach. (A DUNS number is a unique identifier assigned to each business by Dun and Bradstreet.) The use of the DUNS numbers with the customer hierarchy helps manage and report on DUNS numbers and their relationship to the parent customers (i.e., sold-to and ship-to) within the customer database. A common practice is to have Dun and Bradstreet provide a DUNS number in conjunction with SAP's customer hierarchy approach. Then a business intelligence (BI) reporting layer is created to publish real-time reporting to show customers across different sales organizations and product divisions. This allows your company to have product market managers to take an active role in making decisions on information from your core ERP system and use a tool, such as D&B for customer account management.

This section provided recommendations and hints for successful data migration projects. Next, we discuss the evolution of Data Services at National Vision.

6.3 Evolution of SAP Data Services at National Vision

National Vision's use of Data Services evolved over a period of time and is continuing to change with business requirements. When reflecting back over the various projects that extended the use of Data Services, the evolution has (so far) included five phases. This section will discuss each of those phases, explaining how EIM solutions were used to address specific business challenges.

6.3.1 Phase 1: The Enterprise Data Warehouse

Data Services was first introduced at National Vision as the main tool selected to build an enterprise data warehouse. The business challenge being addressed was the requirement to bring together timely, accurate, and actionable data to provide insights into the factors impacting retail sales and customer behavior. The following were the key issues the project contended with:

- Silos of data sources and applications (ERP system, human resources system, store point of sale system, e-commerce system, etc.).
- Limited business user access to information needed to make informed decisions.
- Business users had to wait for IT programmers to create or make changes to mainframe-generated reports. Additionally, business users worked mainly in a Windows environment, and the mainframe interface made it difficult for them to interact with reports.
- Inconsistent definition of key metrics; for instance, the definition of "sales revenue" varied among store brands and channels.

The solutions chosen to address these problems were the Data Integrator capabilities of Data Services and the SAP BusinessObjects Business Intelligence (BI) platform. Using the ETL functions in Data Services, an enterprise data warehouse was created and loaded nightly, consolidating data from disparate sources. This was then exposed through BI to provide improved transparency in the flow of data from the source to the reports for the end users. Figure 6.4 shows how Data Services was utilized to load the data warehouse. Data flowed from applications to the enterprise data warehouse to the SAP BusinessObjects BI platform.

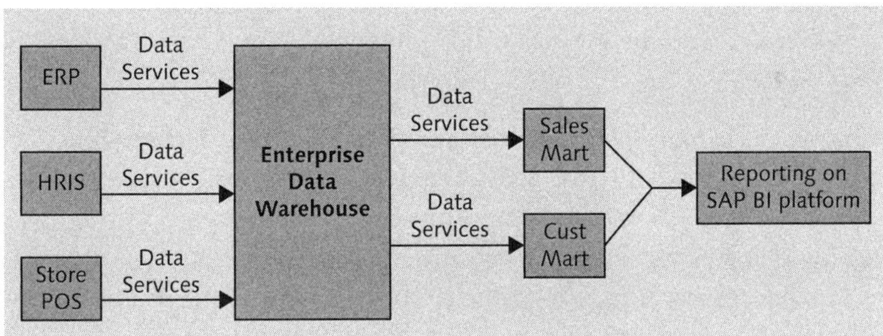

Figure 6.4 Data Services to Load Data Warehouse

Data Services was used to extract data from over 20 applications, such as an ERP system, HRIS (human resources information system), and store POS (store point of sale) system. Once the data was extracted to the enterprise data warehouse, Data Services was again employed to create subject area data marts optimized for reporting. Examples included data marts for customer data, employee data, sales data, and order detail data. The data marts focused on subject area, but benefited multiple functional departments.

6.3.2 Phase 2: Enterprise Information Architecture—Consolidating Source Data

The next business challenge addressed arose from the realization that many applications require and use the same data. The lack of sharing data between applications resulted in duplicate and manual data entry, inefficient processes, and data not kept in sync between applications. Table 6.1 shows an example.

ERP	HRIS	Store POS
Customer data	Store data	Customer data
Sales data	Employee data	Sales data
Store data		Employee data
Product data		Product data

Table 6.1 Same Data Required in Multiple Applications

Much of the same data is stored in and consumed by multiple siloed applications. However, up to this point, the stored data that was shared between the ERP and HRIS systems had not been rationalized or compared. The same was true for employee data, product data, and to some extent, the customer data.

The solution was to extend the use of Data Services beyond just loading the data warehouse. Data Services was engaged to identify a single origin for each data subject, determining which system "owns" the data, then operated as the conduit to push the data to other systems that consume the information. Reusable data flows and transforms (explained in Chapter 9) were created, and the data flows became more focused on each data object (data flows for customer data, for product data, for employee data, etc.).

In the example of the employee data, the HRIS system owned the data, and Data Services was used to replicate it, as shown in Figure 6.5. This figure shows the HRIS system in the middle, where all employee data is maintained and updated. It is then pushed to consumers of employee data, such as the enterprise data warehouse, ERP, training systems, and the store POS system.

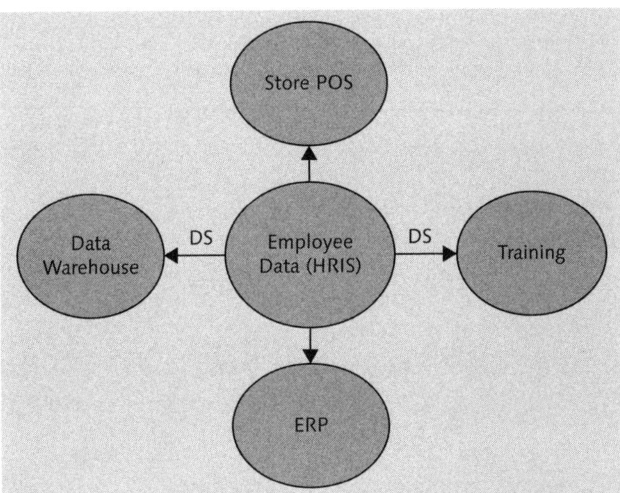

Figure 6.5 Example of Employee Data Owned by HR System and Replicated

Data management evolved through a process of identifying the best source systems and having departments take ownership of the data. The other systems became the recipient systems. This entire process emerged into a master data and governance discipline.

In addition to the governance and master data discipline that transpired from this (albeit sometimes painful) process, this solution also provided better data quality due to less manual data entry and less effort on keeping data in sync between the applications.

6.3.3 Phase 3: Data Quality and the Customer Hub

The third phase in our evolution was the creation of a global view of the customer across original data sources to meet the challenge of measuring retention, lifetime value, and the purchase cycle. This phase was important in addressing the following issues:

- Since many physical stores and the online channels originated customer data, it was stored in hundreds of separate databases.
- There was little consistency in customer data entry; it was only as good as entered.

- Customer address information was out of date as a result of relocations.
- The source system analysis and data profiling on new data sources was manual.

The solution was to use the data quality capabilities within Data Services. The employment of data quality enabled the following:

- Customer data from all sources moves through address cleansing and standardization transforms in Data Services, utilizing the U.S. Postal Service database, which is updated monthly via subscription. (Chapter 9 covers the details of how this works in Data Services.)
- National changes of address (NCOA) are now applied monthly, and addresses are kept updated.
- Updated customer records go through a matching routine in Data Services to determine duplicates. (Chapter 9 covers matching capabilities.)
- All de-duped customers are grouped and assigned a global customer ID, populating the *customer hub* database.
- Geocoded, cleansed customer records, and the global customer ID are pushed from this hub to various applications, such as campaign management, a geospatial application, and the enterprise data warehouse.

Figure 6.6 shows an example of how this works. In this example, William Smith is a customer entered in a specific store *and* Bill Smith originates from the web channel. Data Services realizes both records refer to the same customer and harmonizes them to be William Smith, which is then replicated to the customer hub that owns the customer data. The de-duped customer data is then replicated to multiple applications.

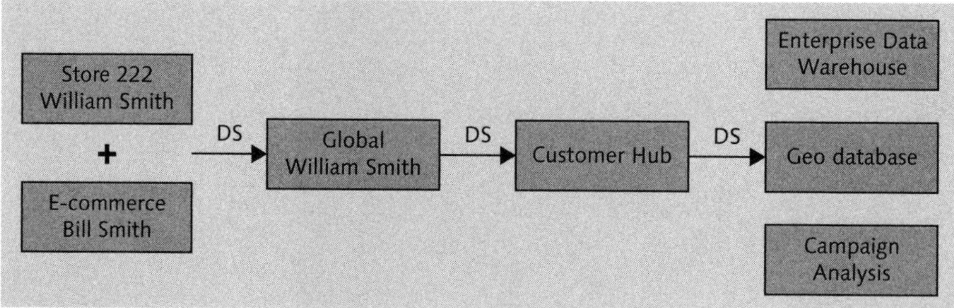

Figure 6.6 Data Services to Cleanse and Remove Duplicates Before Replicating to Multiple Target Systems

Another example of improved data quality relates to the telephone number. This data is important in a business-to-consumer (retail) scenario where you need to call the customer to let them know their order is ready or to follow up their store visit with a customer satisfaction survey. Prior to this phase, the customer phone number was stored in over 125 patterns. After this phase, the phone number across many systems was stored in one pattern, improving data quality and customer service. Data quality supported the project with:

- Cleansed and parsed customer data, including the ability to use existing dictionaries to cleanse data and the ability to create a customized dictionary.
- Standardized names (e.g., Bob, Robert).
- Standardized different entities such as email, telephone numbers, and dates.
- Standardized and validated address data using built-in transforms and the government's address database.
- Geocoded customers based on address, appending latitude and longitude for each customer for placement on maps.
- Universal data cleansing that allowed non-customer data matching by utilizing rule-based parsing and rule editing architecture to achieve better results.
- The flexibility to create its own transform with nonproprietary Python code. (Chapter 9 discusses transforms.)

During this data quality process, it was critical that we match the customer records to remove duplicates. Why go to the trouble of matching data? The easy answers are: in-storage savings by eliminating redundant data, and in-time savings from moving data around between the applications. However, the major benefit of matching data remains the ability to identify and understand all interactions of a customer. Being able to measure the true value and lifecycle of a particular customer or household can potentially change how you interact with that customer. For example, a direct mail or email campaign may contain different messages or targeted offers based on the global customer's previous purchase activity. If that unmatched customer exists as multiple customers, the purchase history would be incomplete, likely resulting in the wrong offer and multiple mailings. For vendors or product-related matching, there are significant savings in consolidating the purchasing of related products and knowing where and what you are spending with each vendor.

6.3.4 Phase 4: Application Integration and Data Migration

The first business challenge addressed in the application integration and data migration phase was to integrate an acquired company's application output, especially from a different point of sale system, into the main company's applications, such as an ERP system, until the systems could be replaced.

The solution was to use Data Services to routinely extract data from the legacy point of sales system; cleanse, transform, and validate the data; and then load it into the ERP system on a daily basis. This was a complex integration project, but was accomplished within three months with the help of Data Services and a now experienced team, ensuring that the acquired stores' products were replenished on a timely basis, and their employees and customers were properly serviced. This project added event-triggered jobs in Data Services.

Later, when legacy systems, such as point of sale and financial/accounting systems from the parent company were being replaced, the new business challenge became the migration of historical, financial, and customer data into the new applications, from the old versions of each.

The solution was to again use Data Services to extract, transform, map, cleanse, remove duplications, and load historical data into new applications. Batch processing or using web service options within Data Services enabled communication and integration between applications. Data Services was used to consume XML messages, perform data cleansing and data standardization, and then output an XML hierarchy. The ability to reuse transforms from earlier projects greatly simplified development.

6.3.5 Phase 5: Next Steps with Data Services

In the case study discussed here, the next plans for Data Services are to cleanse and de-duplicate data at the source, when data is being entered into the system. Additional extensions will target the use of real-time loads to the data warehouse and to include the text data processing capabilities that bring in unstructured data to better understand customer behavior and sentiment.

This section discussed the evolution of Data Services from use as an ETL tool to load a data warehouse, to a data platform to manage and ensure the quality of data globally. Next, we'll discuss recommendations for a master data program.

6.4 Recommendations for a Master Data Program

Companies start managing their master data for a variety of reasons, ranging from increased accuracy and reliability in business intelligence, to operational improvements such as reduced shipping errors. They also start their journey at various levels of maturity. Whatever may be the end benefit, most have to follow a similar sequence of steps to achieve their specific goals. To be successful with managing master data, the following must be defined:

- Common enterprise vision and goals
- Master data strategy
- Roadmap and operational phases
- Business process redesign and change management
- Governance
- Technology selection

In this section, we discuss each of these concepts.

6.4.1 Common Enterprise Vision and Goals

A statement about an enterprise's vision and goals is an articulation of why master data management is important to the enterprise and the end state vision. Typically, this is driven by vision/goal setting workshops that includes multiple business stakeholders; alternatively, it can be created by a smaller operating team that shares it with the larger organization for approval. Having this vision defined and supported by the necessary top management roles is essential for the program's success. Short-term goals that translate the vision into achievable milestones provide concreteness to the sometimes more abstract vision. For example, if the vision is to "transform enterprise data, business processes, and organization into assets that will provide business value," the shorter-term goals could include specific targets such as "Consolidate customer master data for the ERP and CRM systems by end of the second quarter of next year."

6.4.2 Master Data Strategy

For the purposes of this section, the master data strategy specifies the approaches, standards, and methodology for achieving the common enterprise vision. To continue with the example of achieving the vision of "transform enterprise data, business processes, and organization into assets that will provide business value," the approach could be regional, local, or global; the standards could be around data and business process; and the methodology could involve starting with one domain or multiple domains. So one variation of a strategy could be "global centralized management of customer master data by standardizing creation and updating processes and data elements."

6.4.3 Roadmap and Operational Phases

In this planning phase, the strategy is made operational with specific scopes, milestones, and deliverables. This could be based on low-hanging fruit, or the most value that can be delivered to the organization within a given time frame. Whatever the approach, the end result is an operational plan with time-bound deliverables. The operational phase could involve various tasks such as data discovery, business process inventory, new process definition, data quality remediation, and so on. The operational phase is tied to specific systems, data domains, and delivery dates. Master data scenarios typically involve consolidation, harmonization, or centralization. The roadmap and operational phases could outline specific scenarios or styles for individual domains.

6.4.4 Business Process Redesign and Change Management

For ongoing maintenance and upkeep of master data, a certain amount of redesign is typically required with the master data management processes (create, read, update, delete/archive). The usual change management guidelines apply here with periodic communication of changes, training, and executive support. Data quality and process metrics are useful in enforcing these changes. For example, if master data was allowed to be created in various applications prior to a change that resulted in a centralized approach, the users have to be trained to follow the new process and understand the revised service-level agreements, the required data elements, and data quality checks/standardizations built into the process.

6.4.5 Governance

Governance is the glue that holds together the various components of a master data management program. Business driven and enforced, data governance helps organizations in an enterprise come up with processes to manage, measure, and control the quality of master data. Successful master data management programs are all backed by strong business-driven data governance efforts. Depending on the organization profile, data to be managed, and applications landscape, the governance organization can be centralized or decentralized. In most enterprises, the governance function is enforced by a combination of bottom-up effort driven by data stewards and analysts and supported by a top-down data governance council that acts as a final arbiter of data issues and an enforcer of enterprise standards and business processes. Since governance is management and business driven, to a large part, this is dependent on the organizational culture. Since a governance program is an important prerequisite for a successful master data program, starting and nurturing a governance initiative is an important task by itself that needs to be managed with due diligence.

6.4.6 Technology Selection

Technology selection is purposefully presented toward the end of the section, as the previous items are relevant and important to guide this task. While there is no one tool that will do all the required tasks, a combination of tools and technologies is now definitely available in the marketplace to help manage master data. Based on the vision, goals, and master data strategy and a combination of other factors, such as the existing solution and tool landscape and approved technology portfolio, this can be a complex task.

Following these steps will help the enterprise achieve its master data vision. The benefits can vary, but include:

- Operational efficiencies such as improved shipping and billing processes that ensure the right products are sent efficiently to the right customers, suppliers are paid on schedule using the right payment instruments, and the right products are included in the catalog for the correct set of customers or partners.
- Analytic improvements such as the ability to create true profit and loss reports by customer and/or product, identify true spend by suppliers across all the material/product categories, and rationalize the supplier base periodically to have the right mix required to support the enterprise.

Apart from these improvements, a structure that is in place for governing and managing master data can be used to effectively work with business scenarios including mergers and acquisitions, new product introduction, compliance initiatives, and so on.

Next, we discuss recommendations on using SAP Process Orchestration; specifically, SAP Process Integration and SAP Data Services.

6.5 Recommendations for Using SAP Process Integration and SAP Data Services

In this section, we'll discuss the use of SAP Process Integration (a component of SAP Process Orchestration) and the use of Data Services for data integration. This section is intended for companies that have both SAP Process Integration (hereafter SAP PI) and Data Services. This section assumes knowledge of SAP PI and will not introduce this tool. If you do not already have SAP PI, you might want to skip this section.

6.5.1 A Common Data Integration Problem

When integrating data between multiple systems, the integration can include several layers and integration points. When something goes wrong with an integration process, a common problem that occurs in the enterprise is that people always want to "shoot the messenger." From an integration standpoint, this means the blame for poor performance or reliability issues is focused at the middleware. Of course, the middleware is sometimes to blame, but it is important to separate fact from fiction. A case in point is drawn from the timeframe after SAP PI was launched within a large company. SAP PI had a large role in the middleware; it abstracted services from SAP to be available to the rest of the enterprise (for example, get purchase order data, get customer information). Over time, the number of interfaces rose quickly. Data flowing in and out of the SAP backend was going through a messaging chain that included SAP PI.

A chorus of "SAP PI has a performance problem" or "SAP PI is broken" was growing. Further analysis showed that as projects were developing SAP PI interfaces between enterprise systems, they were using them not only for near-real-time data feeds, but also for very large data moves with short durations. Messaging chains through SAP PI and other enterprise web services that worked fine for incremental data transfers collapsed under the load of a huge data moves.

Examples of these types of data moves were large product updates or wide-ranging price updates.

6.5.2 A Data Integration Analogy

As the company tried to explain the differences between ETL processes and incremental near-real-time processes, it became clear that the message wasn't sinking in across teams of developers, architects, and managers. The architects came up with an analogy that helped people understand this difference. It became known as the "concrete and sugar" analogy. Basically, it uses the example of a construction truck moving large numbers of concrete bags compared to a sedan used to move bags of sugar. The truck is a heavy-duty flatbed vehicle with a large bed for transporting material. It has a large diesel motor, a heavy-duty suspension, and big tires. The car is a standard passenger car with a medium-sized motor and has enclosed space for protecting passengers and carrying small items.

Both the truck and the car can move either concrete or sugar (the messaging layer doesn't care about the content), but the volumes that can be moved efficiently are not interchangeable. Trucks are like the large ETL systems. They excel at transforming and moving very large batches. Cars are like middleware that excels at moving smaller volumes repeated many times. The truck is most efficient at moving large numbers of large bags. But it can also carry small bags. It is designed to move a lot of material, but not at a very fast pace. The passenger car can move a couple of bags of concrete or several bags of sugar. It is designed for fast trips carrying small loads. It can even handle a burst of activity and carry a lot of bags of sugar.

You wouldn't say the car has "performance problems" because it can't move a ton of concrete, and you couldn't efficiently use a large construction truck for your regular trips to a grocery store to pick up a few small bags of sugar. Both the car and the truck are best utilized for the type of use case for which they were designed. If you move a couple of bags with the truck, it will work but won't be efficient. And it will take a while (won't be "real time"). If you try to move too much concrete at once, you will either slow down the passenger car or you will break it.

We found that using this analogy helped the developers, architects, and managers better understand the correct usage of SAP PI and Data Services. Next, we'll provide some guidelines in more detail on choosing the right software capability for the integration requirements.

6.5.3 Creating Prescriptive Guidance to Help Choose the Proper Tool

As the conversations on which tools to use continued, one thing that became apparent was that there was still a mindset in the enterprise that thought in terms of executing updates in large batches. But the enterprise architecture in many companies is moving toward smaller, incremental updates in a near-real-time (NRT) fashion. The collision of these two mindsets is where enterprise integration teams hear cries of performance problems and unreliability. As they work with project teams and clearly delineate the line between ETL and NRT, they need to create prescriptive guidance for the use cases and can thereby ease a lot of the problems. Figure 6.7 shows the convergence of ETL and NRT, with data synchronization on one end and multistep processing on the other end.

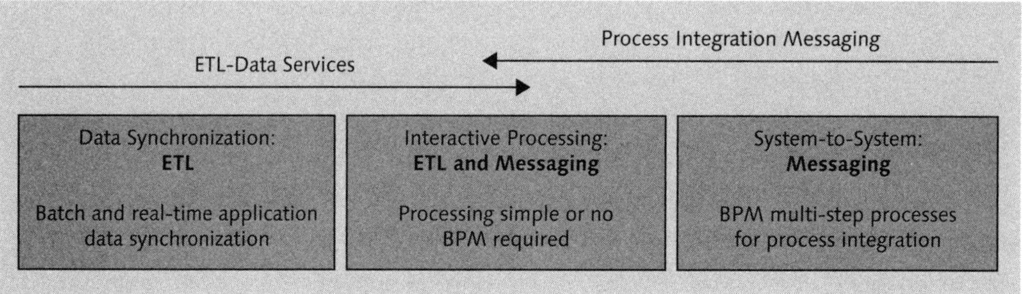

Figure 6.7 ETL and Messaging Spectrum

The following are some use cases where you would choose one method over the other, or use a blend of the two:

- **ETL**
  The same data needs to be in two or more systems; for example, data migration projects to seed new applications.
- **ETL and messaging**
  A transaction needs to be completed across systems. This can also be called a composite application.
- **Messaging**
  A business process where several transactions occur in steps through a predefined sequence across two or more systems and you need to guarantee delivery.

The advantages of ETL lie in use cases that involve processing large amounts of data, use ETL tools already in place, and use complex transformations including data quality, cleansing, validation, de-duplication, enrichment, as well as point-to-point movement of data.

The advantages of messaging lie in uses cases that involve processing a high number of transactions over time, use messaging tools already in place, require little data augmentation but need message transformations, and involve one-to-many and many-to-many data movement.

Another way to look at the overlap between SAP PI and Data Services is by creating a radar map. This type of map plots the fit of each capability along the spokes of a circular radar graph and gives a good visual representation of the strengths of each tool as well as the areas of overlap. SAP has created a radar map for positioning Data Services and SAP Process Integration; it is part of a larger positioning presentation that you can find on the SAP Community Network (SCN).[1]

6.5.4 Complex Examples in the Enterprise

It's not that simple in all cases. If a project team has developed middleware interfaces for data feeds, they of course want to reuse those for the occasional big batch product/price updates mentioned previously. They would ask, "Why should we create a process/tool for the batch updates when we have a perfectly usable interface in place?" This question requires more analysis. An example use case is one where SAP data was being fed near-real-time through SAP PI to another legacy transformation engine and then through a web service that loaded into another database.

This chain performed very well with incremental feeds, but was overwhelmed in the web service layer during large batch loads. As the endpoint overloaded, the problems backed up through the messaging chain, and the integration team ended up with "PI has performance problems" messages in their inboxes from the angry project team.

In reality, SAP PI had so much capacity in the environment that as the source system was pushing large updates out, SAP PI was overwhelming the downstream chain. This use case was not one where the project team had the time or the resources or the need to build an ETL solution for these infrequent data pushes.

---

1 *http://www.sdn.sap.com/irj/scn/go/portal/prtroot/docs/library/uuid/10fbac70-c381-2d10-afbe-c3902a694eaf?QuickLink=index&overridelayout=true*

The solution that the integration architecture team came up with was called "throttle at the source." Through benchmarking, they determined the volume at which the weakest link in the integration chain would break. Using this information, they worked with project teams to determine a throttle rate for the source system that would allow data to flow smoothly and efficiently given the existing capacity of the enterprise systems. This increased the time required to complete the total data movement, but there were some dials that could be controlled on this throttle to minimize the total time.

Throttling the rate at which messages are sent from the source system can be seen in the example of price updates, where a large number of products need to have prices updated in one or more systems. Instead of pushing out product prices as quickly as the system can, it can be controlled so that only *x* number of price updates per hour are sent from the source system for instance. Any mechanism that can control the rate at which messages or updates are sent into the enterprise can be used as an effective throttle.

Other ways to minimize the impact on the systems in the enterprise are as follows:

- Move the pushes to off hours when the systems have more available capacity and do not collide with known peak messaging times.
- Sometimes systems can also be segmented such that hardware can be dedicated in the short term to service the data push without impacting other critical interfaces. SAP PI, for instance, has the ability to segment queues that are used.
- Move interfaces to asynchronous processing. The middleware layer can help with reliability and can make the system less susceptible to failures by using asynchronous processing instead of the more fragile synchronous processing.

6.5.5 When All Else Fails...

In spite of the best architecture efforts, there will still be occasional big batches that are pushed through unexpectedly and that could break somewhere in the integration chain. That is where the final defense needs to be architecting robust systems that degrade gracefully and where there are better monitors in place to proactively detect the problems as early as possible so that there is time to react and protect critical interfaces.

What is graceful degradation? It can be seen in a complex system that instead of reaching complete failure as errors occur continues to limp along and process messages as system monitors are alerting support personnel of the problems so they get the system back up to full capacity. A complex system that uses asynchronous messaging along with hardware and software segmentation greatly improves the chances for graceful degradation during system problems and improves the probability of a happy ending.

6.6 Ensuring a Successful Enterprise Content Management Project by Belgian Railways

This section will discuss SAP Extended Enterprise Content Management by OpenText (hereafter SAP Extended ECM) and its use by Belgian Railways, including how the business case was built and key success factors for the project.

6.6.1 Building the Business Case

The business case for SAP Extended ECM focused on the overall return on investment. A high-level calculation was used that, perhaps surprisingly, considered not document volumes, but rather the number of employees. Because most employees handled paper documents at some point during the day, by determining the cost to handle a paper document, a general conclusion was reached. The following high-level calculation was used without any consideration for document volumes but based on the number of employees:

- Handling cost of one document is approximately 15 EUR.
- Each employee handles at least one document a day and works at least 200 days a year. The average cost is theoretically about 3,000 EUR per employee per year.
- For 10,000 users, this cost is *theoretically* about 30,000,000 EUR a year.
- By combining measures to drastically reduce the use of paper and using SAP Extended ECM, this cost can be reduced by at least 50%.

A detailed budget planning was presented to the board of directors to raise the funds from the government needed for a four-year roadmap, along with the arguments for each of the following corporate objectives defined by the government:

- Cost optimization driven by paper-reduction strategy and lower TCO for a unique central repository
- Enhanced customer services by offering faster response to customer complaints, faster customer contract handling, punctuality of rail services, and standardization of communication
- Improved punctuality of rail services due to valid information (legal procedures, enhanced training materials, weather conditions) to the train conductors; troubleshooting wizard
- Uncompromising safety through accessibility and accuracy of technical drawings and work procedures, better train maintenance operations and audit/traceability, controlled and validated information to train conductors, enhanced training materials, skills management

Our goal with SAP Extended ECM was to not only create a benchmark in terms of document management, but also to add value by enabling content-enriched business processes with new views and perspectives on data and documents.

The following are examples of what has been or is planned to be implemented at Belgian Railways.

Drawing Management for the Maintenance of Rolling Stock

Drawing management is a business activity focusing on the creation, editing, and publishing of 2D/3D designs related to any train part. These designs are provided by third parties or self-made. In the past, drawing management was prone to inconsistencies, duplicates, obsolescence, and inaccuracy due to the use of many decentralized file servers and legacy databases with local versions of drawings. Operational activities were planned and managed in the SAP Business Suite, while the related technical documents such as plans and drawings were managed in collateral environments.

This did not facilitate the integration and planning of operational activities within the company, and this was often the source of the purchase or production of huge amounts of wrong spare parts, with significant money loss.

Today, there is only one repository containing all released 2D/3D designs integrated with bills of materials used in purchases and production. These drawings are managed with drawing management software, and metadata is maintained and synchronized with SAP Extended ECM once a drawing is released. All previous versions are kept to provide traceability and auditability. Tools have been provided to migrate all legacy databases and perform mass upload from third-party drawings needed from time to time. Once a material has been connected to a mark within a drawing, any new version of the drawing is visible from the material, bill of material, and so on. When a document is used in a purchase requisition or in a production order via a material, a snapshot is generated to keep the version used at that time after a last approval from the drawing office to ensure its validity. These documents are also regulated with watermarks to visually inform users about their status.

The immediate benefits include the availability of documents in their latest version (the only version of the truth), a better integration between SAP processes and documents, improved search capabilities, and accurate purchase and production of spare parts leading to more safety on the rail and cost optimization.

Purchasing Transparency

Fraud detection is critical in the public sector, and it starts with the public tenders for the purchase of goods and/or services. The end-to-end business process needs to be auditable, not only in terms of data and approvals/signatures but also in terms of documents. Purchasers deal with all vendors, from the request for quotation until the invoice. All posted mail documents, emails, and files used need to be classified correctly, need to be secured by using legal holds, and need to be fully integrated with the SAP Business Suite and attached to every business process step (business object), automatically if possible.

When a purchase order is created, it goes through a release strategy with workflow to gather digital signatures from the selected hierarchy printed on the released document. SAP Extended ECM enables every printout of a changed purchase order to generate a new version stored in SAP Extended ECM for better traceability and auditability.

Customer Complaints Handling

Customer complaints are treated by a call center using SAP Customer Relationship Management integrated with web, email, and telephone support. Claim forms on paper are sent to the call center and are scanned. All these documents are linked to activities and stored on the SAP CRM system, leading to capacity and performance issues.

All these documents will be migrated to SAP Extended ECM, using its optical character recognition (OCR) capabilities to automate the processing of a claim form. The new process will provide privacy compliance of customer data to comply with governmental legislation and prescriptions. A business workspace (explained in Chapter 13) will be added to SAP CRM's customer interaction center to provide call center personnel with enhanced document management capabilities.

Intelligent Driver Assistant

Intelligent Driver Assistant is a program that will provide the train driver with legal information on a ruggedized tablet replacing a 20-kg backpack full of paper he has to carry every day to perform daily duties. This business transformation has been initiated by the unions having concerns about the impact of the backpack on the train driver's health and safety.

All documents are managed by SAP Extended ECM, providing version management, approvals for publishing, distribution for offline use, and reading confirmation as the train driver needs to know the latest rules, regulations, and requirements prior to the start of his duty with a specific train on a specific train track. The use of the ruggedized tablet will be extended with applications such as a troubleshooting wizard, time and activity registration, a holiday request e-form, a logbook, a weather channel (on train track conditions) to apply safety measures, an energy performance monitor, access to a corporate web portal, and so on.

Revision and Modernization of Rolling Stock

Revision and modernization are two types of maintenance that are managed by projects, as they involve many sequential and parallel activities with the highest level of quality and within tight schedules. To speed up and ease these activities, the technical worker will access all data and documents related to his activities with a tablet or a kiosk in the field. The accuracy of data and documents is critical to avoid safety breaches and can only be ensured by high-quality data and the latest released version of all related documents. Documents are linked to every project component such as functional location, equipment, bill of material, or material. The authoring and publishing of documents is managed by different offices outside the SAP GUI, the structure is managed by the project team via the SAP GUI, and the consumption is done via SAP Enterprise Portal. When a document is linked to a project component, a snapshot is generated to keep the version used at that time. The same snapshot principle is used for traceability and auditability with SAP Plant Maintenance (PM) notifications and orders. You can use task lists and tasks (master data) where the link to documents is dynamic, providing version management.

Wagon Maintenance Services Compliance with Governmental Legislation

The Belgian Railways Wagon Maintenance Services (WMS) is an entity of maintenance shops with central coordinating services for maintaining train cars not only for Belgian Railways but also for other railways. A web portal provides all other railways companies with accurate information about any maintenance activities, coming from the SAP Business Suite. All documents related to these activities will soon also be available via this portal using SAP Portal Content Management by OpenText (discussed in Chapter 13).

The entity in charge of maintenance needs to comply with the following requirements:

- **It manages the maintenance logbooks and ensures correct implementation.**
  This is done for each vehicle that is registered in the National Register of Vehicles as an entity in charge of maintenance. The correct implementation is ensured by checking that the vehicle is maintained in accordance with its maintenance backlog and requirements force, including the Technical Specifications Interoperability (TSI).
- **It provides traceability of maintenance operations.**
  Traceability is performed on each vehicle by managing and keeping up to date the maintenance reports for each vehicle.
- **It analyzes the lessons learned.**
  These include the data from maintenance, accidents, or incidents to update the owner's maintenance logbook adequately.
- **It informs the owner.**
  It informs the owner of all restrictions and specific operation conditions of the cars.
- **It contracts liability insurance.**
  Insurance covers sufficient financial risks arising from its activities.

Moreover, we need to keep track of 40 years of maintenance logs together with their related documents. This will dramatically increase the storage volume.

Therefore, we used SAP Information Lifecycle Management to define proactive data and document archiving strategies with volume management and (legal) retention management capabilities.

Projects and Resource Portfolio Management

The Belgian Railways IT department is managing, implementing, and supporting many SAP and non-SAP projects. To ensure an efficient follow-up, all documents related to resource management, project planning, project implementation, and project support will be managed by SAP Extended ECM using business workspaces (explained in Chapter 13). This way, documents are accessible not only from a project perspective, but also from a business partner perspective or from a support perspective; for example, they are linked to support tickets created in SAP Solution Manager. The storage of documents with SAP Resource and Portfolio Management (RPM) and cProjects is also done with SAP Extended ECM for a global unification, more functionalities, and better accessibility. Figure 6.8 shows how this works.

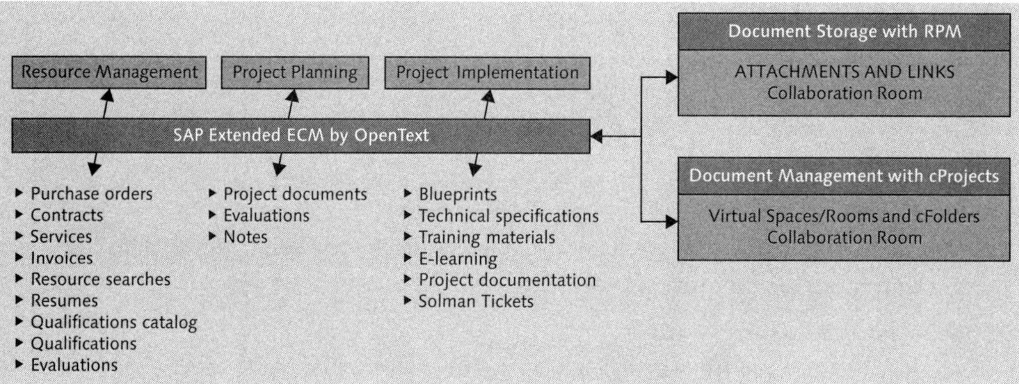

Figure 6.8 Projects and Resource Portfolio Management

Figure 6.8 shows the storing, organizing, and classifying of all project implementation documents, such as blueprints, technical specifications, training materials, project documentation, and SAP Solution Manager tickets. This will also contribute to better business process management when users need to search for relevant information; for example, if they need to locate all contracts related to a particular project. The filing and search capabilities offered by SAP Extended ECM bring significant value with business workspaces' deep integration with the SAP Business

Suite. The workspaces provide team and project rooms, collaboration spaces, forums, and wikis.

Vendor Invoice Management

Prior to SAP Invoice Management by OpenText, purchasing, invoice reception, and accountancy were done at several work locations in Belgium. At that time, there were many lost invoices, double payments, lost discounts, and late payments (above 60 days and sometime up to 1 year). It was not possible to have accurate accruals, and closings were extremely difficult. There was no visibility into costs or vendor performance, as there was no integrated and optimized purchase-to-pay process with clear action at the source to prevent errors.

Then we went live with SAP Invoice Management by OpenText, along with the purchase-to-pay process optimization within the SAP Business Suite. The benefits are paper reduction, central processing within an integrated system, no more backlog, a 67% reduction in time to execute the business process, quality accruals, work distribution, traceability, on-time payments, more effective reporting, cost transparency, and easy closings with high quality.

Our goal is to migrate all scanned invoices to SAP Extended ECM, enabling full text search on all appendices that might contain critical business information. Today, only the invoice financials are optically recognized for efficient processing and to limit license fees per page read. If a purchaser or accounts payable clerk needs to find legal details related to the contract or purchase order within the appendices, he has to go to the MIRO transaction (invoice verification) and read the scanned document attached until he finds the relevant information. Along with the migration, we will provide a business workspace to access documents from a vendor perspective that will grant access to any document within a virtual folder structure generated from purchase requisitions, requests for quotations, contracts, purchase orders, and invoices related to a single vendor. All appendices will go through basic optical character recognition (OCR) to provide full-text indexing and full-text search capabilities. This migration will add more value to the existing vendor invoice management process.

6.6.2 Key Success Factors for Your SAP Extended Enterprise Content Management by OpenText Project

The following outlines key success factors for a successful SAP Extended ECM implementation.

Building a Roadmap

To build a successful roadmap, you first need to select business processes that are already standardized in your SAP Business Suite for which you have the highest number of users and the highest volume of documents, such as SAP Plant Maintenance or SAP Enterprise Asset Management. In parallel, you should select some document processes like the one used in legal services or corporate communication to reach different types of audiences.

Another approach consists of interviewing every business unit, department, plant, and so on to collect information regarding all the document types and associated procedures they are dealing with on a daily basis. The result of these interviews should guide you in trying to standardize their processes.

Project Team Setup

The ideal project team would consist of business analysts, SAP experts, OpenText experts, ECM experts, change management consultants, a system administrator, and a project manager with a strong track record of business process improvement projects.

The ECM experts need to support the role of business analysts to successfully describe the document processes and the way to classify documents at the enterprise level using best practices. The ECM experts set up the governance model to ensure consistency and integrity with the continuous addition of new document types.

The OpenText experts translate the business requirements formulated in the various business blueprints into technical specifications for the configuration of the platform. The OpenText experts need to be consulted at any stage of the blueprint phase to ensure the feasibility of the realization phase and to ensure that standard features are being used.

Change Management

Change management is always a challenge, but it is an even bigger challenge with content management, as you will face the paper syndrome—resistance to change as people try to keep their paper processes as they are today. You may face resistance while converting, cleansing, and migrating your legacy systems and fileservers to the platform, as you will force the use of a unified classification and unique naming conventions for metadata and its possible values. For example, different units or departments working on the same set of data and documents have different ways to classify data and have different naming conventions. A specific example is drawings (2D/3D designs) provided by the drawing office used for purchasing for maintenance operations and for production.

You might also meet user disappointment at the go-live stage in some cases. For example, SAP Invoice Management by OpenText means no more paper invoices. Vendor invoices with their scanned images are distributed through the organization via SAP Business Workflow. This is a big change for people used to an In bin and Out bin from which they could see the work done at the end of the day.

You will also face people printing documents for approval without using the defined workflows. Don't forget to perform your paper reduction strategy by removing printers and copiers from time to time and replacing them with controlled mail/fax rooms.

You will need strong sponsorship and patience to articulate the change even if empowered from the top. However, the different user interface options fully integrated with SAP Extended ECM will help you achieve good user adoption by selecting the right user interface for the right audience: An accounts payable clerk uses the SAP GUI to perform invoice verification, a purchaser uses Microsoft Outlook to manage all vendor correspondence in a purchase process, a technical worker accesses documents in plant maintenance orders using SAP Enterprise Portal, a customer service professional dispatches all customer complaints from a business workspace in the SAP CRM Customer Interaction Center, a legal expert manages records using Microsoft Windows Explorer, and so on. (User interface options with SAP Extended ECM are covered in Chapter 13.)

In the first stage of your roadmap, you'll need to limit the rollout to basic functionalities such as version management and workflow to avoid uncontrolled resistance. People have to abandon the paper culture before you give them functionalities such as forums, collaboration spaces, and wikis.

Governance

You need to set up governance that controls the cohesion and consistency at functional and technical levels. It defines a set of guidelines for the correct use of the platform. Governance spans from governing the portfolio and project prioritization through governance on operational issues, from the updating of models through the help desk experience. The goals of the governance program included reducing administrative overhead, ensuring conformity to regulations, and ensuring a single platform for a single version of the truth.

Once SAP Extended ECM was implemented, its document controls were used to govern content approvals, check in/out, version control, and other document maintenance tasks.

Additionally, governance had to extend to governing the content itself. This included:

- Types of information
- Communication channels
- Establishing what document is the working copy
- Naming requirements
- Multilingualism
- Content templates

There is also governance on configuration such as the folder structure (for example, not more than three levels that will be freely defined) and information metadata.

The governance program increased predictability and the quality of results, reflecting business terminology, creation of name standardization and clarity of reuse of naming, and coordination within a larger architecture as an element of communication between platforms and ensuring correct access for multiple target groups.

The governance guidelines for the architecture included standardization of integration, standardized functionality, and use of standard user interfaces. Included were guidelines for operations; for example, all master data must come from SAP, and global master data must be managed centrally. The governance board was defined at a strategic level, and the governance team was defined at an operational level.

This section has introduced SAP Extended ECM including specific use cases and the value of using SAP Extended ECM. More information on the details of SAP Extended ECM, including business workspaces, is covered in Chapter 13.

Note

You can connect with others involved in enterprise content management by joining the ECM LinkedIn community: *http://www.linkedin.com/groups?gid=3874677.*

Next, we discuss recommendations for creating an archiving strategy.

6.7 Recommendations for Creating an Archiving Strategy

Archiving data is usually the last thing anyone thinks about during an SAP implementation. All of the focus early in an SAP project is usually directed at business process chains, such as sales or procurement processing, and not much attention is paid to retention policies or retirement of data. However, data archiving is just as important as any other process in an SAP system. Eventually, all of those documents and transactions are going to have to be removed from the database. Executing well-defined data archiving projects should be an important part of your overall enterprise information management strategy.

6.7.1 What Drives a Company into Starting a Data Archiving Project?

There are several reasons companies execute data archiving projects. These reasons have changed: It started with *disk drive costs* in the 1990s and then moved to *system performance* gained by the removal of data no longer required. As time progressed, SAP provided support for the *Euro* as well as support for *UNICODE*. The Euro and UNICODE upgrades required converting a lot of data from all of those previous transactions that still resided in the database. Data archiving was used to reduce the amount of data in the database that needed to be converted and shorten the *system down time*.

Legal compliance and *records management requirements* are also major drivers for data archiving. Many companies have records retention policies that specify a life span for business transactions and other data. These policies mandate that expired data be removed from the database and destroyed. As many SAP implementations are now maturing past the retention policies, this is becoming a very common reason for initiating a data archiving project.

Note

SAP Information Lifecycle Management (hereafter SAP ILM) supports both retention policy management and archiving. SAP ILM is discussed in Chapter 12.

We're approaching a new era with SAP HANA. Starting with business warehouses, SAP HANA will transform the performance of those systems, and it will be important to start your migration with a lean system and not retain data that is unnecessary to your business units. You will want to include archiving in your overall SAP HANA strategy.

While the reasons just discussed are examples of a real need to archive, the best time to start your archiving project is when you are first implementing the system. At this time you have the resources engaged to define an entire archiving strategy. If you didn't do that, don't feel bad. You are not alone. Most archiving projects are started well after the deployment teams have dispersed.

Next, we discuss recommendations for getting started with an archiving project.

6.7.2 Who Initiates a Data Archiving Project?

Archiving projects are rarely initiated by the business. The business experts want as much data as possible in the system. Data is value—that's their motive.

The legal department may initiate an archiving project to eliminate risk. If your organization has been live on SAP long enough that documents or transactions are approaching the expiration date per your records retention schedule (you do have one, don't you?), the legal department may approach the IT department and query about your archiving policy. You'll want to be ready for this conversation. So, why would legal worry about archiving so much? Many companies have been sued for a variety of reasons—say, for instance, unfair business transactions. The courts have ordered that the defendant (in this case, your company) must turn over all records pertaining to the case. If you have a retention schedule of say, seven years, and you have not archived any data in the twelve years since your SAP system has been live, you could be forced into turning over much more data than you would have had to if you expunged your records per your retention schedule.

Database administrators are usually the first to inquire about archiving data from the database. They are on the front line and are the first to see the impact of a database that is too large. They look at data archiving from a strictly technical sense. The database administrator's motivations are directly opposite the business units. They use tools such as transaction codes to analyze the size of the tables in the database. They use this as one of the inputs to monitor the health of the database.

Your SAP development teams may also initiate an archiving project because they have been educated by webcasts or user group seminars such as ASUG or DSAG, or maybe they've read some consulting company white papers on archiving SAP best practices. Or it may be a line item or subproject in a conversion or upgrade initiative.

The important take away from this conversation is that you *need* an archiving strategy in your systems roadmap. Be sure to have that 30-second elevator speech ready when your CIO pops the question about your archiving strategy.

6.7.3 Project Sponsorship

As with any project, you will need sponsorship; a data archiving project requires a very strong sponsor. It's not one of those glamorous projects like customer relationship management, supplier relationship management, or any of the other enhance capabilities projects, but it is just as important because it has all of the key project components—risk, expense, and scope. Each of these will be explained next.

Risk

All projects have risk, but an archiving project carries a little more than most projects you may have done in the past. A well-managed data archiving project manages risk at every project milestone. You'll want to evaluate the risk and put a mitigation plan in place for each major milestone in your project plan. For instance, during the project initiation phase, you may notice that there isn't a lot of participation in the project. Don't underestimate the impact on your project when team members don't show up for meetings or think this project is a minor distraction in their day. This is where you need that strong sponsor mentioned above. All team members should be fully engaged.

Another risk is the impact you will be imposing on the business units. After all, you're changing the way they access and use their data. Depending upon your retrieval and/or display plans, you may have to do some significant retraining. There may also be data that will no longer be included in reports. You will need to plan for this training in your change management portion of the project.

Expense

An archiving project can be as expensive as you make it. Depending on the reason you have initiated the project, this is a highly variable figure. If you are planning extensive archiving, then you will most certainly benefit by utilizing consultants to help you along the way. You may need to procure a storage platform for your archive files, whether that resides physically in your data center or, more recently, in the cloud. Depending on your retrieval/display requirements, you may or may not need an external content server. Archiving to a file system is completely supported within SAP but usually not implemented in common practice. Most companies utilize an external content server, especially when implementing SAP Information Lifecycle Management.

You'll want to make sure that you have done your homework during the planning stages of the project and ensure that you manage your project budget accordingly. Of course, the scope of the project will be the key variable that will impact the cost of the project.

Scope

So you've decided to start the inevitable archiving project. What's next?

The previous section stated many reasons you may choose to, or need to, execute an archiving project. The reason will be a major determining factor on how your project will be structured. For instance, there are two methodologies for setting the timeline of a project: left to right and right to left.

- **Left to right planning**
  When setting the schedule of a project, classic project management tells us to carefully plan each step, determine the availability of the required resources, determine the required amount of time needed for each task, sequence the steps and add any dependencies, and finally derive the end date of the project from the resulting Gantt chart. This is often called left to right planning, as the timeline is a direct result of the careful analysis of each step as well as the input received from the expert resources you've consulted for each task.

- **Right to left planning**
  This is when you are forced into an end date as a result of an uncontrolled deadline. In this method, you start with an end date and then work your way back to the left until you get to the present day. Here's an example of this with respect to archiving: It was back in 1997, and we were approaching a top limit of our database just two short years after our go-live. If we didn't immediately reduce the size of the database by archiving, the SAP system we just rolled out was going to come to a complete halt because of a size limitation of the database. Another example might be if you are going to archive because you are planning an upgrade, and that upgrade project requires a lot of data conversion. If you can reduce the amount of data to be converted, you can reduce the system downtime during the data conversion step. Right to left planning can work, but you better do your homework first. There are a lot of opportunities for that unexpected pitfall that will set you back.

So again, why are you doing your archiving project? There are other factors that are part of your project planning as a result of the reason for archiving data. If you're archiving because of a performance problem, then you must first analyze where the problem exists. Are your business users in the sales department complaining about customer programs running slow because of all those billing documents? Are you a retail shop and your material movement documents are slowing you down? (SAP retail systems can generate a tremendous amount of data, and archiving should be considered during your initial blueprinting.) These kinds of questions will help you determine the resources you'll require to bring your project to a successful end.

Resourcing Your Project

To staff your project, you'll need people from the applications that are most impacted (for example, when archiving financial information), but who else will you require to be an active part of the team?

Some choices are obvious: system administrator, database administrator, business expert for the application areas, legal department, tax specialist, project manager, and data warehouse expert. Other recommended project team members may not be as obvious: training, communication, and documentation specialists. These team members are also needed to ensure that users understand the changes that will impact them after the data has been archived. Reports will look different, transactions may look different, and the end users need to understand how they will be impacted by the archiving project.

6.8 Summary

This chapter has provided many real-world examples of using SAP's EIM solutions for specific business needs, and has discussed recommendations for getting started as well as the benefits of EIM.

Now that you have a basic understanding of the concepts of EIM, the EIM solutions offered by SAP, and some real-world examples, Part II of the book covers more details on the specific technical components of EIM in SAP.

PART II
Working with SAP's Enterprise Information Management Solutions

This chapter introduces SAP PowerDesigner as a modeling and design-time metadata management platform for information management designs.

7 SAP PowerDesigner

All enterprises today are or will be faced with a transformative event, such as regulation changes, merger and acquisition activity, or enablement of new business models from new technologies (e.g., cloud and in-memory). You need to be able to treat information as a corporate asset to succeed with such business transformation. This chapter focuses on the discipline of enterprise information architecture (EIA) as part of SAP Enterprise Information Management (EIM), and how tools such as SAP PowerDesigner, a modeling and design-time metadata management platform, enable you to understand your current information landscape, align business information with technical implementation, and plan for change.

Architecture is about planning for, designing, and executing change. SAP PowerDesigner (hereafter PowerDesigner)'s value is best realized when we use the current state information models, captured and documented in the tool, to help us plan the next generation business. Transformation needs a plan, and designing future state versions of data models, aligned to the current conceptual data model (CDM) and business glossary, ensures we make a united step forward in any step along the way.

Adding technical details in logical data models (LDMs) and physical data models (PDMs), together with specialized analytics models, ensures that we can communicate details to the responsible database development teams. PowerDesigner's unique Link and Sync technology streamlines impact analysis and design-time change management, reducing the time, cost, and risk associated with change.

In this chapter, we'll explore enterprise information architecture, including the different model types, the core components of each, and how they work together to make a complete view of information for designers. This chapter will also cover how the repository helps with tasks such as managing model-to-model dependencies and impact analysis. You'll learn the value that architecting, or planning, provides to all organizations that are faced with managing complex change in information systems.

7.1 SAP PowerDesigner in the SAP Landscape

PowerDesigner provides architecture and modeling capabilities to all organizations and is uniquely integrated into many SAP products. PowerDesigner is integrated with SAP Business Suite and the SAP HANA Cloud Platform (HCP). Within the EIM landscape, PowerDesigner is integrated with SAP Information Steward (hereafter Information Steward), SAP BusinessObjects, and SAP Replication Server (hereafter Replication Server). PowerDesigner is also a key element of Intelligent Business Operations powered by SAP.

7.1.1 SAP Business Suite

PowerDesigner can connect to the SAP Business Suite and create a PDM representing the data dictionary by reading the business and technical metadata from SAP Business Suite. This is very useful when looking at SAP Business Suite as the standard definition for any homemade applications built around common data sets, or for when preparing for an enterprise data warehouse and extracting data from SAP Business Suite to populate the warehouse as one of the key sources.

7.1.2 SAP HANA Cloud Platform

SAP HANA has a repository that's used for the development and implementation of data structures that is optimized for helping developers get the most out of SAP HANA's unique in-memory capability. PowerDesigner can write to the SAP HANA repository or read from it. Reading the SAP HANA repository creates or updates a PDM in PowerDesigner. PowerDesigner can also take a PDM that includes SAP HANA-specific attribute and analytic views and create new, or merge with existing, repository objects.

7.1.3 SAP Information Steward, SAP BusinessObjects Universes, and Replication

PowerDesigner's repository is read by Information Steward, enabling people to read metadata from PowerDesigner's PDMs, LDMs, and CDMs. This allows all the known metadata, both operational and architectural, to be visible to the data steward as he manages the quality of information sources in operation.

PowerDesigner's dimensional diagram can create SAP BusinessObjects universes. PowerDesigner can read a universe and create a new, or merge with an existing, dimensional diagram.

PowerDesigner can reverse engineer Replication Server's catalog to create or merge with an existing data movement model. This data movement model can generate new replication definitions. Special patterns exist to streamline use cases of replication and SAP Data Services (Data Services) together to implement real-time loading and other scenarios.

7.2 Defining and Describing Business Information with the Enterprise Glossary

An enterprise glossary helps everyone define and describe information assets and related technology. It lists business terms in business language, independent of any data characteristics. One term can relate to multiple data items (atomic data elements), and a data item can have multiple terms associated with it.

Example

NeedsEIM Inc. defines its information model to have a customer entity that can have a customer address attribute, which is combining the terms *customer* and *address* together to make up its name.

In PowerDesigner, the enterprise glossary is a global service provided by the repository that is available to all users. It contains all terms, synonyms, and related terms, grouped by nested term categories. A glossary term identifies the term (NAME) and provides a standard abbreviation for the term (CODE) and a definition (DESCRIPTION). The glossary term will be created within a category folder (CATEGORY) and may also be further defined in an external system and referenced via a URL (REFERENCE URL). As you can see in Figure 7.1 in the next subsection, the business term "commission" is defined, and every time the word commission appears in the design (such as a table or column name), the standard abbreviation of "CMSN" will be used in the name. You can also see that this term is approved in the STATUS box, so you know it's the right definition for this term.

PowerDesigner's glossary is meant to be a direct reflection of the business glossary in Information Steward. Information Steward is used to capture, define, and manage the glossary terms and relate them to the metadata of operational systems, while in PowerDesigner, the same terms can be imported and then used to standardize names for all new information assets that are defined in any model.

7.2.1 Glossary Terms for Naming Standards Enforcement

Using a common business language ensures that when users collaborate across business units, or outside the company, they're all using the same concepts in the same way. This is a critical part of establishing enterprise information architecture and a key component of any data dictionary. The enterprise glossary (see Figure 7.1) can be used to manage naming standards for all design models in PowerDesigner. The NAME field is used for name lookup, and any name that matches a term is linked to that term. If there are any aliases associated, when you begin to type the alias, PowerDesigner detects the use of an alias and indicates that there is a preferred term to use in lieu of the alias. This helps establish the enterprise use of the preferred term and further increases understandability and readability of all models as everyone will be using the standard terms.

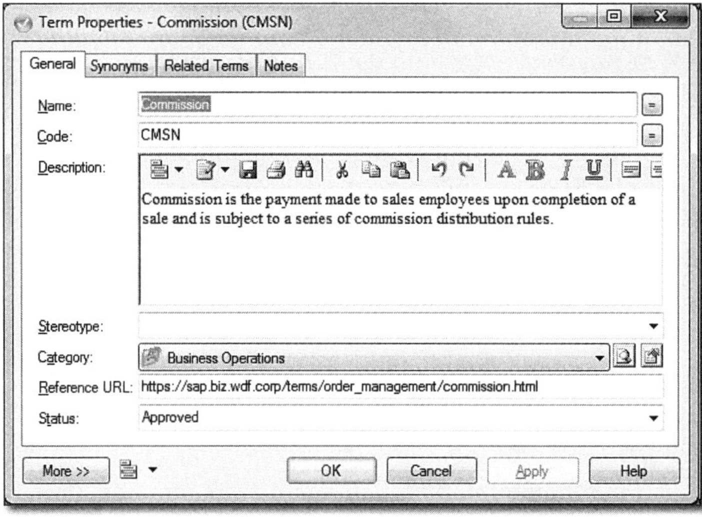

Figure 7.1 A Glossary Term in SAP PowerDesigner

7.2.2 Naming Standards Definitions

PowerDesigner can be configured to use the glossary to ensure all names used throughout a model are found within the list of terms. To configure PowerDesigner to use the enterprise glossary, follow these steps:

1. Select Tools • Model Options, and then select Naming Convention.
2. Check Enable glossary for autocompletion and compliance checking.
3. Select the Name to Code tab, and set Conversion Table to glossary terms.

You can combine multiple terms into one name (e.g., "Customer Address" using terms "Customer" and "Address").

You can also enable automatic conversions of names to implementation concept Code values. In PowerDesigner, the Name field is the business language descriptor, while the Code field represents the name used for the object when converted into any sort of implementation code (e.g., when used in a `CREATE TABLE` statement).

7.3 The Conceptual Data Model

PowerDesigner supports the definition of a CDM. For an organization to treat information as a corporate asset, all information sources should be derived from a common definition, or a core concept. A CDM is meant to model a single definition of any data asset, independent of both the storage paradigm (relational, hierarchical) and the physical characteristics of the systems that will ultimately store them.

The enterprise CDM also represents the sum of all use cases for a given data concept. Any entity defined in the enterprise CDM will have all the attributes needed for all processes or all applications. For example, the enterprise CDM entity for customer will have all attributes together, whether used for order, relationship, support management, and more; while LDMs and PDMs that represent the individual systems will have their own subset of these attributes. This will help ensure that any attributes that are shared between implementations follow a common standard and will reduce the impedance mismatches found when you later need to integrate these data sets together.

Let's review the core components of an enterprise CDM by looking at elements, attributes, data items, and domains in the following sections.

7.3.1 Conceptual Data Elements, Attributes, and Data Items

PowerDesigner manages enterprise CDM concepts such as entities, attributes, data items, and domains. These four concepts make up the core of the CDM, and we'll discuss them in more detail in the following subsections.

Entities

Entities are structured elements that define a core business concept that you need to keep account of, such as product, customer, or delivery. Anything the business as a whole needs to account for and keep records of should be represented by an entity in the CDM. A CDM's entity should represent a single global view of all possible attributes that the concept may need for any given use case or business process.

Attributes and Data Items

In PowerDesigner, entity *attributes* and *data items* are separate but tightly related concepts. Data items in PowerDesigner represent a unique data cell—a single value of a specific type for a specific purpose. Examples of data items are Customer Name, Delivery Date, Product Description, or Phone Number.

Because data items exist independent of the entity attributes they represent, you can use them as a data dictionary, or list of all atomic data managed in the enterprise. This list of data items, or the data dictionary, is useful to communicate with the data stewards to ensure you have the right definition for the data independent of any use in an entity or any physical implementation in a database.

Entity attributes are a relationship, or link, between an entity and a data item. For example, when the Customer entity is related to the Customer Name data item, the Customer entity will have an attribute called Customer Name. Any changes made to the data Item will be reflected in the attribute as well.

Domains

Domains provide another level of data standardization. A domain is a named set of common data characteristics for any number of data items (and therefore all attributes using that data item). For example, a domain called Name can define the data type, length, and other common characteristics of any name type of data item in the model. Anything using "Name" (e.g., Product Name, Customer Name, or Company Name) that is also using the Name domain will share this common characteristic. The key difference between a domain and a data item in PowerDesigner is that the data item is a direct representation of an attribute on one or more entities and carries a name representing a cell of information, while the domain is a common set of data characteristics used by one or more data items and doesn't represent a cell of information itself, just its common structural characteristics.

7.3.2 Separation of Domains, Data Items, and Entity Attributes

The key advantages to this separation of entities, data items, and domains are freedom of expression and improved standardization.

Domains standardize common data characteristics for any information you need to manage for the business, regardless of what you call it. This ensures a consistent use of data structures for all attributes that are of a common concept, such as money, name, or phone number. When data items follow a common standard domain like this, comparing and integrating data is a lot easier. You won't need to create complex transformation code to make the two different data elements match in form and structure, so you can get right to comparing values.

7.3.3 Entity Relationships

The enterprise CDM would not be complete without the relationships that are defined between the entities. The CDM is essentially an Entity-Relationship Diagram (ERD). The relationships between the entities complete the understanding of the business data the CDM represents. There are two major types of relationships in the CDM: the ones that represent how two entities are connected to each other, and the ones that represent entities that are, in essence, a specialization of another.

Relationships that represent the connections between two entities carry cardinality; that is, the frequency of the instances of each side. You can define relationships of cardinality types zero- or one-to-many, many-to-many, and one-to-one (see Figure 7.2, showing a one-to-many between CUSTOMER and ORDER and a many-to-many between ITEMS and ORDER). Relationships representing a supertype/subtype, also known as an "is-a" relationship, may also be defined in the CDM using the inheritance object. When you define an inheritance, or "is-a" relationship, all attributes of the parent are available attributes of each child.

To define a relationship in PowerDesigner, use the RELATIONSHIP tool from the tool palette. Follow these steps:

1. Select the RELATIONSHIP tool, click on one of the entities, and drag to the second entity to link.
2. To change the cardinality settings, double-click on the relationship line, and you can change the following:
   - CARDINALITIES, ONE TO MANY, MANY TO MANY, or ONE TO ONE
   - The ROLE NAME (in both directions) to label the relationship, typically with a verb
   - MANDATORY (on each end), determining whether a parent can exist without any children or not, and whether a child can exist without a parent, or not

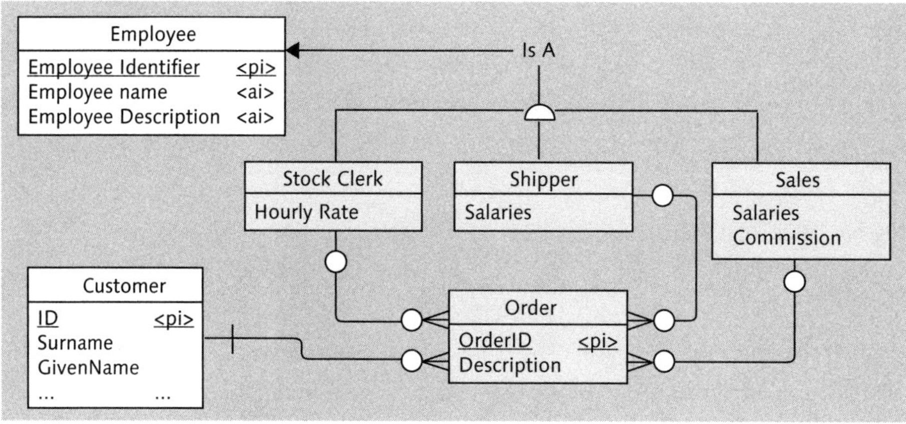

Figure 7.2 An Example CDM

7.3.4 Best Practices for Building and Maintaining an Enterprise CDM

Business details are discovered over time, not all at once. The definitions of business terms evolve as the business evolves. New terms are discovered, old terms obsoleted, and existing terms redefined. In the following subsections, we'll discuss what to keep in mind when defining an enterprise CDM.

Version Terms and the Enterprise CDM

Different versions of the enterprise CDM will be attributed to different projects at different stages in their lifecycle. You can do this in PowerDesigner by setting up a configuration in the repository. Configurations are defined in the REPOSITORY menu, under CONFIGURATIONS. You can create a new configuration and then add specific model versions to it from a select list. Using a PowerDesigner configuration, you can indicate which specific versions of the enterprise CDM are related to which versions of the logical and physical models representing projects and implemented systems.

Don't Overload a Single Concept

Let each data item represent a single concept. For example, break address concepts into their lowest levels of detail (street number, street name, city, etc.). You do this manually in PowerDesigner by creating additional data items for the more granular elements and removing the complex one. This way, the language that's used to identify the data item and the meaning of the information it represents will be crisp and clear.

Keep Definitions Granular

If you need too many examples and too many sentences to describe a single business information concept, then it may be too complex for a single entity or data item to represent it. You should consider simplifying the concept to a common denominator or finding some way to separate it into multiple discrete concepts. In PowerDesigner, you simply create additional entities and attributes to define these more granular concepts.

Use Synonyms Where Possible

Make sure a common concept shares a common language. Assign synonyms to a common term in the enterprise glossary so that the preferred term is always known. You do this in PowerDesigner by double-clicking the term in the glossary browser and selecting the SYNONYMS tab. Any word you enter in the SYNONYMS list will be an alternate term defining the same concept as the term itself (now known as the preferred term). This way, you don't confuse a different name as something with a completely different concept.

Keep Obsolete Concepts

If you have a concept that's no longer needed, it's better to leave the definition in the enterprise CDM, marked as obsolete. You can do this in PowerDesigner by unchecking the GENERATE checkbox, which prevents the concept from moving forward into LDMs and PDMs. This way, any new concepts that are similar won't reuse the old terms and entities, but create new ones. This ensures that there will be no future confusion with older systems using the original definition of that concept.

Don't Redefine and Reuse

This complements the idea that you should keep obsolete concepts around. If something has really changed enough that the definition of the concept deviates from the original idea, then a new term, new data item, or new entity should be defined, and the original one should be kept around for legacy reasons. In PowerDesigner, you can mark the old term as LEGACY in the STEREOTYPE field, and uncheck the GENERATE checkbox. A good test of this is whether the original concept fits within the new definition, or whether the data sets managed by the concept would have to be deliberately segregated to keep them understood.

7.4 Detailing Information Systems with Logical and Physical Data Models

The PowerDesigner LDM and PDM represent the Relational Database Management Systems (RDBMSs) that implement the data concepts from the enterprise CDM. These models differ fundamentally from the enterprise CDM in three key ways: scope, structure, and technical considerations.

7.4.1 Scope

LDMs and PDMs are slivers of the enterprise, representing a specific subset of the concept to be implemented. These models represent a given functional area of the business and their one or more physical databases. While the enterprise CDM has a single "namespace"—a name can only be used once for the entire enterprise CDM—the logical and physical layers allow for multiple namespaces, each one constrained by a given system boundary.

Example

In identifying and managing customer metadata, NeedsEIM Inc. creates an entity for the customer concept that has all attributes, including customer name, address, gender, age range, income bracket, and more. The LDM for the order-to-cash functional area will only take the name and address attributes. A completely separate LDM for customer relationship management will take only the demographic attributes.

LDMs and PDMs design information structures within a given storage paradigm. When targeting an RDBMS, the LDM represents the relational structures and includes relational concepts such as migrated foreign keys. The PDM adds the vendor- and version-specific RDBMS details such as physical data types, triggers and procedures, and more. Other types of LDMs exist, such as a hierarchical representation in canonical data models (XML structures) or an object-oriented representation targeting object-oriented systems design.

7.4.2 Structure and Technical Considerations

LDMs and PDMs contain structure definitions that have nothing to do with business data definitions, and everything to do with technical considerations for implementation. As shown in Figure 7.3, details such as foreign keys to define how relationships will be stored, or link entities storing the keys of many-to-many relationships are foreign to the business; they have no meaning when trying to understand a business concept. PDMs may involve denormalizing; for example, combining multiple tables or duplicating columns in more than one table to reduce the number of joins needed in a query and improve application performance.

The LDM helps us prepare for physical implementation, and represents the data structures for a given functional area. It may represent multiple databases, from multiple vendor/version RDBMSs. The PDM is an abstraction from the actual details of a physical implementation and is useful for application designers and developers to know what information is available. The PDM is there to develop the actual database and adds details such as indexes, views, referential integrity constraints, triggers, stored procedures, and more.

Each PDM is tightly related to a specific relational database vendor and version and is intended to be a 1:1 representation of the actual physical database. The PDM can be created by reverse engineering an existing running database. Any PDM can be used to generate new Data Definition Language (DDL) files to create a new database, or can be compared to an existing database to update using DDL and Data Movement Language (DML) to change the schema while keeping the existing data in place.

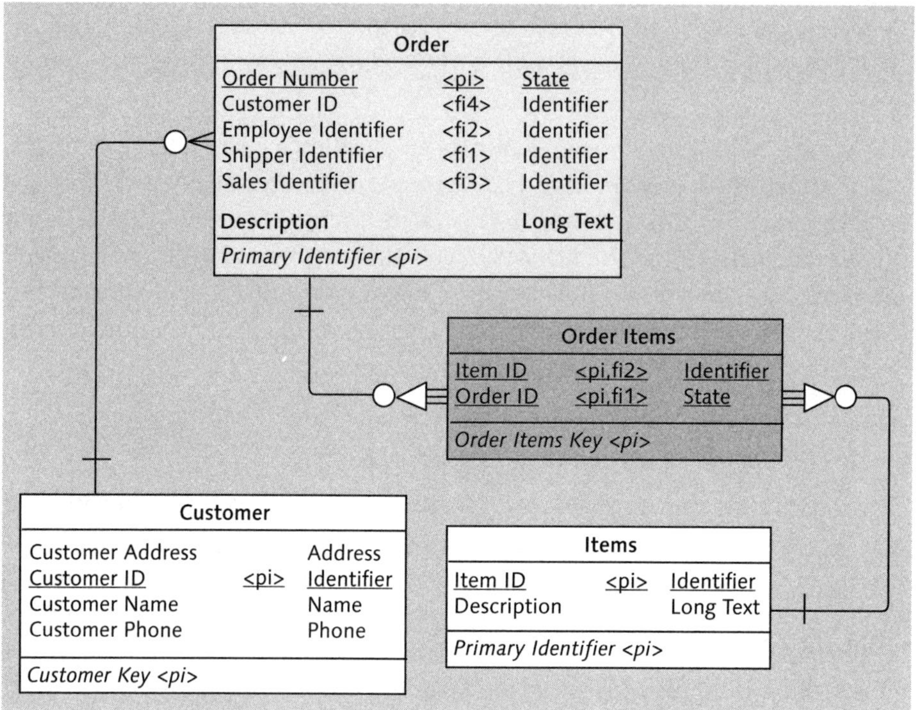

Figure 7.3 Logical Data Model with Migrated Foreign Keys

7.5 Canonical Data Models, XML Structures, and Other Datastores

Enterprise information architecture goes beyond relational databases and includes information in all structures within the enterprise. One common representation of information in nonrelational structures is the XML formatted messages used to communicate between systems. XML Schema Definitions (XSDs) represent the messages and the message structure.

PowerDesigner has a special XML model, shown in Figure 7.4, that represents an XSD directly and can map that model to one or more PDMs to show where the data in messages is read from or written to.

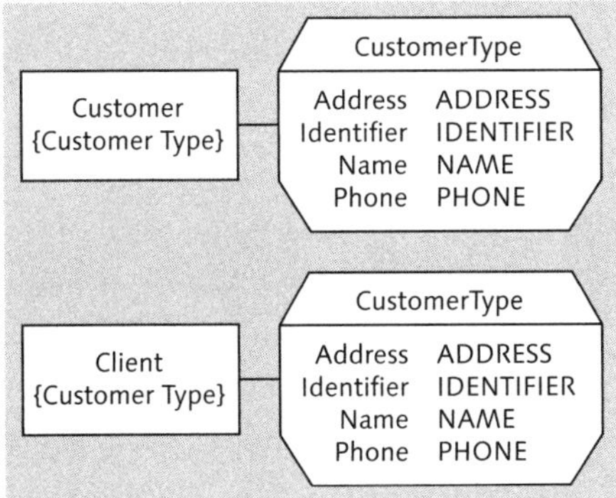

Figure 7.4 XML Model in SAP PowerDesigner showing complex type reuse

Many organizations have worked to standardize the structures of message formats by using a Canonical Data Model, which is an XML model that gathers all the elements of all the messages together and creates a series of XML complex types to define commonly reused data structures. This Canonical Data Model is a sort of data dictionary for the messages themselves.

In PowerDesigner, mappings can be created between the complex type definitions and the data model representing how message content can be stored in one or more physical databases (see Figure 7.5).

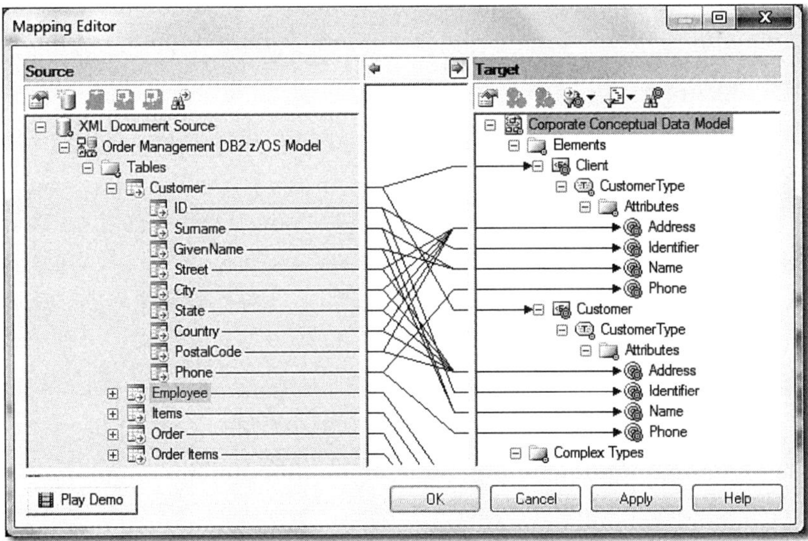

Figure 7.5 XML Model Mappings with a PDM

Use the MAPPING EDITOR from the TOOLS menu to define mappings. Then, create the mapping definitions by dragging the data elements from the left dropping them to the XML structures on the right.

In PowerDesigner, you can also create a library of commonly reused complex types and then use shortcuts to reuse these in any number of XML models representing different sets of messages. To do this, create a new XML model in PowerDesigner, and either reverse engineer an existing XSD with the complex types defined, or use the palette to create new complex types in the model. When you check the model into the repository, click the ADVANCED button, and select LIBRARY in the FOLDER option.

7.6 Data Warehouse Modeling: Movement and Reporting

When you start trying to define and describe the data warehouse and business analytics systems, you need to understand data in motion between source systems and analytics stores. You also want to know the relationship between analytics systems and the underlying data warehouse database. This helps ensure that you've identified the right data sources, that you can answer the business questions needed to help in decision making, and that you know what parts of the system will be affected when changes happen to any given component of the environment.

PowerDesigner data mappings are captured using the MAPPING EDITOR for easy, drag-and-drop identification of the dependencies between transactional systems and analytics systems. Follow these steps:

1. Select MAPPING EDITOR from the TOOLS menu. If this is the first time you've started the MAPPING EDITOR, you'll be prompted to complete a wizard to identify the sources for the mappings.
2. You may identify one or more PDMs to represent the source for the data warehouse or master datastore.
3. Create mappings by dragging a source data element (table or column) from the left-hand side to the destination (table or column) on the right. You can also define mappings between an enterprise data warehouse and a series of data marts.

PowerDesigner table definitions allow you to mark mappings as a FACT or DIMENSION. To do this, go to the GENERAL tab, and select the option from the DIMENSIONAL

TYPE dropdown. At the physical table level, this helps report designers know what tables contain the different types information, which ones represents things the business will measure, and the variables by which we partition them.

In PowerDesigner, you may select MULTIDIMENSIONAL OBJECTS, RETRIEVE MULTIDIMENSIONAL OBJECTS from the TOOLS menu and automatically detect the dimension type based on key structures of each table. For tables that have a compound primary key made up of foreign keys migrated from other tables, the logic determines that it's a likely fact table, and for all other key structures, the table is determined to be a dimension.

Dimensional Modeling

In PowerDesigner, dimensional models represent the analytic reports themselves. The dimensional model is a graphical representation of fact and dimension objects. As shown in Figure 7.6, fact objects represent one or more fact tables coming together to make a single fact concept. Dimension objects represent the dimension tables collapsed into a simpler representation, complete with multiple hierarchies representing drill-up and drill-down opportunities within the attributes.

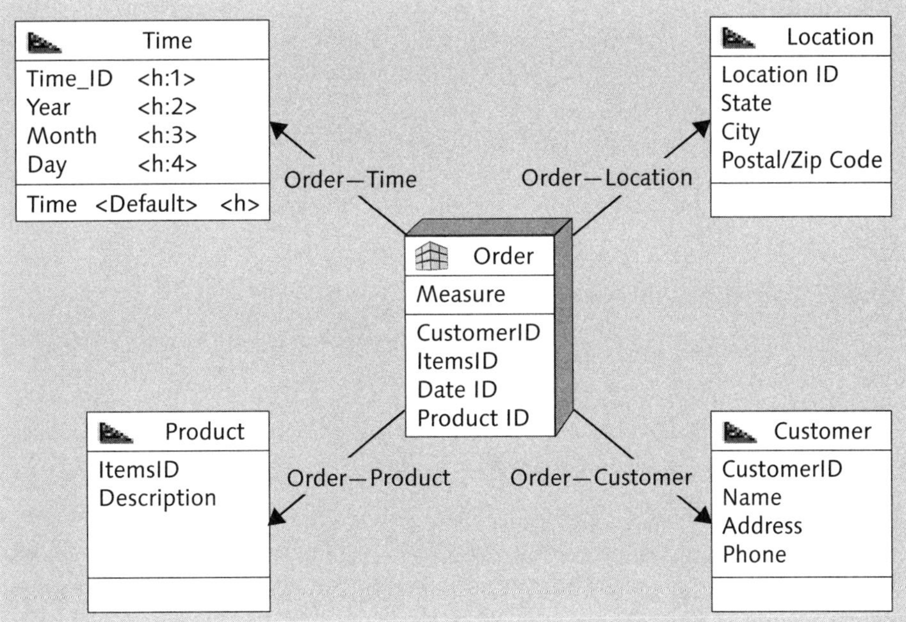

Figure 7.6 Dimensional Model with Facts, Dimensions, and Hierarchies

These models are created either by selecting NEW DIMENSIONAL DIAGRAM from the PDM's context menu, or running the wizard from TOOLS • MULTIDIMENSIONAL OBJECTS • GENERATE CUBE.

Note

While it's useful to mark tables as fact and dimension in order to identify where in the database the structures for analytics systems will likely be finding information, it's not a description of a specific report.

7.7 Link and Sync for Impact Analysis and Change Management

PowerDesigner uses the dependencies that are tracked and managed between models to help facilitate impact analysis and change management. This is known as PowerDesigner's Link and Sync technology. This allows CDMs, LDMs, and PDMs to remain synchronized through iterations of change without requiring designers, architects, and developers to redo their work.

Link and Sync captures the cross-domain dependencies, such as data used by a process step or flow, or the applications that access certain data assets. You can show all business tasks and all applications that interact with enterprise data.

In the following sections, we'll discuss how PowerDesigner can be used to create links between any objects in any models, and how it automatically manages model-to-model synchronization through the model generation engine.

7.7.1 Link and Sync Technology

From the name, you see that Link and Sync has two parts: the Link part and the Sync part.

Linking

Linking is when a modeler recognizes a dependency between any two things in PowerDesigner and creates the link. You can create links between any PowerDesigner model, including models that aren't directly used for data modeling but found in information and enterprise architecture, such as the requirements model or the business process model. Linking between such models happens naturally for the most part; for example, attaching a list of data elements to a process.

When you define a CRUD matrix in a PowerDesigner Business Process Model (BPM) referencing data in a CDM, you're creating links. When you create any type of dependency by drawing a reference, relationship, or inheritance, you're creating a link. You can also create links by opening any object's property sheet, going to the TRACEABILITY LINKS tab, and clicking the NEW button to select any object in any model.

You also establish links when binding requirements to any object through the requirements traceability matrix. This is easily done in PowerDesigner by simply opening the requirements traceability matrix, selecting any empty cell, and pressing the [Space] bar. To remove a link, select a cell that contains a checkmark (identifying the presence of a link), and press the [Space] bar. You can create dependencies between any two objects in PowerDesigner using the dependencies matrix, which looks and operates nearly identically to the requirements traceability matrix, but can be established between any two objects, in the same or in different models. To create a new dependency matrix, simply select NEW TRACEABILITY MATRIX from the model's pop-up menu in the object browser, and specify the object types to use for the rows and columns. You can also select which attribute will be used to identify the link, if more than one way to combine these objects is possible (e.g., reference or inheritance on an entity in a CDM).

Synching

The synchronizing part in PowerDesigner Link and Sync is when one model is generated from another. PowerDesigner keeps track of the transformed objects and their source. When you generate a model from another (for example, when creating a PDM from an LDM), the sync technology remembers everything. If you then make changes to the original model, the second generation isn't a new creation of a new PDM, but a write into the existing one generated the first time. Sync technology publishes only the changes made in the LDM since the last generation. This way, any changes made to the PDM in areas not affected by the LDM change will be preserved.

To initiate a synch process, use the model generator from the TOOLS menu. For example, to synchronize an LDM to a PDM, open the LDM first, and select

Generate Physical Data Model from the Tools menu. This initiates the sync compare and presents you the Compare/Merge dialog. After accepting the changes you want to synchronize, PowerDesigner automatically applies them to the selected PDM and opens the PDM model when complete.

PowerDesigner's Merge Models dialog, shown in Figure 7.7, allows you to manually override any preserved changes if needed, simply by checking the empty checkbox next to the detected difference. This is sometimes useful when implementation starts to deviate too far from the original concept, and a reset in a precise area is needed to get the database design back on track.

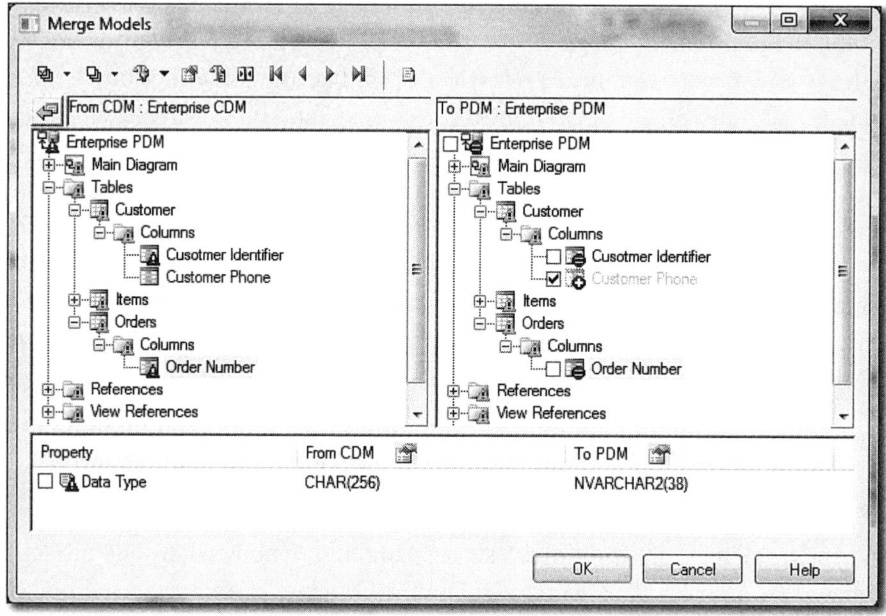

Figure 7.7 Compare/Merge Showing Preserved Differences

Synchronization ensures that models derived from each other remain aware of each other and that dependencies can be tracked at the smallest level. This Sync technology makes it natural and easy for business analysts, technical analysts, architects, designers, and developers to remain in lockstep while managing continuous change at any level of abstraction.

7.7.2 Impact Analysis Reporting

The most important use case for keeping all these models linked and synchronized together is so that you can determine what will happen if you change anything. The Impact Analysis feature in PowerDesigner produces a list of impacted objects with a tree-like structure. Filters and other tools help scope the analysis to areas of interest. To begin an impact analysis in PowerDesigner, follow these steps:

1. Either select IMPACT ANALYSIS from the TOOLS menu or right-click on any object in the browser or diagram area, and select IMPACT AND LINEAGE ANALYSIS from the pop-up menu.
2. Generate a diagram view from the tree view by clicking the GENERATE DIAGRAM button on the IMPACT AND LINEAGE ANALYSIS dialog box, as shown in Figure 7.8. This diagram is very useful to collaborate with others in an easy-to-view format (see Figure 7.9).

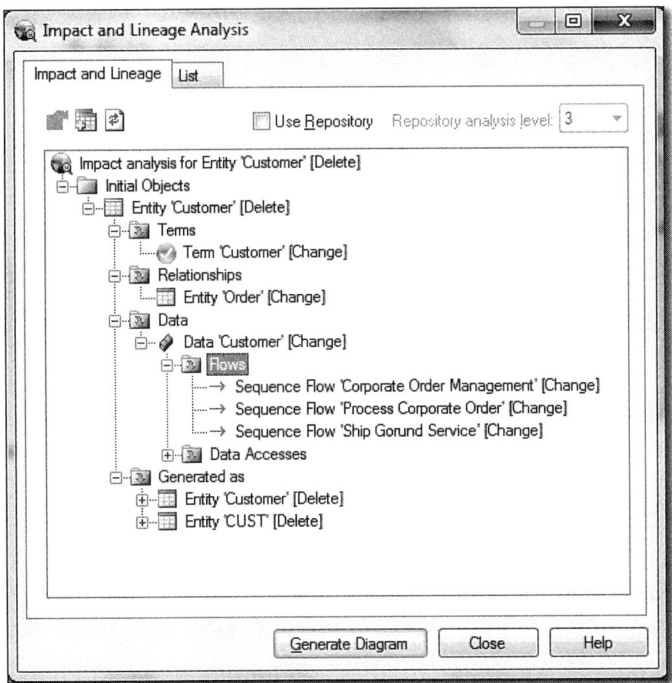

Figure 7.8 SAP PowerDesigner Impact Analysis Dialog

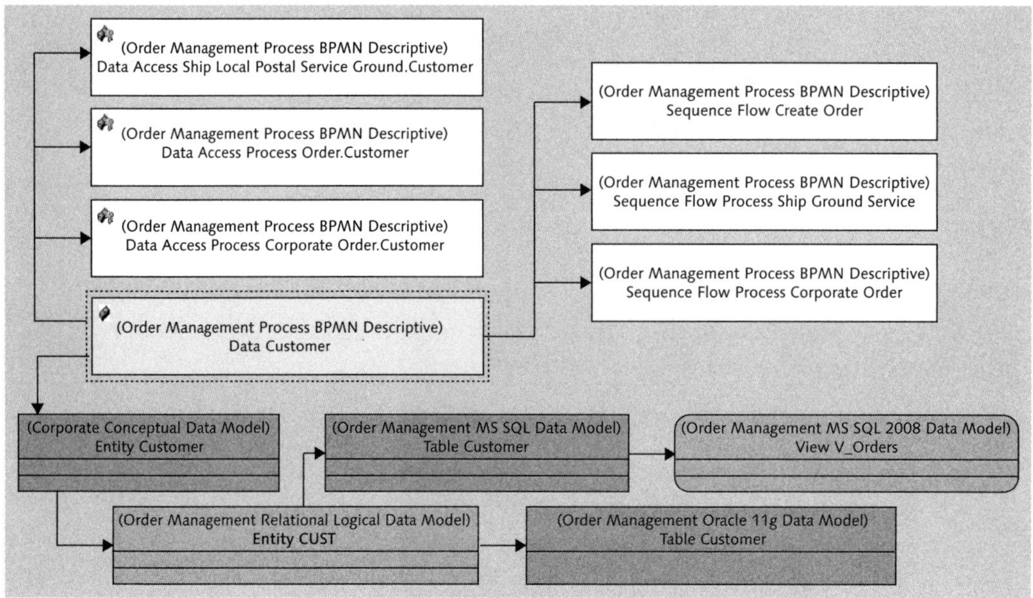

Figure 7.9 SAP PowerDesigner Impact Analysis Diagram

Impact analysis makes sure you won't forget that certain dependencies exist and will take them into consideration on each and every change request from business or technical stakeholders. Downstream, you can see what objects will need to be changed, tested, and verified based on this change. Because you know what databases, applications, and systems will be affected, you can get all the right people involved, and when the change is made to the operational systems, it's done in a way that minimizes any surprises and minimizes the risk of any unplanned downtime.

7.8 Comparing Models

Modeling is a great way to communicate and collaborate with different people on any complex project. To communicate effectively, it's not always practical to open a modeling tool, navigate through multiple models, and read screens. To help share information in any model, PowerDesigner has ways to analyze and report on that information and then share it with all nonmodelers in the enterprise.

Model comparison is used whenever changes are made to a model and the model is checked into the repository. To initiate a compare in PowerDesigner, open the model you want to compare, and select Tools • Compare from the menu. You must choose the other model to compare this one to, and select OK to run the comparison.

Figure 7.10 shows a typical Compare Models dialog for two CDMs. This comparisons feature is also used when generating changes from one model into another when using Preserve Modifications. Compare Between can also be run at any time.

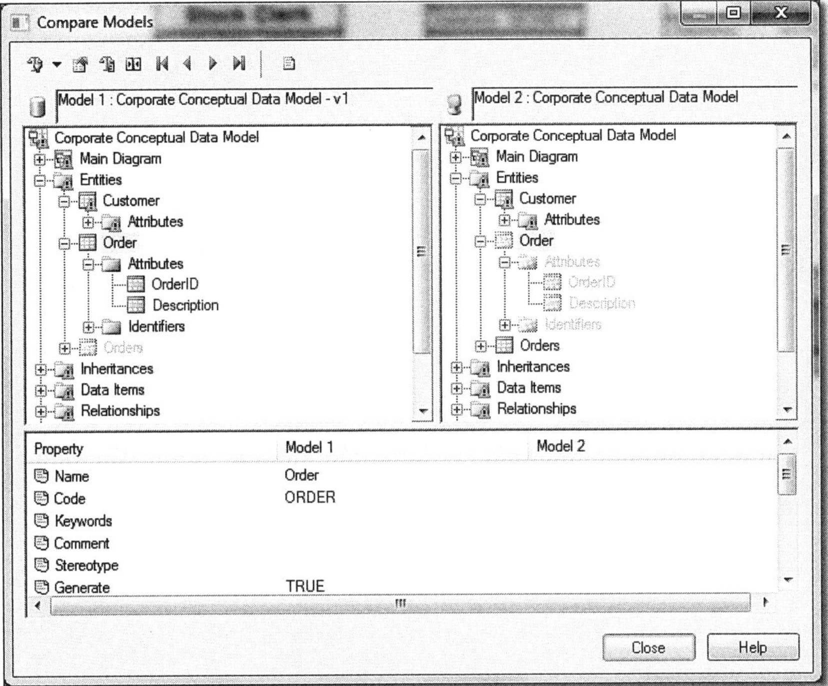

Figure 7.10 SAP PowerDesigner Compare Dialog

Model comparison is useful for several reasons. It's a great way to see if there are any similarities in models from completely different sources. It's also a great way to see what changes are made between two different versions of a model, or for understanding the gap between current and desired future state.

Options allow you to narrow the scope of the compare by excluding comments, data types, or other elements. We may force a compare between two objects that were not found to be the same by using the MANUAL SYNCHRONIZATION function.

Yellow and red flags indicate differences, bold and grayed out indicate presence and absence of whole objects, and the detailed compare window at the bottom shows the exact difference. The compare preview allows you to save the comparison as a Microsoft Excel spreadsheet for further analysis.

7.9 Summary

In this chapter, you learned that using PowerDesigner as an integral part of the SAP EIM solution gives you the power to successfully navigate the pitfalls of business transformation. PowerDesigner provides the right tools to manage information as a corporate asset today and into the future. PowerDesigner's unique integration into the SAP landscape means designs in the models can easily translate directly to physical artifacts in databases, data movement, and reporting technologies.

In the next chapter, we'll discuss SAP HANA Cloud Integration capabilities to connect databases and applications on-premise and in the cloud.

This chapter introduces SAP HANA Cloud Integration for data services, SAP's solution for delivering integration between on-premise and cloud applications. We'll discuss the product and its architecture, and then demonstrate the ease of implementation.

8 SAP HANA Cloud Integration

In this chapter, we'll focus on the data services capabilities of SAP HANA Cloud Integration (which we'll refer to as HCI in this chapter), looking at the simplistic beauty of this cloud integration tool and how it can be leveraged to meet data load demands. For integration and connectivity options, HCI is a tool that's designed to handle data integration use cases for bulk data loads on-demand, as well as on a scheduled basis (e.g., hourly, weekly, quarterly, etc.). HCI supports data integration between on-premise and cloud, as well as cloud to cloud. Today, HCI easily connects to applications on-premise and in the cloud (e.g., SAP Business Suite, SAP Sales and Operation Planning (S&OP), and SuccessFactors), along with databases (e.g., SAP HANA, Oracle, DB2, SQL Server, MySQL) and files. HCI also supports integration between non-SAP systems, targeting any-to-any integrations.

For integration developers, HCI provides a rich web-based user interface (UI) to model integration flows. An integration flow in HCI defines how data is extracted, transformed, and loaded from the source to the target application (we'll cover step-by-step instructions on how integration flows are created in HCI in Section 8.2). HCI provides a rich set of adapters with various connectivity options, including Simple Object Access Protocol (SOAP) and Representational State Transfer (REST) web services, OData, and Secure FTP (SFTP). See Table 8.1 for the wide variety of HCI connectivity that is available today. And this list is ever expanding through the several software releases of HCI each year, keeping ahead of the cloud application industry's rapid pace of innovation.

In this chapter, we'll go into detail on the HCI architecture, capabilities, and how to quickly implement and deploy data integration between on-premise and cloud systems.

SAP Business Suite Applications	Databases	SAP HANA Applications in the Cloud	Other Cloud Applications	Files
▸ Business Content Extractors: standard and custom extractors, including delta queues ▸ ABAP tables: cluster, transparent, pool, Z-tables ▸ SAP BW: direct access to ODS tables	▸ SAP HANA ▸ IBM DB2 ▸ MS SQL Server ▸ MySQL ▸ Oracle	▸ SAP Sales & Operations Planning ▸ SAP Scouting ▸ SuccessFactors Workforce Analytics ▸ Generic SAP HANA database on SAP HANA Cloud platform	▸ SuccessFactors applications (BizX, Employee Central): tables (SFAPI), compound employee, OData ▸ Web services (SOAP and REST)	▸ Delimited files (local files, remote files through SFTP) ▸ XML files (based on XSD, template files)

Table 8.1 SAP HANA Cloud Integration for Data Services Connectivity

8.1 SAP HANA Cloud Integration Architecture

As discussed in the introduction of this book, SAP's Integration Platform as a Service (iPaaS) solution is SAP HANA Cloud Integration, which leverages our leading-edge SAP HANA in-memory DBMS as an integrated feature and is based on the SAP HANA Cloud Platform (HCP). HCP is an in-memory cloud platform for today's increasingly networked, mobile, social, and data-driven world. Based on open standards, it provides access to a feature-rich, easy-to-use development environment in the cloud.

As shown in Figure 8.1, HCP is comprised of three service layers, each with a unique set of tools: Application Services, Database Services, and Infrastructure Services (for more details, see Chapter 3, Section 3.1.7). With HCP, customers have their own secure SAP HANA database in the cloud (a tenant) with many additional services on top. It meets the demands of a high-tech and fast-paced on-demand world with an infrastructure that supports elasticity, an uptime of 99%, failover, and load balancing. The actual setup of a tenant happens very quickly. In a matter of minutes, users can access their cloud system, perform final setup of their source and target data systems, and be ready to develop data flows for loading data to their new environment with HCI.

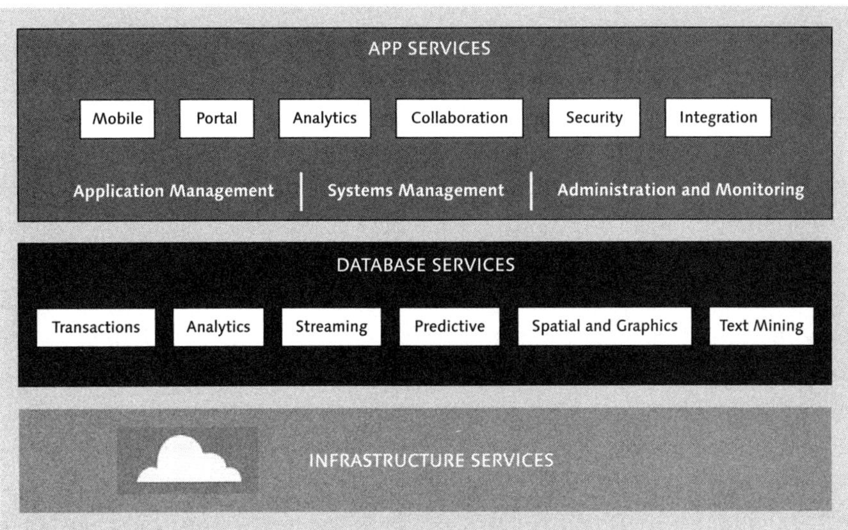

Figure 8.1 SAP HANA Cloud Platform

SAP HANA Cloud Integration for data services consists of two major components, one component running on the SAP HANA Cloud Platform (HCP) and the other component in the customer environment (we'll discuss each of these in more detail, as well as the UI, in the following sections). Leveraging the HCP, HCI offers automated failover, scalability, and subscription-based usage.

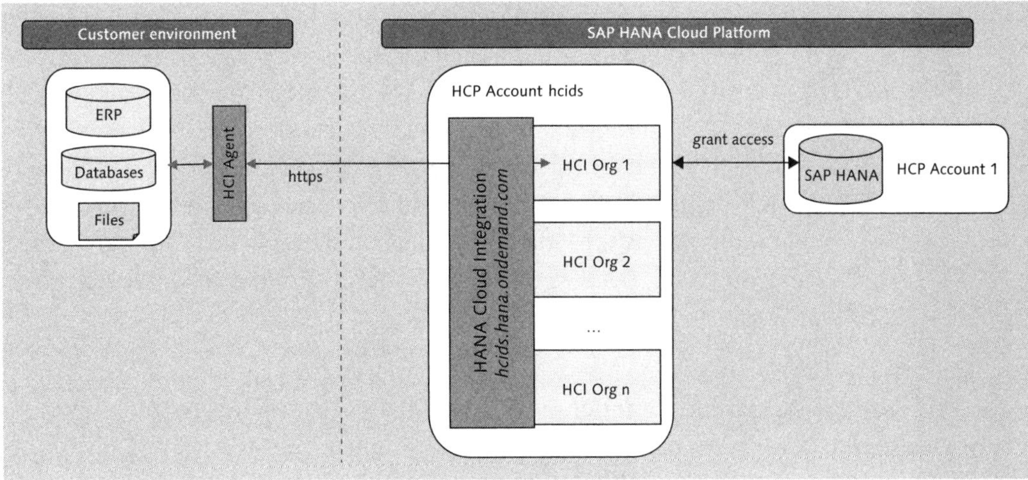

Figure 8.2 SAP HANA Cloud Integration for Data Services Architecture

As you can see in Figure 8.2, there are two environments: the customer environment and the SAP HANA Cloud Platform. In the following sections, we'll discuss the different areas of this diagram.

8.1.1 SAP HANA Cloud Platform

The HCI application runs on the HCP. Each new customer is given a new secure organization (org) as depicted in Figure 8.2. Each organization's metadata (via separate, dedicated SAP HANA database schemas) are strictly separated from each other. With HCI, all SAP customers go to the same URL (e.g., *hcids.hana.ondemand.com*), but depending on their login credentials, only get access to their specific organization. Organizations use HCI to define how their data needs to be extracted from on-premise data sources and loaded into their target application (e.g., an SAP HANA schema on the HCP). Alternatively, HCI can read from an SAP HANA schema on the HCP and write it back to an on-premise system, such as a database or file. Ultimately, the data can flow bi-directionally. Communication is always from the HCI Agent to the HCP. Even if data flows from the HCP to on-premise, the request is always initiated by the HCI Agent. This means, from a network point of view, that it's easy to set up the firewall with only outbound HTTPS required.

8.1.2 Customer Environment On-Premise

As mentioned in the previous section, the on-premise component of HCI is the HCI Agent (as shown in Figure 8.2). The HCI Agent is linked to one HCI org and provides connectivity between on-premise applications or databases and the cloud (see Table 8.1 for a listing of applications, databases, and file types). With the HCI Agent, HCI lends itself naturally to the dynamic adoption model that is characteristic with cloud. With HCI, you can start small using the agent for one cloud application, and as you add other cloud applications to your system landscape, you can use this same agent for integrating with the other cloud applications too.

You'll need to download and install the HCI Agent (on Windows or Linux), which has a small footprint of around 100MB. Once installed, the HCI Agent can be configured to connect to multiple data sources. The HCI Agent will package and compress the data and send it securely over HTTPS to the HCP server, where the data is then loaded into the targeted SAP HANA cloud application. For accessing SAP applications on-premise, it communicates through remote function calls (RFC), which is encryptable via Secure Network Communications (SNC). The HCI Agent uses long polling. It places requests to the server and waits for a response as to when a task is ready to execute. HCI operates without firewall exceptions; communication is always from the HCI Agent to the cloud. In other words, there is no need for a virtual private network (VPN), reverse proxy, or other firewall exceptions.

Note

The HCI Agent is only required for data integration scenarios, not for process integration.

8.1.3 SAP HANA Cloud Integration User Experience

SAP HANA Cloud Integration for data services provides a web-based UI that's accessible by a variety of web browsers. The UI gives the user an intuitive experience to produce and manage data integration tasks. Upon logging into the system, the user is presented with a dashboard. This dashboard graphically displays the production activities that have taken place within this system (see Figure 8.3). A user can request a view of certain time frames (e.g., from the past day, week, or month) or a view of all activities.

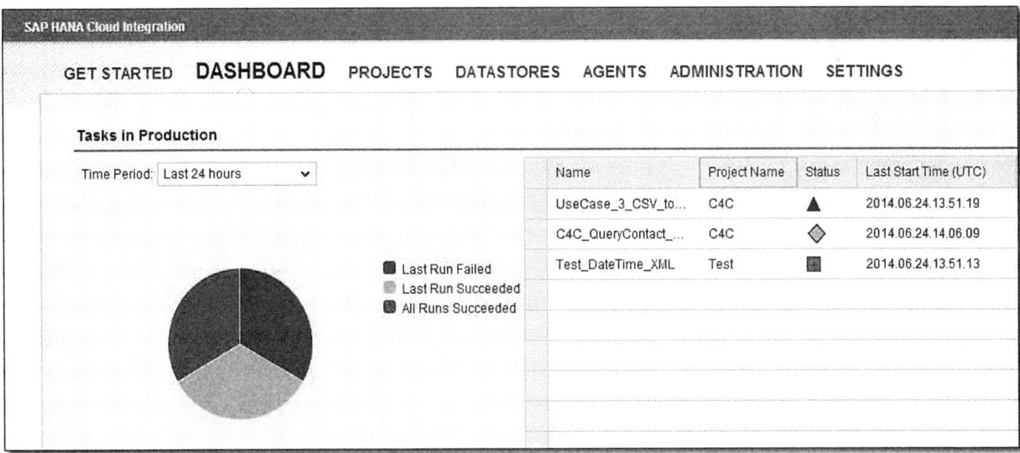

Figure 8.3 SAP HANA Cloud Integration for Data Services Dashboard

HCI provides a simple and straightforward data flow editor. The editor is a graphical editor, with simple drag and drop operations to add transformation steps and connect steps for a complete data flow (see Figure 8.4).

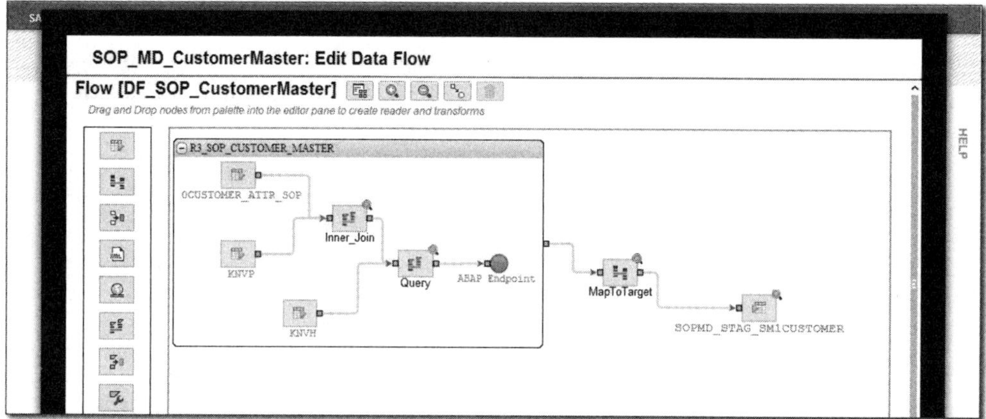

Figure 8.4 Graphical Data Flow Editor

In each transformation step, the mapping details are provided. Again, with simple drag and drop operations, you can map columns, add filters, define aggregation levels, and so on. Figure 8.5 shows an example of a query transform where columns are mapped from source (left) to target (right). More complex mappings are available through the mapping editor with a rich function library of built-in functions.

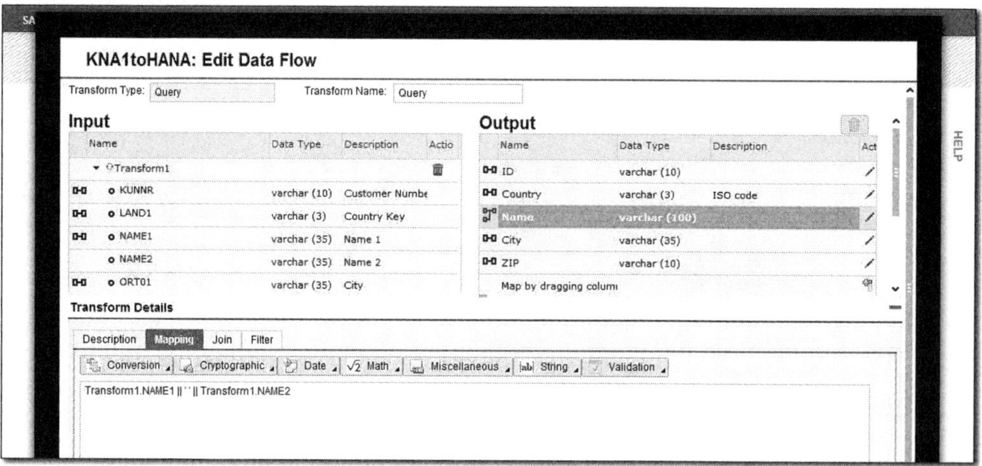

Figure 8.5 Query Transform

After the data flow has been created, the HCI interface supports developers and administrators to easily sequence and replicate data flows, manage multiple versions, schedule and audit production runs, and monitor various integration scenarios.

To log the activity that takes place in HCI, the system provides a detailed security log, including the time of event, the user responsible for the event, and the event itself. This is key for tracking down changes that have occurred within the system.

8.2 Getting Started with SAP HANA Cloud Integration

After logging into HCI, you can click on the GET STARTED tab (as shown in Figure 8.6) to get a full understanding of assets, including the process at a glance, product documentation, user guides, and video tutorials that detail how to get started with HCI.

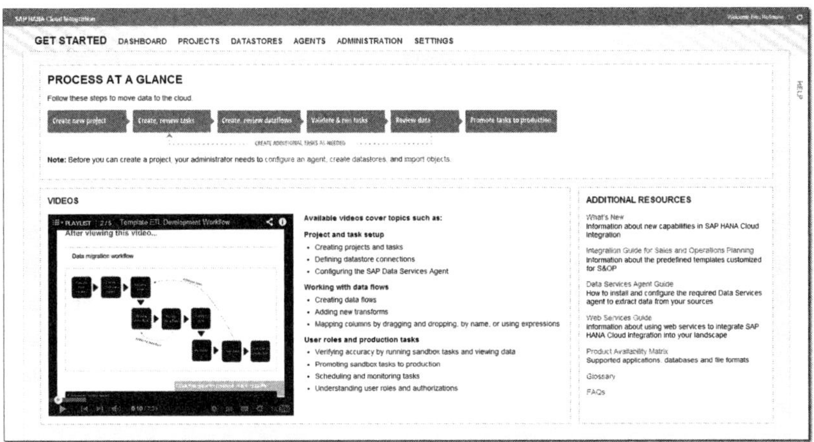

Figure 8.6 Get Started Tab in SAP HANA Cloud Integration for Data Services

In the following sections, we'll discuss the different steps that you should follow before and during an integration.

8.2.1 Blueprinting Phase

To begin the implementation and use of any integration tool, there must be data planning on the frontend, so you understand your data needs and sources. For data planning, you need to build a blueprint of the system tables and data that you want to have and use in your cloud or target solution. Along with an understanding of the data itself, you should identify the desired quality and the granularity of data (dimensions, key figures, planning levels, etc.). You need to also know the final counts for master data types, attributes, and key figures. Also, determine what the data load frequency (by object) will be from the source to the target.

You can leverage the information gathered during this blueprinting phase as your data requirements, helping you to determine what data should be sourced, to specify how many sources must be accessed, and to ensure that the actual data in source systems is available at the desired quality and granularity. In addition, this information is helpful in determining the source-to-target mappings and extraction logic.

8.2.2 Predefined Templates

After this blueprinting is complete, and you have a full understanding of your data needs, you can first review the predefined templates available with HCI for possible use in your implementation. HCI provides prepackaged content to greatly decrease the time-to-value of the solution. The integration packages available are listed in the web-based catalog that comes with every instance of HCI. After a user finds an integration package, the user can select and quickly deploy the package onto his assigned HCI organization. We'll cover this in Section 8.2.6, which explains how to create new tasks.

By using a template, you'll speed up your implementation. Because each implementation is unique, you'll almost always need to customize the out-of-the-box tasks and data flows that you create from the templates. However, using the templates to create tasks and data flows as a starting point has the following advantages over creating tasks from scratch:

- Template tasks provide the framework and thus reduce the integration development time.
- Template tasks contain the global variables required to successfully load and process data into applications such as S&OP and SuccessFactors.
- Preload scripts are configured with default values for these global variables and provide a framework, which eliminates the need to write preload scripts from scratch.
- Master data and key figure template data flows follow best practice design for optimal integration performance.

- Master data and key figure template data flows contain mappings from source systems, such as SAP ERP, which include joins and predefined filters.
- Master data and key figure template data flows contain predefined transformations for source systems such as SAP ERP.

8.2.3 Setting Up Your HCI Tenant

After you've completed the blueprint for your data requirements and have identified what (if any) templates you'll be using, there are a few prerequisites to set up to connect to your HCI organization.

First, SAP Cloud Operations will set up your HCI organization in the cloud. This tenant will consist of a sandbox environment for development as well as a production environment. As part of the on-boarding process, an initial user is created so that this one user can log in, and from that moment onward he can set up other users to perform HCI tasks.

Table 8.2 describes the four user role types in this step.

User	Description
Production Operator	▸ Views tasks, data flow details, and datastore connections ▸ Executes and schedules tasks in the production environment ▸ Monitors running and finished tasks
Administrator	▸ Has all the abilities of a Production Operator ▸ Manages the registration of HCI Agent instances ▸ Creates or modifies datastore connection information in the production environment ▸ Promotes tasks from sandbox to production
Integration Developer	▸ Has access only to the sandbox environment, and can't access production tasks ▸ Creates and modifies tasks, data flows, and datastore connections ▸ Executes jobs in the sandbox environment and views data to verify the results

Table 8.2 User Roles

User	Description
Security Administrator	▸ Creates, activates, and deletes users ▸ Assigns roles to users ▸ Reviews security logs

Table 8.2 User Roles (Cont.)

The next prerequisite item is to download and install the HCI Agent and connect the HCI Agent to its assigned HCI organization.

8.2.4 Setting Up Your Datastore

A datastore is a logical channel that connects HCI to a source or target database/application. A source system is where the data is available in an application, database, or file that you want the application to process. A target system is the database, file, or application where the data is loaded. The following steps explain how to create a new datastore:

1. Go to the DATASTORES tab.
2. Click the NEW DATASTORE button.
3. Fill in the datastore name, datastore type, and any additionally required connection parameters.
4. Click SAVE.

After the datastore is created, you can use the TEST CONNECTION button to test the connection to the application. Either a success message or an error message will be shown.

After the new datastore source and target connections are created, you can use that connection to import the source and target tables and metadata you need to meet the data requirements of the source and target systems.

Follow these steps to import tables:

1. Select the datastore you want to import table metadata from.
2. Go to the TABLES tab.
3. Use the IMPORT OBJECTS button to get a list of available objects.
4. Select one or more tables, and click IMPORT to retrieve the metadata and store it in the HCI repository.

Figure 8.7 shows all the tables and views that were imported from a datastore, along with related metadata.

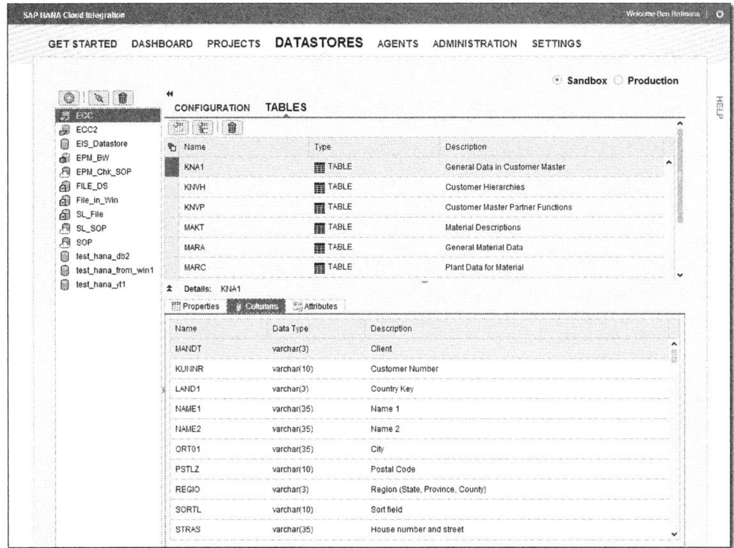

Figure 8.7 SAP HANA Cloud Integration for Data Services Datastores Page

8.2.5 Creating a New Project

Figure 8.8 shows the steps involved in creating a task in HCI. A task is a set of steps executed together; that is, an integration data flow. A task can be run on-demand or scheduled for execution. The first step is to create a new project. A project is a container that's used to group related tasks.

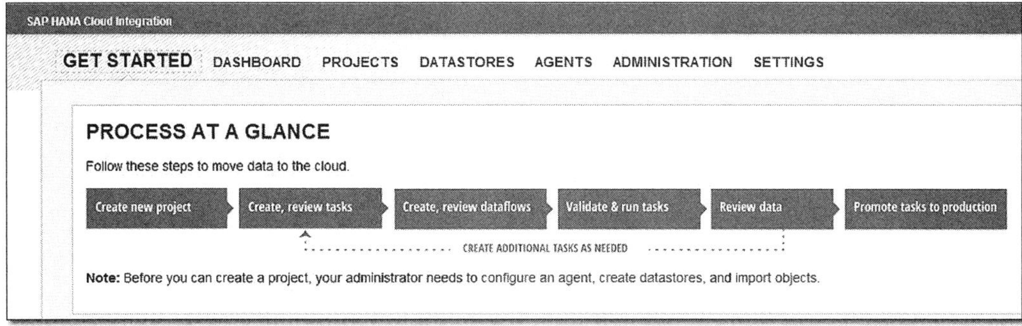

Figure 8.8 Process at a Glance

Execute the following steps to create a new project:

1. Go to the PROJECTS tab.
2. Click on the NEW PROJECT link in the top-right corner.
3. Provide a name and description for the project.

After the project has been created, the user can create a task to move data from a source system to a target system. Within the task are data flows. A data flow is an object that contains the steps to define the transformation of data from source to target. The example in Figure 8.9 shows a data flow with three transforms.

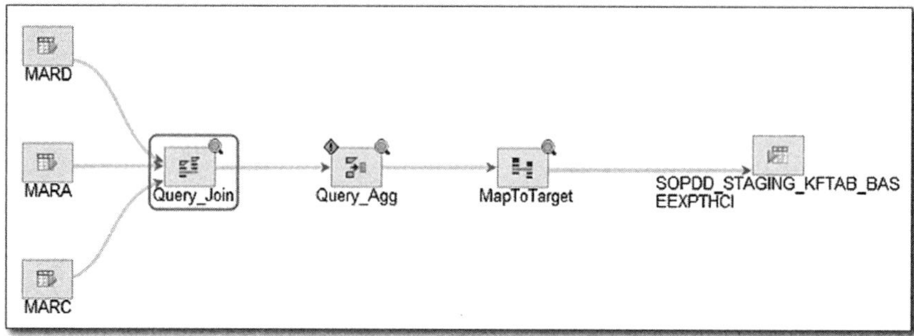

Figure 8.9 Example Data Flow

With HCI, building a task can be very quick and simple. HCI provides a graphical UI and a step-by-step process for building a data flow. In addition, task templates are available to you. The optional task templates are tasks that contain predefined content, which serves as the starting point for populating a data integration project, helping to greatly reduce the integration development time. (Predefined templates are described in detail in Section 8.2.2). To create a task, follow these steps:

1. On the PROJECTS tab, select a project where your task will be created.
2. Click the CREATE TASK button to launch a three-step wizard that will guide you through task creation.
3. In step 1 of the wizard, provide a name and description for the task. You can also select USE TEMPLATE to choose one of the available templates from the catalog. Create the task from scratch by deselecting this option.
4. Click NEXT to select the datastore that will be used as the source for your task.

5. Click NEXT to select which datastore will be used as the target for your task.
6. Click SAVE AND CLOSE or SAVE AND CREATE DATA FLOW. The latter will continue on with creating a data flow in this task.

You can have one or more data flows inside a task. A data flow defines the source object, target object, and sequence of transformation steps to be applied to the source data prior to being loaded into the target.

To create a data flow, follow these steps:

1. Click the ADD TARGET OBJECT link in the top-right corner.
2. From the list of imported objects in the target datastore, select the object that will become the target of this data flow.
3. Click CREATE DATA FLOW.
4. Fill in the main properties of the data flow, such as the NAME and DESCRIPTION, as well as any optional parameters.
5. Click OK.

After clicking OK, the graphical data flow editor will display so you can drag and drop additional source objects, along with transforms to manipulate your source data. HCI provides a selection of transform types for mapping source table columns to target table columns:

- Aggregation and ABAP Aggregation (for an SAP source)
- Custom ABAP
- Query and ABAP Query (for an SAP source)
- Target Query
- XML Map
- Web Services

The ABAP transforms are designed specifically to run very efficiently to pull data from SAP application sources. Leveraging the query transforms, you can also implement mapping expressions, with built-in function support to perform operations such as string manipulation or data type conversion.

Figure 8.9 shows an example of such a created data flow. Data is joined from three tables in an ABAP query transform, then the data is aggregated in an ABAP query transform, and finally, the results are mapped in a target query to the target object (in this example, an SAP HANA table in the cloud for S&OP).

After the data flow has been completed, HCI provides a one-click operation for validating the data flow to check for any configuration issues. After validation is complete, the user can save the data flow and can elect to build another data flow under the same task just completed. If the user elects to build another data flow, the user goes through the same process as before. If a second data flow is complete and validated, HCI provides the ability to sequence these two flows. HCI is also flexible in allowing you to write some additional scripting (pre- and post-load), if required. Scripting is a step in a task that allows you to calculate values to pass to other parts of the task by calling functions, executing if-then-else statements, and assigning values to variables.

8.2.6 Moving a Task from a Sandbox to a Production Environment

If you like the results from your data flow that you created in the sandbox environment, you can simply move this data flow to the production environment with a few simple steps.

To promote a task, follow these steps (note that you need administrator permissions to execute these steps):

1. On the PROJECTS tab, make sure that the SANDBOX option is selected in the top-right corner.
2. Select the task you want to promote to production.
3. Click the MORE ACTIONS button, and then click PROMOTE TASK.
4. In the PROMOTE TASK window that displays, select a project name, and click PROMOTE.
5. Use the option box in the top-right corner to switch to the PRODUCTION repository. You'll see the task that was promoted appearing as the selected project in your production repository.

When the data flow resides in the production environment, you can run this data flow on-demand or schedule this data flow to run at a certain times and dates. To run production tasks outside of HCI scheduler, a user can elect to run their production tasks via an on-premise scheduler. To handle this option, HCI provided the ability to invoke a HCI production task via a web services call.

> **Note**
>
> When using web services to start a task, the web service call is made directly to the HCI server on the cloud, not the agent.

When running HCI tasks in production, the system provides notification functionality for authorized users to be informed via email that a scheduled task failed to run or ran successfully. HCI also keeps an audit trail for actions performed on production data. For jobs that have finished running, a production operator is provided with logs within HCI to see what transpired during the data load run. HCI includes three logs: trace, monitor, and error.

8.3 Summary

In this chapter, we've discussed the key elements of a SAP HANA Cloud Integration for data services as a strategic cloud integration tool. The chapter discussed the HCI architecture, its key features, and how you can easily get started moving data between your on-premise and cloud environments.

In the next chapter, we discuss SAP Data Services as SAP's on-premise solution for extracting, transforming, and loading data across the enterprise.

This chapter introduces SAP Data Services as the data foundation for Enterprise Information Management. You'll find an overview and practical examples of the data integration, data quality, and text data processing capabilities that are delivered with SAP Data Services.

9 SAP Data Services

Chapter 4 introduced SAP Data Services (hereafter Data Services) as the data foundation for EIM. Data Services includes data integration, data quality, and text data processing capabilities. Data Services allows you to integrate, transform, improve, and deliver trusted data to critical business processes across the enterprise for both SAP and non-SAP systems. It provides one development user interface (UI), metadata repository, data connectivity layer, runtime environment, and the management console for administration activities.

In this chapter, we'll offer a basic explanation of extraction, transformation, and loading (ETL), highlighting some of the high-level use cases supported by Data Services. The chapter starts by explaining typical data integration scenarios and then discusses the Data Services architecture. After you understand the architecture, you'll learn how to use the Data Services Designer to extract and load various data sources and targets. With this information in hand, you're ready to start creating your first job and learning about both basic and complex transformations, which are key to Data Services. Finally, you'll learn how to execute and debug a job as well as expose real-time services. To conclude the chapter, capabilities specific to data quality and text data processing are covered in detail.

9.1 Data Integration Scenarios

In a perfect world, you would have a single software application that meets business needs, is easy to use, is fast, and stores all your information—current and past—in a single location. However, we must deal with the fact that most companies have many different software applications from many different software vendors, which all hold different information from different points in time. This is why data integration is necessary.

We introduced NeedsEIM Inc. in Chapter 1 and Chapter 4. This fictional company has several issues that can be addressed with the integration capabilities available in Data Services. Here are a few of them:

- **Integration between disparate systems**
  NeedsEIM Inc. has many different ERP, CRM, and manufacturing systems, resulting in data fragmentation across the enterprise. Moving data between various types of systems can help pull this information together for operational and analytical use cases.
- **Master data management**
  NeedsEIM Inc. is looking to improve its visibility into supplier spend and reduce the number of suppliers it deals with, as well as get more visibility into customer profit and loss (P&L). To do this, the company needs to consolidate all of its supplier and customer master data from its disparate systems into a single repository to understand the current state and start taking action. Data Services can help extract this data for cleansing and consolidation of this information into SAP's solutions for managing master data.
- **Data warehousing/analytics**
  NeedsEIM Inc. is looking to better understand its supplier spend and customer P&L. After the company has harmonized its customer and supplier master data, the company will be able to pull in the related supplier invoices and customer P&L information to perform the needed analytics to make improvements in these areas.
- **Data migration/mergers and acquisitions**
  NeedsEIM Inc. continues to grow its business through acquisition, and thus continuous data migration projects have been ongoing for the past few years to harmonize and move data from the acquired organizations' systems into the NeedsEIM Inc. systems. The SAP Rapid Data Migration rapid-deployment solution, discussed in Chapter 5, uses Data Services and supports NeedsEIM Inc.'s requirements for migration due to acquisitions.

The following provides a holistic list of use cases where data integration is commonly applied, including those covered previously for NeedsEIM Inc.:

- **Provisioning of data for operational use**
  - Integration of data between applications; for example, upload new products or sales orders from one system to another.

    - Integration of harmonized master data (such as customer, supplier, and material master data) to provide a consistent view across the enterprise.
    - Migration and conversion of data from legacy systems.
- **Provisioning of data for analytical use**
    - Aggregation of data from operational systems and collection over time for business analysis in a data warehouse or SAP HANA.
    - Provisioning of generic services for data, allowing organizations to provide a consistent means for accessing, transforming, and loading data in the enterprise that can be provisioned to various departments as a service.

Note

For some of the issues mentioned in the preceding list, SAP provides additional comprehensive solutions (not discussed in the book) that also use Data Services, such as Spend Performance Management and Collaborative E-Care Management.

9.2 SAP Data Services Platform Architecture

This section covers the basic architecture of Data Services, along with the component, services, and UIs that make up this application. Figure 9.1 provides a high-level view of the Data Services architecture. This figure includes closely related components for SAP Information Steward (hereafter Information Steward) and information platform services.

The three major components of the architecture that will be discussed in this section are the UIs/clients, the core server components, and the repositories. These discussions will explain what is shown in Figure 9.1.

The various components of this architecture can and are recommended to be installed (in most cases) across different physical or virtual machines. This provides an architecture that allows for the most reliable system and the ability to scale as your needs grow.

Let's discuss each of the major components of Data Services so you better understand each of the elements of the architecture. We'll start with the UI components, cover the core server components, and then finish with the repository components.

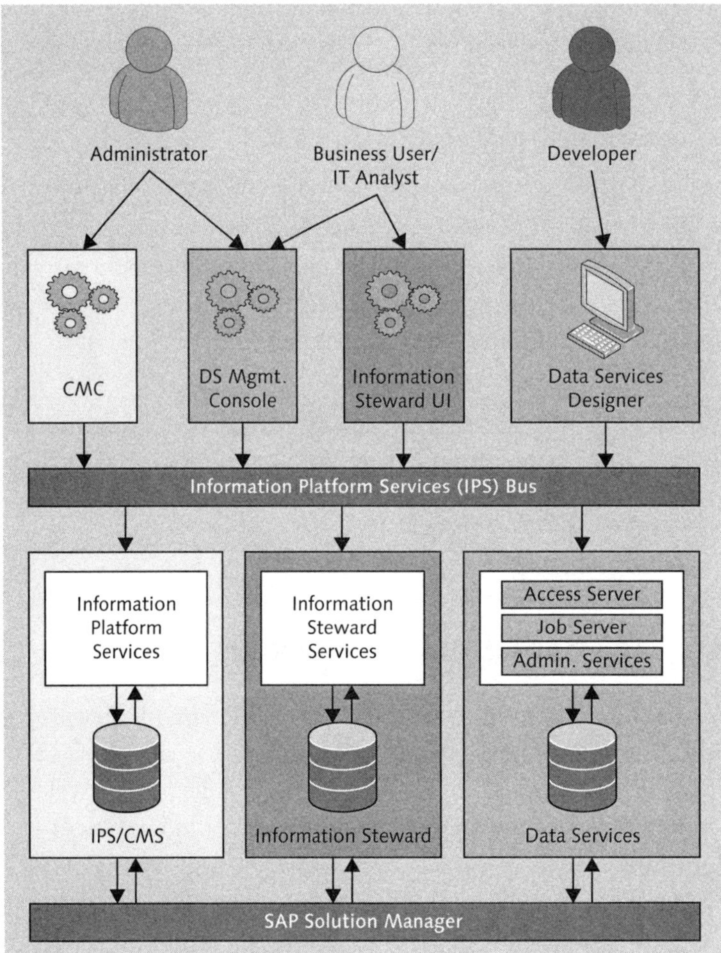

Figure 9.1 Data Services Architecture

9.2.1 User Interface Tier

The UI tier is shown in the top part of Figure 9.1 as CMC, DS Mgmt Console, Information Steward UI, and Data Services Designer. Each of these will be explained in more detail in the following subsections.

SAP Data Services Designer

As indicated in Figure 9.1, the Data Services Designer is used by the developer. The designer is a thick-client, graphical UI that runs on developers' desktop machines and allows them to create the graphical representations of how they want to extract, transform, map, and load data in their organization.

Don't be scared off by the term *developer*. The designer is a very easy-to-use interface, and, in many cases, there are analysts in organizations using this tool to do data transformation. However, it's most commonly used in the IT organization, and, as you'll see next, Information Steward is the UI focused on interaction with data management experts (such as data stewards, who may not be technical IT staff).

The designer provides a workspace where users can define the different sources and targets where data is stored. These source and target objects are placed onto a canvas where a data flow can be defined to perform various mappings and transformations to the data. The objects that are defined in the designer represent metadata that is stored in a repository. The job server uses this metadata definition of the data flow (also shown in Figure 9.1) to execute the data flow that was designed by the developer.

SAP Information Steward User Interface

The Information Steward UI is depicted in Figure 9.1. Information Steward is a product that uses Data Services as a runtime engine. The web-based UI is focused on providing various features around information governance and is specifically designed for the data steward or less technical individuals who are data domain experts. The many capabilities included in the Information Steward solution are discussed in Chapter 10.

SAP Data Services Management Console

The Data Services management console UI is represented in Figure 9.1 as DS Mgmt Console. The management console is a web-based UI that provides the majority of the administration capabilities for Data Services, as well as some metadata and reporting capabilities. Notice that it's used by both the business user/IT analyst and the administrator. The following is a summary of capabilities that are part of this UI:

- **Administration functions**
  - Scheduling, monitoring, and executing batch jobs
  - Configuring, starting, and stopping real-time services
  - Configuring job server, access server, and repository usage

    - Configuring and managing adapters
    - Publishing batch jobs and real-time services as web services
    - Promoting objects among development, test, and production environments
- **Metadata reporting**
    - Impact and Lineage Analysis: This functionality provides dependency information between objects within Data Services, as well as the related source and target information. It allows a user to see what will be impacted by making a change, as well as where data is coming from and potential transformations applied to that data. (Note: Information Steward, discussed in Chapter 10, provides more comprehensive capabilities in this area.)
    - Operational Dashboard: This functionality provides a graphical depiction of Data Services job execution statistics over time.
    - Auto Documentation: This functionality provides an easy way to generate documentation for all of the data integration objects created in Data Services. This capability captures critical information about each job from the metadata and provides a comprehensive summary that can easily be put into PDF or Microsoft Word format for easy sharing.
    - Validation Dashboard: This functionality provides a graphical dashboard summarizing the quality of data based on validation rules applied within a data flow using the validation transform in Data Services.
    - Data Quality: This functionality generates reports for many of the data quality transformations in Data Services to provide a detailed view of your data's quality during processing.

Central Management Console (CMC)

The Central Management Console (CMC) is a UI component of the information platform services that are part of the SAP BusinessObjects Business Intelligence (SAP BusinessObjects BI) platform. This UI is where administrators create and maintain users, groups, and their rights for Data Services.

Other User Interfaces

The repository manager allows administrators to create, upgrade, and check versions of Data Services repositories. The server manager allows administrators to add, delete, or edit the configuration of job servers and access servers.

9.2.2 Server Tier

Figure 9.1 shows three categories of server tier components. Above those three components is the information platform services (IPS) bus. This will be explained in the next section, followed by the Data Services tier and repository tiers.

All of the three categories of server tier components, discussed next, are not required. You must always have the information platform services, and you can have both Data Services and Information Steward as additional tiers, or only Data Services. However, if you have Information Steward, then you must always have all three server tier components.

Information Platform Services (IPS) Server Tier

The information platform services (IPS) components are part of both Data Services and Information Steward. If you're familiar with the SAP BusinessObjects BI platform, you'll recognize IPS. IPS is a subset of functionality from the platform that is used to provide security and infrastructure capabilities for Data Services. If you're already using the SAP BusinessObjects BI platform (version 4.0 or higher), you can use that installation instead of the IPS component delivered with Data Services.

Data Services uses the Central Management Server (CMS) to manage the users and group security. The CMC UI is used for configuration of these services.

SAP Data Services Server Tier

The Data Services server tier includes the server components delivered with Data Services for the execution of Data Services capabilities. These components include the following:

- **Job server**
  The job server is responsible for starting the engines that execute the data integration jobs created with the Data Services Designer. These engines perform the ETL of data in batch processes or process the data provided as part of a service call for real-time jobs that are managed by the access server.
- **Access server**
  The access server acts as a message broker when real-time services are used. Various Application Programming Interfaces (APIs), including web services, are

used to send requests to Data Services, and the access server manages these requests and distributes them to the various engines for each service. The access server is also responsible for scaling up new engines to handle increased loads and distributing those requests across many engines.

- **Administration services**
  Administrative services enable Data Services integration with Information Steward, IPS, and SAP Business Warehouse (SAP BW).

Repository Tier

Data Services has a few types of repositories in its architecture that are managed by a relational database and contain tables with predefined system information, user-created objects, copies of source and target metadata, and transformation rules. There are two types of repositories:

- **Local repository**
  There's a local repository for each developer who is using the Data Services Designer. Each developer has his own instance of a local repository type to store the objects he creates. Normally, there's also one local repository for test efforts and for the production environment.
- **Central repository**
  The central repository is an optional repository that is used for more complex multi-user development environments. Its purpose is to act as a master repository for all objects across all developers. It provides a mechanism for locking an object while a developer is working on it as well as history tracking so users can revert to older versions of objects if necessary.

The IPS repository contains the additional configuration information for all of the services running in the IPS. For Data Services, this is the security information about users, groups, and rights to the various Data Services repositories and features in the application.

9.3 SAP Data Services Designer Overview

This section provides a high-level overview of the Data Services Designer. You'll become familiar with all the major components provided in the designer. The designer is made up of four major areas, as shown in Figure 9.2.

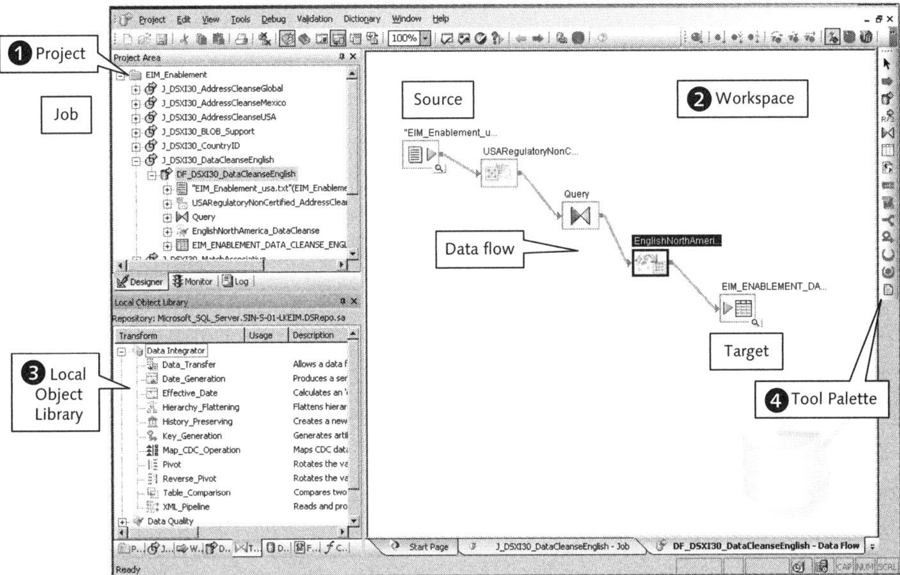

Figure 9.2 Four Areas in the Data Services Designer

Each area is listed and described in Table 9.1.

Area	Description
❶ Project Area	Provides a hierarchical view of selected projects and all objects within those projects (jobs, workflows, data flows, etc.).
❷ Workspace	Provides the open area where you drag and drop objects such as sources, targets, and transformations to operate on data.
❸ Local Object Library	Provides access to objects created and stored in the repository such as jobs, workflows, data flows, and data source and target information. It also provides access to built-in system objects such as transformations.
❹ Tool Palette	Provides shortcuts on the right-hand side of the screen that allow you to quickly add common objects such as data flows and workflows.

Table 9.1 Major Areas of the Data Services Designer

There are many object types in the Data Services Designer. We'll cover just a subset of the main objects. You can always refer to the product documentation for far more detail about each available object.

Data Services contains two broad categories of object types:

- **Single-use objects**
  Single-use objects are created for use in a job and can only be used in the context of that single job; for example, a script.
- **Reusable objects**
  Reusable objects are created once and can be reused many times in different jobs. The majority of the objects in Data Services are reusable. This makes it easy to make a change in one place for an object definition and have it take effect in all places where it's used. This significantly reduces the work around standard definitions of rules, mappings, and transformations.

When objects are created in the designer, they are associated with each other in a logical manner, thus creating a hierarchy. Figure 9.3 shows a high-level set of relationships among the objects you can create with the designer. (Note: This isn't comprehensive.)

The primary objects are the following:

- **Projects**
  Projects are objects that are used to help organize all of the jobs that you develop.
- **Jobs**
  Jobs are the one kind of object that is actually executed. It's a container that can contain many workflows, data flows, scripts, and control logic items that are executed in serial and/or parallel. There are two types of jobs:
  - *Batch jobs* are used to process large volumes of data. Data Services extracts data from one or more source systems and writes it to one or more target systems.
  - *Real-time jobs* are used to expose real-time services. Their purpose is to accept requests to process data from other applications that come to Data Services via an API, web service call, or other transport mechanism—such as an SAP intermediate document (IDoc) or Java Message Service (JMS), for example.
- **Workflow**
  A *workflow* is a container where users can define control operations and decision-making steps around the execution of data flows. A workflow exists inside a job. A typical use of a workflow in a SAP BusinessObjects BI project, for example, would be to control the execution of data flows that load a group of dimension tables and then another workflow to control the loading of fact tables.

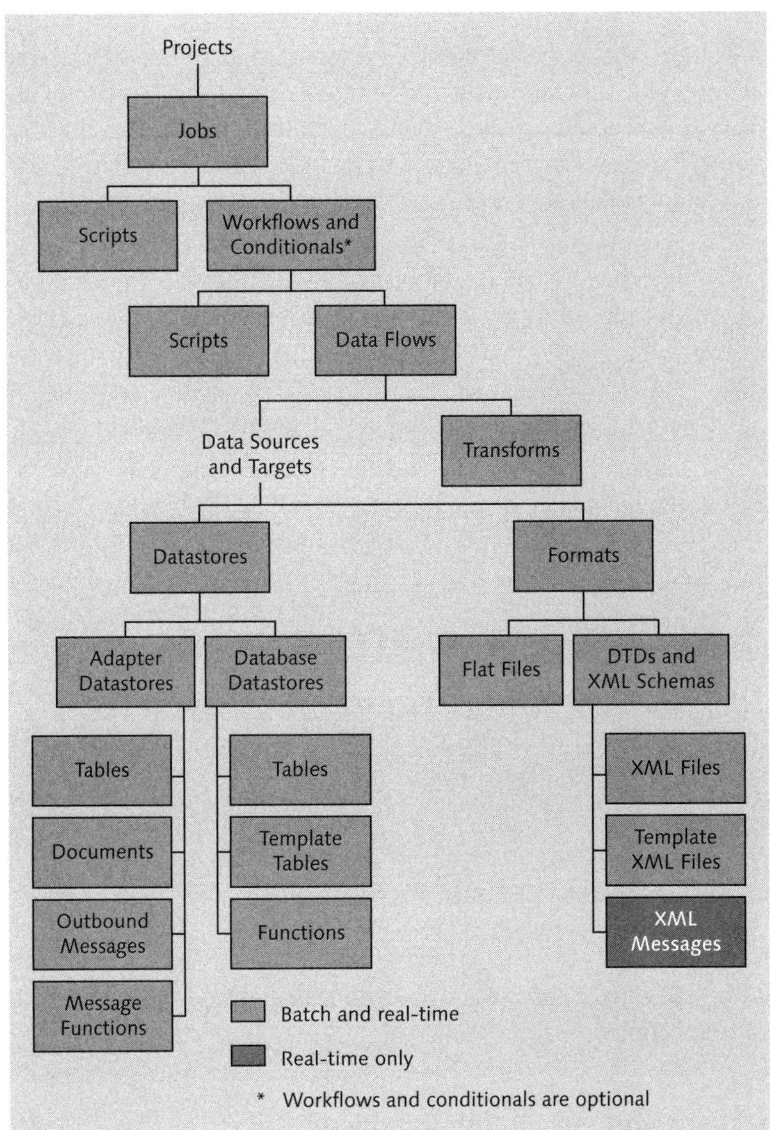

Figure 9.3 Data Services Object Hierarchy

- **Data flow**
  The *data flow* is the workhorse of Data Services. This is where developers define which source(s) to extract from, what transformations to perform, and which target(s) to write to.

- **Transforms**
  Transforms are objects that perform complex operations on data being processed within a data flow. There are four categories of transforms in Data Services: platform transforms (most commonly used), data integrator transforms (usually used for the creation of data marts/warehouses), data quality transforms (for data quality operations), and text data processing transforms (for unstructured text).
- **Formats**
  Formats describe the structure of a file-based source or target, such as a flat file, XML, COBOL Copybook, Microsoft Excel workbook, unstructured text document, or web log.
- **Datastores**
  Datastores contain the information needed to access data in a database or application, such as connection information and configuration options. They also contain a copy of the metadata for the datastore to which they refer.
- **Functions**
  Functions are reusable objects that execute a very specific operation on data. There are several built-in functions as well as the ability to write your own user-defined functions. Functions are discussed in more detail in Section 9.6.

This section provided an overview of the Data Services Designer and the major components of the designer. Now you're ready to dive into more details for using the designer.

9.4 Creating Data Sources and Targets

One of the first steps in Data Services is to create connections to the source and target systems. This section describes the connections that are available, as well as how to create a connection.

9.4.1 Connectivity Options for SAP Data Services

Data Services supports many connectivity options for structured and unstructured data, including SAP applications, databases, other vendor applications, text files, Microsoft Excel, mainframes, and so on.

- **Databases**
  SAP HANA, SAP Sybase ASE, IQ, SQL Anywhere and Replication Server, SAP

PowerDesigner, Microsoft SQL Server, Informix, Teradata, ODBC, MySQL, Netezza, HP Neoview, Oracle, IBM DB2, Hadoop (HDFS, Hive)

- **Applications**
  SAP, SuccessFactors, JD Edwards, Oracle, PeopleSoft, Siebel, Salesforce.com
- **Files/transports**
  Delimited text, fixed-width text, XML, Cobol Copybooks ANSI 85, Excel, HTTP, JMS, JSON, web services (WSDL/SOAP, WS-Security)
- **Mainframe**
  Attunity, ADABAS, ISAM, VSAM, Enscribe, IMS/DB, RMS
- **Unstructured data**
  Any text file (flat files, documents, PDFs, PPTs) supported in 31 languages

Detailed information can be found on the SAP Product Availability Matrix (PAM) at *http://service.sap.com/pam.*

Next, you'll learn how to create datastores to connect to a relational database, as well as how to connect to a file source.

Connecting to a Datastore

Figure 9.4 shows an example of creating a new datastore. In this example, a database datastore was chosen, but remember, there are many options, as described previously.

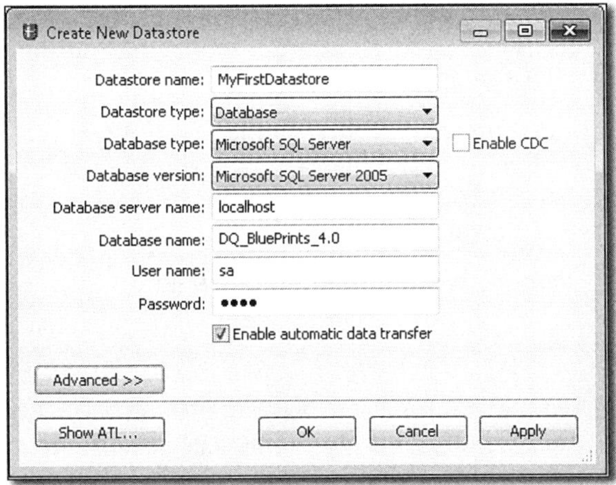

Figure 9.4 Creating a Datastore to Connect to an RDBMS

The following steps describe how to create a datastore:

1. In the Local Object Library on the bottom left, click on the Datastores tab.
2. Right-click and select New.
3. Enter a datastore name. For this example we're using "MyFirstDatastore".
4. For the Database type, select the dropdown list and notice all the database options. Select Database in the dropdown.
5. Enter the details for connecting to the database.

Connecting to a File Source

In addition to databases, Data Services also supports connecting to file sources. Figure 9.5 shows the definition of a new file source. After you provide the file name, it will show the column headers and data in the file (not shown in this figure).

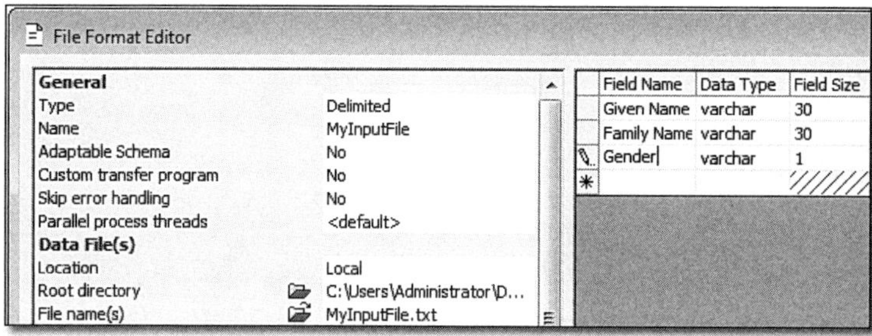

Figure 9.5 Creatign a File Format Definition

To connect to a file source, follow these steps:

1. In the Local Object Library on the bottom left, click on the File Format tab.
2. Expand the Flat File node.
3. Right-click on Flat File, and select New.
4. Enter a format name. For this example, we're using "MyInputFile".

Tip

If something changes in the structure of your datastore or format definition (such as new columns being added), you'll need to change your definition. If your metadata is a datastore, you'll need to re-import the metadata.

9.4.2 Connecting to SAP

When connecting to SAP, you have several options: connection to an SAP application such as SAP ERP or SAP CRM, connection to SAP BW, and connection to SAP HANA. Each of these will be described next.

Connecting to SAP ERP

Data Services provides multiple ways to connect to the SAP Business Suite applications for extracting and loading data. Following is a summary of those methods and a brief description of when to use each method:

- **Read tables via an ABAP program**
  This method uses an ABAP data flow that generates an ABAP program. This should be used when extracting large volumes and performing transformations inside the SAP source (joins, lookups, etc.).
- **RFC_READ_TABLE**
  This method is used when you simply drag a table from an SAP source into a regular data flow, not an ABAP data flow. Use this method when you're reading a single table, and only a few rows are intended to be read.
- **RFC and BAPI**
  Data Services provides a way to call a Business Application Programming Interface (BAPI) in the SAP system. The purpose of this is to reuse SAP logic that's already created inside your SAP system to extract information, instead of reading from a table directly and re-creating the logic in Data Services. This should be used only when retrieving a small number of rows.
- **IDoc (Intermediate Document Type)**
  IDocs can be received from SAP applications and sent to SAP applications from Data Services. SAP uses IDocs to send messages between applications, commonly for synchronization. Data Services can act like any other SAP system to send and receive these types of messages.
- **Extractors**
  Extractors are designed for SAP BW to consume data from SAP applications such as SAP ERP. However, Data Services is also able to use them as a source. Extractors are delivered by SAP, but they don't exist for all information in SAP applications. They are tailored for data warehouse use cases and should only be used for large volumes. You can use extractors to easily get the data you want

from an SAP system and then apply complex transformations such as data quality to that data.

You can find more information on these different methods in the product documents as well as on the SAP Community Network.

Connecting to SAP Business Warehouse

Data Services is integrated with SAP BW in many different ways. First, Data Services can be used to extract and load data with SAP BW. Data Services does the extractions and loads by using SAP BW's Open Hub service.

If you want to read from SAP BW first, some configuration is required in the SAP BW application before Data Services can access the information. You must execute the following steps to enable Data Services to read from SAP BW:

1. Configure an SAP BW open hub destination. This is essentially a table that acts as an interface between SAP BW and Data Services during extraction.
2. Configure an SAP BW process chain. A process chain is required to execute a SAP BW data transfer program (DTP) that is responsible for populating the open hub destination so Data Services can read the data.
3. Create the Data Services data flow. When the datastore is created for the SAP BW source, you'll be able to directly access the open hub destination just like a typical RDBMS table and can drag it onto a Data Services data flow as a source.

Figure 9.6 shows an example of how a data flow with SAP BW works.

When loading SAP BW, you can use Data Services as an external source to SAP BW. First, you need to configure the InfoSource and DataSource in SAP BW so that it can be loaded via Data Services. After this is complete, Data Services will see this object, similar to a normal RDBMS table, and can use it as a target within a data flow. More details about these methods can be found in the product documentation or on the SAP Community Network.

In SAP BW 7.30, users of the SAP BW workbench can directly browse non-SAP sources. Any source Data Services supports can be viewed directly from the workbench. When the user selects the data he wants to extract, the SAP BW workbench auto-generates very simple Data Services data flows and jobs that can then be immediately executed. The user of the SAP BW workbench can now easily access data from non-SAP applications using Data Services without having to launch the

Data Services Designer. Note that transformation logic can't be defined from the SAP BW workbench. The Data Services Designer still needs to be launched to create any complex transformation logic when using this method.

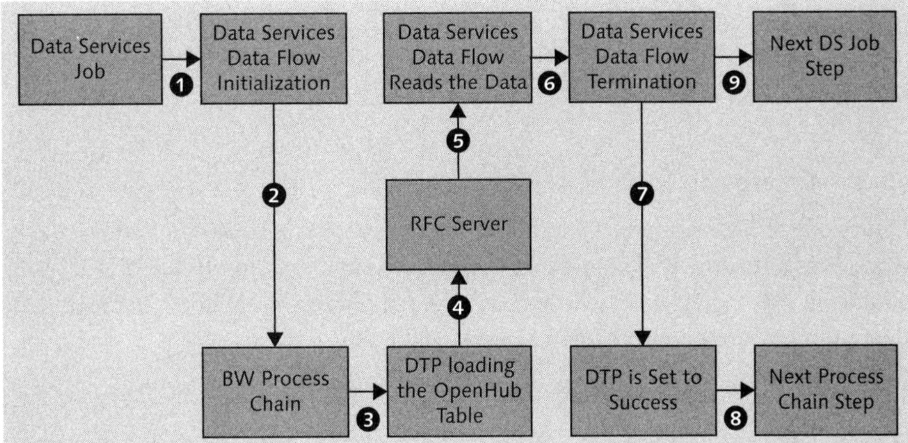

Figure 9.6 Reading Data from SAP BW

Connecting to SAP HANA

Data Services is delivered as part of SAP HANA and provides the primary data integration capabilities to extract data from various upstream systems into SAP HANA. In this case, the SAP HANA database acts as another target for Data Services. Data Services and SAP HANA have been highly optimized to work together, providing capabilities for high-performance loading of massive volumes of data. Chapter 3, Section 3.2 provides more detail on Data Services and SAP HANA.

9.4.3 Connecting to Hadoop

Chapter 3 discussed big data in terms of EIM, SAP HANA, and Hadoop. Data Services provides connectivity to Apache Hadoop, including Hadoop Distributed File System (HDFS) and Hive sources and targets. Data Services uses Pig scripts to read from and write to HDFS, including joins and push-down operations. In addition, Data Services supports text data processing in the Hadoop framework using a MapReduce form of the entity extraction transform. Coupling the Data Services capabilities of data integration, data quality, and text data processing with Hadoop and SAP HANA provides the most comprehensive stack for big data processing and analysis.

9.5 Creating Your First Job

It's time to get down to business and create your first job. In this example, you're going to create the most basic job and build on what you learned in the previous section, where you created a file format and a datastore for a relational database. In this section, you'll create the data flow, add a source, add a query transform, add a target, do some mapping, and create the job.

9.5.1 Create the Data Flow

As previously mentioned, the data flow is the basic object type that does all the work. This data flow will read data from a flat file and load it into a relational database table. The example data flow you'll create is shown in Figure 9.7. Execute the following steps to create the data flow:

1. Click on the DATA FLOWS tab in the LOCAL OBJECT LIBRARY.
2. Right-click in the white/open area on this tab, and select the NEW menu item.
3. Select DATA FLOW.
4. Name the data flow "MyFirstDataflow".
5. Double-click on the data flow you just created to open it in the workspace.

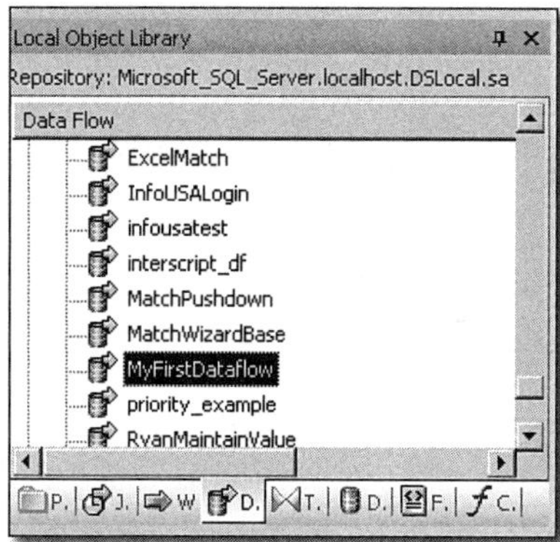

Figure 9.7 Creation of a Data Flow

Now that you've created the data flow, it's time to add your source.

9.5.2 Add a Source to the Data Flow

Adding sources and targets to the data flow connects Data Services to your application, database, file, and so on, using the list of connections previously discussed. In this example, you'll add a flat file as a data source.

Execute the following steps to add a source to a data flow:

1. Click on the File Format tab in the Local Object Library.
2. Open the Flat File node in the File Format tab.
3. Drag the file format you created previously, MyInputFile, into your data flow in the workspace.
4. Select Make Source in the popup dialog.

Now that you've added a source to the data flow, you'll add a query transform.

9.5.3 Add a Query Transform to the Data Flow

The query transform has many uses in Data Services. It can be used to filter data, join data from multiple sources, perform functions on the data, and many other things. In this example, we'll use the query transform to do basic field mapping to tell Data Services which columns from the flat file to populate in columns of the target relational database table.

Execute the following steps to add a query transform to a data flow:

1. Click on the Transforms tab in the Local Object Library.
2. Click on the Platform node on this tab to open the list of transforms.
3. Drag the query transform onto the workspace somewhere to the right of the source object you already created.
4. Connect the source object to the query transform on your workspace. (You do this by clicking on the small output tab on the source object and dragging it to the query transform. You'll see Data Services create a line connecting the two objects.)

Next, you'll add a target to the data flow.

9.5.4 Add a Target to the Data Flow

In this example, we've already created a table in the database that's being used as a target. When we created the datastore, we imported the metadata for the tables we wanted to use as sources and targets. Therefore, we'll use an existing table as a target. Execute the following steps to add a target to the data flow:

1. Click on the DATASTORE tab in the LOCAL OBJECT LIBRARY.
2. Click on the MYFIRSTDATASTORE node to expand it.
3. Click on the TABLES node to expand it.
4. Drag the table MYTARGETTABLE onto the data flow workspace somewhere to the right of the query transform that was added.
5. Select MAKE TARGET in the popup menu.
6. Connect the query transform to the target object.

Now it's time to return to the query transform and do some mapping.

9.5.5 Map the Source Data to the Target by Configuring the Query Transform

Now, you need to map the source data to the target data. As you can imagine, the mapping can range from simple to very complex. The following is a simple mapping example:

1. Double-click on the query transform in the data flow workspace.
2. Drag and drop the source field to the desired target field to do a one-to-one mapping of the fields. You'll then see the mapping editor shown in Figure 9.8.

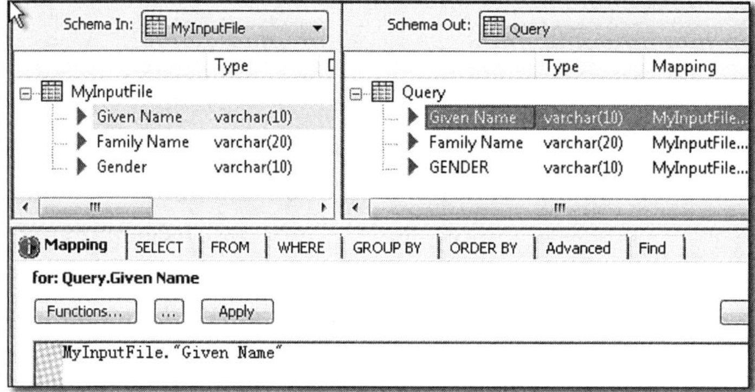

Figure 9.8 Mapping Editor to Map Output Schema Fields to Input Fields

Notice that given name from the SCHEMA IN MYINPUTFILE is mapped to given name in the SCHEMA OUT QUERY. All fields in Figure 9.8 are mapped. This is indicated by the right-pointing arrow in front of each field.

3. Click the SAVE button in the menu bar at the top of the designer to save all your work.

Now that your data flow is created, it's time to finish with the creation of the job itself.

9.5.6 Create the Job and Add the Data Flow to the Job

Remember that the job is the object that is executed and will be the container object for the data flow we just created. The following steps describe how to create a job:

1. Click on the JOBS tab in the LOCAL OBJECT LIBRARY.
2. Click on the BATCH JOBS node to expand it.
3. Right-click on the BATCH JOBS node, and select NEW.
4. Name the job "MyFirstBatchJob".
5. Double-click on this job to open it in the workspace.

Next, add a data flow:

1. Click on the DATA FLOWS tab in the LOCAL OBJECT LIBRARY.
2. Drag the data flow MYFIRSTDATA FLOW to the job workspace.
3. Save the job by clicking the SAVE button in the toolbar.

That's it! You've completed your first job.

9.6 Basic Transformations Using the Query Transform and Functions

In this section, you'll learn how to do some basic transformation of data by using the query transform and the built-in functions in Data Services.

Data Services provides many functions for data transformation, and you can even create your own user-defined functions by using the built-in scripting language in combination with the built-in functions to perform whatever operations you like.

Figure 9.9 shows the built-in function categories in Data Services. You can see a sampling of some of the functions in the STRING FUNCTIONS category. The capabilities are broad, including trimming, matching patterns, conversions to ASCII, and so on.

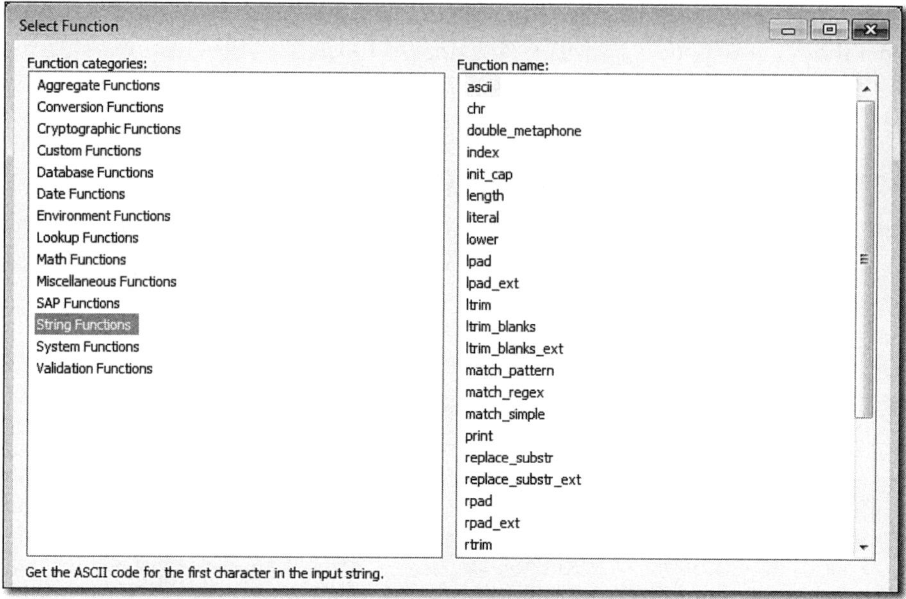

Figure 9.9 Function Wizard

In this next example, we're going to perform a very basic transformation on the data in our flat file. In the source file, there is a GENDER column that contains the full word Male or Female. However, in our target, we want the value to be either M or F.

There are multiple ways that this can be accomplished in Data Services, such as using some basic `if/then` statements, the `search_replace()` function, or the `lookup_ext()` function to look up the values in a database table. Because the `lookup_ext()` function is very commonly used, we'll use that option for this example.

First, we'll remove the current mapping for the GENDER column, and then we'll add a lookup function.

To remove the current mapping for the GENDER column, follow these steps:

1. Double-click on the query transform in the data flow MYFIRSTDATAFLOW.
2. Right-click on the GENDER column representing the target's schema on the right side of the screen.
3. Select DELETE from the popup menu to delete the existing GENDER column.
4. In the SCHEMA OUT area, right-click on QUERY, and select NEW FUNCTION CALL... (shown in Figure 9.10).

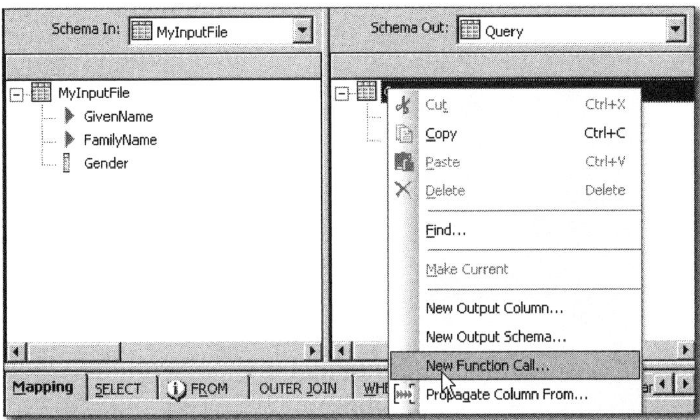

Figure 9.10 Insert Lookup_ext() Function Call

The following steps add a gender lookup using a database table called GENDER-LOOKUP that was created for this example. See Figure 9.11 for the details of the lookup function.

1. Select the lookup function `lookup_ext()`.
2. Click on the NEXT button.
3. At the top of the screen, browse to the lookup table by first selecting the datastore you created (called MYFIRSTDATASTORE), and then the GENDERLOOKUP table, which was created for demonstration purposes.
4. In the CONDITION section, select GENDERLONG in the COLUMN IN LOOKUP TABLE column. Select = for the OP.(&) column (shown in Figure 9.11).
5. Enter "MyInputFile.Gender" in the EXPRESSION column. This tells Data Services that you want to select values where the GENDERLONG column is equal to the value of the GENDER column in your input flat file.

6. In the OUTPUT section, select the column in the lookup table that you want to return from the function call. In this case, you want the short version of the gender, so select the GENDERSHORT column under the COLUMN IN LOOKUP TABLE column of this section.
7. In the OUTPUT COLUMN NAME column, enter the value "Gender".
8. Click on the FINISH button.
9. Select SAVE to save the data flow.

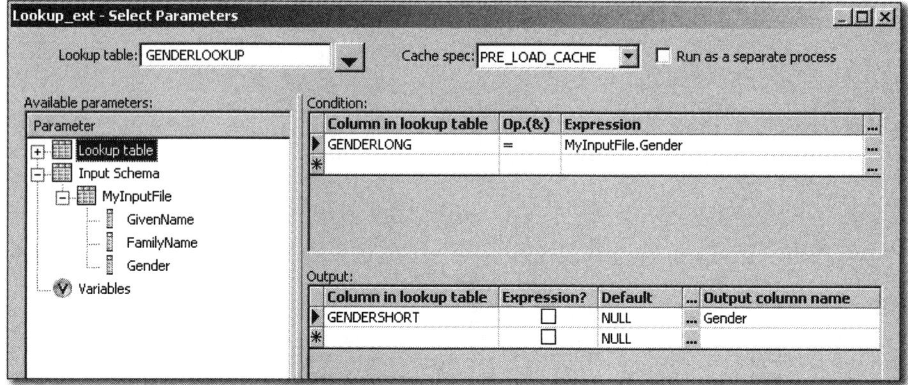

Figure 9.11 Details of the Gender Lookup Function

Now that you understand how to create a simple job with a query transform, we'll introduce a few of the complex transforms.

9.7 Overview of Complex Transformations

Many other transformations are provided as part of Data Services. This section provides a high-level description of some of the most commonly used platform transforms and the data integrator transforms. The data quality and text data processing transforms will be covered in detail in Section 9.10 and Section 9.11, respectively.

9.7.1 Platform Transformations

Platform transformations are core to Data Services. This means that regardless of your scenario or use of Data Services, these are transforms that can always be used and apply to a wide variety of data transformation requirements. The platform transformations include the following:

- **Query**
  The query transform is the most commonly used transform in Data Services and provides several capabilities. The most common use is to express operations on data similar to a SQL statement for data stored in a database, but at a higher level of abstraction (e.g., operations such as joins, ORDER-BY, and GROUP-BY). These operations are automatically converted by the Data Services optimizer at runtime to generate the proper SQL (if RDBMS) based on the sources. If sources other than an RDBMS are used, such as a file or an application interface, these operations may still be "pushed-down" to the source, or the data may be extracted and the operations performed in the Data Services engine.

  Other common use cases include mapping data between different sets of fields, using functions to manipulate a column of data, manipulating hierarchical schemas such as XML, or calling out to a web service.

- **Case**
  Case allows the user to distribute rows of data down different branches in a data flow. Case or decision logic to control the branching of rows is controlled by defining expressions in an expression table in the transform. For example, if you want to select only a subset of the rows you're processing to insert into a table, and the rest go to a flat file, you can use case to write the expression to identify those rows and route them accordingly.

- **SQL**
  SQL allows a user to explicitly define a specific SQL statement to be executed and feed rows into a data flow as a source. This transform should only be used if for some reason complex operations can't easily be accomplished using typical query transforms and datastore tables.

- **Merge**
  Merge combines incoming rows with the transform from multiple branches or sources in a data flow, producing a single output data set with the same schema as the input schemas (e.g., merging customer information from two legacy systems). (Note: The input schemas must be normalized using the query transform to ensure that the schemas are identical prior to using merge.)

- **Data mask**
  Data mask allows the user to anonymize, obfuscate, or mask the data, increasing the ability to share relevant data by protecting sensitive information. This

transform will preserve relationships and keep the data sensible. For example, if you want to mask out all but the last four digits of an identification number but retain the identification formatting, use the data mask transform.

- **Map_Operation**
  Data Services uses what is called an op-code to control the type of operation that should be done for each row when it's being pushed into a particular target. For example, when loading into an RDBMS, the op-code associated with each row of data is used by the loader to determine if a row should be inserted, updated, or deleted from the target. Some transforms automatically manipulate this hidden attribute, and, in this case, the `Map_Operation` transform can be used to explicitly set the op-code for the rows that pass through it.
- **Row_Generation**
  `Row_Generation` is used to generate rows in a data flow. You can control how many rows will be generated. This transform is used for complex schema generation (such as XML) and to generate rows for creating time dimensions within a data warehouse.
- **Validation**
  The validation transform enables you to define data validation rules and filter out rows with data that follow data validation standards. This transform is covered in more detail in Section 9.10.
- **User defined**
  If Data Services doesn't provide a function or transformation that you need, you can create your own. The user-defined transform allows you to extend Data Services with custom transforms to perform any kind of transformation you need. This transform allows you to define custom input fields and output fields for mapping data in and out of the transform. The actual transformation logic is written using the Python scripting language, which is embedded in this transformation. You can create your own named transformation configurations (combination of field definitions and Python scripts) so other users can easily reuse your transform configuration in many different data flows.

9.7.2 Data Integrator Transforms

The group of transformations that is referred to as the *data integrator transforms* perform several operations. Many of them are very commonly used to create data warehouses, and others are used to manipulate data and enhance performance.

The three transforms that we'll discuss are commonly used to easily manage the concept of slowly changing dimensions (SCDs) when building a star schema. Let's briefly discuss what we mean by this before jumping into the transform details. In a star schema, there are dimension and fact tables. The dimension tables typically hold master data entities such as customers or products. When you're loading this type of information, there may be changes to the data, such as a customer moving to a new address or attributes of a product changing over time.

When this happens, you have to decide if you want to maintain the history of those changes over time (depending on whether they are important to the usefulness of your data). There are generally three basic ways of dealing with this, and they are referred to as type 1, type 2, and type 3 slowly changing dimensions:

- **Type 1: no preservation of history**
  Existing rows for a customer, for example, are overwritten with new information.
- **Type 2: unlimited history preservation**
  New rows are generated to represent the attributes of an entity at any given time. A surrogate key is used to reference the correct representation of the entity in other tables at any given time.
- **Type 3: limited history preservation**
  Typically, only the current values and the last set of values for a given set of attributes are maintained. Columns are used instead of rows to store the prior value(s), and an effective date is used to signify when the change in values occurred.

Let's look at how Data Services makes it easy to handle history preservation. Three transforms are used in conjunction to accomplish this. In the following examples, the input table contains the new data coming through Data Services and being loaded into a data warehouse. The comparison table holds the existing data. The output table contains the output from the transformations based on the input table, comparison table, and transformation logic to preserve history.

The op-code column is the attribute for each row that Data Services generates for the loader in the data flow to know what it should do with the row, such as `INSERT`, `UPDATE`, or `DELETE` from the comparison table.

The three transforms used to accomplish this are table comparison, history preservation, and key generation.

Table Comparison

The table comparison transform compares the specified columns in the input with the comparison table to see if there are changes in the data (user defined). If there are, it flags the row with an op-code to update the existing row instead of inserting a new row by default. This transform can be used by itself in situations where history isn't preserved.

Because the same customer was detected (by ID) in Figure 9.12, but the address has changed, Joe and Sid are flagged for UPDATE. Elvis is completely new, so he will be flagged for INSERT.

Input:

ID	Name	Address	Op Code
10	Joe	11 Rehab Street	Normal
20	Sid	13 Cadillac Dr.	Normal
30	Charlie	15 Yukon Lane	Normal
40	Dolly	Goldrush Saloon	Normal
50	Elvis	Graceland, Memphis	Normal

Output:

ID	Name	Address	Op Code
10	Joe	11 Rehab Street	Update
20	Sid	13 Cadillac Dr.	Update
50	Elvis	Graceland, Memphis	Insert

Comparison table:

ID	Name	Address	Op Code
10	Joe	12 Halfway House	Normal
20	Sid	13 Deadhead Road	Normal
30	Charlie	15 Yukon Lane	Normal
40	Dolly	Goldrush Saloon	Normal

Figure 9.12 Table Comparison Output Results

History Preserving

When you want to preserve history, use this transform in conjunction with the table comparison transform. This ensures that the changed rows are inserted rather than updated to ensure tracking of all historical changes.

In Figure 9.13, we want to ensure that we track the history of changed addresses but not changes in names. Row IDs 10 and 20 will be converted from UPDATE to INSERT to preserve the history of the address change. But row 30 has only a change in name and so will remain an UPDATE because we don't track this type of history.

Input (from Table_Comparison):

ID	Name	Address	Op Code
10	Joe	11 Rehab Street	Update
20	Sid	13 Cadillac Dr.	Update
30	Charles	15 Yukon Lane	Update
50	Elvis	Graceland, Memphis	Insert

Output:

ID	Name	Address	Op Code
10	Joe	11 Rehab Street	Insert
20	Sid	13 Cadillac Dr.	Insert
30	Charles	15 Yukon Lane	Update
50	Elvis	Graceland, Memphis	Insert

Comparison table:

ID	Name	Address	Op Code
10	Joe	12 Halfway House	Normal
20	Sid	13 Deadhad Road	Normal
30	Charlie	15 Yukon Lane	Normal
40	Dolly	Goldrush Saloon	Normal

Figure 9.13 History Preserving Transform Output

Key Generation

This transform can be used following the history preserving transform to generate sequential key values for new rows, starting from the maximum existing key value in the target table where the `INSERT`s and `UPDATE`s are happening.

Figure 9.14 shows what a completed data flow may look like using these transformations together to find out which rows have changed, set up the `INSERT` and `UPDATE` operations to properly maintain history, and generate key values for any new rows.

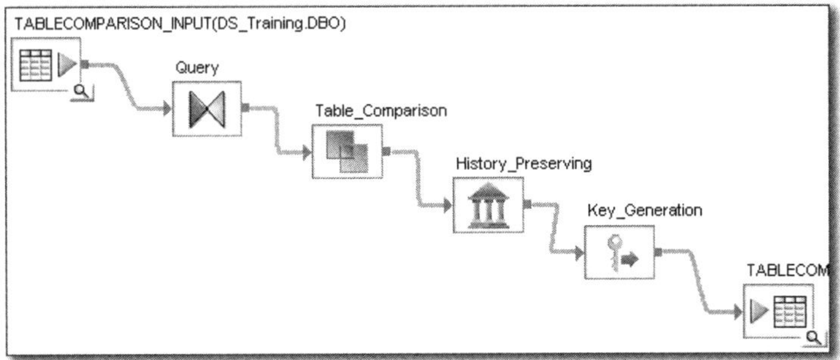

Figure 9.14 Complete Slowly Changing Dimensions Data Flow Example

In addition to these, other transforms include date generation, effective date, flattening, pivot, and several others. For more information on transforms, see the online help at *http://help.sap.com/eim*.

9.8 Executing and Debugging Your Job

After a job is set up, it can be executed in many different ways, from batch to real-time to scheduled to ad hoc. Jobs can be executed from the designer, management console, from the command line using a script, or from a web service. In the designer, a job can be executed in debug mode.

The debugging capabilities allow you to set breakpoints anywhere in a data flow. When the job is executed in debug mode, the data flow stops running when the first row hits the breakpoint location (some point between transformations). The user is then able to click on a magnifying glass icon on any line between transforms to view the data that has travelled through that path. Data Services allows users to view the data in any two paths at a time so they can compare the data in those two points in a data flow. This is shown in Figure 9.15.

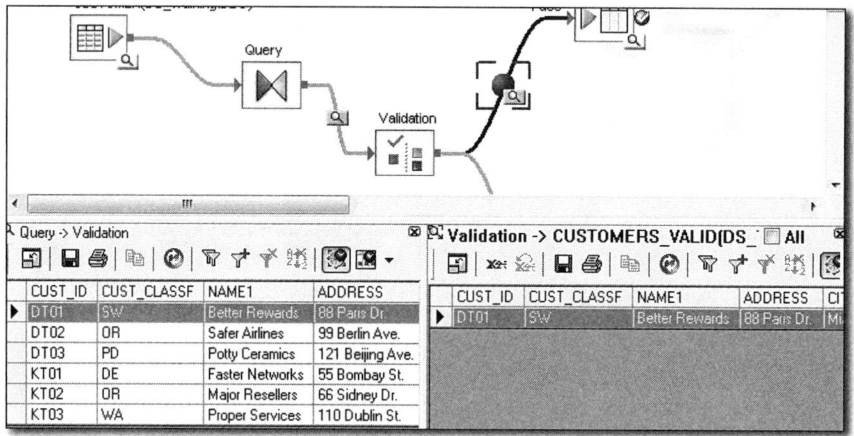

Figure 9.15 View Data between Transforms during Debugging

Notice in Figure 9.15 that you see the data after the query step and prior to the validation step on the left side of the screen. The first record after the validation step is on the right side.

Breakpoints can be configured to be conditional. So instead of the breakpoint causing the execution to pause when the first row hits that point in the data flow, you can configure conditions. Only when a condition is met will the execution stop, and you can examine the data within the data flow. Figure 9.16 shows a conditional breakpoint.

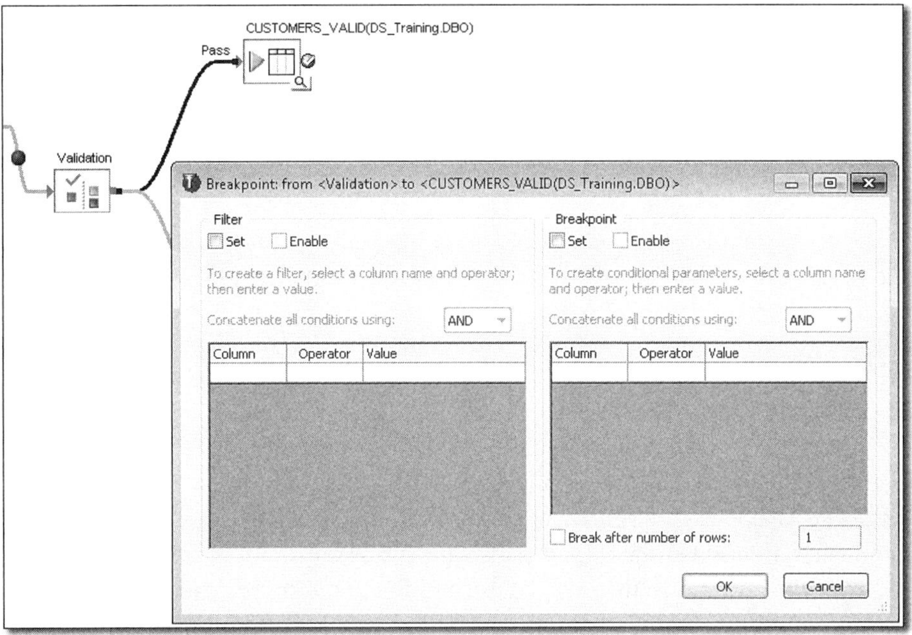

Figure 9.16 Set Up Conditional Breakpoints and Filters

In Figure 9.16, notice the option to filter based on a COLUMN, OPERATOR, and VALUE.

For more information on debugging and administration, see the administrators guide, which is available at *http://help.sap.com*. At the help site, follow the menu path SAP BUSINESSOBJECTS • ENTERPRISE INFORMATION MANAGEMENT • DATA SERVICES.

9.9 Exposing a Real-Time Service

Data Services provides APIs that allow many operations to be performed by other applications through the integration of these APIs. Usually, developers use the web service methodology to integrate with Data Services, but Java and C++ APIs are also provided for some of the more performance-intensive operations. The web service interface has many operations to perform activities, such as execute a batch job and retrieve operational metadata, logs, and current status for an executing batch job, as well as transactional integration and transforming of data.

This section discusses a use case that exposes a real-time service as a web service so that data transformations can be performed as a service. Other applications in the enterprise can then leverage these services. A common use case for this is data cleansing as a service. Many organizations expose services to perform data validation for master data, for example, address cleansing. Others may expose a service to perform matching against their master data to ensure that they are preventing duplicates.

Next, we explain how to create a real-time job and a real-time service and expose the new service as a web service to be called from other applications.

9.9.1 Create a Real-Time Job

The first step is to create a job that's capable of being called as a service such that the consuming application is able to pass data to Data Services, and Data Services is able to return data to the application. To do this, Data Services allows you to define an XML message source and an XML message target. These source and target objects are used in data flows that will be exposed as a real-time job. Whereas in batch jobs, you typically use a database or file as the source and target, here you define an XML message structure.

A schema defines how the XML message structure should look, and it must be defined first. The schema definition will be discussed next, followed by the data flow and the job.

Create a Schema

First, go to the Local Object Library and the Formats tab. From here, you can create schemas by defining a schema name and then importing an XML schema definition (XSD or DTD) that defines the structure. Figure 9.17 shows an example imported schema.

Notes for Creating Schemas

You should create a separate schema definition for your source and your target. Each should have its own unique namespace. Our recommendation is to always define a default namespace and target namespace, and specify the attributes `elementFormDefault` and `attributeFormDefault` for your schema.

Also, if you use the option in a query transform to create an XML schema, it won't automatically add a namespace and the preceding attributes, so you'll need to manually add them to the XML schema file that's generated before importing the new schema into the designer.

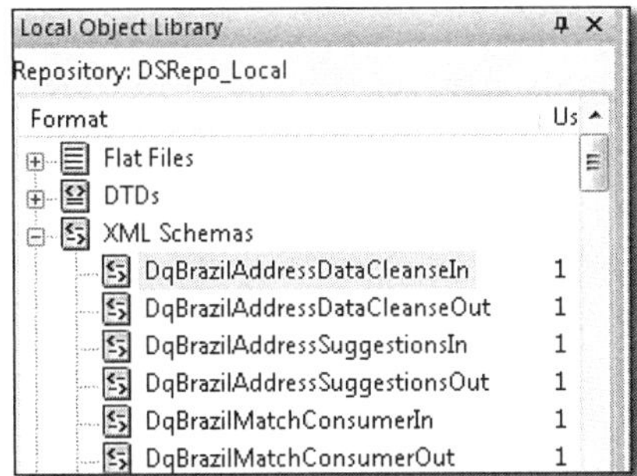

Figure 9.17 Example of XML Schema Definitions

Notice in Figure 9.17 that XML schemas are another format type that's available in the Local Object Library. Next, we describe the creation of the data flow.

Create a Data Flow

The next step is to create a data flow using the schemas: Simply drag the schema onto the designer as your XML message source and XML message target. From there, the process is the same as creating any other data flow. Drag the desired transformations, and perform the mappings. Figure 9.18 shows an example job that's created by using XML schemas a source and target.

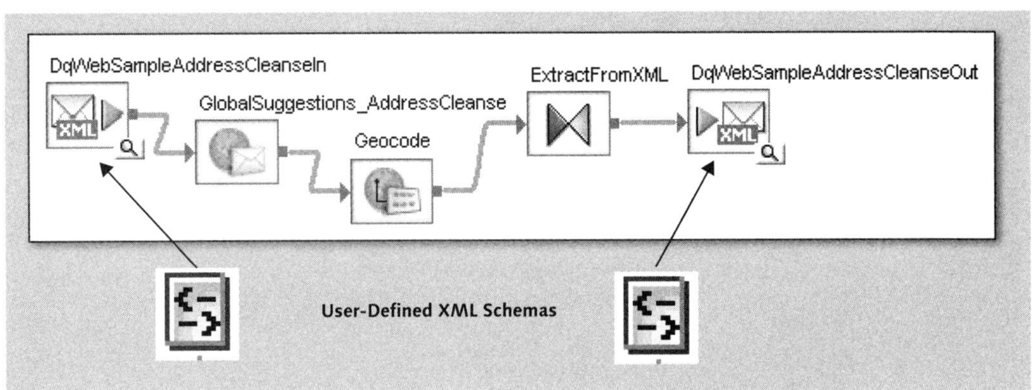

Figure 9.18 Example Data Flow for a Real-Time Job Using XML Schema Source/Target

After this is done, you just need to create the job.

Create the Job

The final step is to create the job. Go to the Local Object Library, and create a new real-time job. You can use the steps described in Section 9.5.6 to create batch jobs, but select Real-Time. Then add the data flow you just created. It's that simple.

9.9.2 Create a Real-Time Service

After you've completed the creation of a real-time job, it's the administrator's responsibility to expose this real-time job as a real-time service. A real-time service is an abstraction layer between the consuming applications and the Data Services job. Most organizations use naming conventions for the objects in their Data Services repository, and this process allows you to create a user-friendly name for the service instead of the job name.

The real-time service construct also allows the administrator to define settings to help ensure the quality of service and scale the solution. It's at this point that the administrator determines on which job server instances the service will be provisioned, and determines settings such as request/response time-outs, how many service providers are required to handle typical loads, and how to scale up automatically when peak loads occur.

To create the real-time service, execute the following steps, shown in Figure 9.19:

1. Log in to the management console.
2. Click on the Administrator icon.
3. Open the following tree: Real-Time • <Access Server Host:Port> • Real-Time Services.
4. Click on the Add button.

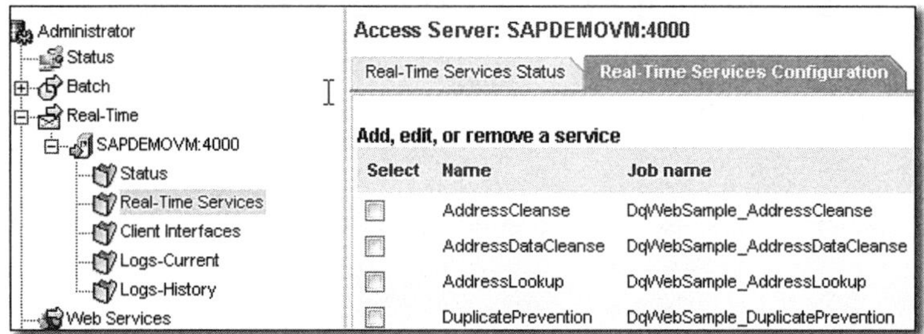

Figure 9.19 Select the Configuration Tab to Create a New Real-Time Service

5. Select the Real-Time Services Configuration tab.
6. Set the service name.
7. Click on the Browse Jobs button to select a job to associate this service with.
8. Click on the hyperlink for the real-time job you created.
9. Click on the Add button to add a job server as your service provider.
10. Click on the Apply button (see Figure 9.20).
11. Click on the Real-time Services status tab at the top to view the list of available real-time services, which should include the new service just added.
12. Select the checkbox next to the real-time service you just created.
13. Click on the Start button to start the service on the assigned job servers.

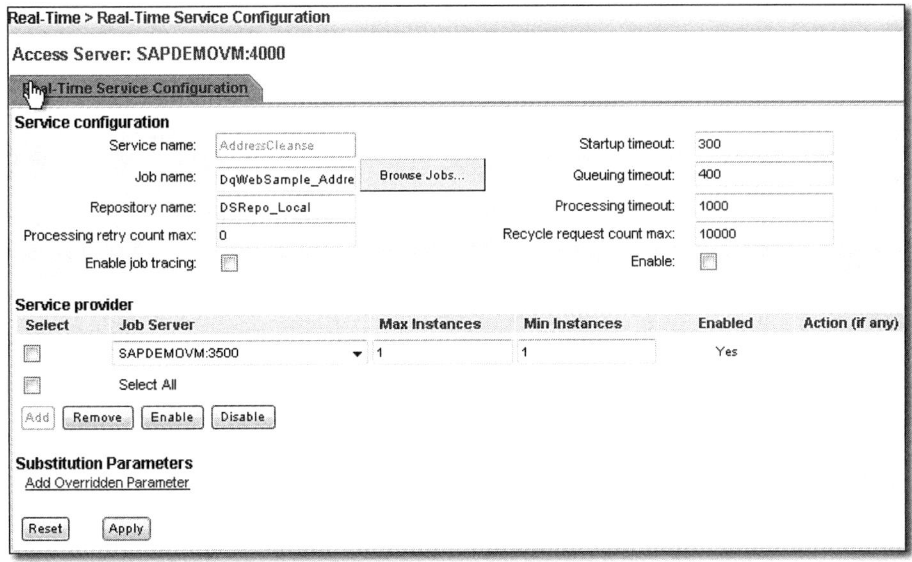

Figure 9.20 Detailed Configuration of a Real-Time Service

Now that you have a real-time service, you can call this service using the Java or C++ Message Client libraries provided with Data Services. If you want to use web services instead of the Java or C++ APIs, see Section 9.9.3. To get more information about these, refer to the *Data Services Integrator's Guide* in the product documentation, which is available at *http://help.sap.com.*

9.9.3 Expose the Real-Time Service as a Web Service

The final step is to expose the real-time service via the web service interface. Data Services supports the Web Service Definition Language/Simple Object Access Protocol (WSDL/SOAP) standards for the web service interface. To expose this real-time service via a web service, execute the following steps:

1. After selecting the ADMINISTRATOR icon when logging in, select the WEB SERVICES hyperlink in the tree on the left-hand side.
2. Select the WEB SERVICES CONFIGURATION tab.
3. In the dropdown box, select ADD REAL-TIME SERVICE.
4. Click on the APPLY button.
5. Select the checkbox next to the real-time service you just created.
6. Click on the ADD button.
7. Click on the WEB SERVICES hyperlink in the tree once again (or the bread crumb trail at the top of the page) to go back to the list of operations exposed as a web service. You should see your new service in the list of web service operations.
8. Select the VIEW WSDL button to launch a web browser with the WSDL file that a software developer can use to consume the web service. It contains all the metadata, including the schema for the source/target XML messages for the real-time job.

Figure 9.21 shows some examples of real-time services exposed as web service operations.

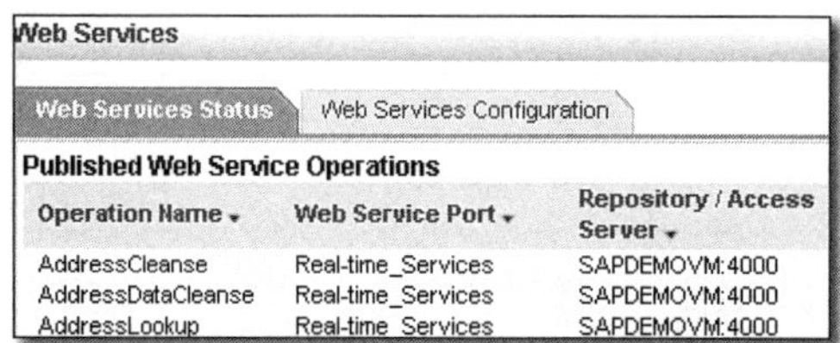

Figure 9.21 Web Service Listing of User-Defined Real-Time Services

A developer can now take the URL to the WSDL and import it into any development application to consume the web service for data transformation. There are two ways that the web service can be executed. The first is by an explicit web service operation named after the real-time service name defined during the creation of the service. With this method, the XML schemas are available in the WSDL so that the consuming application can more intelligently create code to automatically serialize and de-serialize the input XML message and output XML message. This brings a lot of simplicity to the consuming developer, as well as other tools such as SAP Process Orchestration (previously SAP NetWeaver Process Integration). Because the schemas are known, they can provide some automation.

The other method is to use the web service method `Run_Realtime_Service`. This method is more dynamic in the sense that you can use this one operation to execute any real-time service. The parameters for this operation are simply the name of the service, as defined when creating the service, and the XML string for the input conforming to the XML schema imported into the data flow.

9.10 Data Quality Management

The data quality process takes action to guarantee clean and accurate data by automatically correcting your data based on reference data and data cleansing rules, enhancing your data with additional attributes and information, and finding duplicates and merging your records into one consolidated, best record. Figure 9.22 shows the data quality wheel that will be a guide for you throughout this chapter.

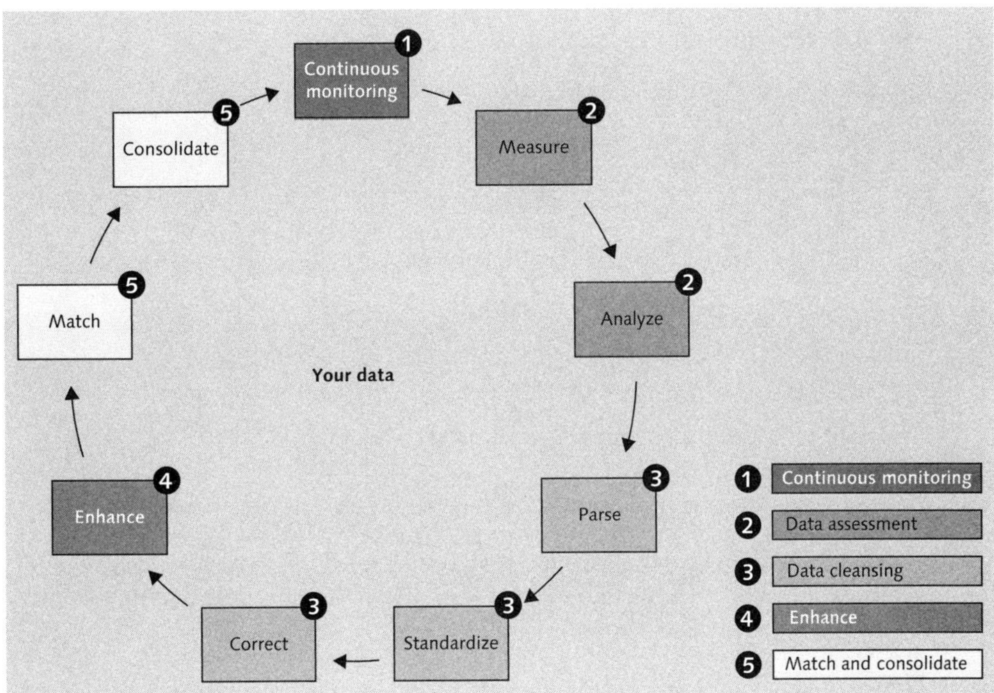

Figure 9.22 Data Quality Wheel

The goal of data quality is to have a single version of the truth. Whether performing a transactional or bulk data load into an SAP CRM system, master data management, or an enterprise data warehouse, you want to have a consolidated view of the customer. Because most organizations put the customer first, we will as well, and focus on using data quality to create a single customer view throughout this section, with some content later that explains how data quality can be adapted to other domain types.

In this section, we'll explain how to maintain data quality using *transforms* in Data Services. We'll start with a discussion of data cleansing and then move on to data enrichment in Section 9.10.2, which is what happens to data after it's cleansed. After that, we discuss data matching in Section 9.10.3, which detects duplicates and can consolidate data records. These first three sections will walk you through each major step required to create a data flow, an example of which is shown in Figure 9.23. This example shows a data quality data flow created in Data Services using the transforms specific to data quality, including the address cleanse, data cleanse, and match transforms, which will also be explained in these first three sections on Data Quality Management.

We'll refer back to Figure 9.23 as we look at each transform in detail, so you might want to bookmark this page.

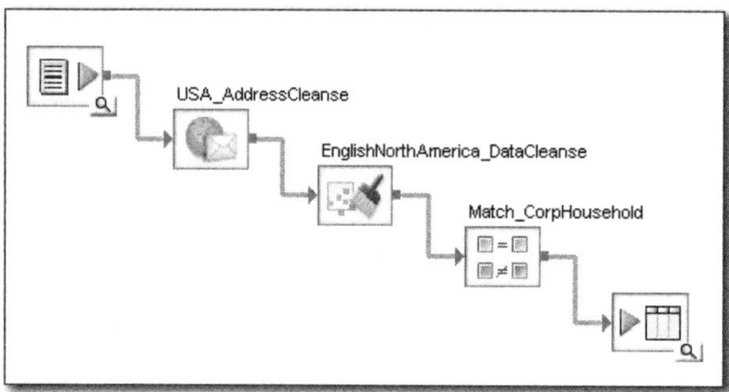

Figure 9.23 Example Data Quality Data Flow in Data Services

> **Note**
>
> For a complete list of data quality transforms, see Appendix A. (All appendices are available for download from the book's page at *www.sap-press.com/3666*.)

9.10.1 Data Cleansing

General data cleansing starts with the base transform, which is used to configure a custom data cleanse transform. The base transform for general data cleansing capabilities is called the data cleanse transform. There are also several sample data cleanse transform configurations of the data cleanse transform shipped with Data Services; for example, ENGLISHNORTHAMERICA_DATACLEANSE is preconfigured to cleanse name, title, firm, date, email, and phone data using English-based data quality rules.

This section also discusses the address cleanse transform for more specialized address cleansing capabilities. Two base transforms are available for address cleansing, the *global address cleanse transform* and the *USA regulatory address cleanse transform*. In addition to the base transforms, there are several sample configurations, including the USA_ADDRESSCLEANSE configured to cleanse address data in the United States (in a nonregulatory mode). Throughout this chapter, we won't refer to specific base or custom transform configurations, but instead more generally to the data cleanse and address cleanse transforms.

Let's get started with cleansing data for NeedsEIM Inc. using the first two transforms shown in Figure 9.23: the address cleanse and data cleanse transforms. The data cleansing process can be broken down into three steps: parsing, standardization, and correction. Validation is a fourth, optional step that is used to validate the data, and this can be done before or after the core cleansing steps. Each of these will be examined closely in its own section.

Data Parsing

As the initial step, data parsing identifies and isolates data elements in data structures. Often, multiple data elements are collected and stored in a database grouped into single fields. Parsing identifies individual data elements and breaks them down into their component parts. It rearranges data elements in a single field or moves multiple data elements from a single data field to multiple discrete fields. Parsing is vital to the data cleansing effort because it provides information about the type of data in each field, which is used later when correcting data as well as matching records. Figure 9.24 shows an example of data parsing with the input record and the output record after the data has been parsed.

Input Record	Output Record	
Mr. Don R. Smith Jr. CPA Account Mgr. Jones Inc. Dept. of Accounting PO BOX 567 Biron, WI 5594	Prename	Mr.
	First Name	Don
	Middle Name	R.
	Last Name	Smith
	Maturity Postname	Jr.
	Honorary Postname	CPA
	Title	Account Mgr.
	Firm	Jones Inc.
	Department	Dept. of Accounting
	Locality	Biron
	Region	WI
	Primary Number	567
	Postal Code	5594

Figure 9.24 Data Parsing Example

To get started with data parsing, you must first understand the makeup and format of the data in your source systems. Profiling can be very helpful in this process of getting to know your data (discussed in detail in Chapter 10) in terms of how the data is fielded, formatted, and populated. Figure 9.25 shows an example of how data is broken down for parsing.

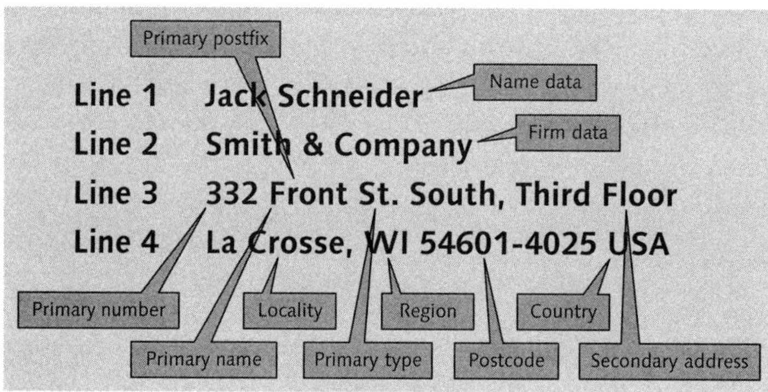

Figure 9.25 Basic Name and Address Components

Focusing on name and address information, Figure 9.25 highlights the basic data components, including the following:

- **Name line (lines 1–2)**
  - Name: the contact name
  - Firm: the company, business, or organization name

- **Address line components (line 3)**
  - Primary range: the premises or street number (e.g., 332)
  - Primary name: the street description, such as Front or Main
  - Primary type: the abbreviated or nonabbreviated type of primary name, such as Street (St.) or Avenue (Ave.)
  - Primary postfix: the abbreviated or nonabbreviated directional, such as south (S) or northwest (NW)
  - Secondary address: the floor (e.g., third floor), unit, stairwell, or wing data
- **Last line components (line 4)**
  - Locality: the city, town, or suburb, such as La Crosse or Chicago
  - Region: the state (e.g., WI), province, territory, or region
  - Postcode: the postal code, including primary (e.g., 54601) and secondary (e.g., 4025) postal codes
  - Country: the country name, such as USA or Germany

These data components can be represented in a discrete, multiline, or multiline hybrid format. With a discrete format, data elements appear in the same field arrangement from record to record, meaning that a locality field will always contain city data, and a postcode field will always contain postcode data. In a multiline format, data isn't consistently located in the same arrangement in all records. That is, data items "float" among fields, or data components may appear in different fields from one record to another. Multiline hybrid is a format that includes a combination of both discretely fielded and multiline formatted data in the same record. Figure 9.26 is an example of the discrete format.

Field	Record 1	Record 2	Record 3
Firm			Dupong S.A.
Address1	MikroElektronik GmbH	Nybroveg 120	225 rue de Bragance
Locality1	Baumschulgasse 25	Lyngby	Luxembourg
Region1	Weinheim		
Postcode	69469	2800	1449
Country	Germany	Denmark	Luxembourg

Figure 9.26 Discrete Format

Figure 9.27 shows an example of the multiline format. In this figure, notice that both the first and last name are in a multiline field. Also notice the difference of use for MULTILINE4. For RECORD 1, it has an address, and for RECORD 3, it has the name of a company.

Field	Record 1	Record 2	Record 3
Multiline1	Lance Robinson		Peter Grant
Multiline2	Information Services Plc	Gran Via de Carles S.A.	
Multiline3	Cornwall House	Ibarra Campilo	
Multiline4	56 Henley Road		United Car Rental Ltd.
Multiline5		48010 Bilbao	
Multiline6	London		
Multiline7	NW2Y 5DM		3150 S. Larkin Rd. Suite 10
Multiline8			Etobicoke, ON M9C4T9
Multiline9	United Kingdom	Spain	Canada

Figure 9.27 Multiline Format

Figure 9.28 shows an example of the hybrid multiline format.

Field	Record 1	Record 2	Record 3
Multiline1	Lance Robinson		
Multiline2	Information Services Plc	Gran Via de CarlesS.A.	Azko Chemicals
Multiline3	Cornwall House	Ibarra Campilo	
Multiline4	56 Henley Road		Moreelsepk 24
Multiline5			
Locality1		Bilboa	
Locality2	Harlow		
Region1	Essex		
Postal Code	CM19 5AE	48010	
Last line			3511 EP Utrecht
Country	United Kingdom	Spain	Netherland

Figure 9.28 Hybrid Multiline Format

While Figure 9.26 through Figure 9.28 show examples of address data, this concept extends beyond address data. You also should become familiar with how your other data components are being fielded and formatted. For example, do you have a discrete first name and last name field or a single name field? If you have both a first name and last name, how are middle names or initials handled (e.g., consistently at the end of the first name field, at the beginning of the last name field, or a combination of both)? Do you have multiple phone number or email fields, and are some more frequently populated than others? How consistently formatted are those fields? Ultimately, understanding the makeup and format of your data will help you later on when configuring various data cleanse operations.

Let's look at NeedsEIM Inc.'s supplier data from one of its sources. The data, shown in Table 9.2, includes several discretely fielded data components (Name, Organization, City, Region, Postalcode) along with multiline data (Address1, Address2, Lastline). In addition, there are also nondiscrete data components represented as miscellaneous data fields with a mix of email, phone, date, and identification information (Miscellaneous1, Miscellaneous2).

Note

Note that the data in Table 9.2 hasn't been standardized or corrected yet as a part of the data cleansing process, so you'll note errors in the information. Standardizing and correction are covered in subsequent sections.

	Record 1	Record 2
Name	Mr. Robert L King Jr	Chris C Henderson C.P.A
Organization	PRODIGY	LTD
Address1	208 South Akard Street	5000 BRDWAY ST S STE300
Address2	Suite 150	<Blank>
City	Dalas	Kansas City
Region	TX	Montana
Postalcode	75020	<Blank>
Country	<Blank>	US
Miscellaneous1	PROPERTY MGR	Jan 24 1984
Miscellaneous2	robertk@prodigy.net	800.223.1212 EXT 879

Table 9.2 Example Supplier Data for NeedsEIM Inc.

To highlight the parsing capabilities in Data Services, we'll now discuss the address cleansing transforms and the data cleanse quality transforms. The address cleansing can be done using either the global address cleanse or the U.S. regulatory address cleanse. In this example, we'll use the global address cleanse transform.

Global Address Cleanse Transform

Look at Figure 9.23 again. In this example, you'll learn how to parse data using the global address cleanse, which is the first transform shown in the example data flow in Figure 9.23. The global address cleanse transform enables you to parse data by mapping the input data to the transform's discrete and mutltiline input to do the data parsing. Follow these steps:

1. Drag the global address cleanse transform to the canvas, and connect the source data to the transform. The address cleanse transform will be used to parse the address fields from Table 9.2.
2. When you double-click on the transform, there are three major sections in the Transform Editor: Schema In, Schema Out, and a bottom configuration pane that includes Input, Options, and Output tabs (see Figure 9.29). The Schema In area relates the source data shown in Table 9.2.

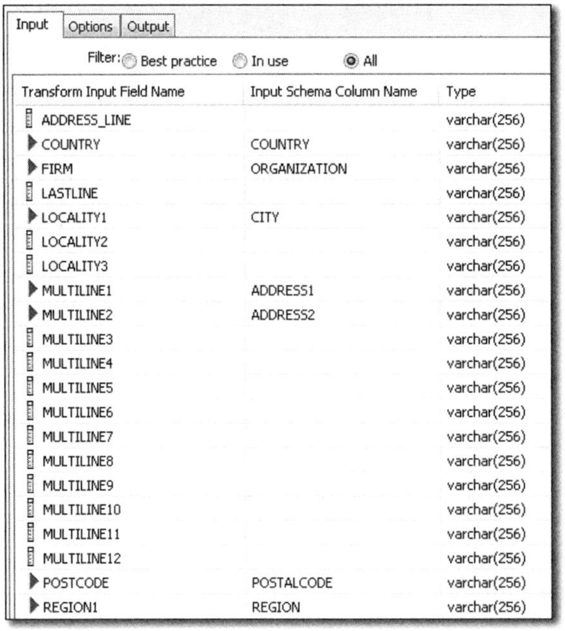

Input | Options | Output

Filter: ○ Best practice ○ In use ◉ All

Transform Input Field Name	Input Schema Column Name	Type
ADDRESS_LINE		varchar(256)
COUNTRY	COUNTRY	varchar(256)
FIRM	ORGANIZATION	varchar(256)
LASTLINE		varchar(256)
LOCALITY1	CITY	varchar(256)
LOCALITY2		varchar(256)
LOCALITY3		varchar(256)
MULTILINE1	ADDRESS1	varchar(256)
MULTILINE2	ADDRESS2	varchar(256)
MULTILINE3		varchar(256)
MULTILINE4		varchar(256)
MULTILINE5		varchar(256)
MULTILINE6		varchar(256)
MULTILINE7		varchar(256)
MULTILINE8		varchar(256)
MULTILINE9		varchar(256)
MULTILINE10		varchar(256)
MULTILINE11		varchar(256)
MULTILINE12		varchar(256)
POSTCODE	POSTALCODE	varchar(256)
REGION1	REGION	varchar(256)

Figure 9.29 Global Address Cleanse Transform Input Tab

3. Map the input schema columns to both discrete and multiline input fields that are recognized by the transform on the TRANSFORM EDITOR'S INPUT tab. In Figure 9.29, ORGANIZATION, ADDRESS1, ADDRESS2, CITY, REGION, POSTALCODE, and COUNTRY are mapped to the TRANSFORM INPUT FIELD NAME address cleanse transform in the leftmost column. The arrow icon indicates which fields are mapped.
4. On the OUTPUT tab, all of the parsed output fields are listed that are available to you (Figure 9.30 shows just a sampling of the available fields). For example, notice that the primary number, name, prefix, postfix, type, and secondary information of the address are all available as parsed, discrete output fields.

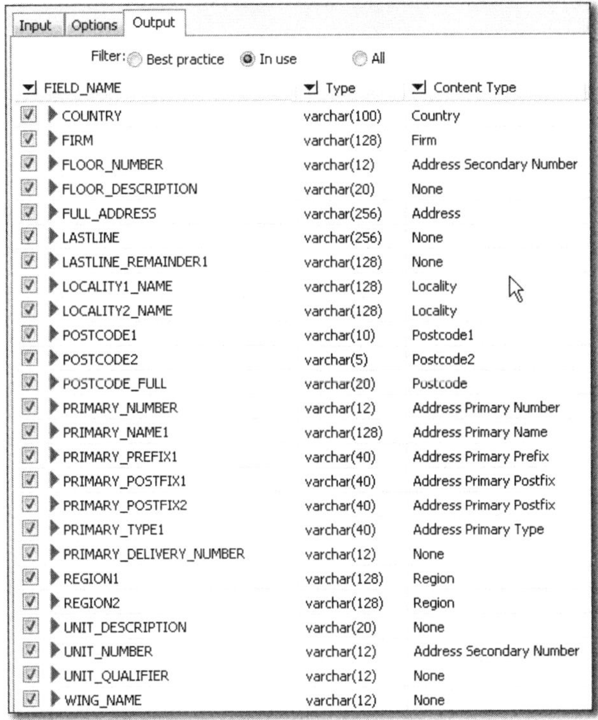

FIELD_NAME	Type	Content Type
COUNTRY	varchar(100)	Country
FIRM	varchar(128)	Firm
FLOOR_NUMBER	varchar(12)	Address Secondary Number
FLOOR_DESCRIPTION	varchar(20)	None
FULL_ADDRESS	varchar(256)	Address
LASTLINE	varchar(256)	None
LASTLINE_REMAINDER1	varchar(128)	None
LOCALITY1_NAME	varchar(128)	Locality
LOCALITY2_NAME	varchar(128)	Locality
POSTCODE1	varchar(10)	Postcode1
POSTCODE2	varchar(5)	Postcode2
POSTCODE_FULL	varchar(20)	Postcode
PRIMARY_NUMBER	varchar(12)	Address Primary Number
PRIMARY_NAME1	varchar(128)	Address Primary Name
PRIMARY_PREFIX1	varchar(40)	Address Primary Prefix
PRIMARY_POSTFIX1	varchar(40)	Address Primary Postfix
PRIMARY_POSTFIX2	varchar(40)	Address Primary Postfix
PRIMARY_TYPE1	varchar(40)	Address Primary Type
PRIMARY_DELIVERY_NUMBER	varchar(12)	None
REGION1	varchar(128)	Region
REGION2	varchar(128)	Region
UNIT_DESCRIPTION	varchar(20)	None
UNIT_NUMBER	varchar(12)	Address Secondary Number
UNIT_QUALIFIER	varchar(12)	None
WING_NAME	varchar(12)	None

Figure 9.30 Global Address Cleanse Transform Output Tab

5. To build the SCHEMA OUT for the transform, select the parsed values to be generated by the transform from the OUTPUT tab, including the address line as a whole (the PRIMARY_SECONDARY_ADDRESS output field includes both primary and secondary address information) as well as the discretely parsed

components, primary name and number, unit number, city, state, and primary and secondary postcode information.

6. To pass input fields (from the SCHEMA IN pane) through the transform, drag and drop the input fields from SCHEMA IN to SCHEMA OUT. *Pass through* refers to input fields that are unrelated to the current cleansing process (e.g., a customer ID that is unrelated to address cleansing) and fields for which you want to maintain the original content for later use. In our example, we're passing the contact name and miscellaneous fields through the address cleanse transform. These fields will be used later as input into the data cleanse transform.

Note

You can get help with the input or output fields that are available to you by viewing the embedded help. If help isn't visible, mouse over the right-hand side of the TRANSFORM EDITOR to access it (see Figure 9.31).

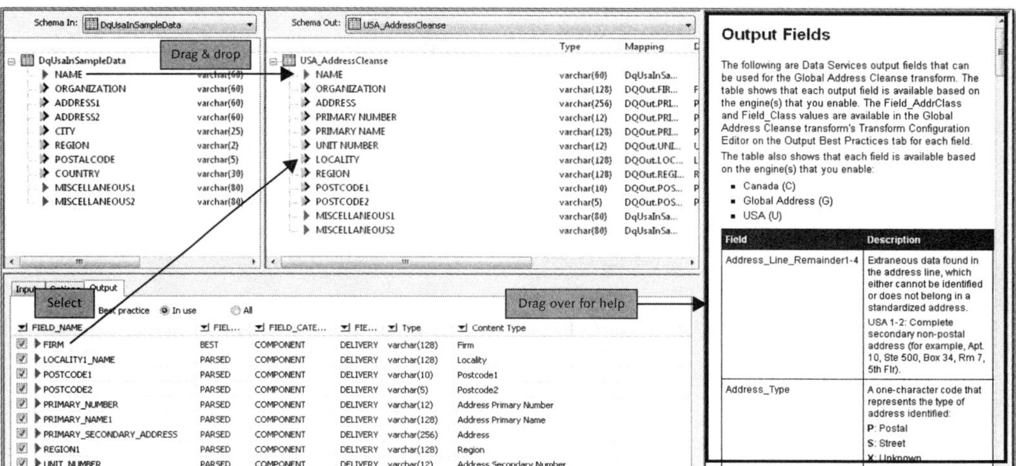

Figure 9.31 Global Address Cleanse Transform Editor

7. After the address cleanse step has executed, the parsed output will look like what's shown in Table 9.3.

Note

Note that the data in Table 9.3 is parsed only. Standardization and correction as a part of the data cleansing process are covered in subsequent sections.

Pre-Parsed Data		
Address 1	208 South Akard Street	5000 BRADFORD ST S STE300
Address1	Suite 150	<Blank>
City	Dalas	Kansas City
Region	TX	Montana
Postalcode	75020	<Blank>
Parsed Data		
Primary Number	208	5000
Primary Name	Akard	BRADFORD
Primary Prefix	South	S
Primary Postfix	<Blank>	<Blank>
Primary Type	Street	ST
Unit Number	150	300
Unit Description	Suite	STE
Locality	Dalas	Kansas City
Region	TX	Montana
Postalcode	75020	<Blank>

Table 9.3 Address Parsing Example

Now that you've parsed the address data using the global address cleanse transform, you'll see an example of parsing the nonaddress data using the data cleanse transform.

Data Cleanse Transform

The *data cleanse* transform takes discrete or miscellaneous, multiline data and parses out date, email, firm or company, phone number, Social Security number, name, and title information into discrete fields. In addition, users also can define custom parsers to go beyond the recognized content types just listed to be able to parse out and identify numbers (for example).

For each content type, *data cleanse* gives the user the option to further break the type down into smaller components. For example, name data can be parsed into first (given name 1), middle (given name 2), and last (family name) components along with prename and honorary (e.g., CPA) and maturity (e.g., Jr.) postnames. Email data can be further parsed into user, domain, and host. Name data is parsed differently depending on the cultural norm. For example, for Spanish, Portuguese, and Japanese names, it's considered a norm to have two last names or family names. As such, data cleanse outputs to both a family name 1 and family name

2 output field. Appendix A (available for download from the book's page at *www.sap-press.com/3666*) has an example of differences in name parsing logic to support various cultures and international data sets.

Refer to Figure 9.23 for the next example, which builds on the second step in the data flow. When using the data cleanse transform, we're using the delivered variation of the transform, called EnglishNorthAmerica_DataCleanse.

The following steps describe how to use the data cleanse transform to parse data into discrete components such as first name, last name, title, organization, and so on:

1. Drag the data cleanse transform to the canvas, and connect the global address cleanse transform to this transform. The data cleanse transform will be used to parse the nonaddress fields from Table 9.2.
2. On the Input tab, we'll map the name, organization, and miscellaneous 1 and 2 data fields as input into data cleanse and pass through the parsed address components that were output from the preceding global address cleanse transform.

Input | Options | Output

Filter: Best practice | In use | All

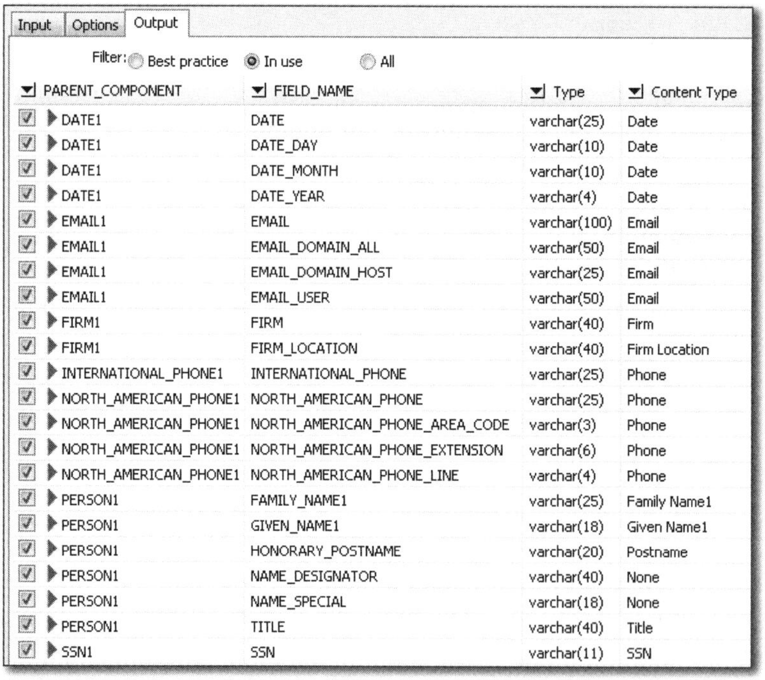

PARENT_COMPONENT	FIELD_NAME	Type	Content Type
DATE1	DATE	varchar(25)	Date
DATE1	DATE_DAY	varchar(10)	Date
DATE1	DATE_MONTH	varchar(10)	Date
DATE1	DATE_YEAR	varchar(4)	Date
EMAIL1	EMAIL	varchar(100)	Email
EMAIL1	EMAIL_DOMAIN_ALL	varchar(50)	Email
EMAIL1	EMAIL_DOMAIN_HOST	varchar(25)	Email
EMAIL1	EMAIL_USER	varchar(50)	Email
FIRM1	FIRM	varchar(40)	Firm
FIRM1	FIRM_LOCATION	varchar(40)	Firm Location
INTERNATIONAL_PHONE1	INTERNATIONAL_PHONE	varchar(25)	Phone
NORTH_AMERICAN_PHONE1	NORTH_AMERICAN_PHONE	varchar(25)	Phone
NORTH_AMERICAN_PHONE1	NORTH_AMERICAN_PHONE_AREA_CODE	varchar(3)	Phone
NORTH_AMERICAN_PHONE1	NORTH_AMERICAN_PHONE_EXTENSION	varchar(6)	Phone
NORTH_AMERICAN_PHONE1	NORTH_AMERICAN_PHONE_LINE	varchar(4)	Phone
PERSON1	FAMILY_NAME1	varchar(25)	Family Name1
PERSON1	GIVEN_NAME1	varchar(18)	Given Name1
PERSON1	HONORARY_POSTNAME	varchar(20)	Postname
PERSON1	NAME_DESIGNATOR	varchar(40)	None
PERSON1	NAME_SPECIAL	varchar(18)	None
PERSON1	TITLE	varchar(40)	Title
SSN1	SSN	varchar(11)	SSN

Figure 9.32 Data Cleanse Transform Output Tab

3. On the OUTPUT tab, the available parsed output fields are listed (Figure 9.32 shows just a sampling of the available fields). Select various parsed components, including PRENAME, HONORARY and MATURITY_POSTNAME, GIVEN_NAME1 (first name), GIVEN_NAME2 (middle name), FAMILY_NAME1 (last name), TITLE, PHONE, EMAIL, DATE, SSN (Social Security number), and FIRM (organization), for parsing.
4. To pass input fields (from the SCHEMA IN pane) through the transform, drag and drop the input fields from SCHEMA IN to SCHEMA OUT. In our example, we're passing the address-related fields from the global address cleanse process through the data cleanse transform. This is shown in Figure 9.33.

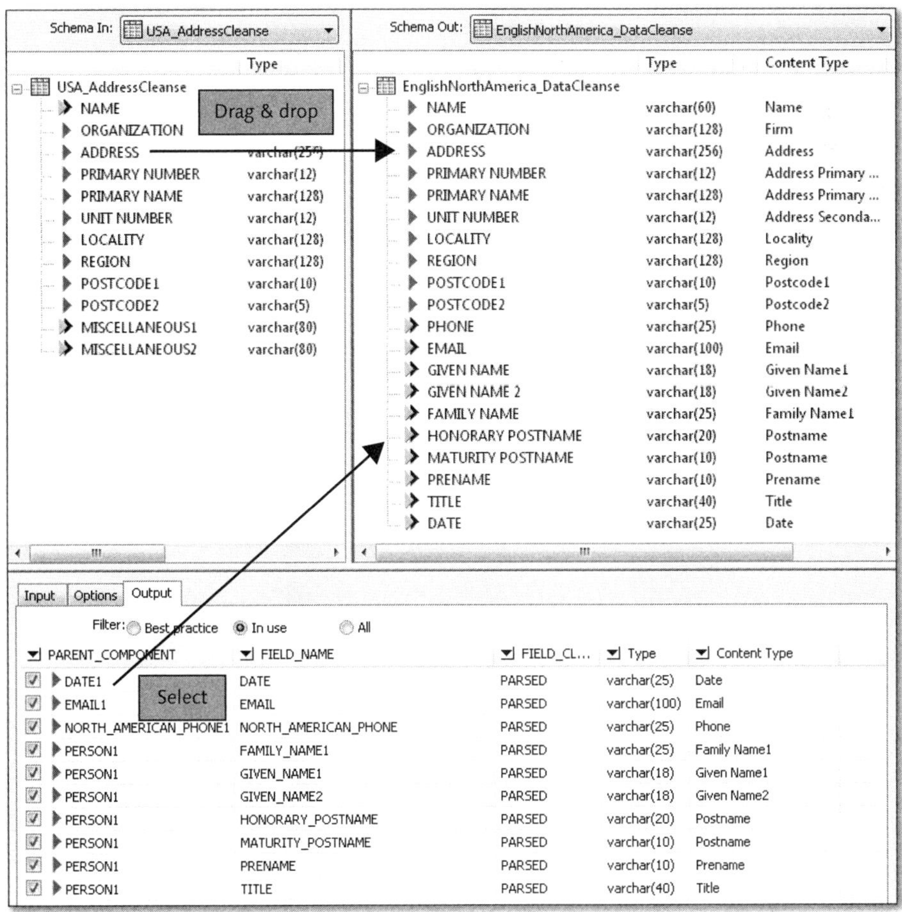

Figure 9.33 Data Cleanse Transform Editor

After the data cleanse step has executed, the parsed output will look like Table 9.4.

Pre-Parsed Data		
Name	Mr. Robert L King Jr	Chris C Henderson C.P.A
Organization	PRODIGY	LTD
Miscellaneous 1	PROPERTY MGR	Jan 24 1984
Miscellaneous 2	robertk@prodigy.net	800.223.1212 EXT 879
Parsed Data		
Prename	Mr.	<Blank>
Given Name 1	Robert	Chris
Given Name 2	L.	C
Family Name	King	Hendersen
Maturity Postname	Jr	<Blank>
Honorary Postname	<Blank>	C.P.A
Organization	PRODIGY	LTD
Title	PROPERTY MGR	<Blank>
Phone	<Blank>	800.223.1212 EXT 879
Email	robertk@prodigy.net	<Blank>
Date	<Blank>	Jan 24 1984

Table 9.4 Name and Data Parsing Example

We mentioned earlier that data cleansing includes data parsing, data standardization, and data correction. Now that the data has been parsed, you'll learn about data standardization next.

Data Standardization

After your data has been parsed, the next step is to ensure consistency across all of your records. This is necessary to prepare the data for validation, correction, and accurate record matching. Data standardization includes business rules concerning formats, abbreviations, acronyms, punctuation, greetings, casing, order, pattern matching, and so on. Each of these are examples of elements you can control to meet your business requirements. Figure 9.34 shows an example of data standardization.

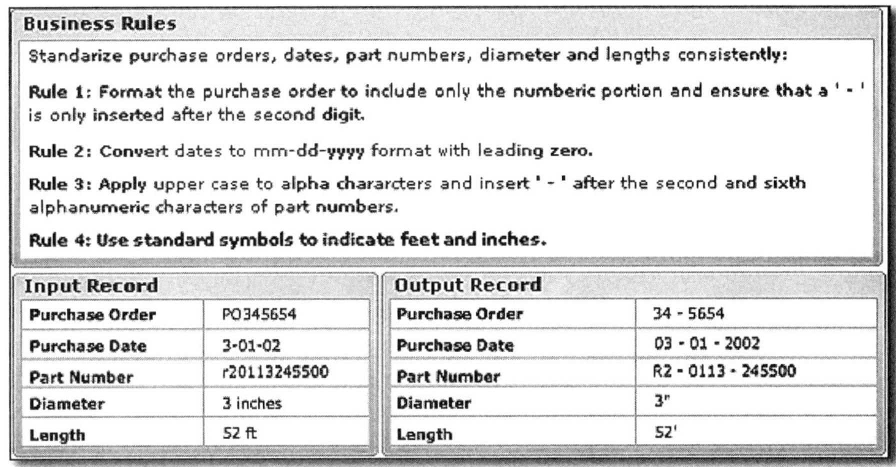

Business Rules

Standarize purchase orders, dates, part numbers, diameter and lengths consistently:

Rule 1: Format the purchase order to include only the numberic portion and ensure that a ' - ' is only inserted after the second digit.

Rule 2: Convert dates to mm-dd-yyyy format with leading zero.

Rule 3: Apply upper case to alpha chararcters and insert ' - ' after the second and sixth alphanumeric characters of part numbers.

Rule 4: Use standard symbols to indicate feet and inches.

Input Record

Purchase Order	PO345654
Purchase Date	3-01-02
Part Number	r20113245500
Diameter	3 inches
Length	52 ft

Output Record

Purchase Order	34 - 5654
Purchase Date	03 - 01 - 2002
Part Number	R2 - 0113 - 245500
Diameter	3"
Length	52'

Figure 9.34 Data Standardization Example

Take a look again at the data examples in Table 9.2 and Table 9.3. We can see that the data has been parsed into discrete components, but not always in a consistent, standardized manner. As examples:

- Primary Name, Primary Type, and Unit Description were output in mixed case as well as uppercase (e.g., Akard and BRADFORD; Street and ST; Suite and STE).
- Primary Prefix, Primary Type, and Unit Description were output using the full as well as abbreviated forms (e.g., South and S; Street and ST; Suite and STE).

Looking at the OPTIONS tab of the global address cleanse TRANSFORM EDITOR, you can see several standardization options to control the way your address data is output (how your address data will look). Figure 9.35 shows just some of the standardization options that are available.

Input | Options | Output

Filter: ○ Best practice ◉ All

Option Name	Option Value
⊟ Standardization Options	
⊟ Country	
⊟ Options	
Capitalization	MIXED
Directional Style	SHORT
Directional Punctuation	NO
Primary Type Style	SHORT
Primary Type Punctuation	NO
Secondary Description Style	SHORT
Secondary Description Punctuation	NO

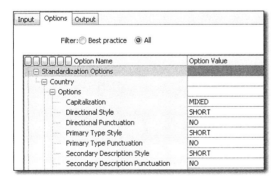

Figure 9.35 Global Address Cleanse Standardization Options

There are options to control the capitalization, the style of the directional or primary type information (SHORT or abbreviated, LONG or spelled out, or PERSERVE as exists within your source data), the type of punctuation, the region and country style, and so on.

On the address cleanse transform's OPTIONS tab, there are some similar standardization options for things such as capitalization and punctuation, but also some specific options for standardizing person, firm, phone number, dates, and so on (see Figure 9.36).

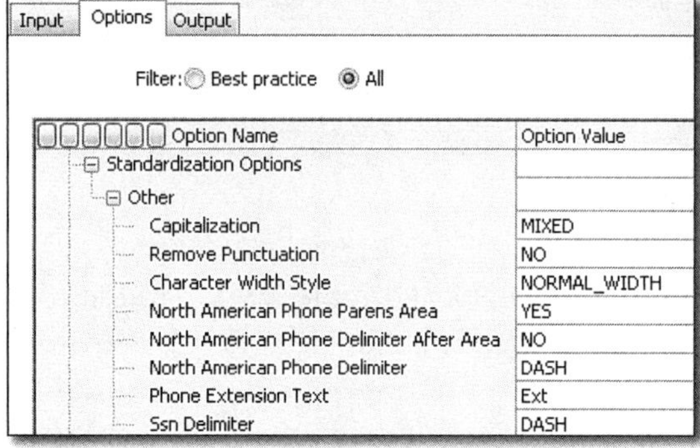

Figure 9.36 Data Cleanse Standardization Options

Note

You can get help with the available standardization options by viewing the embedded help. If help isn't visible, mouse over the right-hand side of the TRANSFORM EDITOR to access it.

After you set up the standardization options on the address cleanse and data cleanse transforms in the OPTIONS tab, and after you adjust the data quality transform to select standardized output fields (instead of parsed-only data), the output changes to be more consistent, as shown in Table 9.5 and Table 9.6.

Pre-Parsed and Standardized Data		
Address 1	208 South Akard Street	5000 BRDWAY ST S STE300
Address 2	Suite 150	<Blank>

Table 9.5 Address Standardization Example

Parsed and Standardized Data		
Primary Number	208	5000
Primary Name	Akard	Brdway
Primary Prefix	S	S
Primary Postfix	<Blank>	<Blank>
Primary Type	St	St
Unit Number	150	300
Unit Description	Ste	Ste

Table 9.5 Address Standardization Example

Pre-Parsed and Standardized Data		
Name	Mr. Robert L King Jr	Chris C Henderson C.P.A
Organization	PRODIGY	LTD
Miscellaneous 1	PROPERTY MGR	Jan 24 1984
Miscellaneous 2	robertk@prodigy.net	800.223.1212 EXT 879
Parsed and Standardized Data		
Prename	Mr.	<Blank>
Given Name 1	Robert	Chris
Given Name 2	L.	C.
Family Name	King	Hendersen
Maturity Postname	Jr.	<Blank>
Honorary Postname	<Blank>	CPA
Firm	Prodigy Inc.	Limited
Title	Property Manager	<Blank>
Phone	<Blank>	(800) 223-1212 Ext 879
Email	robertk@prodigy.net	<Blank>
Date	<Blank>	1/24/1984

Table 9.6 Name and Data Standardization Example

Notice the following changes shown in the previous tables:

- Capitalization is mixed-case throughout.
- The primary prefix and type information along with unit description is abbreviated.

- Phone and date information has been formatted.
- Punctuation is consistent throughout.

Note

To output parsed data, select output fields that have a FIELD_CLASS = PARSED on the data quality transform's OUTPUT tab.

To output parsed and standardized data in the data cleanse transform, select output fields that have a FIELD_CLASS = STANDARDIZED on the transform's OUTPUT tab.

To output parsed and standardized data in the address cleanse transform, select output fields that have a FIELD_CLASS = BEST on the transform's OUTPUT tab.

To output additional details about the type of parsing and standardization that has occurred with the data cleanse transform, use the following:

- **Information codes**
  These are available via the INFO_CODE DATA CLEANSE output field and provide information about how parsing occurred.
- **Status codes**
  These are available via the <OUTPUT_FIELD>_STD DATA CLEANSE output fields and represent how the data was standardized or that a specific standard could be used on the data during processing.

The other place where standardization rules are represented is in data cleansing packages. Cleansing packages are dictionaries that contain the rules that define how data will be parsed and standardized. Data Services offers an out-of-the-box predefined, global cleansing package for person and firm parsing and standardization that can be used with the data cleanse transform. The person and firm cleansing package is tuned to support various language nuances and cultural standards across the globe. As the name implies, the cleansing package provides support to parse and standardize firm, or company, data as well as the names and titles of your contacts and customers. It will give NeedsEIM Inc. a way to standardize supplier names on standard forms, for example, standardizing "Limited" instead of "LTD", as in Table 9.6. Standardizing supplier names will ultimately help NeedsEIM Inc. get to that consolidated view of its suppliers because it will allow accurate consolidation to occur.

The SAP-supplied person and firm cleansing package also contains powerful name, title, and firm alias information that serves as input into the matching process (discussed in Section 9.10.1) to overcome the challenge of different representations of the same data in a customer or supplier database. Think about trying to match "Mr. Dan R. Smith Jr., CPA" against another record in your database that represents that same person as "Daniel Smith Junior." The predefined person and firm cleansing package allows you to output match standards to help overcome issues with identifying matching records due to alternative spellings (e.g., Catherine and Katherine), abbreviations (e.g., IBM and Intl Business Machines), nicknames (e.g., Pat and Patrick), and multiple scripts. Match standards are available for the following:

- Family_Name1 and Family_Name2 (supports alternative script type; e.g., a Japanese family name represented in kanji as well as kana renditions)
- Firm and Firm Location
- Given Name 1 and Given Name 2
- Honorary Postname
- Maturity Postname
- Prename
- Title

Table 9.7 shows the match standards, or name aliases that would be generated by the data cleanse transform leveraging the SAP-supplied person and firm cleansing package for a first or given name of "Al."

Output Field	Value
GIVEN_NAME1	Al
GIVEN_NAME1_MATCH_STD1	Albert
GIVEN_NAME1_MATCH_STD2	Alexander
GIVEN_NAME1_MATCH_STD3	Alphonse
GIVEN_NAME1_MATCH_STD4	Alan
GIVEN_NAME1_MATCH_STD5	Alfred

Table 9.7 Match Standards Example

The matching standards will be discussed in the upcoming section on data matching (Section 9.10.3). Now that data has been parsed and standardized, it can be corrected, which is discussed next.

> **Note**
>
> You can install and use the SAP-supplied person and firm cleansing package without modification. You can also adapt that SAP-supplied cleansing package to meet your specific person and firm data cleansing requirements and standards by leveraging the Cleansing Package Builder capabilities in SAP Information Steward.

Data Correction

Let's finish up with the last step of the data cleansing process (refer to Figure 9.22)—data correction. Data with incorrect elements is known as *dirty* data. Cleansing dirty data involves verifying the data, correcting it, and adding missing elements such as directional or primary type information to an address. Depending on the data type, you can remove or correct dirty data using sophisticated algorithms and rules in conjunction with referential data. A data correction example is shown in Figure 9.37.

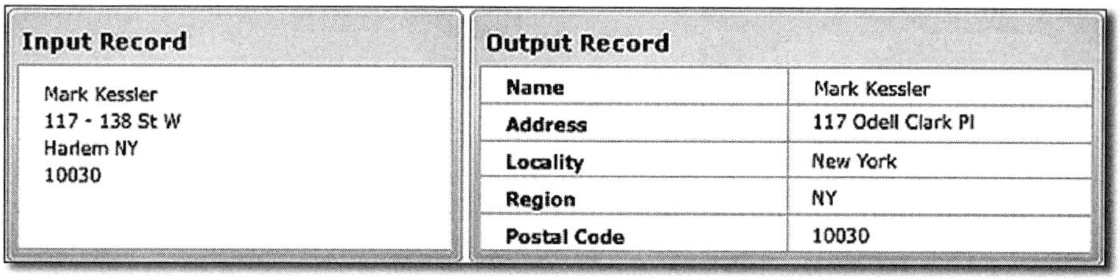

Input Record

Mark Kessler
117 - 138 St W
Harlem NY
10030

Output Record

Name	Mark Kessler
Address	117 Odell Clark Pl
Locality	New York
Region	NY
Postal Code	10030

Figure 9.37 Data Correction Example

The correction process leverages reference or "truth" data sets. For the address cleanse transform, these are referred to as *address directories*. There is an *all-world address directory* that supports last line (city, region, postal code, and country) parsing, standardization, and correction, as well as *country-specific directories* for more precise address correction capabilities. For each country that you want country-specific support, you need a corresponding address directory that contains the detailed reference data necessary. With the country-specific address directories, reference data suppliers are picked carefully and in many cases are the local postal authorities. Country-specific directories give you finer-grained address assignment and accuracy with the ability to cleanse, in addition to last line information:

- Secondary information: unit, floor, or stairwell information
- Primary range: house number
- Primary name: street name

Note

The Data Services installation doesn't install address directories. Address directories are licensed on an annual subscription basis and are downloaded and installed separately from the product. They are updated monthly or quarterly, depending on the source.

The location of your address directories is set using the REFERENCE FILES • DIRECTORY PATH parameter of the address cleanse transform's OPTIONS tab.

To realize data correction benefits, just adjust the address cleanse Transform Editor's OUTPUT tab to select corrected output fields (instead of parsed- and/or standardized-only data). Table 9.8 shows how the data components have been affected. After address correction, you can see several corrections that have taken place, including correction of street name, locality or city name, and postcode, as well as the creation of the missing postal codes.

Pre-Cleansed Data		
Address 1	208 South Akard Street	5000 BRDWAY ST S STE300
Address 2	Suite 150	<Blank>
City	Dalas	Kansas City
Region	TX	Montana
Postal code	75020	<Blank>
Cleansed Data		
Primary Address	208 S Akard St	5000 Broadway St
Secondary Address	Ste 150	Ste 300
Locality	Dallas	Kansas City
Region	TX	MO
Postcode 1	75202	64111
Postcode 2	4229	2413

Table 9.8 Address Correction Example

Note

To output *corrected data*, select output fields that have a FIELD_CLASS = CORRECT on the address cleanse transform's OUTPUT tab. These fields output the complete and correct value found in the address directories and are standardized according to any setting that you define in the standardization options group in the OPTIONS tab.

To output additional details about the type of correction that has occurred, use the following:

- **Information codes**
  These are available via the INFO_CODE GLOBAL ADDRESS CLEANSE output field and explain why an address was unassigned or uncorrected.
- **Status codes**
  These are available via the STATUS_CODE GLOBAL ADDRESS CLEANSE output field and represent the corrections made to the address during processing.
- **Quality codes**
  These are available via the QUALITY_CODE GLOBAL ADDRESS CLEANSE output field and relay additional information about the quality of the address.

For more details about address cleansing, including unique capabilities of the U.S. regulatory address cleanse transform and global address cleansing capabilities, see Appendix A (available for download from the book's page at *www.sap-press.com/3666*).

So far, you've learned how to cleanse data starting with data parsing, data standardization, and data correction. After the data is cleansed, the next step is data validation.

Data Validation

You can use data validation up front, before data cleansing, to route only specific records to the data cleansing process—records where you've identified anomalies in the incoming data through the data assessment process. Alternatively, you can use data validation after correction has occurred to continue with only a subset of the parsed, standardized, and corrected records into the next phases of the data quality process: enrichment, matching, and consolidation. The validation transform in Data Services allows you to define rules that sort the good data from the bad. This can permit you to write the nonconforming data to a table or a file for subsequent review or route it to a set of transforms for continued or specialized processing.

For example, suppose your business rules dictate that all phone numbers in the United States should have the format (999) 999-9999. However, the profiling results show that records have varying formats—anything from 9999 to 9999999 to 999.999.9999. You can use a validation transform to identify rows containing the unwanted formatting. Then you can correct the data using the data cleanse transform to conform to your business rules and reload it. As another example, the address cleanse transform includes the ability to output various information, status, or quality codes that explain why an address was unassigned, represent corrections made, or relay additional information about the quality of the address. These codes can be used with the validation transform to route only the cleansed or quality addresses to the de-duplication process.

The following steps describe how to use the validation transform to validate a telephone number against a specific pattern:

1. Drag the validation transform to the canvas, connecting it to the previous data source or transform requiring data validation.
2. Double-click on the validation transform to open the Rule Editor. Set the Name and Description for the validation rule and select Action on Fail. Select the column to validate and the condition that must be met. In the example in Figure 9.38, we're creating a rule which validates that the format of a phone number matches the pattern (999) 999-9999. If the rule fails, records are routed to a separate failure output stream (see Figure 9.39).

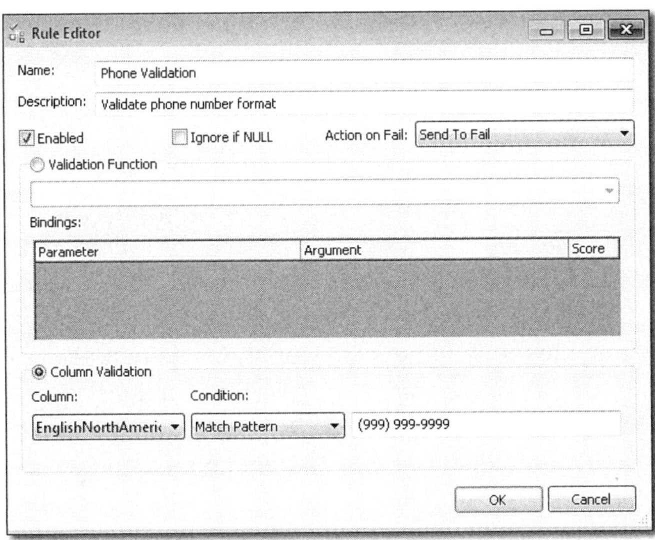

Figure 9.38 Validation Transform Rule Editor

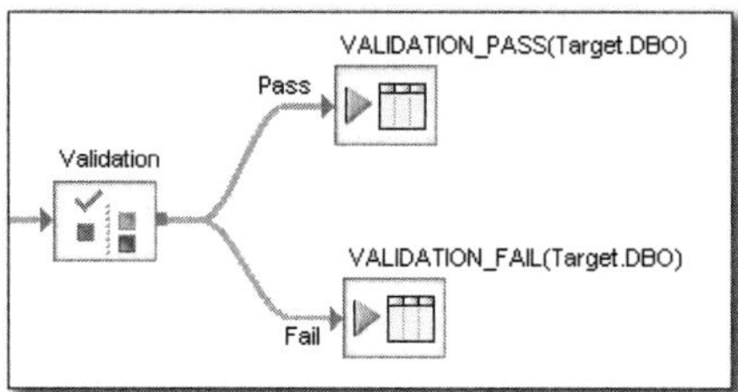

Figure 9.39 Validation Transform Data flow

You now have a good idea of how data parsing, standardization, correction, and validation work in Data Services and the role they each play for data cleansing. Next, we discuss the enrichment of data after it's been cleansed.

9.10.2 Data Enhancement

Returning to the data quality wheel (refer to Figure 9.22), let's take a look at data enhancement. Enhancement is the process of enriching your existing data set by appending additional data fields or attributes to it. This provides a more complete view of your data, which can be valuable for analysis, insight, and other business purposes. Enhancement options in Data Services include the following:

- Providing full international postal information
- Assigning longitude and latitude information to records
- Assigning geospatial information such as tax jurisdiction identifiers
- Assigning gender and prenames
- Using third-party referential data to enhance records

As discussed in the previous section on data cleansing (Section 9.10.1), the address correction process includes enhancing customer or supplier data with missing common address information, such as the street name, directional, city, state, or postcode. You can also append missing address information that is critical for mail delivery, such as a ZIP+4®, delivery point bar code (DPBC), or carrier routes that are available from the postal address directories. In addition, the U.S. regulatory address cleanse transform provides USPS®-certified options such as DPV (Delivery Point Validation) and RDI (Residential Delivery Indicator), as well as interfaces with the USPS LACSLink™ (Locatable Address Conversion System), SuiteLink™, and NCOALink™ (National Change of Address), which provide a wealth of data enrichment options for U.S. addresses. Appendix A (available for download from the book's page at *www.sap-press.com/3666*) has more details on the U.S. regulatory address cleanse. Geospatial data is also available via the address cleanse transforms. Geospatial assignment of customer addresses can be useful for determining tax jurisdictions and insurance-rating territories and identifying insurance hazards. Data enhancement is accomplished by posting data from the data quality transforms via designated output fields.

From the data cleanse transform in Data Services, it's possible to output gender and prename information. Names in the SAP-supplied name, title, and firm cleansing packages have a gender associated with them (ambiguous, strong male, strong female, weak male, or weak female). Gender can be output using the GENDER output field from the data cleanse transform. When the Assign Prenames option is set to Yes on the Options tab of the Transform Editor, the data cleanse populates the PRENAME output field with a prename (e.g., Mr. or Mrs.) when a strong male or female gender is assigned to a name.

Geocoding information, longitude and latitude, can be posted to records for business processes or policies (e.g., a marketing initiative) that are geographically based. The Data Services geocoder transform can enrich location data with varying degrees of precision:

- **Primary number exact**
  The finest depth of assignment available, to the exact location.
- **Primary number**
  The second most precise, with assignment to the midpoint of a primary address range (e.g., 100–500 Main St).
- **Postcode or locality level**
  The most general output level, with assignment to a city, town, suburb, or postcode.

Adding location awareness to the analytical process helps many companies make better business decisions. For example, imagine that a company is thinking about opening a new retail store. Some of the key factors to consider include the following:

- Number of new customers that can be targeted for the new store
- Proximity of competing businesses
- Distribution of complementary services (e.g., opening a fast-food restaurant next to a large strip mall)

Consider an example in a mobile environment: Imagine being able to determine and track your customers' locations and then make them real-time offers based on location awareness.

Example

For NeedsEIM Inc., knowing the location of all the suppliers can be critical when doing disaster planning. For example, if a natural disaster occurs, and a supplier must suspend its business, NeedsEIM Inc. might want to know what other suppliers are in the same area and thus might be impacted. Additionally, the company may need to quickly identify alternate suppliers outside the disaster zone. There is tremendous business value to having the tools to take advantage of the context of location.

Along with longitude and latitude, the geocoder transform also supports point-of-interest (POI) geocoding, returning a list of all locations that meet the POI search criteria within a geographical area. This allows you to search for POIs (more than 65 categories are supported) within a radial range from or closest to a particular location. The geocoder transform also supports reverse geocoding, which identifies the closest mailing address (POI or residential) based on an input latitude and longitude. Going back to our previous example, POI geocoding and geospatial search capabilities help a business identify what other businesses, competitive and complementary, are already in a given area.

Like address cleansing, the geocoding enrichment process leverages reference data sets referred to as *geo directories*. Geo directories are country specific. So for each country that you want geocoding support, you need a corresponding geo directory that contains the necessary detailed reference data.

Note

The Data Services installation doesn't install geo directories. Geo directories are licensed on an annual subscription basis and are downloaded and installed separately from the product. They are typically updated quarterly, depending on the country.

The location of your geo directories is set in the Reference Files • Directory Path parameter of the geocoder transform's Options tab.

Another form of data enrichment is demographic data. To append demographic information, you need a demographic database from a third-party data provider. When you obtain one, you can use the Data Services matching process to match your records to the demographic database and append the demographic information into your records.

9.10.3 Data Matching

We're almost around the wheel (refer to Figure 9.22), and the next step is a big one: match and consolidate. Matching and consolidation are essential for the following:

- Business intelligence (BI) initiatives where your goal is a single version of the truth
- Migration of data from legacy systems or systems gained through acquisition
- Leveraging third-party content such as do-not-mail, prison, or decreased consumer lists to avoid marketing to certain demographics

Example

For NeedsEIM Inc., obtaining legal entity or corporate hierarchy information may prove very useful in the effort to get a consolidated view of its suppliers.

To start, look at Figure 9.40, which shows an example of matching.

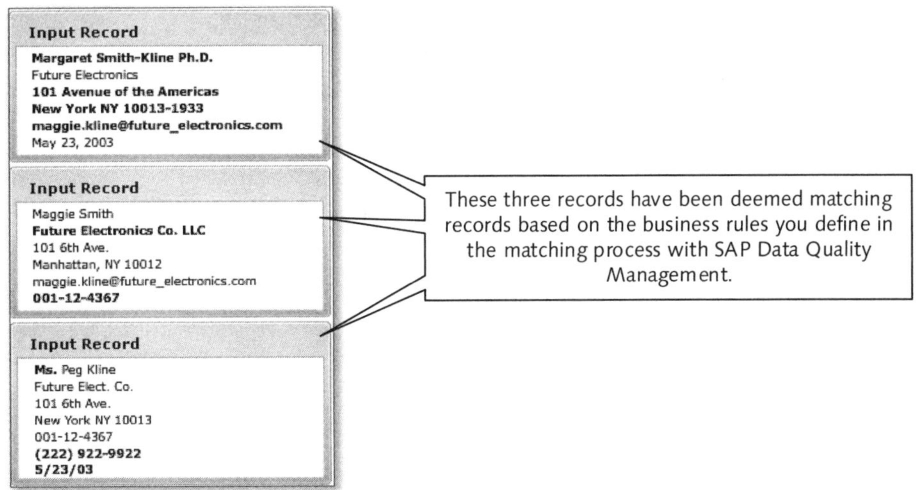

Figure 9.40 Matching Example

Duplicate records often exist in one or more source systems. The goal of matching is to determine whether records refer to the same entity. This involves evaluating how well the individual fields, or attributes, of the records match each other. SAP Data Quality Management matching capabilities allow you to use various fields for comparisons, to compare records in multiple directions, and then join the intersections. SAP Data Quality Management employs powerful matching algorithms to account for data entry errors, character transposition, and other data inaccuracies to match records. Table 9.9 describes some of the typical use cases for matching.

Use Case	Description
Consumer householding	Duplicate detection based on person names and addresses at various levels, such as household, family, and individual. Can be used for targeted marketing campaigns.
Corporate householding	Duplicate detection based on organization names and addresses at various levels, such as firm, department, and individual. Can be used for partner or supplier consolidation when multiple contacts exist.
Identity resolution	Duplicate detection based on person names and addresses, and perhaps other attributes such as account numbers or identification numbers. Useful for fraud prevention. Duplicate prevention at point of entry. Used in SAP CRM and SAP ERP systems when adding a new entity to the master database to detect whether the record already exists.
Direct marketing	Duplicate detection typically based on person names and addresses using customer lists and in batch mode. Used for the following: ▸ To eliminate redundant communication or shipping costs ▸ To leverage purchased or rented customer lists ▸ To pull in additional third-party demographic information for targeted marketing ▸ With geocoding to match to a specific geographic proximity (e.g., within 50 miles of a particular retail store)
Master data management	Duplicate detection in existing master records or duplicate prevention when a new record or entity is added. Used to establish and maintain a single version of the truth.
Business intelligence	Duplicate detection when pulling multiple sources together to create a data warehouse for BI initiatives. Used to establish and maintain a trusted, single version of the truth.

Table 9.9 Typical Match Use Cases

With data originating from different sources and systems and from different lines of the business with varying business processes and polices, identifying duplicates can be difficult. The example in Figure 9.40 shows the importance of data cleansing upstream of the matching process with all of the possible variations and inaccuracies that can exist in the data. We need to parse, standardize, and correct the information to improve the matching results.

Example

NeedsEIM Inc.'s finance department was finding it difficult to get at a customer-level P&L statement because the data lives in so many applications and datastores, and procurement wants to reduce the number of duplicate suppliers in its system to improve process efficiency. Now that the necessary data cleansing has occurred to parse, standardize, and correct the supplier data, it's time to tackle matching to identify duplicates and get to the consolidated view of major suppliers that finance and procurement is after.

Before we get into NeedsEIM Inc.'s solution, let's spend some time covering some of the core concepts of matching. First, what is a duplicate? Records may look different, but for business purposes they are the same record. A duplicate is going to be different for different users, different data domains, and different business goals. Sometimes it just depends on who you ask and what type of data is under review, for example:

- For names, *William, Will,* and *Bill* are duplicates. But *Bill* and *Billiards* are not.
- For names, *Mary Jones-Smith* and *Mary Jones* are duplicates.
- For addresses, *First Street* and *1st St* are duplicates. But *First Street* and *Frost St* are not.
- For firms, *International Business Machines*, *IBM,* and *intl bus mach* are all duplicates.
- For firms, *Midtown water and power* and *Midtown power and water* are duplicates, but *Midtown shipping* is not.
- For SSNs, *123-45-6789* and *122-45-6789* are not duplicates.
- For part descriptions, *40bar, 350Hp* and *350HP, 40bar* are duplicates, but *45bar, 350HP* is different.

Ultimately, you need to determine a matching strategy to decide what constitutes a duplicate and what type of results you want out of the matching process. Work with the business to determine the matching strategy for a data domain or data warehouse. Take a look at Table 9.10 for some examples of questions to consider.

Question	Example
What attributes does my data consist of?	Customer data, vendor data, international data, and so on.
What fields or attributes are important in the comparison process?	Last name, firm, address, unique identifier, and so on.
What are the relative strengths and weaknesses of the data in the comparison fields?	The consumer address data may tend to be inaccurate or incomplete; however, email addresses are usually populated and accurate.
What end result do I want when the matching job is complete?	Depending on the use case (direct marketing versus master data management) the end result will be different—one record per family, per firm, and so on.

Table 9.10 Developing a Matching Strategy

Tip

As mentioned a few times now, you'll get better results if you cleanse your data before matching. If data attributes that are important to the comparison process are missing, and if you need to go to a third-party vendor to acquire that data, data enhancement may also improve matching results.

Also, data profiling can help you answer some of these questions, especially to understand the relative strengths and weaknesses of the data.

Getting back to a technology perspective, many types of matching techniques and algorithms can be applied to determine duplicates. The Data Services match transform performs rule-based similarity matching. Duplicate detection is based on *similarity scoring*, a scoring system that determines what percentage of the data or content is alike. A similarity score is derived using the edit distance method, calculating how many corrections are required to make two strings identical, and then determining the score based on the string length and corrections required.

In the example in Table 9.11, a similarity score of 100 means that the match transform is 100% sure that the two records are the same (person). A similarity score of 80 means that match is 80% sure that the two records are the same. (Another way of interpreting a similarity score of 80 is that there is a 20% deviation between two records' measured content). This is a simple and straightforward matching example; however, many *match comparison options* are available with the match transform that can affect the similarity of the records and improve the flexibility and power of the matching capabilities. These match comparison options are explored in detail in Appendix A (available for download from the book's page at *www.sap-press.com/3666*).

Record 1	Record 2	Similarity Score
Smith	Smith	100
Smith	Jones	20
Smith	Smitt	80

Table 9.11 Simple Similarity Score Example

Let's cover some of the basic aspects of matching using the match transform. A match transform in your Data Services data flow represents a *match set*. Each match set can have its own break groups, match criteria, and prioritization (concepts we'll get to soon). A match set has three main purposes:

- To allow only select data into a given set of match criteria for possible comparison (excluding blank SSNs, international addresses, etc. from the comparison process)
- To allow related match scenarios to be stacked, creating a multilevel match set
- To allow multiple match sets to be considered for association in an associate match set

A *match level* is an indicator of what type of matching will occur, such as on an individual, family, resident, firm, and so on. The purpose of the family match type is to determine whether two people should be considered members of the same family; the result of the match is one record per family. The purpose of the individual match type is to determine whether two records are for the same person; the result of the match is one record per individual. The same concept applies to a residence, firm, and person at a firm; the result is one record per each. There can be multiple levels of matching. Only records that are found in a match group at the first level are fed to the second level, and so on.

Match criteria are the fields or attributes that you want to match on. You can use match comparison options to specify business rules for matching on each of these fields or attributes, depending on the data type. *Match thresholds* allow you to control how close to exact the data needs to be for that data to be considered a match or a nonmatch.

Match groups are groups of records that the match transform has found to be matching, based on the criteria you've created. The *master record* is the first record in the match group. The master is sometimes referred to as the *surviving* or *highest-priority* record. You can control which record this is by using a group prioritization operation before the best record operation (data consolidation, or best record creation, is covered in an upcoming subsection "Data Consolidation"). *Subordinate* records are all of the remaining records in a match group. This is sometimes referred to as the *nonsurviving* or *lower-priority* record from a master.

For each match criteria you define in your match set, there are three ways to prioritize the match criteria identified:

- **Rule-based matching method**
  All criteria for matching are given the same amount of importance (or weight). The method relies solely on the match and no-match scores to determine matching within criteria. If any criteria fail to meet the specified no-match threshold, the records don't match.
- **Weighted scoring matching method**
  This method relies on a total contribution score to determine matches based on contribution values that have been set per criteria. Individual match criteria can be given higher weightings or contribution values to raise their priority in the match process.
- **Combination matching method**
  This combines rule-based and weight scoring methods. A no-match occurs when any criteria fails to exceed the no-match threshold. A match is determined only by comparing the total contribution score against the weighted match score.

Let's walk through an example of each method. After the matching, you'll learn about consolidating data from the matching process.

Match Configuration

Match criteria and methods, including match and no-match thresholds, are set up using the Match Editor or optionally with the help of the Match Wizard. The upcoming subsection "Data Matching" describes a matching example for NeedsEIM Inc.

Rule-Based Matching Method

In Figure 9.41, the first name, last name, and email have been identified as match criteria. Looking at Record A and Record B, with a similarity score of 100 and the Match threshold and No-match threshold set, the First Name is determined a match. The Last Name criteria similarity score of 80 is in the gray area (between the no-match and match threshold), so it will depend on the next criteria to determine whether the records are a match. Email is the last criteria, and is a match with a similarity score of 91, so the records are a match.

Match Criteria	Record A	Record B	No-match threshold	Match threshold	Similarity score
First Name	Mary	Mary	82	95	100
Last Name	Smith	Smitt	74	95	80
Email	*msmith@ abcdef.com*	*mary.smitt@ abcdef.com*	79	80	91

Figure 9.41 Rule-Based Matching Method Example

Weighted Scoring Matching Method

The next technique is the weighted scoring method. Note that the no-match and match thresholds of -1 and 101 imply that these thresholds won't be used. Instead, a contribution value or weight for each match criterion is set. The contribution score for each match criterion is calculated as the similarity score multiplied by the contribution value. Then the contribution scores are added together to determine a total contribution value. In the example in Figure 9.42, the contribution scores of the First Name, Last Name, and Email are added together for a total contribution score of 91.

Match Criteria	Record A	Record B	No-match threshold	Match threshold	Similarity score	Contribution value	Contribution score
First Name	Mary	Mary	-1	101	100	25%	25
Last Name	Smith	Smitt	-1	101	80	25%	20
Email	*msmith@ abcdef.com*	*mary.smitt@ abcdef.com*	-1	101	91	50%	46
						Total contribution score	91

Figure 9.42 Weighted Scoring Matching Method Example

If the weighted match score threshold set in the match transform is 90 or less, then all records with a contribution score higher than 90 will be considered a match. These records will be determined a match because the total contribution score is higher than 90.

Combination Matching Method

A combination of the previous two techniques can also be used. In the following example (Figure 9.43), a similarity score of 22 for the Last Name match criteria was below the no-match threshold, so records fail the match test. No further processing is required. In the second example (Figure 9.44), none of the match criteria fail to meet the no-match threshold. So the total contribution score of 91 determines whether or not the records are matches. Again, if the weighted match score threshold set in the match transform is 90 or less, then these records will be determined to be a match because the total contribution score is higher.

Match Criteria	Record A	Record B	No-match threshold	Match threshold	Similarity score	Contribution value	Contribution score
First Name	Mary	Mary	59	101	100	25	25
Last Name	Smith	Hope	59	101	22	25	N/C
Email	*msmith@ abcdef.com*	*mary.hope@ abcdef.com*	49	101	N/C	50	N/C
						Total contribution score	N/C

Figure 9.43 Combination Matching Method Example 1

Match Criteria	Record A	Record B	No-match threshold	Match threshold	Similarity score	Contribution value	Contribution score
First Name	Mary	Mary	59	101	100	25	25
Last Name	Smith	Smitt	74	101	80	25	20
Email	*msmith@ abcdef.com*	*mary.smith@ abcdef.com*	79	101	91	50	46
						Total contribution score	91

Figure 9.44 Combination Matching Method Example 2

Another important concept in matching is a *break group*. A break group controls the number of comparisons required to complete the matching process. Break groups directly affect the performance of matching. When the number of comparisons is reduced, the time required to complete the matching process is also reduced. A typical break key in a customer scenario uses the postcode, and more specifically, the first three digits of the postcode.

Using this example, only records with the same first three digits of their postcode would be compared. This means John Smith who lives in Seattle (98406) would be compared to John Smith who lives in Tacoma (94816), but neither of these two would be compared to John Smith in Denver (80204). A break group consists of driver and passenger records. The first record serves as the driver. All remaining records in the break group serve as passengers and are compared against the driver to find matches. After a passenger is found to match a driver, it's no longer used in the matching process. The next passenger in the break group that hasn't been found as a match is used as the second driver and is compared against any remaining nonmatched passenger records in the break group. The match process iterates through all records in a break group in this manner to identify matches. When finished with one break group, the process continues to the next break group and repeats the above iterations.

Match performance is improved when the break key creates many break groups with only a few data records in each break group. However, as more and more break groups are created, the risk of a missed match increases because you're comparing fewer and fewer records, and the matching process doesn't get the opportunity to match data records in different data collections. Match accuracy is improved when the break group compound results in a few data collections with many data records in each. Nevertheless, the disadvantage is that the matching process takes more time due to many comparisons in each data collection. Ultimately, you need to be careful to balance performance with results. The objective is to maximize the speed without compromising the accuracy of your matching process. You may need to use some degree of trial and error to find the right balance.

Data Matching

Getting back to NeedsEIM Inc., it's time to take the next step toward that consolidated view of its suppliers by identifying duplicates in the supplier data.

Example

To match suppliers, the business owners have decided to take a first crack at de-duplication using match criteria focused on the organization and the contact's email address' domain host (e.g., "sap" in the case of *joex@sap.com*).

The first thing we need to do is go back to the data cleanse transform and configure it to output the firm match standards and email domain host needed to support Needs-EIM Inc.'s matching strategy.

Match standards help you overcome matching problems related to alternative spellings or representations and acronyms. For example, HP is the match standard or alias for Hewlett Packard. If the data cleanse cleansing package doesn't have an alias entry for a given firm or organization, then the output field(s) are empty.

Referring back to Figure 9.23, the following example demonstrates the third step in the data quality data flow, using the Match Wizard and the Match Editor:

1. Double-click on the data cleanse transform to open the TRANSFORM EDITOR. Go to the OUTPUT tab to select the FIRM_MATCH_STD output fields for output to supply match standards for firms along with the EMAIL_DOMAIN_HOST parsed and standardized output component (see Figure 9.45).

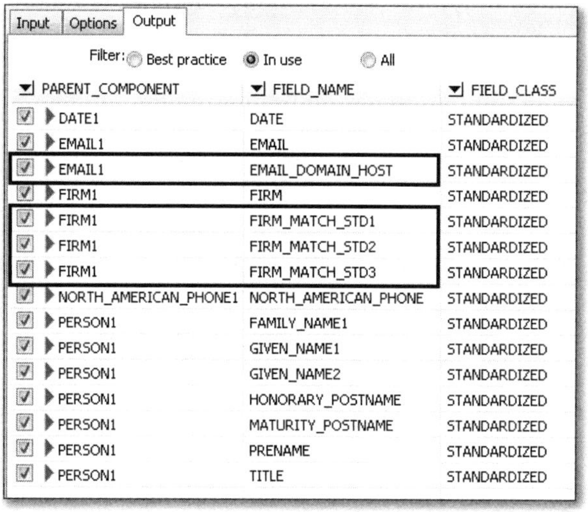

Input | Options | Output

Filter: Best practice | In use | All

PARENT_COMPONENT	FIELD_NAME	FIELD_CLASS
DATE1	DATE	STANDARDIZED
EMAIL1	EMAIL	STANDARDIZED
EMAIL1	EMAIL_DOMAIN_HOST	STANDARDIZED
FIRM1	FIRM	STANDARDIZED
FIRM1	FIRM_MATCH_STD1	STANDARDIZED
FIRM1	FIRM_MATCH_STD2	STANDARDIZED
FIRM1	FIRM_MATCH_STD3	STANDARDIZED
NORTH_AMERICAN_PHONE1	NORTH_AMERICAN_PHONE	STANDARDIZED
PERSON1	FAMILY_NAME1	STANDARDIZED
PERSON1	GIVEN_NAME1	STANDARDIZED
PERSON1	GIVEN_NAME2	STANDARDIZED
PERSON1	HONORARY_POSTNAME	STANDARDIZED
PERSON1	MATURITY_POSTNAME	STANDARDIZED
PERSON1	PRENAME	STANDARDIZED
PERSON1	TITLE	STANDARDIZED

Figure 9.45 Preparing the Data Cleanse for Matching

2. Use the MATCH WIZARD in Data Services to get a jump start on configuring the match. Right-click on the data cleanse transform, and select RUN MATCH WIZARD.
3. Start by selecting the CORPORATE HOUSEHOLDING match strategy (Figure 9.46).
4. Select LOOK FOR CORPORATE-LEVEL MATCHES, and then choose FIRM and EMAIL (Figure 9.47).

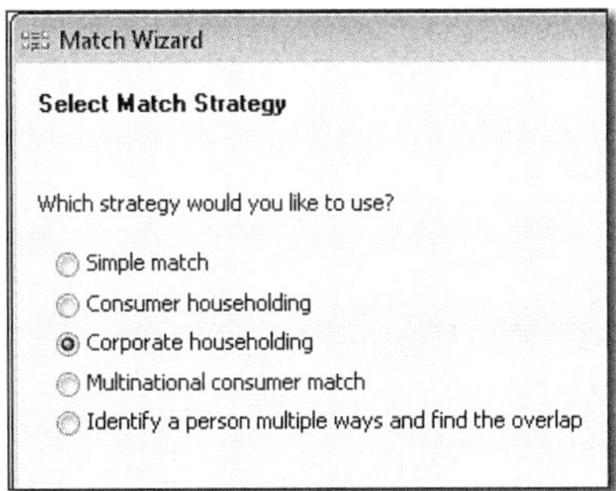

Figure 9.46 Match Wizard – Select Match Strategy

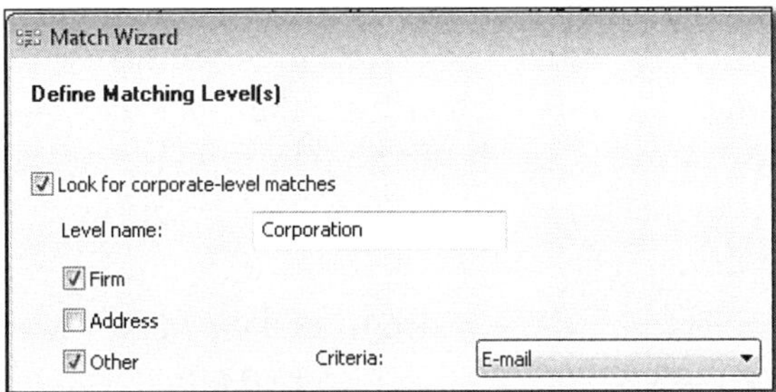

Figure 9.47 Match Wizard – Define Matching Levels

5. Set up the match criteria fields, mapping in the appropriate FIRM, FIRM_MATCH_STD, and EMAIL fields from the data cleanse (Figure 9.48). We're going to skip the break key definition (we'll need to set it up later to tune the matching process).

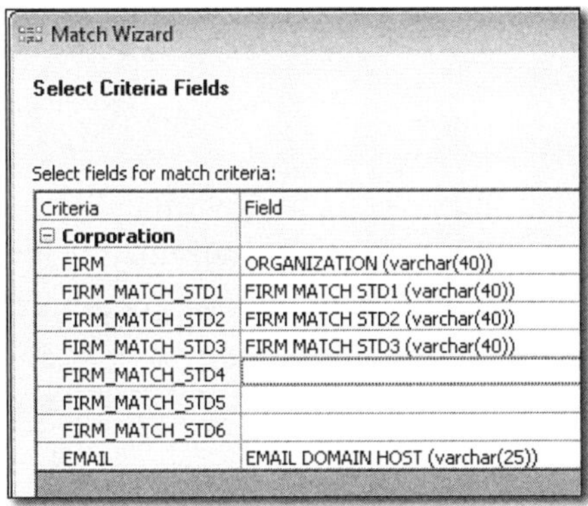

Figure 9.48 Match Wizard – Select Criteria Fields

6. Click on FINISH. The result is a newly generated match transform with the basic match setup configured (Figure 9.49).

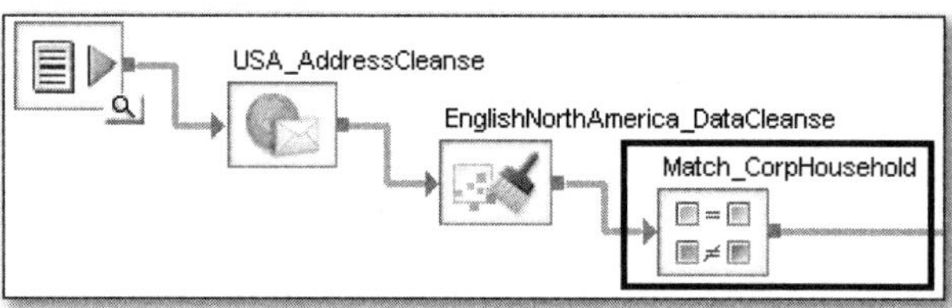

Figure 9.49 Data Quality Data flow with Match Transform

7. Double-click on the match transform that was generated to make some initial adjustments to the matching configuration. When opening the match transform, you'll notice a few things that are different from the other data quality transforms. In particular, the OPTIONS tab of the match transform isn't editable. Match has a specialized TRANSFORM EDITOR. To access it, click on the EDIT OPTIONS button on the OPTIONS tab.

8. In the MATCH EDITOR, you can review the match criteria that the MATCH WIZARD set up by selecting MATCH CRITERIA in the left pane (Figure 9.50).

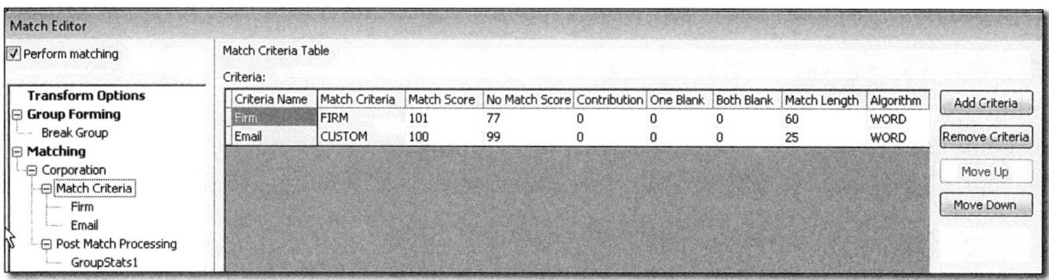

Criteria Name	Match Criteria	Match Score	No Match Score	Contribution	One Blank	Both Blank	Match Length	Algorithm
Firm	FIRM	101	77	0	0	0	60	WORD
Email	CUSTOM	100	99	0	0	0	25	WORD

Figure 9.50 Match Editor – Match Criteria Table

9. Double-click on the individual criteria, and select the OPTIONS tab to see detailed match comparison options as a result of the MATCH WIZARD (see Figure 9.51). For more information on the match comparison options, see Appendix A (available for download from the book's page at *www.sap-press.com/3666*). Having profiled their data during the data assessment phase of their data quality initiative, NeedsEIM Inc. knows that their email contact data is less complete than they would like. So we want to make an adjustment to their match criteria to accommodate null or blank email fields.

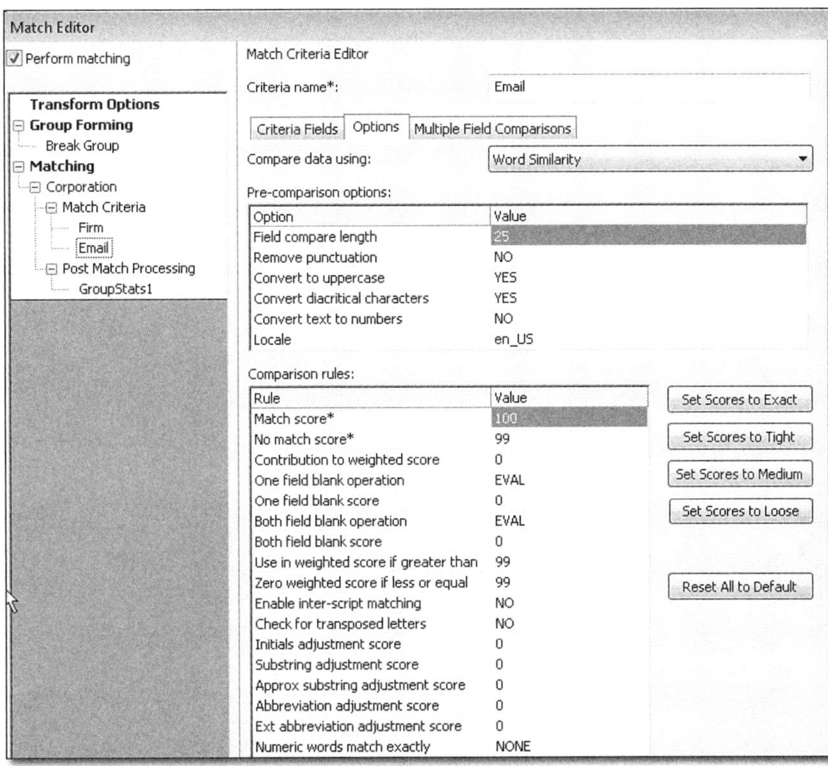

Figure 9.51 Match Criteria Editor

Tip

If you want help with the MATCH WIZARD or MATCH EDITOR options, mouse over the right pane of the wizard or editor to access the embedded online help.

10. In the MATCH CRITERIA EDITOR area, the ONE/BOTH FIELD BLANK OPERATION comparison rules should be set to IGNORE, so the email match criteria is ignored in the comparison process if the email field is blank in one or both of the records (see Figure 9.51). Because we're using a rule-based matching strategy, in the case of blank email fields, it will fall completely to the firm match criteria to determine whether or not two records match.

11. Another adjustment that is needed is to lower the match score for the firm criteria. Currently, the MATCH WIZARD has set the match score to 101, which means the criteria by itself is never enough to consider two records a match.

Lower the match score to 90 (in the MATCH CRITERIA EDITOR area, shown in Figure 9.51) so that if data in two records is 90% similar or higher, the records will be considered a match. The email match criteria will then determine a match if the firm similarity score is somewhere in the gray area (in this case, between 77 and 90) or eliminate a match if two nonblank email fields are not an exact match.

Table 9.12 shows the results of the matching process. Match group numbers, match scores for each subordinate record, the match group count, and a match group rank (M = master record and S = subordinate record) are all available to post as output from the match transform as long as the *group statistics* post-matching operation is enabled. An example of group statistics is GROUP_ORDER. With GROUP_ORDER, the master record receives a value of 1. Subordinate records receive a value of 2 through the number of records in the match group.

Group Number	Group Count	Match Score	Match Group Rank	Organization	Email Domain
10	2	<Null>	M	Grossman Forgals Inc.	Grossman
10	2	97	S	Grossman Forgal	Grossman
11	4	<Null>	M	Precision Woodwork	<Null>
11	4	100	S	Precision Woodwork	Precision
11	4	98	S	Precision Woodwork Co.	<Null>
11	4	93	S	Precision	<Null>
12	6	<Null>	M	M & I Bank	Mibank
12	6	92	S	M&I Bank	<Null>
12	6	92	S	M & I Bank	<Null>
12	6	100	S	M&I Bank of Beloit	Mibank
12	6	100	S	M&I Bank of Beloit	<Null>
12	6	92	S	MI	Mibank
13	2	<Null>	M	Smith & Harris Mach.	<Null>
13	2	92	S	S & H Mach.	<Null>
14	2	<Null>	M	Valk & Fragger	Vaulkfrager
14	2	99	S	Valk & Frager	<Null>

Table 9.12 Match Transform Example Output

Based on the initial results, NeedsEIM Inc. can make adjustments to the match criteria, comparison options, and/or match and no-match thresholds to fine-tune the match result set. For information on additional options for supporting your matching business requirements and tweaking your match results, see Appendix A (available for download from the book's page at *www.sap-press.com/3666*).

After the matching has occurred, the data must be consolidated, which we discuss next.

Data Consolidation

Data consolidation eliminates, filters, or combines duplicate records using configurable rules. After matches have been identified, data from the match groups can be salvaged and posted to form a single best record, or posted to update all matching records. Best record selection is based on your data priorities—in terms of source, frequency, completeness, timeliness (most current or up-to-date), and so on. Consolidation can also build reference keys to track individual records and their associations across multiple databases or sources. Figure 9.52 shows an example of data consolidation across three records in the same match group.

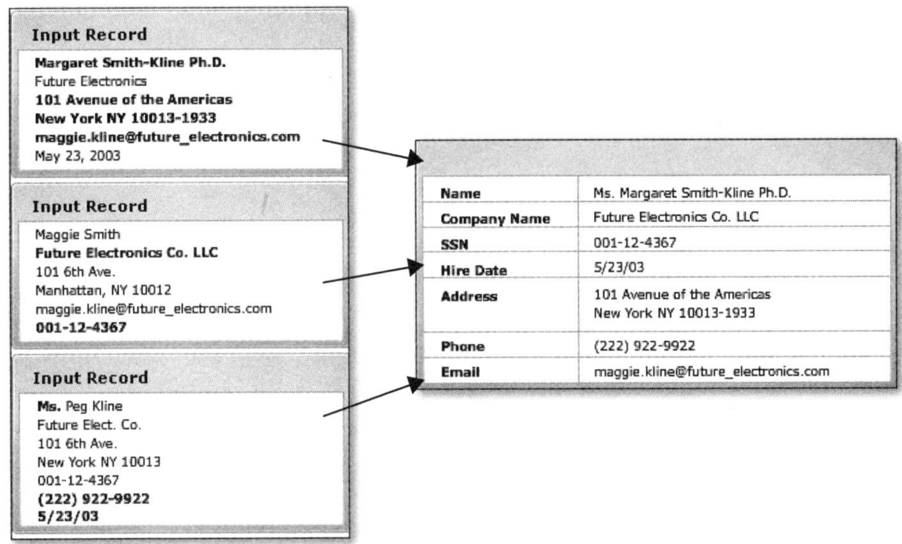

Figure 9.52 Data Consolidation Example

You can perform data consolidation by adding a best record post-match operation. The functions you perform with the best record operation involve manipulating or moving data contained in the master and subordinate records of match groups.

Table 9.13 shows a match group. As you can see, each record is slightly different. Some records have blank fields, some have a new date, and all have different phone numbers. An example of a best record strategy that could be applied would be to move the most current (based on date) phone data to all of the records in the match group (master and subordinate records).

Record	Name	Phone	Date	Group Rank
1	John Smith		11 Apr 2001	Master
2	John Smyth	608-788-8700	12 Oct 1999	Subordinate
3	John E. Smith	608-788-1234	22 Feb 1997	Subordinate
4	J. Smith	608-788-3271		Subordinate

Table 9.13 Best Record Creation Example

Another example might be to salvage useful data from matching records before discarding them. For example, when you run a driver's license file against your house file, you might pick up gender or date-of-birth data to add to your house record.

Using the best record operation, you can control when to populate a specific data element, whether data is populated in the master and/or the subordinate records in the match group, and how to populate a specific data element. Data Services provides strategies to help you set up the more common best record operations quickly and easily. If the prebuilt strategies don't meet your needs, you can always create a custom best record strategy. In our example of updating a phone field with the most recent data (Table 9.13), we can use the date strategy with the newest priority to update the master record with the latest phone number in the match group. This latter part (updating the master record with the latest phone number) is the action. You can also update all of the records in the match group (master and all subordinates) or only the subordinates. The best out-of-the-box record strategies include the following:

- **Date**
  With priority on the newest or oldest date in the strategy field.
- **Length**
  With priority on the shortest or longest string in the strategy field.

- **Priority number**
  With priority on the highest or lowest number in the strategy field.
- **Priority string**
  Priority on the string with the most ascending or descending string order in the strategy field.
- **Non-blank**
  Bases the strategy on the completeness of the data in the strategy field.

After the best record strategy and strategy priority are selected, just choose a field that contains the data that you need to execute your strategy on and whether you want to post to the master only, subordinates only, or all records in a match group.

Example

To work toward a goal of consolidated supplier data, NeedsEIM Inc. will need to implement a best record strategy to work toward a single "golden" master record. You can take a step in that direction by adding a post-match operation to the match transform.

The following steps show a best record strategy using the post-match processing option:

1. Double-click on the match transform. Click on the EDIT OPTIONS button on the OPTIONS tab.
2. Right-click POST MATCH PROCESSING in the left pane of the MATCH EDITOR, and select ADD and then BEST RECORD.
3. Select a best record strategy based on NON_BLANK data in the EMAIL_DOMAIN_HOST strategy field to be posted to the EMAIL_DOMAIN_HOST destination field in the master record of each group. Figure 9.53 shows the settings described.

After rerunning the data flow, you can see that the master records of each match group are now more complete with the addition of email data for each supplier (see Table 9.14). NeedsEIM Inc. would go through a similar process for those data fields or attributes that they want to consolidate in their match groups to form a best record view of each of their suppliers, based on finance and procurement business needs.

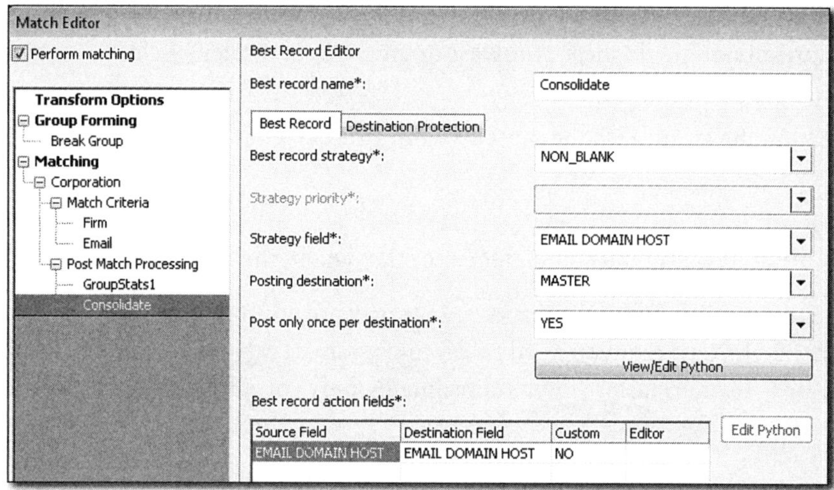

Figure 9.53 Best Record Editor

Group Number	Group Count	Match Score	Match Group Rank	Organization	Email Domain
10	2	<Null>	M	Grossman Forgals Inc.	grossman
11	4	<Null>	M	Precision Woodwork	precision
12	6	<Null>	M	M & I Bank	mibank
13	2	<Null>	M	Smith & Harris Mach.	<Null>
14	2	<Null>	M	Valk & Fragger	vaulkfrager

Table 9.14 Best Record Example Output

Note

This section provided details on data quality and how to get started using data quality transforms. For more details, including information about getting started with data quality blueprints, see Appendix A, available for download from the book's page at *www.sap-press.com/3666*.

9.10.4 Using Data Quality beyond Customer Data

For the examples in this section, the focus was on cleansing party data (e.g., consumer, customer, supplier, business partner). Let's shift gears and take a look at data quality for data that isn't made up of names and addresses (commonly referred to as *nonparty data*). There is a unique challenge to cleansing nonparty data such as product or operational data. The problem is that SAP can't necessarily ship you predefined cleansing packages that represent your products, services, or operations. These are unique to your business. Instead, there needs to be a way for your organization to describe and define custom cleansing rules that represent your business.

Imagine that you're a part of an office supply store chain. You offer a variety of paper products. In your systems, your paper product data is represented in an assortment of formats and descriptions. The box below shows a common example of how such data looks. However, the business is building a new website, and as a part of the requirements, there needs to be the ability to browse products by manufacturer. How are you going to make the link between manufacturers and what is in your various point-of-sales systems that describes your company's products?

Product Data

Office Max multipurpose paper, 96 bright, 20 lb. paper, 2500 sheets, 8.5 x 11 inches, OM44011

The answer is data quality—parsing and standardizing your business' product data stored in your point-of-sales systems to meet your new business requirements. And the critical piece of the solution is a tool in Information Steward called the *Cleansing Package Builder*. Cleansing Package Builder allows you to develop the necessary custom data parsing and standardization rules to cleanse your business's unique product and operational data. Cleansing Package Builder provides a UI that allows a data steward to visualize how the data is parsed and standardized and evaluate the impact of the customized logic.

Cleansing Package Builder automatically creates the data dictionary, rules, and patterns that make up a cleansing package, which is then consumed by a Data Services data cleanse transform to parse, standardize, and cleanse business data such as account numbers, product codes and descriptions, part numbers, SKUs, and so on. After the custom data parsing and standardization rules are in place to perform data cleansing on the product data, data cleanse can output discrete, standardized data attributes (such as manufacturer), which can be used in the matching process to support business goals around consistent, quality data to support that single view across the enterprise.

9.11 Text Data Processing

Text analytics, or text data processing, is the process of taking unstructured text data and turning it into something you can analyze and act on. It allows you to deal with information overload by mining very large bodies of text and making sense of all the information without having to read every sentence. Simply put, text analytics automates research analysis from data sources that were previously unprocessable.

Text analytics can assist the enterprise by pinpointing the who, what, where, when, and how much in unstructured text. The primary benefit of locating these atomic elements and transforming them into structured types is that businesses can spend more time analyzing and less time searching text. IT can unlock trends, issues, and opportunities concealed by unstructured text data. This information discovery facilitates enterprise decision-making processes by extending the value of your BI investments that report from structured data.

Chapter 4 mentioned a few use cases for text data processing. Table 9.15 provides a more comprehensive list.

Use Case	Description
Electronic discovery	Accelerate the process of analyzing documents for evidence in discovery to avoid expensive legal costs. (Discovery is a pretrial phase in a lawsuit, in which each party makes information available to the other.)
Brand monitoring	Determine what people are saying about products and brands. Are they creating a "buzz," and is it positive or negative?
Employee morale	Use sentiment analysis of collaboration spaces to detect employee problems early.
Investigative case management	Analyze criminal records to discover connections among suspects, organizations, and events.
Innovation management	Evaluate ideas using this labor-intensive process. Find related variances and group them together.
Patent research	Classify invention disclosure forms (IDF) according to topic maps.
Customer service	Optimize call center operations by routing topics in questions to the right person.

Table 9.15 Use Cases for Text Data Processing

Use Case	Description
Information governance, risk, and compliance	Detect leaks of confidential data.
Recruiting	Help HR departments best match applicants to open positions.
Public sector	Analyze field reports for connections among people, organizations, bank accounts, and so on to discover terrorist networks and other threats.
Life sciences and pharmaceutical research	Aid scientists in finding related research documents.
Health care informatics	Scrutinize patient records to assist hospitals with identifying drug dosages from freeform notes.
Personalized newsfeeds	Use reader interests to identify news articles they may want to read.
Customer satisfaction	Predict customer churn and detect product defects from customer complaints.
Contract management	Author, negotiate, audit, and continuously improve contracts to help organizations establish strategic long-term agreements.

Table 9.15 Use Cases for Text Data Processing (Cont.)

In the following sections, you'll find an introduction to the text data processing capabilities that are provided by SAP. After that, we'll dive into the details of the entity extraction transform, which is the transform for text data processing capabilities.

9.11.1 Introduction to Text Data Processing Capabilities in SAP Data Services

As mentioned, Data Services is a unified, fully integrated platform for doing data integration and data quality on unstructured text data as well as structured data. This unique data foundation enables businesses to gain insights and make decisions on the basis of high-quality, reliable data that leverages both structured and unstructured sources.

In Data Services, text data processing (TDP) refers to transforms that extract information from unstructured data in multiple languages and create structured data that can be used by BI tools. TDP analyzes text and automatically identifies the language of the text, extracts entities, including people, dates, places, organizations, and so on. It also looks for patterns, activities, events, and relationships among entities and enables their extraction. Identifying such information tells you what the text is about.

TDP goes beyond conventional string matching tools for information retrieval and seeks exact or fuzzy matches for specific sequences of characters. Data Services includes language modules for the languages supported by TDP. The language modules enable TDP to perform linguistic analysis and extraction of unstructured text in a given language.

TDP can be configured to automatically identify the language of input text. It evaluates a short snippet of text against all supported languages and identifies the best-fit language. If the best-fit language can't be identified, TDP uses the default language defined as part of its configuration. After the language of the input text is determined, TDP uses the respective language module and applies full linguistic and statistical techniques to ensure that the entities and relationships that get returned are correct.

First, TDP performs grammatical parsing on the input text, for example:

- Can we *bill* you?
- *Bill* was the president.

As a result, it linguistically figures out if the word *bill* is a verb or a noun in the first bullet and not a person. In the second bullet, *Bill* is a proper noun.

Second, TDP performs semantic disambiguation, which is the process of resolving conflicts that arise when a term is ambiguous. For example:

- I talked to *Bill* yesterday.
- The duck has a *bill*.
- The *bill* was signed into law.

As a result, TDP figures out which noun is a person and core entity. In the first bullet, *Bill* is a proper noun, which is the name of a person. In the second bullet, *bill* is a common noun with one meaning. In the third bullet, *bill* is a common noun with a completely different meaning.

TDP automates the extraction of key information from text sources to reduce manual review and tagging. Access to relevant information in unstructured text can help streamline operations and reduce unnecessary costs by enabling you to understand important insights hidden in text.

Earlier in the chapter, you learned that there are several types of transforms in Data Services. There are transforms for cleansing, data validation, querying, and so on. TDP capabilities are also tied to a transform—the entity extraction transform. Next, we'll provide an overview of the entity extraction transform and discuss how it works.

9.11.2 Entity Extraction Transform Overview

Extracting entities and relationships among entities from unstructured text is accomplished in the Data Services Designer using the entity extraction transform under the Text Data Processing folder. This is shown in Figure 9.54. The entity extraction transform is another transform found in the Transform tab in the Local Object Library in Data Services.

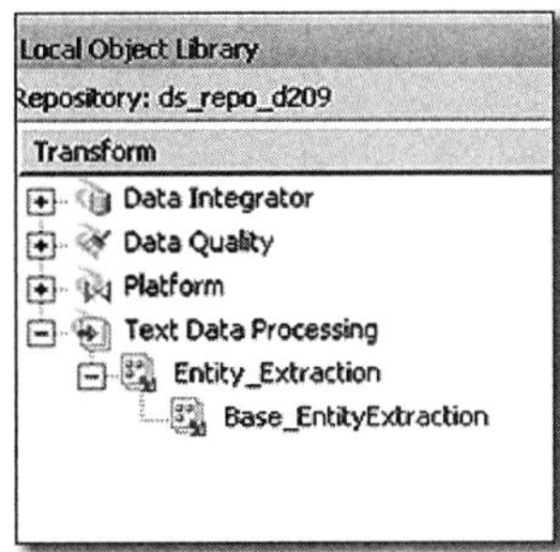

Figure 9.54 Entity Extraction Transform in the Local Object Library in the Data Services Designer

Extraction involves grammatically parsing and semantically disambiguating the text, discovering entities of interest, classifying them to the appropriate type, and providing this metadata in a standard format. By using dictionaries and rules, you can customize your pattern extraction output.

Entities denote names of things that can be extracted and categorized by type. Entities may have subtypes that indicate further classification; this is a hierarchical specification of an entity type that enables the distinction between different semantic varieties of the same entity type. A subtype can be described as a subcategory of an entity.

Here are some examples of entities and subtypes:

- Boeing 747 is an entity of type VEHICLE with a subtype AIR.
- BMW X5 is an entity of type VEHICLE with a subtype LAND.
- SAP is an entity of type ORGANIZATION with a subtype COMMERCIAL.

Note

The naming conventions of entity types are aligned with the classifications of the various data quality transforms in Data Services.

Facts are umbrella terms that cover extractions of more complex patterns, including one or more entities, a relationship between one or more entities, or some sort of state involving an entity. Entities by themselves only show that they are present in the text corpora, but facts provide information on how these entities are related. Facts are extracted using custom extraction rules. Fact types identify the category of a fact, such as sentiments and requests.

Here are some examples of facts:

- *Business Objects acquired Inxight in a friendly takeover.* This is a relationship of type MERGER AND ACQUISITION.
- *Ms. Jane Smith is very upset with her reservation.* This is a relationship of type SENTIMENT.

Note

Data Services provides, by default, out-of-the-box fact extraction for sentiments, events, and relationships from text in several languages. You can get more details about these language modules in the TDP Language Reference Guide at *http://help.sap.com/boeim.*

9.11.3 How Extraction Works

The extraction process uses its inherent knowledge of the semantics of words and the linguistic context in which these words occur to find entities and facts. It creates specific patterns to extract entities and facts based on system rules. You can add entries in a dictionary, as well as write custom rules to customize extraction output. The following sample text and sample output (Table 9.16) show how unstructured text data can be transformed into structured information for further processing and analysis.

> *Steven Paul Jobs (born February 24, 1955) was an American business magnate and inventor. He is well known for being the co-founder and chief executive officer of Apple. Jobs also previously served as chief executive of Pixar Animation Studios; he became a member of the board of The Walt Disney Company in 2006, following the acquisition of Pixar by Disney.*

Entities	Type
Steven Paul Jobs; Jobs	PERSON
February 24, 1955; 2006	DATE
Co-founder; chief executive officer; chief executive; member of the board	TITLE
Apple; Pixar Animation Studios; Pixar; The Walt Disney Company; Disney	ORGANIZATION@COMMERCIAL
American business magnate; inventor; acquisition	NOUN_GROUP or Concept
Facts	**Type**
Jobs also previously served as chief executive of Pixar...	EXECUTIVE JOB CHANGE
Acquisition of Pixar by Disney	MERGER AND ACQUISITION

Table 9.16 Conversion of Unstructured Text to Structured Entity and Fact Types

The entity and fact extraction process is based on the use of dictionaries and rules:

- **Dictionary**
  A dictionary for TDP is a user-defined list of entities. It allows for specifying entities that the entity extraction transform should always extract while processing text. The information is classified under the standard form and the variant of an entity. A standard form may have one or more variants. For example, *American Telephone and Telegraph* may be the standard form for a company, and *AT&T* is a variant of the same company. However, many would agree it's the other way around.
- **Rule**
  A rule for TDP defines custom patterns to extract entities, sentiments, events, and other relationships between entities that are together referred to as facts.

You write custom extraction rules to perform extraction that is customized to your specific domain, for example, to identify entities in unusual or industry-specific language, such as the use of the word *crash* in computer software versus insurance statistics.

9.11.4 Text Data Processing and NeedsEIM Inc.

Now that you have a general understanding of the technology, uses cases, and content, the following step-by-step example will get you started with TDP in Data Services.

The entity extraction transform can extract information from any text, HTML, or XML content and generate structured output. You can use the output in several ways: You can use it as an input to another transform or write to multiple output sources such as a database table or a flat file.

The following sections provide an overview of this functionality in light of some challenges facing NeedsEIM Inc.

9.11.5 NeedsEIM Inc. Pain Points

NeedsEIM Inc. has seen an uptick in product quality issues as reported through the warranty channels in its complex supplier network. Fearing that this could lead to a widespread product recall, which would result in lost revenues and damage the brand, the risk management team must evaluate and mitigate the risks.

However, the company's data warehouse doesn't contain any information about the root cause of the quality issues, which is locked inside field technicians' free-form text notes. NeedEIM Inc. also doesn't have the staff to read every repair log file and tag them for root causes.

After IT processes the text data fields using the TDP entity extraction transform to detect root causes, the dashboard shown in Figure 9.55 enables the risk management team to drill down into the results, explore the data, and discover correlations between products and models and the top 10 quality issues affecting them. Notice the most common concepts, by product line, which TDP has detected and extracted from the technicians' comment fields. TDP has pulled these concepts into a new field, making analysis of the root causes possible, where there was no visibility before.

Figure 9.55 shows an example of what a report might look like.

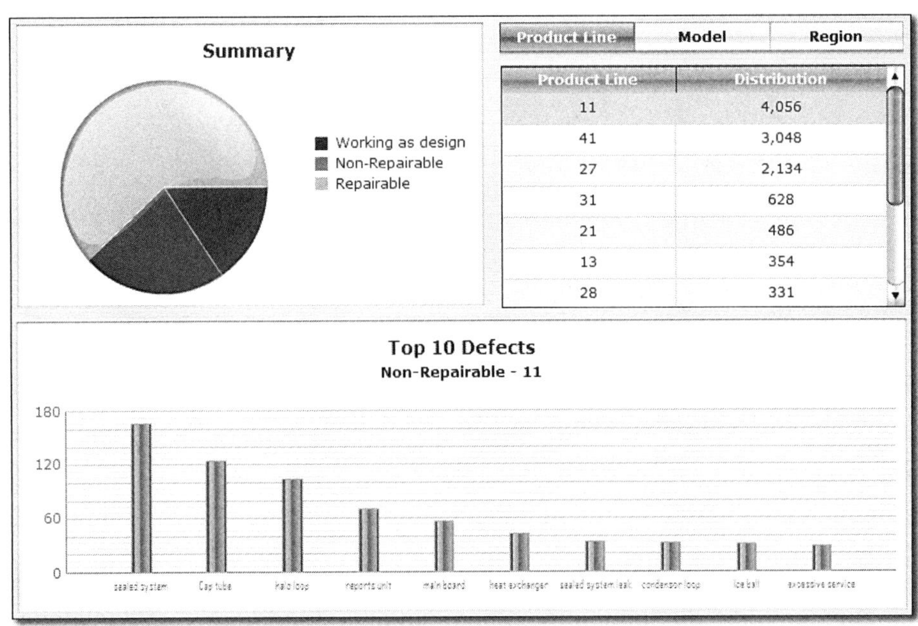

Product Line	Distribution
11	4,056
41	3,048
27	2,134
31	628
21	486
13	354
28	331

Figure 9.55 Top Defects Report Extracted from Technicians' Free-Form Notes

In Figure 9.55, notice the list of the top 10 defects and a summary of the types of defects. Data Services made this possible by performing the following tasks:

- Integrating the warranty repair data into the warehouse
- Processing the text data to discover the most mentioned concepts
- Matching the discovered concepts to determine the most common root causes

Figure 9.56 shows a job in Data Services that is used for TDP to create the dashboard shown in Figure 9.55.

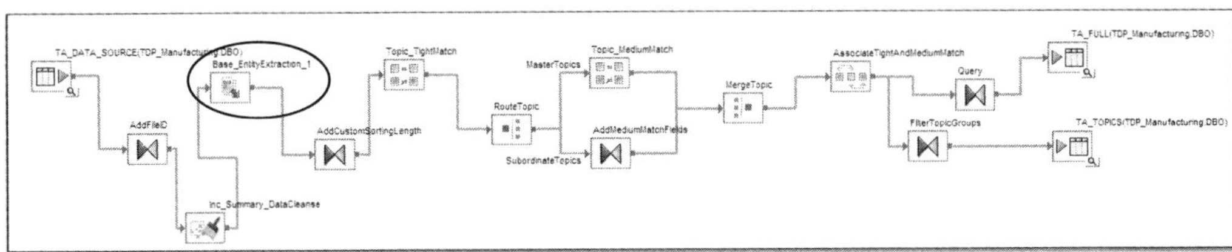

Figure 9.56 Data Flow in Data Services That Extracts Entities from the Technicians' Integrated Repair Log

Figure 9.56 is the entire job required to extract, cleanse, match, process, and prepare the data for the dashboard. Next, we describe how the TDP transform highlighted in Figure 9.56 was built, including the key requirement for TDP, the entity extraction transform.

9.11.6 Using the Entity Extraction Transform

From a very high level, NeedsEIM Inc. requires processing of unstructured text data from a database that IT set up to integrate all the repair logs. To do this, the company has to do the following:

1. Configure a connection to the database via a datastore.
2. Build a data flow with the database table as the source, an entity extraction transform, and a target.
3. Configure the transform to process the text.

In the following subsections, we describe the step-by-step instructions on how to use the entity extraction transform. This includes adding it to a data flow, configuring the transform, and hints for working with the entity extraction transform.

How to Add an Entity Extraction Transform to a Data Flow

This section describes the steps that are necessary to add an entity extraction transform to a data flow.

> **Note**
>
> A transform configuration is preconfigured with best practices for input fields, output fields, and options. These are useful if you repeatedly use a transform with specific options and fields. You can also create your own transform configuration, either by replicating an existing configuration or creating a new one.

The following steps use an out-of-the-box transform configuration for the entity extraction transform. This transform configuration is called BASE_ENTITYEXTRACTION.

1. Open a data flow object.
2. Open the LOCAL OBJECT LIBRARY if it's not already open.
3. Go to the TRANSFORMS tab.

4. Expand the TEXT DATA PROCESSING folder, and select the transform or transform configuration that you want to add to the data flow.

   In Figure 9.57, ENTITY_EXTRACTION is the transform, and BASE_ENTITYEXTRACTION is the transform configuration.

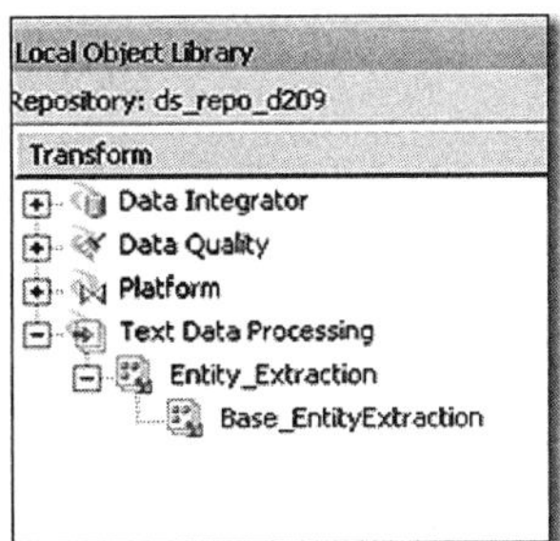

Figure 9.57 Entity Extraction Transform and Transform Configuration as Base_EntityExtraction

5. Drag the ENTITY_EXTRACTION transform or the BASE_ENTITY-EXTRACTION transform configuration onto the data flow workspace.
6. Draw the data flow connections.
7. Double-click on the name of the transform. This opens the TRANSFORM EDITOR, which lets you complete the definition of the transform.
8. In the SCHEMA IN field, select the input field that you want to map, and drag it to the appropriate field in the INPUT tab, as shown in Figure 9.58.
9. This maps the input field to a field name that the transform recognizes so that the transform knows how to process it correctly. For example, an input field that is named TEXT would be mapped to the TEXT input field. It's important to know that the TEXT input field for input mapping can have the data type LONG, BLOB, or VARCHAR. The content to be processed must be in text, HTML, XML, or one of the supported binary formats, such as PDF.
10. In the OPTIONS tab, select the appropriate option values to determine how the transform will process your data (see Figure 9.59).
11. Make sure that you map input fields before you set option values.
12. If you change an option value from its default value, a green triangle appears next to the option name to indicate that you made an override. The settings are shown in Figure 9.59.

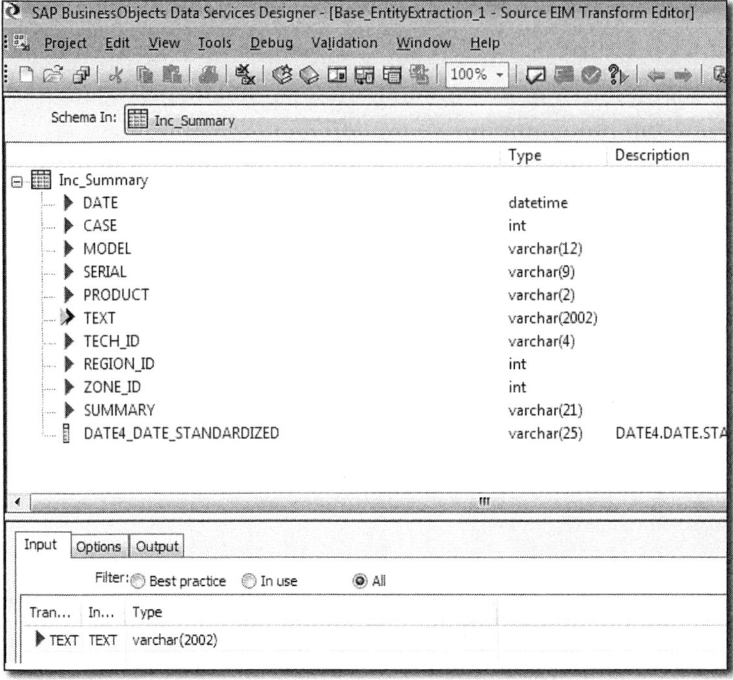

Figure 9.58 Mapping of the TEXT Input Field for the Entity Extraction Transform

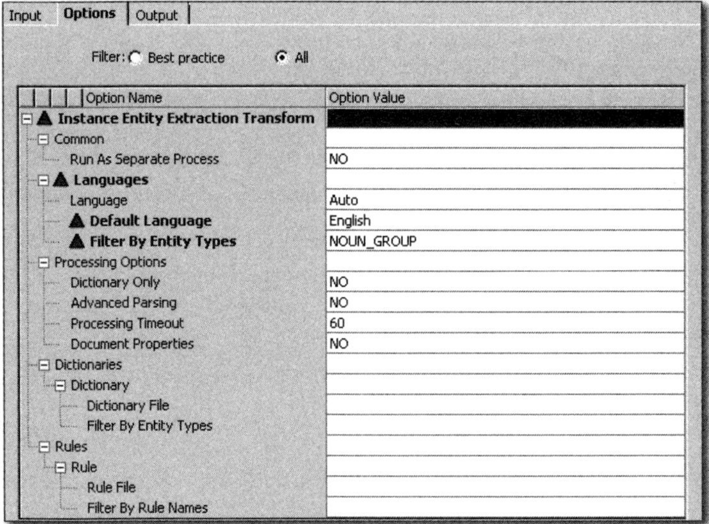

Figure 9.59 Configuring the Options of the Entity Extraction Transform

The following are some hints for configuring the transform:

- Run as Separate Process
  Choose to spawn the entity extraction transform as a separate process or keep it as a single, possibly multithreaded, process.
- Language
  Use this to specify the language of your input data. The default language setting is Auto, which causes the entity extraction transform to automatically identify the language of input text. You can select a language from the list of available languages in the dropdown menu and override automatic language identification. If the transform can't identify the language of input text, it uses the setting of the Default Language option.
- Filter By Entity Types
  Use this setting to limit the extraction output to include only selected entities for this language.
- Dictionary Only
  Limit the extraction process to use entities defined only in the specified dictionaries. You must specify a dictionary file to use this option. TDP includes the dictionary schema file *extraction-dictionary.xsd*. By default, this file is installed in the *LINK_DIR/bin* folder, where *LINK_DIR* is your Data Services installation directory. Refer to this schema to create your own dictionary files.
- Advanced Parsing
  Use this setting to produce metadata for richer noun phrase structure, noun phrase coordination, and syntactic attributes that can be leveraged in custom rules. This is only available in English.
- Document Properties
  Extract document properties of a binary document, if they are present in the document. Document properties are extracted as entities.

Configuring the Output Tab of the Entity Extraction Transform

To configure the Output tab, follow these steps:

1. In the Output tab, double-click on the fields that you want to output from the transform. The transform can generate fields in addition to the input fields that the transform processes, so you can output many fields (see Figure 9.60).

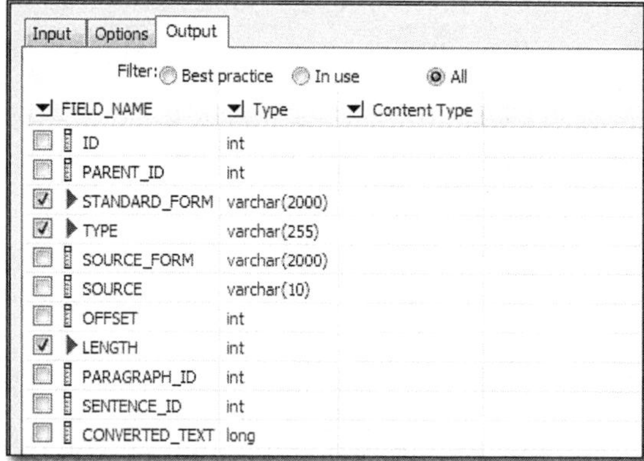

Figure 9.60 Output Fields That You Can Use in the Output Mapping for the Entity Extraction

2. Make sure that you set options before you map output fields.
3. The selected fields appear in the output schema. The output schema of this transform becomes the input schema of the next transform in the data flow.

The following are hints for working with output fields:

- STANDARD_FORM
  The official or normalized name associated with the value of the corresponding TYPE.
- TYPE
  The type of entity or fact. It may also represent subtypes.
- LENGTH
  The character length of an entity or a fact.

At this point you have done the following:

- Configured a connection to the database via a datastore
- Built a data flow with the database table as the source, an entity extraction transform, and a target
- Configured the transform to process the text

Now you can run the job so that TDP parses the unstructured text input in the field technicians' notes, identifies the concepts mentioned, and pulls these concepts into a new field, making analysis of root causes possible. You can now access a qualitatively different type of information, where there was no visibility before. First, look at the example input data that's shown in Figure 9.61.

TA_DATA_SOURCE(TDP_Manufacturing.DBO)

DATE	CASE	MODEL	SERIAL	PRODUCT	TEXT
2006.11.27	3103441	ZIC360NMBLH	ZDO30595	11	"leaking from fill tube at ba...
2006.11.29	3103473	JT952BFBB	ML608657Q	21	lot of grease on the oven fl...
2006.11.28	3103472	GSS22QGMWW	FD224746	11	tech reports new doors wer...
2006.11.29	3103475	ZISB360DRB	LG033436	11	"Warm ff. Check all the ba...
2006.11.29	3103479	SCA1001KSS02	TL900491K	27	"The cavity is dented on th...
2006.11.30	3103480	PDW9800J10BB	RH717747	41	"Leaking from the top tub s...
2006.11.28	3103482	JVM2070SK02	FL903119B	27	tech reports control freezes
2006.11.29	3103485	SCA2000BAA	AZ900092	27	"new smart board not oper...
2006.11.29	3103484	FUF20DPJRWH	SL171980	13	consumer complains of moi...
2006.11.25	3103489	GSD4330Z00WW	HT752896B	41	"tech reports harness caug...
2006.11.25	3103488	GSD5500G02CC	LG800836B	41	"tech reports that call was ...
2006.11.28	3103490	FCM20DPFWH	LL171525	13	"tech 582 reports he replac...
2006.11.29	3103496	PDW8280J10SS	RL825724B	41	"left side hinge failed on fra...
2006.11.24	3103500	PFS22SISBSS	VH047253	11	"REPAIRABLE Tech state...
2006.11.29	3103503	GTS18FBSWW	RH778315	11	"There was a leak in the e...
2007.01.02	3193507	JVM1851BD002	GD994218S	27	"Bob. Burnt wave guide. u...
2007.01.02	3193508	JVM1441WD	TA919262S	27	"glass broke, repairable ...
2006.12.01	3103442	SCA1000HWW04	GL901955K	27	"tech states the unit was dr...
2006.11.28	3103502	JVM1790WK01	RL901683	27	tech 332 reports that tone ...

Figure 9.61 Input Data from the Technicians' Notes in the Text Column

In Figure 9.61, notice the unstructured input data from the field technicians' notes in the TEXT column; for example, the NEW SMART BOARD NOT OPER... record. This record has a serial number, product number, and text. In Figure 9.62, notice how this changes after the execution of TDP in Data Services.

TA_FULL(TDP_Manufacturing.DBO)

DATE	CASE	MODEL	SERIAL	PRODUCT	STANDARD_FORM	TYPE	LENGTH
2006.11.29 00:00:00.0000...	3103485	SCA2000BAA	AZ900092	27	new smart board	NOUN_GROUP	15
2006.11.29 00:00:00.0000...	3103485	SCA2000BAA	AZ900092	27	NON REPAIRABLE o/w	NOUN_GROUP	18
2006.11.29 00:00:00.0000...	3103485	SCA2000BAA	AZ900092	27	return unit	NOUN_GROUP	11
2006.11.29 00:00:00.0000...	3103484	FUF20DPJRWH	SL171980	13	environmental issues	NOUN_GROUP	20
2006.11.25 00:00:00.0000...	3103489	GSD4330Z00WW	HT752896B	41	caught fire	NOUN_GROUP	11
2006.11.25 00:00:00.0000...	3103488	GSD5500G02CC	LG800836B	41	top rack binding	NOUN_GROUP	16
2006.11.28 00:00:00.0000...	3103482	JVM2070SK02	FL903119B	27	known suggestions	NOUN_GROUP	17
2006.11.28 00:00:00.0000...	3103482	JVM2070SK02	FL903119B	27	smart board	NOUN_GROUP	11
2006.11.28 00:00:00.0000...	3103482	JVM2070SK02	FL903119B	27	vent louver motor runs	NOUN_GROUP	22
2006.11.28 00:00:00.0000...	3103472	GSS22QGMWW	FD224746	11	consumer uses alot	NOUN_GROUP	18
2006.11.28 00:00:00.0000...	3103472	GSS22QGMWW	FD224746	11	crushed ice	NOUN_GROUP	11
2006.11.28 00:00:00.0000...	3103472	GSS22QGMWW	FD224746	11	air leaks	NOUN_GROUP	9
2006.11.29 00:00:00.0000...	3103475	ZISB360DRB	LG033436	11	cold air return	NOUN_GROUP	15
2006.11.29 00:00:00.0000...	3103479	SCA1001KSS02	TL900491K	27	left side wall	NOUN_GROUP	14
2006.11.30 00:00:00.0000...	3103480	PDW9800J10BB	RH717747	41	top tub seams	NOUN_GROUP	13
2006.11.28 00:00:00.0000...	3103472	GSS22QGMWW	FD224746	11	new doors	NOUN_GROUP	9
2006.11.28 00:00:00.0000...	3103490	FCM20DPFWH	LL171525	13	returned appl	NOUN_GROUP	13
2006.11.28 00:00:00.0000...	3103502	JVM1790WK01	RL901683	27	possible volume levels	NOUN_GROUP	22
2006.11.28 00:00:00.0000...	3103502	JVM1790WK01	RL901683	27	middle volume level	NOUN_GROUP	19
2006.11.28 00:00:00.0000...	3103502	JVM1790WK01	RL901683	27	OVEN LIGHT	NOUN_GROUP	10

Figure 9.62 Extracted Entities from the Technicians' Notes in the STANDARD_FORM Column Limited to NOUN_GROUP as Indicated in the TYPE Column

In Figure 9.62, notice that after processing the technicians' free-form notes, the entity extraction transform has pulled out the concepts or NOUN_GROUP entities into a new field. For example, on the top row in the STANDARD_FORM column, the new smart board concept is highlighted. We now have the information that the smart board is a return unit and is nonrepairable.

Without processing the text fields, our reporting could only work with the structured fields in the data: Date, Model Number, Product Line, and Region. There was nothing explaining root cause, severity, or what was done to address the issue. This has changed since performing TDP. Figure 9.63 shows a dashboard aggregating the entities, including their various variations.

The use of TDP enables companies such as NeedsEIM Inc. to turn service technicians' logs into proof-points of product quality issues they are facing. Trends and issues can now be addressed without requiring the staff to read every repair log file and tag them for root cause.

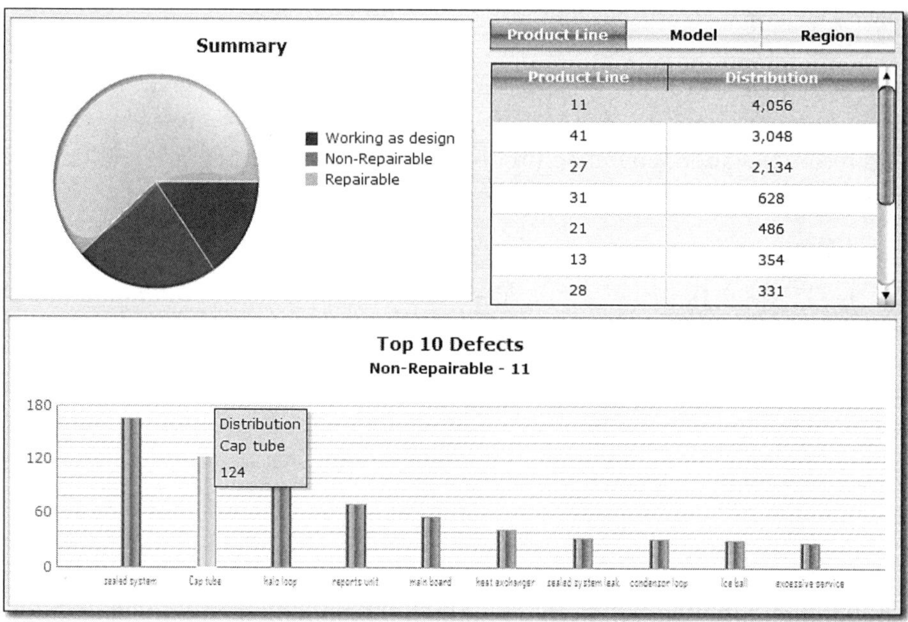

Figure 9.63 Top 10 Defects Extracted from NeedsEIM Inc. Technicians' Free-Form Text

9.12 Summary

In this chapter, we started off by discussing the different use cases for data integration, from data migration to BI to master data management. Data Services provides a multitier architecture with different UIs for the different roles in the enterprise that may interact with this solution during data governance activities.

We covered the different UIs, with a primary focus on the Data Services Designer for the technical user. You learned that a developer can use many objects to access data, transform that data, and load it into its ultimate target. You learned in detail how to create a job that extracted data from a flat file, performed a basic transformation (data lookup), and loaded that data into an RDBMS. Data Services is a powerful tool that not only provides batch processing capabilities but also provides a way to expose data transformation as a web service to support your service-oriented architecture (SOA).

This chapter also provided a detailed look at data quality and TDP and how to get started using data quality and TDP transforms.

Data Services provides SAP's data management platform and supports many solutions from SAP. The next chapter will discuss SAP Information Steward, which is a complementary solution with Data Services in supporting your data quality and information governance initiatives.

SAP Information Steward enables you to understand the details of your data, where it's stored, and how good or bad the data really is, while also supporting you in the improvement process and allowing you to monitor the ongoing health of your data.

10 SAP Information Steward

When starting a project to assess critical business data, you start with an *as-is* analysis and then define what you want to achieve. You need to start by determining what data should be included in the project. You obviously won't be profiling all of your data, so you need to determine what data is most important to you. Examples of where to start include assessing the quality of your plant assets, examining customer data from a recent acquisition, and examining sales order data to determine why shipments are chronically late.

In this chapter, we'll focus on the data quality profiling and assessment capabilities of SAP Information Steward (hereafter Information Steward) and explore how they support information governance. Information Steward can be leveraged to support the following three components of an information governance program:

- **Discover**
  Discover and understand your enterprise data by using data profiling and metadata management capabilities, as well as creating a central catalog all of your data assets.
- **Define**
  Define the data quality requirements as validation rules or cleansing rules to document and implement the quality targets that you want to reach. Set up and maintain your organization's central business term glossary to ensure that everyone in the organization has the same understanding of key terms and definitions.
- **Monitor**
  Apply the validation rules to the data to measure the current state of data quality once, and apply the same validation rules on an ongoing schedule to monitor

your data over time and monitor how your data quality level and the financial impact of that quality level changes.

Information Steward has five major areas of capabilities:

- Data profiling and data quality monitoring
- Cleansing rules
- Match review
- Metadata analysis
- Business term glossary

This chapter will start by introducing metadata management capabilities to identify and catalog your data assets and their relationships, as well as capture business-related concepts and definitions. You'll learn how to profile your data by creating Data Insight projects. You'll also learn how to use validation rules to monitor and assess the quality of your data, including the major steps in creating a data quality scorecard. In addition, we'll discuss quick starting data quality initiatives with the Data Quality Advisor.

10.1 Cataloging Data Assets and Their Relationships

One of the initial activities that's required to learn about your data is the central documentation and collection of all the technical metadata of your existing data assets. The goal of a metadata management repository is to consolidate technical metadata from individual data sources and applications into one central location. Getting metadata information together and linking information about the table structure—for example, names and columns, as well as additional information about data mapping or movement information from extraction, transformation, and loading (ETL) tools—enables you to identify similar redundant data objects that exist in different databases or applications. By linking physical data objects with the data mapping information, it's also possible to track how data is moved from different sources to target systems. This analysis provides data lineage, answering questions such as "From what source system is the data within my data warehouse coming?" A metadata management repository also enables impact analysis, answering questions such as "What reports are using the data from my operational source system?" This analysis improves trust and confidence in the system landscape.

To integrate metadata information from several solutions, you must first set up the required metadata integrators and the necessary connection parameters to access the source systems and execute the metadata integration collection. *Metadata integrators* read metadata from multiple systems. They read the table headers, columns, ETL jobs, and other technical information about the data in your landscape. This is an important first step toward learning what data is stored where, and how many different names you use for the same data.

In this section, we give step-by-step instructions to set up a metadata integrator source and to execute and/or schedule a metadata integration job.

10.1.1 Configuring a Metadata Integrator Source

Follow these steps to configure a metadata integrator source:

1. Log on to the SAP BusinessObjects Business Intelligence (SAP BusinessObjects BI) platform or information platform services (IPS) Central Management Console (CMC), and go to the INFORMATION STEWARD section.
2. Add a new integrator source by clicking on the MANAGE button.
3. Define all the necessary connection options for NEW INTEGRATOR SOURCE. Depending on the integrator type that you choose from the dropdown menu, the layout and requested parameters change.
4. Test the connection to the metadata source by clicking on the TEST CONNECTION button.
5. Click on the SAVE button to save and close the new metadata integrator source definition.

In Figure 10.1, a connection is made to a sales warehouse by selecting SAP BUSINESSOBJECTS ENTERPRISE in the INTEGRATOR TYPE field. The integrator types connect to the database directly. Other integrator types include Common Warehouse Modeling, SAP PowerDesigner, SAP BusinessObjects Data Federator, SAP HANA, SAP Business Warehouse (SAP BW), SAP Data Services (hereafter Data Services), and a relational database integrator. When connecting to SAP application systems, the relational database integrator is used.

In addition to the integrator types provided by SAP, there is also a third-party metadata integrator (Meta Integration Model Bridge by MITI) that allows you to connect more than 50 applications, including data modeling tools and other ETL tools.

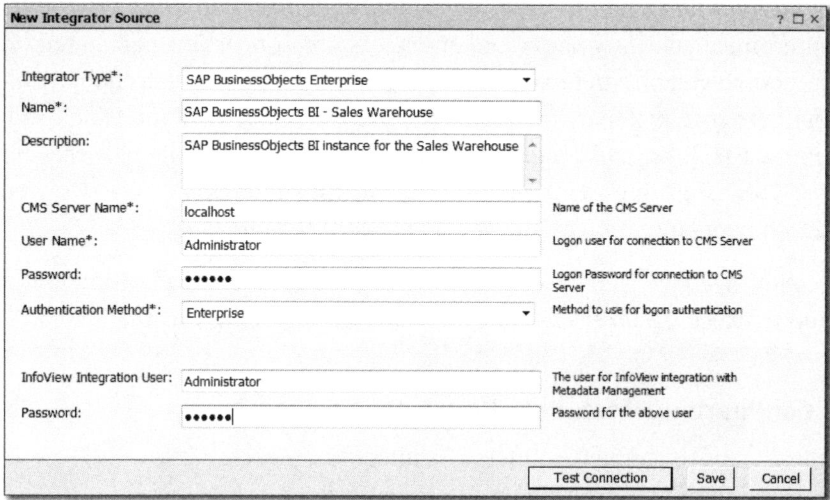

Figure 10.1 Creating a New Metadata Integrator Source

After setting up connections for all systems, the system administrator can review the list of all defined integrator sources by following the menu path INFORMATION STEWARD • METADATA MANAGEMENT • INTEGRATOR SOURCES in the CMC.

Central Management Console

The CMC is a web-based tool that offers a single interface for day-to-day administrative tasks, including user management, content management, and server management. The CMC is used by the SAP BusinessObjects platform, Data Services, and Information Steward.

The next activity is to either execute each integrator source once, or set up an appropriate schedule for executing ongoing metadata integration tasks. The execution will collect and consolidate all technical metadata descriptions. The integration tasks collect the following information:

- **Database system information**
  Includes the description of the table names, field names, and data types. This includes information from an SAP application database.
- **Data modeling**
  Includes the description of the relationship between different models.
- **Data movement and ETL systems**
  Includes the description of the data movement jobs from target to source sys-

tems. This information is available when connecting to Data Services as a metadata integrator source.

- **Business intelligence and data warehouse systems**
  Includes the description of queries and reports.

The metadata integration tasks include all information in its central repository. Relationships between the different metadata objects are automatically determined by Information Steward's relationship service.

10.1.2 Executing or Scheduling Execution of Metadata Integration

Follow these steps to execute metadata integration:

1. Highlight one of the integrator sources from the INTEGRATOR SOURCE LIST in the CMC.
2. Choose RUN NOW from the ACTIONS dropdown list to run the metadata integrator immediately.
3. Choose SCHEDULE from the ACTIONS dropdown list to open the scheduler configuration window.

Figure 10.2 shows an example of the results of this job.

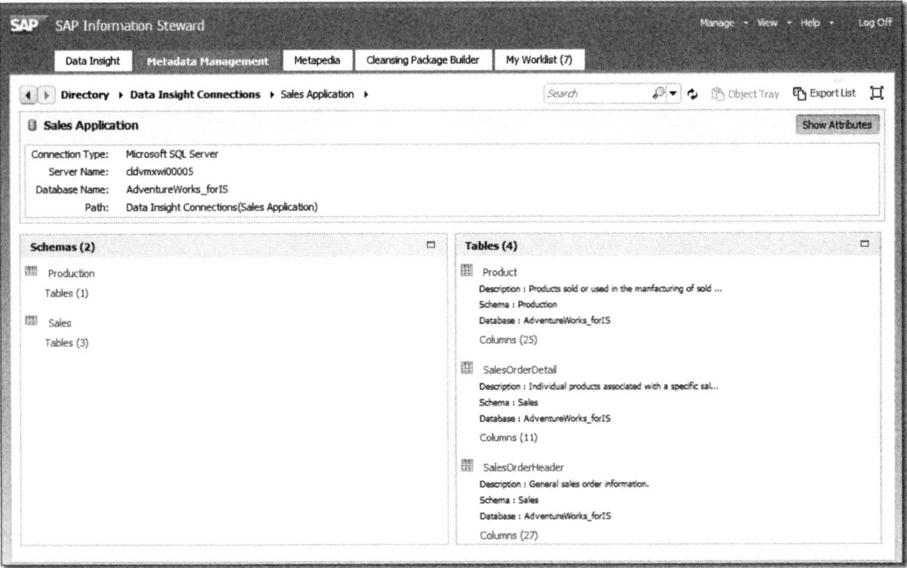

Figure 10.2 Data Catalog for Data Insight Connection Database Sales Application in Metadata Management

Figure 10.2 shows the METADATA MANAGEMENT tab of Information Steward. In the results for the job, you can see that there are two database schemas and four tables. You can see the number of columns for each of the tables. You can also drill down into each level to see column names and other information such as field attributes.

The consolidated and enriched metadata information allows the data analyst or business user to review, search, and browse the complete metadata catalog, including all data objects as well as related information on descriptions, synonyms, or associated business terms. Another perspective allows the user to view the data lineage or impact analysis representation in either tabular or graphical form to see how information is moving from source to target systems within the system landscape. This helps you to understand where the data is coming from and how it's being transformed (data lineage), as well as assess the impact of change to downstream systems and reports (data impact). Figure 10.3 shows an example of the graphical representation of data lineage.

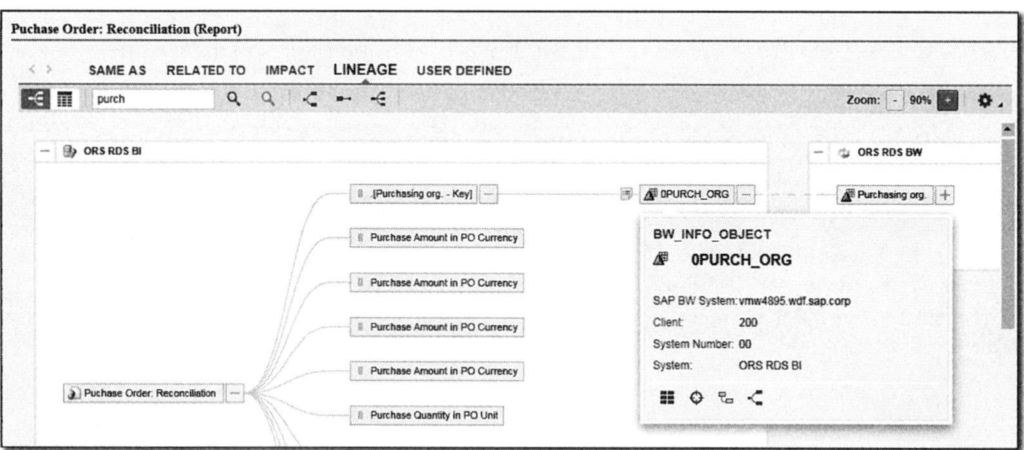

Figure 10.3 Metadata Management Data Lineage Example

10.2 Establishing a Business Term Glossary

Information Steward's Metapedia promotes proactive information governance with common understanding and agreement on business taxonomies that are related to your data. With Metapedia, users have a central location in which they can define standard business vocabulary of words, phrases, or business concepts, and then relate that terminology to the metadata objects (e.g., systems, tables, reports) that were discussed in the previous section, as well as to Data Insight quality rules and scorecards that we'll discuss in subsequent sections. After the business glossary is established, business users can easily search the content and concepts using familiar business vocabulary and synonyms, as well as access related terms from data quality rules and scorecards (see Figure 10.4), from SAP BusinessObjects BI reports via an integration with BI Launchpad, and really from just about anywhere using the Metapedia web service (refer to the Information Steward Integrator Guide for details on web service support at *http://help.sap.com*).

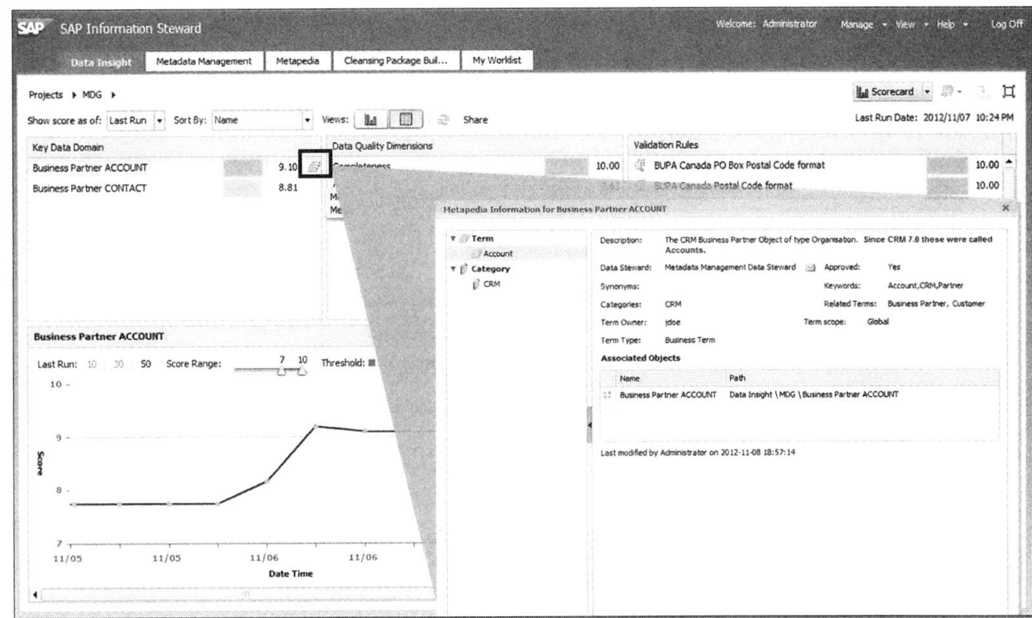

Figure 10.4 Metapedia Term Association to Data Quality Scorecard

Many techniques can be applied within Metapedia to organize and describe your business terms. These techniques will improve both the understanding and the access to the established taxonomy. The techniques are illustrated in Figure 10.5 and discussed in more detail in the following list.

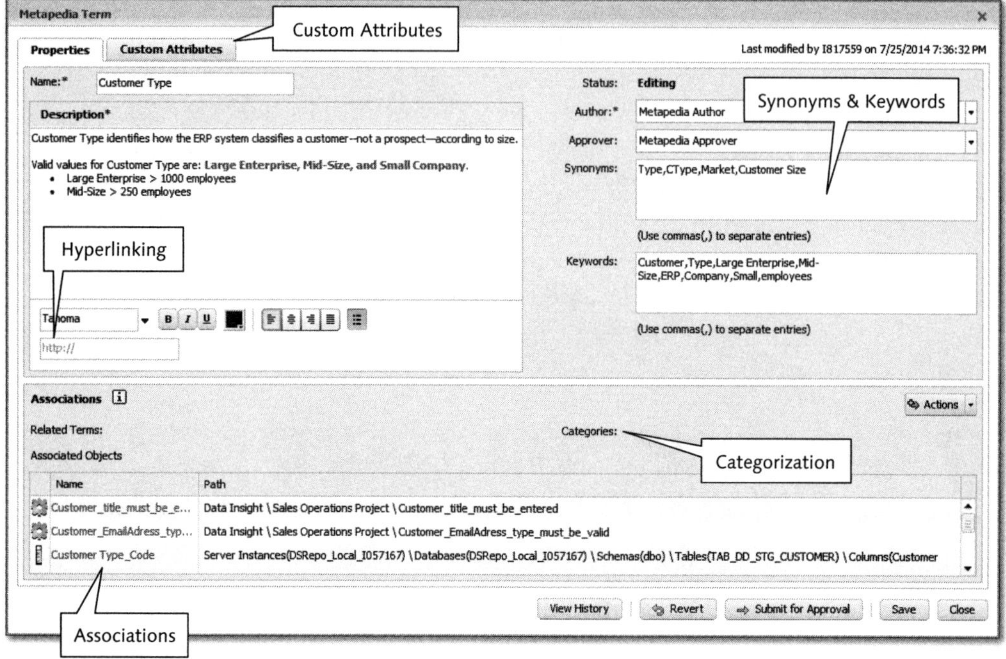

Figure 10.5 Metapedia Term Categorization and Associations Techniques

- **Categories**
  Multiple levels of categories can be created to establish term hierarchies by subject area, data domain, business unit, business process, and so on to denote commonalities. A Metapedia term can be associated with more than one category or subcategory.
- **Related terms**
  After two or more terms have been created and approved, an author can relate the terms. As an example, the terms "Gross Revenue" and "Net Revenue" could be related so when a business user searches for one of the terms, the metadata information about the other is also available.
- **Hyperlinks**
  A hyperlink can be added to the description of a term to point to additional information, specifications, or supporting documentation.
- **Synonyms and key words**
  Synonyms and key words may be specified to enhance search capabilities. For example, let's say you create the term "Net Revenue" and place it in a category

called "Financial". However, in your organization, many business users refer to "Net Revenue" as "profit," which you don't intend to use as a Metapedia term. In the creation of the "Net Revenue" term, the author could apply the word "profit" as a synonym. Then, when a business user searches Metapedia for "profit", Metapedia returns the term "Net Revenue".

- **Custom attributes**
  You can enhance your terms and categories with custom-defined attributes. For example, you might add a customer attribute to capture details such as the business process (where used), comments, reference documents, and so on.
- **Associated objects**
  Data assets cataloged as a part of Information Steward's Metadata Management (e.g., data column, table, universe, BI report, etc.) and objects created as a part of Data Insight projects (e.g., data sources, validation rules, or scorecards) can be associated to Metapedia terms. See Figure 10.4 for an example of a term and category that has been associated with a data quality scorecard.

10.3 Profiling Data

Dealing with data in an unknown environment can be a challenging, if not daunting, task. Even if you have documentation for the metadata of the different data assets, including the schema, table names, and column names, you shouldn't rely on the headlines of the columns and expect to find exactly the content that the headline implies. You definitely need to drill into the table columns and analyze what information is really stored in those fields.

Information Steward provides easy access to helpful statistical information about the data that is stored in any database system, application, or file. Using statistical information and a user-friendly user interface (UI) to drill down into details, even down to the individual rows, will provide the data analyst with insight about what the content behind the labels and headlines in the tables *really* is.

Executing data profiling on the existing databases, applications, or files of a company is essential to find the hidden rules that are only visible within the data itself. An example of a hidden rule is the discovery that 95% of the time when an order is placed for the Northeast region, the order is set to a rush order. This may not be a documented policy or instruction, but a discovery made while analyzing the data. It could be that if 95% of the time a pattern emerges, it should also happen the other 5% of the time, so a new rule is needed to document the unspoken policy.

Data profiling is a fast way to identify suspicious data or outliers that should be used to establish further data quality rules based on the finding of the data profiling. This can be used to enforce service-level agreements within a governance project (governance projects with service level agreements are discussed in Chapter 2). Data profiling can also be used to assess data quality requirements from external regulations or already documented internal data quality requirements.

Note

This chapter focuses primarily on Data Insight projects in Information Steward, and how they're used to define separate projects for different functional areas in a company, ensuring that users access only the projects to which they have been assigned.

Data profiling first requires you to create a Data Insight project for data profiling. Then, within the project, you select the source system for the profiling and drill down to select the specific tables and files that should be included in your Data Insight project. You start by gaining some statistical information on the data content, executing some basic profiling, and then focusing on relationships between fields and columns.

10.3.1 Configuration and Setup of Connections and Projects

After the project team has identified what database tables, applications, or files should be used for initial data profiling activities, the IT administrator provides the access to those systems for Information Steward. Information Steward is able to directly connect to a large number of databases or applications; however, whether a company wants to execute the data profiling and data quality monitoring directly on its production system or on a snapshot or staging area of the data is a system design question.

To allow the data analysts to access the necessary tables of files in their Data Insight projects, connections in the CMC are configured to the necessary application, database, or file directories. Besides giving the connection a unique name, further system parameters such as the database name and user credentials are set up, and the general access is tested.

Data profiling projects are called *Data Insight* projects in Information Steward. The following describes how to set up a connection for a Data Insight project. An administrator normally performs this task. This includes setting up the connection to the source system for the Data Insight project, creating the new project, and adding information on the data you want to profile (e.g., the specific tables and/or files that should be included).

Setting Up a Connection for Data Insight Projects

When getting started with Data Insight projects, you first need to set up a connection for the project by following these steps:

1. Log on to the CMC.
2. Go to the INFORMATION STEWARD section.
3. Follow the menu path MANAGE • NEW • CONNECTION.
4. Define all the necessary options for the new connection. Depending on the connection type you choose from the dropdown menu, the layout and requested parameters change.
5. Test the connection to the data source by clicking on the TEST CONNECTION button.
6. Save and close the CREATE CONNECTION configuration window.

In addition to the different connections that provide access to the data, multiple individual Data Insight projects can be defined on an Information Steward installation. Projects are dashboards that are composed of several related scorecards. A project, for example, can represent different application areas, different data domains, and different regions or business processes. Data analysts working with Information Steward are granted only specific user rights to their Data Insight project(s). This allows the system administrator to explicitly limit access to Data Insight projects to those users who are allowed to see the data.

Setting Up a Data Insight Project

After the connections are done, you set up the Data Insight project itself. This includes providing a project name and description, as follows:

1. In the CMC, go to the Information Steward section.
2. Follow the menu path Manage • New • Data Insight Project.
3. Enter a project name and project description in the New Data Insight Project configuration window.
4. Save and close the New Data Insight Project configuration window.

After the IT administrator has set up the basic technical configuration required for Information Steward, the data analysts are able to log on to a web browser-based UI and start working on their Data Insight projects. The users can add files or tables from the technical connections to the file directories, database systems, or applications. Using the integrated metadata browsing capability, the data analyst will get an overview of all available files and tables, including tables from SAP applications, and the technical names and business names or descriptions of the embedded tables.

Adding Tables or Files to a Data Insight Project

This example describes how to add tables or files to your new Data Insight project. Follow these steps:

1. In the Data Insight tab, click on your project's workspace link.
2. Go to the Workspace Home tab.
3. Click on the Add button, and choose the type of data object (table or file) you want to add to your project.
4. In the Browse Metadata window, select the preconfigured database connection where you want to add tables.
5. Select the tables that you want to add from this connection. You can take a look at the data before adding it to the project by clicking on the View Data button, shown in Figure 10.6. Notice the selection of Sales Application and then the Person.Address table.
6. Click on the Add to Project button to add all selected tables from this data source to your project.
7. Close the Browse Metadata window.

After the tables are added, you can start to profile and collect information about the data content.

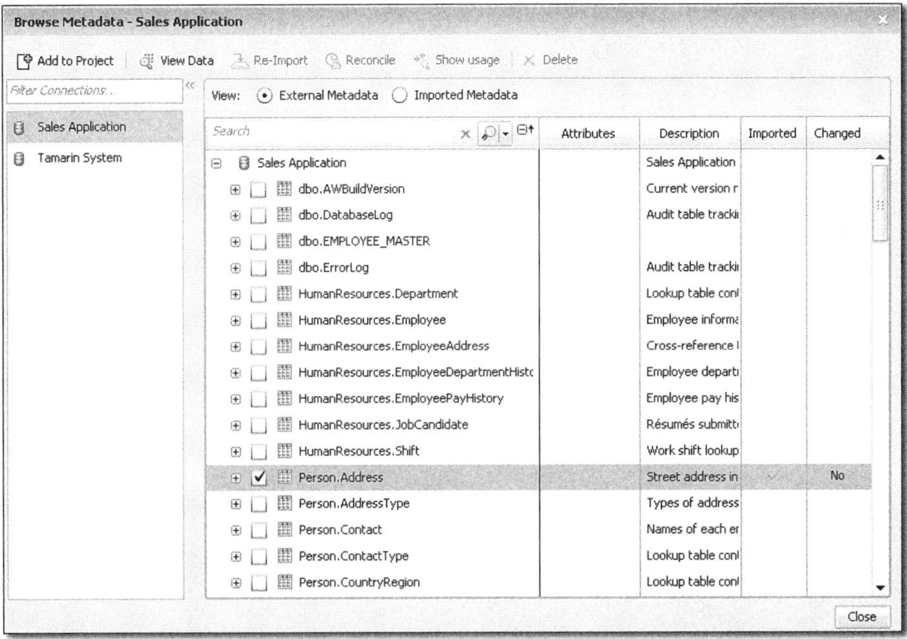

Figure 10.6 Browsing the Metadata Catalog to Add Tables to Your Data Insight Project

10.3.2 Getting Basic Statistical Information about the Data Content

The easiest way to get some initial insight into the content of a table or columns in a spreadsheet is by applying sorting or filtering capabilities. It's amazing to see how even some simple information such as the smallest and largest value of a column can give a data analyst hints about potential data quality issues.

Example

NeedsEIM Inc. has issues with its supplier data. When examining the supplier email field, the analyst quickly sees +180062545, which looks like a telephone number. While this type of basic profiling can be done with a spreadsheet application, when it comes to the analysis of large data sets, more mature and sophisticated solutions are required to support data analysts in their interactive analysis.

You can set up a basic data profiling task for any of the files and tables that are added to a Data Insight project. Within basic data profiling, you can define details on the data sample size and the detail level of data profiling statistics as well as determine if the basic profiling task should be executed immediately or be scheduled.

The next example describes how to define, execute, and review the results of a basic data profiling task.

Define and Execute a Basic Profiling Task

The following steps show how to create a simple column profiling task:

1. Go to the WORKSPACE HOME tab in your Data Insight project.
2. Check the file, table, or view for the basic profiling.
3. Click on the PROFILE button, and choose the COLUMNS option.
4. In the DEFINE COLUMN PROFILING TASK window, give this task a unique name, and set the required options for the profiling task (described in more detail next and shown in Figure 10.7).

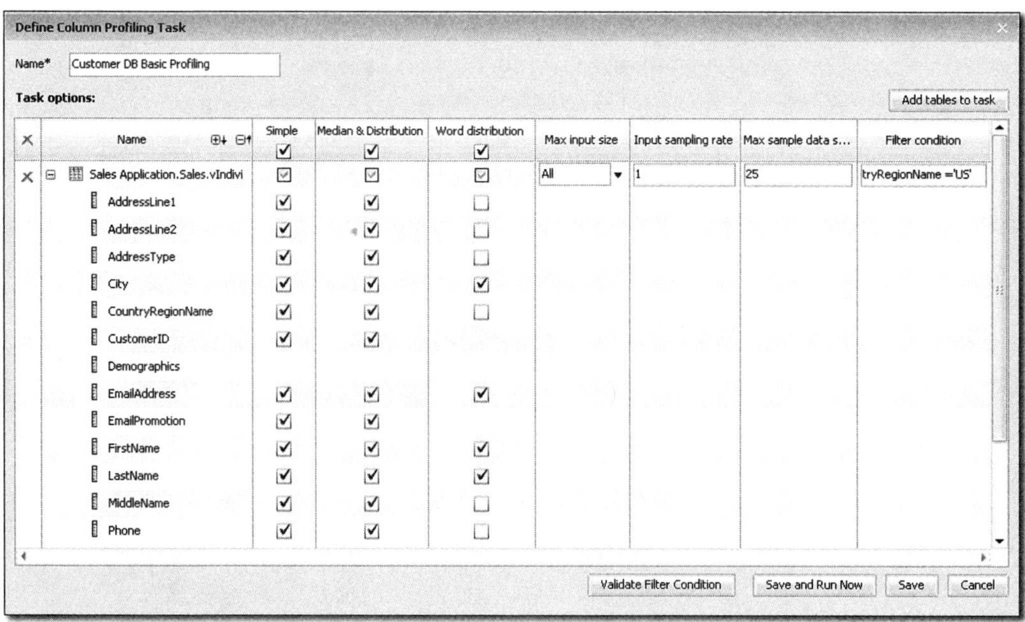

Figure 10.7 Defining and Immediately Executing a Column Profiling Task

5. If you've defined a filter condition, click on VALIDATE FILTER CONDITION to see if you used the correct syntax.
6. Click on the SAVE AND RUN NOW button to immediately execute the profiling task, or click the SAVE button to save the task for later execution or scheduling.

After executing the basic profiling task, you can view results for every table profiled. The following list describes what is available with basic profiling:

- **Summary**
The summary column (untitled) includes icons for data design information such as primary keys, sparsely populated columns, and so on, where the data analyst can get detailed information when he moves the mouse over the icon.
- **Advisor**
The ADVISOR column will include an icon to inform you as to whether validation and/or cleansing rules can be recommended based on the results of profiling. Clicking on the appropriate icon will launch either the Data Validation Advisor or Data Cleansing Advisor. These tools are a part of the Data Quality Advisor covered in more detail in Section 10.6.
- **Content type**
If you selected a CONTENT TYPE profiling task, you'll see the suggested content types. If you think that the generated content type is incorrect, you can highlight the content type and click ASSOCIATE CONTENT TYPE to change it. To view other content type suggestions for a column, click the content type to open the side pane. The currently assigned content type (if one exists) along with the confidence of the match is listed first. Other potential content types and their confidence scores are listed in descending order by percentage. The confidence percentage can add up to more or less than 100 because they are suggested values. For example, a certain piece of data might be suggested as both a phone number and a material number if the material number custom content type has a similar pattern to a phone number. Note that content type profiling is leveraged by the Data Quality Advisor to make validation and cleansing rule recommendations.
- **Value (min, max, average, median)**
The VALUE columns include information about the minimum and maximum values of the column, as well as the average and median values for numeric values. Even if there are only two values for a column, such as the minimum and maximum for a field, those two values can be a hint about existing internal data quality problems that should be tracked further with a validation rule and ongoing assessment. Clicking on the hyperlinked numbers in the VALUE columns opens a separate data review area that shows the corresponding data record sample. An example of what you can see could be colors for a particular article of clothing. You would easily be able to see how many color values,

including articles that have no color assigned (null values in columns where there should be a value).

- **String length (min, max, average, median)**
  The String Length columns include information about the minimum and maximum string length stored in the column, as well as the average and median string length. The maximum string length information in particular can be very helpful together with the data type definition of the column.

  If the maximum string length is equal to the field length definition, this might indicate a truncation problem; for example, if a user copies data from one data source to another, truncation could occur if the source field is longer than allowed in the target field. By clicking on the hyperlinked numbers in the String Length columns, a separate data review area opens where the corresponding data record sample is shown.
- **Completeness (Null %, Blank %, Zero %)**
  The Completeness columns include detailed information about how many records of the data source include either technical null values or empty blank strings or zero in a numeric data field. You should look closely to see if any mandatory columns have null or empty values. By clicking on the hyperlinked numbers in the Completeness columns, you can see the corresponding data record sample.
- **Distribution (Value, Pattern, Word)**
  The Distribution columns include information about the number of distinct values in the data source column. The Value column shows the number of distinct values for the complete data field, while the Word column shows the number of distinct values for a string field content when the individual words within a long string are counted individually. The Pattern column shows the number of distinct patterns in the column, where digits are represented by 9 and characters by A. You can get more details on the frequency distribution of the values, pattern, or words in a separate distribution list by clicking on the hyperlinked number.

Using Hyperlinked Numbers in Information Steward

This chapter will often refer to selecting a hyperlinked number in Information Steward to drill down to create validation rules or view sample data, failed data, and so on. In Information Steward, the hyperlinks are blue—even though the screenshots in the print version of this book are in grayscale and thus don't reflect this. Color figures are viewable in the online version of the book, which can be accessed at *www.sap-press.com/3666*.

Reviewing the Basic Profiling Results

This example describes how to view the results of the profiling task. Figure 10.8 shows the example results.

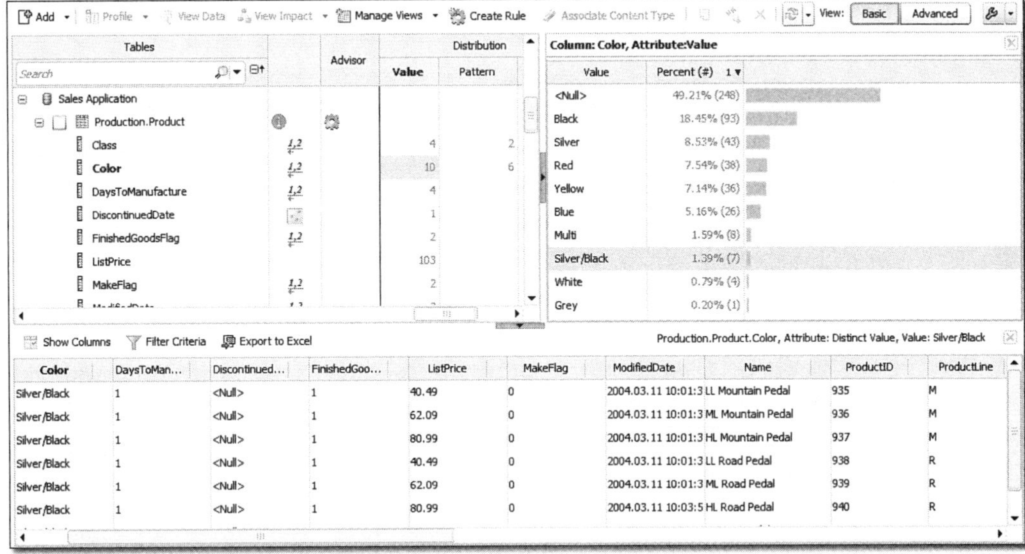

Figure 10.8 Basic Profiling Results—Frequency Distribution and Failed Record Sample Data

To view the results, follow these steps:

1. Go to the Workspace Home tab in your Data Insight project.
2. Click on the Profile Result tab.
3. Change the view to Basic.
4. Expand the database connection entry in the Tables column.
5. Expand the table entry where you want to review the basic profiling results.
6. Click on the hyperlinked numbers to either drill down to a frequency distribution overview, or go directly to the records that are counted for this number.

   On the right side of the screen shown in Figure 10.8, Information Steward displays colors and the frequency distribution. For example, the most-used color is no color (set to null), and the second color in the list is black. This area is the frequency distribution. When you're in the frequency distribution area, you can click on the hyperlinked numbers to get to the corresponding records.

7. Reduce the number of columns, filter the number of records that are presented, or click on the EXPORT TO EXCEL button to save the records for external processing in a Microsoft Excel spreadsheet.

What kind of information might this reveal to users? To understand this, let's turn to our NeedsEIM Inc. example.

Example

The NeedsEIM Inc. data analyst is reviewing the data profiling basic results for the supplier master data table. In the REGION field, the results show that the minimum value is 1 and the maximum value is WY. Because the expected result is to have only two-character region codes, this is an indicator that further analysis of the REGION field is needed (e.g., reviewing the pattern distribution in the basic data profiling).

In the basic data profiling, it's discovered that the email address field of the supplier master data table isn't always populated, and there are a small number of null values within this field. Additionally, it's discovered that there are several records with the same supplier names. Finally, the frequency distribution of the words shows that among the 25 most common words in the SUPPLIER NAME field are Limited, Lim., and Ltd., which are all legal forms of companies but should be standardized to one single representation.

The example we just discussed shows profiling within a single column. Next, we discuss the profiling of cross-field and cross-column data relationships.

10.3.3 Identifying Cross-Field or Cross-Column Data Relationships

The basic profiling activity provides information on a single field or column content. For cross-column or cross-table profiling, extended functionalities are provided in the advanced profiling area. The next example discusses how to create an advanced profiling task, which includes defining an advanced profiling task and reviewing the results.

Define and Execute an Advanced Profiling Task

Advanced profiling offers several options for profiling. Follow these steps to create an advanced profiling task:

1. Go to the WORKSPACE HOME tab in your Data Insight project.
2. Check the file, table, or view for extended profiling.

3. Click on the PROFILE button, and choose the ADDRESS, DEPENDENCY, REDUNDANCY, or UNIQUENESS option (explained in more detail in the next bullet list).
4. In the DEFINE PROFILING TASK window, give this task a unique name, and set the required options for the profiling task.
5. Click on the SAVE AND RUN NOW button to immediately execute the profiling task, or click on the SAVE button to save the task for later execution or scheduling.

The following describes the types of profiling that are available:

- **Address profiling**
  Address profiling allows validation against the backend address directories from global address cleansing in Data Services. For any data domain that includes address-relevant information, you can map the corresponding data fields and see a pie chart representation of how many addresses are already correct, how many are wrong but can be automatically corrected in a Data Services-based address cleansing job, and how many are wrong and can't be corrected automatically.
- **Dependency profiling**
  Dependency profiling identifies if there are business dependencies between two or more columns; for example, there might be a dependency between the locality name and the region name of an address, or between a product name and a product class. With dependency profiling, you can review if a given value in one column only exists when a specific value in another column exists.
- **Redundancy profiling**
  Redundancy profiling detects missing data that should be multiple tables (e.g., expected redundancies between a table with customer data and a table with address data). Redundancy profiling detects where there are customers without addresses and addresses without customers.
- **Uniqueness profiling**
  Uniqueness profiling detects if a primary key is sufficient to uniquely identify a record or if multiple fields are really needed to identify unique records. For example, in a product database, a primary key might be a product name, but if a uniqueness profile on product_name, product_color, and product_size indicates that only 95% of records are unique, this means that 5% of products are redundant but have different primary keys.

After executing the advanced profiling task, you can find the results for every table that was selected for profiling. The next example shows how to view the results.

Reviewing the Advanced Profiling Results

Follow these steps to see the results of an advanced profiling task:

1. Go to the Workspace Home tab in your Data Insight project.
2. Click on the Profile Result tab.
3. Change the view to Advanced.
4. Expand the database connection entry in the table's column. You can click on each profiled column to get to the next detail level, which shows the results of the advanced data profiling activity.

Figure 10.9 shows the result of advanced profiling. This screen indicates that most of the addresses are incorrect. The bottom part of the screen shows the addresses that will be valid if corrected. Not shown in the screenshot are the data quality codes that indicate the problem with the data.

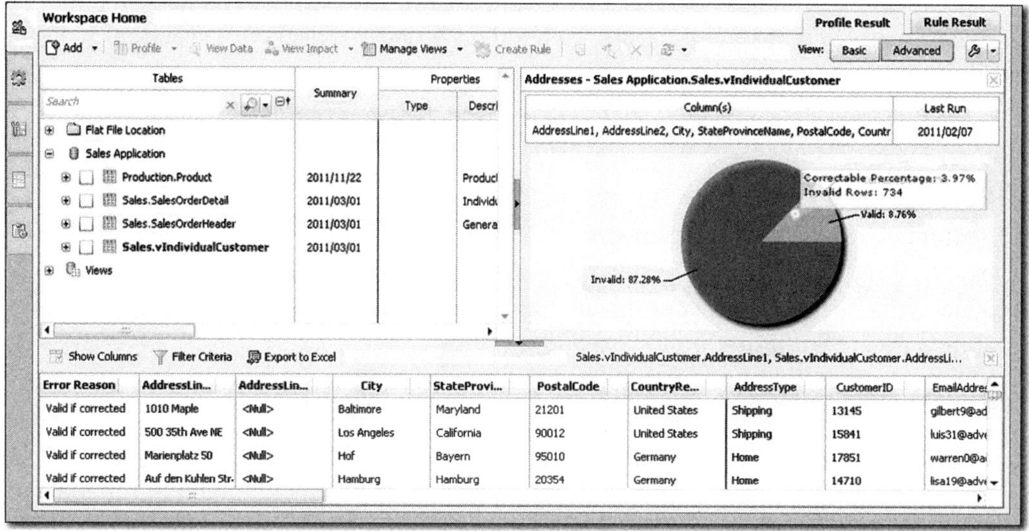

Figure 10.9 Advanced Profiling Results—Address Profiling with Drill-Down to Automatically Correctable Address Records

Example

When relating this to NeedsEIM Inc., this graphic identifies that almost 4% of the company's addresses aren't correct according to the official reference data, but most can be automatically corrected using the global address cleanse solution in Data Services. Chapter 9 covers global address cleanse and other data quality functions.

10.4 Assessing the Quality of Your Data

For assessment and the ongoing monitoring of current data quality, it's essential to implement a solution that provides a repeatable way to apply business rules and requirements to your data assets. Getting permanent insight into the current data quality level, as well as identifying early trends and changes, enables you to react quickly to potential data quality issues.

Information Steward includes the ability to define *validation rules* that are managed and approved by data analysts, business users, or data stewards. Validation rules represent technical requirements or business rules that are essential for an organization's business execution.

Examples of a centrally defined and reusable validation rule include the following:

- Ensuring that required fields contain values and that those values are valid, such as a postal code that contains a four-digit extension.
- Checking to make sure a purchase order contains a valid product.
- Ensuring compliance with regulatory requirements or adhering to industry standards, such as having a 9- or 13-digit ISBN number for a book.

A validation rule consists of the following elements:

- **Unique name**
  Each validation rule needs to have a unique name. Organizations might apply their own naming conventions to categorize or group their rules.
- **Description**
  The rule description provides more detail about the core definition or content of the validation rule.

- **Author and approver**
  Every validation rule needs to have an author and an approver. When the initial definition of the validation rule has been saved, the validation rule is in the EDIT status and can be submitted for approval. At this point, the rule is submitted to the approver who was indicated, and a rule approval task appears in the approver's worklist.
- **Quality dimension**
  Each validation rule can be linked to a specific quality dimension that is used for hierarchy, grouping, or use on the *data quality scorecard* setup. (Section 10.5 covers data quality scorecards in detail.)
- **Financial impact per failure**
  For each rule, you can optionally configure associated costs. These estimates result in a total amount that represents the financial impact value of that rule per failure. You can select from a variety of resource-independent and resource-dependent cost types or create your own. You can later manipulate these values in the business value analysis what-if scenario view, if you believe the cost is different from what was originally estimated in the rule. See Section 10.5.5 on business value analysis for more information.
- **Parameters**
  A validation rule can have one or multiple input parameters dependent on the complexity of the business rule. If a parameter is only used for filtering or dependency condition checking and should not be assigned a score value, this needs to be configured in the validation rule editor. A validation rule can also optionally be assigned to a content type. Using a content type in your rule helps to automatically generate rule recommendations for other tables or data sources with the selected content type (see Section 10.6 on the Data Quality Advisor).
- **Expression**
  The validation rule expression represents the data quality requirements for the parameters. The rule definition editor includes a basic rule editor with a set of predefined validation functions (e.g., IS NOT NULL) that allows easy setup of simple rule expressions. Additionally, there's an advanced rule editor with wizard-style support. Text editor capabilities are also an option to create the native scripting for any kind of complex validation rule expression. The transformation of the validation rule expression into the native Data Services scripting language is always shown in a preview window.

The elements of a validation rule support an important Information Steward concept: Validation rules should represent an organization's requirements independent of the data assets to which they are applied. For example, a validation rule stating that all product names must follow a certain nomenclature is an organizational requirement. This rule can be applied to products and services of different types across different application systems. Another example is that all email fields can't be null. This could be applied to customers, suppliers, contact persons, and so on.

After the responsible person approves the validation rules, the next step is to bind or link the generic validation rules to one or multiple data objects within the organization. Then the validation rules are executed based on the defined bindings on the data sources to calculate the individual quality score values.

In the next section, you'll learn how to define validation rules that meet business requirements for data quality. You'll also learn how to link those roles to specific data sources (called *binding* in Information Steward) and how to execute the validation rules and view the results.

10.4.1 Defining Validation Rules Representing Business Requirements

Validation rules are the essential and central component for the ongoing monitoring and assessment of the data quality level in an organization. The sources for the validation rule expressions are manifold, and some of the examples discussed here will explain the two general ways of creating and defining a new validation rule. We'll demonstrate how validation rules can be created either directly from the data profiling results based on the findings of the statistical analysis of the existing data assets, or from scratch, directly in the rules editor. Creating validation rules directly in the rules editor is important for rules that are based on external regulative requirements, common industry standards, or internal company policies. You'll also learn how to test a validation rule.

Setting Up Validation Rules Based on Data Profiling Results

As discussed in Section 10.3, profiling results are a valuable source for interactively identifying outliers or data quality issues. This insight can then be used to set up the validation rules for ongoing data quality assessment. You can create validation rules directly from the data profiling results panel by following these steps:

1. Figure 10.8 showed the results of a basic data profiling task. To create a validation rule, click on a hyperlinked number (e.g., the null percentage number).
2. Click on the Create Rule button.
3. In the validation Rule Editor, a new rule is created, including context-relevant information such as the input parameter $Color, the expression Is Not Null, and so on (see Figure 10.10).
4. Add the unique validation rule name, the data quality dimension, and the validation rule description.
5. Save the rule after you've defined the expression, and click on the Validate button to validate the expression syntax.

In the example validation rule shown in Figure 10.10, notice that the rule is about the color; it should not be null. However, at this point, the rule isn't tied to any specific application or table. This enables the rules to be based on business requirements and later be technically bound to the specific data element(s) for the rule.

By building the rule from the data profiling results, you can immediately transfer data profiling findings into potential data validation rules for ongoing data quality monitoring.

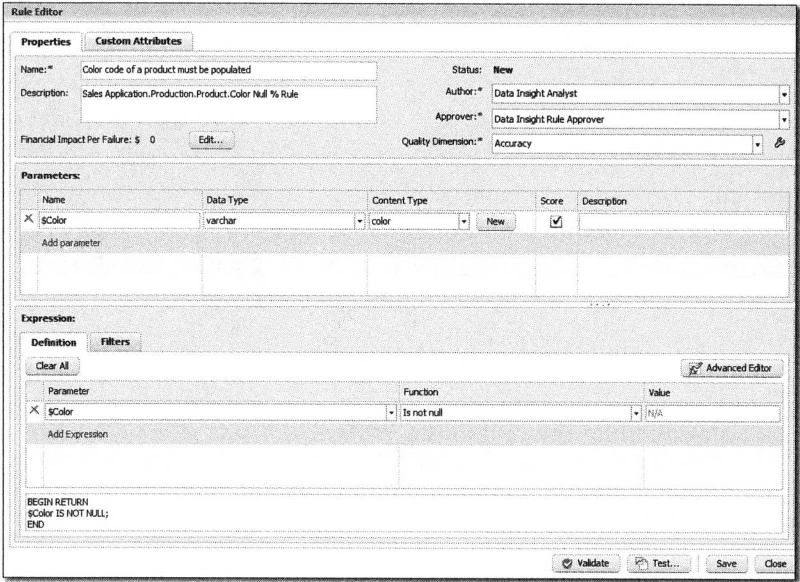

Figure 10.10 Example Validation Rule

Example

NeedsEIM Inc. has identified in the initial data profiling activity that the EMAIL_ADDRESS field is empty for some of its suppliers. From the PROFILING RESULT tab, the NeedsEIM Inc. analyst clicks on the hyperlinked number of null percentage values and then chooses CREATE RULE to directly open the rule editor window that already includes the prepopulated name, description, parameter, and expression information.

Up to this point, we've discussed the creation of validation rules based on data profiling results. Rules can also be created separately from the profiling results; for example, when creating a rule to enforce an industry format for an ISBN number. The steps are the same as described previously; the only difference is that no data profiling is done before creating the validation rule, so you must provide parameters for the rule. Rules can also be created via the Data Validation Advisor, which is covered in Section 10.6.

Figure 10.11 shows the RULES overview, where you can create a new rule or edit an existing rule separately from the profiling results.

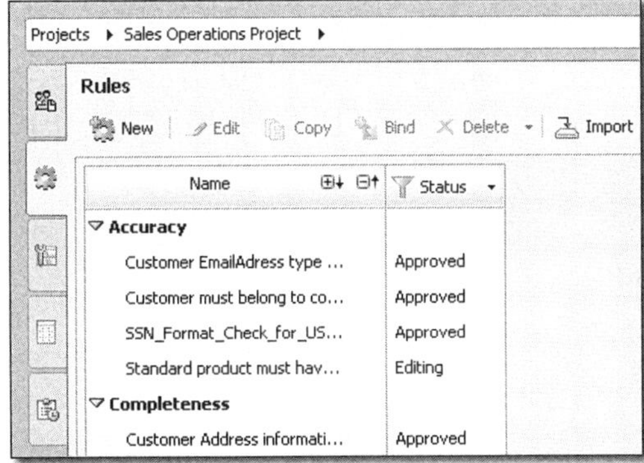

Figure 10.11 Rules Overview

Creating a Validation Rule Directly in the Rule Editor

The following steps describe how to create a validation rule directly in the rule editor. This is required for industry rules or external policies that you need to enforce in the data.

1. Go to the RULES tab in the Data Insight project.
2. Click on the NEW button to open the rule editor.

3. Enter the name, quality dimension, and description information for the new validation rule. It will look like the screen shown earlier in Figure 10.10.
4. Click on the ADD PARAMETER hyperlink to add a new parameter to the rule, define the parameter type, and add a description. Deselect the score box if the calculated score for a rule should not be attached to this parameter.
5. Create the rule expression that's based on the parameters defined. You can either use functions on the list of predefined functions (such as IS NOT NULL) for simple rule expressions or click on ADVANCED EDITOR to open a wizard-style editor, where you can define the expressions in a script language style.
6. Save the rule after you've defined the expression, and click on the VALIDATE button to validate the expression syntax.

Testing a Validation Rule

During the definition of a validation rule, it's important to validate and test the correctness of the validation rule expression. This is especially true for complex validation rules. After saving a validation rule, you can test the rule by executing the following steps:

1. Click on the TEST button in the RULE EDITOR window to open the TEST RULE window (see Figure 10.12).

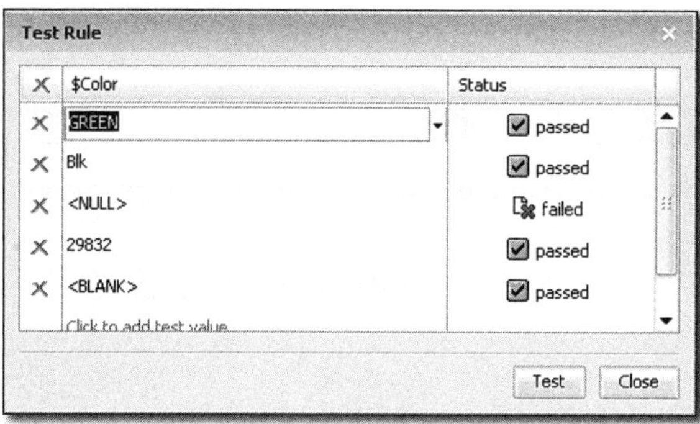

Figure 10.12 Testing a Validation Rule

2. Each rule is represented as a column. You can add multiple test records in the TEST RULE window. If you want to test <Null> or <Blank> as test data, you can choose them from the dropdown in the field.

3. Click on the TEST button to execute the test run immediately.
4. The TEST RULE window shows the status (passed, failed, or filtered) of the entered samples of the test run.
5. Close the TEST RULE window by clicking on the CLOSE button.

It's important to mention that the test values and statuses are stored with the validation rule, so that they are available for later testing after a validation rule update.

10.4.2 Binding Rules to Data Sources for Data Quality Assessment

In an enterprise, a validation rule is defined, managed, approved, and stored in the central repository. From this central repository, a validation rule is reused and linked in multiple projects and to multiple data sources. The linking of the rule to a data source is called *binding*. There are two ways to bind validation rules to data sources, both of which we describe next.

Manual Rule Binding

Manual rule binding is done for validation rules that have been defined from scratch and stored in the general RULES tab, or for rules where an existing rule is bound to an additional table. To manually bind a generic validation rule to a data source and its columns, execute the following steps:

1. Go to the RULES tab in the Data Insight project.
2. Highlight the rule that you want to bind to a table or a file, and click on the BIND button to open the Rule Binding Editor.
3. Select the SOURCE dropdown list to choose the database table, view, or file to which you want to bind the rule (see Figure 10.13).
4. Information Steward tries automatically to bind the similar columns form the source you've selected to the rule parameter. Check the suggestion and change the column name if necessary by choosing the right column name from the dropdown box.
5. A data quality score is between 0 and 10. You can determine what the thresholds are for green, yellow, and red indicators. For example, you could say everything below 5 is red. Here, you can define the low and high threshold

marks. The thresholds are used for showing traffic light color coding. Move the sliders to the values you want.

6. Save your new rule binding by clicking on the SAVE AND CLOSE button.
7. Review your new rule binding in the RULES tab.

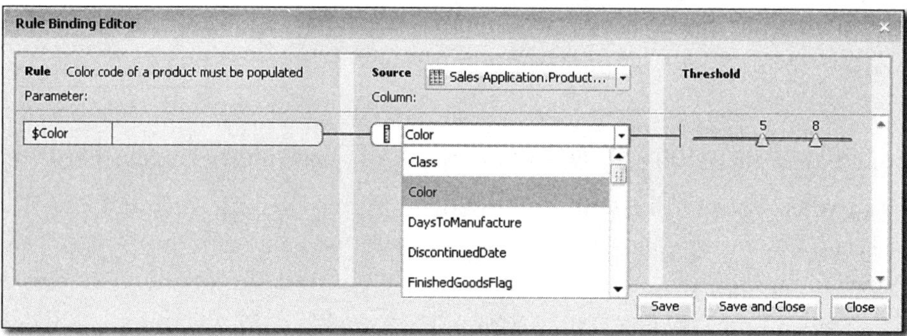

Figure 10.13 Binding a Validation Rule to a Data Source

Notice in Figure 10.13 that the rule is bound to a specific source—in this case, the sales application database and the product table. The column is selected for the variable $COLOR.

Rule Binding Based on Data Profiling Results

If a validation rule is defined directly from the data profiling result area and saved and closed, the rule is automatically bound to the new validation rule based on the context of the data profiling results. A status window is shown where you just need to confirm that it should be automatically bound. You can check the automatic binding by going to the RULES tab in your Data Insight project.

> **Example**
>
> At NeedsEIM Inc., the data stewards centrally define a validation rule that validates the format of an email address field: "An email address needs to have a specific pattern." This validation rule is centrally stored and approved by the responsible data steward. As multiple data domains such as customer, supplier, and employees are stored with email address fields in the master database system, the validation rule is bound to the corresponding EMAIL_ADDRESS field in each of the three data sources.

10.4.3 Executing Rule Tasks and Viewing Results

In the previous section, we described how the validation rules are created and how they're bound to the individual data sources. This represents the important task of transferring business knowledge and expertise, as well as business requirements into technical rules and linking them to different data assets. The next step is to apply those validation rules to existing data and calculate the quality scores that represent how many records of a data source are compliant with or violate a specific validation rule.

Rule tasks can be executed interactively by a user or automatically executed by using an integrated scheduler or an external scheduler. This supports the easy execution of the same set of validation rules on the same data sources over time to get historical trend information about data quality-level changes.

Next, we describe how to execute a rule task. Specifically, we explain how to execute a rule task, how to create and view a table-based data quality dashboard based on the rule, and how to create a rules data quality dashboard.

Executing a Rule Task

To calculate quality scores immediately or to create a rule task, execute the following steps:

1. Go to the Workspace Home tab in your Data Insight project.
2. Click on the Rule Result tab.
3. Check the file, table, or view for which you want to calculate the score.
4. Click on the Calculate Score button.
5. Complete the following parameters (shown in Figure 10.14):
   - Name
     Every rule task is assigned a unique default name, including the current creation date. This name should be changed to your own naming conventions.
   - Email notification
     An email address is used for notification if the score drops below the low threshold.
   - Save all Failed data to
     The failed record database allows you to store all failed records in an external database. This enables other external applications to directly access failed

record information in their own system and integrate this into data cleansing or data remediation processes.

- TASK OPTIONS
  TASK OPTIONS include the number of input records that should be used for the rule task execution, as well as for the optional input sampling rate. Additionally, you can set the size of the sample data.

6. When all parameters for the rule task have been defined, you can choose SAVE or SAVE AND RUN NOW.
7. Go to the TASK OVERVIEW tab in your WORKSPACE HOME tab and review the status and the execution of the rule task.

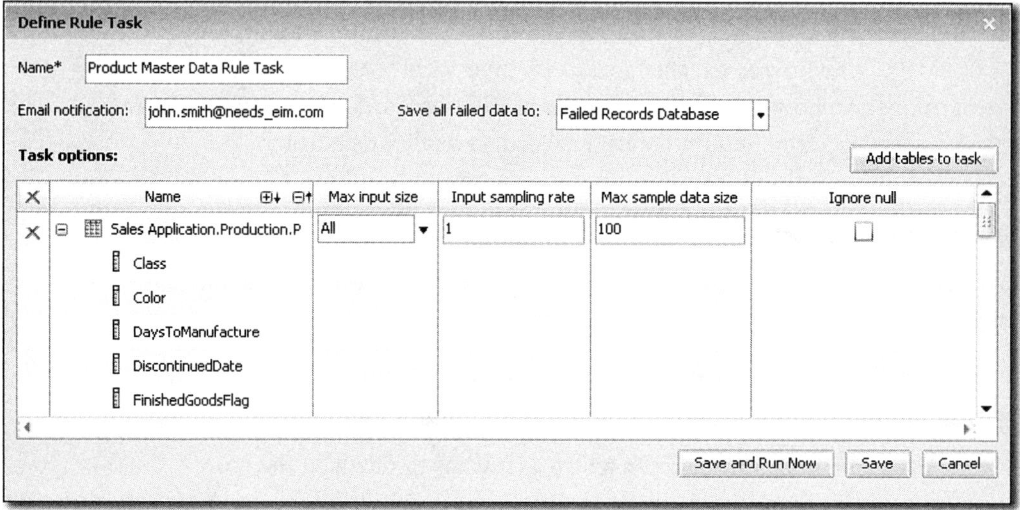

Figure 10.14 Defining a Validation Rule Task

For automatic ongoing measurement of the data quality scores, you can use the internal scheduler of the CMC. All defined task objects have a properties section that includes an option to schedule the execution of the task based on calendar schedules.

After successful execution of a rule task, the rule result panel is automatically updated with the most recent rule results and statistical information, as shown in Figure 10.15.

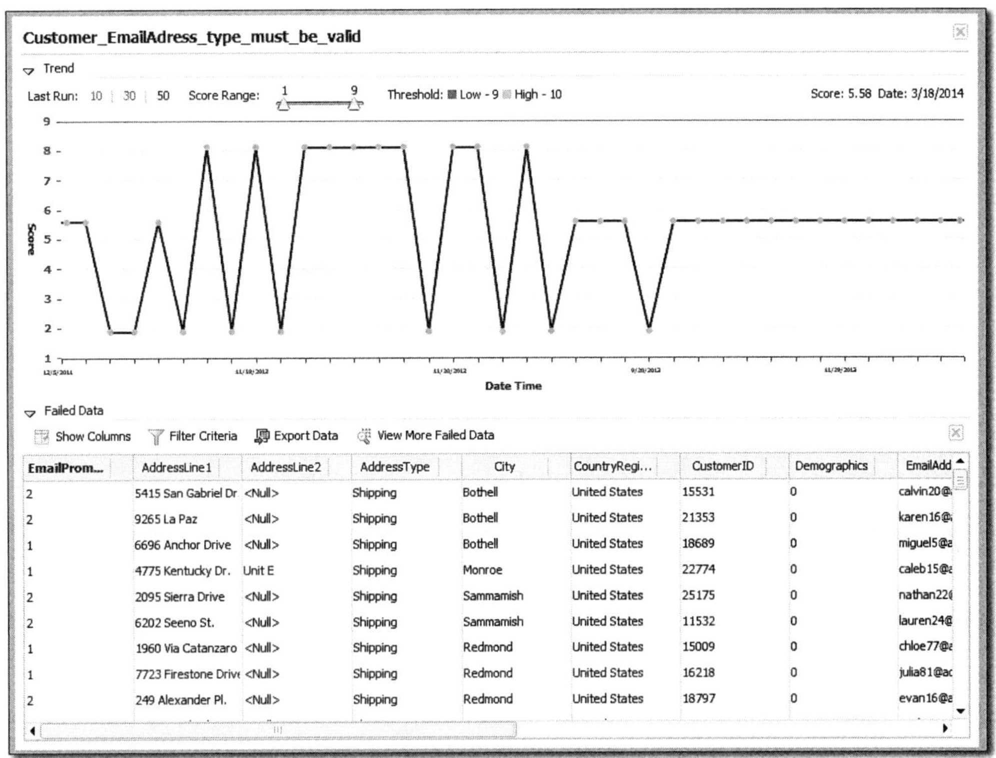

Figure 10.15 Validation Rule Score Trend Chart and Failed Record Sample Data

Figure 10.15 shows a *table-based data quality dashboard* that's based on the customer email address validation rule. Here, you can review the quality score, the change from the last run, and the number of failed and successfully passed records for all data sources (table, view, or file) in tabular form. You can also drill down into the statistics for the fields in the sources down to the individual rules bound to the fields. Both the data quality score trend and the failed record sample data can be accessed from this scorecard.

Creating and Viewing a Table-Based Data Quality Dashboard

A table-based data quality dashboard is important if you want to get specific insight into the data quality of a specific table. The following steps describe how this is done:

1. Go to the Working Set tab in your Data Insight project, and click on the Rule Result tab.

2. Expand the flat file location, sales application, or views group to view the individual data sources.
3. Expand the data sources to see the individual columns.
4. Expand the columns to see the bound validation rules.
5. Review the score and further details, such as the change from last run and the number of failed and total records.
6. Click on the hyperlinked score value to drill down to individual trend charts and failed record sample data.
7. Click on the SHOW COLUMNS or FILTER CRITERIA button or on the individual headlines for sorting options to format the failed record sample data.
8. Click on the EXPORT DATA button to save your failed record sample data into a spreadsheet for external processing.

This dashboard supports users who are responsible for technical objects, such as a specific database system or files, and who want to get an insight into the overall data quality level of these technical assets.

Creating a Rules Data Quality Dashboard

In addition to the table-based data quality dashboard, there is also a rules data quality dashboard. The rules data quality dashboard is shown in Figure 10.16. Notice the list of all the rules on the left and the data quality score for a selected rule on the right.

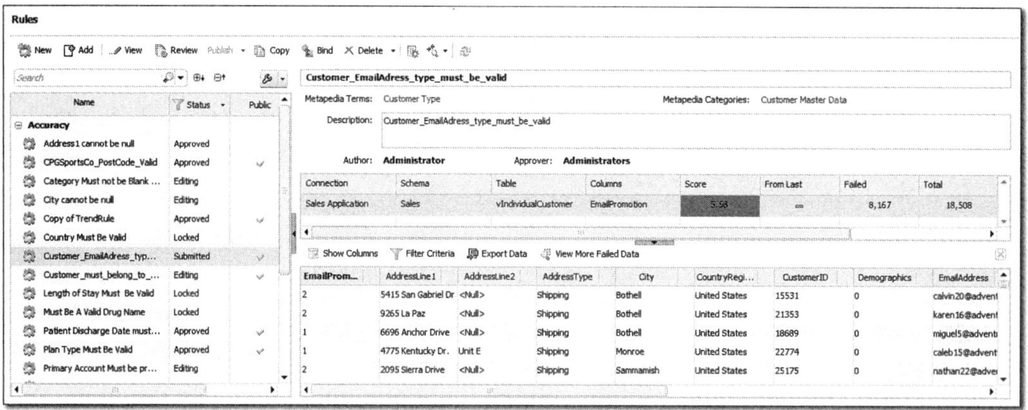

Figure 10.16 Overview of Validation Rules, Bound Data Sources, and Failed Record Sample Data

The rules data quality dashboard enables you to view all rules in a specific Data Insight project. The user can review each defined validation rule and the quality scores for each individual rule binding to the different data sources in tabular form. The user can also see the trend of the quality score from the last rule task execution, as well as information on the low and high threshold definition. For each quality score, the failed record sample data can also be analyzed. This perspective supports users who are responsible for individual validation rules independent of the different data objects they are assigned to and who want to gain insight into the data quality level of the different datastores based on their data quality requirements.

A rules data quality dashboard enables you to review the result of a rule execution in a dashboard. The following steps describe how to review the result of a rule execution:

1. Go to the RULE tab in your Data Insight project.
2. Select one of the validation rules from the rules list.
3. Review the individual binding of the validation rule to multiple data sources, the score, and failed and total record numbers.
4. Click on the SCORE value to drill down to the failed record sample data.
5. Click on the SHOW COLUMNS or FILTER CRITERIA button or on the individual headlines for sorting options to format the failed record sample data.
6. Click on the EXPORT DATA button to save your failed record sample data into a spreadsheet for external processing.

10.5 Monitoring with Data Quality Scorecards

The previous section introduced validation rules in Information Steward to measure the current status of data quality. The validation rules created in Information Steward can be executed either directly from Information Steward, or they can be exported to Data Services to be used in data quality jobs. In Data Services, the validation transform uses the validation rules. The validation transform is discussed in Chapter 9.

So far, we've discussed the ad hoc and scheduled execution of validation rules to get the most current information about the level of quality. This allows a user to review the data quality level from a technical perspective, answering questions such as the following:

- How good is the data content in the database system, application, or table that I'm responsible for?
- What is the overall quality level for the file that we've processed during an ETL batch job?

But beyond the data quality scores associated with individual technical objects such as database tables, applications, or batch jobs, the business users in a company need to visualize and drill down along other paths of information, answering questions such as these:

- Can I immediately see the overall quality level of our product master data, independent of where it's stored?
- What are the different data quality levels of my customer records by regions?
- What is the financial impact of having low-quality supplier data on my business?
- How did the data quality level change over time for my product data? Can I identify early drops of quality level before it's recognized by operational processes?

Information Steward answers these kinds of questions with *data quality scorecards.* A data quality scorecard allows a data steward—for example, the person responsible for the supplier data at NeedsEIM Inc.—to get one central starting point to immediately see the consolidated data quality score of the supplier data *independent* of all applications that contain supplier data. This includes the most current data quality score and associated cost, as well as historical trends. From this high-level overall score and cost data, the data steward can drill down into further details such as the data quality dimensions, the individual rules, and the technical objects to which the rules have been bound, as well as perform a what-if analysis of financial impact.

This section will go through the major steps in creating a data quality scorecard using NeedsEIM Inc. as an example to monitor supplier and customer data. In addition to data quality monitoring discussed in this chapter, there are also some reports for data quality available in Data Services. These reports are discussed in Appendix A (available for download from the book's page at *www.sap-press.com/3666*).

10.5.1 Components of a Data Quality Scorecard

Data quality scorecards are based on the consolidation of individual data quality scores calculated during the rule task execution. One data quality scorecard with multiple key data domains can be defined for each Data Insight project. A data quality scorecard consists of at least of one tile that is linked to a specific key data domain. Additional key data domains can be included, each with their own tile. Figure 10.17 shows one tile linked to the CUSTOMER data domain.

The number of tiles that are used on the data quality scorecard depends on the multiple key data domains or data entities that are used in the project. Customers also create different data quality score tiles for departmental or regional separation of the same data entities; for example, customers might define key data domains for customers in different regions such as North America, Europe, the Middle East and Africa (EMEA), and Asia Pacific Japan (APJ).

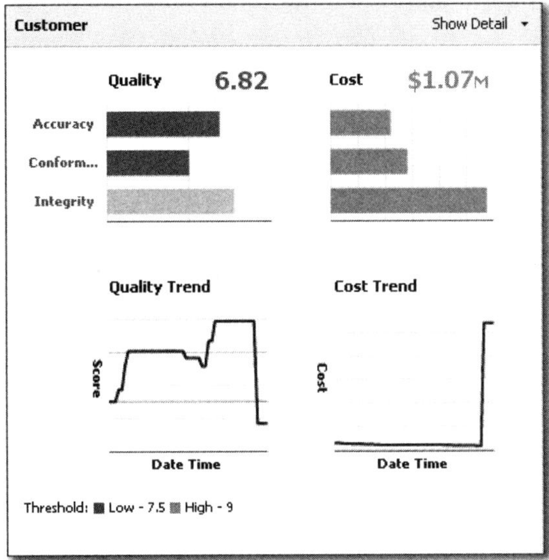

Figure 10.17 General Data Quality Scorecard Tile with Cost

Each data quality scorecard tile includes the name of the key data domain as a headline and the quality score that has been aggregated based on the calculation formula defined during the data quality scorecard setup. The data quality scorecard has three major aspects, as shown in Figure 10.17 and described here:

- **Scores**
  The overall data quality score and cost in terms of financial impact are displayed at the top of the scorecard. The scorecard includes traffic light color-code information based on the low-to-high thresholds defined for excellent, acceptable, and bad quality scores for the overall quality score. In the example in Figure 10.17, the overall scorecard (the quality score) is 6.82 and red. The scorecard also includes an overall cost figure, if cost information is available. The business value analysis will be covered in more detail in Section 10.5.5.

- **Dimensions**
  The next level of detail information is based on the different quality dimensions that have been configured for the key data domain. The quality-related dimensions are color-coded for quick information. Both quality and cost dimensions support tooltip information on the individual score and cost value when the user moves the mouse over the bars. In Figure 10.17, each data quality dimension's color is based on the quality score. ACCURACY is red (i.e., below acceptable quality), CONFORMITY is red, and INTEGRITY is yellow (i.e., close to falling below acceptable quality).

- **Trend**
  In the bottom area, the quality and cost trend diagram shows how the quality score and cost have changed over time.

Color Figures

Although the print version of this book is in black and white, the online and e-book versions have full-color figures. Please visit *www.sap-press.com/3666* for online book access.

From this high-level representation, you can see the most important information about the current quality status. You can drill down into a further detailed representation of the data quality score or business value analysis by clicking on the SHOW DETAIL dropdown in the upper-right corner of each data quality scorecard tile. After you drill into further detail of the data quality scores, you see a detailed view as shown in Figure 10.18.

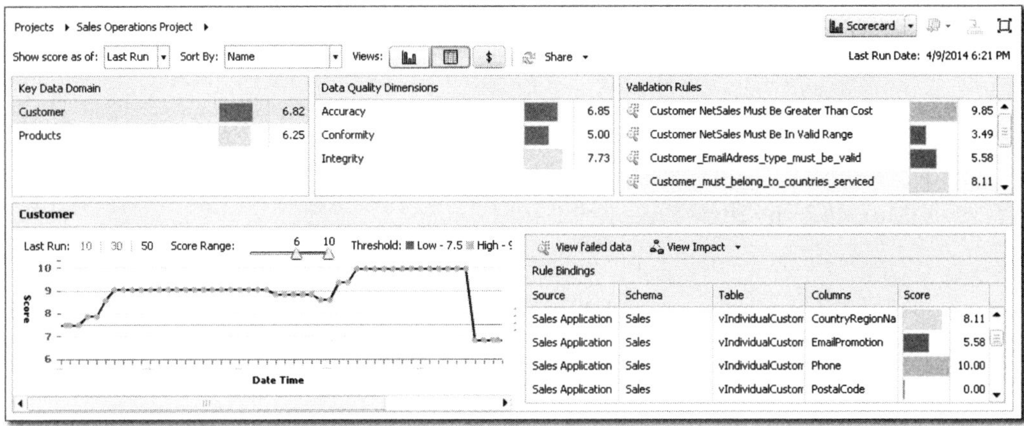

Figure 10.18 Data Quality Scorecard Detail View

The detail screen has a drill-down hierarchy starting on the highest level with the key data domains of the data quality scorecard. By clicking on the individual levels on one of the entries, you can filter the next level of information to get from the key data domain to the linked data quality dimensions, to the linked validation rules, down to the individual rule bindings for the filtered validation rule. For all areas, the quality score itself and the color-coded category is printed, which allows you to get a quick visual picture to easily identify the biggest data quality issues. The bottom-left area represents the quality trend over time for the highlighted hierarchy level.

On the most detailed level of the scorecard, you can either view the failed data or view the impact or the data lineage of the bound data fields that are based on the metadata management information that's collected for the data source.

We'll discuss the detailed view of the business value analysis in Section 10.5.5.

10.5.2 Defining and Setting Up a Data Quality Scorecard

The starting point for the definition and setup of a data quality scorecard is determining what key data domains should be used for individual scorecard components. You must define which individual data quality scores related to the defined validation rules and data assets in the Data Insight project should be consolidated and aggregated to the key data domain.

In this section, we'll start by explaining how to model the high-level data quality domains and map these domains to data quality dimensions. Then you'll learn how to add validation rules, and finally, how to bind the data sources to the data quality scorecard.

Modeling the High-Level Key Data Domains

The key data domain is the highest level of the whole data scorecard perspective. For each key data domain, a separate data quality scorecard element will be added to the overview. There are several options to define these key data domains and create side-by-side tiles that visualize the data quality level of these business-related data domains. Examples of domains used to create scorecards include the following:

- Classical data objects such as customer, supplier, employee, product, and financial data
- Regional data domains such as North America, South America, EMEA, and APJ
- Department, line of business (LoB), or brand data domains such as finance, sales, marketing, and human resources

This definition of the first level of separation of individual data quality scores depends on your business requirements and the data that will be assessed.

The following steps explain how to define the key data domains for a data quality scorecard:

1. On the Data Insight tab, choose the project for the new scorecard, and click on the Workspace hyperlink.
2. Click on the Scorecard Setup tab.
3. Click on the Add button in the key data domain to open the Key Data Domain Definition window.
4. Enter the key data domain Name and Description, and edit the lower and higher threshold for the traffic light color coding of the calculated score.
5. Click on the Save button to close the Key Data Domain Definition window.

Figure 10.19 shows an example of the customer key domain for a data quality scorecard.

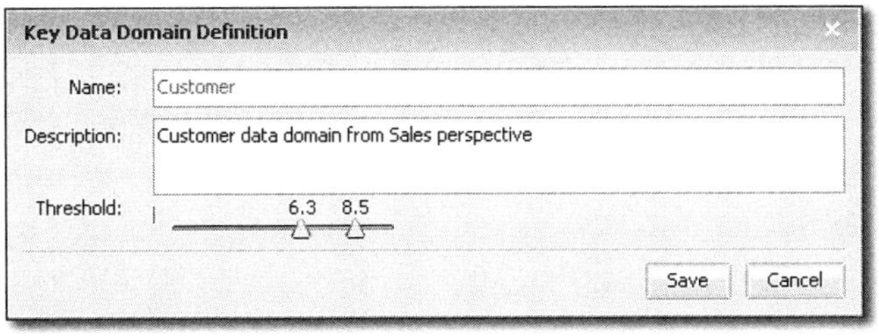

Figure 10.19 Defining a Key Data Domain for a Data Quality Scorecard

Notice the name, description, and threshold settings in Figure 10.19. Although it isn't pictured in the print version of this book, red is the color up to score 6.3, then yellow between 6.3 and 8.5, and green for any score above 8.5. (Again, you can access a full-color online book at *www.sap-press.com/3666*.)

Defining Data Quality Dimensions for the Key Data Domains

After setting up the key data domain for the scorecard, you defined the data quality dimensions to calculate the overall data quality score. Remember that the data quality dimensions have already been assigned to the individual validation rules (see Section 10.4.1). The data quality dimensions represent the next level grouping of calculated data quality scores. For a data steward who's responsible for a specific data domain, it's important to be able to drill down into multiple dimensions for further details to identify where the biggest problem areas for his overall data quality score are.

The predefined data quality dimensions are described here:

- ACCURACY
  Determines the extent to which data objects correctly represent the real-world values for which they were designed. For example, the sales orders for the Northeast region must be assigned a Northeast sales representative.
- COMPLETENESS
  Determines the extent to which data isn't missing. For example, an order isn't complete without a price and quantity.
- CONFORMITY
  Determines the extent to which data conforms to a specified format. For example, the order date must be in the format YYYY/MM/DD.

- CONSISTENCY
  Determines the extent to which distinct data instances provide nonconflicting information about the same underlying data object. For example, the salary range for level 4 employees must be between $40,000 and $65,000.
- INTEGRITY
  Determines the extent to which data isn't missing important relationship linkages. For example, the launch date for a new product must be valid and must be the first week of any quarter, because all new products are launched in the first week of each quarter.
- TIMELINESS
  Determines the extent to which data is sufficiently up to date for the task at hand. For example, hats, mittens, and scarves are in stock by November.
- UNIQUENESS
  Determines the extent to which the data for a set of columns isn't repeated. For example, the new product name must be unique (the same name can't be in the product master table).

Note

Information Steward provides a built-in custom attribute named QUALITY DIMENSION, which contains default values (those just listed) by which you can group validation rules. You can delete a default value (such as TIMELINESS) if it's not relevant to your data. Or you can add a value (such as RELEVANCY) to make the list more meaningful to your organization.

You can also define completely new custom attributes to provide more information or better categorize your rules (such as GEOGRAPHIC LOCATION, BUSINESS PROCESS, or IMPACT).

You can modify quality dimensions and create custom attributes from either MANAGE • CUSTOM ATTRIBUTES in the top menu bar of Information Steward or by clicking the MODIFY CUSTOMER ATTRIBUTE icon in the RULE EDITOR.

The following steps show you how to associate quality dimensions for a key data domain.

1. Highlight the key data domain in the SCORECARD SETUP tab where you want to add the quality dimensions.
2. Click on the ADD button in the QUALITY DIMENSIONS area to open the ASSOCIATE DIMENSIONS FOR: window.

3. Check the quality dimensions you want to add, as shown in Figure 10.20.

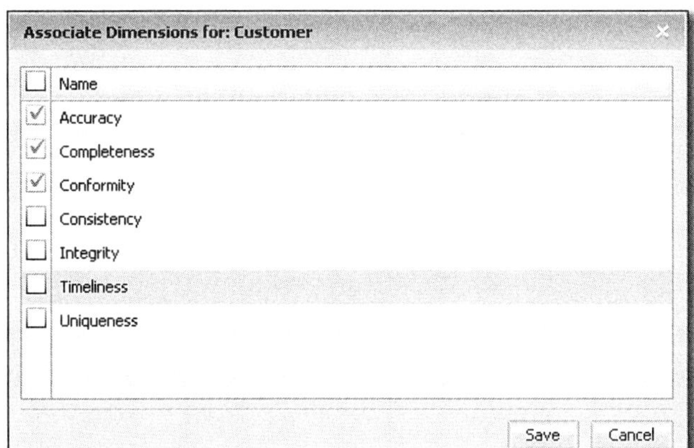

Figure 10.20 Associating Quality Dimensions to a Key Data Domain of a Data Quality Scorecard

4. Click on the SAVE button to close the ASSOCIATE DIMENSIONS FOR: window.
5. Review the weighting that you want to assign to the individual quality dimensions. By default, it's an equal weighting, but you can also set up fixed weighting by changing from AUTO to FIXED and editing the fixed value. (Note: Weighting is also discussed in the next section.)

Example

NeedsEIM Inc. has defined two key data domains for the data quality scorecard—one for the supplier data domain and one for the customer data domain. For each of the two key data domains, the data steward adds the following quality dimensions: ACCURACY, COMPLETENESS, and CONFORMITY.

Adding the Validation Rules and Quality Dimensions for a Key Data Domain

The next step of the data quality scorecard setup is to add all the generic validation rules that you want to use for calculating the data quality scorecard. During the definition of the generic validation rules, the data quality dimensions were assigned to the rule. This means that within the data quality scorecard setup, the set of available validation rules to be added to a specific key data domain and possible data quality dimensions are limited based on the assignment done during the validation rule creation.

The following steps explain how to associate rules for a quality dimension:

1. Select the quality dimension in the SCORECARD SETUP tab where you want to add the validation rule.
2. Click on the ADD button in the RULES area to open the ASSOCIATE RULES window.
3. The ASSOCIATE RULES window shows all the validation rules that have been defined for the quality dimensions you've selected. Check the rules you want to add from the list.
4. Click on the SAVE button to close the ASSOCIATE RULES window.
5. Review the weighting that you want to assign to the individual rules. By default, it's an equal weighting, but you can also set up fixed weighting by changing from AUTO to FIXED and editing the fixed value. Figure 10.21 shows an example.

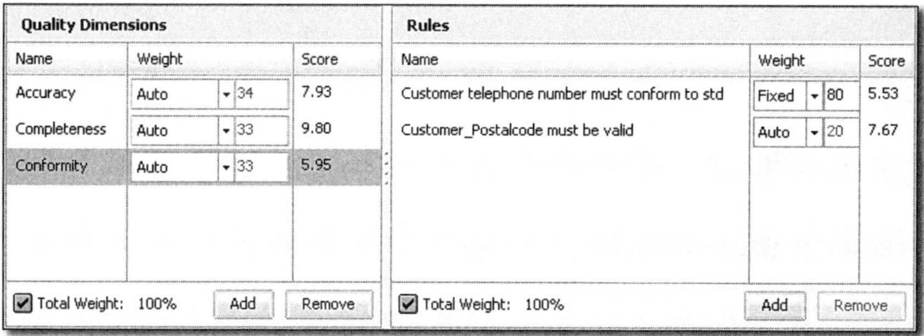

Figure 10.21 Reviewing the Weighting of Validation Rules for a Quality Dimension on a Data Quality Scorecard

In Figure 10.21, notice that the quality dimension CONFORMITY has two rules, one for the telephone number conformity and a second for the zip code. Also notice that the weight for the postal code is automatically set to 20, and the telephone number rule has a fixed rating of 80. You can also see the existing score of the rule. This score is from the last execution of the validation rules.

Example

NeedsEIM Inc. can use this capability to define a generic "An email address needs to have a specific pattern" validation rule, which is linked to the CONFORMITY data quality dimension. The data steward creating the data quality scorecard adds this validation rule to the CONFORMITY data quality dimension for the key data domains for supplier and customer.

Binding the Data Sources to the Data Quality Scorecard

After the validation rules are added to the data quality dimensions for each key data domain, the last step is to bind the data sources to the individual validation rules. Information Steward allows companies to define and approve the validation rules once and publish them as "public" to be able to manage them centrally, abstracted from specific data sources. These validation rules are then bound to individual data sources that can be stored in multiple locations throughout the enterprise. For the data quality scorecard setup, the same validation rule might be used for multiple key data domains, but only bindings to individual data sources and the data quality scores from these data sources should be used to calculate the overall score of a key data domain.

The following steps explain how to associate a validation rule with a specific data source:

1. Select the rule in the SCORECARD SETUP tab where you want to add the rule binding. In Figure 10.22, the rule about the telephone number has been selected.
2. Click on the ADD button in the RULE BINDINGS area to open the ASSOCIATE RULE BINDINGS window.
3. The ASSOCIATE RULE BINDINGS window shows all the source connections that have been defined for the rule you've selected. Check the rule bindings that you want to add from the list.

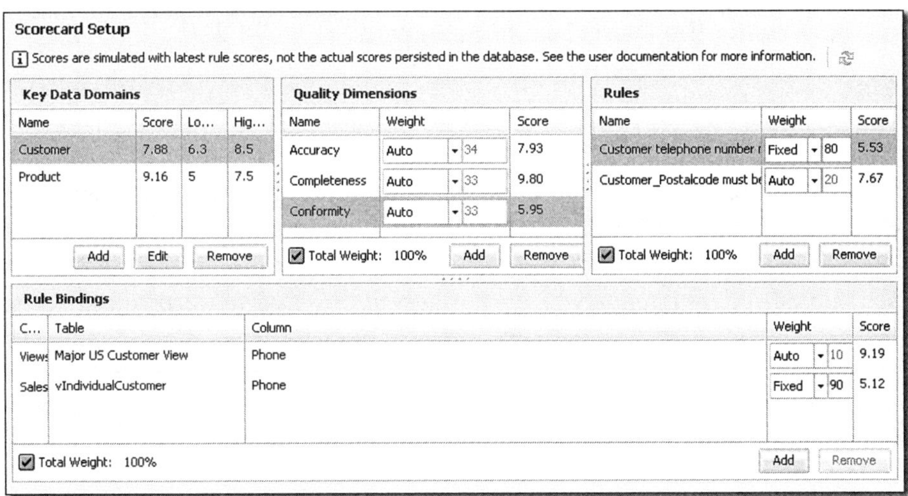

Figure 10.22 Data Quality Scorecard Setup

4. Click on the SAVE button to close the ASSOCIATE RULE BINDINGS window. Figure 10.22 shows the results where the telephone number rule has been associated with two views: the major U.S. customer view and the individual customer view.
5. Review the weighting that you want to assign to the individual rule bindings. By default, it's an equal weighting, but you can also set up fixed weighting by changing from AUTO to FIXED and editing the fixed value.

You've successfully completed the data quality scorecard setup if none of the elements on the scorecard setup panel has a warning symbol indicating that the next hierarchy level hasn't been set up.

Example

NeedsEIM Inc. has bound the public "An email address needs to have a specific pattern" validation rule to the email columns of the customer, supplier, and employee database tables. For the data quality scorecard, the company has chosen to represent only the supplier and the customer key data domain. The data steward at NeedsEIM Inc. added the "An email address needs to have a specific pattern" validation rule to the CONFORMITY data quality dimension for each of the two key data domains, customer and supplier, and bound them to the respective tables. This automatically ensures that the data quality scores calculated for the generic validation rule on the different database tables will be correctly assigned to the right data quality scorecard tile.

10.5.3 Viewing the Data Quality Scorecard

The data quality scorecard is the central entry point to gain quick insight into the current and historical data quality level of specific data domains. From the data quality scorecard, you can drill down to detailed-level information, even down to the failed record sample data. The data quality scorecard includes an additional perspective on the data quality scores calculated during the rule task execution. Compared to the more technical perspectives of assessment through validation rules, scorecards are intended for the business user or data steward who wants to view data for a given data domain, independent of the technical objects and tables where the corresponding data is stored within the applications and databases.

After the scorecard is set up, you just select the SCORECARD link in the Data Insight project. An example is shown in Figure 10.23 for the CONFORMITY data quality dimension for the postal code rule.

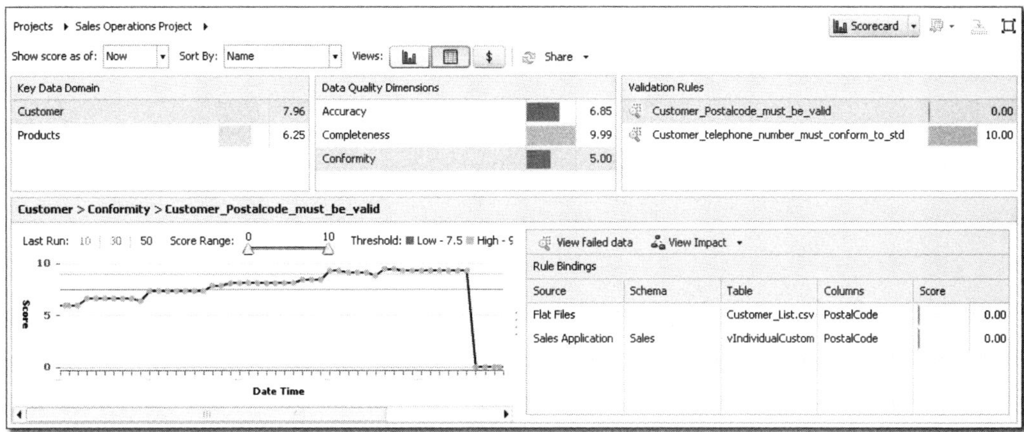

Figure 10.23 Drilling Down to the Individual Rule Binding Level in the Data Quality Scorecard Detail View

For each of the key data domains, you can now review the overall quality score value between 0 and 10 with a quick indicator of traffic light colors that are based on the defined thresholds. This gives you a very good first insight into the current level of data quality of the data related to the key data domain. As the quality score is calculated from the different quality dimensions, you can see the status of those quality dimensions in a bar chart as well. While the diagram shows only the color codes for quick insight, you can move the mouse over the individual bars to get detailed information from the tool tips. The quality trend for the quality score of the key data domain is also presented on this data quality scorecard tile, giving you information about how the quality score has changed over time and the last data quality assessments. This also gives you an early indicator if the quality score has increased (e.g., after a data cleansing activity) or decreased (e.g., after a new data load) over time.

This section explains how to drill into the scorecard details and analyze the failed record sample.

Drilling Down into Data Quality Scorecard Details

Follow these steps to drill down into the data quality scorecard details:

1. Click on the Show Detail dropdown in the key data domain scorecard tile, and select Data Quality Score.

2. Review the quality score of each of the key data domains.
3. Select the key data domain into which you want to drill down further, and view how the rest of the information on the scorecard is filtered based on your selection. You'll see only the data quality dimensions, validation rules, and rule bindings that are assigned to your selected key data domain. Also, the score trend chart now represents the trend over time for your selected key data domain.
4. Select the data quality dimension in which you want to drill down further, and view how the rest of the information on the scorecard is filtered based on your selection. You'll only see the validation rules and rule bindings that are assigned to your selected data quality dimension. Also, the score trend chart now represents the trend over time for your selected data quality dimension.
5. Select the validation rule into which you want to drill down further, and view how the rest of the information on the scorecard is filtered based on your selection. You'll see only the rule bindings that are assigned to your selected validation rule. Also, the score trend chart now represents the trend over time for your selected validation rule.
6. Select the rule binding into which you want to drill down further, and view how the trend chart changes. Hover the mouse over the score value for the rule binding and get further information on the number of failed and total records for score calculation.

From the scorecard in Figure 10.23, you can see that the quality trend of the postal code rule has steadily increased over the time measured, but a recent event has caused the quality to plummet.

Analyze Failed Record Data

At this point, you need to analyze the failed records. The steps for this process are as follows:

1. Click on the View failed Data button to view the failed record sample data in a separate window (shown in Figure 10.24).
2. Click on the column headlines to sort the records, or click on the Show Columns or Filter Criteria buttons to change the layout of the table.
3. Click on the Export Data button to save the table to a spreadsheet for further review or processing.

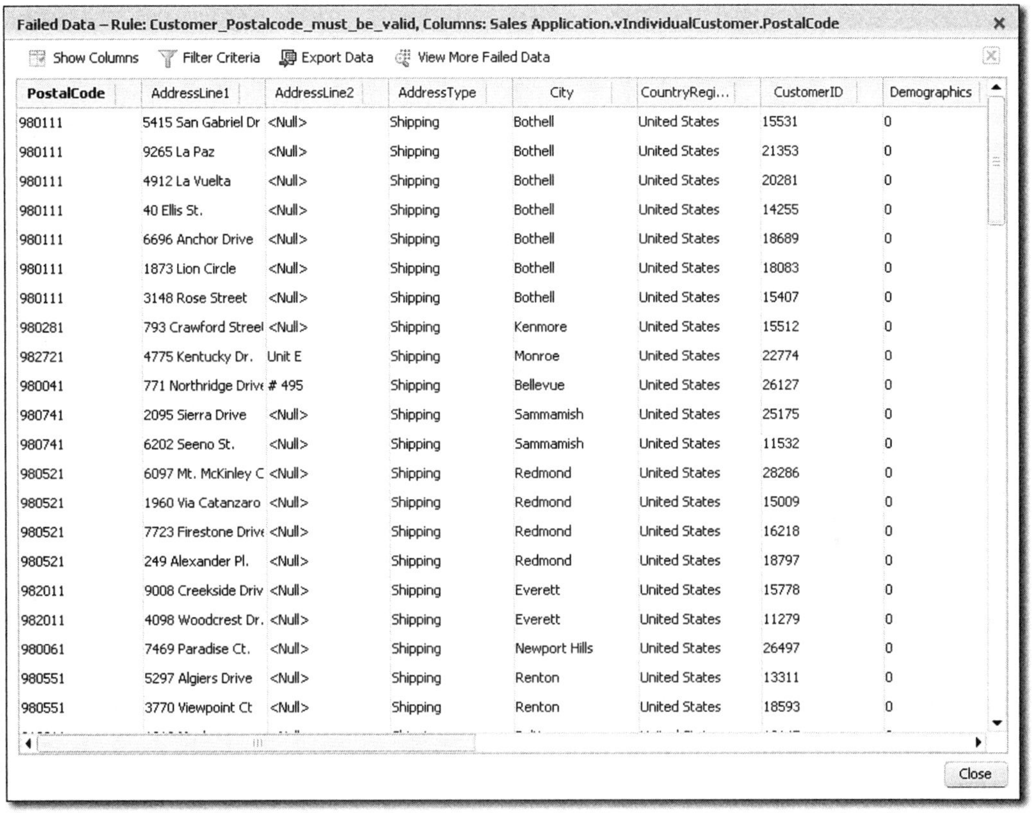

Failed Data – Rule: Customer_Postalcode_must_be_valid, Columns: Sales Application.vIndividualCustomer.PostalCode

Show Columns Filter Criteria Export Data View More Failed Data

PostalCode	AddressLine1	AddressLine2	AddressType	City	CountryRegi...	CustomerID	Demographics
980111	5415 San Gabriel Dr	<Null>	Shipping	Bothell	United States	15531	0
980111	9265 La Paz	<Null>	Shipping	Bothell	United States	21353	0
980111	4912 La Vuelta	<Null>	Shipping	Bothell	United States	20281	0
980111	40 Ellis St.	<Null>	Shipping	Bothell	United States	14255	0
980111	6696 Anchor Drive	<Null>	Shipping	Bothell	United States	18689	0
980111	1873 Lion Circle	<Null>	Shipping	Bothell	United States	18083	0
980111	3148 Rose Street	<Null>	Shipping	Bothell	United States	15407	0
980281	793 Crawford Street	<Null>	Shipping	Kenmore	United States	15512	0
982721	4775 Kentucky Dr.	Unit E	Shipping	Monroe	United States	22774	0
980041	771 Northridge Drive	# 495	Shipping	Bellevue	United States	26127	0
980741	2095 Sierra Drive	<Null>	Shipping	Sammamish	United States	25175	0
980741	6202 Seeno St.	<Null>	Shipping	Sammamish	United States	11532	0
980521	6097 Mt. McKinley C	<Null>	Shipping	Redmond	United States	28286	0
980521	1960 Via Catanzaro	<Null>	Shipping	Redmond	United States	15009	0
980521	7723 Firestone Drive	<Null>	Shipping	Redmond	United States	16218	0
980521	249 Alexander Pl.	<Null>	Shipping	Redmond	United States	18797	0
982011	9008 Creekside Driv	<Null>	Shipping	Everett	United States	15778	0
982011	4098 Woodcrest Dr.	<Null>	Shipping	Everett	United States	11279	0
980061	7469 Paradise Ct.	<Null>	Shipping	Newport Hills	United States	26497	0
980551	5297 Algiers Drive	<Null>	Shipping	Renton	United States	13311	0
980551	3770 Viewpoint Ct	<Null>	Shipping	Renton	United States	18593	0

Close

Figure 10.24 View the Failed Record Sample Data from the Data Quality Scorecard Detail View

After you've viewed the failed data, you can use this information to fix the data issues, as well as identify the root cause and impact of the poor data quality in your enterprise.

Failed Data Repository

By default, Information Steward will output only a sampling of failed data to the Information Steward repository. To capture all failed data for later viewing, further analysis, or custom reporting, you must set up a failed data repository (see the Information Steward Administrator Guide section on "Data Insight Connections" and the User Guide section on "Accessing Additional Failed Data Information" for more details).

Note that each rule task can use a different failed data connection.

10.5.4 Identifying Data Quality Impact and Root Cause

As mentioned previously, you can drill down from the data quality scorecard to the individual validation rule scores and inspect the failed record sample data. This provides insight into the content of the data source that's assessed by the data quality project and allows you to identify how good or bad the data in the data sources really is.

But successfully managing data quality doesn't just mean identifying that the data in a specific datastore isn't meeting the given requirements. It's also important to identify what impact this bad data has on any other application or system in the enterprise. With the direct linkage of data quality monitoring and metadata management capabilities, it's possible to follow how data elements are moved between or within different applications.

This means, for example, that you can drill down in a data quality scorecard to the current quality scores on the staging area of an SAP BW system to analyze the impact of the bad data in the warehouse down to the report level. This section explains the process of reviewing the data quality issue impact on downstream processes or reports, as well as analyzing the data quality root causes.

Follow these steps to determine the data quality issue impact on downstream processes or reports:

1. In the data quality scorecard Detail View, select the Rule Binding, including the data source and column to see the impact information.
2. Click on View Impact. This opens a separate screen, including the impact analysis diagram representing the relationships among the technical objects such as the tables, mappings, queries, and reports.

Figure 10.25 shows an example of an impact analysis for a healthcare-related validation rule. Here, the impact analysis shows what data fields have been selected based on the rule binding and the quality score that has been measured for the field. Notice that the link is mapped to Data Services from the application source for the ETL relationships, which is then mapped to an SAP BusinessObjects Enterprise instance. This was done based on the metadata information that has been integrated into Information Steward. This impact analysis can help answer the following questions:

- What ETL tool or process is moving data from this data field to other databases or applications? How is the data being transformed?
- What reports are affected by the data quality of the source data field?

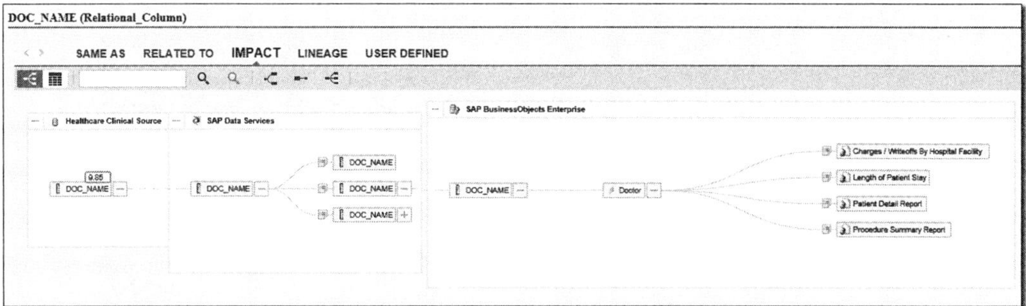

Figure 10.25 Data Quality Issue Impact Analysis

Based on this impact analysis diagram, you can precisely track down which other applications further downstream in the data flow or process chain are using the identified bad data. This allows you to identify the priority of necessary data cleansing or improvement activities on the bad data. For example, the data quality issue impact analysis shows that some of the most important business processes or reports are using data from data source fields that have a very low data quality score.

Another important use case for the direct linkage between the data quality scorecard and metadata management is the data quality root-cause analysis. While a data steward is drilling down into the detail view of the data quality scorecard for a master data table, he can choose to view the lineage analysis functionality from metadata management directly from the data quality scorecard as well. In this case, the lineage analysis diagram shows the highlighted data field from the rule binding area on the right-hand side of the diagram and also shows how this field was populated by an ETL solution from any data source system (including the mapping and data movement information). This allows you to track back and determine from what source field the bad data was populated. Based on this data quality root-cause analysis, further data quality assessment activities or data cleansing activities at the entry point of the bad data can be set up to improve the overall data quality level.

Example

This type of root-cause analysis is important to NeedsEIM Inc. The company starts by drilling down the data quality scorecard of the supplier data to the binding of the "An email address needs to have a specific pattern" validation rule to the supplier master table. Because the quality score is quite low, the view lineage functionality is used to identify how the data field EMAIL_ADDRESS has been populated by Data Services, and from what operational source systems the data has been extracted. This allows the company to get insight into where the bad data can come from. The data lineage graph indicates that two Data Services jobs have moved email address information from the operational SAP ERP Central Component (ECC) system, as well as from the additional Microsoft SQL Server database system. As a next step, the company can initiate a data quality assessment on these source systems to verify if only one or both systems include bad email address information. NeedsEIM Inc. just needs to add these systems to the Data Insight project and apply the already defined validation rules to the operational systems.

10.5.5 Performing Business Value Analysis

Poor data quality can affect businesses in many ways. The impact can be financial, customer perception, operation efficiency, brand recognition, regulatory compliance, and so on. Table 10.1 includes some examples of issues that can arise due to bad data and the possible impact on your business. Many more such issues can arise from specific industries and business processes as well.

Data Quality Issue	Impact
Determine the right recipients for marketing campaigns is difficult.	Operational efficiency
Inaccurate order information causes delayed or lost shipments and lower customer satisfaction.	▸ Financial ▸ Customer Satisfaction
Sales representatives aren't able to identify relevant accounts.	Operational efficiency
Costs are high due to account duplication, while response rates are low.	▸ Financial ▸ Operational efficiency ▸ Customer Acquisition
Potential customers are annoyed by redundant mail, emails, and phone calls.	Customer Satisfaction

Table 10.1 Business Impact of Poor Data Quality

Data Quality Issue	Impact
Total revenue and profitability of products and services is reduced.	Financial
Reporting uses the wrong data, which leads to wrong conclusions and decisions.	▸ Financial ▸ Operational Efficiency ▸ Customer Satisfaction
Inaccurate statutory reporting occurs.	Legal
Carrier stops charges for incorrect or incomplete addresses.	▸ Financial ▸ Customer Satisfaction
Misalignment between vendors and defined terms occurs due to system inaccuracies.	Financial
Poor spend visibility is due to unstandardized, duplicate data.	Operational Efficiency
Inability to find the right product/material is caused by unstandardized, duplicate data.	▸ Financial ▸ Operational Efficiency
Items are purchased off contract at premium prices due to poor quality supplier data.	▸ Financial ▸ Operational Efficiency

Table 10.1 Business Impact of Poor Data Quality (Cont.)

To change an organization's culture around managing data quality, it's important to understand, quantify, and demonstrate how bad data impacts the top and bottom line of the business. By assigning a dollar amount to poor data quality, the business awareness of what poor data quality is costing the organization isn't only increased, it's validated. It puts value on clean, accurate data and can be used to justify additional funding for your information governance initiatives. An organization may know in theory that there is a cost associated with bad data, but to be able to put actual numbers behind it can really give the data quality cause the credibility it needs.

Information Steward's Business Value Analysis enables business-orientated data stewards (or data stewards in collaboration with LoB representatives) to connect financial return on investment (ROI) to the organization's data quality and information governance initiatives. Figure 10.26 shows an example of the dashboard available to an organization to demonstrate the financial impact of poor data quality.

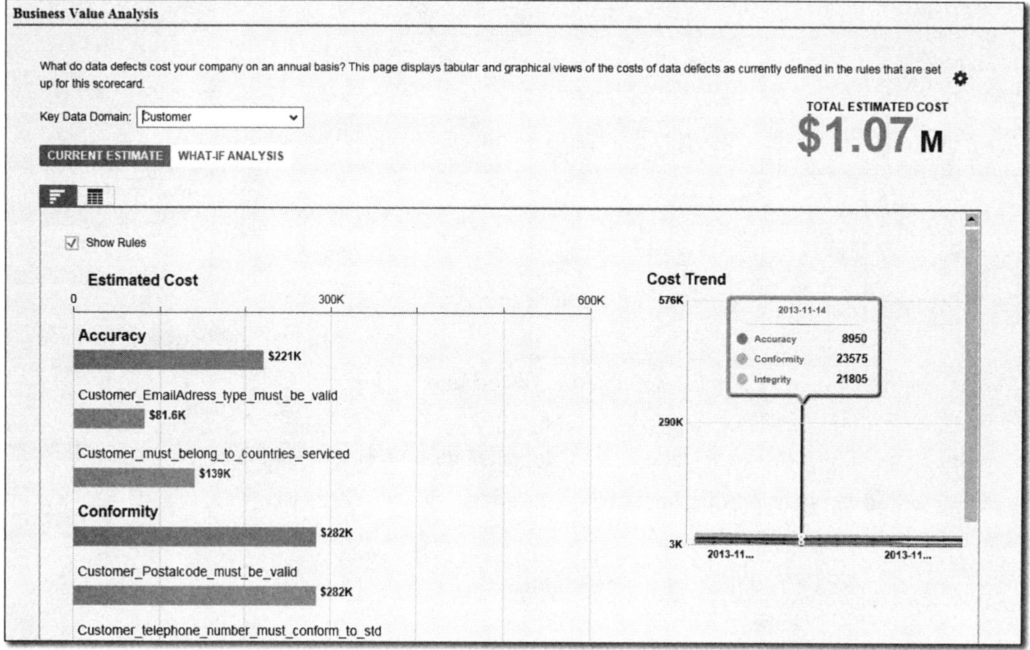

Figure 10.26 Business Value Analysis

Information Steward's Business Value Analysis features also allow the organization to see the overall trend for the cost of poor data at various levels for root-cause analysis. The business can perform what-if analysis to identify potential savings if it cleans the bad data and accordingly focuses its data quality efforts in the areas that will benefit the company most.

Defining and Setting Up Financial Impact

The process of validation rule development includes defining itemized cost per failure. This cost indicates the cost the business will incur due to the data quality issue being validated by this rule. This isn't something that's necessarily easy to arrive at in all cases, and you may need to spend some time researching the actual impact and figuring out a method to calculate. This time is likely spent working closely with the appropriate LoB representatives to arrive at some agreed upon numbers. In most cases, an exact cost to the final cent may not be achievable because it's subjective and depends on individual judgment. The idea is to be in the vicinity of the expected cost. You can always do a what-if analysis later (see the subsequent section "Performing What-If Analysis") and get a different impact by tweaking this cost parameter.

There are two types of costs that can be considered when you calculate the cost per failure. Some costs are incurred in terms of a human resource spending time on addressing the issue or performing root-cause analysis. These are called resource-dependent costs. Then, there are costs that are resource-independent in nature. Table 10.2 lists some examples of the different cost types. This is by no means an exhaustive list. The idea is to provoke thinking about such costs when trying to understand impact.

Resource-Independent Costs	Resource-Dependent Costs
▸ Cash flow: Additional costs incurred to the organization's cash flow, such as delays in recognizing revenue or making supplier payments ▸ Fees: Costs associated with any additional expenses or direct fees, such as those resulting from regulatory compliance failures ▸ Fixed overhead: The fixed overhead cost distributed per failure, such as storage costs due to returned shipments ▸ Revenue: Loss of direct revenue, such as lost customers or new sales ▸ Sales: Additional costs associated with selling goods, such as sales organizations following erroneous leads ▸ Other: User-supplied costs	▸ Labor: Costs associated with the loss of productivity, for example, a resource or person will have to spend a specified amount of time to capture and remediate quality issues ▸ Other: Costs that aren't covered by the existing types

Table 10.2 Resource-Independent and Resource-Dependent Costs per Failure

The following steps describe how to add financial impact per failure to a validation rule from the rule editor.

1. Go to the RULES tab in the DATA INSIGHT project tab.
2. Click on the NEW button or the EDIT button to open the rule editor.
3. Click on the EDIT button within the rule editor to set the FINANCIAL IMPACT PER FAILURE within the BUSINESS VALUE WORKSHEET.

4. If applicable, add one or more resource-independent costs. Choose the appropriate cost type from the dropdown (valid values include Cash Flow, Fees, Fixed Overhead, Revenue, Sales, and Other), a description, and estimated cost incurred per failure. See Figure 10.27 for an example.
5. If applicable, add one or more resource-dependent costs. Choose the appropriate cost type from the dropdown (valid values include LABOR and OTHER), a description, number of people involved, the labor rate, and the number of hours per person needed to address the data defects. See Figure 10.27 for an example.
6. Review the subtotals and totals for accuracy.
7. Click OK.

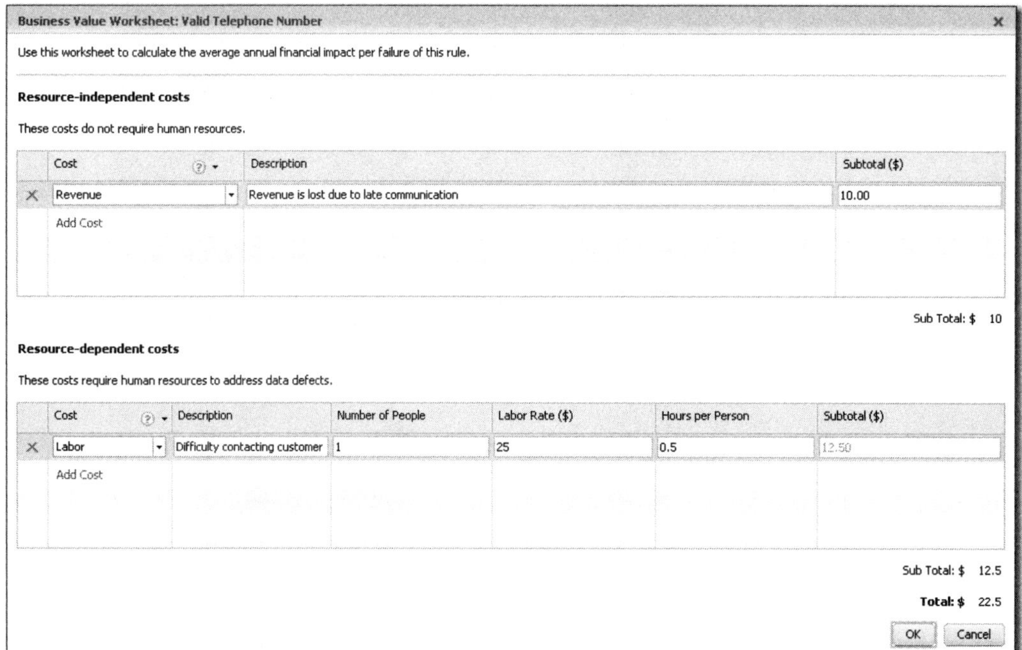

Figure 10.27 Business Value Worksheet

> **Note**
>
> You can change the currency that's shown on the various Business Value Analysis related screens to the currency of your choice as a part of the Information Steward PREFERENCES, available via the main MANAGE menu.

Viewing the Business Value Analysis

As a part of your Data Quality Scorecard, the financial impact that has been assigned to the associated rules and the data that failed against those rules are immediately taken into account. The formulas that you'll use to calculate cost are fairly straightforward. For each rule, it's a multiplication of actual failure and failure row count. Then, it's aggregated at the quality dimension level and then at the key data domain level.

The results of the Business Value Analysis are available only in the Scorecard view. After you've set up the cost per failure for various rules and run the tasks to calculate the data quality score and cost, open the data quality scorecard to see the financial impact as a part of the scorecard. You can either select the BUSINESS VALUE ANALYSIS ($) view button or the SHOW DETAIL dropdown menu's BUSINESS VALUE ANALYSIS option to get to the detailed information.

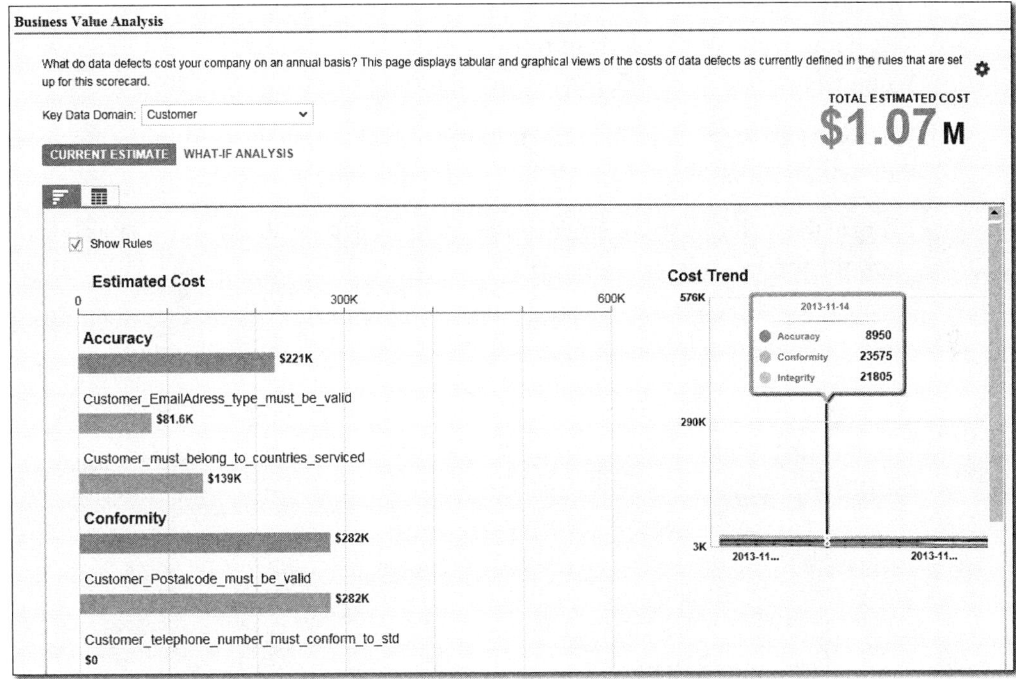

Figure 10.28 Business Value Analysis Dashboard

Figure 10.28 shows the default graphical view when you open the Business Value Analysis. On the left side, it shows the current estimated cost based on actual failure of validation rules and cost per failure input by the data steward. You can select the desired key data domain and then choose either CURRENT ESTIMATE or WHAT-IF ANALYSIS. The top-right area shows the overall cost for the key data domain selected. It's rounded to the closest thousand, million, billion, and so on. You can toggle between graphical and tabular views of the analysis. Blue bars are for quality dimension summaries, which is an aggregate of all rules underneath. On the right side, it shows the cost trend for each of the dimensions.

These results can also be exported to Excel. Note that if you perform what-if analysis, that information is also saved in the Excel spreadsheet.

Performing What-If Analysis

Sometimes, users who are looking at the Business Value Analysis aren't the same users who set the initial cost parameters. Or, maybe the same user may have a new and different perspective. What-if analysis allows you to quickly change the cost parameters and understand potential savings (or losses) due to change in actual failure rate or cost per failure for different rules.

The following steps describe how to perform what-if analysis from the Business Value Analysis dashboard:

1. From the Business Value Analysis dashboard, click the WHAT-IF ANALYSIS button on the top-left side of the screen.
2. Hover over a rule, and a CHANGE button will appear. Click on CHANGE to bring up a pop-up window with failure and cost details (see Figure 10.29).

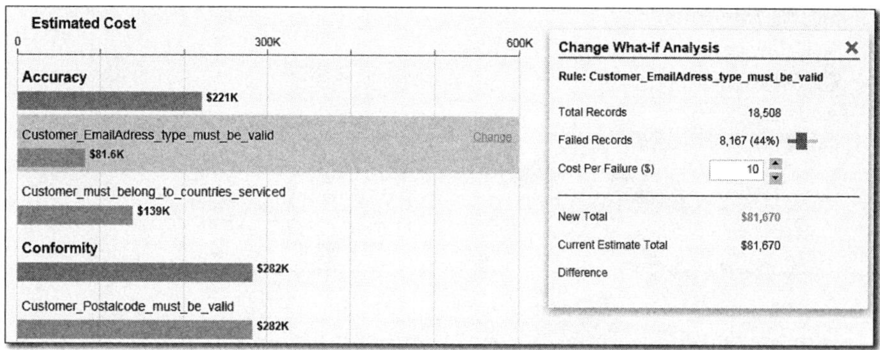

Figure 10.29 What-If Analysis

3. Use the various controls on the CHANGE WHAT-IF ANALYSIS pop-up to adjust costs.
   - Use the slider to change the FAILED RECORDS (%).
   - Use the spinner to change the COST PER FAILURE ($).
4. Click on the EDIT button within the rule editor to set the financial impact per failure within the Business Value Worksheet.

As soon as you change any of these values, new totals and difference due to the change are made available for the rule. The bar chart and the total on the top-right of the screen are immediately changed as well. You can hover over it to see exact values. The bar chart itself has some visual indicators to show increase or decrease in the cost. If the cost increases, the bar chart has a white marker to indicate the original. If the cost decreases, the change is indicated with a lighter shade.

10.6 Quick Starting Data Quality

The Data Quality Advisor encompasses several Information Steward capabilities that guide data stewards to rapidly develop a solution to measure and improve the quality of their information assets. Data stewards can use the Data Quality Advisor features to assess their data and get a recommendation on validation and cleansing rules with additional capabilities to review and tune the cleansing rules to better meet their business needs. Data Quality Advisor includes the following features:

- Data Insight's content type profiling feature provides suggested meaning that's based on the data in the column. Identifying content types enables the software to suggest context-appropriate validation and cleansing rules after running a content-type profiling task.
- Data Insight's Data Cleansing Advisor feature recommends a data cleansing solution based on the content type profiling results and SAP best practices for a particular data domain. You can accept the recommendation or tune it to better meet your needs, and then publish the solution for use in the Data Services Workbench.
- Data Insight's Data Validation Advisor feature suggests the application of new or existing rules to the data based on statistical analysis and content type profiling results.

The following is a high-level overview of the Data Quality Advisor process.

10.6.1 Assess the Data Using Column, Advanced, and Content Type Profiling

The Data Quality Advisor starts with the data, leveraging the results of data profiling and content type discovery to get an understanding of the data to make a recommendation in terms of data validation, cleansing, and matching rules. Column profiling and advanced profiling provide a statistical analysis of the data, which gives insight into data abnormalities that could be prevented or data standards that could be enforced. Content type profiling provides suggested meaning based on the data and the metadata attributes in the column, establishing context for the recommendations that are being made.

10.6.2 Receive Validation and Cleansing Rule Recommendations

To better define best practices regarding the implementation of validation, cleansing, and matching rules, use the Data Validation Advisor and Data Cleansing Advisor. After profiling, users can view the generated validation rule recommendations by launching Data Validation Advisor (see Figure 10.30).

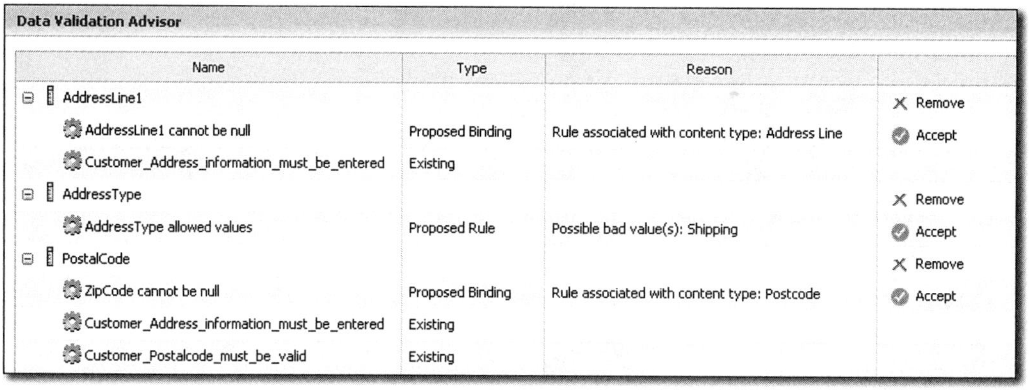

Data Validation Advisor

Name	Type	Reason	
AddressLine1			Remove
AddressLine1 cannot be null	Proposed Binding	Rule associated with content type: Address Line	Accept
Customer_Address_information_must_be_entered	Existing		
AddressType			Remove
AddressType allowed values	Proposed Rule	Possible bad value(s): Shipping	Accept
PostalCode			Remove
ZipCode cannot be null	Proposed Binding	Rule associated with content type: Postcode	Accept
Customer_Address_information_must_be_entered	Existing		
Customer_Postalcode_must_be_valid	Existing		

Figure 10.30 Data Validation Advisor Rule Recommendations

These rules are automatically suggested, based on the content type profiling results and statistical analysis of the data. Then, data stewards determine if they want to use the validation rule on the profiled data. Likewise, if an existing rule is available for a defined content type, Information Steward suggests using the rule on other profiled data that has the same content type.

The Data Cleansing Advisor is a feature within Data Insight that simplifies the data cleansing process by intelligently recommending a data cleansing solution for your data. The recommended data cleansing solution is based on your data's content type identification results and SAP best practices for a specific data domain. A data cleansing solution is a collection of cleansing and matching rules for *party data* (e.g., customer, supplier and vendor data) that you can publish for use in the Data Services Workbench.

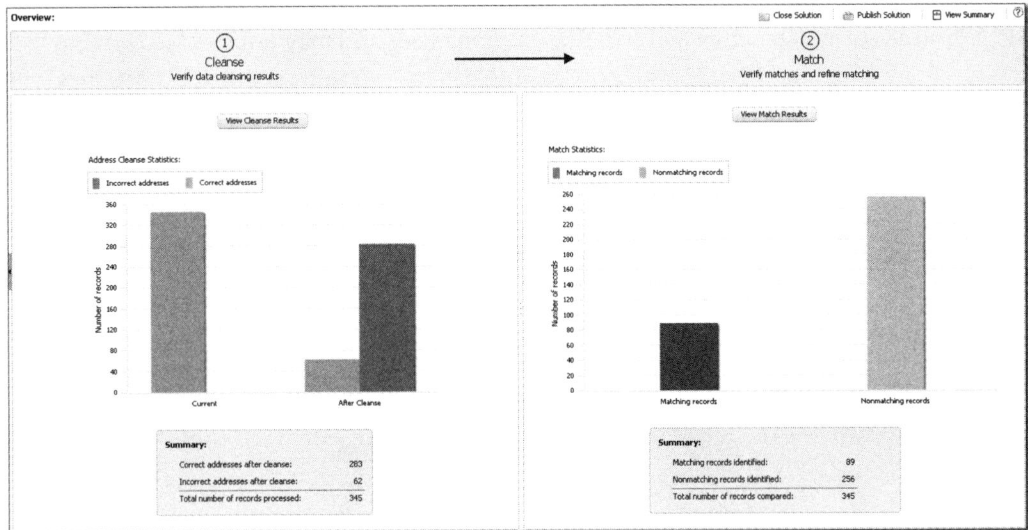

Figure 10.31 Data Cleansing Advisor Recommendation Overview

For example, in Figure 10.31, the Data Cleansing Advisor was able to determine that the input source contains 100% incorrect addresses (82% or 283 of which are correctable) and over 25% (89) duplicate records. You don't need to have technical knowledge on how to configure the Data Services address cleanse or match transforms; Data Cleansing Advisor will create the cleansing and match rules for you. At the point the rules are recommended, you can simply publish those rules to Data Services (by clicking the PUBLISH SOLUTION button in the upper-right corner of the Data Cleansing Advisor's OVERVIEW screen) to leverage the cleansing solution as a part of a Data Services data flow or take the next step of further reviewing and tuning the rules.

10.6.3 Tune the Cleansing and Matching Rules Using Data Cleansing Advisor

In Data Cleansing Advisor, you can see the data cleansing solution's effect on your data by viewing cleanse and match results, including statistics, graphs, and a data preview. If the analysis reveals unsatisfactory results, you can change option settings and see a new preview of the results on your data.

The Data Cleansing Advisor gives you options to review and fine-tune the results. The first is a chart that allows you to drill down into the results by creating filters to view the data that is most important to you. Figure 10.32 shows the match results divided by the match confidence (HIGH, MEDIUM, or LOW). HIGH confidence matches are close to being exact matches and may not need to be reviewed. MEDIUM and LOW confidence matches are considered to be suspect matches, and you may want to review these record groups to see if there is additional tuning of the match rules that can take place to eliminate the suspect matches.

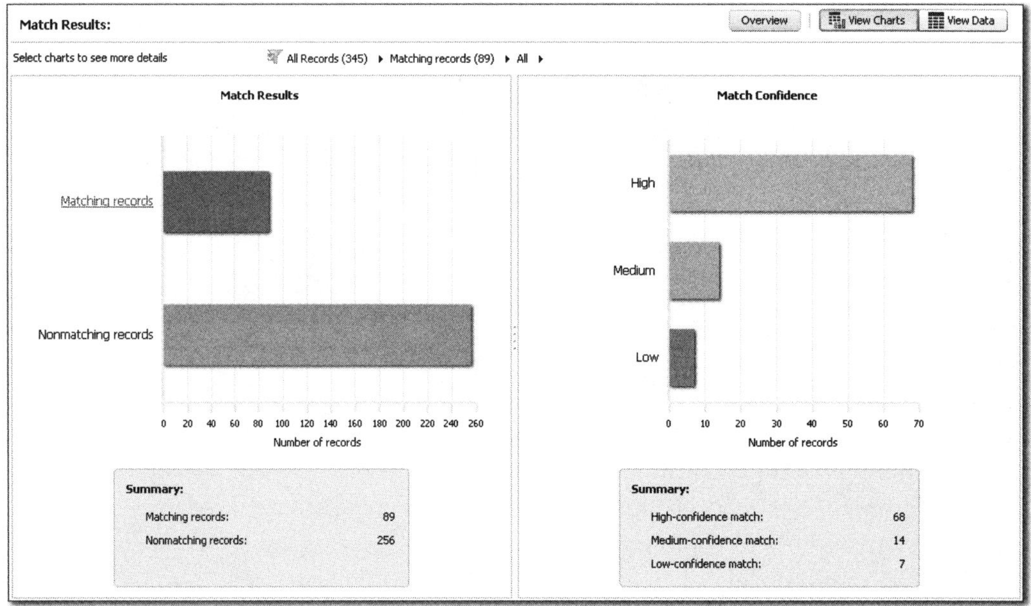

Figure 10.32 Reviewing Match Rules in the Data Cleansing Advisor

When making changes to the match rules, the user is presented with a preview of the impact of those changes and an opportunity to preview the effect on the data (see Figure 10.33). Similar capabilities are available to review and tune the results of cleansing.

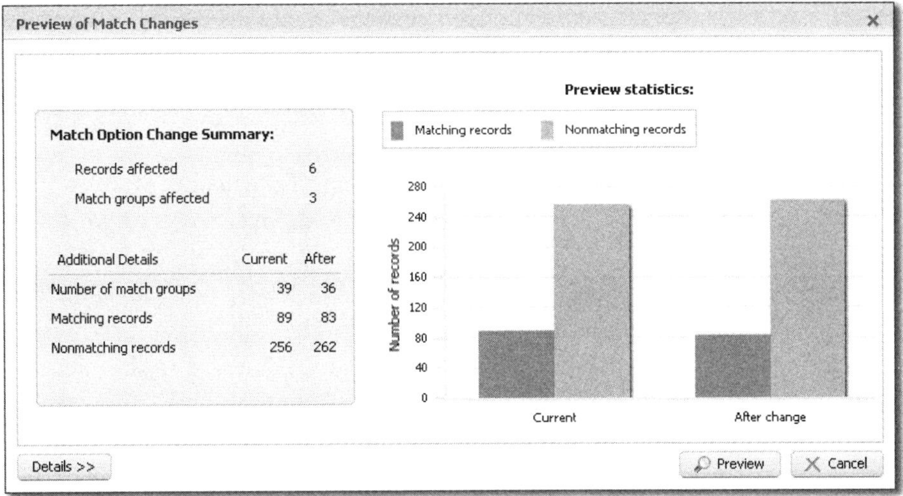

Figure 10.33 Preview of Match Changes

> **Note**
>
> The data changes that you preview in Data Cleansing Advisor are temporary and for planning purposes only. Data Cleansing Advisor creates staged data based on your data and works on the staged data. Nothing is changed in your actual data until the job is processed in the Data Services Workbench.

10.6.4 Publish the Cleansing Solution

As mentioned previously, when you're satisfied, you can publish the data cleansing configuration, allowing the Data Services developer to consume that solution within the context of a Data Services data flow.

See Chapter 9 for more information on the Data Services data quality capabilities.

10.7 Summary

In this chapter, you learned how to view, profile, and assess data quality for specific data domains or critical elements of a business process from within Information

Steward. Information Steward can be used to support the business case for building an information governance organization, investing in master data management, or implementing additional data management procedures using business process management technologies. And by measuring data quality over time, Information Steward can provide evidence that investments in technologies, processes, and procedures are paying off, and it can indicate where more investment or adjustment is needed.

We covered the concept of data quality scorecards in Information Steward. Data quality scorecards allow business users to get easy and direct access to the quality score of the key data domains for which they are responsible. In addition to the overview, data stewards can drill into various detail levels, down to individual data sources violating the defined validation rules. They can browse and review the failed record sample data, and, with the integrated linkage to the metadata management capabilities, they can also identify either from what source system failed data is populated into the systems or where the bad data is being used. This provides an organization with information about the content quality level of their data assets, as well as transparency and confidence in the data used by its operational applications. It allows an organization to know it can track where its data is coming from, as well as the quality of that data. The Business Value Analysis feature of the data quality scorecards was also discussed, supporting efforts to understand, quantify, and demonstrate how bad data impacts the top and bottom line of the business.

Finally, we covered the Data Quality Advisor as a tool to rapidly develop a solution to measure and improve the quality of a company's information assets.

In the next chapter, we'll discuss SAP Master Data Governance, SAP's solution for managing the quality of your master data.

This chapter introduces out-of-the-box, domain-specific master data governance to centrally create, maintain, and distribute master data, with a focus on the SAP Business Suite.

11 SAP Master Data Governance

Most organizations face complex master data governance challenges. Without an integrated and centralized approach to master data governance, companies have ad hoc and unplanned data processes that aren't sufficiently controlled or guided. Managing corporate master data in such cases can become quite time-consuming, slow, and error-prone.

Companies need correct and complete master data to maximize the efficiencies of their business processes. Availability of such data across the business network needs to be accelerated. Fortunately, *SAP Master Data Governance* (SAP MDG) can help by providing prebuilt scenarios for centralized governance of master data domains. The prebuilt scenarios can be customized and extended, and new scenarios can be developed. Because SAP MDG also allows for customized processes, it ensures a consistent definition and governance of master data in the organization. This, together with the distribution of the master data to the relevant business systems in the landscape, can replace the often error-prone process of manually maintaining master data in multiple systems.

Note

Although the focus of this chapter is SAP MDG, SAP's master data management offering covers broad customer needs with a comprehensive portfolio of master data infrastructures and applications. This includes SAP NetWeaver Master Data Management (SAP NetWeaver MDM) with a proven multi-domain infrastructure for analytical master data scenarios, and SAP Data Services (hereafter Data Services) to support integration and data quality improvements such as address cleansing and duplicate detection.

SAP MDG runs on the SAP Business Suite and uses existing business logic and customer-specific configuration to ensure the quality of master data at the point of creation. It supports centralized maintenance processes that ensure the master data is always fit for use in a company's business processes. The native integration into SAP Business Suite means that SAP MDG is capable of reusing the existing data models, validations, business logic, and configurations for managing master data from the underlying SAP applications. There is no need to rewrite all of these from scratch.

Note

All master data that's managed through SAP MDG is ready for use in the SAP Business Suite's business processes. However, it's important to note that this data can be validated for non-SAP usages and distributed and used in non-SAP systems as well.

SAP MDG works very well with other SAP solutions for Enterprise Information Management (EIM). SAP MDG complements the capabilities of SAP NetWeaver MDM, for example, when customers want to consolidate master data from disparate sources, and use SAP NetWeaver MDM as the hub for integration and consolidation of globally relevant master data. Later in this chapter, you'll also learn how SAP MDG natively uses Data Services and SAP Information Steward (hereafter Information Steward).

This chapter starts by introducing SAP MDG, including the key concepts and a typical process flow. You'll learn how to get started with key configuration that's required in SAP MDG. After learning about the default governance processes that are provided, we'll discuss governance for custom objects and walk through an example of master data governance for a custom object. We'll introduce the concept of a rules-based workflow and then provide an example of the integration of SAP MDG and Information Steward.

11.1 SAP Master Data Governance Overview

SAP MDG enables collaborative governance of master data through integrated workflows by using a *change request process*. The workflows orchestrate the governance process across multiple users who each contribute their knowledge to the creation or change of master data. It starts with a request to maintain master data, continues with validation and processing by various stakeholders, and ends with approval or rejection by authorized experts. This entire process is supported by SAP Business Workflow, together with the Business Rules Framework Plus (hereafter BRFplus), which is an ABAP-based rule engine.

Note

For more information on SAP Business Workflow and BRFplus, refer to the third edition of *Practical Workflow with SAP* by Jocelyn Dart, Sue Keohan, and Alan Rickayzen (SAP PRESS, 2014).

The change request process ensures that the data needs to be maintained only once centrally. After this, it's replicated to all connected systems in the landscape. SAP MDG comes with a *data replication framework* (DRF) that supports the organization and execution of this data replication and eliminates the need for manual maintenance multiple times in different systems. It's important to note that by providing DRF, SAP MDG hasn't invented a new way of performing data replication. Rather, the intention is to better support customers in managing the replication they already do today. DRF sits on top of the established replication mechanisms, such as application link enabling (ALE), intermediate documents (IDocs), and enterprise services. The purpose of SAP MDG's DRF is to keep track of what data needs to be distributed where and what has been distributed successfully or not, regardless of the replication mechanism. In the DRF, systems can also subscribe to the distribution of master data based on certain filter criteria; for example, only materials for plant 1000 with material type finished goods should be distributed to a system TRN.

SAP MDG comes with prebuilt applications for master data domains such as customer, supplier, material, or financial data. The domain-specific scenarios provided out of the box have been built using the *master data governance application framework*. This framework is also available for customers to build their own custom-defined SAP MDG scenarios that are based on their own master data models. These custom models can be completely self-defined by the customer, can be extensions of the standard models in SAP MDG, or can be based on standard SAP data domains where there isn't yet standard SAP MDG content for the data domain.

Customers can use the framework to define the appropriate data models and then generate the persistence and user interfaces (UIs) based on these models. They can define appropriate workflows and the roles that will provide access to the UIs. They can use the DRF to distribute the data that has been maintained. Also, they can build their own validations or extend existing ones based on BRFplus. Finally, Business Add-Ins (BAdIs) are also provided to include custom ABAP code in SAP MDG's processes. In Section 11.3, you'll see a simple example of configuring a custom-defined object from scratch in SAP MDG.

SAP MDG supports flexible deployment options. It can be deployed either as a standalone system or on top of an SAP ERP system. An end user can access SAP MDG using either the SAP Enterprise Portal or the SAP NetWeaver Business Client.

In this section, we'll introduce some of the most important elements of SAP MDG, including deployment options, change request and staging, and an example process flow.

11.1.1 Deployment Options

SAP MDG was delivered starting with SAP ERP 6.0, EHP5. As shown in Figure 11.1, there are two typical ways for customers to deploy SAP MDG in relation to their existing system landscape.

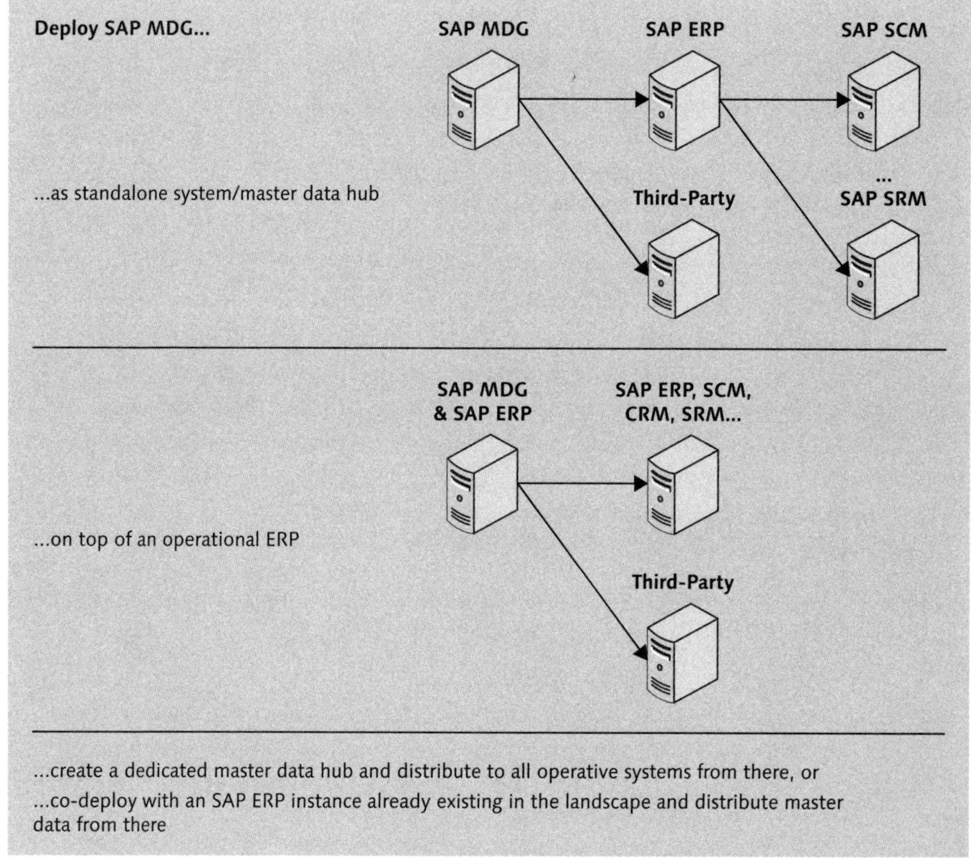

Figure 11.1 Deployment Options for SAP MDG

The first way is to introduce a completely new system as a dedicated master data hub, using only the master data governance functionality in this system and distributing the master data from it to other SAP or third-party systems that run the various business processes. This approach has the advantage that SAP MDG can be deployed without disturbing the existing system landscape. Existing SAP ERP systems don't require an upgrade to a release supporting SAP MDG, as the hub itself handles distribution of governed master data to older SAP or third-party systems in the landscape.

The second approach is to run SAP MDG on an existing SAP ERP system. All governed and approved data from SAP MDG is then directly available to the business processes running on that system, and is also distributed to all other systems that need it.

A special flavor of the second case could be customers who only run one SAP ERP system. In such cases, SAP MDG can be deployed with that single SAP ERP system by upgrading it to at least EHP5 and turning on SAP MDG's business functions. Even if you don't want to distribute the master data to any receiving system (which would rarely be the case), SAP MDG will still allow you to do the following:

- Separate incomplete or not-approved data from the production data.
- Use workflows to distribute maintenance of data to multiple people.
- Enhance validations beyond the existing business process rules.
- Benefit from the improved prevention of duplicates and data quality enrichment.
- More easily track key performance indicators (KPIs) for master data creation, and maintain an audit trail of all master data changes.

Both deployment options allow customers to efficiently govern their corporate master data. The approach that a company chooses will depend on its specific business needs and cost considerations.

For more details on deployment considerations, refer to System Landscape Recommendations for SAP MDG at the SAP Community Network (search for "Master Data Governance" on *http://scn.sap.com*).

11.1.2 Change Request and Staging

Now that you understand the deployment options in SAP MDG, let's talk a little more about some of the most important concepts involved in SAP MDG. The data that's governed in SAP MDG goes through a change request process involving an approval workflow. Until the changes are approved, they must be kept separate from the data that's used in the business process. Such changes must become visible to the business processes only after they are approved. In other words, you need to separate data entry from data approval.

This is where the concepts of change request and staging come into the picture. Change request and staging are core concepts for SAP MDG and are used to drive collaboration between the various users, such as the requester of changes and the approver.

A *change request* is a container for new and changed master data of one change process. It determines the approval process flow and the processors. Changes are carried by the change request until they are approved, for example, by a data steward. You can configure change request processes to add or remove steps or processors, include objects to be changed at request creation, or handle multiple or single master data object instances.

Figure 11.2 shows the steps that are involved in a typical change request process. An example is the maintenance of master data, its validation and approval, and finally its replication to the various target systems in the landscape.

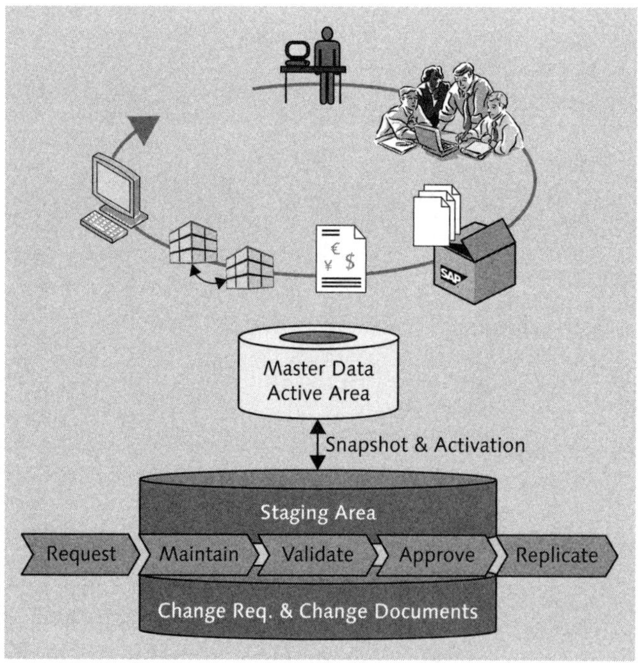

Figure 11.2 Change Request and Staging

Data that's still in process is stored in a separate temporary repository known as the *staging area*. The staging area can only be accessed by SAP MDG; business processes can't access this unapproved data. A complete audit trail of changes is maintained by the system. After the changes are finally approved, the data is transferred to the productive master data, which is known as the *active area*. All business processes and applications refer only to the master data that is held in the active area. From SAP MDG's active area, the data can be distributed to other systems to be used there.

SAP MDG provides two modes for active area persistence:

- **Reuse active area (reuse mode)**
  In this mode, existing database tables of the related applications are used for storing the active master data. For example, SAP MDG for materials uses the MARA table and others in SAP ERP ECC. Reuse mode is best suited for customers who want to use the existing ABAP Data Dictionary structures provided by SAP, including extended or previously created custom structures.
- **Generated active area (flex mode)**
  In this mode, new database tables generated by SAP MDG are used to store the active data. This mode provides additional flexibility, as it doesn't need any additional ABAP Data Dictionary structures to be created. Customers can simply model the attributes in SAP MDG and then SAP MDG generates the active area. You don't need to change any structures or tables in the SAP ERP system. This is particularly useful if you want to maintain and store data centrally but rather for distribution to other SAP or non-SAP systems.

11.1.3 Process Flow in SAP Master Data Governance

Figure 11.3 shows a typical process flow in SAP MDG using the scenario Create Material or Change Material. This is one example of the standard content shipped with SAP MDG.

In SAP MDG for Material, the default approval process follows the two-man rule:

- The process begins with a *business user* requesting creation of a material or change of material data. After completing his input, the business user *submits* the request.
- The *master data expert* is notified of this new request through his work list. He reviews the changes, after which he may add further changes or enhancements and send the review back to the business user for *revision* or clarification.

- The *business user* can decide to *cancel* the request (e.g., in cases where a suitable material already exists) or adjust the data and *resubmit* his request.
- The *master data expert* can again review and revise the request. If the data is complete and correct, he approves the request and *activates* the data.

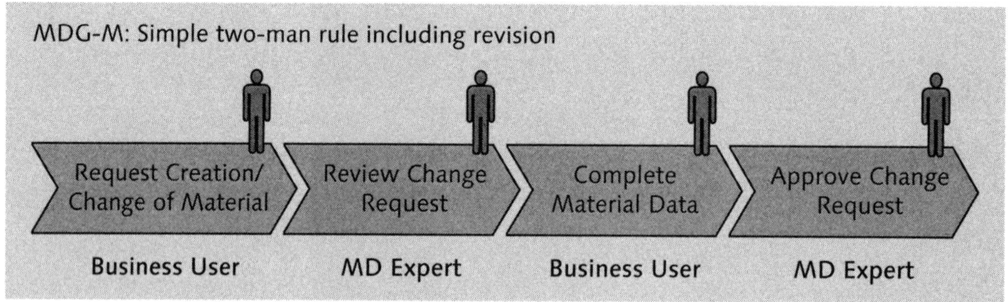

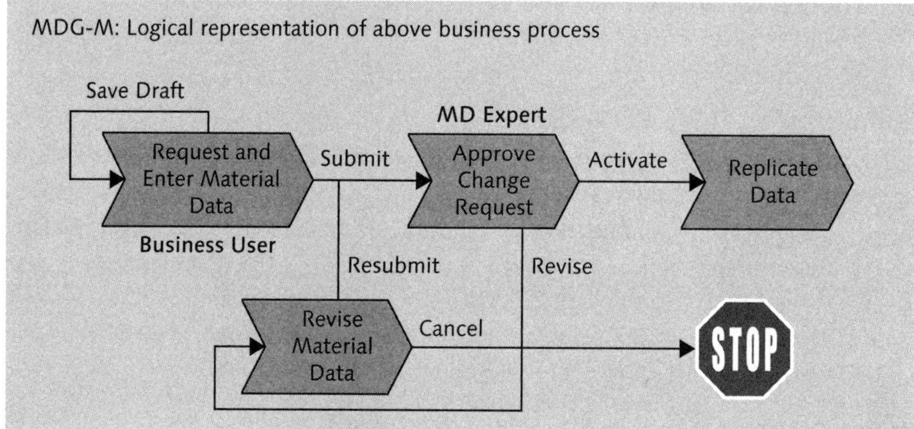

Figure 11.3 Material Governance Process

All changes are carried by a change request, as discussed in the previous section. The proposed changes are validated for correctness against the existing business logic, using the validations defined in the underlying SAP Business Suite. In addition to these, external validations may be used as well. Custom validations may be modeled using BRFplus or programmed using code lists or simple coding checks. After the data has been validated and found to be error free, it's approved by a master data expert and moved to the active area.

The active data can then be replicated to all connected systems in the landscape. The replication can be automatic as part of the last step in the workflow, or it can be triggered manually by the user.

The entire governance process is controlled by adaptable workflows that can be configured based on business requirements. In Section 11.4, you'll learn how the workflow can be configured.

After the data has been replicated to other systems, it can be adapted or enriched in the local client systems, typically adding attributes that aren't under central governance.

11.1.4 Use of SAP HANA in SAP MDG

SAP MDG can be deployed on top of any database, with SAP HANA being an optional component. However, using SAP HANA for SAP MDG provides significant advantages. To benefit from these advantages, you can either run SAP MDG directly on SAP HANA configured as the primary database, or you can have SAP HANA running next to your SAP MDG system as a secondary database, which will be provided with master data governance data by near real-time replication.

In both cases—whether you have the SAP MDG data in the primary SAP HANA database, or the data is replicated into it—you can benefit from SAP HANA's ranked similarity search on that data. With this, you can provide users with additional information in search result lists, for example, the degree of similarity of all found records compared to the search criteria. The result list is sorted by similarity, so the users find the closest matches at the very top. You can also use the calculated similarity rank for a better assessment of potential duplicates. The rank indicates how likely certain entries are to be duplicates.

In addition, because SAP HANA is a columnar database, it shows you how many instances of each attribute value exist in your complete master data with very short response times. For example, you could use this function to find out how many customers have the attribute value for GERMANY in the attribute COUNTRY. This is one of the features provided by the SAP MDG *multi-attribute drill-down* application. This highly interactive application enables you to slice and dice the complete set of master data by selecting filter values for attributes and by drilling into the structure of the master data. For example, you can easily determine how the customer categories are distributed in one particular zip code, or how many organizations versus people there are in a certain state. This is a completely different approach to searching, because you always find data according to available attribute values, and you never type and search based on terms that may not exist in your data. This also gives you a completely new insight into the implicit structures in your master data, and it supports you in finding potential data quality issues you might have overlooked earlier.

Based on the master data governance data in SAP HANA, SAP MDG also allows for the analysis of SAP MDG processes with *SAP Smart Business*. This provides a very easy and intuitive access to information, for example, KPIs of exceeded processing times, overdue or long-running requests, average processing times, or the total number of successfully executed processes. Users can then navigate from the KPIs to a more detailed analysis for issue resolution. Customers can freely define SAP Smart Business KPIs in their environment based on SAP HANA views and according to their business needs.

11.2 Getting Started with SAP Master Data Governance

You can get SAP MDG up and running quickly and with minimal configuration. The required settings can be found in the Implementation Guide (Transaction SPRO) by following the path Cross-Application Components • Processes and Tools for Enterprise Applications • Master Data Governance.

This section provides an overview of the most important configuration steps.

11.2.1 Data Modeling

Establishing the data model is the first step in getting started with SAP MDG. A data model represents the master data in the system. It consists of entity types and relationships to enable modeling master data structures of any complexity in the system. You have the options to use the data models provided, to enhance existing data models, or to create your own data models.

There are a few key terms you need to know when working with data models. The first is *entity types*. Entity types are collections of fields and substructures in a data model. For example, the data model Material (MM) has multiple entity types that relate to a material. One entity type relates to the material basic data and contains fields such as weight, material group, and base unit of measure. Each SAP MDG data model contains multiple entity types with different characteristics and the relationship types. Some of these entity types will be available to directly process them in SAP MDG change requests. Other entity types won't be available for processing in a change request. Think of those as if they were look-up values that should never be changeable in an SAP MDG process. An example might be the international article number (EAN). And there are also entity types that only make sense in the context of another entity type. For example, the plant-dependent data of a material can only appear in the context of that material and not in isolation. These characteristics of the entity type are defined by its storage and use type. The system generates database tables for each entity type that's required for processing the master data in SAP MDG. The storage and use type determines whether and how master data can be changed in SAP MDG and the type of tables that are generated by the system for storing the master data.

Recommendations for SAP MDG Data Models

- Use the SAP-delivered data models when possible; this will save implementation time.
- Extend the SAP data model when needed.
- Before creating your own data model, check the SAP roadmap of data models in the SAP MDG area of the SAP Community Network.

The validity of entity types can be restricted using *editions*. An edition is important if the master data object has some time dependency. Editions are delivered by default for the financial domain; for example, for cost centers, profit centers, and cost elements. You may want to add a time dependency to General Ledger (GL) accounts, companies, and/or consolidation structures. Using an edition requires some additional configuration in the model so that the time dependency is included in the persistence layer. (You can find more details on editions by performing a search for "MDG editions" at the SAP MDG documentation at *http://help.sap.com.*)

Entity types can be linked using *relationships*. Relationships can be of types Leading, Qualifying, or Referencing. A Leading or Qualifying relationship specifies the From-Entity type on a higher level than the To-Entity type. The From-Entity type is automatically taken as the key in the generated tables. A referencing relationship specifies the From-Entity type as an attribute of the To-Entity type. An example is material leading to a global trade number (GTIN) where the material becomes part of the key field for the GTIN entity. An example of a referencing relationship is a COUNTRY CODE that is checked for a supplier address, but isn't part of the key field. For more information, again see the SAP MDG documentation.

11.2.2 User Interface Modeling

UI modeling is done when defining the UI configuration of the web UI for creating and processing a change request. If you want to use the existing UI models, no further configuration is required for the UI. You only need to do the UI modeling if you choose to customize existing models or create your own.

For example, you can specify whether the system hides certain entity types and fields on the selection screens, in the results of a search, or in data cleansing. The settings for UI modeling can be found in SAP MDG Customizing under GENERAL SETTINGS • UI MODELING.

In addition to using the delivered UI logic, you can use BAdIs to change the UI for individual processing of an entity type. Changes can be made in the following areas:

- Adjust the definition of attributes, or add new attributes.
- Initialize the displayed data (e.g., when creating a new entity).
- Restrict the values displayed in a dropdown box or selection field group.
- Restrict the values displayed in the input help.
- Dynamically control the visibility of fields on the UI and of the property that determines if fields are required or display-only.
- Define navigation destinations of UI elements of the type hyperlink or push-button.
- Check if the lead selection of a table may be changed.

UI modeling will be discussed in more detail in Section 11.3.

11.2.3 Data Quality and Search

Several important configurations for data quality and search are done in this step. First, *validations* and *derivations* are defined for the data models. Just as with the other areas, no configuration is required if you want to use the validations and derivations provided out of the box. Validations ensure that the master data is consistent. Derivations are used to calculate values for some attributes based on the values entered in other attributes, thereby simplifying data entry. For example, the tax jurisdiction code for a business partner is derived from the address.

The customizing activity GENERAL SETTINGS • DATA QUALITY AND SEARCH • DEFINE VALIDATION AND DERIVATION RULES is used to configure validation and derivation rules. In addition to this, a BAdI is provided to create customer-specific checks on entities and change requests. This BAdI can also be used to define that certain field values are to be derived from the values of other fields in the master data.

The second aspect is that search providers that should be available for the different types of search used in SAP MDG are defined in this step. The available search applications are Business Address Search (BAS), Database Search, Enterprise Search, and Remote Key Search.

Types of Searches Available in SAP MDG

- BAS enables you to search by an address, including fuzzy search based on similarity ranking.
- Database Search is an exact search method based on values or ranges stored in a database.
- Enterprise Search is for free text and fuzzy search.
- Remote Key Search searches from a remote client system into the central SAP MDG system.

The third important feature in this customizing activity is the configuration for duplicate checks. On the basis of the data model (e.g., business partner or material), you can define which search mode the system will use and which thresholds (percentages) to apply to determine duplicates.

Records that have a matching score that's lower than the low threshold aren't considered duplicates. Records that have a matching score that lies between the defined low and high thresholds are considered potential duplicates. Records that have a matching score higher than the high threshold aren't allowed by the system, as they are identified as duplicates.

Note

Data quality duplicate checks and thresholds are discussed in more detail in Chapter 9.

Finally, the enrichment capabilities are defined in this customization activity. An example is an external address directory for address cleansing. Both internal and external service calls are supported. For example, for enrichment of the address data, SAP Data Services can be called as an external service.

11.2.4 Process Modeling

Process modeling defines the relationships among the business activity, change request types, the workflows, and the entities. The customizing activities for process modeling include creating editions, configuring business activities, creating change request types, and workflows. Process modeling configurations can be found under GENERAL SETTINGS • PROCESS MODELING.

A *business activity* is a business operation you can perform in SAP MDG. Examples of delivered business activities are CREATE MATERIAL, DISPLAY MATERIAL, CREATE SUPPLIER, BLOCK/UNBLOCK SUPPLIER, and so on. Additional business activities can be created using the configuration under GENERAL SETTINGS • PROCESS MODELING • BUSINESS ACTIVITIES • CREATE BUSINESS ACTIVITY.

A *change request type* defines one dedicated governance process. Change request types are assigned to specific data models, and a business activity can be associated with one or more change request types. Each change request type can have a different workflow template and different service-level agreement and is capable of processing single or multiple objects. For example, the business activity CREATE SUPPLIER can be associated with change request type CREATE SUPPLIER and change request type CREATE SUPPLIER, SIMPLIFIED WORKFLOW.

If you use the data model for business partner or material, the business activities (such as Create, Change, Approve) are already defined and assigned to the data models; you only need to assign the right people to the workflow in the process modeling configuration steps. The customizing activity for creating business activities allows you to create your own business activity and assign it to a data model. This is meant for cases in which you want to process your own entity types, and SAP doesn't deliver a suitable business activity.

Customizing activities are available in the process modeling node for configuring a rules-based workflow and defining steps in it. When you configure a rules-based workflow, separate settings are provided for each change request type. SAP delivers BRFplus decision tables as example content for each change request type. This SAP-proposed content is imported into client 000. To use this content, you can export the decision tables from client 000 to Microsoft Excel and then import them into your client. The decision tables in the customer system are then filled with the example content. It's also possible to define the decision tables manually. If the Excel import is recorded in a customizing request, it can also be used to then transport these decision table entries to other systems. SAP also delivers predefined change request steps for rules-based workflows with corresponding application scenarios.

11.2.5 Data Replication

The customizing activities for data replication are used to specify how data is replicated to one or more target systems. For example, the filters for selecting data to be transferred can be specified here (e.g., only materials for plant 1000 will go to a dedicated system). Using the customizing activities for data replication, you can define the business object settings and the communication-relevant settings (e.g., services, ALE, IDocs) for business systems involved in data replication, and you can create replication models. Each replication model can consist of one or more outbound implementations. For the configuration of data replication, existing outbound implementations are referenced or new user-specific ones are defined.

To add custom implementations, BAdIs are available to change the default system behavior for transferring language-dependent texts, formatting the file for downloading data from SAP MDG, uploading master data to SAP MDG, and creating SAP MDG change pointers from ALE change pointers for selected message types.

11.2.6 Key and Value Mapping

Mapping is needed in various scenarios where the same business object is created in different systems with different identifiers. *Key mapping* is when the primary key for an object (such as business partner or material) is different in various systems; the key mapping ensures that we know which object IDs represent the same thing in different systems. *Value mapping* is used when codes used in master data attributes are different between systems, and they should be translated when distributing data between systems.

The following are two typical use cases showing the relevance of key mapping:

- **Use Case 1**
  A business partner is created in the SAP MDG system (A) with business partner ID 4711. Afterward, it's replicated to a second system (B) with internal

number creation for business partners. In this system, the business partner is created with number 0815. Using key mapping, it's possible to store the information and know that partner 4711 in system A is the same as business partner 0815 in system B. Later, when replicating changes regarding this business partner, the changes will be sent to system B using the correct ID, so that the same business partner is updated in system B and a new business partner isn't created.

- **Use Case 2**
  One material was distributed to several systems and was given different IDs in each system. For analytic reasons, it's necessary to accumulate the information from all systems about this material (e.g., all quantities in stock). Therefore, the analytic report needs to know all the different identifiers of the various systems. This information can be retrieved out of the key mapping data in SAP MDG.

The configuration settings for key mapping can be used to do the following:

- Change the default key mapping settings.
- Extend key mapping settings for existing business objects, typically by adding new object IDs.
- Extend key mapping settings for new business objects.

Common examples of value mapping include payment terms and country codes (USA versus US versus United States in different systems). Value mapping is an alternative to synchronizing the customizing entries and their corresponding master data across all systems. Table 11.1 shows a use case in which the Form of Address customizing element uses one set of codes in SAP MDG and a different set of values in another system.

Form of Address	Code Value in SAP MDG	Code Value in System B
Mr.	0001	0004
Ms.	0002	0003
Company	0003	0002
Mr. and Ms.	0004	0001

Table 11.1 Example of Different Code Values between Systems

11.2.7 Data Transfer

SAP MDG supports import of data from the master data client systems. These inbound channels are a part of the data transfer functionality. The following three capabilities are provided for data transfer:

- **Export master data**
  To export various types of master data from client systems in enterprise service XML format.
- **Import master data**
  To import various types of master data (available in enterprise service XML or IDoc formats) into SAP MDG.
- **Convert master data**
  To convert various types of master data (available in non-XML or third-party formats) into enterprise service XML format for subsequent import into SAP MDG.

Through the customizing activities in the data transfer area, you set up the ABAP class that should be called to convert to the proper XML format. In addition, you configure the service call such as the message type, and the import sequence for objects with dependencies.

In the customizing for data transfer, you need to define a subset of all logical directories set up for the system. Only these selected logical directories can then be used by the SAP MDG data transfer applications as the destination for exported XML files and the source for files to be imported or converted. After the system has imported or converted files for a selected object type, they are moved to an archive directory that must also be defined in the customizing for each object type used in data transfer.

11.2.8 Activities beyond Customizing

A few other activities are required beyond customizing to get started with SAP MDG. These are primarily related to the creation and maintenance of user roles and configuration of SAP Enterprise Portal or SAP NetWeaver Business Client. The roles need to be assigned to users. Data model UI configurations are assigned to the roles. For SAP Enterprise Portal, several business packages are available as templates.

After these settings have been made, you can start using SAP MDG.

11.3 Governance for Custom-Defined Objects: Example

As mentioned earlier, customers can extend SAP MDG by adding their own business logic or even using SAP MDG for governance of their own objects. For example, in the context of standard SAP MDG domains (financials, supplier, material, etc.), subordinate entity types that aren't yet delivered with the data model may be added. You can include Z-tables, additional fields, and other customer enhancements (including non-SAP data) to the SAP MDG data model. You can also extend an existing model with additional reference data, such as bank codes, additional material information sales, or plant data.

An important decision is where the active area should reside. When extending a data model, you typically have to follow the approach chosen for the extended data model, as the active area is defined per entity type. For example, if you extend the MM data model by adding a customer-defined attribute (z-field) to the entity type MATERIAL, you must store the attribute's data in the reuse area and can't use the active area provided by SAP MDG.

In the previous section, we discussed at length the various configuration options available. Now you'll learn how to use these options for configuring a custom-defined object in SAP MDG based on an example scenario to govern airline data. This simple data model should use the active area provided by SAP MDG, which includes the following fields and attributes as defined by the respective data element:

- ID, data element `S_CARR_ID`
- Description, data element `USMD_TXTMI`
- URL, data element `S_CARRURL`
- Currency, data element `S_CURRCODE`

In the next sections, we explain the basic steps to set up this scenario.

11.3.1 Plan and Create Data Model

Planning the data model is the first step toward implementing this custom-defined object in SAP MDG. This involves asking questions such as the following:

How many and what entity types are needed? What is their relationship? Which of the fields are automatically available via an entity type, and which additional fields need to be modeled? What is the active area? After these questions are answered, data modeling can be performed.

Plan the Data Model

In this example, the data model consists of one entity type for the airline, for which we pick the name CARR. As CARR should be governed with SAP MDG, and the staging and active area should be provided by SAP MDG, the storage and use type must be CHANGEABLE VIA CHANGE REQUEST; GENERATED DATABASE TABLES, and the active area should be defined in the system as MDG. This means that the ID will be derived from the assigned data element, and a field to cover the description can automatically be provided. An attribute is required to store airline URLs. For CURRENCY, the data element `S_CURRCODE` defines a list of valid values by using a check table. You can either model CURRENCY as another attribute or as a dedicated entity type with a referencing relationship to CARR. For demonstration purposes, we use the latter. In this case, another entity type CURRENCY is required. As it should not be possible to modify the contents of the check table with SAP MDG, the storage and use type is NOT CHANGEABLE VIA MDG; NO GENERATED TABLES.

Create the Data Model

First, you need to create a new data model and choose MDG as the active area in the customizing activity GENERAL SETTINGS • DATA MODELING • EDIT DATA MODEL.

Create Entity Types

Create entity type CARR as shown in Figure 11.4 by choosing the following properties:

- ENTITY TYPE: CARR
- STORAGE/USE TYPE: CHANGEABLE VIA CHANGE REQUEST; GENERATED DATABASE TABLES
- DATA ELEMENT: S_CARR_ID
- MEDIUM TEXT LENGTH: 20

For other properties, leave the default values. Finally, add an attribute URL with data element S_CARRURL.

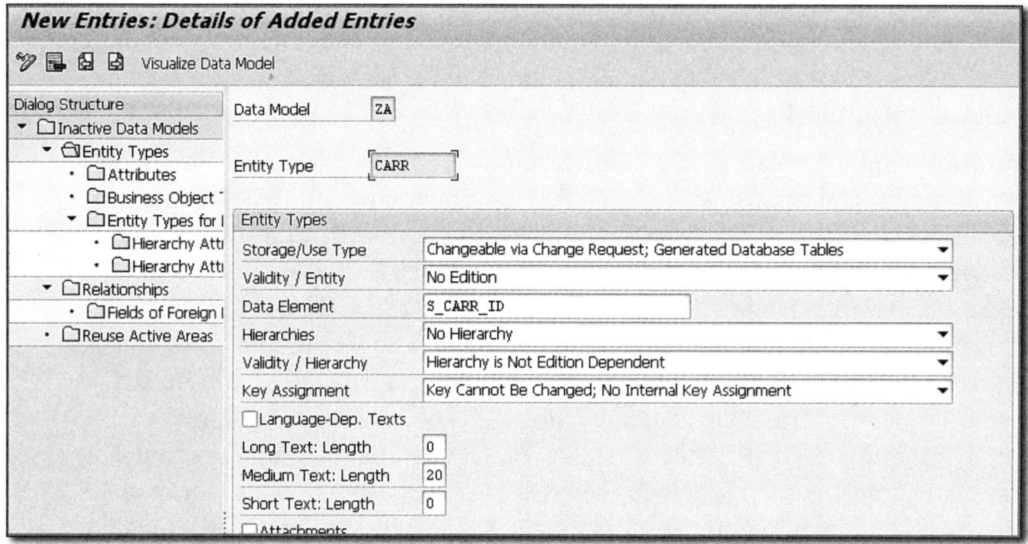

Figure 11.4 Define Entity Type CARR for the Data Model

Typically, several entity types belong together and form a business object that is processed in a UI or replicated to another system, so you need to designate one entity type as the root of a business object. In this example, CARR and CURRENCY together form the business object, and CARR is the root entity type. In the BUSINESS OBJECT TYPE view, enter the respective business object type code, and set the ROOT indicator. For a custom business object, you may need to add a new type code in the customizing activity GENERAL SETTINGS • DATA REPLICATION • ENHANCE DEFAULT SETTINGS FOR OUTBOUND IMPLEMENTATIONS • DEFINE BUSINESS OBJECTS AND OBJECT IDENTIFIERS • DEFINE BUSINESS OBJECTS.

Proceed by creating the entity type for CURRENCY with the following properties as shown in Figure 11.5:

- ENTITY TYPE: CURRENCY
- STORAGE/USE TYPE: NOT CHANGEABLE VIA MDG; NO GENERATED TABLES
- DATA ELEMENT: S_CURRCODE

New Entries: Details of Added Entries

Visualize Data Model

Dialog Structure
- Inactive Data Models
  - Entity Types
    - Attributes
    - Business Object
    - Entity Types for I
      - Hierarchy Att
      - Hierarchy Att
  - Relationships
    - Fields of Foreign I
  - Reuse Active Areas

Data Model: ZA

Entity Type: CURRENCY

Entity Types

Storage/Use Type	Not Changeable via MDG; No Generated Tables
Validity / Entity	No Edition
Data Element	S_CURRCODE
Hierarchies	No Hierarchy
Validity / Hierarchy	Hierarchy is Not Edition Dependent
Key Assignment	Key Cannot Be Changed; No Internal Key Assignment
Language-Dep. Texts	
Long Text: Length	
Medium Text: Length	
Short Text: Length	

Figure 11.5 Define Entity Type CURRENCY for Data Model

Create Relationship

To combine CARR and CURRENCY into one business object, create a relationship between the two by entering the following values in the RELATIONSHIPS view, as shown in Figure 11.6:

- FROM-ENTITY TYPE: CURRENCY
- RELATIONSHIP: CARR_CURR
- TO-ENTITY TYPE: CARR
- RELATION. TYPE: REFERENCING
- CARDINALITY: 1:N
- DATA ELEMENT: S_CURRCODE

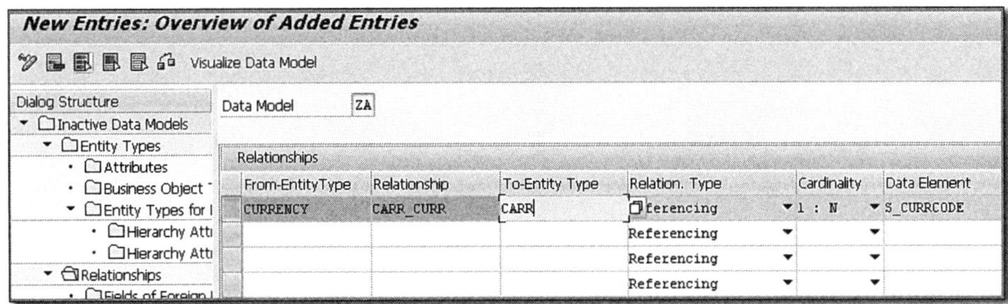

Figure 11.6 Define Relationship from CURRENCY to CARR

Activate Data Model

Finally, save and activate the data model, which generates the tables for staging and active area.

You can visualize the created data model by selecting the data model name and choosing VISUALIZE DATA MODEL. The result is shown in Figure 11.7.

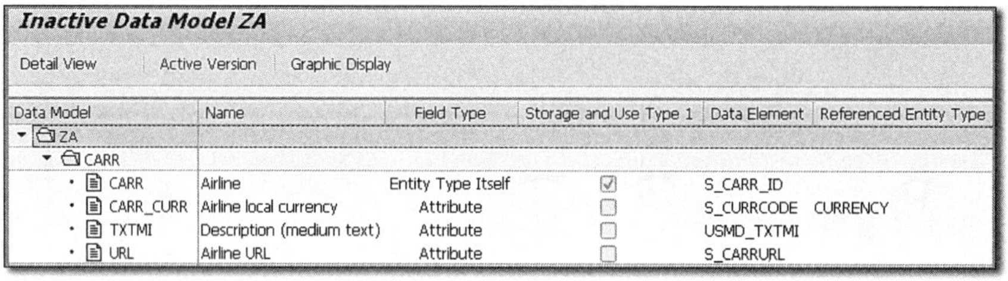

Inactive Data Model ZA

Detail View | Active Version | Graphic Display

Data Model	Name	Field Type	Storage and Use Type 1	Data Element	Referenced Entity Type
ZA					
CARR					
CARR	Airline	Entity Type Itself	☑	S_CARR_ID	
CARR_CURR	Airline local currency	Attribute	☐	S_CURRCODE	CURRENCY
TXTMI	Description (medium text)	Attribute	☐	USMD_TXTMI	
URL	Airline URL	Attribute	☐	S_CARRURL	

Figure 11.7 Data Model Visualization

You see that the entity type CURRENCY is effectively available as an attribute of the entity type CARR with the name CARR_CURR. For the description, an attribute TXTMI was automatically added.

Choose Actual Entity Type for Business Object

There can be multiple data models and entity types that describe the same business object. However, at runtime, there can only be one that is actually used. In customizing, follow the path GENERAL SETTINGS • DATA MODELING • DEFINE ENTITY TYPE TO BE USED BY BUSINESS OBJECT TYPE to create an entry for your business object, and enter your data model and the entity type CARR as the actual values.

Generate Structures

The system requires several data structures that are specific to the data model. After the data model is activated for the first time, and also after every change to the data model, these structures need to be generated. Use the GENERAL SETTINGS • DATA MODELING • GENERATE DATA MODEL-SPECIFIC STRUCTURES customizing activity for all entity types to generate those structures as shown in Figure 11.8 for the following entries of the WHERE USED column:

- MAPPING OF REUSE ACTIVE AREA
- SEARCH APPLICATION

- Field Control for Attributes
- Field Properties for Attributes and Key Fields
- Key Fields of an Entity Type

Change View "Structures": Overview

New Entries | BC Set: Change Field Values | Generate Selected Structures

Dialog Structure: Data Models; Structures; Mapping

Data Model: ZA

Structures

Entity Type	Where Used	Name of Structure	Package
CARR	Mapping of Reuse Active Area	PP_CARR	$TMP
CARR	Search Application	ES_CARR	$TMP
CARR	Field Control for Attributes	FC_CARR	$TMP
CARR	Field Properties for Attributes and Key Fields	FP_CARR	$TMP
CARR	Key Fields of an Entity Type	KF_CARR	$TMP

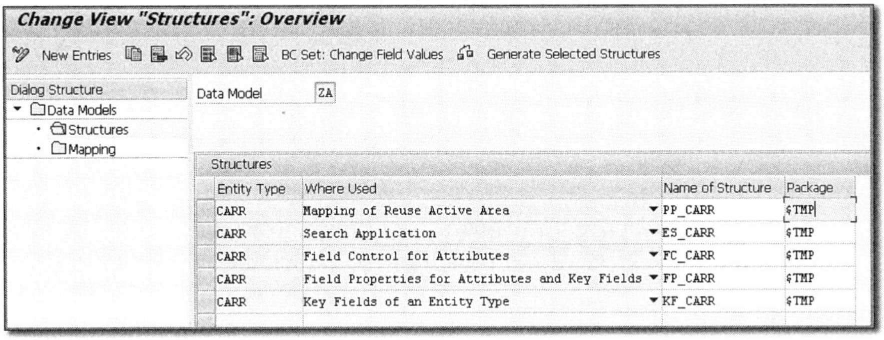

Figure 11.8 Generate Data Model-Specific Structures

11.3.2 Define User Interface

After the data model has been created in SAP MDG, the next step is to define a UI for the single-object maintenance of an airline with a change request. The UIs for SAP MDG are based on ABAP Web Dynpro. They are built with the Floor Plan Manager (FPM) using its Business Object Layer (BOL)/Generic Integration Layer (genIL) technology, which enables creation of UIs that are loosely coupled to the SAP MDG-specific processes, and are highly flexible.

The UI for single-object maintenance contains at least one page. At least one section of the page contains UI building blocks (UIBBs). UIBBs are reusable components that support lists, forms, and special user interaction such as pop-ups, search input, and search results. They help in achieving a uniform look and feel across all SAP MDG UIs. Most UIBBs enable the processing of business object data on the UI. On the single-object maintenance UI, these UIBBs are configured for all entity types that belong to the business object. In addition to this, the SAP MDG framework provides the following UIBBs:

- The change request UIBB displaying the change request properties, such as description, due date, notes, and attachments
- The validity UIBB displaying the time validity for edition-based entities

These UIBBs aren't explicitly a part of the configuration of the Web Dynpro application, but they are added at runtime by the SAP MDG communicator, which has overall responsibility for the change request process. The SAP MDG communicator controls the availability of change request actions, which are represented as buttons in the global toolbar.

If you need an object-specific search, the UI can include an initial screen with an FPM search UIBB to enter search criteria and a list UIBB to display search results.

Set User Personalization

The UI configuration is based on the active version of an SAP MDG data model. At design-time, when you create a UI configuration or customize a UI, the relevant data model is determined by the standard data model from the user profile. You set the standard data model in the following way, depicted in Figure 11.9:

1. Run Transaction SPERS_MAINT.
2. Select Edit Objects.
3. From the displayed list, choose SAP Master Data Governance – R_FMDM_MODEL.
4. In the pop-up, set the value of the Standard Data Model field to the model that you want to use for UI processing.
5. Confirm and save.

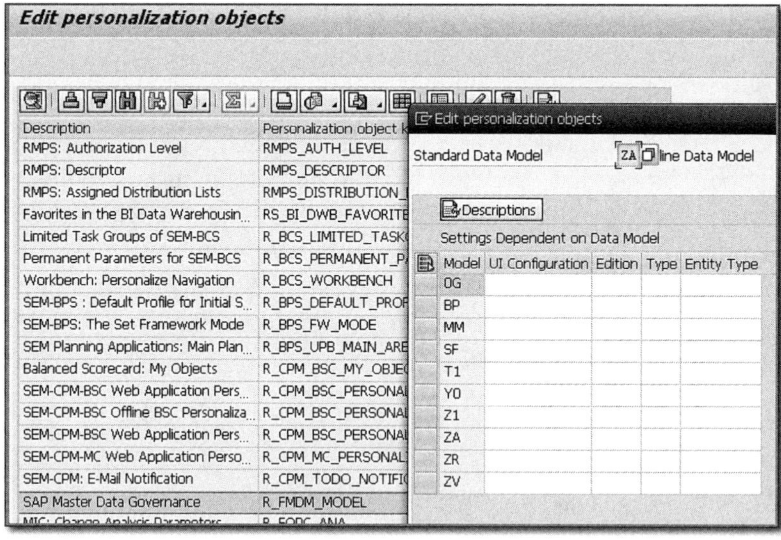

Figure 11.9 Edit Personalization Objects

Create Form UIBB

The SAP MDG framework application delivers templates so that you don't need to create everything from scratch. Therefore, you can create a new Airline Form UIBB for airline data by simply copying the template component configuration FPM_FORM_UIBB_GL2_TEMPLATE (see Figure 11.10).

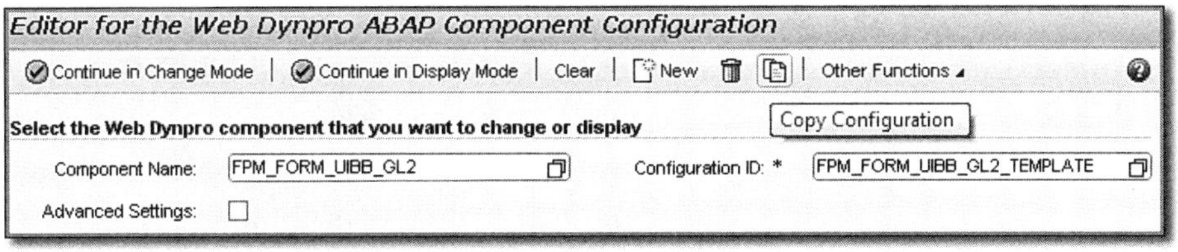

Editor for the Web Dynpro ABAP Component Configuration

Continue in Change Mode | Continue in Display Mode | Clear | New | Other Functions

Copy Configuration

Select the Web Dynpro component that you want to change or display

Component Name: FPM_FORM_UIBB_GL2

Configuration ID: * FPM_FORM_UIBB_GL2_TEMPLATE

Advanced Settings:

Figure 11.10 Copy Template Configuration

Copy it as a local object with Configuration ID of say, ZA_AIRLINE_FORM02, and the generic SAP MDG feeder class for forms CL_MDG_BS_GUIBB_FORM is automatically assigned to it as shown in Figure 11.11. For feeder class parameters, enter the generic SAP MDG model as the component and the entity type Carr as the object name. Save this configuration.

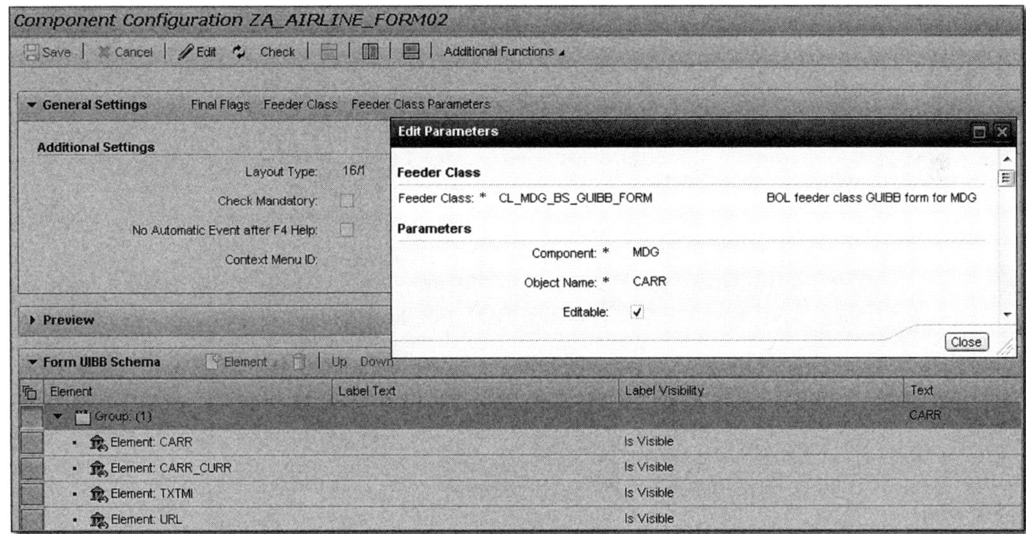

Figure 11.11 New Component Configuration for Airline Form UIBB

Copy Form UIBB into an Existing Configuration

Now you can reuse your newly created Airline Form UIBB in an existing UI configuration. For this example, the UI configuration ZA_USMD_SF_CARR_OVP_10 is used, which was created in the following way:

1. Navigate to the customizing activity General Settings • UI Modeling • Manage UI Configurations.
2. For data model SF, an application configuration USMD_SF_OVP_CARR is available for the generic SAP MDG Web Dynpro application USMD_OVP_GEN. Select this row, and choose Copy.
3. In the next screen, deselect all the form and list UIBBs that are auto-selected for copy from the existing configuration. These aren't needed, because you're creating the new UI configuration with your own Airline Form UIBB created previously.
4. Click on Change Affixes to change the prefix and suffix of the target configuration IDs. In this example, the prefix used is Za, which is the name of the data model, and the suffix entered is 10.
5. Choose Start Deep-Copy to create the new application configuration and UI configuration. Choose the newly created application configuration ZA_USMD_SF_OVP_CARR_10, and set its application parameter Usmd_Otc to the BO Type of the Type 1 Entity Carr. In this example, the Usmd_Otc parameter is set to value Z_Za.
6. Display the UI configuration ZA_USMD_SF_CARR_OVP_10 after it has been created.
7. To add the new Airline Form UIBB component ZA_AIRLINE_FORM02 to it, choose UIBB • Form component. In the Wire Schema tab, select the Connector class CL_MDG_BS_CONNECTOR_BOL_CR_REL.
8. Save the configuration.

Please see Figure 11.12.

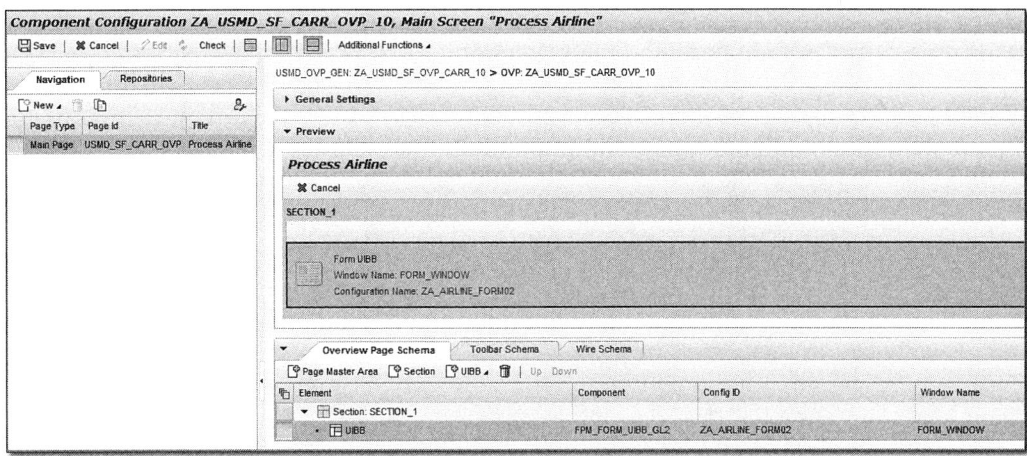

Figure 11.12 Copying Airline Form UIBB into the Existing UI Configuration

Create Communicator Settings

The SAP MDG communicator is part of the SAP MDG framework. It has the overall responsibility for the change request process and controls the availability of the change request actions, which are represented as buttons on the global toolbar. You connect your UI configuration to the SAP MDG Communicator to ensure that you can dynamically integrate the SAP MDG change request UIBB and its wiring into your application.

Open the Web Dynpro component MDG_BS_GOV_COMMUNICATOR, and create a new component configuration for it. While doing this, it's important to give the new component configuration for the communicator setting the same name as the Web Dynpro application configuration of your existing UI configuration (in this case, ZA_USMD_SF_OVP_CARR_10).

In the component configuration ZA_USMD_SF_OVP_CARR_10, maintain the attributes for the element CRWIRES as shown in Figure 11.13. Enter the same page ID of your main page as entered for the UI configuration in Figure 11.12, and define the relevant wiring information, including the connector class and the source configuration name.

This completes the UI configuration for the new airline change request UI.

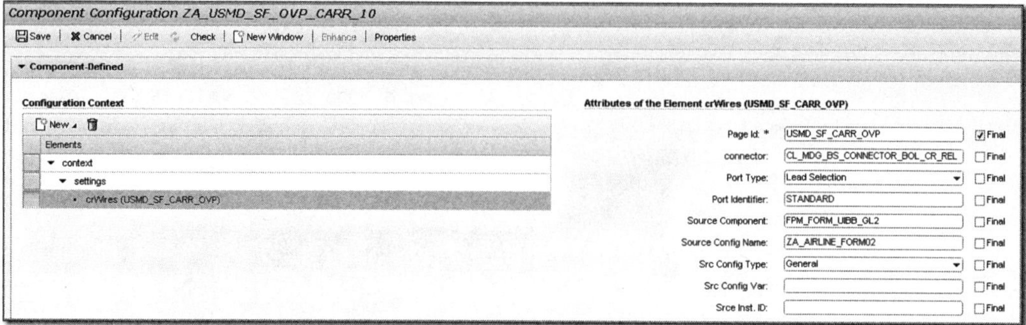

Figure 11.13 Create SAP MDG Communicator Settings

11.3.3 Create a Change Request Process

Now that the data model and UI configuration have been created, we need to define a change process for the maintenance of the airline with an SAP MDG change request. The definition of the change process consists of the following:

- Submission of request for changes to the airline data.
- Processing by a data expert to enhance the airline data.
- Final check by an approver.
- Revision potential if the approver rejects and sends the request back to the initiator.

We begin by creating a change request type that will be linked to an SAP Business Workflow template (described in more detail in Section 11.4):

1. Access the customizing activity for creating a change request type, which can be found at General Settings • Process Modeling • Change Requests • Create Change Request Type.
2. Create a change request type ZACRTYP. Name the new change request type ZA Airline (Single). A new change request type is created for data model ZA using this customizing activity as shown in Figure 11.14.
3. Enter "CARR" in the Main Entity Type column, and enter "WS75700040" under Workflow.

New Entries: Overview of Added Entries

Dialog Structure
- Type of Change Request
  - Entity Types
    - Scope on Entity Ty
  - Business Activities
  - Service Level Agreeme

Type of Change Request

Type of Chg. Request	Data Model	Description (medium text)	Objects Required	Single Object	Parallel	Main Entity Type	Workflow
ZACRTYP	ZA	ZA Airline (Single)	☐	☑	☐	CARR	WS75700040
			☐	☐	☐		
			☐	☐	☐		

Figure 11.14 Create Change Request Type

Navigate to the customizing activity, General Settings • Process Modeling • Change Requests • Configure Properties of Change Request Step. Select your change request type, and go to User Interface per Change Request Step. Enter the UI application name and configuration ID as shown in Figure 11.15.

Change View "User Interface per Change Request Step": Overview

Dialog Structure
- Type of Change Request
  - Change Request Step
    - Enhancements and Checks per Change Re
    - Entity Types per Change Request Step
      - Attributes per Change Request Step
  - User Interface per Change Request Step

Type of Chg. Request: ZACRTYP

User Interface per Change Request Step

Step	UI Application Name	Configuration ID	Highlight Changes
00	USMD_OVP_GEN	ZA_USMD_SF_OVP_CARR_10	☐
01	USMD_OVP_GEN	ZA_USMD_SF_OVP_CARR_10	☐
02	USMD_OVP_GEN	ZA_USMD_SF_OVP_CARR_10	☐
03	USMD_OVP_GEN	ZA_USMD_SF_OVP_CARR_10	☐

Figure 11.15 Assign the User Interface to the Change Request Step

11.3.4 Assign Processors to the Workflow

The next step to configure the airline object in SAP MDG is to assign processors to workflow steps. Navigate to the customizing activity, General Settings • Process Modeling • Workflow • Other MDG Workflows • Assign Processor to Workflow Step Number (Simple Workflow), as shown in Figure 11.16.

New Entries: Overview of Added Entries

Assignment of Processors to Workflow Step Number

Type of Chg. Request	Step	Description (medium)	Ob	Agent ID	Complete name
ZACRTYP	0	Submission	US	SINHAAK	Akshay Sinha
ZACRTYP	1	Processing	US	SINHAAK	Akshay Sinha
ZACRTYP	2	Final Check	US	SINHAAK	Akshay Sinha
ZACRTYP	3	Revision	US	SINHAAK	Akshay Sinha

Figure 11.16 Assign Processors to Workflow Steps

In Figure 11.16, notice that there are four steps and that for this example, we assigned the same user ID to all steps. You may also choose to assign these to a position, job, or organizational unit.

Standard Workflow versus Rules-Based Workflow

This example uses a standard workflow, which always includes steps for reviewing, approving, and revising the change request. In this example, a person, job, or organizational unit is assigned as a processor. Later, you'll learn about using a rules-based workflow, which extends the standard delivered workflow.

This completes the configuration for the airline object. You can now test the creation of the airline in SAP MDG using the change request type defined previously, which is discussed next.

11.3.5 Test the New Airline Change Request User Interface

For testing, you can launch the new AIRLINE change request UI from the SAP MDG generic search application USMD_SEARCH. Figure 11.17 shows how the newly created AIRLINE change request UI looks.

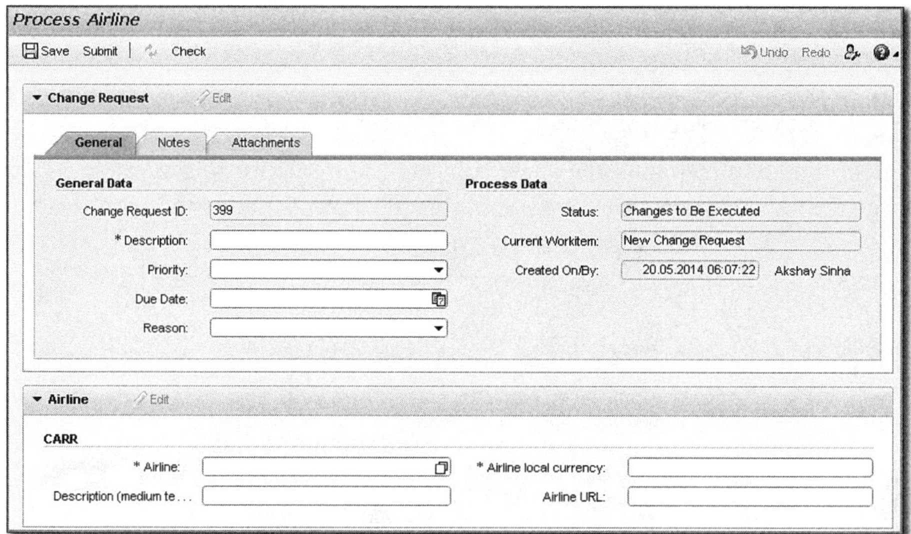

Figure 11.17 Airline Change Request UI

Notice that the Airline UIBB (created in the previous sections) appears below the CHANGE REQUEST UIBB in the newly created UI. You may now provide values for the new airline code to create airline local currency, description, and airline URL, and then submit the form to create a change request in SAP MDG. This change request is routed to the inbox of the processing agent. The various steps to process this change request can now be performed, thereby completing the process of governance for the airline master data change request.

Approval or rejection of the change request can be performed on the UI shown in Figure 11.18. The processor may also navigate to the WORKFLOW LOG or the CHANGE DOCUMENTS from this screen to know more about this change request. After approval, the new airline code is created in the active area and is ready for use by business processes.

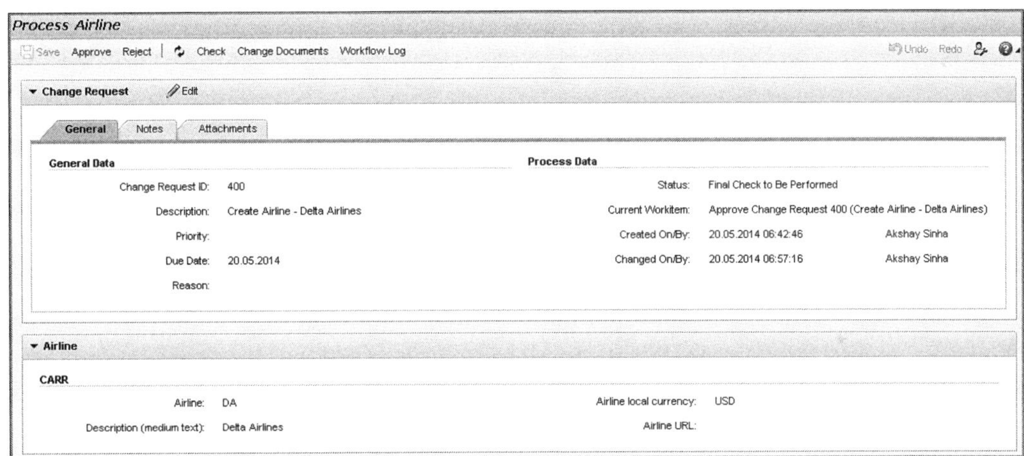

Figure 11.18 Approve/Reject Change Request

11.4 Rules-Based Workflows in SAP Master Data Governance

This section provides an overview of how SAP MDG uses SAP Business Workflow and BRFplus for workflows that are dynamically controlled at runtime by decisions that are based on rules.

Details of SAP Business Workflow and BRFplus

This section only provides a general overview of SAP Business Workflow and BRFplus. If you would like to know more about these solutions, refer to the following SAP books:

- *Practical Workflow for SAP*, third edition (Jocelyn Dart, Sue Keohan, and Alan Rickayzen, SAP PRESS, 2014); see the dedicated chapter on SAP MDG
- *BRFplus—Business Rule Management for ABAP Applications* (Thomas Albrecht, Carsten Ziegler, SAP PRESS, 2011)

Workflows are critical to managing master data, because without the right level of process control, the management of master data is often completely unstructured and neither guided nor controlled. Workflows guide users through the master data process, help monitor the progress, and provide governance. Change processing and issue resolution, integrated with workflow, keeps data, process, and issue resolution in one place. Expensive, hard-coded, inflexible, semi-automated processes can be replaced by a flexible process, especially if the workflow is based on integrated rules management.

SAP MDG provides a predefined set of default workflows for master data governance processes. These processes and roles can be adapted and tailored based on customer needs, and can span the enterprise to accommodate your master data governance requirements.

This section uses a concrete example based on a default workflow process that's provided by SAP for material governance. This section also includes information about how to get started with the required SAP MDG-specific configuration.

11.4.1 Classic Workflow and Rules-Based Workflow Using SAP Business Workflow and BRFplus

SAP MDG allows companies to use workflow in two flavors. One option is to use traditional SAP Business Workflow and to model all workflow branches for one governance process in the workflow modeling environment. The other option is to combine SAP Business Workflow with the capabilities of BRFplus. Using BRFplus enables the use of one generic workflow template with parallel branches across all processes. At runtime, BRFplus defines which of the parallel branches to execute. The runtime decisions happen iteratively based on the current state of the workflow, the status of the change request, and user interactions. The flow is determined by decision tables. This combination of SAP Business Workflow and BRFplus is often referred to as *rules-based workflow*.

Rules-based workflow is a good match for master data governance processes, because a rules-based workflow provides flexible processing and easy configuration. The following are typical requirements for master data governance processes that require this flexibility and ease of configuration:

- Adding or removing a workflow step (e.g., adding an additional approval or notification step)
- Changing the order of workflow steps (e.g., moving an approval step before a special data enhancement step to avoid detailed work on approved requests)
- Skipping workflow steps based on certain rules (e.g., a Material Create request coming from an SAP Product Lifecycle Management (PLM) system may skip an approval step)
- Routing rules based on the change request type (e.g., regional data enhancements/approvals)
- Routing rules based on the content of the master data (e.g., secondary approval for special customer payment terms)

These configurations are usually driven by business users who want to make changes to the master data governance processes over time. The combination of SAP Business Workflow and BRFplus fulfills the requirement for a powerful yet easily configurable governance process.

SAP Business Workflow is the core technical engine used to run the process. It's used to trigger the execution and distribution of the steps of the workflow. BRFplus is the coordinator and decision maker for every step of the workflow. Before executing the next step, the rules engine determines the next step and the next processor (who should perform the step, whether human or the system).

To allow for this flexibility, the generic workflow template for rules-based workflows in SAP MDG has been designed as shown in Figure 11.19. The process starts when a change request is created. At that time, some preparation is done based on the change request type and other variables. Then the decision tables are read. Based on the decision tables, a workflow task is created using the parallel processing branch, and it's either executed as a backend process activity (executed automatically) or sent to a user for execution. After one step is completed, the rules engine is used to determine the next step. This happens iteratively until the process is completed, cancelled, or requires error handling.

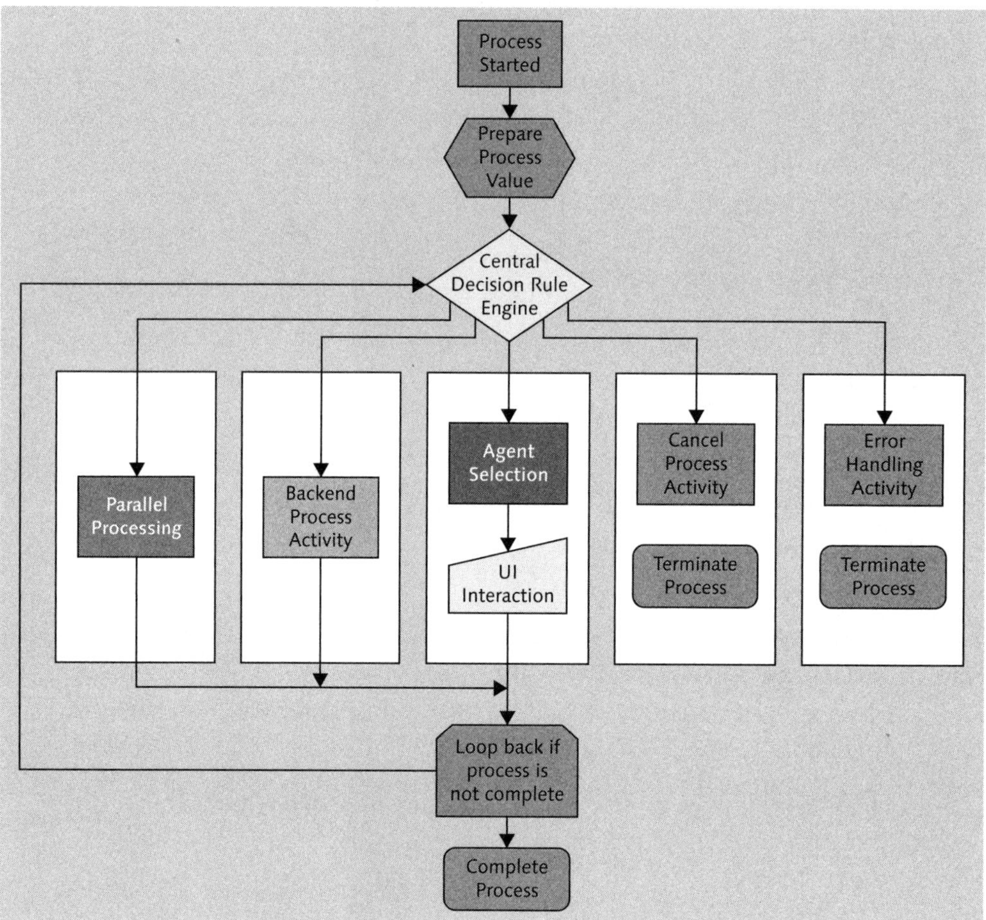

Figure 11.19 Flow of Rules-Based Workflow

The rules engine requires several inputs for the decisions:

- **Object type and request type**
  For example: Object type MATERIAL, request type CREATE or CHANGE.
- **Request status**
  For example: TO BE CONSIDERED AND APPROVED, CHANGES TO BE EXECUTED, or TO BE REVISED.

- **Previous step and rule/role**
  For example: The previous step was requested by the data steward, or the previous step was rejected by the plant manager.
- **Data entered in the request**
  The data includes attributes that can be used for routing tasks to users, for example, MATERIAL TYPE or MRP CONTROLLER.
- **Initiator**
  This is the user who initiated the request.
- **User action**
  For example: APPROVE, REJECT, or FINALIZE PROCESSING.

All design-time configuration of the process is reflected in BRFplus decision tables, which can be maintained by nontechnical users. At runtime, each process loops back to the rules engine to decide on the next step. The content maintained in the decision tables reflects your governance process.

Three decision tables are available:

- Single-value decision table (DT_SINGLE_VAL_<CR_type>)
- User agent decision table (DT_USER_AGT_GRP_<CR_type>)
- Nonuser agent decision table (DT_USER_AGT_GRP_<CR_type>)

It's critical to understand these three tables and how they work together, because all three are required for decision processing in BRFplus. The text in parentheses in the table names is the technical name of the table. The appendage of <CR_type> indicates that there's a different set of tables for each change request type. This is important because the workflow template is common across all change requests. The same workflow leverages the rules for all change request types. It's the content of the decision tables for each change request type (CR_type) that differentiates one governance scenario from another. For example, change request type MAT01 is a change request type to create a material. Change request type MAT06 is a change request type to mark a material for deletion. The decision table is related to the change request type; for example, DT_SINGLE_VAL_MAT01 has the single-value decisions for the material creation process. Decision table DT_SINGLE_VAL_MAT06 has the single decision values for the mark material for deletion change request.

Each of the three decision tables will now be discussed in more detail.

Single-Value Decision Table or DT_SINGLE_VAL_<CR Type>

The single-value decision table reflects the governance process flow. The combination of previous step and previous action determine the next step and the next change request status. Examples of the change request status include CHANGES TO BE EXECUTED, FINAL CHECK APPROVED, and TO BE REVISED.

The single-value decision table also holds the link between the three tables, which is referred to as a *condition alias*. Each condition alias needs at least one processor. The processor can be a person, or it can be the system (meaning the next step will be processed automatically with no human interaction required). For each condition alias, there needs to be a related entry in one of the other decision tables. For condition aliases requiring a person, the link is in the user agent decision table. For condition aliases pointing to an automated step, the link is in the nonuser agent decision table.

User Agent Decision Table or DT_USER_AGT_GRP_<CR_Type>

The user agent decision table holds the users and the type of steps they execute. The user can be defined as an actual user ID, a role, or an organizational unit. Examples include "data stewards approve," "plant managers revise," or "Bob checks the data." In this case, "data steward" and "plant manager" could be positions in the organizational structure or a role such as an authorization role. And Bob, of course, is an actual person.

The agents are assigned to the following step types: CHECK, APPROVE, PROCESS, REVISE, and ACTIVATE. In the example where data stewards approve, the step type APPROVE is assigned to the data steward role.

This means that a condition alias in the single-value decision table could point to a processor as a data steward. The user agent decision table indicates that the data steward is a specific role and that data stewards approve. The result is that users with the role data steward receive an approval task. Likewise, if the condition alias has Bob as a processor, then the user agent decision table knows that Bob is a specific user ID, and he will receive a task to check data.

Nonuser Agent Decision Table or DT_NON_USER_AGT_GRP_<CR_Type>

Just as the user agent decision table links the user to the step type, the nonuser agent decision table links the automatic steps (not requiring user action) to the type of action that needs to be performed. In this case, the action is referred to as a process pattern. Process patterns are abstractions of business activities. Some examples of process patterns include the following:

- Background processing pattern (call of a service, function, etc.)
- Error-handling pattern
- Notification pattern (sending a notification to a user or system)

The configuration of the rules content via the three tables can be done by uploading Excel files. This allows a business user to work in a known environment rather than learning a new UI to configure a master data governance process. A summary of how the decision tables build the process workflow is shown in Figure 11.20.

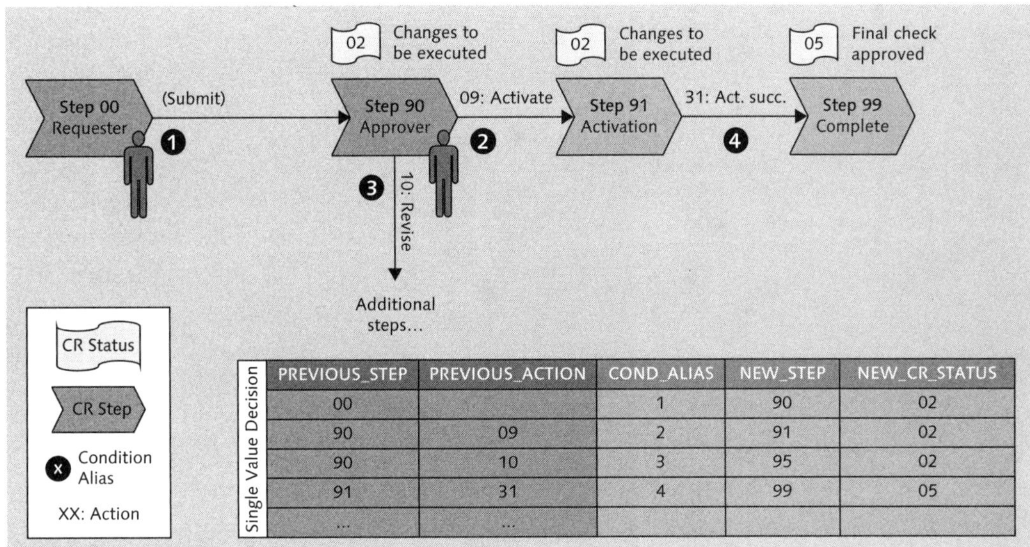

PREVIOUS_STEP	PREVIOUS_ACTION	COND_ALIAS	NEW_STEP	NEW_CR_STATUS
00		1	90	02
90	09	2	91	02
90	10	3	95	02
91	31	4	99	05
...	...			

Figure 11.20 Example Process Flow Defined by Excel Tables

Figure 11.20 shows an example of the Excel process that's used to define a workflow and update the single-value decision table. In the table shown in Figure 11.20, the previous step is 00, there is no previous action, the condition alias is 1, the new step is 90 (which is FINAL CHECK, explained in the next section), and the new change request status is 02. This all means that in the single-value decision table, after step 00, the next step should be step 90, and the new change request status should be 02. Note in the workflow that step 90 is APPROVE and change request status 02 is CHANGES TO BE EXECUTED. In the second row, if the previous step is 90, which is the APPROVE step, and the previous action is 09, which is ACTIVATE, then the next step should be 91, which is the activation of the change request. In the third row, if the previous action is 10 (action 10 is SEND FOR REVISION), then the next step is 95 (not shown in the figure, but it's a step to REVISE). By configuring the previous step and next step in the Excel spreadsheet, the user can configure the workflow. This means that users can change the flow of the workflow with less IT involvement.

As an example of changing the flow without IT involvement, let's say that in Figure 11.20, you want to add an additional expert to review the material. Assuming that there is a step type and user assigned for this additional review step in the user agent decision table (e.g., check by MRP controller), you just need to update the Excel spreadsheet or update the single-value decision table, as shown in Figure 11.21.

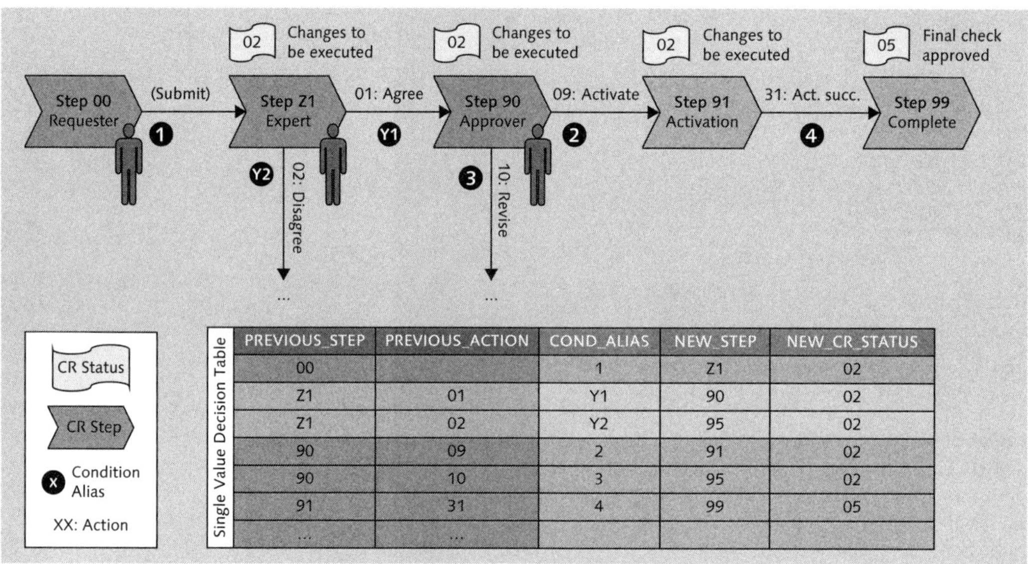

PREVIOUS_STEP	PREVIOUS_ACTION	COND_ALIAS	NEW_STEP	NEW_CR_STATUS
00		1	Z1	02
Z1	01	Y1	90	02
Z1	02	Y2	95	02
90	09	2	91	02
90	10	3	95	02
91	31	4	99	05
...	...			

Figure 11.21 Enhance Process Flow

Figure 11.21 shows new step Z1, previous action 01, and condition alias Y1. Assuming Y1 is defined in the user agent table to check by the MRP controller, just by adding Z1 to the single-value decision table or the Excel spreadsheet, the workflow is enhanced with a new step for review. Remember that the condition alias will link Z1 and 01 to the user agent table for check by the MRP controller. If the step Z1 has an action of 02, which is DISAGREE (actions are described in the next section), then the next step is now different, and the user involved is different as well.

11.4.2 Designing Your First Rules-Based Workflow in SAP Master Data Governance

This section explains the most important steps involved in getting started with the configuration of your own rules-based workflow. A more detailed step-by-step process is included in the online help and guides available (search for "Extensibility Options for SAP Master Data Governance" on the SAP Community Network). This section provides an overview of the key areas involved in the creation of your own rules-based workflow in SAP MDG.

Before You Start, Configure Basic Workflow Settings

Before using SAP Business Workflow or a rules-based workflow, some configuration is required in the IMG. This includes basic configuration of SAP Business Workflow and extended configuration of SAP MDG. These settings can be found under SAP NETWEAVER • APPLICATION SERVER • BUSINESS MANAGEMENT • SAP BUSINESS WORKFLOW, and in the SAP MDG customizing section, GENERAL SETTINGS • PROCESS MODELING • WORKFLOW.

Before designing your own rules-based workflow, you need to understand a couple of basics. From the preceding discussion, you know that the design of a rules-based workflow requires building the three decision tables: single value, user agent, and nonuser agent. The update to these tables determines the process, actions allowed, step types, and agents. You also must understand the following:

- There are specific step types and actions that you'll use to design your rules-based process. The allowed step types and actions are listed in the following section.
- Each change request type has a defined set of change request steps and numbers associated with each step.

Next, we discuss step types/actions and change request types in more detail.

Step Types and Actions

The user agent decision table contains the users and the step types they can execute. In the earlier example, the data stewards could approve, where APPROVE was the step type defined for the data steward in the user agent decision table. Examples of step types and actions are provided in Figure 11.22.

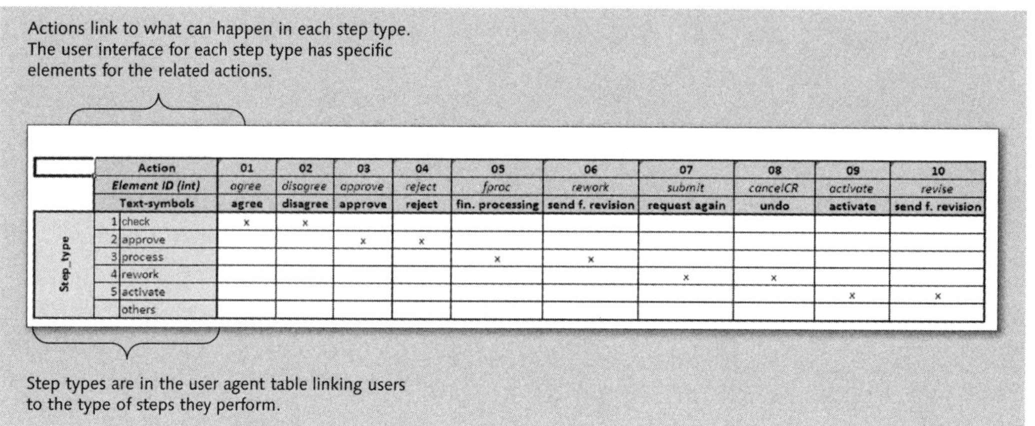
Actions link to what can happen in each step type. The user interface for each step type has specific elements for the related actions.
Step types are in the user agent table linking users to the type of steps they perform.

	Action	01	02	03	04	05	06	07	08	09	10
	Element ID (int)	*agree*	*disagree*	*approve*	*reject*	*fproc*	*rework*	*submit*	*cancelCR*	*activate*	*revise*
	Text-symbols	**agree**	**disagree**	**approve**	**reject**	**fin. processing**	**send f. revision**	**request again**	**undo**	**activate**	**send f. revision**
Step_type	1 check	x	x								
	2 approve			x	x						
	3 process					x	x				
	4 rework							x	x		
	5 activate									x	x
	others										

Figure 11.22 Step Types, Actions, and User Interface

The step types are used in the user agent decision table. The actions are used in the PREVIOUS ACTION column of the single-value decision table. Back in Figure 11.20 and Figure 11.21, the actions shown are 09, 10, and 31. In Figure 11.22, you can see that 09 means Activate, and 10 means Send for Revision. Action 31 (not shown in the table) is the outcome of an automated step and stands for Activation Successful.

Each of the step types determines the UI and the related action options the users will have. For example, for step type 1 (CHECK), the UI gives the user two options: Agree and Disagree. For step type 2 (Approve), the user can approve or reject. For step type 5 (Activate), the user can activate or send for revision. When you configure the step types, you're actually configuring the UI options for the user.

Change Request Type and Change Request Steps

It's also important that you know the change request steps allowed for each change request. Table 11.2 shows an example for the change request type Create Material (MAT01).

Type of Change Request	Change Request Step	Description
MAT01 (create material)	00	Processing
MAT01	90	Final check
MAT01	91	Activation
MAT01	92	Revision
MAT01	93	Validation
MAT01	95	Revision processing

Table 11.2 Material Change Request Step

Table 11.2 shows that for change request type MAT01 (Create Material), the allowed steps are 00, 90, 91, and so on. The table indicates that 90 means Final Check and 91 means Activation. These steps are delivered by SAP, are used for configuring the single-value decision table, and used in BRFplus to configure the workflow (as shown in Figure 11.20 and Figure 11.21).

If you have a customer-defined change request (such as the request for new airlines described in Section 11.3), you'll define which change request steps you want for your change request. In the configuration for SAP MDG, you'll add entries similar to those shown in Table 11.2 for your change request type.

Now that you understand the major configuration steps involved, you can begin to design your own rules-based workflow. Following are the steps that need to be performed:

1. Design the flow, and decide which steps and loops are needed. This should be done with the data stewards and business experts who know what is needed for a particular change request type.
2. Decide which step types are needed, understanding that each step type relates to the options the users will have (Approve, Reject, Activate, etc.).
3. Enhance the flow diagram with the resulting actions of each step. This is where you start to tie in the numbers. So if a resulting action is Send Back for Revision, this is mapped to action 10.
4. Enhance the flow diagram with the condition alias. Remember that the condition alias defines who will perform the action by linking to the other decision tables.

5. Enhance the flow diagram with change request statuses such as To Be Considered and Approved, Changes to Be Executed, or To Be Revised.
6. Build the decision tables in SAP MDG configuration (single-value decision table, user agent table, and nonuser agent table). The decision tables can also be built with the Excel upload.

> **Note**
>
> For more details on workflow configuration, refer to the online help and guides available in the SAP MDG extensibility center on the SAP Community Network.

11.5 NeedsEIM Inc.: Master Data Remediation

Now that you have a better understanding of SAP MDG and have seen how it works, we'll apply the capabilities of SAP MDG to NeedsEIM Inc. (introduced in Chapter 1).

Cleansing supplier master data is one of the requirements outlined by the procurement business function at NeedsEIM Inc. The problem is that until now, supplier naming in this organization has been all over the board, with no rules in place. This has led to dissatisfaction on the part of the suppliers, as their names and general information are incorrectly printed in correspondence. Moreover, payments to suppliers have failed in the past because the supplier name wasn't legally correct. NeedsEIM Inc. wants to correct the supplier data as part of an overall effort to reduce the number of total suppliers and increase the percentage of discounts the company receives from its top-tier suppliers. To overcome these issues, a new process has been introduced at NeedsEIM Inc. to standardize the names of all new and existing suppliers.

One of the rules that's part of this new process is that supplier names may not contain special characters. Therefore, the supplier master data needs to be cleaned up by removing any special characters used in the name fields. The changed names will have to be approved before they can be used in any business transaction. Therefore, this activity not only needs a large number of master data changes, but also collaboration between the data specialist, who is responsible for making the name changes, and the approver. A combination of Information Steward and SAP MDG provides a perfect solution for this problem.

Figure 11.23 shows how Information Steward can be integrated with SAP MDG. Information Steward sits on top of Data Services and provides an end-user environment for visualizing data quality analysis results. The core of Information Steward is a set of rules defined by the user. Information can be exported from a master data source and be imported into Information Steward. After this import, the information can be checked for compliance against the set of rules defined by the user. The integration of SAP MDG and Information Steward is available as a rapid-deployment solution (SAP Rapid Deployment solutions were introduced in Chapter 5).

At NeedsEIM Inc., the source of this master data is the vendor master table. Data is exported from this table, imported into Information Steward, and matched against a set of user-defined rules.

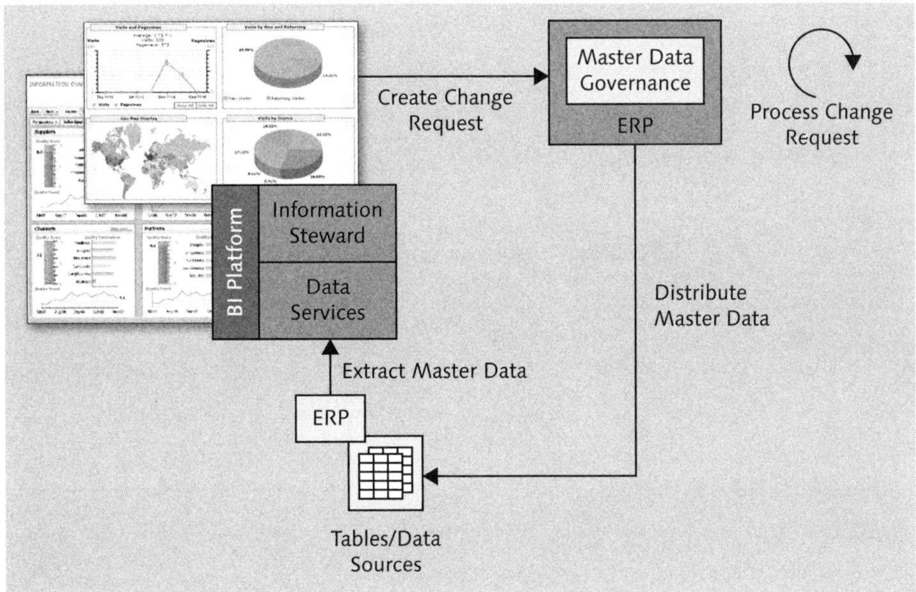

Figure 11.23 Integration of Information Steward with SAP MDG

The result of the data quality evaluation is available as a scorecard in Information Steward. A *scorecard* is an aggregation over several quality dimensions. One quality dimension consists of one or more validation rules. A failed record database table holds information about which records failed which rules. This is basically a list of vendor numbers.

For the records that don't comply with a validation rule, a change request can be created directly in SAP MDG. The change request is processed in SAP MDG, and during this period, the changes are stored in the staging area, as explained earlier. After approval, the changes are activated and are reflected back into the vendor master table. Upon looking at the updated data in Information Steward, it's possible to see the data quality improvements in the dashboard.

Figure 11.24 shows a data quality work center in SAP MDG. At the top of Figure 11.24 are the validation rules (discussed in Chapter 10). The failed records for each validation rule can be viewed in the table at the bottom. The validation rule and failed record information is read from Information Steward using a web service call. The CREATE CHANGE REQUEST button above the failed records enables the creation of a change request in SAP MDG for one or more selected records.

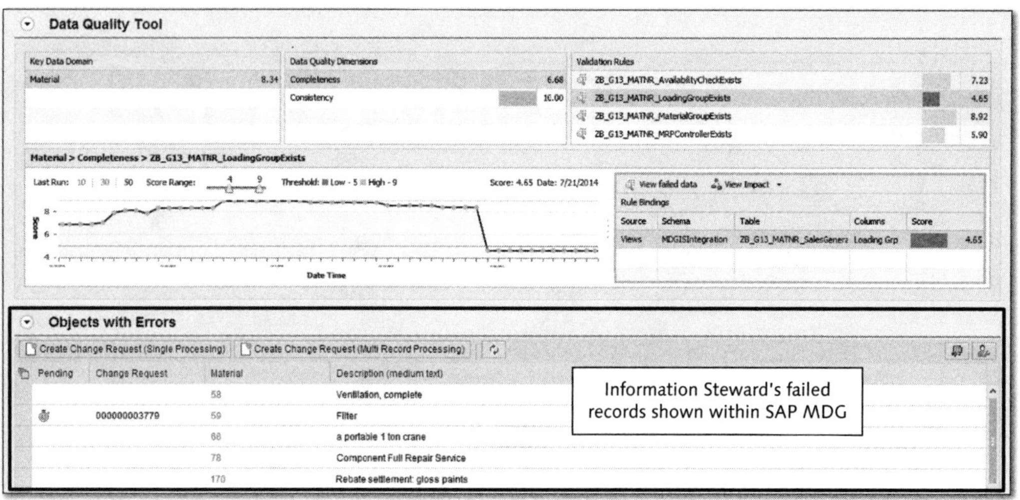

Figure 11.24 Data Quality Work Center in SAP MDG

At this point, the failed records are stored in SAP MDG, which provides many options for interacting directly with the SAP MDG APIs. For each failed record, you can see whether it's a part of another change request and, if so, what the status of that change request is. What follows is a normal change request approval workflow process, at the end of which corrected data becomes available in the active area. Thus, using this technique, remediation of the supplier master data at NeedsEIM Inc. can be performed efficiently.

11.6 Summary

This chapter covered SAP MDG and how it provides centralized governance for selected master data domains (e.g., supplier, material, customer, and financials). In addition to the standard master data domains, this chapter also discussed how you can extend SAP MDG for custom-defined objects. You also learned how SAP MDG provides a very flexible workflow that can easily be adapted to business needs, as well as how the combination of Information Steward and SAP MDG supports the clean-up of existing master data. For all new master data not yet in the system, SAP MDG ensures that the data is entered correctly during the creation process. To learn more about SAP MDG, see the Master Data Governance site on the SAP Community Network.

The next chapter discusses data archiving, retention management, and system decommissioning available with SAP Information Lifecycle Management.

In this chapter, you'll learn how to leverage SAP solutions for information lifecycle management (ILM) to establish a holistic ILM strategy for your organization that covers the entire information universe: structured and unstructured content, SAP and non-SAP systems, and live and legacy systems.

12 SAP Information Lifecycle Management

Saying that we're living in an information age or information society may sound like a cliché, but it's absolutely true. And it becomes more obvious every day as the influx of information, particularly that companies have to deal with, increases at an amazing speed. Therefore, every organization needs a strategy to cope with the challenges of managing the lifecycle of its business information.

Such an information lifecycle management (ILM) strategy must be holistic in a way that takes into account several factors, such as managing information from both live and legacy systems, and covering both structured and unstructured information. And, of course, it must be compliant with legal retention requirements.

SAP solutions for information lifecycle management support you in building a holistic ILM strategy that covers the entire spectrum of information management: information of structured and unstructured types, from live and legacy systems, and from SAP and non-SAP systems. SAP therefore truly considers itself a "one-stop shop" for companies that are seeking to establish a holistic ILM solution for their business.

SAP Information Lifecycle Management (SAP ILM) contains the following capabilities:

- **Retention management**
  Enables you to set retention rules and retain business records for different periods of time according to policy or legal requirements. This holds true for all previously mentioned information types and systems. You also can collect and preserve records related to ongoing legal cases.

- **System decommissioning**
  Supports the decommissioning of legacy systems. This includes the transfer of data from the legacy system to the retention warehouse and reporting on this data using SAP Business Warehouse (SAP BW) or local reporting. Retention management actions can also be applied to legacy data residing in the retention warehouse.

In addition to the core capabilities of retention management and system decommissioning included in SAP ILM, it also uses the following products within the retention management and system decommissioning capabilities:

- **SAP Data Services (hereafter Data Services)**
  Data Services enables the integration, transformation, improvement, and delivery of trusted data to support critical business processes and decisions. In a system decommissioning scenario, this product also provides the required extraction, transformation, and loading (ETL) capabilities for decommissioning non-SAP systems.
- **SAP Archiving by OpenText**
  SAP Archiving by OpenText provides archiving functionality for the storage of data and documents via SAP ArchiveLink. The product contains the OpenText Enterprise Library, which implements the web-based Distributed Authoring and Versioning (WebDAV) interface of SAP ILM and secures the retention of data files stored with SAP ILM.
- **SAP Document Access by OpenText**
  SAP Document Access by OpenText is an Enterprise Content Management (ECM) solution that provides easy access to SAP data, such as archive files and SAP ArchiveLink documents for both live and legacy content. It also includes basic extended content management functions, such as scanning, optical character recognition (OCR), and bar-coding.
- **SAP LT Replication Server (hereafter SAP LT)**
  SAP LT is the real-time replication tool for most data provisioning scenarios for SAP HANA. As a cornerstone in most SAP HANA landscapes, it has evolved to become a proven replication technology that can also be used beside SAP HANA (e.g., SAP BW). In SAP ILM scenarios, it's used to extract retention-relevant data from systems to be retired and transfer to the SAP ILM retention warehouse.

Note on Terminology

SAP ILM is the core component in the suite of SAP solutions for information lifecycle management. Therefore, in this chapter, most processes and examples refer to this solution.

In this chapter, we'll provide more insight into how to use the SAP solutions for information lifecycle management to implement a solid ILM strategy and meet your ILM goals. Specifically, we discuss the history of SAP ILM, offer a brief general introduction to the tool, and then take a closer look at managing the information lifecycle in your SAP systems, both for legacy systems and during a system decommissioning.

Given the limited space available in this book, this chapter can only provide you with a brief overview of the SAP solutions for ILM. For more in-depth information, you can refer to the official SAP ILM documentation on the SAP Help Portal, or attend the training course BIT665.

Note on Versions

The information, screenshots, and examples provided in this chapter are mostly based on SAP ILM 7.40, delivered with SAP NetWeaver 7.40 and SAP ERP 6.0 EHP7. You can also use previous versions of SAP ILM if you're on the following releases: SAP NetWeaver 7.0 EHP3/SAP ERP 6.0 EHP6 and SAP NetWeaver 7.0 EHP2/SAP ERP 6.0 EHP5.

12.1 The Basics of Information Lifecycle Management

Let's discuss what ILM means and then consider why it's needed. Over the past few years, ILM has transformed from being a mere buzzword to representing a solid strategy and concept with a clear definition that most agree upon. According to the definition at SAP today, *information lifecycle management* is comprised of the policies, processes, practices, and tools used to align the business value of information with the most appropriate and cost-effective IT infrastructure from the time information is created through its final destruction. This definition reflects an application-centric, rather than technology-centric, approach.

The ILM approach wasn't is a result of various developments and global trends over the past decade (e.g., the high cost of data management, increased legal risks associated with information management, and poor system usage and performance). The drivers that make ILM necessary can be grouped into two categories: external drivers and internal drivers. We discuss both of these next.

12.1.1 External Drivers

Due to disasters such as 9/11 and economic scandals such as Enron and WorldCom, the number of laws and regulations governing the retention of information has increased dramatically on a worldwide scale—and so have related lawsuits. This clearly shows that there is a huge demand for this kind of data handling (e.g., e-discovery and legal hold management, both features that are included in SAP ILM).

12.1.2 Internal Drivers

One of the major internal drivers can be labeled *system landscape harmonization*. In today's highly globalized economy, the number of mergers and acquisitions (M&A) increases on a worldwide scale, making it necessary for the parties involved to consolidate their IT landscape accordingly. The selling party, for example, needs to hand data pertaining to the sold business over to the buyer and—provided that all legal retention obligations are met—can then shut down the system. But system landscape harmonization isn't only about M&A, it has also to do with a company's need to reduce the complexity of its system landscape to keep it manageable.

The bottom line for all internal drivers is cost. It's a waste of money and resources to maintain systems that aren't needed for operational use and that are only accessed sporadically. Relocating retention-relevant data from old systems to a safe place and shutting down these systems for good can save companies large amounts of money in terms of hardware, energy, and personnel costs.

12.2 Overview of SAP Information Lifecycle Management

SAP ILM hasn't emerged out of the blue. Its foundation was laid years ago in close cooperation with the Americas' SAP Users' Group (ASUG). Several of the basic functions were partly designed in conjunction with the ASUG ILM Influence Council. Through this close cooperation with its customers, SAP was able to obtain specific feedback on the pain points that companies face in their ILM and legal compliance strategies. As a result, development of the new retention management and system decommissioning functions has been directly aimed at solving these pain points and has been developed with a special focus on enhancing or building on existing capabilities.

SAP ILM addresses many of the pain points associated with ILM (discussed in Section 12.1 and shown in Figure 12.1). It does this by providing adequate tools and processes that enable you to control the lifecycle of your data from the time it's created until its final destruction at the end of its life. When this data is no longer needed for daily operations, it's moved from the database to the archive to keep the database volume at a reasonable level. While the data resides in the archive, retention policies ensure that it's retained and deleted in a legally compliant way. SAP ILM also enables you to decommission obsolete systems and move retention-relevant data to the ILM retention warehouse for long-term storage.

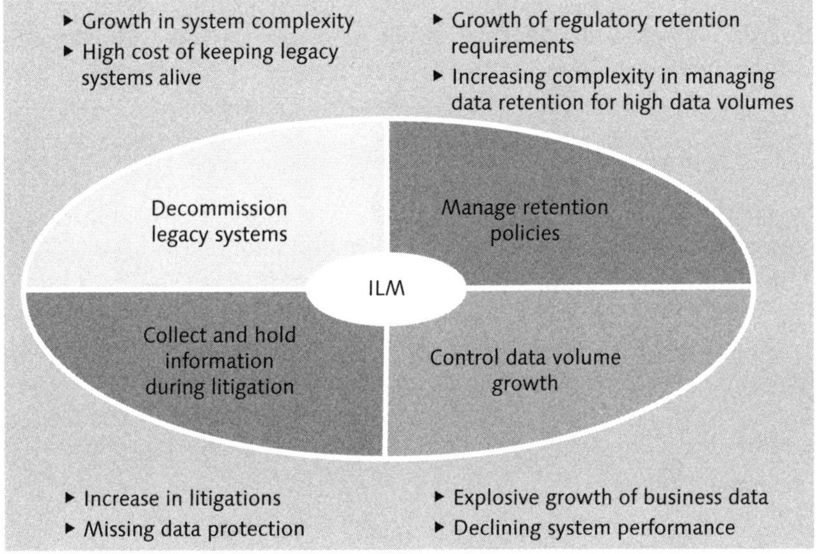

Figure 12.1 Customer Pain Points and How SAP ILM Helps

Next, we'll introduce the major capabilities that are included with SAP ILM.

12.2.1 Cornerstones of SAP ILM

SAP ILM includes the following cornerstones:

- SAP Data Archiving
- Retention management
- System decommissioning

We discuss each of these in more detail in the following subsections.

SAP Data Archiving

This cornerstone is at the heart of SAP ILM and focuses mainly on managing database volumes. SAP Data Archiving is a tried and tested standard method for relocating business-complete data from the database to the archive. With more than 1,000 archiving objects across the SAP Business Suite having been developed in the past 18 years, it's an indispensable means for fighting data growth, reducing storage costs, and ensuring the performance of applications. With SAP ILM, the classical data archiving functions have been enhanced to support new ILM requirements; for example, data destruction or the archiving of data from open business processes (snapshots, which are copies of data from the database). The archive files created as a result of an SAP ILM process have the same format as files created in classical data archiving (ADK files, see Section 12.2.2).

Retention Management

This cornerstone supports the business scenario for *end-of-life data*. It's aligned with the typical lifecycle of data in an SAP application and involves functions to control the retention of data from creation to destruction, based on policies and rules defined in SAP ILM. It also allows you to perform e-discovery actions and place legal holds on data that needs to be protected from destruction for litigation reasons.

System Decommissioning

This cornerstone focuses on the business scenario for an *end-of-life system*. Using a standardized methodology for system decommissioning, it enables you to shut down obsolete systems for good. This includes extracting retention-relevant data from the legacy system, transferring it to the ILM retention warehouse, and applying the ILM retention rules to it. And finally, it enables you to report on the retained data; for instance, during a tax audit.

12.2.2 Data Archiving Basics

As mentioned already, SAP ILM is deeply rooted in SAP Data Archiving, the de facto standard for data archiving in an SAP environment. To avoid the negative effects of large data volumes on costs, performance, and system availability, *business-complete data*—which is nonchangeable data that's no longer needed in everyday business processes—needs to be removed from the database and stored in such a way that it can be accessed in read-only mode at a later time. SAP Data Archiving is the only method supported by SAP for this process and is particularly suited for processing mass data. Before we look at the data archiving process in more detail, let's briefly define some technical terms:

- **Archiving object**
  The archiving object is a logical grouping of related business data. In other words, it contains the definition of the logical units in business processes. It also contains the programs necessary for processing the data (primarily, write and delete programs), as well as the definition of the required customizing settings. In the context of SAP ILM, the concept of archiving objects has transformed into the notion of the *ILM object*, which in most cases corresponds 100% to the underlying classical archiving object (e.g., FI_DOCUMNT).
- **Archive Development Kit (ADK)**
  The vast majority of archiving objects are based on the Archive Development Kit (ADK) technology. ADK is the fundamental technology on which SAP Data Archiving is built (for the ABAP environment). It provides the necessary runtime environment for all archiving processes and programs and is used by both SAP development and customers to develop new archiving objects. In addition, it's responsible for ensuring, for example, that data is retrieved correctly when accessed in the archive, irrespective of the application release at the time of archiving. It can handle data that's archived before and after a Unicode conversion. Other technical issues, such as the compression of the data that is archived and file handling, also fall under the responsibility of ADK.

As of SAP Web Application Server 6.40, SAP offers an additional technology that's especially designed for XML-based archiving. Both ADK-based and XML-based archiving is performed using Transaction SARA (Archive Administration). Archive Administration is the main tool that's used for most user activities in data archiving, such as scheduling write and delete jobs, building and deleting the archive index, and storing or retrieving archive files.

ILM Work Centers

As of SAP NetWeaver 7.40 SP04, you can use the new ILM work centers as a complementary or alternative tool to Transaction SARA for managing your data archiving-related SAP ILM activities. These work centers have been designed according to the latest usability guidelines, and are targeted to SAP ILM administrators who would like to use a modern, intuitive, and state of the art archiving tool for their daily work. By using the work centers, administrators have access to all related activities at one place, which makes their job more efficient.

The following work centers are available:

- **Archiving work center**
  Supports all activities around data archiving, such as scheduling and monitoring jobs; managing variants; displaying the job log, job spool, or application log; and more. The *personal work list* is the entry point for these activities. It provides a personalized view for the administrator and is fully customizable.
- **Reporting work center**
  Helps the administrator monitor table growth and track the efficiency of data archiving. For example, the administrator can determine the current size of or growth of a particular table as well as the currently largest tables or archiving objects. All statistics can be selected by time intervals, such as weeks, months, or years. Users can choose to have a graphical or tabular view of the data. These features are particularly useful for management reporting and for demonstrating the efficiency of data archiving projects.

You have two options to set up the Archiving work center and related personal work list:

- **Option 1**
  Start NetWeaver Business Client, select one of the two predefined template roles, and adapt it to your needs:
  - SAP_BC_ILM_ADMIN_RM
  - SAP_BC_ILM_ADMIN_RM_V3
- **Option 2**
  Configure the work center as a web application. To do so, define the personal work list as a favorite using the parameter `APPLID` with the value `ILM_WORKCENTER`.

The Data Lifecycle

It's important to visualize the typical lifecycle that data records follow that have been created in an SAP application. Figure 12.2 shows the lifecycle and the frequency with which SAP data is usually accessed over its lifetime.

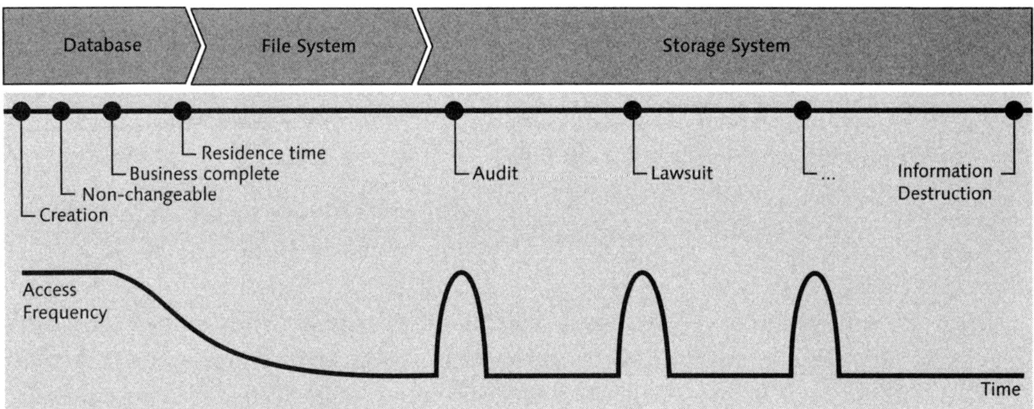

Figure 12.2 The Lifecycle of Data

When a business document, such as an accounting document or a sales order, is created in an SAP application, it's stored in the database, from where it can be accessed any time. After its creation, the document is usually accessed quite frequently; however, as the business process to which the document belongs is completed, it will be less frequently accessed, then may only require read-only access, and perhaps should eventually be destroyed. There are some important terms related to these time periods that you should understand:

- **Residence time**
  In SAP Data Archiving, this is the length of time that must be exceeded before application data can be archived.
- **Retention period**
  This is the length of time up to the point at which the data or documents can be destroyed. In SAP ILM, we also speak of minimum and maximum retention periods. The minimum retention period is the least amount of time that data has to be kept due to legal requirements before it can be destroyed. The maximum retention period is the amount of time data has to be kept before it must be destroyed due to legal or other requirements.

Residence Time versus Retention Period

In regards to the retention time, it doesn't matter where the data resides (either in the database or a storage system). Therefore, the residence time always falls within the retention period.

In the context of the entire lifecycle, data is only modifiable and relevant for operational use for a short period of time. The largest portion of the lifecycle is the retention period, during which the data can't be deleted due to legal requirements. In this period, the data is only accessed infrequently, due to a tax audit or a product liability issue, for instance.

From an EIM perspective, data also has its own lifecycle with regard to the investment required for managing the data during its life. In the on-boarding phase, right after the data is created or when it arrives in the system—for instance, due to a migration or consolidation project—the investment effort is low. Most activities are performed during the active use of the data. For example, the data is subject to data quality or data governance activities, or it's loaded into the data warehouse for reporting. After its active use, the data is only processed infrequently, mainly during archiving or retention management activities or when the system is decommissioned. (Refer back to Figure 1.2 in Chapter 1 for a visual image of this process.)

Data Archiving Process

Figure 12.3 depicts the basic process of data archiving in an SAP system, which can be divided into the following steps:

1. **Write data to archive files.**
   The data to be archived is read from the database and written sequentially to newly created archive files. This step is performed by the write program of the archiving object.
2. **Delete data from the database.**
   The delete program deletes the data from the database after it has been completely written to the archive files. To ensure the integrity of the archived data, the delete run isn't started until the created archive files have been read and confirmed.
3. **Store archive files.**
   The archive files that were created during the write phase can be moved to storage systems or to tertiary storage media. The storage phase isn't part of the actual archiving process. As an option, the user can start the storage phase before the deletion phase.

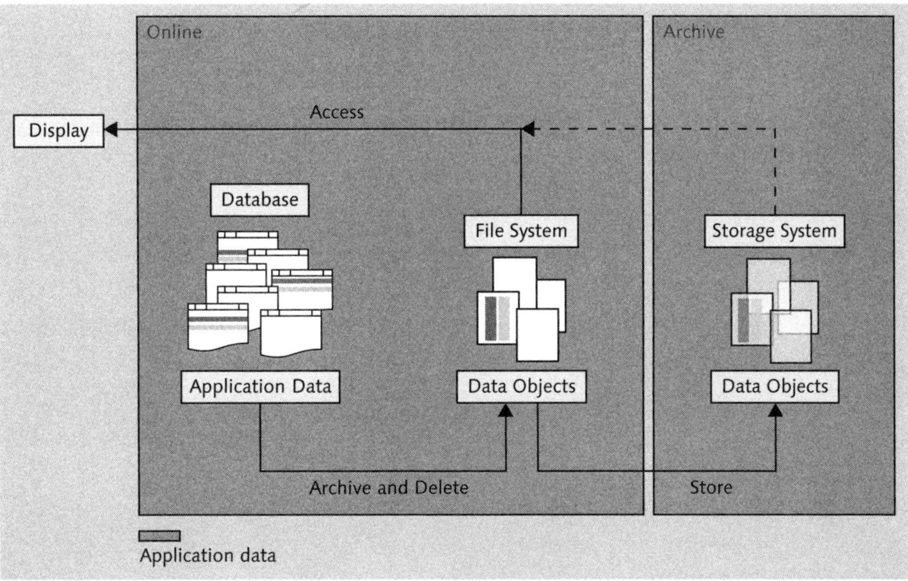

Figure 12.3 Data Archiving Process

12.2.3 ILM-Aware Storage

An ILM strategy would be incomplete without taking into account the storage of the data in a secure environment that prevents the data from being deleted or manipulated in any way. To comply with legal rules and regulations, SAP ILM uses a concept called *ILM-aware storage*.

ILM-aware storage is based on the new WebDAV interface, which, in contrast to SAP ArchiveLink, has the ability to create complex storage hierarchies and to attach properties to each node in the hierarchy and the content (archive file) itself. SAP ILM uses an ILM-enhanced WebDAV interface for information transfer between the application system and the storage system. This ensures that not only is the actual content passed to the storage, but also metadata in the form of WebDAV properties, such as expiration dates or legal holds.

For the storage system to understand and allow actions on the stored data based on the retention rules, it must be able to receive this metadata and act accordingly. If it does, it's considered ILM-aware. Storage vendors can obtain an ILM certification from SAP to show their customers that their system is ILM-aware. New certifications are currently based on version ILM-BC 3.0.

To fulfill the requirements of ILM, the storage system must meet certain criteria. On the one hand, it must ensure that the data it harbors is protected against deletion, as long as its retention time hasn't expired. On the other hand, it must support the destruction of data on request. WORM-like magnetic storage technology is particularly suited for this purpose.

From an ILM perspective, unstructured documents, such as scanned invoices, incoming or outgoing documents, or print lists, are as important as structured data because the information they contain also needs to be retained, as it complements the information included in structured data. SAP ILM supports the handling of SAP ArchiveLink documents and print lists that are stored on a storage system using the SAP ArchiveLink interface. SAP ArchiveLink documents are linked to their corresponding structured documents (the link information is stored in the TOAx tables); hence, they are often referred to as attachments. SAP ArchiveLink documents are handled in both the retention management and the system decommissioning scenarios.

While structured data (archived data) managed by SAP ILM is stored on an ILM-aware storage system, unstructured documents (such as .pdf, .tif, .jpg, etc.) are stored as before via SAP ArchiveLink. In SAP ILM, only the references to the SAP ArchiveLink documents are stored in the archive hierarchy (see Figure 12.4).

Print lists may be difficult to locate and retrieve because of the restricted set of available selection criteria. SAP Document Access by OpenText provides for easier print list retrieval through its virtual folder technology, generated indices, and the ability to add search fields and grouping definitions.

Figure 12.4 shows how structured and unstructured data is stored in separate hierarchies based on retention rules.

With the ILM-enhanced WebDAV interface, the archive files and snapshots (copies of data from the database) are stored in a hierarchy that reflects the parameters determined by the SAP ILM retention rules and that is built at the time of storage. The system distinguishes between archived data and snapshots. As you can see in Figure 12.4, archived data is stored under the node AD, whereas snapshots are stored under the node SN.

References to SAP ArchiveLink documents and print lists are stored in a "shadow" hierarchy that corresponds to that of the structured data. This way, the unstructured data is placed opposite of its corresponding structured data and inherits the same lifecycle metadata. In Figure 12.4, you can see that SAP ArchiveLink documents are stored under the node AL, and print lists are stored under the node DL (DL stands for the German word *Drucklisten*).

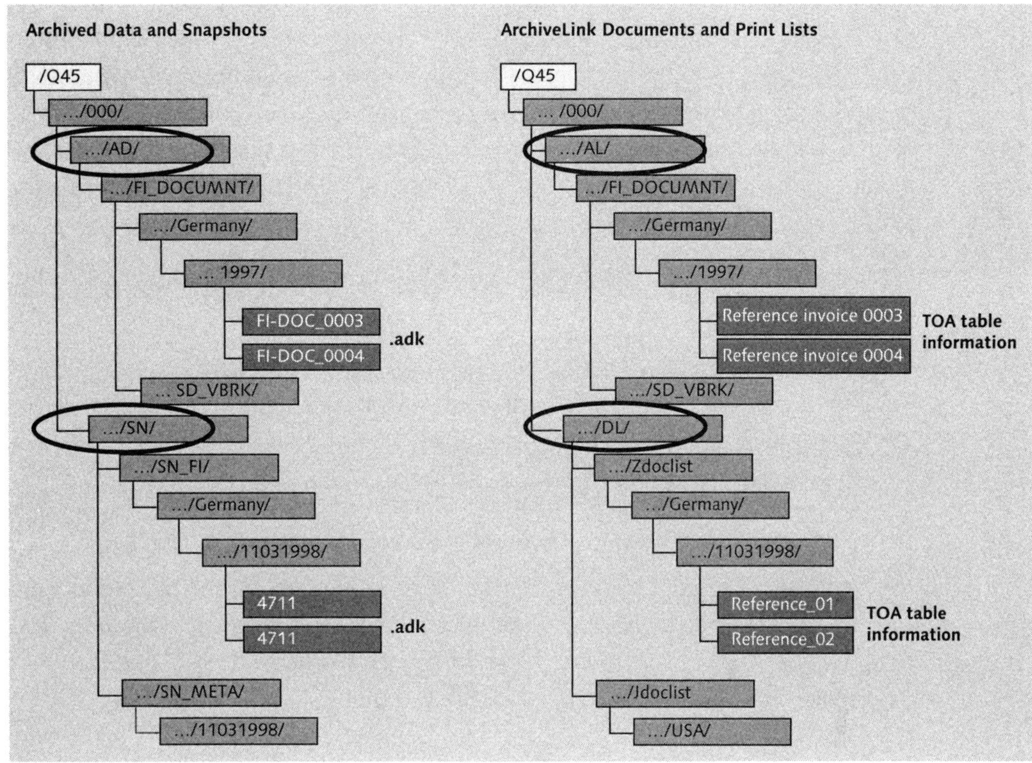

Figure 12.4 ILM-Aware Storage: Archive Hierarchy Based on Retention Rules

The archive hierarchy is built according to the rules specified in SAP ILM and the type of data archived.

SAP ILM Database Storage Option

The SAP ILM database storage option provides you with an alternative way to store your archived data in a secure environment. Instead of using a conventional third-party WORM-like or SAP ArchiveLink data store, you store the data in a SAP IQ database. In subsequent releases of this solution, other databases, such as SAP HANA, may be supported. In this new solution, the full retention management capabilities of SAP ILM, such as propagation of expiration dates, legal hold support, and rule-based destruction, have been combined with the column-based architecture of SAP IQ.

SAP IQ is a highly optimized analytical platform that's particularly designed to process and report on large amounts of data. Thanks to its columnar table design, you can benefit from high compression rates for the data, improved search capabilities, and increased performance for archiving and reporting (faster IO because the database is directly connected to the SAP application system, which results in fewer software layers to be accessed) compared to a conventional third-party store.

With the SAP ILM database storage option, you can store the following items in SAP IQ:

- **Archive indices**
  These are ZARIX structure tables created by the Archive Information System (AS). Archive indices are normally created and built up in the database of your SAP application during or after data archiving. This adds to the size of the database and diminishes the effect of data archiving. By storing the archive indices in columnar tables on SAP IQ, you benefit from the high compression rate (up to 90%) and keep the strain on the data volume at a minimum. To use this functionality, you simply need to create a connection to a secondary database (SAP IQ) in the Archive Information System via Transaction DBCO. This feature is available as of SAP NetWeaver 7.31 SP07.
- **Archive files**
  These are ADK files created with SAP ILM-enabled archiving objects and as a result of data archiving in a live SAP application environment or data taken over from legacy systems in the course of decommissioning. The files are stored as binary large objects (BLOBs) in the write-once space of the IQ database. In SAP ILM policy management (Transaction IRMPOL), you simply need to enter the SAP ILM store that points to SAP IQ. This feature is available as of SAP NetWeaver 7.31 SP10 and 7.40 SP05.

The next innovation cycle of the SAP ILM database storage option aims to also support the storage of SAP ArchiveLink attachments (unstructured content) in SAP IQ, which will enable you to dispense with the SAP ArchiveLink store from your system landscape.

To make the most out of your investment in SAP IQ, you can also use the same SAP IQ instance used for SAP ILM to store your SAP BW data using the SAP BW Near-Line Storage (NLS) interface. SAP delivers a native ABAP-based implementation of the SAP BW NLS interface, but you can also use partner implementations. This enables you to simplify your IT landscape by consolidating your storage infrastructure on a single platform and thus substantially reducing your storage-related costs. For more information on how to obtain SAP BW NLS, see SAP Note 1796393.

12.2.4 Architecture Required to Run SAP ILM

The core functions of SAP ILM are provided with SAP NetWeaver enhancement packages, whereas the application-specific content, such as the SAP ILM-enabled archiving objects, is contained in SAP ERP enhancement packages (see SAP Notes 1168187 and 1494347). Figure 12.5 and Figure 12.6 provide an architectural overview of the SAP ILM scenarios, including the system components and landscape layers involved.

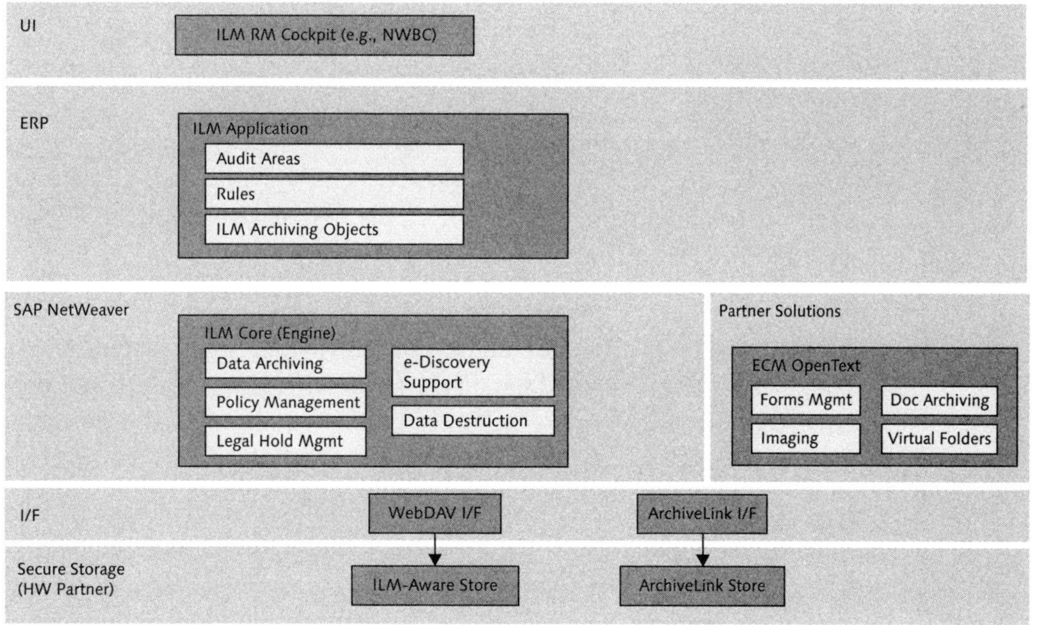

Figure 12.5 Architecture of the Retention Management Scenario

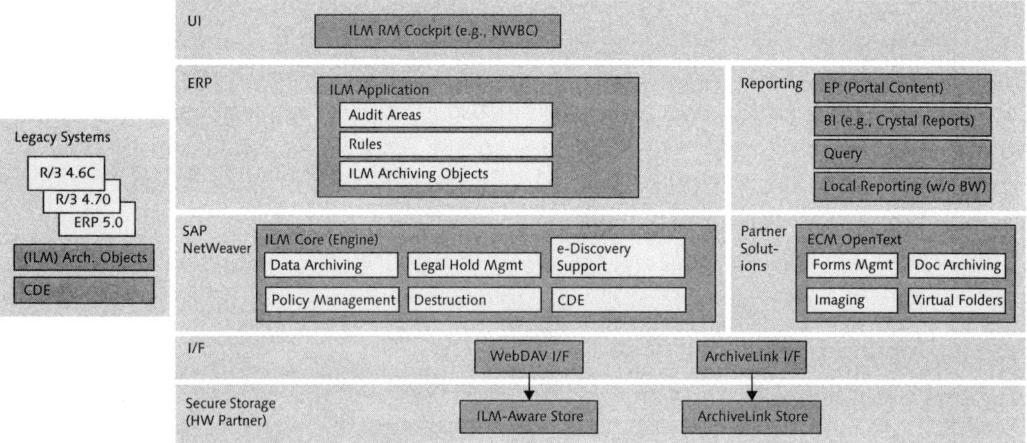

Figure 12.6 Architecture of the System Decommissioning Scenario

To use SAP ILM, you need to activate the relevant SAP ILM business functions in the switch framework (Transaction SFW5), depending on the SAP ILM scenario. The activation of SAP ILM can't be revoked.

Retention Management

You use the SAP ILM retention management functions in a live SAP ERP application system (AS ABAP) that uses SAP NetWeaver 7.40 as its technology platform. To control the communication of the ABAP application instance with the external SAP ILM store, you require a storage service. You have the following options:

- You can use the storage and retention service (SRS) that runs on the application system (AS ABAP). The SRS can run either locally on the application system or centrally on a different AS ABAP instance. In the latter case, several application systems can share it.
- You use the XML data archiving service (XML DAS) that runs on an application server in Java (AS Java). Select an appropriate system with the usage type AS Java from your system landscape. Several AS ABAP instances can share the XML DAS running on this system.

System Decommissioning

To manage the lifecycle of legacy data in the SAP ILM retention warehouse, you need to set up a dedicated system (AS ABAP) with the latest software version; that is, SAP ERP 6.0 EHP7 based on SAP NetWeaver 7.40. You also need SAP BW for reporting and an SAP ILM-aware storage system. For the administration of the SAP ILM store, the same options apply as described for retention management.

12.3 Managing the Lifecycle of Information in Live Systems

SAP ILM enables you to control the lifecycle of information in a live SAP environment. This includes online data that is still available in the database and nonoperational data that has been moved to the archive. SAP ILM includes the following retention management capabilities:

- **Manage audit areas**
  - Create audit areas at the beginning of the process.
- **Manage and enforce retention policies**
  - Set policies for automatic data retention and subsequent destruction.
  - Retain data according to set policies.
  - Responsibly destroy data when the expiration date has been reached.
- **Maintain separate archives per retention period**
  - Create multiple archive files for each calculated expiration date.
- **Perform e-discovery**
  - Search for information in response to legal requests.
- **Apply legal holds on data**
  - Automatically prevent data destruction.
  - Apply hold to online and archived data.

In the next sections, we explain some basic concepts, such as audit areas, data destruction, and legal hold management.

12.3.1 Audit Area

The audit area is another central concept in SAP ILM. It bundles data according to the reason for keeping the data. For example, financial data needs to be kept for tax reasons and would therefore belong to the audit area TAX. SAP delivers the following audit areas with SAP ERP 6.0 EHP7:

- **TAX**
  Covers the minimum scope for tax auditing in the United States or Germany. This scope was defined with the help of SAP user groups. The German *Braunschweig* model can be used from a reporting perspective as a guideline for the scope of the TAX audit area.
- **PRODLIABIL**
  Contains the data required for processing product liability claims. The scope of this audit area includes pick lists and batch where-used lists reports. The audit areas for tax and product liability also include objects for SAP for Utilities and SAP for Oil & Gas.
- **DEMO**
  This is a sample audit area to which the SAP ILM object FLIGHT_BOOKINGS is assigned. It also contains a DEMO policy. This audit area can be used for test purposes because it doesn't deal with business-relevant data. Therefore, it's not assigned to a switch, and no SAP BW queries are delivered for it.
- **GENERAL**
  This audit area is delivered empty, which means no SAP ILM objects are assigned to it. The aim is to assign objects to this audit area that aren't assigned to a different audit area. This approach is ideal if you want to have the retention rules from different application areas in a consolidated form. Any objects assigned to the GENERAL audit area can't be assigned to another audit area.

Standard audit areas delivered by SAP can't be modified. To use these audit areas, you can copy them into the customer namespace and edit them as required.

Using the policy management or "policy engine" component, you can specify policies and rules according to which data will be segregated into different files during archiving, as shown in Figure 12.7. This holds true for structured data and unstructured documents. Archive files created before the implementation of SAP ILM can also be integrated. A conversion tool helps you "re-archive" such files, thereby applying the retention rules on them.

Simply put, *policy management* (in previous releases of SAP ILM, this was also referred to as the *information retention manager*, or IRM) lets you define the amount of time data will be kept and the location where it will be stored. Apart from retention rules, you can also define residence rules to specify how long data resides in the database before it can be archived.

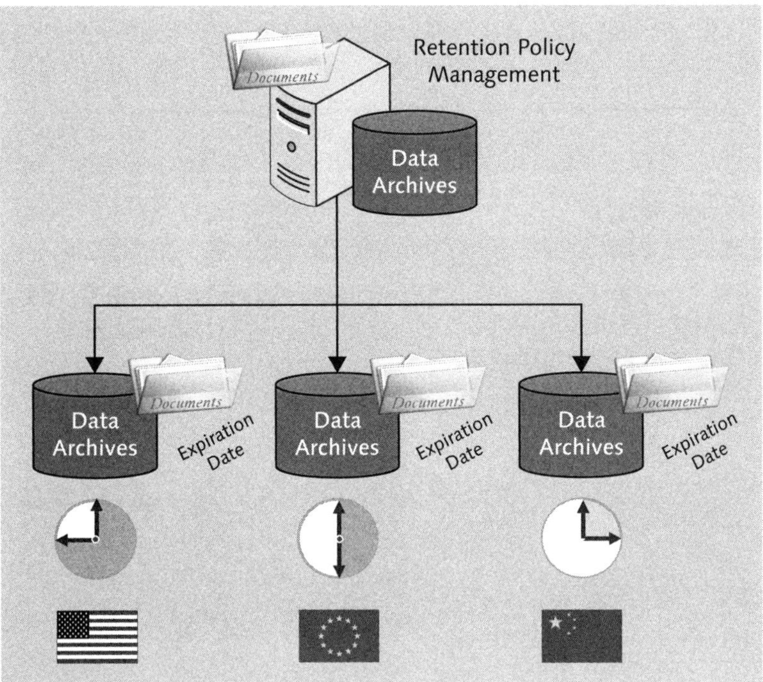

Figure 12.7 Creation of Archive Files according to Set Rules

Section 12.5 will show how to set up a policy and define rules. In the example, this is shown from the perspective of system decommissioning, but the same procedure applies for live systems.

Retention Management of Unstructured Data

In SAP ILM, retention rules can also be applied to unstructured documents linked via SAP ArchiveLink. However, they aren't applied to the documents themselves, but rather to their references as stored in the archive hierarchy of the SAP ILM-aware storage (see Section 12.2.3). That way, unstructured documents can inherit the retention times of their parent object. If, for example, an accounting document receives a retention time of seven years, the corresponding scanned invoice would also receive a retention time of seven years.

You can propagate retention times for SAP ArchiveLink documents and print lists in the store by running the following reports:

- ARLNK_SET_PROXYS_ALDOCUMENTS
- ARLNK_SET_PROXYS_PRINTLISTS

As a prerequisite for the enforcement of retention times, the storage system must have the correct compliance class. This means, for example, that a document will be destroyed when it has reached its expiration date *only* if the SAP ArchiveLink storage system supports the destruction of documents and understands the SAP destroy command.

12.3.2 Data Destruction

Retention management would be incomplete without being able to destroy data whose minimum retention period has passed or whose maximum retention period has been reached. With SAP ILM, you can destroy data in the database and also archived data and SAP ArchiveLink documents that are kept in the store. In either case, data can't be destroyed if it has a legal hold placed on it. In the destruction function, you can select online data, archive files, attachments, and print lists whose retention period has expired, transfer them into a destruction work list, and execute the destruction run.

To destroy data in the database of a live system, you simply choose the DATA DESTRUCTION option offered in the write program variant of SAP ILM-enabled archiving objects (shown in Figure 12.8).

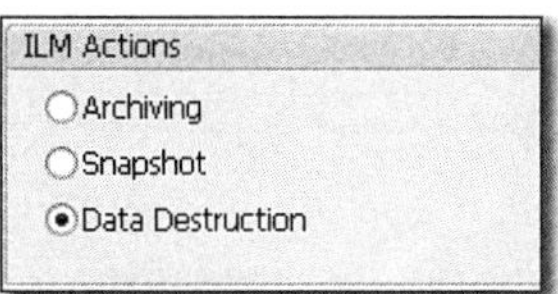

Figure 12.8 Data Destruction in the Live Database (Transaction SARA)

Destruction of data in the database is carried out with an archiving write run and a subsequent delete run. In this process, temporary archive files are created and then deleted at the end of the delete phase. These files, together with the administration data that relates to them, are automatically deleted by the system.

With SAP ILM, you can also destroy data in the archive, including attachments and print lists. For more information, refer to Section 12.5.

12.3.3 Legal Hold Management

Legal hold management is a tool specially developed for use in SAP ILM scenarios. Although it provides functions similar to SAP Case Management, it can be used independently from the latter. With legal hold management, you can create legal cases, place legal holds on archived data business object repository (BOR) objects and SAP ArchiveLink documents, and run e-discovery reports. Together with the BOR objects to be locked, you can also display the related attachments and include them in the hold.

Let's assume that your company is currently going through a lawsuit and that the related data, including a specific accounting document, has been secured by placing a legal hold on it. In this case, the system would not allow you to destroy the document, even if it has reached its expiration date and is ready for destruction.

Legal hold management comes with a history function that allows you to find out, for example, which reports have been executed or which objects have been deleted. By using a personalization function, you can specify which object types will be used in the e-discovery search.

Note

The SAP ILM-specific function for setting legal holds (as an alternative to SAP Case Management) is currently available only for use in live application systems. The complete availability of this function in the retention warehouse system (system decommissioning scenario) is planned for future deliveries.

The following is a summary of the retention management functions provided by SAP ILM:

- Audit area management
- Policy and rule management
- Archiving programs that integrate with the policy and rule management functions
- Destroy function (for databases, archiving, and attachments)
- Legal hold management
- ILM-aware storage for secure and legally compliant retention of data
- An ILM-certified storage system

Retention management always occurs in a live system environment. To use the latest version of the retention management functions, you must be on SAP ERP 6.0 EHP7. Also, see Section 12.2.4 for more about retention management.

12.4 Managing the Lifecycle of Information from Legacy Systems

SAP ILM provides a standardized method for decommissioning legacy systems, including SAP and non-SAP systems. As a basic principle, you first need to analyze the data in the legacy system you want to decommission (part of the preliminary project steps). Then you transfer the selected data from the legacy system to the SAP ILM retention warehouse system, where you apply retention rules on it to ensure legally compliant storage. From the store, the data can be accessed at any time (e.g., to respond to tax audits or to create financial reports). Figure 12.9 shows the basic process, including the system prerequisites.

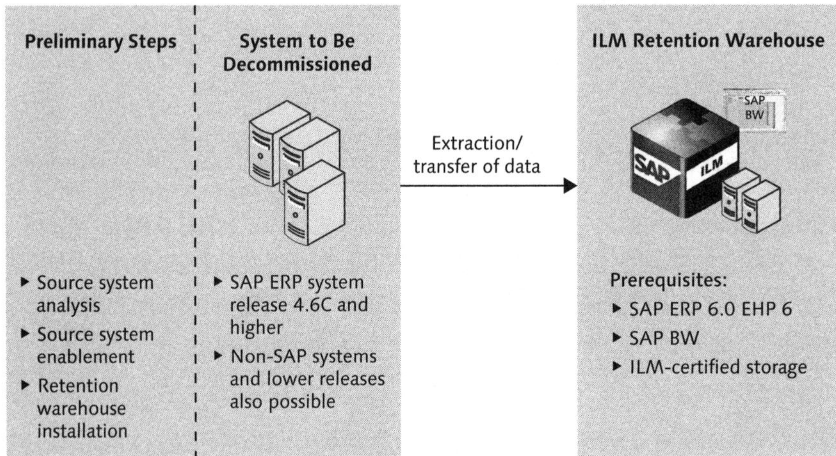

Figure 12.9 Process Overview and System Prerequisites

In the following sections, we go through the main steps that are required to decommission legacy systems.

12.4.1 Preliminary Steps

Before you start to decommission a legacy system, several preliminary steps need to be completed, as discussed next.

Analyze the Data in the Legacy System

Typically, you only want to extract data from the legacy system that needs to be retained (e.g., for legal reasons). In this step, you analyze the data volume in your legacy system to identify exactly which data is eligible for extraction.

Questions to be answered include the following:

- What data does the legacy system contain?
- What data is relevant for reporting (e.g., for tax audits or product liability claims)?
- Are the relevant archiving objects available in the system?

In the SAP system, you can find a variety of tools that help you analyze the content of your system:

- Database analysis (Transaction DB02)
- Database tools such as SAPDBA and BR for Oracle and Informix
- Tables and archiving objects (Transaction DB15)
- Table analysis (Transaction TAANA)

SAP also offers services to support you in your system analysis. As a result of your analysis, you should have a clear picture of what data must be transferred to the retention warehouse and what data can be left behind.

Enable Your Legacy System for SAP ILM

Because your legacy system doesn't have any ILM functions, you must enable it for use with SAP ILM. This includes importing SAP ILM-enabled archiving write programs and the context data extractor (CDE) extraction services.

You need to implement SAP Notes to install the CDE (see SAP Note 1089434) and SAP ILM-enable any archiving objects (see SAP Note 1180653) to cover all the data you need to transfer to the retention warehouse.

If your legacy system is on SAP R/3 4.6C or SAP R/3 Enterprise 4.70, you can use the related SAP ILM add-on to import this content:

- BC-ILM-ADO-46C: see SAP Note 1402693
- BC-ILM-ADO-47: see SAP Note 1614029

For other releases or non-SAP systems, contact the SAP System Landscape Optimization (SLO) group at *http://service.sap.com/slo.*

Configure the Retention Warehouse System

Before you can start reporting on the data transferred from the legacy system, you need to configure the retention warehouse system. To do so, you need to install and set up an SAP ERP 6.0 EHP7 system and connect it to an SAP ILM-aware storage system. The main step here is setting up and configuring the archive store, as described in the SAP ILM documentation. You also need an SAP BW system for reporting. Also, see Section 12.2.4 for an overview of the required architecture.

The process of managing the lifecycle of information from legacy systems requires different steps in each phase and for each system involved. Figure 12.10 provides an overview of the process steps involved in system decommissioning.

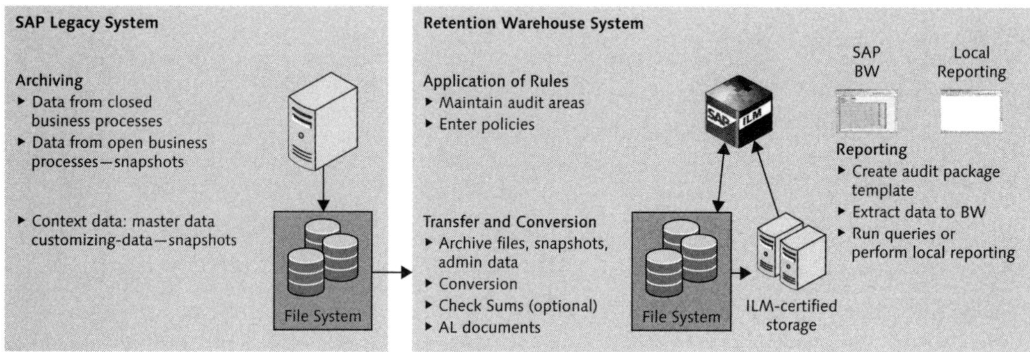

Figure 12.10 System Decommissioning Process Steps

After the preliminary steps of analyzing the data and preparing the legacy system for SAP ILM are completed, the next step is to archive the data, which is discussed next.

12.4.2 Steps Performed in the Legacy System

Before shutting down the legacy system for good, you have to ensure that you've archived all the data that you need to retain. This entails archiving business-complete data (i.e., data from closed business processes) as well as data from still open processes that might be worth keeping for retention reasons. Apart from this transactional data, you also need to archive context data, such as master data, and metadata such as ABAP Data Dictionary records, customizing settings, and so on. You use different functions for each of these types:

- **Business-complete data**
  Standard archiving objects.
- **Business-incomplete data**
  Snapshot option provided by SAP ILM-enabled archiving objects.
- **Master data for which an archiving object exists**
  Snapshot option provided by SAP ILM-enabled archiving objects.

- **Master data for which no archiving object exists**
  CDE extraction services.
- **Metadata**
  CDE extraction services.

12.4.3 Steps Performed in the Retention Warehouse System

In addition to the steps in the legacy system, several steps must be done in the retention warehouse in SAP ILM:

- **Define audit areas and retention policies**
  To ensure that the data coming from the legacy system will be stored safely according to its retention time, you must define adequate audit areas and retention policies. You can then transfer the data from the legacy system and apply the retention rules to it.
- **Transfer the data from the legacy system to the retention warehouse system and convert the data**
  You can now transfer the archived (structured) data and the SAP ArchiveLink information (for the unstructured data) to the retention warehouse system and convert it for use in SAP ILM (SAP ILM conversion). You must also transfer the related archive administration data so that archiving sessions are made available to the retention warehouse system. After the data has been transferred, you can start the ILM conversion, during which the retention rules are applied to the data. As an optional step, you can create checksums to compare the data before and after conversion.
- **Use reporting in SAP BW or use local reporting**
  After you've decommissioned the legacy system, you can use the data stored in the retention warehouse to report on it. This can be done using either SAP BW or local reporting, a function that doesn't require SAP BW.

SAP ILM Cockpit Roles for the SAP NetWeaver Business Client

To help you perform the process steps of the SAP ILM scenarios (retention management and system decommissioning) faster and in the recommended order, SAP delivers the following SAP ILM cockpit roles for the SAP NetWeaver Business Client (NWBC):

- **Retention Management Cockpit—Administrator**
  Contains all steps an administrator needs for all retention management functions.
- **Retention Management Cockpit—Line of Business**
  Contains only those functions that are relevant for line of business (LoB) staff (e.g., accountants).

- **System Decommissioning Cockpit—Administrator**
  Contains all steps an administrator needs for all system decommissioning functions performed in the retention warehouse.
- **System Decommissioning Cockpit—Line of Business**
  Contains only those functions that are relevant for LoB staff (for example, accountants), with a main focus on reporting.

Using the SAP ILM cockpits, you don't have to remember all the transactions that are required in an SAP ILM scenario; the cockpits will guide you through the process in the right sequence. The cockpit roles are delivered as templates and can be adjusted as needed. It's still possible to use the transactions in the system (e.g., Transaction SARA).

Figure 12.11 shows the SAP ILM cockpits in NWBC. The SAP ILM RETENTION WAREHOUSE cockpit for administrators has been opened.

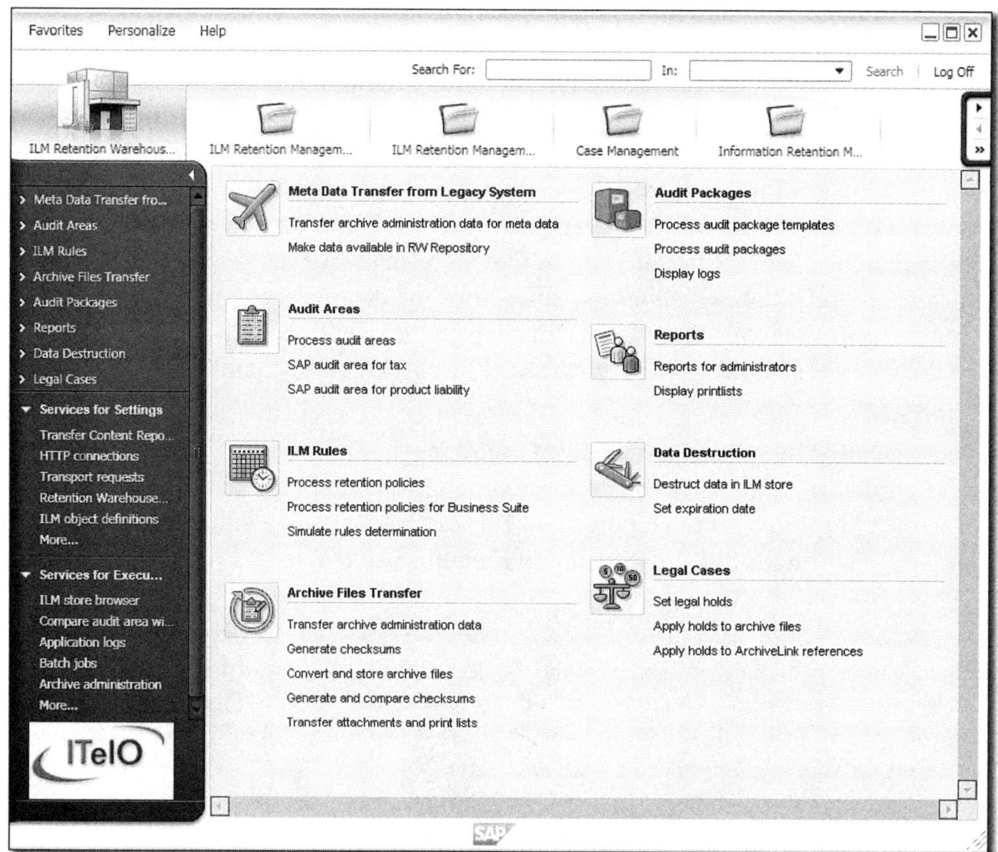

Figure 12.11 SAP ILM Cockpits in SAP NetWeaver Business Client

12.4.4 Handling Data from Non-SAP Systems During Decommissioning

The SAP solutions for ILM also support the decommissioning of non-SAP systems. The main difference from SAP system decommissioning is the handling of the original data to be extracted from the legacy system. Because the definition of this data may follow a data model that's totally different from that of SAP data, the legacy data needs some special treatment before it can be transferred to the retention warehouse for further use.

By leveraging the ETL capabilities of Data Services, it's possible to extract the data from a non-SAP system, map it onto SAP structures, and convert it into Archive Development Kit (ADK) archive files with an identical format, such as archive files created from native SAP data. The ADK mapping is performed using adapted ADK write programs (non-SAP write programs), in which, for instance, the archiving checks are disabled. Data Services does the technical profiling and data auditing to help assess the state of the data from the data conversion and archiving readiness. Additionally, Information Steward can be used for business data assessment on the legacy system as well as a single view of data lineage and impact analysis.

After the data from the non-SAP system has been processed this way, you can use it in the retention warehouse in a similar way as you would do with native SAP data. For example, you would apply retention rules to the freshly created ADK files and move them to the store for long-term preservation. For reporting, you would simply load the data into SAP BW and use predefined queries for tax audits or product liability. Of course, you can also use the local reporting tool.

12.4.5 Streamlined System Decommissioning and Reporting

To speed up the process of system decommissioning and reduce the overall project risk, duration, and costs, SAP has enhanced the tools that are used and considerably increased the level of automation.

In this section, we'll introduce a new concept that uses SAP LT Replication Server (SAP LT) software, combined with the new generic Content Data Extractor tool (CDE, part of SAP ILM) to achieve this goal. The primary purpose of SAP LT is to assist customers in adapting their system landscapes to recurring transformation needs, such as M&A, divestitures, carve-outs, and so on. But the tool is also perfectly suited for supporting system decommissioning with SAP ILM, particularly for non-SAP systems or old SAP releases.

What's Special about Generic Context Data Extractor?

Basically, the job of CDE is to enable the extraction of content from a legacy system not covered by existing archiving objects. Typically, this covers context information such as customizing or master data, but in fact any kind of data, including transactional data, can be processed.

By default, the Generic CDE considers all tables in the system and doesn't require extensive customizing. This simplifies the process and helps better leverage SAP LT. Key benefits include the following:

- No manual activity, such as creation of a structure, required
- Can be invoked either from the system to be decommissioned or from the SAP ILM retention warehouse
- Uses a sophisticated grouping logic, based on the application component of the package, for easy identification of archiving objects

Figure 12.12 depicts the general system decommissioning process.

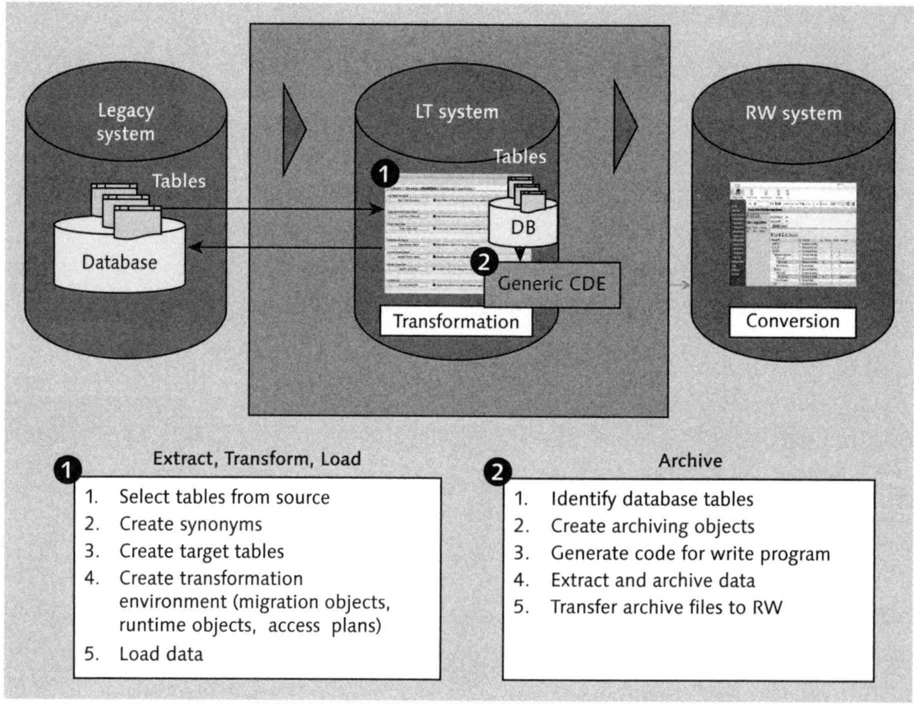

Figure 12.12 System Decommissioning with SAP LT and Generic CDE

The process steps are performed in the SAP LT system, which acts as a staging system. We'll go over each process step in the following subsections.

❶ Transformation of Legacy Data (Extract, Transform, Load)

These steps are performed using standard SAP LT functionality, which has been adapted to ILM needs:

1. **Select tables from source.**
   Select all tables from the source system to be extracted. Only entire tables can be selected, but individual tables can be omitted from the selection.
2. **Create synonyms.**
   Create mapping information (synonyms) between the source and target tables (to be created in the SAP LT system).
3. **Create target tables.**
   Create the tables to be used for the data load. The system uses technical names (according to SAP LT nomenclature) that have nothing to do with the table names in an SAP system.
4. **Create transformation environment.**
   This step includes the definition of migration objects for the tables created, the generation of runtime objects to be used for the data transfer, and the calculation of access plans (indices used to distribute data based on specific criteria, such as keys).
5. **Load data.**
   In the final step, the system transfers the actual data from the source tables in the legacy system to the target tables in the SAP LT system. In principle, the legacy system can now be switched off, but we recommend you keep it up and running until you've verified that no data was left behind.

❷ Extraction of Legacy Data (Archive)

As a result of the transformation process, the data from the legacy system now resides in the newly created technical tables in the SAP LT system. To be available for use in the SAP ILM retention warehouse, the data needs to be processed using the Generic CDE. The process includes the following steps:

1. Group the context tables and identify the related transactional tables.

2. Create the archiving objects for snaphots (*SN) and for transactional tables.
3. Run the archiving objects, and write the transactional data, context data, and metadata into archive files.
4. Transfer the resulting archive files to the SAP ILM retention warehouse.

Accelerated Reporting

By selecting the Optimized Retention Warehouse option in retention warehouse customizing, you can enable additional features for the optimized use of retention warehouse. As a result, a new data provisioning layer is created in the application database. During BI extraction or local reporting, the system extracts the data from the database tables created in the data provisioning layer. Thus you can significantly increase the performance during data loading and reporting. This feature is available as of SAP NetWeaver 7.40 SP03.

The Optimized Retention Warehouse option is the basis for another enhancement called *accelerated reporting*. Accelerated reporting simplifies the extraction of data from the legacy system and allows for an alternative way of performing reporting using the data persistency introduced previously. This feature is available as of SAP NetWeaver 7.40 SP07 (see also SAP Note 1974000) and 7.31 SP11 (see also SAP Note 1942476).

12.5 System Decommissioning: Detailed Example

Now that you're familiar with the SAP ILM retention warehouse and know the basic concept of system decommissioning, we'll present a detailed example of how the process works in the system. Given the large number of steps that a system decommissioning project may involve, we'll only focus on the most important steps.

For this scenario, we assume that you've analyzed the data in your legacy system and that you've enabled the system for use with SAP ILM. You've also configured the retention warehouse system as needed. For more information, see Section 12.4.1.

In this section, we explain the steps that are required to extract data from the legacy system, transfer it to the retention warehouse, and report on this data.

12.5.1 Data Extraction

To be compliant with legal or business requirements, it's necessary to extract the transactional data, master data, and context data from the legacy system before it's shut down.

We recommend that you perform the necessary archiving steps in the following order:

1. Archive business-complete data (transactional data).
2. Archive business-incomplete data (transactional data).
3. Archive master data for which archiving objects exist.
4. Archive master data for which no archiving objects exist and other context information.
5. Archive all other data not covered in the preceding steps.

Let's start with archiving the transactional data. This includes both the settings to archive transactional data and to archive the related context using the CDE.

Archive Transactional Data

In this step, we first archive business-complete data by using the standard write program, and then we archive business-incomplete data via the snapshot function. In this example, we archive financial accounting documents using the archiving object FI_DOCUMNT.

1. In Transaction SARA, create a variant for the write program and specify the archiving range (as shown in Figure 12.13):
   - Company Codes: 1000
   - From Fiscal Year: 2000
   - Document Numbers: 100001350 to 100001399

   Note the ILM Actions section. It only appears for SAP ILM–enabled archiving objects. To archive data from closed processes, select Archiving. Enter a comment on the archiving session in the Comment on archiving run text box to make it easier to spot later on in archive management.
2. Specify that the archiving session should run in productive mode and request a detailed log. Then schedule the session as usual.

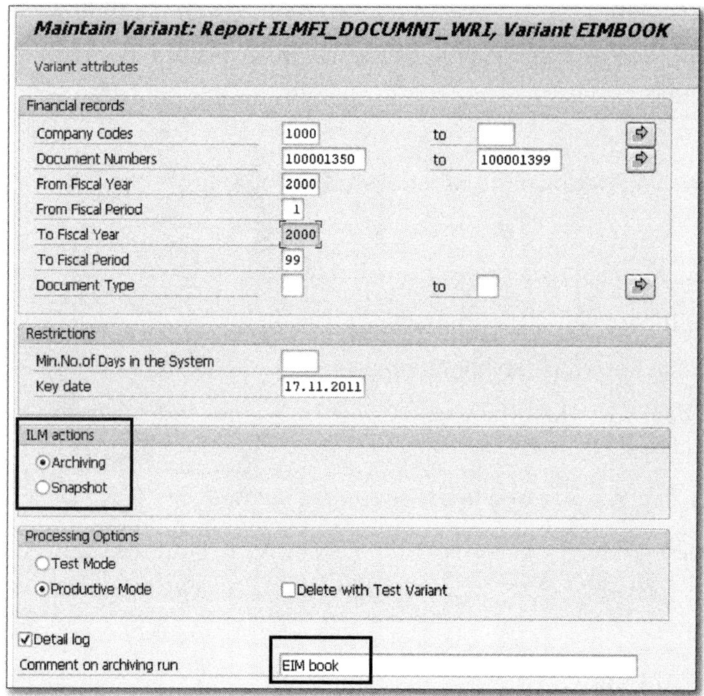

Figure 12.13 Maintain the Write Program Variant

3. After the write job is finished, check in the log to see whether the documents are archived (Figure 12.14).

17.11.2011 Archiving of Financial Reords: Write Program 2

Log (Summary)

Message	Obj. Disp.	Object (Example)
Document archived	12	1000/2000/0100001351
Document has open items	11	1000/2000/0100001350

Figure 12.14 Log of Write Program

As you can see, 12 documents were archived, and 11 documents could not be archived because they have open items. We now need to archive these 11 documents using the snapshot function:

1. In Transaction SARA, use the same variant for the write program as used previously.

2. Choose SNAPSHOT in the ILM ACTION section, and execute the run as you would normally do.
3. After the write job is finished, check in the log to see whether the documents are archived (Figure 12.15).

17.11.2011 Archiving of Financial Reords: Write Program 2

Log (Summary)

Message	Obj. Disp.	Object (Example)
Document archived	11	1000/2000/0100001350

Figure 12.15 Log of Write Program—Snapshots

The log states that the remaining 11 documents with open items were also archived. Remember that snapshots are taken with no archivability checks on. This enables the archiving of data that, in classical archiving, would not be eligible for archiving.

In this example, we chose to have the delete program start automatically when the write job is finished (START AUTOMATICALLY checkbox in ARCHIVING-OBJECT SPECIFIC CUSTOMIZING). Therefore, we don't need to schedule a delete run right now.

Next, we need to archive the context information.

Archive Data Using the Context Data Extractor

After you've archived the transactional data, you must ensure that the associated context information that is required for the later interpretation of the transactional data is also transferred to the retention warehouse. This is done by using the CDE discussed earlier. In this example, we archive context data from Financial Accounting (FI) in SAP ERP and the fiscal year 2004.

1. Call Transaction ILM. Select ARCHIVE DATA FOR ILM from the EXTRACTION folder.
2. Enter the required parameters (e.g., enter "FI" in the APPLICATIONS text box). Figure 12.16 shows an example.
3. Execute your run. The archiving object that is used in the background is SN_FI (snapshot of FI data).
4. In archive management (access via Transaction SARA), the CDE run is listed as a complete archiving session (Figure 12.17).

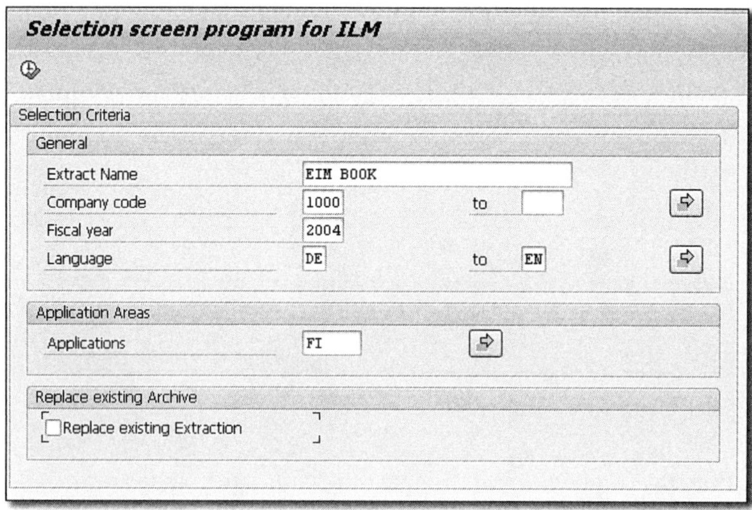

Figure 12.16 CDE Selection Screen

Archive Administation: Archiving Session Overview

Spool list | Storage system | Customizing | Database tables | Information system

Archiving object SN_FI FI segments for Information Lifecycle Management

Sessions and files for archiving object	Note
Complete archiving sessions	
734 - 797 (11.08.2011 - 17.11.2011)	
797 - 17.11.2011	EIM book 1000 2004 DE EN
000797-001SN_FI	
782 - 18.10.2011	1000 2002 DE EN
781 - 18.10.2011	1000 2001 DE EN
755 - 25.08.2011	1000 1998 DE
749 - 24.08.2011	1000 1997 DE
739 - 16.08.2011	1000 2000
734 - 11.08.2011	1000 2000

Figure 12.17 CDE Session in Archive Management

By taking a look at the statistics, you'll see that you've archived 135 data objects (Figure 12.18).

5. To view the result of the CDE run, call Transaction ILM, and select Data Extract Browser from the Extraction folder.

   The content of your CDE extract is displayed in the DART_Browser (Figure 12.19). You can see that in your session, you've extracted context data related to transactional data and master data, both from FI.

Selection screen program for ILM

Statistics of archived objects

Archive file: 000797-001SN_FI Number of objects: 135
Size in MB: 0,566

Table	Number	Description
TXI_CONTROL	135	Control Record for ILM archives
TXI_FM01	5	Financial Management Areas
TXI_FMFPO	1.130	FIFM: Commitment Item
TXI_INDEXD	3	Index definition (security index)
TXI_LFBK	267	Vendor Master (Bank Details)
TXI_PTRV_DOC_HD	69	Transfer Travel -> FI/CO: Header o
TXI_PTRV_DOC_IT	280	Transfer Travel -> FI/CO: Lines of
TXI_PTRV_DOC_TAX	90	Transfer Travel -> FI/CO: Tax line

Figure 12.18 Statistics of Archived Objects

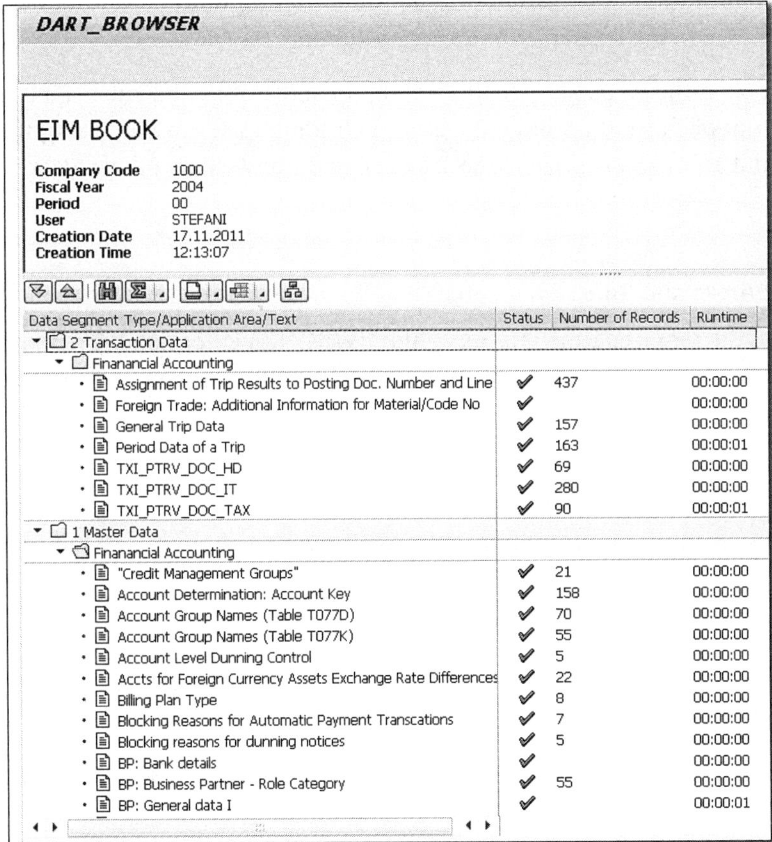
DART_BROWSER

EIM BOOK

Company Code 1000
Fiscal Year 2004
Period 00
User STEFANI
Creation Date 17.11.2011
Creation Time 12:13:07

Data Segment Type/Application Area/Text	Status	Number of Records	Runtime
2 Transaction Data			
Finanancial Accounting			
Assignment of Trip Results to Posting Doc. Number and Line	✔	437	00:00:00
Foreign Trade: Additional Information for Material/Code No	✔		00:00:00
General Trip Data	✔	157	00:00:00
Period Data of a Trip	✔	163	00:00:01
TXI_PTRV_DOC_HD	✔	69	00:00:00
TXI_PTRV_DOC_IT	✔	280	00:00:00
TXI_PTRV_DOC_TAX	✔	90	00:00:01
1 Master Data			
Finanancial Accounting			
"Credit Management Groups"	✔	21	00:00:00
Account Determination: Account Key	✔	158	00:00:00
Account Group Names (Table T077D)	✔	70	00:00:00
Account Group Names (Table T077K)	✔	55	00:00:00
Account Level Dunning Control	✔	5	00:00:00
Accts for Foreign Currency Assets Exchange Rate Differences	✔	22	00:00:00
Billing Plan Type	✔	8	00:00:00
Blocking Reasons for Automatic Payment Transcations	✔	7	00:00:00
Blocking reasons for dunning notices	✔	5	00:00:00
BP: Bank details	✔		00:00:00
BP: Business Partner - Role Category	✔	55	00:00:00
BP: General data I	✔		00:00:01

Figure 12.19 Content of CDE Archive File

Now that you've archived all the data (business-complete data, business-incomplete data, and context data) from the legacy system that you need to retain for later access, you're ready to transfer the resulting archive files to the retention warehouse and, after they've arrived there, apply retention rules on them in the SAP ILM conversion step.

12.5.2 Data Transfer and Conversion

Before you start transfer and conversion, you need to set up audit areas and retention rules. During conversion, the rules will be applied to the transferred data to make sure it's stored with the appropriate expiration date in the SAP ILM-aware storage. Remember that only the retention warehouse has the SAP ILM functionality required to perform these steps; the legacy system is totally unaware of SAP ILM (with the exception of the SAP ILM-enabled archiving objects and the CDE extraction services being available in the legacy system).

Let's take a look at the steps involved in setting up audit areas and rules. First is the actual set up of the audit areas and rules, then the transfer of data using the audit areas and rules, and, finally, the transfer and conversion of the data to archive files.

Set Up Audit Areas and Rules

You can access the required functions using the NWBC ILM Retention Warehouse cockpit for administrators, under Audit Areas and ILM Rules. You can also use the corresponding transactions.

Before you can create policies, you must have at least one audit area set up. For this example, we've copied the standard audit area TAX and created the new audit area ZILMTAX in the customer namespace. We've assigned the following SAP ILM objects to the new audit area:

```
FI_DOCUMNT, AL_DOCUMENTS, SN_META, SN_GEN, SN_GENC, SN_FI, SN_FIC
```

These SAP ILM objects belong to our example. We need them to view a complete SAP BW query at the end of the process, including the original documents:

1. To create a policy, go to Audit Areas • Process Audit Areas, or use Transaction IRMPOL.

2. Make the necessary entries as shown in Figure 12.20, and then choose New.

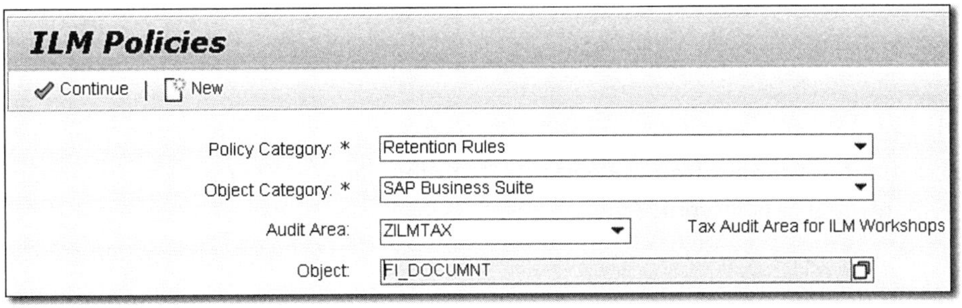

ILM Policies

Continue | New

Policy Category: * Retention Rules

Object Category: * SAP Business Suite

Audit Area: ZILMTAX Tax Audit Area for ILM Workshops

Object: FI_DOCUMNT

Figure 12.20 Define a New Policy

Because this example is about managing the retention of data, we choose the Policy Category Retention Rules. SAP ILM policy management also supports the policy category Residence Rules, which lets you define residence periods for your archiving objects.

3. Enter a Policy Name (in this example, "EIMBOOK").
4. Select the field BUKRS (company code), and then use the Add Item arrow to move it into the Selected Condition Fields table (see Figure 12.21). We'll need this field later in the reporting phase.

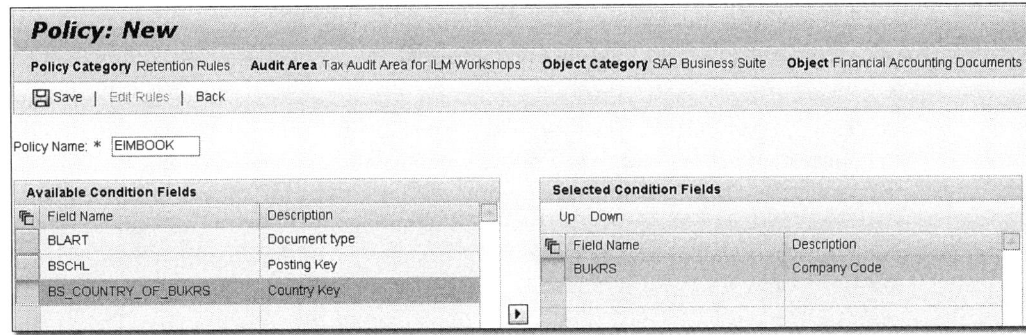

Figure 12.21 Define a New Policy (Cont.)

5. Save your new retention policy. You need to have a customizing transport request ready.
6. For your new policy, enter a retention rule like the one we created for this example (see Figure 12.22).

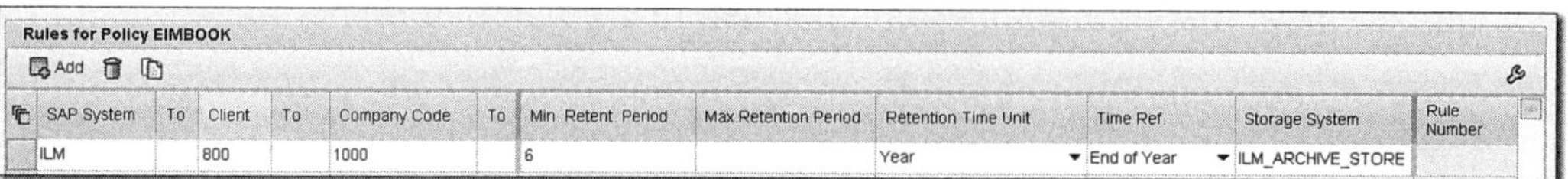

Figure 12.22 Define a Rule

7. After you've saved your retention rule, select CHANGE STATUS to set the policy status to live (shown in Figure 12.23).

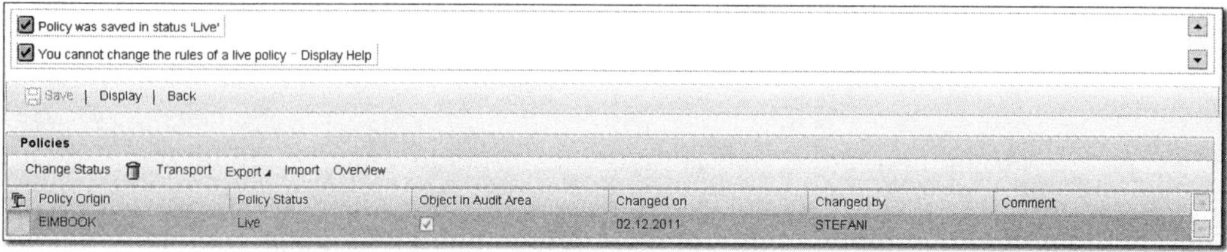

Figure 12.23 Set the Policy Status to Live

What You Should Know about Retention Rules

When you create a new retention policy, you can choose the fields that are to appear during rule maintenance. There are mandatory fields (e.g., system, client) that are always part of the rule, and other fields that can be selected from a list of available fields, such as the company code. The available fields are set up in Customizing by SAP development, and vary per SAP ILM object. If you create your own SAP ILM objects, you must also set up available fields in Customizing (Transaction IRM_CUST).

For the system to determine the expiration date during archiving, you must specify certain criteria when setting up a new rule. It's possible to enter a minimum and a maximum retention period, as well as a retention time unit (e.g., year, day, and month) and a time reference. The minimum retention period indicates the least amount of time the data must be kept. The maximum retention period indicates after what date the data must be destroyed. The time reference criterion tells the system from what point in time the retention times are to start counting (e.g., end of year, end of fiscal year).

By entering a storage system, you specify the location at which the data will be stored in the SAP ILM-aware storage.

Your retention policy and rule have now been activated, which means that during archiving, the system will route the data to the correct storage location and will store the calculated expiration date.

Transfer and Convert the Archive Files

In the next phase, you transfer the actual data and the archive administration data (information about the archiving sessions, such as session number, etc.) from the legacy system to the retention warehouse. If the legacy system and the retention warehouse system are connected to the same file system, it's only necessary to transfer the administration data. You also transfer the link information of SAP ArchiveLink attachments and propagate the retentions onto the references. This will enable you to include your attachments in your SAP ILM strategy.

After you've transferred all the data, you apply the retention rules that you set up earlier to the data using the SAP ILM conversion function. An important part of this process is filling the repository from the *SN_META* file. This file contains the necessary metadata that allows for the interpretation of the data after the original system has been shut down.

> **Note**
>
> As an optional step, you can use the checksum function to compare the data before and after the rules have been applied. We don't cover this step in this example.

Figure 12.24 shows the steps of the data transfer process.

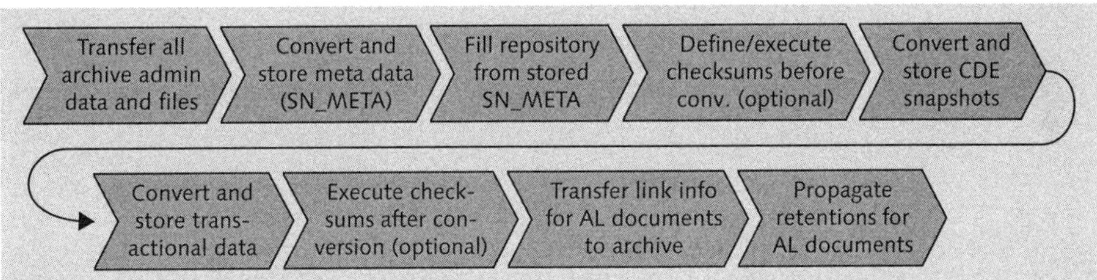

Figure 12.24 Transferring Data Step-by-Step Process

The transfer is triggered from within the retention warehouse system and requires a remote function call (RFC) connection between the legacy system and the retention warehouse system. In this example, we perform the transfer from the NWBC ILM Retention Warehouse cockpit for administrators. Our retention warehouse system and the legacy system share the same file system, so we only need to transfer the archive administration data.

To transfer the archive administration data for the archiving sessions performed in the legacy system, proceed as follows:

1. Go to Archive Files Transfers • Transfer Archive Administration Data (Transaction ILM_TRANS_ADMIN_ONLY).
2. Double-click on the legacy system (in our example, "ILM" is the name of the legacy system we want to decommission) to call up the work list of available archiving objects and sessions (see Figure 12.25).

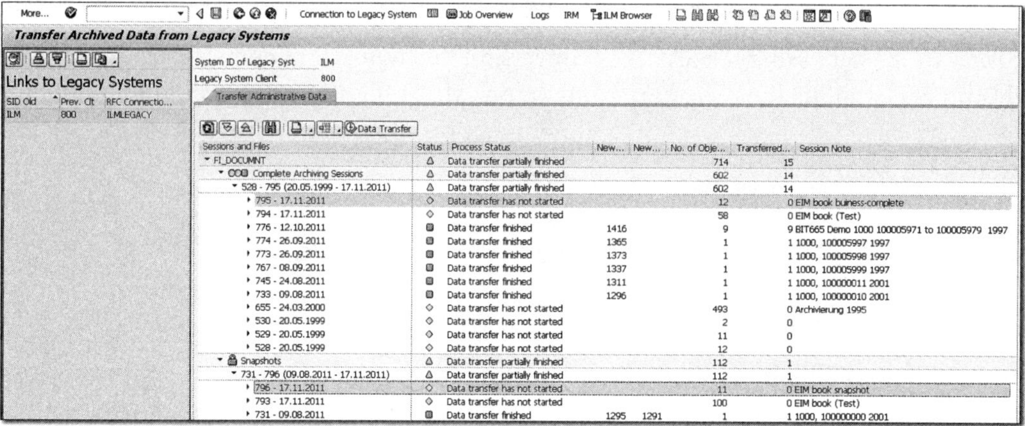

Figure 12.25 Transfer Archive Administration Data

In Figure 12.25, we've highlighted the two archiving sessions that we created in the legacy system. The first one contains the business-complete data, and the second one contains the snapshot data (shown in the bottom portion of Figure 12.25). You can see that the transfer of these sessions hasn't started.

3. To start the transfer, select the required sessions (multiple selection is possible by holding down the [⇧] or [Ctrl] key on your keyboard), and choose Data Transfer.
4. Fill in the pop-up screen with the required information, and schedule the run in live mode. When the job is finished (see Figure 12.26), you can see in the overview screen that two new sessions have been created during the transfer: 1453 and 1454.

Transfer Administrative Data

Data Transfer

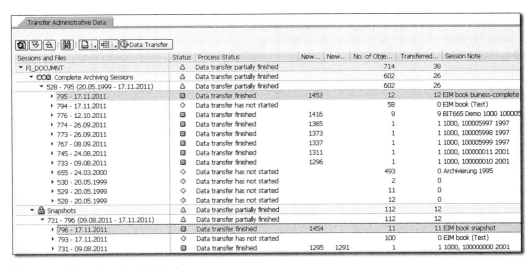

Sessions and Files	Status	Process Status	New...	New...	No. of Obje...	Transferred...	Session Note
FI_DOCUMNT	△	Data transfer partially finished			714	38	
Complete Archiving Sessions	△	Data transfer partially finished			602	26	
528 - 795 (20.05.1999 - 17.11.2011)	△	Data transfer partially finished			602	26	
795 - 17.11.2011	■	Data transfer finished	1453		12	12	EIM book buiness-complete
794 - 17.11.2011	◇	Data transfer has not started			58	0	EIM book (Test)
776 - 12.10.2011	■	Data transfer finished	1416		9	9	BIT665 Demo 1000 100005
774 - 26.09.2011	■	Data transfer finished	1365		1	1	1000, 100005997 1997
773 - 26.09.2011	■	Data transfer finished	1373		1	1	1000, 100005998 1997
767 - 08.09.2011	■	Data transfer finished	1337		1	1	1000, 100005999 1997
745 - 24.08.2011	■	Data transfer finished	1311		1	1	1000, 100000011 2001
733 - 09.08.2011	■	Data transfer finished	1296		1	1	1000, 100000010 2001
655 - 24.03.2000	◇	Data transfer has not started			493	0	Archivierung 1995
530 - 20.05.1999	◇	Data transfer has not started			2	0	
529 - 20.05.1999	◇	Data transfer has not started			11	0	
528 - 20.05.1999	◇	Data transfer has not started			12	0	
Snapshots	△	Data transfer partially finished			112	12	
731 - 796 (09.08.2011 - 17.11.2011)	△	Data transfer partially finished			112	12	
796 - 17.11.2011	■	Data transfer finished	1454		11	11	EIM book snapshot
793 - 17.11.2011	◇	Data transfer has not started			100	0	EIM book (Test)
731 - 09.08.2011	■	Data transfer finished	1295	1291	1	1	1000, 100000000 2001

Figure 12.26 Data Transfer Finished

5. By taking a look at the job log, you can see the two new session numbers, 1453 and 1454, which were created for the transferred sessions 795 and 796, respectively (see Figure 12.27).

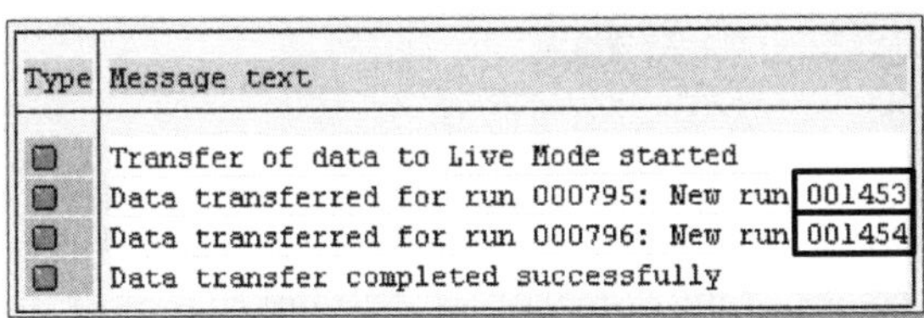

Type	Message text
■	Transfer of data to Live Mode started
■	Data transferred for run 000795: New run 001453
■	Data transferred for run 000796: New run 001454
■	Data transfer completed successfully

Figure 12.27 New Sessions Created during the Transfer

Now you need to convert and store your newly created archiving sessions:

1. Proceed as described previously for the transfer, but choose CONVERT & STORE TRANSACTIONAL DATA.
2. In the CONVERT FILES tab strip, select your sessions, fill in the required information (select the WITH CONVERSION checkbox), and schedule the job in live mode.
3. In ARCHIVE MANAGEMENT, in the section with complete archiving sessions, you can see the names of the new sessions after conversion (see Figure 12.28).

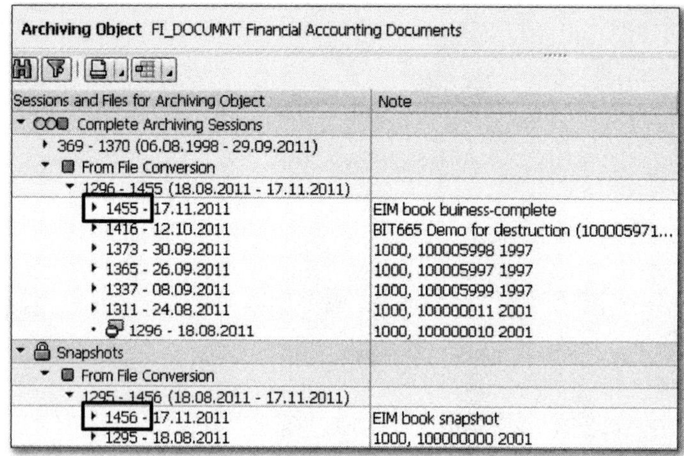

Figure 12.28 New Sessions Created during Conversion

The old sessions that were replaced, 1453 and 1454, appear in the section with replaced archiving sessions (Figure 12.29).

Replaced Archiving Sessions	
365 - 1454 (06.08.1998 - 17.11.2011)	
1454 - 17.11.2011	EIM book snapshot
1453 - 17.11.2011	EIM book buiness-complete

Figure 12.29 Replaced Archiving Sessions

Each of these steps created new archiving sessions. This is the standard procedure in data archiving to ensure full tracking of the entire process and to guarantee that the original sessions and files aren't modified.

In this example, we chose to have the storage start automatically when the conversion is finished (START AUTOMATICALLY checkbox in ARCHIVING-OBJECT SPECIFIC CUSTOMIZING). Therefore, we don't need to store the data at this stage. You can also store your archiving sessions manually by clicking on the FILE STORAGE button in the STORE FILES tab of the transfer tool (see Figure 12.30).

When the storage job has finished, you can see that sessions 1455 and 1456, which we created during conversion, have now been stored.

This is also indicated accordingly in ARCHIVE MANAGEMENT under COMPLETE ARCHIVING SESSIONS • FROM FILE CONVERSION.

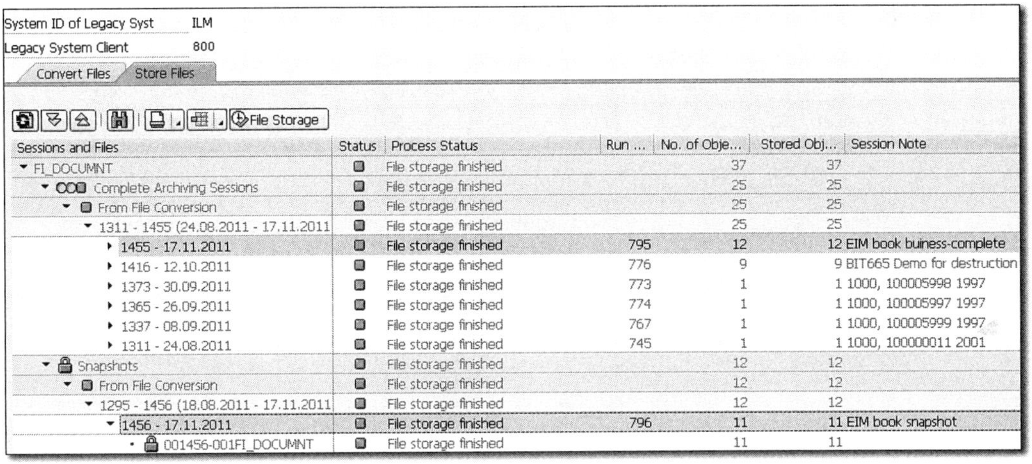

System ID of Legacy Syst ILM
Legacy System Client 800
Convert Files Store Files
File Storage

Sessions and Files	Status	Process Status	Run ...	No. of Obje...	Stored Obj...	Session Note
FI_DOCUMNT		File storage finished		37	37	
Complete Archiving Sessions		File storage finished		25	25	
From File Conversion		File storage finished		25	25	
1311 - 1455 (24.08.2011 - 17.11.2011		File storage finished		25	25	
1455 - 17.11.2011		File storage finished	795	12	12	EIM book buiness-complete
1416 - 12.10.2011		File storage finished	776	9	9	BIT665 Demo for destruction
1373 - 30.09.2011		File storage finished	773	1	1	1000, 100005998 1997
1365 - 26.09.2011		File storage finished	774	1	1	1000, 100005997 1997
1337 - 08.09.2011		File storage finished	767	1	1	1000, 100005999 1997
1311 - 24.08.2011		File storage finished	745	1	1	1000, 100000011 2001
Snapshots		File storage finished		12	12	
From File Conversion		File storage finished		12	12	
1295 - 1456 (18.08.2011 - 17.11.2011		File storage finished		12	12	
1456 - 17.11.2011		File storage finished	796	11	11	EIM book snapshot
001456-001FI_DOCUMNT		File storage finished		11	11	

Figure 12.30 File Storage Finished

The transfer of data from the legacy system to the retention warehouse storage system is now complete. There, the data is stored safely and can be accessed any time the need arises.

12.5.3 Reporting

If you need to access archived data—for example, due to an upcoming audit or if end users need to view historic data—you can run reporting operations on the data in the archive using different reporting options:

- SAP BW using any BW frontend, including SAP Crystal Reports
- Local reporting (without SAP BW)

In the reporting phase, you select the data from the archive and extract it into SAP BW structures or the table browser for the local reporting functions. The data selection is based on the previously defined audit area through the audit package template. The data is extracted through the audit packages and transferred from the archive files into the BW structures. Based on the audit package, you can view the data either in SAP BW or in local reporting. In SAP BW, you can use the queries that SAP predelivers to support tax audits.

Figure 12.31 provides an overview of the steps required for both reporting options.

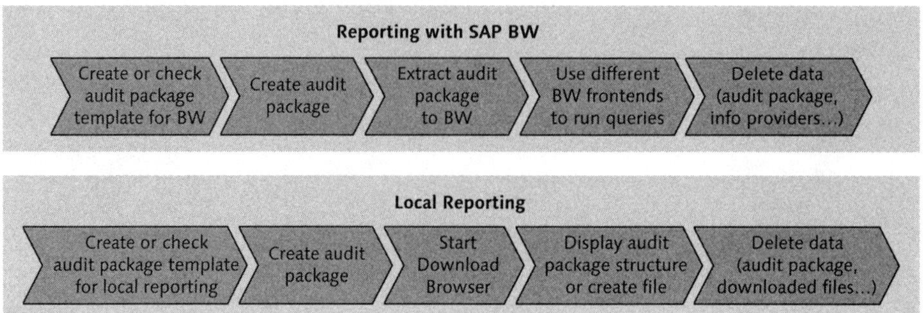

Figure 12.31 Process Steps for Reporting

Reporting with SAP BW

For this example, we assume that an audit package template has already been created for the upcoming audit. An audit package template contains a subset of the objects, tables, and fields of the corresponding audit area, with relevance for the audit.

Next, we go through the main steps required for reporting.

Create Audit Package

Create an audit package using the audit package template previously set up by following these steps:

1. From the NWBC ILM Retention Warehouse cockpit for administrators, choose Audit Packages • Process Audit Packages.
2. Choose New, and enter the required information, such as the audit package template and the source system details.
3. In the second step of this guided procedure, select the archived data to be processed. In this example, we want to report on FI data (FI_DOCUMNT), so we need to specify the document type, the company code, and the fiscal year.
4. In the next screen, you enter additional parameters, such as the name of the audit package, whether it will be used for SAP BW reporting or local reporting, and the execution type.
5. Now you have the opportunity to review your entries and finally create the audit package.

6. The newly created audit package (EIMBOOK in our example; see Figure 12.32) should now appear with the status NEW in the AUDIT PACKAGE HANDLING overview screen.

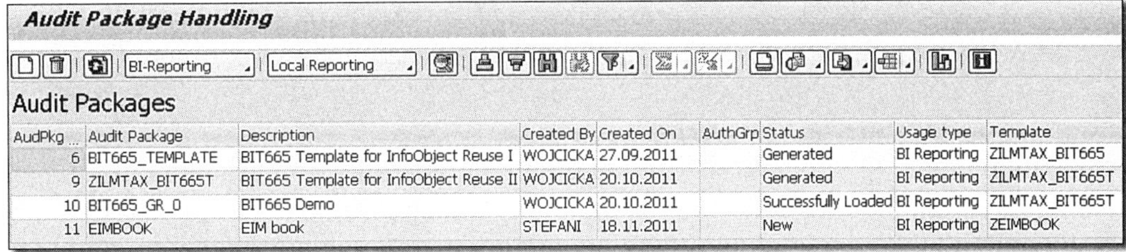

Audit Package Handling

BI-Reporting | Local Reporting

Audit Packages

AudPkg ...	Audit Package	Description	Created By	Created On	AuthGrp	Status	Usage type	Template
6	BIT665_TEMPLATE	BIT665 Template for InfoObject Reuse I	WOJCICKA	27.09.2011		Generated	BI Reporting	ZILMTAX_BIT665
9	ZILMTAX_BIT665T	BIT665 Template for InfoObject Reuse II	WOJCICKA	20.10.2011		Generated	BI Reporting	ZILMTAX_BIT665T
10	BIT665_GR_0	BIT665 Demo	WOJCICKA	20.10.2011		Successfully Loaded	BI Reporting	ZILMTAX_BIT665T
11	EIMBOOK	EIM book	STEFANI	18.11.2011		New	BI Reporting	ZEIMBOOK

Figure 12.32 New Audit Package Created

Extract Audit Package to BI

To extract an audit package to BI, proceed as follows:

1. From the AUDIT PACKAGE HANDLING overview screen, select your audit package. Choose BI REPORTING • EXTRACT AUDIT PACKAGE TO BI.
2. In the next steps of the guided procedure, you define technical parameters, such as the target SAP BW structure (datastore object or InfoCube), and you analyze the results of your selection and define the job parameters, such as server group and start time. Schedule the job as required.

When the extraction job has successfully finished, your audit package appears with the status SUCCESSFULLY LOADED in the AUDIT PACKAGE HANDLING overview screen (see Figure 12.33).

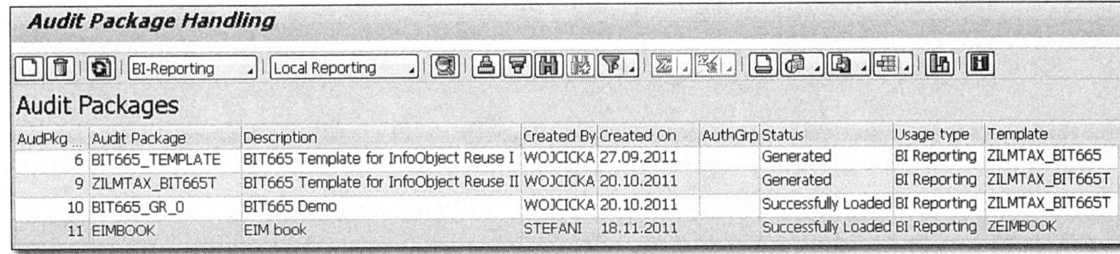

Audit Package Handling

BI-Reporting | Local Reporting

Audit Packages

AudPkg ...	Audit Package	Description	Created By	Created On	AuthGrp	Status	Usage type	Template
6	BIT665_TEMPLATE	BIT665 Template for InfoObject Reuse I	WOJCICKA	27.09.2011		Generated	BI Reporting	ZILMTAX_BIT665
9	ZILMTAX_BIT665T	BIT665 Template for InfoObject Reuse II	WOJCICKA	20.10.2011		Generated	BI Reporting	ZILMTAX_BIT665T
10	BIT665_GR_0	BIT665 Demo	WOJCICKA	20.10.2011		Successfully Loaded	BI Reporting	ZILMTAX_BIT665T
11	EIMBOOK	EIM book	STEFANI	18.11.2011		Successfully Loaded	BI Reporting	ZEIMBOOK

Figure 12.33 Audit Package Loaded to SAP BW

Run Reporting in SAP BW

Now that the archived data is available in SAP BW, you can use the predelivered queries to view the data:

1. Use the query ACCOUNTING DOCUMENT HEADERS to display the accounting documents from the decommissioned system. You'll find it from within the NWBC ILM Retention Warehouse cockpit for LoB under BI REPORTING • TAX REPORTS • ACCOUNTING DOCUMENT.
2. After you've called up the query, the ACCOUNTING DOCUMENT HEADERS window with the subtitle VARIABLE ENTRY appears. Select your audit package and execute.

   Now, in Figure 12.34, you see the accounting document headers from the legacy system according to your previous selections.

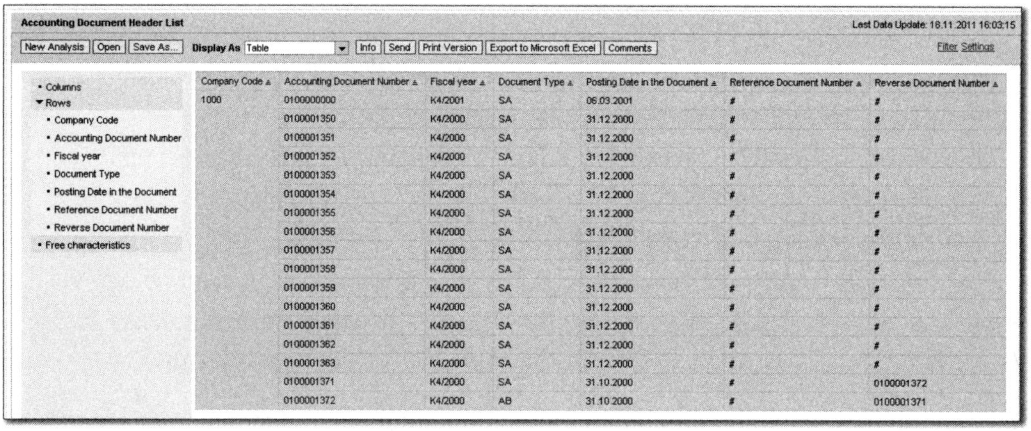
Accounting Document Header List
Last Data Update: 16.11.2011 16:03:15
New Analysis
Open
Save As...
Display As
Table
Info
Send
Print Version
Export to Microsoft Excel
Comments
Filter
Settings
Columns
Rows
Company Code
Accounting Document Number
Fiscal year
Document Type
Posting Date in the Document
Reference Document Number
Reverse Document Number
Free characteristics
Company Code | Accounting Document Number | Fiscal year | Document Type | Posting Date in the Document | Reference Document Number | Reverse Document Number
1000 | 0100000000 | K4/2001 | SA | 06.03.2001 | # | #
0100001350 | K4/2000 | SA | 31.12.2000 | # | #
0100001351 | K4/2000 | SA | 31.12.2000 | # | #
0100001352 | K4/2000 | SA | 31.12.2000 | # | #
0100001353 | K4/2000 | SA | 31.12.2000 | # | #
0100001354 | K4/2000 | SA | 31.12.2000 | # | #
0100001355 | K4/2000 | SA | 31.12.2000 | # | #
0100001356 | K4/2000 | SA | 31.12.2000 | # | #
0100001357 | K4/2000 | SA | 31.12.2000 | # | #
0100001358 | K4/2000 | SA | 31.12.2000 | # | #
0100001359 | K4/2000 | SA | 31.12.2000 | # | #
0100001360 | K4/2000 | SA | 31.12.2000 | # | #
0100001361 | K4/2000 | SA | 31.12.2000 | # | #
0100001362 | K4/2000 | SA | 31.12.2000 | # | #
0100001363 | K4/2000 | SA | 31.12.2000 | # | #
0100001371 | K4/2000 | SA | 31.10.2000 | # | 0100001372
0100001372 | K4/2000 | AB | 31.10.2000 | # | 0100001371

Figure 12.34 Display Accounting Document Headers from SAP BW

From this screen, you also have direct access to any original documents that are attached to the accounting documents. These attachments must also have been made available to the retention warehouse storage system. Simply select the line with the document header in question, and choose DOCUMENTS • DISPLAY DOCUMENTS from the context menu (right-click).

After you're done with reporting, you can delete the audit package in the SAP BW system to release the occupied storage space.

Local Reporting

With local reporting, you can view the data from the archive in a table browser format. You don't need SAP BW for this option. Here also, the retrieval starts with the creation of an audit package template and then an audit package. You can view the contents of the audit package in the download browser and then decide which tables you want to view. Data can only be viewed per table.

An important aspect of local reporting is that you can export data in the SAP Audit Format (AIS). This is important for tax audits, as many financial authorities require companies to hand over tax-relevant data for evaluation in their own tools (such as IDEA in Germany).

Due to the limited space in this chapter, we don't cover local reporting in this example.

12.5.4 Data Destruction

Data destruction isn't one of the core activities that's performed during a system decommissioning project. However, because legacy data that resides in the retention warehouse is subject to the same aging process as data in a live system, it's just as important to control the lifecycle of legacy data as it is for live data. This includes the destruction of archived data that has reached its expiration date.

You can reach the data destruction function for archived data through the link in the NWBC ILM cockpit role for the scenario you're using. You can also call up the function directly by using Transaction ILM_DESTRUCTION. This is regardless of whether data is to be destroyed in a live system environment or in the retention warehouse.

In this example, we want to destroy accounting documents from legacy system ILM, client 800, that we archived and moved to the retention warehouse as part of the system decommissioning process (see Figure 12.25, earlier in the chapter).

1. From the NWBC ILM Retention Warehouse cockpit for administrators, choose Data Destruction • Destroy Data in ILM Store.
2. Choose Archive Files (ADK), and specify the ILM Object Type, the SAP System, and the Client (see Figure 12.35).

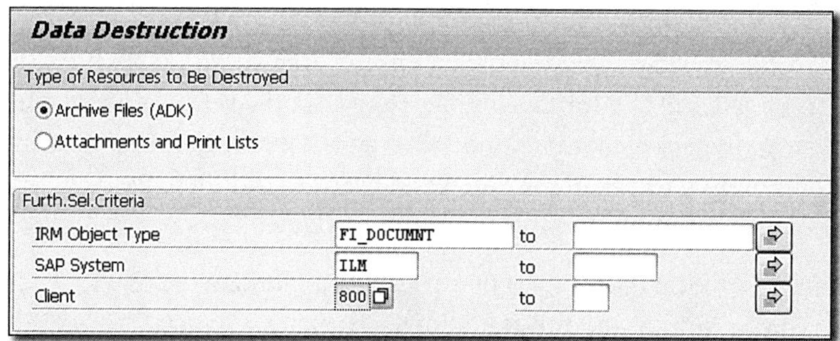

Figure 12.35 Data Destruction Selection Criteria

3. Choose EXECUTE.
4. In the screen with expired resources, drill down to find the archive files you want to destroy (see Figure 12.36). You won't see snapshots, because they have an unknown expiration date and are therefore not shown here. (A special function allows you to set the expiration date of snapshots to TODAY. As a result, these snapshots can be destroyed through the standard destruction transaction on the next day.)

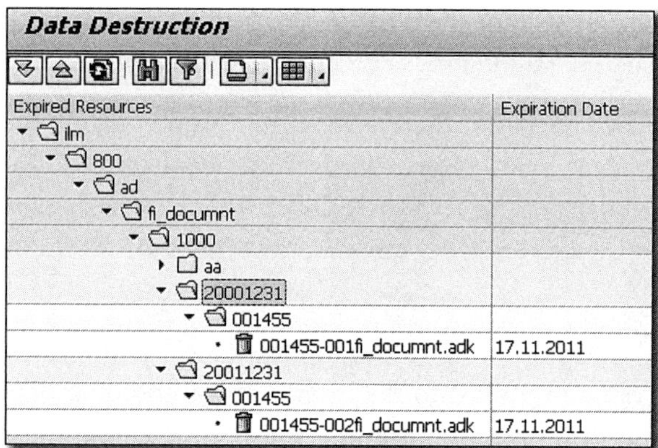

Figure 12.36 Archive Files Eligible for Destruction

Remember that the archive files of session 1455 were created as a result of the file conversion (refer to Figure 12.28). The trash can symbol indicates that the archive file has reached its expiration data and is ready for destruction.

5. In the Data Destruction main screen (see Figure 12.37), select the archive file to be destroyed, and drag it to the Creation of Destruction Worklist container (see Figure 12.38). Save your destruction work list.

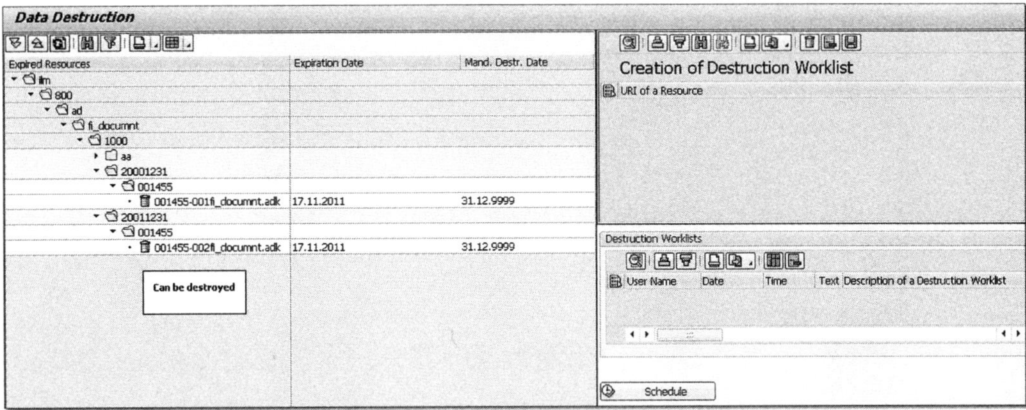

Figure 12.37 Data Destruction Main Screen

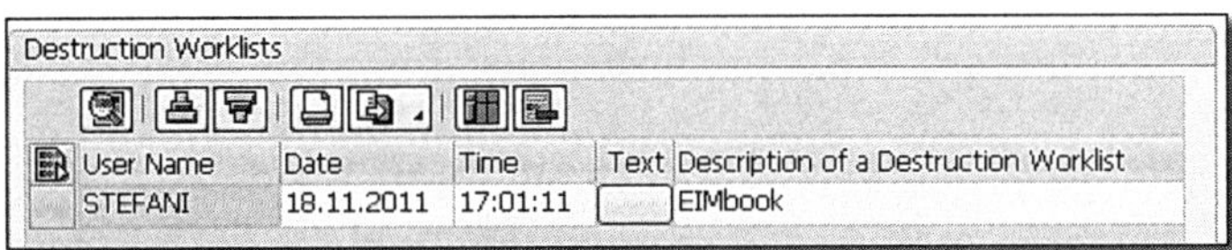

Destruction Worklists

User Name	Date	Time	Text	Description of a Destruction Worklist
STEFANI	18.11.2011	17:01:11		EIMbook

Figure 12.38 Destruction Work List

6. In the lower Destruction Worklist container, select your destruction work list, and schedule the destruction job in live mode.

Security Considerations

To comply with security standards, two individuals can perform the compilation of the work list and the execution of the destruction run steps ("four-eye principle"). This concept is supported by suitable user roles provided with the SAP ILM software.

7. When the job is finished, you can verify the destruction result in the SAP ILM Store Browser or in Archive Management, as shown in Figure 12.39.

The destroyed archiving session is listed as complete, but it's marked with a special icon to signal that its archive files have been destroyed.

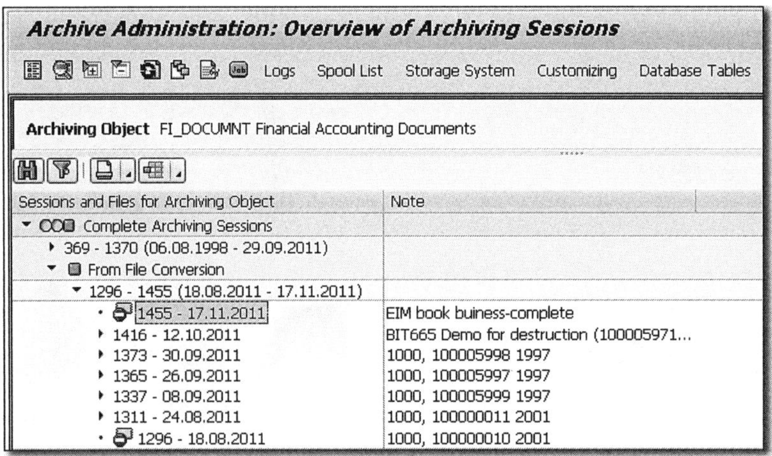

Figure 12.39 Destruction Result in Archive Management

12.6 Summary

In this chapter, we provided you with an overview of the SAP solutions for ILM and showed you how you can best leverage them to build a holistic ILM strategy. With SAP ILM being the pivotal component of this solution suite, we took a more thorough look at the features and inner workings of this product. By following our practical examples, complemented by screenshots from a real system environment, you saw see how SAP ILM works in real life. No matter whether you want to manage the lifecycle of your data in a live system environment, or you need to retire an SAP or non-SAP system in a standardized and legally compliant way, the SAP ILM solutions will help you succeed.

Any company that wants to be successful in today's globalized world needs to ensure that its IT-related costs don't go over the top. It must also ensure adherence to an ever-increasing number of laws and regulations. Therefore, to stay on the safe side, having a holistic ILM strategy in place isn't an option but a must.

Note

For more information on getting started with data archiving projects, see Appendix C (available for download from the book's website at *www.sap-press.com/3666*).

This chapter provides an overview of the business process for managing unstructured content such as pictures, word documents, mails, spreadsheets, and so on.

13 SAP Extended Enterprise Content Management by OpenText

Enterprise content management (ECM) is a broad area that includes capturing, managing, preserving, and delivering content and documents to organizations and business processes. Chapter 4 provided a high-level description of SAP's offering for ECM. This chapter will focus on ECM as it relates to the business process, which we'll call *integrated* ECM. Integrated ECM allows you to associate and manage unstructured information (such as documents or emails) with structured information (such as application data) in the context of business processes.

Integrated ECM has a twofold meaning. The obvious one is that ECM supports seamless integration of unstructured content with application data. The second meaning is that ECM offers content management capabilities within an application system.

Twofold Meaning of Integrated ECM

- *Integration* as support of unstructured content with application data or application systems
- ECM capabilities as *integrated within* an application system

Along with data integration (Chapter 9), data quality (Chapter 9 and Chapter 10), and master data governance (Chapter 11), integrated ECM plays an important role in improving business processes and, in the end, is the underlying strategic key performance indicator (KPI) by which the efficiency and efficacy of those processes are measured.

An example from the German telecom industry can help to illustrate how poor content management can hurt a business process. Suppose Franz wants to remodel his house, but would like to disconnect his home phone during construction. He writes a letter to the phone company (a letter is required in Germany when changing telephone service) explaining that he will need to disconnect his phone during construction.

A week later, Franz gets a message from the phone company—on the answering machine for the line he wants disconnected. He calls the phone company call center, and the agent asks why he is disconnecting his phone service, worried that he has a complaint about their service.

Franz tells the agent that he wrote a letter explaining his need to have the phone disconnected due to demolition and construction, but the call center agent can't see the letter because the telephone company doesn't have integrated ECM. Franz must again explain why he must discontinue phone service and supply his temporary address, and the time of both Franz and the call center agent is wasted. Furthermore, the call center agent changes his home address to the temporary address he has given but unfortunately neglects to update his billing address, resulting in his invoices being sent to the wrong address.

Because the call center agent wasn't able to see all of the documents associated with Franz's account, the net result was poor customer service and damage to the customer relationship. Documents and unstructured content play an important role not only in call center scenarios but also in all customer-centric business processes.

And that's true not only for business processes that rely on customer data, but also for any business process where unstructured content is relevant.

Example

Think back to NeedsEIM Inc. (introduced in Chapter 1). It outsources manufacturing and has a diverse supplier network. ECM tools are needed in various business areas to cover important business challenges, especially in those areas where unstructured content plays an important role, such as contracts, engineering drawings, specification designs, invoicing, and so on.

In addition to better-run business processes with unstructured content, managing the unstructured content is also important for meeting internal and external compliance and reporting demands.

A single, reliable version of truth for both structured and unstructured content, with careful version and access control, should be available for any part of a business process or end-user decision point. Both types of information should also be part of a thoughtful strategy for retention management. These principles, which assure compliance and minimize legal fines, are the foundation of effective, process-centric information management.

SAP Extended Enterprise Content Management by OpenText (hereafter SAP Extended ECM) delivers the basis for the seamless and frictionless integration of unstructured content into the business processes supported by the SAP Business Suite and should be an integral part of any information management initiative.

This chapter describes integrated ECM based on SAP Extended ECM. The discussion includes details of what is offered, core components, and technical integration options supported, and explains how to get started using a workspace, which is a key concept for SAP Extended ECM. (Chapter 6 includes examples of real-world use of SAP Extended ECM.)

13.1 Capabilities of SAP Extended ECM

SAP Extended ECM is a complete ECM solution. Even though it's offered by OpenText, it's a complete solution extension provided by SAP. SAP Extended ECM, as well as the other solutions offered by OpenText, has dedicated product teams on both sides, adheres to SAP requirements for support and upgrades, has deep technology integration with SAP, and includes committed codevelopment efforts.

Figure 13.1 shows an overview of the core capabilities required to deliver an integrated ECM project. These capabilities are delivered with SAP Extended ECM.

Each of the capabilities shown in Figure 13.1 is described in the following list, starting with the bottom and moving toward the top:

- **Archive**
  Refers to data and document archiving. In this context, an archive is the secure storage for all unstructured content.
- **Records management**
  Controls the complete lifecycle of unstructured content with functionality certified by the U.S. Department of Defense (DOD) 5015.2 certification.
- **Content access**
  Enables users to have a personalized view of unstructured content. This includes retrieval of content from authorized sources and viewing of content through a choice of user interfaces (UIs).

- **Document-centric workflow**
  Enables electronic document approval and signing processes.
- **Document management**
  Enables basic content-handling capabilities such as retrieval, storage, versioning, check-in/check-out, metadata handling, and security handling.
- **Capture**
  Enables scanning of paper documents.
- **Collaboration**
  Enables users to brainstorm, develop, share, and comment about document and file collaboration in the SAP business process context.

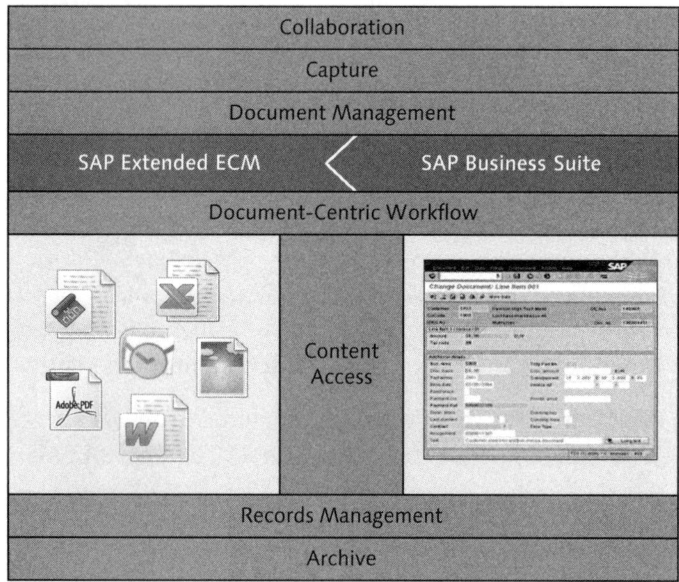

Figure 13.1 Overview of Capabilities Provided with SAP Extended ECM

Each of these is so important that it warrants further discussion of how the capability works and the business problem it addresses.

13.1.1 Data and Document Archiving

All unstructured content must have a repository for storage. OpenText provides this storage to store content such as images, scanned documents, manuals, and all content that is associated with an SAP business process.

As mentioned in Chapter 4 and again in Chapter 12, archiving also refers to the removal of information that is no longer required. SAP Extended ECM also supports retention policies and the archiving of information that is no longer required for productive use. It works with SAP Information Lifecycle Management (SAP ILM) (discussed in Chapter 12) to archive data that's no longer needed. SAP ILM handles the archiving of all structured documents, as well as SAP ArchiveLink documents associated with the SAP business context. This means that if you scan invoices for Financial Accounting (FI) documents, associated documents and manuals with equipment, or associated résumés and pictures with employees using SAP Extended ECM, then when it's time to retire that data, SAP ILM will retire both the SAP structured content and the associated SAP ArchiveLink documents. If you're already using SAP Extended ECM, then you can use the OpenText repository as the SAP ILM-aware storage discussed in Chapter 12. Section 13.3.1 discussed SAP ArchiveLink as the service inside the SAP NetWeaver Application Server ABAP for linking archived documents and the application documents entered in the SAP system. SAP ArchiveLink is fully supported by OpenText, as well as by SAP ILM.

13.1.2 Records Management

Records management is the discipline of managing the lifecycle of documents in physical and electronic format, from creation to deletion. Records management is relevant for all industries to support compliance with financial reporting, auditing standards, and Sarbanes-Oxley requirements.

Records management also plays an important role in many business processes and industries: developing new products, managing public health and public organization records, and managing all records required for government compliance.

The U.S. Department of Defense (DOD) 5015.2 certification is the gold standard for software solutions supporting records management. Even though this certification is only compulsory for organizations associated with the DOD in the United States, it's also used as the records management benchmark in other public sector and nonpublic sector organizations globally.

SAP Extended ECM is certified to the DOD 5015.2 standard and also complies with the international ISO 15489 standard for records management systems. Records management is applied to any document created by any process in SAP Extended ECM. This includes the support of all documents in a classification scheme that defines document types, document lifecycles, and security information for all related documents.

13.1.3 Content Access

Content needs to be made available to the end user, in the user's preferred interface, and independent of the application that initially generated the content. For example, as mentioned previously, a call center agent needs access to all content related to a customer, including content that originated from paper, emails, calls, or other sources.

13.1.4 Document-Centric Workflow

Document-centric workflow is an important capability of SAP Extended ECM to support document-driven processes.

Example

For NeedsEIM Inc., contracts for each outsourced manufacturer and each supplier must be created in a collaborative fashion and go through a series of approvals before being sent to the supplier or manufacturer for their signature.

Document-centric workflow templates can easily be created in a graphical interface and conveniently used by the end user. All workflow steps and decisions are logged in a complete audit trail, so before a contract is sent out, all changes to the contract and the approval process can be tracked in SAP Extended ECM.

13.1.5 Document Management

Document management is the core element of SAP Extended ECM. Document management delivers basic content-handling capabilities such as retrieval, storage, versioning, check-in and check-out, metadata handling, and security handling.

Document management is where you start when moving away from storing your files in various file shares or on laptops, which often makes it impossible to find the latest version of a file. Versioning in file shares is often managed by file name, so names such as *contract_final.doc*, *contract_final_final.doc*, and *contract_final_final_last.doc* are often found in a file share location, and often hierarchies are very complicated. With SAP Extended ECM, versions of files/documents can be easily managed, and the change history easily understood. Major and minor versioning is supported, and access rights can be easily managed.

It's well known that employees spend a significant amount of time searching for documents. Support for users to search for documents is a key functionality of SAP Extended ECM. When searching for a document, you often may only know the author or a key word from the content. Searching by both document metadata and by full text is fully supported in SAP Extended ECM.

Document management is extended by records management to all the compliance regulations supported by records management.

13.1.6 Capture

Capture is a key element of SAP Extended ECM. Capture refers to the scanning of documents in formats such as TIF, PDF, and JPG; indexing the document; providing metadata for search and discovery; attaching the document to the right transaction or business process; and generating searchable PDF documents using optical character recognition (OCR).

SAP Extended ECM supports bar code scenarios out of the box, and all SAP ArchiveLink capture scenarios are supported as well. This will be discussed in more detail in the next section.

The following explains one specific bar-coding example for outgoing documents that is supported by default: Many scenarios, such as contract signing and closing documents, require paper copies to be sent by mail and may require a handwritten signature. Computer-generated signatures are not allowed in some scenarios; for example, in correspondence with public-sector organizations. The approval workflow in SAP Extended ECM supports hand signatures. The user prints the document with an automatically generated bar code and signs it. Before being mailed, the signed document is scanned and automatically added as a signed version.

13.1.7 Collaboration and Social Media

Collaboration is very important for knowledge workers. It happens with or without a system in place to support it. SAP Extended ECM enables the capture of the collaboration to be associated with a business process. This includes social media behavior such as commenting, activity feeds, user notification, users following other users, and so on.

SAP Extended ECM moves collaboration out of email tools and into a true collaborative environment for tasks such as creating a contract for a new supplier or manufacturer.

13.2 How SAP Extended ECM Works with the SAP Business Suite

As explained in the introduction, integrated ECM has a twofold meaning: supporting seamless integration of unstructured content with application data, and offering ECM capabilities as an integrated part of an application system.

Figure 13.2 shows the integration of SAP Extended ECM with the SAP Business Suite.

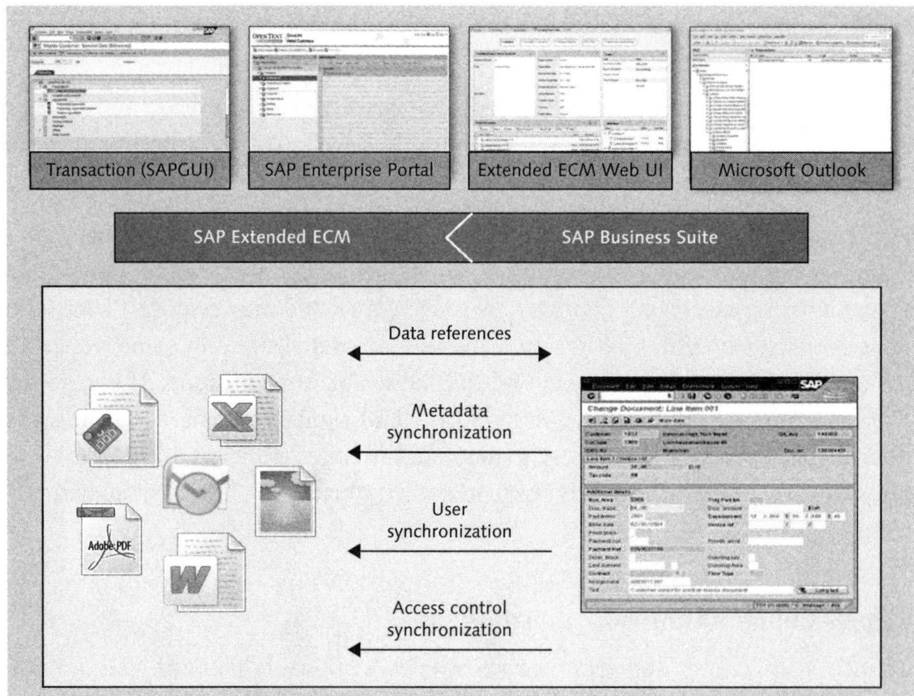

Figure 13.2 Integrated Unstructured Content

Figure 13.2 can be divided into three sections: UI, application integration, and detailed application synchronization. The UIs at the top of the figure reference the types of user experiences available to interact with the content associated with the SAP Business Suite. SAP Extended ECM unstructured content can be associated with application data—for example, a hierarchy of customer documents—and displayed together with the application data in UIs used by the SAP Business Suite (SAP GUI, SAP CRM WebClient, SAP Enterprise Portal, SAP Supplier Relationship Management [SAP SRM]) as well as with non-SAP UIs such as Microsoft Outlook, Lotus Notes, Microsoft Windows Explorer, and SAP Extended ECM's native web interface. Integration of unstructured content with application data is brought to any user via the interface best fitted to the role and task.

The middle portion of Figure 13.2 depicts SAP Extended ECM and SAP Business Suite in the same box, because they are so seamlessly integrated as to appear as the same application.

The lower part of Figure 13.2 shows synchronization details of the integrated platform approach of SAP Extended ECM together with the SAP Business Suite. This includes tight integration and synchronization of data references, metadata, users, and their security access and controls. Each of these is explained next in more detail:

- **User synchronization and SAP Single Sign-On (SSO) support**
  Ensures a consistent and seamless user experience for end users. It also lowers the cost of maintaining various user identities in different systems.
- **Access control synchronization**
  Ensures that access control rights maintained in the SAP Business Suite are also applied on SAP Extended ECM. For example, when a user isn't allowed to see certain customer data in an SAP CRM system, the user also can't access the same details in SAP Extended ECM. SAP authorization objects are synchronized with the access policies in SAP Extended ECM.
- **Metadata synchronization**
  Pushes SAP application data to SAP Extended ECM. This means that SAP Extended ECM is always up to date and in sync with the SAP application data. This tight synchronization ensures high-quality document and folder attribute data and enables searching in offline scenarios, such as providing customer data offline for a sales visit.

- **Data references**
  Ensure referential integrity of the data in SAP Extended ECM and the SAP Business Suite. For example, the unstructured content for a specific supplier is associated with the correct supplier in SAP ERP. It also provides the representation of SAP object relationships, such as the equipment hierarchy or project hierarchy in the SAP Extended ECM UI. The result is that ECM users can leverage the "business model" of SAP applications for browsing, searching, and content classification, providing them the business context for content.

13.3 Integration Content for SAP Business Suite and SAP Extended ECM

SAP Extended ECM supports various options to integrate content in the SAP Business Suite: SAP ArchiveLink, the SAP ECM integration layer, and workspaces within SAP Extended ECM. (SAP ArchiveLink and the SAP ECM integration layer are part of the SAP core offering, and workspaces are part of SAP Extended ECM.) We discuss these three options in this section.

13.3.1 SAP ArchiveLink

SAP ArchiveLink is a building block of SAP Extended ECM. The SAP ArchiveLink interface was the first integration approach developed by SAP to attach documents and scanned images to transactions in SAP; for example, you can attach scanned invoices to financial transactions in SAP ERP. It creates a link in SAP to associate content stored in a document archive repository (see Figure 13.3).

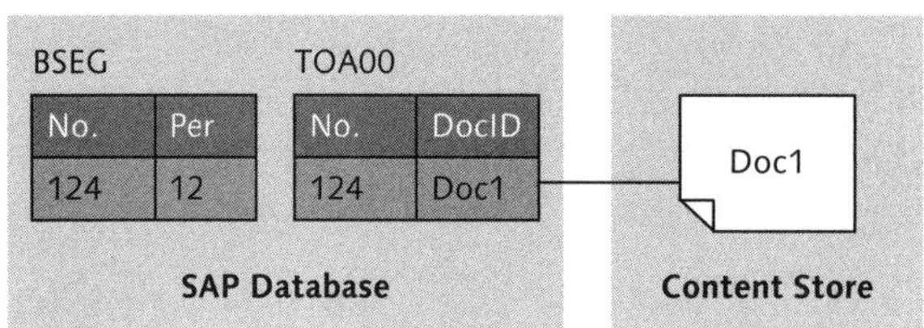

Figure 13.3 SAP ArchiveLink Integration

Figure 13.3 demonstrates the link between the SAP database and the content store. In this example, a document is stored in the application Table BSEG. SAP ArchiveLink creates a reference to this in Table TOA00. This table stores the link between the object in SAP and the document in the content store. With SAP ArchiveLink, a user must be logged in to the SAP system to access the content. The SAP system and the external content store communicate via a standardized HTTP interface.

Hint

SAP ArchiveLink is used for associating content with business objects. SAP ArchiveLink also supports SAP Data Archiving, which relocates information from production systems (discussed in Chapter 12).

The basic architectural guidance for SAP ArchiveLink is to enable attaching one or more documents (such as scanned images) to an SAP transaction. The content is stored not in the SAP database, but in an external content store designed to hold unstructured content.

There are several advantages to using external storage for storing content:

- External content stores reduce the size of the SAP database.
- External content stores are designed to manage unstructured content.
- External content stores support any sort of physical storage media.
- External content stores often come with their own viewer technology.

SAP ArchiveLink supports many scenarios, including the following most common ones:

- Automated storage and management of incoming documents based on SAP Business Workflow.
- Automated linkage and storage of incoming documents using bar codes.
- Ad hoc processing of incoming documents.
- Storage of outgoing documents such as SAP Smart Forms or Adobe print forms. SAP ArchiveLink can attach the outgoing document to the SAP business object, whether it's printed, faxed, or emailed.
- Print lists (reports), for example, an annual report. Examples of print lists are account update logs in finance, warehouse stock, and logs.

SAP Extended ECM enhances the base SAP ArchiveLink capabilities with the use of metadata management, version support, audit trails, searching, and other capabilities, to provide full management of all content that's associated with SAP.

13.3.2 Content Management Interoperability Standard and SAP ECM Integration Layer

Content Management Interoperability Services (CMIS) is an OASIS open standard that works to standardize "a web services interface specification that will enable greater interoperability of Enterprise Content Management (ECM) systems. CMIS uses web services and Web 2.0 interfaces to enable rich information to be shared across Internet protocols in vendor-neutral formats, among document systems, publishers and repositories, within one enterprise and between companies."[1]

To understand how this is supported with SAP Extended ECM by OpenText, refer to Figure 13.4. Notice that the UI on the top represents the UIs that are supported by SAP. The UI on the bottom represents the UIs that are supported by the document management system. Next, notice the SAP ECM integration layer; SAP provides the ECM integration layer as ECM support for all ECM vendors. Also notice the ECM store within the SAP Business Suite; this store is required if you wanted to leverage the ECM integration layer without an external content store. Finally, notice that the CMIS protocol is used to integrate with the document management system.

In Figure 13.4, the ECM integration layer also enables customers to leverage the features of document management systems for documents that are created in their SAP applications. Documents created by an SAP business application should be accessible not only via the business application, but also via the UIs and services provided by the third-party document management system.

To use the powerful features of a document management system such as searching, document-centric processes, or classification mechanisms, you have to enrich the documents stored in the third-party systems with additional metadata from the business application. This metadata enables a user, working directly in the document management system, to understand the business object or business process to which a document belongs without launching the business application. In addition, the application assigns properties to documents or folders that can be used for searching or classification of documents. An application can even add access rights to the documents created in the external system to ensure that only authorized actors are able to access the documents in the third-party system.

The SAP ECM integration layer is supported from SAP NetWeaver 7.03 and on. SAP also provides a Java version for the integration layer, which will be used by

1 Source: *http://www.oasis-open.org/committees/tc_home.php?wg_abbrev=cmis*

SAP Process Orchestration (including SAP Business Process Management) and is supported with SAP NetWeaver 7.2, Java Application Server 7.2, and higher.

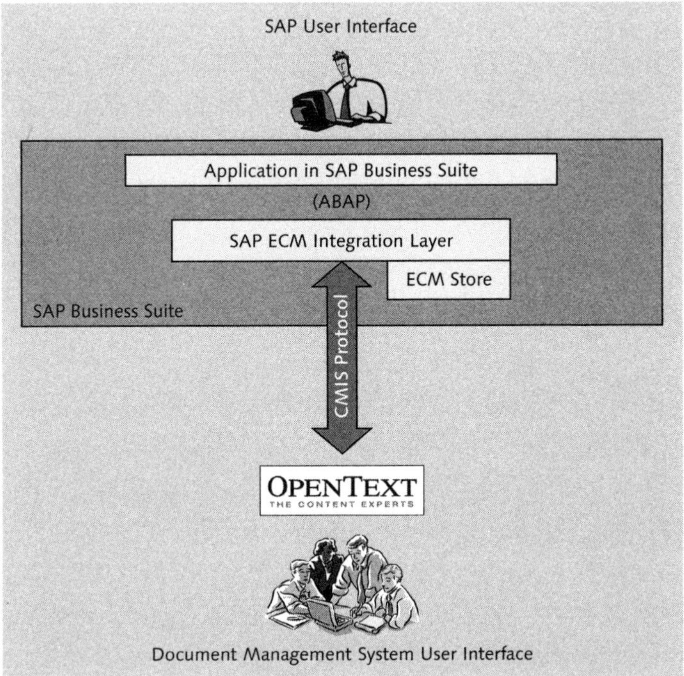

Figure 13.4 SAP ECM Integration Layer and CMIS Standard

13.3.3 SAP Extended ECM Workspaces

Extended ECM's most advanced and innovative integration option with SAP is based on the ECM workspace. While the term *ECM workspace* is well known in the ECM market, our reference to ECM workspaces will be specific to the workspaces provided by the *ECMLink* technology from OpenText.

Figure 13.5 shows an example of a workspace for a piece of equipment. Each workspace is attached to an SAP object and links all relevant content. This includes SAP ArchiveLink documents, non-SAP documents, images, and emails. All content is provided in a single view. The power of workspaces lies in the ubiquitous access from all relevant SAP UIs, including the SAP GUI, SAP Enterprise Portal, SAP GUI for HTML, and specific web UIs provided by SAP CRM, SAP SRM, and the SAP NetWeaver Business Client. In addition to SAP UIs, non-SAP UIs include the SAP Extended ECM web interface, Microsoft Windows Explorer, Microsoft Office, and email clients such as Microsoft Outlook and Lotus Notes.

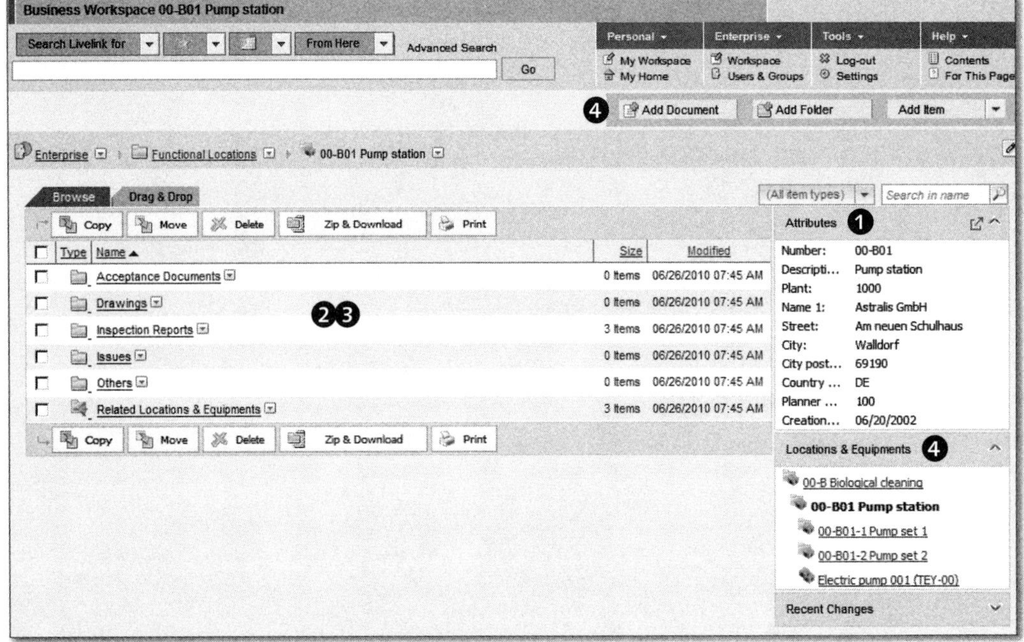

Figure 13.5 SAP Extended ECM Workspace

In Figure 13.5, the workspace includes metadata, folder structures, and documents and forms, as explained here:

❶ Metadata

Metadata provides information about the object that can be displayed in SAP and non-SAP UIs. The metadata is used to identify the workspace in non-SAP UIs as well. Metadata defined for a workspace is available in the web UI of SAP Extended ECM. Metadata is data duplicated from SAP to the SAP Extended ECM UIs. Examples of metadata in Figure 13.5 include the attributes on the pump such as the pump number, description, plant, and so on.

❷ Folder structures

Folder structures reflect how the content is organized. Default folder structures are provided out of the box, and you can create your own as well.

❸ **Documents and forms**
These include all related documents for the workspace, such as pictures, scanned images, videos, contracts, and so on. Additionally, the forms in the workspace can be used as templates to create other documents, for example, an email draft to send to a customer.

❹ **Business relationships**
Business relationships allow you to link the business workspace to predefined business object structures in the SAP system. An example is the relationship of a customer to sales orders. In Figure 13.5, the business relationships shown are the relation of the pump to locations and equipment. Document activity feeds display activities such as NEW DOCUMENT CREATED and NEW VERSION CREATED by certain users.

The full content of a workspace (metadata, folder structure, and business relationships) is dependent on the user's business role. The business role in SAP Extended ECM depends on the user's authorizations in the SAP system.

Example

For NeedsEIM Inc., there is a workspace for each manufacturer, including detailed specifications, drawings, and so on. Internally, the design engineers can only access workspaces for the projects they are assigned to with external manufacturers. An employee working in the contract department would only see the contract-relevant document/folder in the workspace.

Each workspace provides core ECM capabilities, such as collaboration, document-centric workflow, document management, records management, and capture capabilities, each discussed in the previous section. The layout of the ECM workspace for a certain SAP business object is based on fully configurable business workspace templates that define the folder structure, metadata structures, roles, permissions, and UI elements.

SAP Extended ECM supports three workspace types: *business workspaces, case workspaces,* and *binder workspaces*. Case workspaces have additional characteristics, such as a status field used to define a beginning and end of the workspace. Case workspaces support defined phases and typically have a list of processors. They are used to support collaboration, including follow-up actions such as setting a reminder to review a document in two weeks. Binder workspaces only allow attaching a folder structure to SAP objects.

To give you a better understanding of an ECM workspace, Figure 13.6 shows an equipment business workspace in the WebGUI for SAP Extended ECM. We've chosen to show a business workspace, as this is the most commonly used ECM workspace type.

The user can see the folder structure and the attached documents in the middle and all relevant SAP data and the related SAP objects on the right-hand side. On the left, all changes to documents in the business workspace are shown as document and folder activities and feeds. In addition, a powerful faceted full-text search within the documents in a business workspace is available.

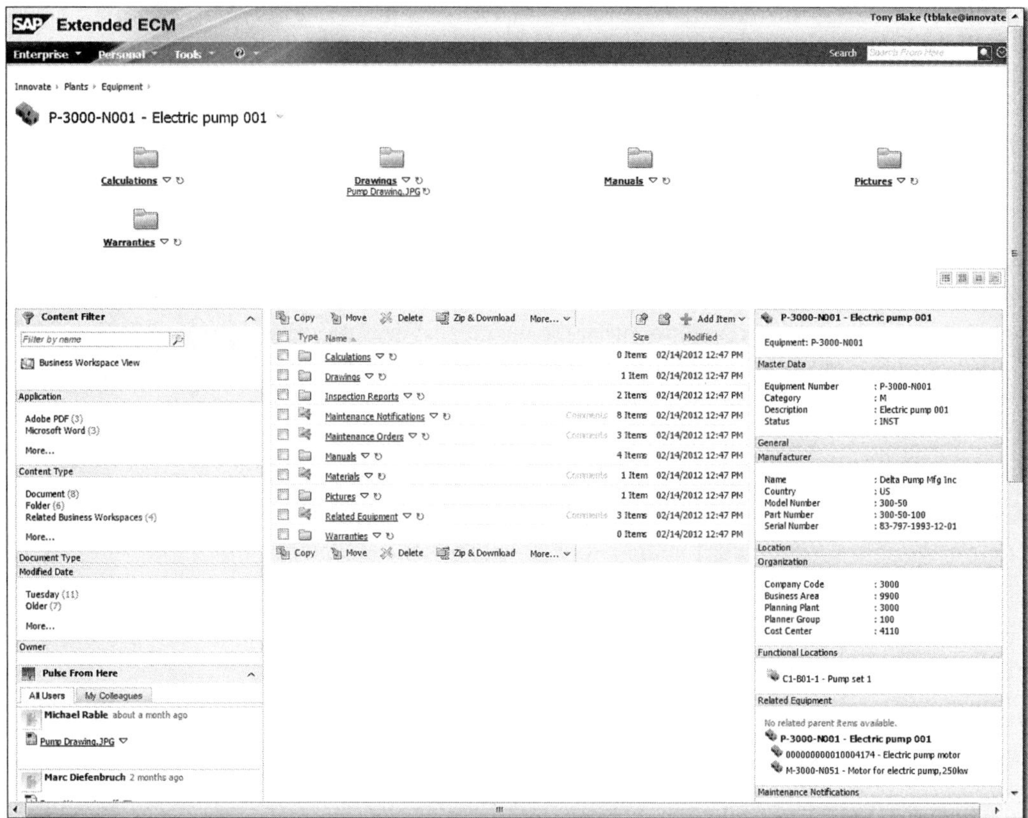

Figure 13.6 Business Workspace for Equipment in SAP Extended ECM WebGUI

As shown in Figure 13.7, the same information can be accessed via the Windows Explorer frontend. Documents can be easily added in the Windows Explorer by drag and drop. All functions that are available in the WebGUI can be performed in this frontend via context menus. For example, the user can display and maintain document attributes in the Windows Explorer frontend.

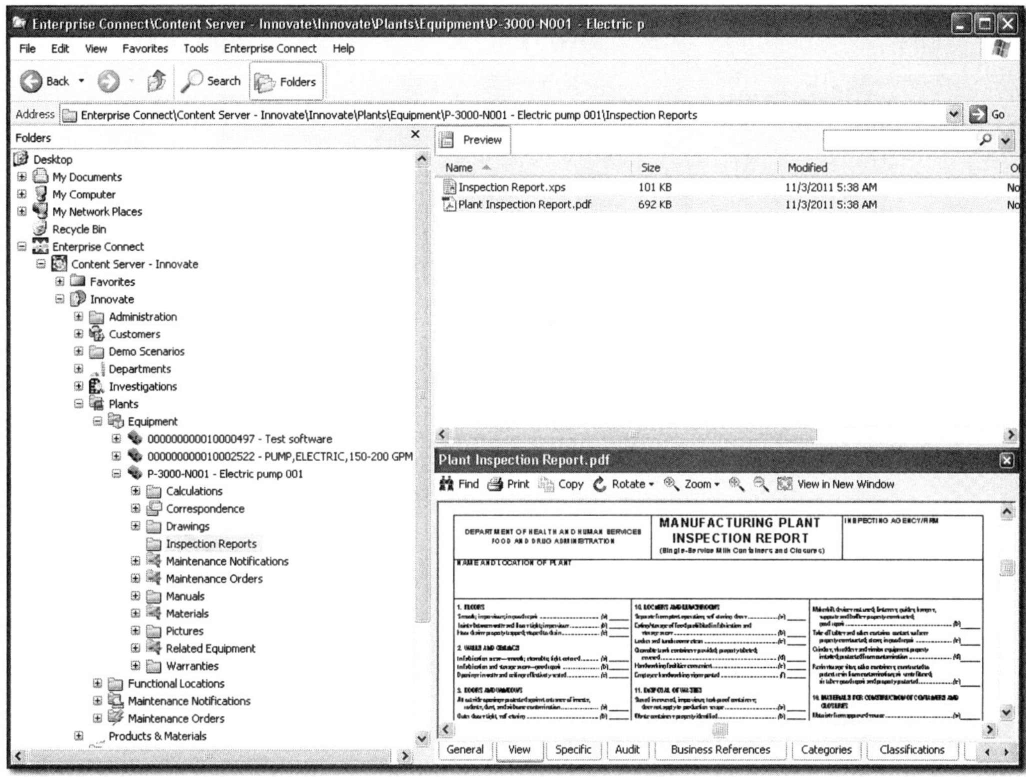

Figure 13.7 Business Workspace for Equipment Displayed in Microsoft Windows Explorer

The same information is available for a user accessing the information via a transaction in the SAP system, as displayed in Figure 13.8. The pump information is now displayed in the SAP GUI, including all content, such as the manufacturing plant inspection report shown in Figure 13.8.

As you get started with SAP Extended ECM, customizing the workspace is a very common activity. Therefore, we'll discuss the basics of how to create your own workspace and where you can get a step-by-step example of workspace creation in the next subsection.

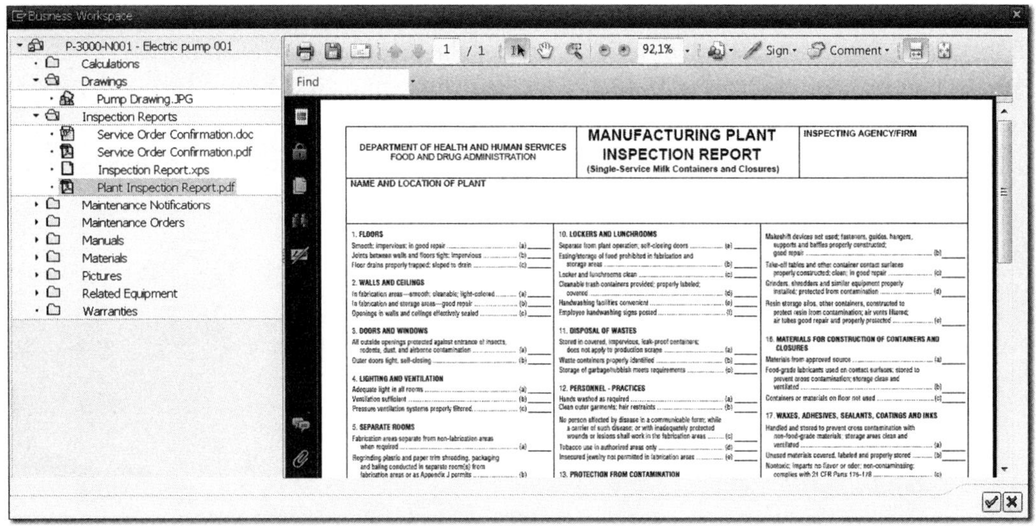

Figure 13.8 Business Workspace for Material via SAP GUI

Configuring Your Own Workspace in SAP Extended ECM

When designing a workspace, you need to know the objects (e.g., material, equipment, vendor) that require workspaces. You need to define the data that should be metadata for the workspace. Remember that the metadata will be displayed in all UIs. Folder structures are provided for you, but you can also customize your own. You also need to consider security aspects, document types, and relationships between workspaces.

Step-by-step instructions for configuring a workspace can be found in the OpenText Knowledge Center. The guide for creation of workspaces can be found here: *https://knowledge.opentext.com/knowledge/piroot/erx/v100000/erx-acs/en/erx-acs-en.pdf*.

After the base configuration is done, business users can create workspaces from the SAP GUI, the SAP Extended ECM UI, the SAP CRM WebClient, or the SAP CRM Interaction Center WebClient. Figure 13.9 shows an example of how a user can create a workspace from the SAP GUI.

If you're already familiar with the generic object services available in the SAP NetWeaver Application Server ABAP, you'll notice how workspaces are associated with the generic object services.

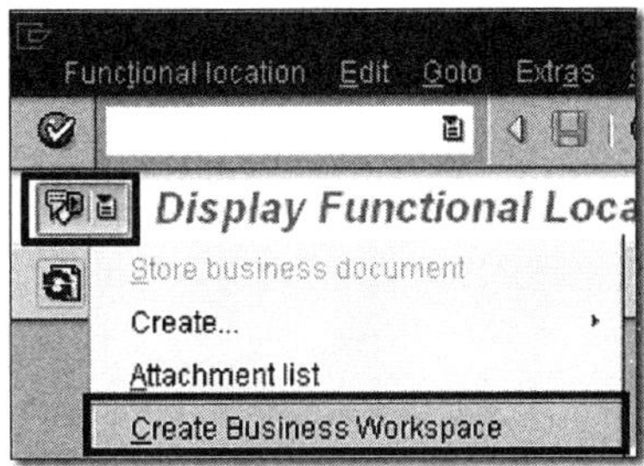

Figure 13.9 Creating a Workspace from the SAP GUI

Workspaces can be generated manually (as shown in Figure 13.9) or automatically. Automatic creation is common if you want to create a workspace for each business object of a certain type, for example, objects used in a Plant Maintenance (PM) application in an SAP system. The configuration for workspaces does require some setup in the SAP IMG (Transaction SPRO) as well as in SAP Extended ECM. After a workspace is created, it can easily be viewed in the SAP GUI, as shown in Figure 13.10.

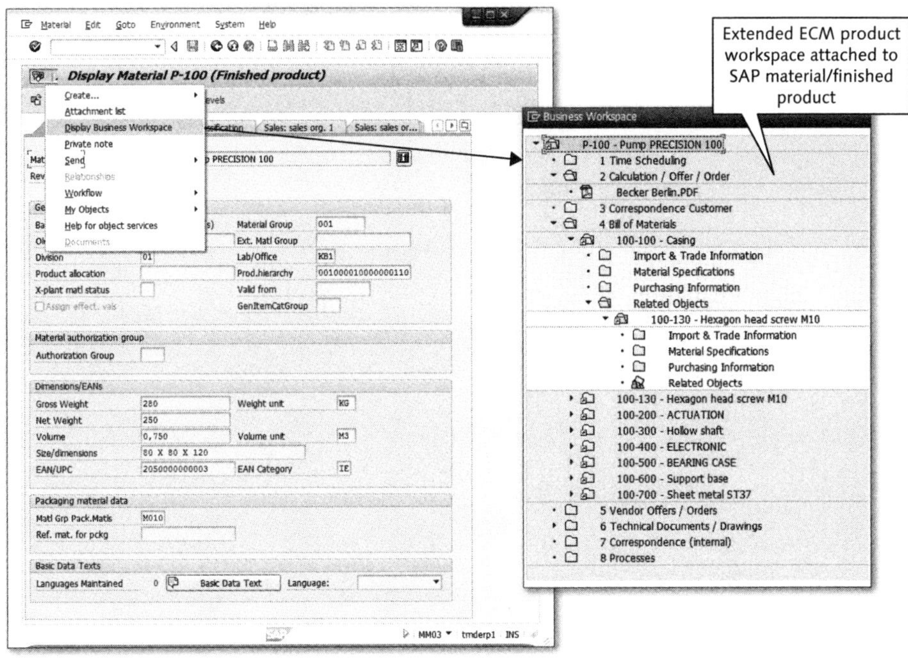

Figure 13.10 Easy Navigation to Workspace in SAP GUI

In Figure 13.10, notice that the user can use the generic object services and select DISPLAY BUSINESS WORKSPACE while viewing any transaction in the SAP system that has a workspace. In Figure 13.10, the example shows a workspace from a material. The user is in the material for the pump and selects to view the workspace. He can immediately see documents stored in SAP Extended ECM related to the material.

13.4 Summary

In this chapter, you learned that SAP delivers integrated ECM. You now understand that SAP ArchiveLink is an important foundation for SAP Extended ECM. You learned about the role of the ECM integration layer and the CMIS OASIS standard for content. You learned about the major features of SAP Extended ECM and how to get started using and configuring workspaces to relate content to the SAP business processes.

This chapter, combined with the ECM discussion in Chapter 6, by Belgian Railways, gives you a good starting point for understanding ECM.

The Authors

Corrie Brague is the director of Data Quality Product Management for SAP, where she defines software solutions that help businesses assess, improve, and monitor their data quality. She participates in ASUG and works with a broad range of customers and partners to support market-driven product direction, as well as enhance the insight of the customer and market space within the development organization. She has more than 15 years of experience in data quality and mail automation software solutions gained through positions in software engineering, project management, development management, and product management.

George Bryce is an enterprise data architect at Procter & Gamble, which has more than 300 consumer brands marketed in 160 countries with global sales exceeding $85 billion annually. He has been a leader in P&G's master data capabilities, with more than 20 years of experience architecting, designing, and supporting the management of data as an asset through the creation of a single global master data client. His current focus is the creation of an enterprise architecture that enables business-led data governance with clear accountability for data ownership.

Ryan Champlin has more than 14 years of experience in the field of information management, having worked within both engineering and product management organizations. At Business Objects and SAP, he played an instrumental role as a product manager on the industry's first single platform for data quality and data integration: SAP Data Services. He currently works as the director of engineering within the SAP HANA team at SAP, where he is responsible for driving new innovations on the SAP HANA platform around information management and the data quality management solutions for various SAP applications (e.g., SAP ERP, SAP CRM, and SAP MDG).

Frank Densborn is a product manager for SAP Rapid Deployment solutions in the technology area, focusing on data migration and cloud integration. Frank is the package owner of SAP's Rapid Data Migration rapid-deployment solution packages and is also working on integrating SAP's cloud solutions with the on-premise world. He joined SAP in 2004 holding various roles in development, education, support, and product management.

David Dichmann is director of product management for SAP's enterprise architecture and modeling tool, PowerDesigner. David manages the product management team, driving next-generation modeling and architecture. David has more than 24 years of industry experience in both technical and business roles, working with small, start-up, and established businesses. David has been published in industry magazines and is a regular speaker at industry events.

Srikant Dharwad is an enterprise data architect for Lexmark International Inc., responsible for developing solutions for customer/vendor master data management and the enterprise data warehouse. He has more than 15 years of experience in solution development/architecture, technology consulting, product development, and EIM solution development for industry verticals. Prior to joining Lexmark, he worked at Teradata Corporation in various roles, including product development and solutions consulting.

Dr. Andreas Engel is an expert in Enterprise Information Management, focusing on integrated Enterprise Content Management. He has more than 15 years of experience in the software industry. Currently working as a solution expert in the SAP Global Center of Expertise for SAP HANA, he drives innovation from market requirements to market adoption.

Ina L. Felsheim is a director of solution management for SAP's EIM products. She has been with SAP since 1997, and currently works on information governance and end-to-end use scenarios. She has managed a diverse set of EIM products and is the SAP point person for both the Data Governance and Data Management SIGs, as well as the EIM Influence Council.

Will Gardella leads the Cloud and Big Data technology innovation team at SAP Labs in Palo Alto, California. He is the technical advisor for SAP's global Big Data strategy, and he has focused on applying Hadoop technology in the enterprise context since 2010.

Ginger Gatling has been with SAP since 1997 and has experience that ranges from teaching Basis and technical courses, to working in solution management, covering topics from SAP Business Workflow to data migration. She co-authored the second edition of *Practical Workflow for SAP* (SAP PRESS, 2009), which has donated more than $20,000 to Doctors Without Borders. She is an active member of her local North Texas ASUG chapter.

Simer Grewal joined SAP in 2004 as an application developer in the ERP master data area, and he has since worked as an architect, project manager, and product owner. As a member of the North America EIM Center of Excellence, he has product knowledge spanning the EIM portfolio, with specialization in the MDM/MDG area. His current focus is to help customers understand their business processes and build an enterprise-wide information governance strategy.

Stéphane Haelterman has been working with SAP since 1997, leading process improvements, process automation, and invoice management projects in Europe. After successfully implementing SAP Invoice Management by OpenText to optimize the purchase-to-pay platform at Belgian Railways, he was asked to build a vision and strategy to bridge the gap between business processes and the most tangible asset left behind: the business documents. He now leads the four-year implementation program for SAP Extended Enterprise Content Management by OpenText.

Eric Hamer has worked at Intel Corporation for 28 years and has experience in wafer fab lithography engineering and factory automation software development and architecture. Currently, he is an enterprise architect for IT solutions. His contribution to Chapter 6, Practical Examples of EIM, reflects his own opinions and experiences, and does not necessarily represent Intel's positions, strategies, or opinions.

Ben Hofmans joined BusinessObjects in 2002 and came to SAP through the acquisition in 2007. For the past eight years, Ben was the product manager for SAP Data Services, with the past two years having a special focus on the cloud version, known as SAP HANA Cloud Integration for data services. Before joining product management, he gained deep technical knowledge in EIM as a consultant and software trainer. Ben has a master's degree in mathematics from the University of Leuven in Belgium.

Rob Jackson has more than 14 years of experience archiving SAP documents and data, and he was the founder and chairman of the ASUG Data Archiving and ILM Special Interest Group from 1998 to 2012. As part of the ASUG Influence Council, he was very involved in the joint initiative with SAP for the creation of SAP ILM. He has worked as an imaging systems engineer at Eastman Kodak Company and as a solutions architect at Owens Corning, and he is currently a solutions architect at a consulting company that specializes in imaging and data archiving projects.

Mike Keilen is a vice president of solution management in the EIM group at SAP, and has been with SAP since 1991. Over this time, Mike has provided leadership across both the EIM and ECM topics in various engineering, product, solution, and partner management roles. Mike is globally responsible for SAP's EIM portfolio covering information governance, master data management, information life cycle management, data migration, data integration, data quality, and ECM solutions.

George Keller holds a BS degree in technical management and has more than 20 years of experience in the field of information management, having worked within engineering, business applications, and product management organizations. He has also served as a professional delivery project manager for a number of Fortune 100 clients. He has extensive experience in cloud integration, master data management, data warehousing, ERP, finance, and customer relationship management. At SAP, he served as a product manager for SAP HANA Cloud Integration for data services and served as an expert consultant and evangelist for master data services.

Markus Kuppe is vice president and chief solution architect for SAP Master Data Governance. Since joining SAP development in 1997, he led various programs across the SAP Business Suite in topics such as analytics, user experience, or architecture—always in close collaboration with customers. He is a frequent author and speaker at business events. Markus holds a degree with distinction in mathematics (Dipl. Math.) from the University of Darmstadt, Germany.

Terry McFadden is the principle enterprise architect responsible for enterprise information architecture at Procter & Gamble, which has more than 300 consumer brands marketed in 160 countries with global sales exceeding $85 billion annually. Having moved from corporate data architect to enterprise architect, his focus is now on Enterprise Information Management. He also leads P&G's Global Business Services benchmarking practice.

Paul Medaille has worked with SAP for more than 15 years, covering Basis (SAP system administration), Process Integration, and SAP EIM solutions. He graduated from UC Davis with a degree in mathematics, and he is well known to the SAP community through his blogs, conference presentations, webinars, and articles. He also contributed to the second edition of *Practical Workflow for SAP* (SAP PRESS, 2009).

Philip On is an industry veteran for Enterprise Information Management with more than 13 years of experience on this topic working for SAP, Business Objects, and Oracle. He is currently the senior director of marketing at SAP, and is responsible for the entire EIM portfolio, as well as strategy and solutions for the cloud.

Hemant Puranik is a product manager for the SAP Enterprise Information Management product portfolio. He has more than 15 years of experience in the field of structured and unstructured data management gained through positions in software development, engineering management, and product management. In his current position, Hemant works closely with customers, driving wide adoption of current SAP products, as well as engaging with customers to influence new product development initiatives within SAP.

Louann Seguin has worked for National Vision, an Atlanta-based optical retailer with more than 700 locations and e-commerce, since 2003. She is currently the vice president of Information Technology and Strategy, and is responsible for overseeing all corporate applications and development, enterprise data/information architecture and management, business intelligence, and web development.

Akshay Sinha holds a master's degree in software systems from Birla Institute of Technology & Science in Pilani, India. He has been working at SAP since 2006 and has extensive software development experience on SAP technologies. He currently plays the role of an associate architect for the SAP MDG development team at SAP Labs.

Helmut Stefani joined SAP in 1997, working on the documentation, product management, solution management, and roll-out of data archiving, Enterprise Content Management, and information lifecycle management topics. He has authored several publications, including a book on data management, data archiving, and ILM. He can be reached at *helmut.stefani@sap.com*.

Eric Stridinger has been a leader in IT, supply chain, business intelligence, and data management for 22 years. In addition to holding several technical and functional positions and leading many high-profile global SAP projects, he has been involved with ASUG and worked as the chairman of the Data Governance Committee for a global tooling manufacturer. He is currently the director of the SAP supply chain for a global pharmaceutical company.

Anthony Waite is the product manager for text analytics products, and works out of the SAP Labs office in Cambridge, Massachusetts. He has been involved in SAP's EIM solutions for more than four years, evangelizing data integration and data quality on structured and unstructured data at SAP. Before joining SAP, he worked for seven years as an OLAP product manager at Oracle.

Niels Weigel is a member of the Global SAP HANA Platform EIM Center of Excellence team, and he works closely with SAP customers on their broader information governance initiatives and how SAP's solutions support these business transformations. Prior to this appointment, Niels was the product manager for the global address cleanse solution within SAP Data Quality Management and solution manager for SAP Information Steward.

All authors have chosen to donate their royalties from this book to Doctors Without Borders/*Médecins Sans Frontières*.

Doctors Without Borders/Médecins Sans Frontières (MSF) is an international independent medical humanitarian organization that delivers emergency aid to people affected by armed conflict, epidemics, natural and man-made disasters, and exclusion from health care in more than 60 countries. A private, non-profit organization, Doctors Without Borders was founded in 1971 as the first non-governmental organization to both provide emergency medical assistance and bear witness publicly to the plight of people it assists. The work of Doctors Without Borders is based on the humanitarian principles of medical ethics and impartiality. The organization is committed to bringing quality medical care to people caught in crisis regardless of race, religion, or political affiliation, and operates independently of any political, military, or religious agendas. The organization received the Nobel Peace Prize in 1999.

Index

A

B

C

D

H

I

J

K

L

M

N

O

P

Q

R

S

T

U

V

W

X

Y

Z

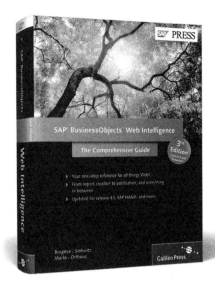